A Handbook
of
Critical Approaches
to Literature

A Handbook
of
Critical Approaches
to Literature

SIXTH EDITION

⌐

Wilfred L. Guerin
Louisiana State University in Shreveport

Earle Labor
Centenary College of Louisiana

Lee Morgan
Centenary College of Louisiana

Jeanne C. Reesman
University of Texas at San Antonio

John R. Willingham
Late of the University of Kansas

New York   Oxford

OXFORD UNIVERSITY PRESS

2011

Oxford University Press, Inc., publishes works that further Oxford University's
objective of excellence in research, scholarship, and education.

Oxford   New York
Auckland   Cape Town   Dar es Salaam   Hong Kong   Karachi
Kuala Lumpur   Madrid   Melbourne   Mexico City   Nairobi
New Delhi   Shanghai   Taipei   Toronto

With offices in
Argentina   Austria   Brazil   Chile   Czech Republic   France   Greece
Guatemala   Hungary   Italy   Japan   Poland   Portugal   Singapore
South Korea   Switzerland   Thailand   Turkey   Ukraine   Vietnam

Published by Oxford University Press, Inc.
198 Madison Avenue, New York, New York 10016
http://www.oup.com

Oxford is a registered trademark of Oxford University Press

Library of Congress Cataloging-in-Publication Data

    A handbook of critical approaches to literature / Wilfred L. Guerin...
[et al.].—6th ed.
        p. cm.
    Includes index.
    ISBN 978-0-19-539472-6 (pbk.)
    1. Criticism.   I. Guerin, Wilfred L.
    PN81.G8   2011
    801'.95—dc22   2009051991

Printing number: 9 8 7 6 5 4 3 2 1

Printed in the United States of America
on acid-free paper

TO OUR FIRST CRITICS
Jeannine Thing Campbell
Carmel Cali Guerin
Rachel Higgs Morgan
Sylvia Kirkpatrick Steger
Grace Hurst Willingham

CONTENTS

PREFACE

˷

This book, now in its sixth edition, has been from the first the product of our shared conviction that the richness of great literature merits correspondingly rich responses—responses that may be reasoned as well as felt. These happen most readily when the reader appreciates a great work from as many perspectives as it legitimately opens itself to. Nothing, of course, replaces the reader's initial *felt* responses: the sound of poetry or the visions of fiction in the mind's eye. But human responses seldom remain dead-level: they reverberate through multiple planes of sensibility, impelled toward articulation—in short, toward criticism. In response to the inevitable classroom question, "Why can't we simply enjoy this poem [story, novel, play] instead of criticizing?" we would answer, "The greatest enjoyment of literary art is never simple!" T. S. Eliot observed that "criticism is as inevitable as breathing, and that we should be none the worse for articulating what passes in our minds when we read a book and feel an emotion about it."

Eliot's observation was instrumental in the genesis of the first edition of the *Handbook*. At that time the four original coauthors, colleagues in the English Department at Centenary College of Louisiana, had become sensitive to the problems of teaching literary analysis to college students in the absence of a comprehensive yet elementary guide to some of the major critical approaches to works of literature. No work of that sort existed, yet students clearly could have profited from a more formalized and contemporary introduction to the serious study of literature than they generally had received in lower levels of education. Even students whose exposure to literature had been extensive often possessed only a narrow and fragmented concept of such interpretive approaches. Consequently, one of our first aims—then and now—has been to help establish a healthy balance in the student's critical outlook through offering the most useful approaches to literary criticism.

We have been gratified with the success of this aim, indicated by the acceptance of the book by our colleagues and by hundreds of thousands of students, now for more than half a century. The book has been published in Spanish, Portuguese, Japanese, Chinese, and Korean, and used in classes from high school to graduate school.

NEW IN THIS EDITION

We hope that in this sixth edition we have preserved that versatility, and we have worked strenuously to improve upon it. Since the publication of our first edition, we have witnessed a veritable expansion and revision of the literary canon. These developments have prompted corresponding revisions in each succeeding edition of our handbooks, including extensive updates in this edition:

- What were previously Chapters 2 through 4, on traditional approaches, historical/biographical approaches, and moral/philosophical approaches, have been condensed and combined into a new Chapter 2 that covers all of these approaches. Thus we have made room for more contemporary theories while retaining the vital information from our original introductory chapters. Chapter 2 retains the plot summaries of our six selected texts.
- We have added three new chapters, including Materialisms (Chapter 4), Literature and Linguistics (Chapter 5), and Postcolonial Studies (Chapter 10), with new readings of our six texts; in these chapters Marxism is given fuller treatment, and some of the newest theory and criticism is presented, including ecocriticism, Literary Darwinism, spatial studies, third-wave feminism, and black maternal theory.
- Chapter 9, Cultural Studies, has been reconceived and reorganized into United States Ethnic Studies, Postmodernism, and Popular Culture. Our previous Chapter 10, Additional Approaches, has been eliminated and its content redistributed into new chapters.
- Throughout, we have condensed some material, supplied updates to all critical approaches, and substituted for older examples texts which today's students would be more likely to recognize.
- We have incorporated many more images into the book and expanded our discussions of film and visual examples of texts. This new edition includes exercises involving the famous painting *Las Meninas* by Diego Velázquez (1656), which are designed to help transition students from their pervasive visual cultures into literary analysis.
- We have added summaries of key points at the end of each chapter and a glossary of literary terms at the back of the text. Literary terms are bold-faced the first time they are used in each chapter; by referring to the glossary, students will find it much easier to master these terms and their applications. The Quick Reference bibliographies have been updated and expanded.
- There is now a companion website to this handbook, www.oup.com/us/guerin, featuring essay assignments, self-quizzes, PowerPoint presentations for each chapter, and links to related websites.

In all of our revisions, we have remained sensitive to the needs and practices of instructors and students—both in preserving the widely praised comprehensiveness, student-friendliness, and clarity of previous editions and in anticipating the interests of a new generation of students and instructors.

METHODOLOGY

Our aim here is still much the same as it was in the first five editions: to provide a basic introduction to the major critical-interpretive perspectives that a reader beginning a serious study may bring to bear on literature. This book describes and demonstrates the critical tools that have come to be regarded as indispensable for the sensitive reader; these tools are what we call "approaches." Furthermore, because this is a *handbook* of critical approaches, we have tried to make it suggestive rather than exhaustive. We make no claim to being definitive; on the contrary, the book's value lies, in part, in opening students' eyes to *the possibilities* in literature and criticism. Today we read much about **heuristics**, the process of discovery. This sense of discovery was important in the previous editions, and it continues to be important here.

But heuristics can be guided, and for that reason we have selected several main approaches to literary criticism, all of which we consider viable not only for the critical expert but also for the critical neophyte. Our chapters begin with an introduction to and definition of a particular interpretive approach, followed by a detailed application of that approach to the same six major works—three British and three American, one of which is African-American—representing the genres of poetry, drama, novel, and short story. Each chapter also includes comments on other literary works cited as occasional illustrations, thereby effectively extending the handbook's application beyond the six works treated more extensively, while at the same time permitting students to apply the various critical approaches to the works thus briefly mentioned. There is no rigid sequence from chapter to chapter, and the six major works are not all treated with the same degree of detail in each chapter, since not all works lend themselves equally well to a given approach. Consequently, one important aspect of our treatment of critical reading should be the student's recognition of the need to select the most suitable approach for a given literary work.

The six works were chosen because they lend themselves exceptionally well to multiple interpretations and because they will make students aware of the joys of reading at increasingly higher levels of ability. Three of the works—*Frankenstein, Adventures of Huckleberry Finn,* and *Hamlet*—are easily available in paperback, if not in a literature anthology. The other three—"To His Coy Mistress," "Young Goodman Brown," and "Everyday Use"—are included in this book.

And we hope that the book will serve as a model or guide for the interpretation of many literary works, not just these. In short, while our handbook possesses an integrity of its own, it may also be used as a complementary text in conjunction with an anthology or a set of paperbacks.

TEACHING FROM THIS TEXT

This handbook may be read from cover to cover as a continuous unit, of course, but it has been organized for both flexibility and adaptability. For example, although it is primarily organized by "approaches" rather than **genres**, at the beginning of a course the instructor may assign the introductory section of each chapter, later assigning the sections dealing with a certain genre. Thus, the instructor who decides to begin with the **short story** may assign "Young Goodman Brown" and "Everyday Use" along with the introductory sections of selected chapters and the accompanying discussions of these two stories. Another possible strategy is to have students read several literary works early in the term and discuss them in class without immediate recourse to this handbook. Then they might read this text, or pertinent sections of it, and bring their resulting new insights to bear on the literature read earlier, as well as on subsequent readings. This double exposure has the advantage of creating a sense of discovery for the perceptive reader.

ACKNOWLEDGMENTS

For the continuing success of this handbook over the past five decades, we owe many thanks. Our debt to the canon of literary scholarship—the breadth and depth of which is reflected in the Quick Reference sections of the text—is obvious, and we acknowledge it with gratitude. Equally considerable is our debt to the many friends and colleagues whose assistance and suggestions have helped to ensure this success. To these we give special thanks: Laurence Perrine, William B. Allmon, James A. Gowen, Donald F. Warders, Arthur Schwartz, Richard Coanda, James Wilcox, Kathleen Owens, Czarena Stuart, Irene Winterowd, Yvonne B. Willingham, Mildred B. Smith, Melinda M. Carpenter, Alyce Palpant, Jeanette DeLine, Betty Labor, Ruby George, Mary McBride, Robert C. Leitz III, Stephen J. Mayer, Karl-Heinz Westarp, Donna Hannah, Ellen Brown, Bernard Duyfhuizen, Michael L. Hall, David H. Jackson, Kyle Labor, Phillip Leininger, Bettye Leslie, Teresa Mangum, Barry Nass, Steven Shelburne, Frederick C. Stern, Keith G. Thomas, David Havird, John Hardt, Harry James Cook, Donald Kummings, Earl Wilcox, Kevin Harty, James Lake, Sue Brown, Helen Taylor, Sura Rath, Larry Anderson, Ed Odom, Garry Partridge, Elia DeLeon, Douglas Bruster, Gena Dagel Caponi, John Kucich, Louis Mendoza, Denise Walker, Kim Chapman, Bridget Drinka, Linda Woodson, Susan Streeter, Alan E. Craven, Patty Roberts, Chris Brown, Dave Foley, Mona Narain, Becky Palmer, Debbie López, Terri Pantuso, Evan Campbell, Roberta Barki, and Melissa Whitney.

Once again we wish to express our appreciation for the constant and thoughtful support from the staff of Oxford University Press, particularly our editor, Jan Beatty; assistant editor, Lauren Mine; and our production editor, Jaimee Biggins.

We also wish to thank the reviewers commissioned by Oxford University Press, who contributed significantly to our revisions: Anthony Amore, University of Rhode Island: Monica Ayuso, California State University, Bakersfield; Thomas Cassidy, South Carolina State University ; June Chung, DePaul University; Charles Cunningham, Eastern Michigan University; Fayeza Hasanat, University of Central Florida; Kristin Jacobson, Stockton College; Brian Lennon, Pennsylvania State University; James Mardock, University of Nevada, Reno; Keith Newlin, University of North Carolina at Wilmington; Peter Sands, University of Wisconsin-Milwaukee; Reiner Smolinski, Georgia State University; Mark Thompson, University of Illinois; Nancy Tuten, Columbia College; and Jolanta Wawrzycka, Radford University.

On a final note, we are especially indebted to Gayle Labor for her editorial efforts, to Greg Guerin for technical assistance, and to Jeff Hendricks for critical insights. We also acknowledge with gratitude the contributions of our late colleague, John R. Willingham, to the first five editions of this handbook.

A NOTE ON TEXTS

There are many good editions of *Hamlet* available to students today. For *Adventures of Huckleberry Finn,* we refer to the only authoritative text, that sponsored by the Mark Twain Project of The Bancroft Library, edited by Victor Fischer and Lin Salamo (Berkeley: University of California Press, 2002). For *Frankenstein,* we prefer the 1818 version and use the Norton edition edited by J. Paul Hunter (New York: W. W. Norton, 1996).

Other useful editions include the Oxford World's Classics editions of *Adventures of Huckleberry Finn* (ed. Emory Elliott, New York: Oxford, 2008) and *Frankenstein* (ed. M. K. Joseph, New York: Oxford, 2008), and the Oxford School Shakespeare edition of *Hamlet* (ed. Roma Gill, New York: Oxford, 2009).

Getting Started: The Precritical Response

It may come as a surprise to contemporary students to learn that well into the nineteenth century, courses in British and American literature were not offered in universities. For centuries in western Europe, only the literature of classical antiquity was thought to have sufficient merit for systematic study. Yet it was inevitable that literature should one day become a part of the academic curriculum. Anything that could so move and interest large numbers of people, including the most cultivated and enlightened, and that had such obvious and pronounced didactic uses was in the judgment of academicians bound to be worthy of intellectual analysis. Such a view may well have motivated educators to make literature an academic subject: it "taught" something; it was a source of "knowledge." In any event, once literature was established in the curriculum, it was subjected to the formal discipline of criticism, which ultimately consisted of taking it apart (and putting it back together again) to see how and why as well as what it was and meant.

A popular opinion has it that because literary "technicians" have so rigorously pursued their studies, many "common readers" (a term that Dr. Samuel Johnson contributed to the lexicon) shy away from the rich and pleasurable insights that balanced, intelligent literary criticism can lead to. Whatever the reason, many students not innately hostile to literature may well have come almost to despise it, certainly to dread it in school.

Some professional critics have apparently sympathized with this negative view of the effects of criticism: in 1964, for example, Susan Sontag in "Against Interpretation" mounted a frontal attack on most kinds of contemporary criticism, which, she maintained, actually usurp the place of a work of art (13–23). In her free-swinging assault Sontag was at once defending a precritical response somewhat similar to the one elaborated in this chapter and asserting that critical analysis was the desecration of an art form. She saw art as the uninhibited creative spirit in action, energetic and sensual. She saw criticism—at least, most of it—as a dry-as-dust intellectual operation, the intent of which is to control and manage art and the method of which was to reduce the work of art to *content* and then to interpret that. Her approach is highly provocative and stimulating. Yet despite some last-minute disclaimers that she is not condemning all critical commentary and some advice to critics to pay more attention to *form*, it is difficult to escape the conclusion that in her opinion interpretation impoverishes art and that its practice for a number of decades by most academic and professional critics had been unquestionably harmful. She concluded with the pronouncement that "in place of a **hermeneutics** we need an erotics of art."

Such a view would seem to place her in general agreement with Leslie Fiedler, who, addressing a national convention of the College English Association in the early 1970s, advocated "ecstatics" as a response to literature. Professor Fiedler would make the gut reaction the be-all and end-all of art. The traditionally accepted standards and classics were in his view elitist, academic opinions and productions that had been forced on the reading public, who demonstrably prefer sentimental literature, horror stories, and pornography—all of the popular variety. Such popular writings produce almost exclusively emotional effects—particularly feelings of pathos, terror, and sexual titillation. They cause readers, said Fiedler, "to go out of control, out of [their] heads." He continued by pointing out that

> we do have a traditional name for the effect sought, and at its most successful achieved, by Pop; the temporary release from the limits of rationality, the boundaries of the ego, the burden of consciousness; the moment of privileged insanity[;] that traditional name is, of course, "Ekstasis," which Longinus spoke of in the last centuries of the Classic Era, not in terms of Popular Art or High Art, which in fact cannot be distinguished in terms of this concept; but of *all* art at its irrational best—or, to use his other favorite word, most "sublime."

That political principles underlie Fiedler's position is clear in his closing remarks:

> Once we have made *ekstasis* rather than instruction or delight the center of critical evaluation, we will be freed from the necessity of ranking mass-produced and mass-distributed books in a hierarchal order viable only in a class-structured society, delivered from the indignity of having to condescend publicly to works we privately relish and relieved of the task of trying to define categories like "high" and "low," "majority" and "minority" which were from the beginning delusive and unreal.

Sontag and Fiedler express in intellectualized terms what many a student has simply asserted, "All this criticism and analysis take all the fun out of reading!"

Among the earliest spirited rebuttals to such subjective interpretation were J. Mitchell Morse's "Are English Teachers Obsolete?," Ann Berthoff's "Recalling Another Freudian Model—A Consumer Caveat," and Eva Touster's "Tradition and the Academic Talent." In the second edition of *How Does a Poem Mean?* John Ciardi emphatically condemns appreciation and free association in discussing poetry in the classroom, calling the one "not useful," the other "permissive and pointless," and both together "dull" (xix–xxi). In an impressive list of works ranging from *Literary Theory: An Introduction* (1983) to *After Theory* (2004), Terry

Eagleton has argued that all literature expresses political philosophy. More specifically, he believes that Marxist theory and not subjectivity can explain any literary work. Responses to Eagleton have taken the form of the defense of beauty itself, as in the work of Wendy Steiner (*Venus in Exile: The Rejection of Beauty in Twentieth-Century Art* [2002] and *The Scandal of Pleasure: Art in an Age of Fundamentalism* [1997]) and Elaine Scarry (*On Beauty and Being Just* and *Dreaming By the Book* [both 2001]), who describe a broader, subtler array of how beauty exists within our lives than "erotics" or "*ekstasis*" can.

Sontag's, Fiedler's, Eagleton's, Steiner's, and Scarry's diverse points of view are instructive for readers interested in familiarizing themselves with the variety of critical responses to a literary work. Whether one subscribes to them in their entirety or in part or disagrees with them categorically, they are invigorating polemics that can spark further intellectual exchange on the issue in the classroom, in learned journals, and in magazines and newspapers, as well as on web sites, chatrooms, and blogs.

Perhaps as a result of such controversy, a dilemma has arisen in the classroom for some teachers of literature, namely, whether to discuss material in an essentially subjective manner—the extreme of which could be relativistic and nonrational—or whether to employ the tools of logical and intellectual analysis. We believe that these options do not necessarily constitute a dilemma.

There is unquestionably a kind of literary analysis that is like using an elephant gun to shoot a gnat. It is practiced by riders of all kinds of scholarly hobbyhorses and may manifest itself in such ways as ascertaining the number of **rhymes** in *The Rape of the Lock* or instances of trochees in book 4 of *Paradise Lost*. The early pages of Charles Dickens's *Hard Times* illustrate the imagination-stifling effect of one such technique. Thomas Gradgrind, patron of a grammar school in an English industrial town, is listening to a class recite. He calls on one of the pupils, "girl number twenty," for the definition of a horse. "Girl number twenty" (in Gradgrind's world there is no personal identity) cannot produce the expected rote answer. A better-conditioned classmate can: " 'Quadruped. Graminivorous. Forty teeth, namely twenty-four grinders, four eye-teeth and twelve incisive. Sheds coat in the spring; in marshy countries sheds hoofs, too. Hoofs hard, but requiring to be shod with iron. Age known by marks in mouth.' 'Now girl number twenty,' said Mr. Gradgrind, 'You know what a horse is.' " It hardly needs pointing out that such a definition would not do justice to the likes of famous horses like Pegasus, Seabiscuit, or Black Beauty. But absorption with extraneous, irrelevant, or even overly practical considerations that detract from aesthetic perception seems to be an occupational disease of many literary critics. This appears to be a problem, however, rather than a dilemma, and its solution is among the several aims of this book.

Our purpose in this chapter is to show that the precritical response is not only desirable but indeed essential in the fullest appreciation of literature. In doing so, we do not mean to suggest that analysis or expertise detracts from aesthetic sensitivity any more than we mean to suggest that a *precritical* response is an unworthy one. It is a truism to say that our senses can sometimes mislead us, hence the need to analyze literature that is being studied as well as read for pure pleasure. This book is predicated on the assumption that knowledge and the intelligent application of several interpretive techniques can enhance the pleasure the reader can derive from a piece of literature.

Let us illustrate with an analogy. A college student decides to take in a film on a Friday evening as a reward for a week of grinding study. She rounds up a group of friends, and they head for a nearby mall, the site of a huge theater where often over two dozen films are being shown simultaneously in different auditoriums. The sheer joy of weekend freedom is heightened by the sight of hordes of other students laughing and clowning about their release from labs and libraries into the world of the movies. America's future business and professional leaders are stocking up on buttered popcorn and mammoth cups of soft drinks before disappearing into dark caverns full of luxuriously upholstered reclining theater seats, there to thrill vicariously to torrid love scenes, gory detective brutality, wild and crazy comedy, complex psychological drama, and science fiction. Everything combines to immerse them in a pool of sensation.

Not far away from these avid fans, a smaller, somewhat less ebullient group of students are making their way into one of the auditoriums, but they lack none of the other group's excitement and anticipation. They are members of one of the college's film classes, and they are accompanied by their professor. They are informed on the history of moviemaking; they know both classic and contemporary films; they understand some of the technical operations of the camera and its myriad effects; they are familiar with many acting styles, past and present. On the level of sense experience, they are receiving the same impressions as the other group of students. But because of their special knowledge, they *comprehend* what they are witnessing. Their knowledge does not dim their pleasure; it does not nullify any precritical, amateur response. It may even intensify it; it certainly complements it. For there is no real opposition of responses here. These more knowledgeable moviegoers do not say to themselves at one point, "Now we're *feeling*," and at another, "Now we're *knowing*." By this stage the knowing is almost as instinctive as the feeling.

What the academic critic needs to keep in mind is that the precritical response is not an inferior response to literature. (After all, we may be sure that Shakespeare did not write *Hamlet* so that scholarly critical approaches to it could be formulated.) Rather, the precritical response employing primarily the senses and the emotions is an indispensable one if pleasure or delight is the aim of art. Without it the critic might as well be merely proofreading for factual accuracy or correct mechanical form. It may be said to underlie or even to drive the critical response. To illustrate the point, we cite the experience of a colleague of ours who gave a birthday party for her 11-year-old son. She chose to take him and eight of his friends to see the film *The Village* (2004). She and another mother sat behind the boys as they watched the film. The moment it was over, a certain George M. jumped to his feet, whirled around to the mothers, and loudly announced, "That

Reading *Las Meniñas* by Diego Velázquez

As our commitment to analogies from film throughout this handbook emphasizes, literary critics today must acknowledge the importance of visual culture for teaching and employing approaches to any art, including literature. Throughout our chapters we draw comparisons between visual and verbal interpretations of texts, particularly for what is possibly the most popularly reproduced literary image in the world, the image of the Creature from Mary Shelley's *Frankenstein* (see Chapter 9). In a few interpretive exercises instructors using Chapter 1 of this handbook may turn to visual aids to convey the literary ideas of basic elements of narrative such as setting, character, and style. We have found that one mysterious painting is especially appropriate for this beginning segue of visual interpretation into verbal: Diego Velázquez's *Las Meniñas* (1656), ostensibly a Spanish court painting but also a teasing instance of art asking viewers for multiple and conflicting interpretations. Throughout our handbook we introduce Pablo

Figure 1.1. Diego Velázquez, *Las Meniñas* (1656).
Getty Images/Imagno.

Picasso's reinterpretations of this seminal painting as representative of a modern approach to understanding its complexities. We are not art critics nor do we claim that techniques to interpret an oil portrait from the seventeenth century are necessarily the guide to reading world literature of many periods. But we suggest using visual metaphors to teach literary ones, visual or cinematic situations to illuminate those in literary works, and the drawing of parallels among many forms of world art. Often students who are not English majors will especially appreciate such an approach; for example, the scientific diagrams, social projections, and cultural icons we offer to illustrate the importance of *Frankenstein* as a world phenomenon (Chapter 9) furnish a concentrated sample of images, but with the famous painting *Las Meniñas* we can offer a few parallel exercises in "reading"; these are further explored on the web site for *A Handbook of Critical Approaches to Literature*, at www.oup.com/us/guerin.

totally sucked! It was so lame!" Then he caught himself, realizing that he was sharing his opinion with his hostess. He shamefacedly shuffled out of the theater along with his friends. Our colleague, when she quit laughing, told him not to worry: his language may not have been proper, but his opinion was absolutely correct! We tell this story to show the importance of having the gut reaction that George had, and also the need for precise critical language to move beyond "it sucked."

We are now about to take our first steps into academic criticism. Whenever students begin to think and talk about setting, plot, character, structure, and so on, they have moved from merely amateur responses to literature toward more analytical commentary on such questions as what, how, and why. But the elements of literature are also sources of pleasure—a plot is suspenseful, a setting scary, a character noble. In subsequent chapters, we examine in detail the various approaches that may be applied to a work of literature.

I. SETTING

The students' precritical response to a film parallels the common reader's precritical response to literature. The unforgiving Alaskan wildnerness of the film *Into the Wild* (2007) corresponds to the *setting* of the work of literature: the antebellum South of *Huckleberry Finn*; Puritan Massachusetts in "Young Goodman Brown"; Cavalier England in "To His Coy Mistress"; eleventh-century Denmark in *Hamlet*; the Deep South of the 1970s in "Everyday Use"; the Arctic desolation of *Frankenstein*.

Precritical responses to settings in the works to be dealt with in this handbook are likely to be numerous and freewheeling. One reader of *Huckleberry Finn* will respond to the nostalgia of an earlier, rural America, to the lazy tempo and idyllic mood of Huck and Jim's raft trip down the Mississippi. Still another will delight in the satiric description of the aristocratic Grangerfords's bourgeois parlor furnishings or the frontier primitivism of Arkansas river villages and the one-horse plantation of the Phelpses. Yet a third will feel repelled by the violence and racism that unfolds. The **Gothic** texture of the New England forest in "Young Goodman Brown" will sober some readers, as will the dark and brooding castle of *Hamlet*. The actual setting of "To His Coy Mistress" must be inferred (a formal garden? the spacious grounds of a nobleman's estate?), but romantically **connotative** settings such as the "Indian Ganges" and the "tide of Humber" are alluded to, as are macabre or mind-boggling places like "marble vaults" and "deserts of vast eternity." The simple living conditions of the Johnsons in "Everyday Use" will seem historically distant to most modern young readers.

The multiple settings of *Frankenstein* enhance the theme and the plot of the novel. The raging storms of the rugged Alpine mountains, the shocking sights in Frankenstein's laboratories, the remote wind-swept Orkney Islands, the frozen wastelands of the polar North—all play a most important role.

II. PLOT

The students' uncomplicated view of an individual film equals the reader's precritical response to the *conflict* (plot) involving **protagonist** and **antagonist** (Hamlet versus his uncle; Batman versus the Joker). Readers who delight in action will thrill to the steps in Hamlet's revenge, even when it lights on the innocent, and will feel the keen irony that prevents him from knowing his Ophelia to be true and guiltless and from enjoying the fruit of his righteous judgment. Such time-honored plot ingredients as the escape, the chase, the capture, the release—sensationally spiced with lynching, tar-and-feathering, swindling, feuding, murder, and treachery—may form the staple of interest for precritical readers of *Huckleberry Finn*. Such readers will also be rooting for the white boy and his black slave friend to elude their pursuers and attain their respective freedoms. Enigma and bewilderment may well be the principal precritical response elicited by the plot of "Young Goodman Brown": is Brown's conflict an imaginary one, or is he really battling the Devil in this theological *Heart of Darkness*? Or in "To His Coy Mistress," will the young Cavalier prevail with his Coy Mistress to make love before they are crushed in the maw of Time? In Mary Shelley's classic thriller *Frankenstein,* will the young scientist befriend, control, or kill the monster he has created, or will the monster wreak vengeance on the world for his "miscreation"?

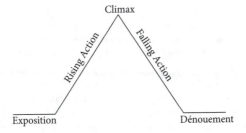

Figure 1.2. Freytag's pyramid.

Gustav Freytag (1816–1895), a German dramatist and novelist, invented what was later called "Freytag's Pyramid." He organized his study of ancient Greek and Shakespearean *drama* into five plot sections and illustrated them with a pyramid with lines extended outward from each side: **exposition**, **rising action**, **climax** (or turning point), **falling action**, and **dénouement** (**comedy**) or **catastrophe** (**tragedy**).

The exposition provides the background information needed to properly understand a story, such as the protagonist, the antagonist, the basic conflict, and the setting, ending with the inciting moment. The inciting moment sets the remainder of the story in motion, beginning with the rising action. During rising action, the basic conflict is complicated by the introduction of other conflicts, such as setbacks, adversaries (called antagonists), or obstacles that frustrate the protagonist. The climax, or turning point, marks a major change for the protagonist. In comedies, things are difficult at first for the protagonist but improve. In tragedy, the protagonist will face his ultimate test at the climax. During the falling action, the protagonist wins against or loses to the antagonist. The falling action might contain a moment of final suspense, during which the final outcome of the conflict is in doubt. Comedy ends with a dénouement (conclusion, or wrapping up) in which the protagonist is better off than at the story's outset. Tragedy ends with a **catastrophe** in which the protagonist is destroyed in some way. Although Freytag's analysis of dramatic structure is based on dramas of five acts, it can be applied to short stories and novels as well.

Reading *Las Meniñas*

Diego Velázquez's famous painting *Las Meniñas* has occasioned centuries of interpretation, from the moment it was unveiled in Madrid in 1656. Hugh Honor and John Fleming have described it as "Velázquez's supreme achievement, a highly self-conscious, calculated demonstration of what painting could achieve, and perhaps the most searching comment ever made on the possibilities of the easel painting" (447). Today it is the subject of web sites, blogs, and documentaries, and endless dissertations and chapters in art books because of its influence on and reinterpretations by subsequent artists (especially Spanish ones). Its mathematics have been uncovered, its physics, its characters' lives, its place in Velázquez's oeuvre, its place in Baroque painting, its historical detail. But it is most famous for what it doesn't offer: an easy interpretation. Indeed, *Las Meniñas* is thought of as a very mysterious painting—hence its long history of attempts at interpretation.

One of its most assiduous interpreters was Pablo Picasso (1881–1973), who made 58 studies of it, while he lived in Cannes, France, from August through December of 1957. These paintings currently occupy the *Las Meniñas* room of the Museu Picasso in Barcelona, Spain. The authors of this handbook tend to use many examples from film to illustrate literary analysis, and in this new edition we add some exercises in criticism using this painting. As noted earlier, many students are more comfortable undertaking literary analysis if they have a few visual analogues. (Please see the *Handbook of Critical Approaches to Literature*, 6th edition web site at www.oup.com/us/guerin.) The last of and the most famous of Picasso's interpretations of *Las Meniñas,* we include in the Epilogue. It dramatically contrasts the front cover's "traditional" version with Picasso's modernism, showing the transitions that have taken place in the arts over the last 400 years and suggests some of the innovations in literary criticism and theory discussed in this handbook.

Throughout the handbook we scatter images of *Las Meniñas* and its interpretations by Picasso, as well as a brief essay on Michel Foucault's famous analysis of the painting. We hope that these visual moments will enhance students' readiness to look deeply and carefully at elements in literary art including setting, character, history, power relations, formal relationships and motifs, symbols, and so on.

III. CHARACTER

The young moviegoers assess, after a fashion, the roles of the actors. Although these are frequently cultural stereotypes, they bear some analogy to the common reader's commonsense character analysis of literary figures (the self-effacing, sacrificial nature of Sidney Carton in *A Tale of Two Cities,* the matter-of-fact courage and resourcefulness of Robinson Crusoe, the noble but frustrated humanity of John Savage in *Brave New World* or Sethe in Toni Morrison's *Beloved*). Precritical reactions to the characters in "To His Coy Mistress" will no doubt vary with the degree to which the reader subscribes to situation ethics or adheres to a clearly articulated moral code. Some will judge the male aggressor a "player" and the woman a tease. Feminists will deplore the male-chauvinist exploitation that is being attempted. In *Huckleberry Finn,* a precritical perusal of the characters will probably divide them into good (those basically sympathetic to Huck and Jim) and bad (those not). Similarly, the **dramatis personae** of *Hamlet* will be judged according to whether they line up on the side of the tormented Hamlet or on that of his diabolically determined uncle. In more complex character analysis, the simplistic grouping into good and bad will not be adequate; it may in fact necessitate an appreciation of **ambiguity**. From this viewpoint, Gertrude and Polonius and Rosencrantz and Guildenstern appear more weak and venal than absolutely vicious. Complexity also informs the character treatment of Dee and her mother in "Everyday Use." The former is not merely the stock figure of the young black civil rights leader of the 1970s any more than her mother is a latter-day female Uncle Tom. Just as ambiguity was prominent in the plot of "Young Goodman Brown," so does it figure in a reader's precritical evaluation of character. Brown may appear to be a victim of trauma, an essentially shallow man suddenly made to seem profoundly disturbed. In the case of *Frankenstein,* we find two conflicted characters who are enmeshed in a web of self-horror.

IV. STRUCTURE

The students' awareness of the major complications and developments of a lengthy plot such as that of *The Lord of the Rings,* the Harry Potter series of books and the importance of each to the outcome is akin to *plot structure,* the relatedness of actions, the gradual buildup in suspense from a situation full of potential to a climax and a resolution (as in Macbeth's rise to be king of Scotland through foul and bloody means and the poetic justice of his defeat and death by the one he had wronged). A precritical response to the structure of "To His Coy Mistress" could certainly involve the recognition of the heightening intensity, **stanza** by stanza, of the lover's suit—from the proper and conventional complementary forms of verbal courting to more serious arguments about the brevity of life, and finally, to the bold and undisguised affirmation that sexual joy is the central goal of the lover's life. The common reader can discern the plot development in *Hamlet* step by step, from mystery, indecision, and torment to knowledge, resolute action, and **catharsis**. He or she may be fascinated by the stratagems that Hamlet and Claudius employ against each other and amused by the CIA-like techniques of Polonius to ferret out Hamlet's secret. Horror and, later, cathartic **pathos** are possible emotions engendered by the climax and dénouement of this **revenge tragedy**. The episodic plot of *Huckleberry Finn* is somehow coherent even though precritical readers must confront in rapid order thrill, suspense, danger, brutality, outrage, absurdity, laughter, tears, anger, and poetic justice as they respond to Huck and Jim's attempts to elude capture; the charlatanism as well as the sinister and criminal behavior of the King and the Duke; wrecked steamboats; tent revivals; feuding, shooting in the street, and thwarted lynching; and finally the mixed triumph of the heroes. The structural stages in "Young Goodman Brown" may result in ambivalent reactions by the reader: on the one hand, plain recognition of the destructive effects of the events of the plot on Brown; on the other, bewilderment as to whether the events really took place or were all hallucination.

V. STYLE

The acting technique in a film may be realistic, as is Clint Eastwood's) in *Mystic River* (2003), or it may be stylized, as is Johnny Depp's in the *Pirates of the Caribbean* films (2003–07). It has its counterpart in the verbal *style* of a literary work: the spare, understated prose of Hemingway; the sophisticated wit of Oscar Wilde's *The Importance of Being Earnest;* the compressed, highly allusive idiom of poets like Eliot and Yeats; the earthy plain talk of Alice Walker's *The Color Purple* and Kurt Vonnegut's *Slaughterhouse-Five*. The precritical reader hears it in the Pike County dialect of *Huckleberry Finn*, its vocabulary and rhythms ringing true in every line; in the urbane diction, learned **allusion**, and polished **couplets** of "To His Coy Mistress"; in the magnificent **blank verse** of *Hamlet*, alternately formal and plain, yet somehow organic and right for both dramatic action and philosophical **soliloquy**; in the solemn, cadenced phraseology of "Young Goodman

Brown," echoing what one imagines Puritan discourse to have been like, both in and out of the pulpit, its lightest touches still somehow ponderous; and in the wry, folksy dialogue and internal commentary of "Everyday Use." The prose style of *Frankenstein* is formal in the extreme, both in the author's exposition and in the **dialect** of the characters; of the latter it is safe to say, no person ever spoke such periods. Even the descriptive passages lose much of their effect because the diction is so learned as to appear artificial.

VI. ATMOSPHERE

Defined as the mood or feeling that permeates an environment, *atmosphere* consists of several factors: in Mel Gibson's *The Passion of the Christ* (2004), the brutality and violence, the acting itself; in a literary work, such similar factors as the eerie locales and stormy weather in Emily Brontë's *Wuthering Heights*, the panic of the green troops in Stephen Crane's *Red Badge of Courage*, the suspense and terror in Edgar Allan Poe's "Tell-Tale Heart," the indifference and listlessness of the characters in William Faulkner's "That Evening Sun."

The six works that we are emphasizing for precritical responses afford interesting possibilities here. "To His Coy Mistress," which on the surface seems to have fewer overt atmosphere-producing elements, in fact has a fairly pronounced atmosphere (or atmospheres, since there are shifts). The atmosphere results from the **diction** and the tone the speaker employs. The formal honorific "Lady" and its implied politeness create, if not a drawing-room atmosphere, a stylized one where there is romantic badinage, where gallants wax hyperbolic in a formulary way, and where women drop their eyes demurely. It is a mannered, controlled, ritualistic atmosphere. But in the second stanza, compliments give way to a professorial lecture as the aggressive male grows impatient with coyness carried too far, hence a dispiriting philosophical discussion about the brevity of life and the nothingness of afterlife. Finally, in the third stanza, the atmosphere becomes electric and potentially erotic and violent.

In *Huckleberry Finn*, on a very obvious plane, setting contributes to atmosphere. The Mississippi River, sleepy villages, small towns, one-horse plantations, Victorian parlors: all combine to present an essentially "normal" nineteenth-century Americana. Diction, character, and costume, however, also function to add troubling features to the atmosphere: especially the casual use of expressions like "nigger"; the toleration and acceptance of inhumanity observable in conversation and exposition; the radical inconsistency of basically decent, religious people breaking up slave families while evincing genuine affection for them and concern for their welfare. The amalgam of their shocking and sometimes contradictory attitudes and actions results in an utterly convincing if chaotic atmosphere.

The atmosphere of *Frankenstein*, one of the novel's most pronounced features, almost figures as a character. It constantly borders on and often overtly causes sheer horror. Alpine mists, Arctic wastes, ocean fogs, thunder, lightning, deluges—all dominate the outdoors. Eerie castles; mysterious laboratories full of body parts; and dark, rural hovels give indoor settings an air of omnipresent terror. This atmosphere perfectly complements the plot.

Similarly, both setting and plot make for a gloomy, foreboding atmosphere in *Hamlet* and "Young Goodman Brown." The play opens with sentries walking guard duty at midnight on the battlements of a medieval castle where a ghost has recently appeared. It is bitter cold and almost unnaturally quiet. Though later the scene changes many times, this atmosphere persists, augmented by the machinations of the principals, by dramatic confrontations, by reveries on death, by insane ravings, and finally by wholesale slaughter. In only slightly less melodramatic form, Hawthorne's story takes the reader to a witches' sabbath deep in the forests of seventeenth-century Massachusetts, where a cacophony of horrid sounds makes up the auditory background for a scene of devilish human countenances and eerie, distorted images of trees, stones, clouds. The protagonist's ambiguous role in the evil ceremony, which ruins his life, adds to the dark atmosphere pervading the story. In "Everyday Use," setting (a humble cabin in modern rural Georgia) and tension (between conservative rural blacks and their "emancipated" kinswoman) combine to form an atmosphere of latent and ultimately overt conflict.

VII. THEME

The often rich and varied underlying idea of the action is the *theme*. In a low-budget film, theme may be no more than "Bust those drug dealers!" "Zap those aliens!" "Go for it!" In a literary work, theme may be as obvious as the message in *Uncle Tom's Cabin* that "Slavery is cruel and morally degrading and must go" or the implicit point of *Robin Hood* that "Some rich folks deserve to be taken from, and some poor folks need to be given to." These scarcely compare with such profound thematic implications as those in *Macbeth, The Scarlet Letter,* or "The Love Song of J. Alfred Prufrock." As theme is a complex aspect of literature, one that requires very intentional thinking to discern, it is not likely to elicit the precritical response that the more palpable features do. This is not to say that it will not be felt. Twain's criticisms of slavery, hypocrisy, chicanery, violence, philistine aesthetic taste, and other assorted evils will move both the casual reader and the scholar. The poignancy of young Hamlet's having to deal with so many of life's insolubles at once and alone is certainly one of the play's major themes, and is one available at the precritical level of response. There are others. Despite complexity and ambiguity, the precritical reader will sense the meaning of faith and the effects of evil in "Young Goodman Brown" as two of the more urgent themes in the story. So will he or she perceive the ambivalence in accepting and rejecting one's heritage in "Everyday Use." Certainly a dominant theme in *Frankenstein* is the forbidden knowledge wherein science combines with the unholy desire to play God by creating life. Destruction awaits whoever would seek and practice forbidden knowledge, knowledge that seemingly empowers the seeker with abilities reserved for God alone. Another theme is the parental abandonment of the Creature by his

God and Father, Victor. In our analyses in the following chapters we shall return to the twin themes of parenting and revenge.

• • •

None of the elements discussed above, whether at a movie or in private reading, is contingent upon a technical knowledge of motion pictures or a graduate degree in the humanities. Without either, people may appreciate and respond precritically to both Oscar-award-winning films and the cold setting of Jack London's "To Build a Fire," to the sequence of events that causes Oedipus to blind himself, or to the phantasmagoric atmosphere of horror pervading Poe's "Masque of the Red Death."

In short, regardless of the extent to which close scrutiny and technical knowledge aid in literary analysis, there is no substitute for an initial personal, appreciative response to the basic ingredients of literature: setting, plot, character, structure, style, atmosphere, and theme. The reader who manages to proceed without that response sacrifices the spontaneous joy of seeing any art object whole, the wondrous sum of myriad parts.

Elements of Narrative in *Las Meninas*

Setting

In a high-ceilinged room in what must be a grand house or palace, the center seems to be a girl clothed on white. Very well-dressed children and adults, plus an artist and a man coming in through a back door, are represented. Light comes into the picture from the large windows to the right. The overall setting is luxurious or even royal. There are many pictures on the walls, but only one really shows up-what appears to be a mirror with a white line around it. Oddly, however, no one is looking at the mirror or the painting the artist is working on. The mirror, exactly half-way down, penetrates into the whole field of representation, restoring visibility to something outside our point of view.

Questions: What are the light and dark elements? What is at the center? Where is the viewer? What key elements are shown?

Plot

The plot seems to be observation and representation, the painter of the royal couple, the couple themselves, and the various other characters in the foreground and background. The Infanta (the princess in the white dress) seems to be trying to draw attention to herself, which she also seems to be successfully receiving from her court maids. But though she seems to be the main subject, she is actually standing in front of her parents, and her back is to the painter (so she cannot be the subject of his painting). Her parents are the (absent) subject reflected in the mirror. Did Velázquez himself have some sort of plot in mind, at least in the form of a visual joke? That is, as court painter, was he having a bit of fun with his usual subjects and their power over him?

Other questions: What is the meaning of the title? What is the most important image portrayed? Who or what is being observed, and by whom?

Character

The historical characters portrayed are, from left to right: Velázquez, Doña Maria Augustina Sarmiento de Sotomayor, the Infanta Margherita, Don José Nieto de Velázquez (the Queen's quartermaster or chamberlin), Doña Isabel de Velasco, Duenna Marcela de Ulloa, an unidentified gentleman (possibly a bodyguard), a dozing mastiff, dwarves Maribarbola and Nicolaso Pertusato. In the mirror are King Philip IV (1605–65) of Spain and his Queen, Mariana, Archduchess of Austria (1634–96). Who is in the middle? Draw an X to find the center of the painting. Is there more than one center? Who is looking at whom? Note groupings by twos: one of each group is looking at the Infanta and one looking straight out at us.

Questions: List and describe the characters portrayed. Is anyone missing? What do you suppose to be their relationships with each other? What difference does it make that Velázquez was the court painter to the king of Spain? What is each character doing? How does this reveal the character's place in the world of the court?

Structure

The painting is famous for its careful placement of structural elements. For example, its figures are grouped into two's and three's, some of which overlap (e.g., painter, maid of honor on left, princess, as well as the princess and her two maids of honor). The large canvas on the left is balanced by the large window on the right and the paintings on the right wall. The room itself moves from the darkness of the ceiling and rear of the room toward the floor and the front. Symmetrically arranged paintings fill the room, though their details are lost. A line of white around the mirror emphasizes its importance.

Let us look more closely at the lines of sight in the painting. Some figures look out of the canvas toward the viewer, while others interact among themselves. Of the twelve figures depicted, five are looking directly out at the royal couple, or the viewer. Their glances, along with the king and queen's reflection, affirm the royal couple's presence outside the painted space. To the rear and at right stands Don José Nieto Velázquez—the queen's chamberlain during the 1650s and the head of the royal tapestry works—who may have been a relative of the artist. Nieto is shown pausing, with his right knee bent and his feet on different steps. We cannot be sure whether he is "coming or going," adding a sense of mystery to the background. Nieto is seen only by the king and queen, who share the viewer's point of view, and not by the figures in the foreground. He is rendered in silhouette and appears to hold open a curtain on a short flight of stairs, with an unclear wall or space; this tends to lure our eyes and our imaginations to the back of the room instead of looking merely at the royal couple or the Infanta. But as we look to the back, the royal couple's reflection seems to push us back in the opposite direction.

The composition of the painting, then, is very complex: the painted surface is divided into quarters horizontally and sevenths vertically; this grid is used to organize the elaborate grouping of characters and was a common device at the time. Depth and dimension are rendered by the use of linear perspective, by the overlapping of the layers of shapes, and through the use of tone. This compositional element operates within the picture in a number of ways, such as the source of light and the question of who is being illuminated.

It is possible to draw lines from the four corners to explore perspective: if one draws an X from the four outer corners of the painting, ironically, the center is in a blank spot on the back wall, which violates one of the rules of such a painting, rules that insist upon the most important object occupying the center of the lines of perspective. However, if one draws an X starting a bit farther down, from the top of the canvas portrayed and the opposite wall, the center is on the Infanta's bright forehead, another ruse, since she is not the subject of the painting the artist is working on.

Style

Seventeenth-century Dutch and Spanish realistic-style paintings were classically influenced by Titian, yet are part of the period of Baroque painting. In *Las Meniñas,* Velázquez was interested in showing a kind of truth behind the official truth not often seen or suggested. Is his work perhaps a parody of court painting? To analyze this, students would need to research the artist and Baroque painting, as well as how European history and royalty were painted at the time.

Atmosphere

There is a self-conscious, in some parts almost supercilious attitude expressed by the artist in this painting; after all, he is making fun of the usual rules of court painting by not even picturing the ostensible subjects of his portrait. His portrait is mysteriously hidden, a sense of the unknown heightened by the entry of the dark silhouette through the back door and the fuzziness of the adult courtiers/chaperones to the right. Instead, light is amply shed on the false center of the picture, the brilliant white dress and face of the Infanta. Yet in the corners of the room lurk shadows and half-seen pictures (see our discussion of structure, above).

Questions: What is the mood? What visual devices does Velázquez use to build atmosphere? How is irony used in the painting?

Theme

What does it all mean? "It" is not "about" a singular subject, but about representation itself. Most works of art are complicated, especially in structure and point of view, and there is almost never a single right interpretation or "theme." But interpretations must be defended—why doesn't a work of art mean "anything I want it to mean," as the Queen of Hearts tells Alice. Meanings exist within communities. We persuade others of our interpretations within a common ground of discourse. Interpretation of meaning is what literary critics, like art critics, do.

Questions: Could there be a theme of mocking authority? After all, as the court painter Velázquez was supposed to portray the king and queen in noble positions of authority, not relegate them to an absence by using a mirror. This painting emphasizes mostly powerless people, children, court jesters, and even a dog. In addition, the Infanta's drawing attention to herself may be a comment on parents and children and the child's need to assert herself in front of her powerful parents.

QUICK REFERENCE

Berthoff, Ann. "Recalling Another Freudian Model—A Consumer Caveat." *The CEA Critic* 35 (May 1973): 12–14.

Ciardi, John. *How Does a Poem Mean?* 2nd ed. Boston: Houghton Mifflin, 1975.

Eagleton, Terry. *Literary Theory: An Introduction.* Minneapolis: University of Minnesota Press, 1996.

——. *After Theory.* New York: Basic Books, 2003.

Fiedler, Leslie. "Is There a Majority Literature?" *The CEA Critic* 36 (May 1974): 3–8.

Honour, Hugh, and John Fleming. *A World History of Art.* London: Macmillan, 1982.

Morse, J. Mitchell. "Are English Teachers Obsolete?" *The CEA Critic* 36 (May 1974): 9–18.

Scarry, Elaine. *Dreaming By the Book.* Princeton, NJ: Princeton University Press, 2001.

——. *On Beauty and Being Just.* Princeton, NJ: Princeton University Press, 2001.

Sontag, Susan. "Against Interpretation." *The Evergreen Review,* 1964. Reprinted in *Against Interpretation and Other Essays.* New York: Dell, 1969.

Steiner, Wendy. *The Scandal of Pleasure: Art in an Age of Fundamentalism.* Chicago, Ill.: University of Chicago Press, 1997.

——. *Venus in Exile: The Rejection of Beauty in Twentieth-Century Art.* Chicago, Ill.: University of Chicago Press, 2002.

Touster, Eva. "Tradition and the Academic Talent." *The CEA Critic* 33 (May 1971): 14–17.

~

Traditional Approaches

I. A NOTE ON TRADITIONAL APPROACHES

The study of literature was once only the study of Greek and Roman classics. When literature in English began to be taught toward the end of the nineteenth century, it was viewed then not as entertainment but as a source of moral uplift, history, and biography. (American literature was not taught in universities until the 1920s.) If "To His Coy Mistress" were taught, students would learn all about Marvell's pol- *A themes itics, religion, character, and career. His historical milieu would be noted and the *in Lt competing worlds of the monarchy and the commonwealth would be mentioned. This sort of traditional approach is today called the "old" historicism, as opposed to recent theories such as the "new" historicism (more on this in Chapter 4). Suffice it to say that today when the traditional approaches of biographical and historical interest are invoked, they are contrasted to a more nuanced, politicized, and socially aware sense of history and literature in our postmodernist times. Different conceptions of historical criticism are followed today, which can be biographical in orientation, can judge the work according to its **mimetic** accuracy, or can explore the difficulties of transhistorical interpretation. Once upon a time, referring to poetry of "the Elizabethan Age," a "Georgian" or "Victorian" poet, or a "Restoration" dramatist was a way of definitively classifying a text by the particular king or queen who happened to be upon the throne, so that authors were identified with periods of literature that corresponded to cycles of political, national, and royal periods. Another preoccupation was what is called "source study." Not the poem itself but the **allusions** to other, older literary works was considered important. Shakespeare could best be understood, for example, by his literary ancestry: Aristotle, Sophocles, the Bible, Seneca, Chaucer, and so on. However, as literature became more and more studied for itself, and not for what it reflects about a time in history or the life of the author, the traditional approaches were replaced by more text-centered analyses such as formalism, most often called the "New Criticism" in honor of its mid-twentieth-century innovators. And then eventually, as historical cycles always teach us, things changed again; theoretical and critical trends left the notion of the text as an independent aesthetic entity and returned to a renewed interest in contexts. As we will see, later approaches, especially new historicism, cultural and ethnic studies, and postcolonialism, return to history and biography but with significantly revised ideas of what texts tell us about their contexts—indeed, how "context" can be seen as a primary fact about any given text. Other traditional approaches, such as textual studies or source study, have remained fairly constant in literary criticism as foundations for further analysis, just as the precritical approach is a foundation for everything that comes after.

The New Criticism emerged in the mid-twentieth century to approach the text formalistically as a separate entity divorced from extrinsic considerations; this became the dominant concern of scholars. The New Critics insisted that scholars concentrate on the work itself, on the text, examining it as art. This method revolutionized the study of literature. It frequently divided critics and teachers into opposing factions: those of the older school, for whom literature provided primarily an opportunity for exercising what they perceived to be the really relevant scholarly and cultural disciplines (for example, history, linguistics, and biography) and the New Critics, who maintained that literature had an intrinsic worth, that it was not just one of the means of transmitting biography and history. New Criticism put into clearer focus what a poem or play or piece of fiction is trying to do; it has unquestionably corrected many wrongheaded interpretations resulting from an unwise use of the older method. To this extent it has expanded our perception and appreciation of literary art.

Nevertheless, in their zeal to avoid the danger of interpreting a literary work solely as biography and history, many twentieth-century followers of New Criticism were guilty of what may well be a more serious mistake, that of ignoring any information not in the work itself, however helpful or necessary it might be. Fortunately, the most astute critics have espoused a more eclectic approach and have fused a variety of techniques. They have certainly insisted on treating literature as literature, but they have also sought further illumination from nonformalist approaches such as New Historicism and Cultural Studies. Oscar Cargill, in the introduction to his *Toward a Pluralistic Criticism,* endorsed the eclectic approach unequivocally. "The critic's task is to procure a viable meaning appropriate to the critic's time and place. Practically, this meant employing not any one method in interpreting a work of art but every method which might prove efficient" (xii–xiv).

As Art Beyer, in *From the New Criticism to Deconstruction: The Reception of Structuralism and Post-Structuralism,* and others have pointed out, many of the most influential (and current) theories of literary criticism owe at least part of their inspiration to formalism and the New Critics, including structuralism (especially in the United States), poststructuralism, and deconstruction. (Even new historicists have made reading closely—as in between the lines—their first step in approaching a text.) For example, the "play of language" prized by followers of deconstructionist Jacques Derrida is first and foremost dependent upon (very) close reading. However, the New Critics seem almost simplistic when contrasted

Las Meniñas: Traditional Perspectives

Diego Velázquez (1599–1660) was a Spanish Baroque painter and the official artist of the court of King Philip IV. Besides many paintings of historical and cultural significance, he painted dozens of portraits of the Spanish royal family, other notable European figures, and commoners. His masterpiece, *Las Meniñas,* painted near the end of his life, is one of the most widely analyzed works in Western painting.

Painters in seventeenth-century Spain were thought of mostly as craftsmen, as distinct from an "artist" of poetry or music. However Velázquez became close to the king and arose through the ranks to gain the title of palace chamberlain (*Aposentador mayor del palacio*), which offered him security and material reward; as chamberlain, he was in charge of all the art in the Alcázar, the Spanish royal palace in Madrid. Velázquez was widely respected in Spain as a connoisseur. Much of the collection of the Prado museum in Madrid today—including works by Titian, Raphael, and Rubens—was acquired and assembled under Velázquez's curatorship.

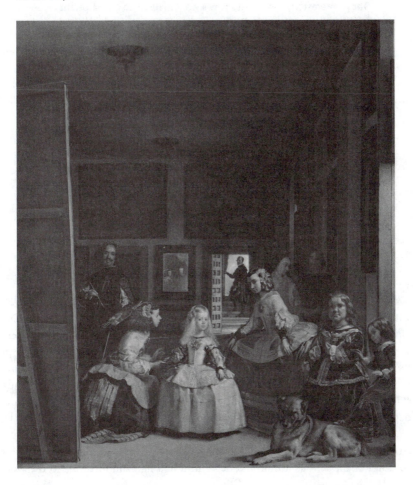

Velázquez painted many portraits of Queen Mariana and her children, but the king himself refused to be painted in his old age, though he did allow Velázquez to include him in *Las Meniñas*. He loaned Velázquez the Pieza Principal ("main room") of the late Prince Baltasar Carlos's living quarters, then serving as the palace museum, to use as his studio. It is here that *Las Meniñas* is set. Philip would sometimes sit in and watch Velázquez at work. He mourned him when he died.

This work, painted in 1656, was in the Alcázar of Madrid until the fire of 1734; later it went to the Palacio Nuevo rebuilt on the site. At the beginning of the nineteenth century, it was placed in the Real Museo de Pintura y Escultura (Museo del Prado), together with other works coming from the royal collections. Royals called the painting many names: "La Señora Emperatriz con sus damas y una enana" and "La familia del Señor Rey Phelipe Quarto." Once in the museum, it was catalogued as "*Las Meniñas*." Meniñas is a Portuguese word used to name the maids of honor of royal children in the seventeenth century. This title is significant, since technically it does not refer to the Infanta (or princess) in the center of the painting, but rather to her ladies in waiting, Doña Isabel de Velasco and Doña Maria Augustina Sarmiento.

Those interested in source study will want to research an important influence on Velázquez, Jan van Eyck's *Arnolfini Portrait* (1434), which by Velázquez's time hung in Philip's palace; thus it would have been familiar to Velázquez. The *Arnolfini Portrait* also has a mirror positioned at the back of the pictorial space, reflecting two figures who seem to be standing in the doorway. *Las Meniñas* was a strong influence on another Spanish painter, Francisco Goya (1746–1828), who etched a print of *Las Meniñas* in 1778. In 1879, American painter John Singer Sargent (1856–1925) painted a small-scale copy of *Las Meniñas*, and in 1882 painted a homage to the painting in his *The Daughters of Edward Darley Boit*. In 1957, Pablo Picasso painted his versions of *Las Meniñas*.

Questions: All of the characters in the painting correspond to real persons, except possibly the unidentified chaperone. What can we find out about these people? What are their individual biographies and histories, and how would these help us interpret the painting? What were their interrelationships? What was Philip IV best known for, and what were the cultural and historic conditions of his reign? As court painter, what was Velázquez's attitude toward his patron? In terms of art history, the painting is in the Baroque style. What were the conventions of this style, and how does the painting both fulfill them and challenge them?

---

with the intellectual gymnastics of deconstructionists—even more, the New Critical belief in elements that composed a unified text is refuted by the deconstructionist assertion that there is no such thing as a single or unified text, despite its formal intricacies. Contrary to the New Criticism, deconstruction sets out to identify not how the text before us is complete and an end unto itself, but to understand that no text is ever "complete" in and of itself, that every text's "meaning" depends on many other texts before and beyond it in a limitless linguistic web of competing signs and **tropes** and allusions and borrowings. Thus the deconstructionist, though influenced by New Criticism, wishes to move outside of the confines of the text as a unit and delve into its linguistic relations to the world, expanding the purview of the "text itself" and showing that there is a lot more going on in reading than is immediately or traditionally apparent.

In any event, if literature is primarily art, art does not exist in a vacuum. It is a creation by someone at some time in history, and it is intended to speak to other human beings about some idea or issue that has human relevance. Its greatness comes from the fact that when sensitive minds bring all their information, experience, and feeling to contemplate it, they are moved and impressed by its beauty, by its unique kind of knowledge, and by its nonaesthetic values. It is surely dangerous to assume that a work of art must always be judged or looked at or taught as if it were disembodied from all experience except the strictly aesthetic. Many literary classics are autobiographical, propagandistic, or topical (that is, related to contemporary events). These concerns are, in fact, central to the most recent theoretical approaches.

✗ Treat literature as an art not a science

II. TEXTUAL SCHOLARSHIP, GENRES, AND SOURCE STUDY

A. Textual Scholarship: Do We Have an Accurate Version of What We Are Studying?

1. General Observations

Before we embark upon any interpretive ventures, we should look to that branch of literary studies known as textual criticism. In the words of James Thorpe, author of one of the best modern books on the subject, *Principles of Textual Criticism*, textual criticism has as its ideal the establishment of an *authentic* text, or the "text which the author intended" (50). This aim is not so easy to achieve as one might think, however, and it is a problem not only with older works, where it might be more expected, but also in contemporary literature. There are countless ways in which a literary text may be corrupted from what the author intended. The author's own manuscript may contain omissions and errors in spelling and mechanics; these mistakes may be preserved by the text copyists, be they scribes, or compositors, or scanners, who may add a few of their own. Or, as has often happened, copyists or editors may take it upon themselves to improve, censor, or correct what the author wrote. If the author or someone who knows what the author intended does not catch these errors during proofreading, they can be published, disseminated, and perpetuated. (Nor does it help matters when authors themselves cannot decide what the final form of their work is to be but actually release for publication several different versions or, as is frequently the case, delegate broad editorial powers to others along the line.) So many additional mishaps can befall a manuscript in the course of producing multiple copies for the public that, to quote Thorpe again, the "ordinary history of the transmission of a text, without the intervention of author or editor, is one of progressive degeneration" (51).

We frequently assume that the text before us has come down unchanged from its original form. More often than not, the reverse is the case; what we see is the result of painstaking collation of **textual variants**, interpretation, and **emendation** or conjecture. Because it is pointless to study inaccurate versions of anything, from economic theories to works of literature, except with a view to ascertaining the true (that is, the authorial) version, our debt to textual criticism is well-nigh incalculable. For example, the student who uses the eight-volume Chicago edition of *The Canterbury Tales,* a collation of scores of medieval manuscripts, should certainly appreciate the efforts of precomputer scholars. Similarly, over the years the studies of W. W. Greg, A. W. Pollard, Fredson Bowers, Charlton Hinman, Stanley Wells, Garry Taylor, and a host of others have gone far toward the establishment of a satisfactory Shakespearean text. This type of scholarship should create in the student a healthy respect for textual criticism and expert editing, and well it might, for as Thorpe has aptly phrased it, "where there is no editing the texts perish" (54).

Textual criticism plays an especially important role in studying the genesis and development of a piece of literature. Thus it has enabled us to see how Ezra Pound's editorial surgery transformed T. S. Eliot's *The Waste Land* from a clumsy and diffuse poem to a modern classic. The poem still presents textual problems, however, because Eliot himself authorized versions containing substantive differences (students may be familiar with the concept of a "director's cut" of a film—the principle is similar.) Other, famous textual cases include Dickens's two endings for *Great Expectations:* after seeing the first "unhappy" ending in proof, Dickens wrote another and authorized only it. Later editors have published the first version as having more aesthetic integrity, but Dickens never approved it. Thomas Hardy made so many substantive character and plot alterations in the four versions of *The Return of the Native,* all of which he authorized for publication between 1878 and 1912, that James Thorpe understandably asks, "Which is the real *Return of the Native*?" (34). Henry James revised all of his work toward the end of his life in the New York Edition; it makes a great difference which text, early or late, of a given James story or novel one reads. Controversy over which of several texts is the "authentic" text of Mary Shelley's *Frankenstein* continues today. Moreover, textual criticism is, contrary to what ill-informed people may think, anything but an essentially mechanical operation. Although its practitioners are very much concerned with such matters as spelling, punctuation, capitalization, italicization, and paragraphing (**accidentals**, as they are called in textual criticism) in the establishment of an authentic text, they deal with much more than close proofreading. They must be highly skilled in linguistics, literary history, literary criticism, and **bibliography**, to mention only the most obvious areas.

However, though textual critics must and do make aesthetic judgments, not only in accidentals but also in **substantives** (actual readings), they do so in order to establish by means as scientific as possible an authentic text for the literary critic, who may then proceed to interpret and evaluate. Textual criticism is therefore treated in this book not as a traditional interpretive approach to literature but as an indispensable tool for further meaningful analysis. This relationship between textual and strictly interpretive criticism may be expressed in a surgical **metaphor**: textual critics are the first in a team of critics who prepare the literary corpus for further study. Nevertheless, we should not push any analogy between textual criticism and science too far. Textual critics are not and should not be considered scientists. They have no predetermined or inviolable laws that they can use to come out with an authentic text. Perhaps it would be more accurate to concede that textual critics are scientists of sorts; they simply are not exact scientists. They are, more precisely, a combination of scientist and artist. As A. E. Housman says, textual criticism is the "science of discovering error in texts and the art of removing it" (2).

Thorpe, however, is highly critical of any scientific claims for textual criticism. Indeed, one of the main points of his book is the failure of textual studies to measure up to their alleged scientific status. Somewhat resignedly he concludes:

> It would be cheerful to be able to report that a mastery of sound principles, an application of effective methods, and an exercise of conscientious care will enable the textual critic to reach the ideal which is incorporated in the first principle of his craft. But it would not be true. In textual criticism, the best that one can do is to cut the losses, to reduce the amount of error, to improve or clarify the state of textual affairs, to approach the ideal. After all has been done that can be done, however, the results of textual criticism still are necessarily imperfect. (55)

All critics can agree on one thing: it is far more preferable to have a version of a literary work that textual criticism can make available to us than to have one that has not been subjected to the rigorous methodology of that discipline.

Another especially thorough and incisive discussion of this subject is D. C. Greetham's *Textual Scholarship: An Introduction*. In addition to a narrative account of the history of the field, there are explanations and illustrations covering the spectrum of textual scholarship. And, though it deals with such technical material as enumerative and research bibliography, descriptive and analytical bibliography, **paleography** and **typography**, historical and textual bibliography, textual criticism and textual theory, and scholarly editing, Greetham's book is as accessible to the nonspecialist undergraduate as it is to the literary scholar and editor.

2. Text Study in Practice

a. "To His Coy Mistress" Textual problems in Andrew Marvell's "To His Coy Mistress" set the stage for our consideration of the poem. One of these problems is the last word in this **couplet**:

> Now therefore, while the youthful hue
> Sits on thy skin like morning dew.

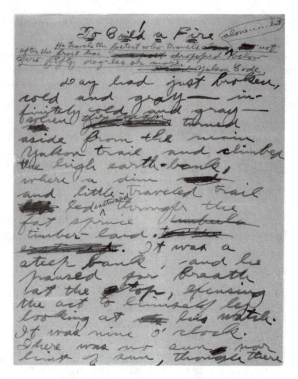

Figure 2.1. Manuscript page one of Jack London's "To Build a Fire" (1908).
Courtesy of the Huntington Library.

Instead of "dew," the first edition of the poem had "glew," which we now know is a dialectal variant of "glow," although it was earlier thought to be another spelling of "glue," a senseless reading in the context. "Lew" (dialectal "warmth") was also suggested as a possibility. But when someone conjectured "dew," probably in the eighteenth century, it was apparently so happy an emendation that virtually all textbooks have long printed it without any explanation. The first edition of this handbook followed those textbooks. But two modern texts restore the earliest reading. Both Louis Martz's *Anchor Anthology of Seventeenth-Century Verse* and George de F. Lord's *Andrew Marvell, Complete Poetry* print "glew" (meaning "glow") as making more sense in the context and being quite sound linguistically. Two other words in the poem that must be explained are "transpires" and "instant" in this couplet:

> And while thy willing soul transpires
> At every pore with instant fires.

In each case, the word is much nearer to its Latin original than to its twenty-first-century meaning. "Transpires" thus means literally "breathes forth," and "instant" means "now present" and "urgent." Admittedly, this sort of linguistic information borders on the technical, but an appreciation of the meaning of the words is imperative for a full understanding of the poem.

b. Hamlet Few literary works have received the amount and degree of textual study as Shakespeare's *Hamlet*. There are some obvious reasons for this. To begin with, in Shakespeare's day copyright laws did not always protect authors. When a manuscript of his play was produced upon the stage, people would attend again and again and try to copy down the words and stage directions, then print up their version and sell it. **Quarto**-sized editions of his plays appeared, some sanctioned and some not. Sometimes printed versions were changed by the compositor (the person who selected each letter of type for each line on pages that were to be printed). It is interesting to note that illiterate compositors were preferred, exactly so that they would not do this. Not until after Shakespeare's death was the first "authentic" text published by his friends and called the *First Folio*. But even the earliest crude printings, shot through with the grossest errors, revealed a story and a mind that excited and challenged viewers, producers, readers, critics, and scholars—so much so that the scholars decided to do everything possible to ascertain what Shakespeare actually wrote. The other reasons are all related to this one. Shakespearean editors ever since have realized the importance of establishing an accurate text if students and audiences are to discover the meaning of *Hamlet*.

It is difficult at this remove in time for college students embarking on a serious reading of *Hamlet* to realize that the beautiful anthology or the handy paperback before them, each edited by an eminent authority, contains the product of nearly four hundred years of scholarly study of four different versions of *Hamlet* and that it still includes some moot and debatable readings. Besides questionable readings, there are a number of words whose meanings have changed over the years but that must be understood in their Elizabethan senses if the play is to be properly interpreted. To be sure, modern editors explain the most difficult words, but occasionally they let some slip by or fail to note that reputable scholars differ. Obviously, it is not possible to point out all the variants of a given passage or to give the seventeenth-century meaning of every puzzling construction, but the student can catch at least a glimpse of the multiplicity and the richness of interpretations by examining some of the more famous ones.

One of the best-known examples of such textual problems occurs in act I, scene ii: "O that this too too solid flesh would melt." This is perhaps the most common rendering of this line. The word "solid" appears in the first **folio** edition (1623) of Shakespeare's complete works. Yet the second quarto edition (1604–5), probably printed from Shakespeare's own manuscript, has "sallied," a legitimate sixteenth-century form of "sully" (to dirty, or make foul). These words pose two rather different interpretations of the line: if one reads "solid," the line seems to mean that Hamlet regrets the corporeality of the flesh and longs for bodily dissolution in order to escape the pain and confusion of fleshly existence. If, on the other hand, one reads "sullied," the line apparently reveals Hamlet's horror and revulsion upon contemplating the impurity of life and, by extension, his own involvement

Figure 2.2. William Shakespeare, *First Folio* (1623).
Courtesy Fine Books Division, Dallas Public Library.

in it through the incest of his mother. In 1935, J. Dover Wilson, in *What Happens in "Hamlet,"* saw "sullied flesh" as the clue to many significant passages in the play (Hamlet's line "foul as Vulcan's stithy," his preoccupation with sexuality, particularly with the sexual nature of his mother's crime; and his strange conduct toward Ophelia and Polonius). This view becomes even more credible when one considers Hamlet's seemingly incomprehensible remark to Polonius in act II, scene ii, where he calls the old man a "fishmonger" (Elizabethan slang for "pimp"); implies that Ophelia is a prostitute by referring in the same speech to "carrion" (Elizabethan "flesh" in the carnal sense); and warns Polonius not to let her "walk i' the sun" (that is, get too close to the "son" of Denmark, the heir apparent, he of the "sullied flesh" and "foul" imagination). Wilson explains Hamlet's ambiguous remark as obscene because Hamlet is angry that Polonius would stoop to "loose" his daughter to him (as stockmen "loose" cows and mares to bulls and stallions to be bred) in order to wheedle from him the secret of his behavior, and he is angry and disgusted that his beloved would consent to be used in this way. Hence his later obscenities to her, as in act III, scene i, when he tells her repeatedly to go to a "nunnery" (Elizabethan slang for "brothel").

One final example must suffice to illustrate the importance of textual accuracy. In the second quarto the speeches of the officiant at Ophelia's funeral are headed "Doct." This is probably "Doctor of Divinity," the term that one editor of *Hamlet,* Cyrus Hoy, inserted in the stage directions (86). The "Doctor of Divinity" reading was one reason for J. Dover Wilson's asserting positively that Ophelia's funeral was a Protestant service, contrary to the way directors often stage it. Indeed, the point seems to be relevant, because it affects one's interpretation of the play. Although Shakespeare used anachronisms whenever they suited his purpose, a careless disregard of facts and logic was not typical of him. For example, both Hamlet and Horatio are students at Wittenberg. That this university was founded several hundred years after the death of the historical Hamlet is beside the point. What does seem important is that Wittenberg was the university of Martin Luther and a strong center of Protestantism. It is not unreasonable to assume, then, that Shakespeare wanted his audience to think of eleventh-century Denmark as a Protestant country (it was so in his day)—indeed that he wanted the entire drama to be viewed in contemporary perspective.

c. Huckleberry Finn To Twain's good ear and appreciation of the dramatic value of **dialect** we owe not only authentic and subtle shadings of class, race, and personality, but also, as Lionel Trilling has said, a "classic prose" that moves with "simplicity, directness, lucidity, and grace" (xvii). T. S. Eliot called this an "innovation, a new discovery in the English language," an entire book written in the natural **prose** rhythms of conversation, what is called the **vernacular**. This linguistic innovation is certainly one of the features to which Ernest Hemingway referred when he said that "all modern American literature comes from one book by Mark Twain called *Huckleberry Finn*" (22). If we agree with Hemingway, we can think of Twain as the "father of modern American literature."

Huckleberry Finn has an interesting textual history that space will allow us only to touch on here. Writing in a frontier dialect, Twain was trying, with what success we have just seen, to capture in both pronunciation and vocabulary the spirit of the times from the lips of contemporary people. Nevertheless, some of his editors (for example, Richard Watson Gilder of the *Century Magazine,* William Dean Howells, and especially Twain's wife Olivia) **bowdlerized** and prettified those passages they thought "too coarse or vulgar" for Victorian ears, in certain cases with Twain's full consent. It is a minor miracle that this censoring, though it has taken something from the verisimilitude of the novel, seems not to have harmed it materially. Hamlin Hill and Walter Blair's *The Art of "Huckleberry Finn"* is an excellent succinct treatment of the textual history of this novel. Also, Henry B. Wonham provides an examination of Twain's use of his own life and his earlier works in *Huckleberry Finn,* a discussion with intriguing textual implications.

The definitive critical edition of Mark Twain's writings—fiction, letters, notes, private papers—is that of the University of California Press. Begun in the early 1970s at the university's Bancroft Library, the Mark Twain Project will ultimately include an estimated seventy volumes, of which more than thirty are in print early in the twenty-first century. The *Huckleberry Finn* volume of 2003, edited by Victor Fischer and Lin Salamo, contains complete textual information.

d. "Young Goodman Brown" Textually, "Young Goodman Brown," first published in 1835 in the *New England Magazine,* presents relatively few problems. Obsolete words in the story like "wot'st" (know), "Goody" (Goodwife, or Mrs.), and "Goodman" (Mr.) are defined in most desk dictionaries, and none of the other words has undergone radical semantic change. Nevertheless, as we have seen, although a literary work may have been written in a day when printing had reached a high degree of accuracy, a perfect text is by no means a foregone conclusion. With Hawthorne, as with other authors, scholars are constantly working toward more accurate texts.

For example, the first edition of this handbook used a version of "Young Goodman Brown" that contained at least two substantive variants. About three-fourths of the way through the story the phrase "unconcerted wilderness" appeared. In 1962, David Levin pointed out that nineteen years after Hawthorne's death, a version of the story edited by George P. Lathrop printed "unconcerted" for the first time: every version before then, including Hawthorne's last revision, had had "unconverted." In that same paragraph the first edition of this handbook printed "figure" as opposed to "apparition," the word that Levin tells us occurred in the first published versions of the story (346, n.8). Obviously, significant interpretive differences could hinge on which words are employed in these contexts.

e. "Everyday Use" "Everyday Use" is an exceptionally well-crafted piece of writing. By the time of its publication in 1973, authors had long been submitting to commercial presses polished typescripts generated on electric typewriters.

Consequently, we do not have textual variants of "Everyday Use" in different editions over a span of time as was common in earlier periods. The closest thing we have to a critical edition of the story—like the Norton Critical Editions—is from Barbara T. Christian's *Women Writers Series*. This edition includes an introduction to and a chronology of Alice Walker's work, the text and background of the story, six critical essays, and a bibliography. The popularity of the story is attested by the frequency with which it appears in collections. Between 1975 and 2000, no fewer than twelve anthologies carried it, including *Major American Short Stories*, edited by A. Walton Litz. It could be interesting to note whether this frequency leads to unintentional textual variants in the future.

f. Frankenstein A discussion of textual matters in *Frankenstein* raises a number of provocative issues. There are two principal editions of the novel, one in 1818 and one in 1831. The authors of this handbook have chosen to cite the first one in our discussions.

The 1818 edition, according to James Rieger, bore witness to the influence of Mary Shelley's husband, the poet Percy Bysshe Shelley, at every stage of its composition—in the correction of grammatical errors, the polishing of the **diction**, even the train of the narrative. One such suggestion led to Victor Frankenstein's going to England to create a female mate for the monster. Percy also made changes in the last half dozen pages of the novel, wrote the Preface to the book, and in 1817, before the book finally went to the publisher, received from his wife "carte blanche to make what alterations you please." Rieger concluded that "[Percy's] assistance at every point in the book's manufacture was so extensive that one hardly knows whether to regard him as editor or minor collaborator" (xviii).

This is not the reason we prefer the 1818 version, for to the contrary, Mary wrote in the Introduction to the other principal edition of the novel (1831) (somewhat disingenuously to be sure), "I certainly did not owe the suggestion of one incident, nor scarcely of one train of feeling, to my husband..." (quoted in Rieger 229). She did except the Preface, which was "*As far as [she could] recollect....* entirely written by him" (emphasis ours). Yet Rieger labels even this claim a "distortion" (xvii).

Rieger collated the first and second editions and demonstrated that significant variants radically changed the second. Even though it is a convention in textual scholarship that an author's final changes produce the most authentic text, in this case Rieger opts for the first edition, judging Mary's emendations "slightly FOR THE WORSE." Rieger does concede that the philosophical question of textual editing in this instance is "perhaps insoluble" (xliii– xliv).

Rieger's more recent argument for using the 1818 edition comes from materials included by J. Paul Hunter in his edition of the 1818 text. In his preface Hunter states emphatically that "Scholarship now strongly prefers the first edition..." (xii). He directs our attention to two essays of a textual nature that he includes in his volume: M. K. Joseph, "The Composition of *Frankenstein*," and Anne K. Mellor, "Choosing a Text of *Frankenstein* to Teach." Particularly helpful in alerting us to the challenges of textual study and pointing to the usefulness of the 1818 text is the following passage from Mellor, who took the extra step of reviewing the manuscript:

> The remarkable shifts in both diction and philosophical conception between the three versions of *Frankenstein*—the manuscript, the 1818 edition, and the 1831 edition—make this an ideal text for use in courses in either text editing or the theory of the text itself. From the perspective of deconstructive literary criticism, *Frankenstein* exemplifies what Julia Kristeva has called "the questionable subject-in-progress," both a text and an author without stable boundaries. For students who have time to consult only one text, the 1818 text alone presents a stable and coherent conception of the character of Victor Frankenstein and of Mary Shelley's political and moral ideology. (166)

In contrast to Rieger, by comparing the three versions, including the manuscript, Mellor persuasively argues that Percy's intrusions into the manuscript departed from what she perceives as Mary's main purposes, mainly by making changes designed to elevate Mary's prose and, most importantly, to lessen Victor's blame. Yet the 1818 edition, she believes, is still closer to Mary's personal and political experiences of the early part of the century; by the 1831 edition, she notes, Percy was dead, and Mary seemed to want to memorialize him and further ameliorate the situations in the book that cast blame on Victor, whom she associated with Percy. Even more recently, in order to present the earliest recoverable version of the novel, in 2008 Charles E. Robinson published the original two-volume version of 1816–1817 from Mary's original manuscripts housed at the Bodleian Library at Oxford University. Robinson's book contains two sections: first, the manuscript draft with Percy's editing, then Mary's original draft.

B.   Matters of Genre: What Are We Dealing With?

1.   An Overview of Genre

No better overview of **genre**, at least in a traditional and historically significant way, can be gleaned than what we gain from a study of Aristotle's *Poetics* (fourth century B.C.). Few works of literary criticism can hope to wear so well, or so long. Our theories of **drama** and of the **epic**, the recognition of genres as a way of studying a piece of literature, and our methodology of studying a work or group of works and then inducing theory from practice—all can find beginnings in the *Poetics*. More specifically, from the *Poetics* we have such basic notions of **tragedy** as **catharsis**; the characteristics of the tragic **hero** (the noble figure; tragic pride, or **hubris**; the tragic flaw); the formative elements of drama (action or plot, character, thought [theme], diction, melody, and spectacle [special effects]); the necessary unity of plot; and, perhaps most significantly, the basic concept of mimesis, or imitation, the idea that works of literature are imitations of actions, the differences among them resulting from means, objects, and manner.

In practice, readers may be Aristotelian when they distinguish one genre from another, when they question whether Arthur Miller's Willy Loman can be tragic or affirm that Melville's Ahab is, when they stress plot rather than character or

diction, or when they stress the mimetic role of literature. In formal criticism, readers will do well to study Matthew Arnold's 1853 preface to his poems as a notable example of Aristotelian criticism in the nineteenth century. In the twentieth century one critic, Stanley Edgar Hyman, has said that the "ideal critic" would be neo-Aristotelian if he or she "scrupulously [induced] from practice" (387).

In fact, in the first half of the twentieth century, there was something of a revival of what might be called Aristotelian criticism, centered at the University of Chicago during the 1940s. Reacting against the rise of the New Critics as "critical monists" (see Chapter 3, on formalist criticism), the movement called for an openness of critical perspectives, a "plurality" of methods, and advocated using Aristotle's principles comprehensively and systematically enough to be developed beyond what Aristotle himself had set down. (For essays that bear on this effort, see those collected by Ronald S. Crane, *Critics and Criticism: Ancient and Modern.*)

Having thus grounded ourselves, if ever so slightly, in Aristotelianism, let us now pursue the topic of genres a bit more.

Genre criticism—criticism of "kinds" or "types"—is a traditional way of approaching a piece of literature. However, like some other traditional approaches, genre criticism has been given revitalized attention in modern times, modifying what was accepted as genre criticism for some two thousand years.

Since the time of the classical Greeks and especially during the **neoclassical** period of the eighteenth century, it was assumed that if readers knew into what genre or form a piece of literature fell, they knew much about the work itself. Is it a drama, **novel,** or **short story**? Put simply, Athenian citizens going to see a play by Sophocles knew in advance that the story would be acted out by a small group of actors, that they would be seeing and hearing a **chorus** as part of the production, and that a certain kind of music would accompany the chorus. When Virgil set out to write an epic for Augustan Rome, he chose to work within the genre that he knew already from Homer. According to the conventions of epic, he announced his theme in his opening line, he set his hero out on journeys and placed him in combat situations, he saw to it that the gods were involved as they had been in the *Iliad* and the *Odyssey,* and in the two halves of his *Aeneid* he even provided actions that were roughly parallel to the actions of the *Odyssey* (journey) and the *Iliad* (warfare). Because Alexander Pope and his readers were schooled in the classics, and the genres of classic literature, his neoclassical **parody** of the epic was easily recognizable in his mock-epic, *The Rape of the Lock.* Pope took the conventions of the epic genre and deliberately reversed them: the epic theme is "mighty contests" arising from "trivial things"; the hero is a flirtatious woman with her appropriate "arms"; the journey is to Hampton Court, a place of socializing and gossip; the battle is joined over a card table, with the cards as troops; the epic weapon is a pair of scissors; the epic boast is about cutting off a lock of hair.

Such are the kinds of observations that traditional genre criticism could provide. It held sway through the eighteenth century. It was less vital as a form of criticism in the nineteenth century, although the conventional types, such as drama, **lyric,** and **romance,** were still recognized and useful for terminology, as they still are. In more recent times, however, new interest has been developed in genre criticism, especially in theoretical matters.

Of major significance is Northrop Frye's *Anatomy of Criticism*. In his introduction Frye points to our debt to the Greeks for our terminology for and our distinctions among some genres, and he also notes that we have not gone much beyond what the Greeks gave us (13). This he proposes to correct in his anatomy. Although much of his book is **archetypal** criticism, and hence has relevance for Chapter 7, much of it—especially the first essay, "Historical Criticism: Theory of Modes," and the fourth essay, "Rhetorical Criticism: Theory of Genres"—also bears upon genre criticism. Calling attention to the "origin of the words drama, epic and lyric," Frye says that the "central principle of genre is simple enough. The basis of generic distinctions in literature appears to be the radical of presentation. Words may be acted in front of a spectator; they may be spoken in front of a listener; they may be sung or chanted; or they may be written for the reader" (246–47). Later he says, "The purpose of criticism by genres is not so much to classify as to clarify such traditions and affinities, thereby bringing out a large number of literary relationships that would not be noticed as long as there were no context established for them" (247–48). On the face of it these passages, though helpful, are not much different from what Aristotle offered in the *Poetics*, but on such bases Frye ranges far and wide (much more than we can here suggest) in his study of modes and genres, classifying, describing, dividing, subdividing.

Monumental as the work is, it provoked mixed responses, and we may cite two works that differ from Frye's, sometimes explicitly, as they also offer other insights into genre criticism.

E. D. Hirsch's *Validity in Interpretation* makes only small reference to Frye and presents (among other things) a quite different approach to genre criticism (Chapter 3, "The Concept of Genre"). Less concerned with the extensive anatomizing of literature and of literary criticism (Hirsch implies that Frye's classification is "illegitimate" [110–11]), Hirsch insists on the individuality of any given work. More important, he shows again and again how the reader's understanding of meaning is dependent on the reader's accurate perception of the genre that the author intended as he wrote the work. (Hirsch is not, however, thinking simplistically of short story, for example, in contrast to **masque**, epic, or the like.) If the reader assumes that a work is in one genre but it is really in another, only misreading can result: "An interpreter's notion of the type of meaning he confronts will powerfully influence his understanding of details. This phenomenon will recur at every level of sophistication and is the primary reason for disagreements among qualified interpreters" (75). And again: "Understanding can occur only if the interpreter proceeds under the same system of expectations" as the speaker or writer (80). Readers of Jonathan Swift's "A Modest Proposal" who did not understand his use of **satire** probably thought him a madman for advocating English consumption of Irish babies. For if readers do not recognize conventions, they are reading at best at a superficial level. As Hirsch says, "every shared type of meaning [every genre] can be defined as a system of conventions" (92). Elsewhere, Hirsch is helpful in showing that when we read a work with which we are not previously familiar or read a work that is creating a new genre, we operate ("triangulate") by moving back and forth from what we know to what we do not know well yet.

Still another work that qualifies Frye's treatment of genres while offering its own insights (though basically on fiction) is Robert Scholes's *Structuralism in Literature.* Scholes's discussion (117–41) is closer to Frye's than is Hirsch's, but it brings to the treatment not only qualifications of Frye's classifications but also the influences of recent work in structuralism (see Chapter 5), whereas Frye's emphasis is archetypal and rhetorical.

All three of these works—those of Frye, Hirsch, and Scholes—although they are challenging and stimulating, are sometimes difficult. Part of the difficulty when they are dealing with genres derives from the fact that pieces of literature do not simply and neatly fall into categories or genres (even the folk **ballad**, seemingly obvious as a narrative form, partakes of the lyric, and of the drama, the latter through its dialogue). This difficulty arises from the nature of literature itself: it is original, imaginative, creative, and hence individualistic. But regardless of literature's protean quality, our interpretation of it is easier if we can recognize a genre as a sort of road map, if we can therefore be provided with a set of expectations and conventions, and if we can then recognize when the expectations are fulfilled and when they are imaginatively adapted. One of the most beneficial aspects of engaging in genre criticism is that, in our efforts to decide into what genre a challenging piece falls, we come to experience the literature more fully. As Allen Rodway observes, "how we finally categorize the poem becomes irrelevant, for the fact of trying to categorize—even through the crudest approach—has brought us near enough to its individual qualities for genre-criticism to give way to something more subtle" (Rodway 91). In response to Jacques Derrida's 1980 attack on genre, more recent inquiries into genre have been carried out in the books and articles of Gérard Genette, Gary Saul Morson, Wendy Steiner, Daniel Chandler, Hayden White, Amy Devitt, and Carolyn Williams.

2. Genre Characteristics in Practice

a. "To His Coy Mistress" Most critics are careful to ascertain what literary type or genre they are dealing with, whether a poem (and if so, what particular kind), a drama, a novel, or a short story. This early step—the question "What are we dealing with?"—is highly necessary, because different literary genres are judged according to different standards. We do not expect, for example, the sweep and grandeur of an epic in a love lyric, nor do we expect the extent of detail or episodes in a short story that we find in a novel. From a technical and formal standpoint, we do expect certain features in particular genres, features so integral as to define and characterize the type (for example, **rhythm**, rhyme, narrative devices such as a **focal character**, and dramatic devices such as the **soliloquy**). The lyric, the genre to which "Coy Mistress" belongs, is a fairly brief poem characterized primarily by emotion, imagination, and subjectivity.

Having ascertained the genre and established the text, the employer of traditional methods of interpretation next determines what the poem says on the level of statement or its paraphrasable content. The reader discovers that this poem is a proposition, that is, an offer of sexual intercourse. At first it contains, however, little of the coarseness or crudity usually implied in the word *proposition*. On the contrary, though impassioned, it is graceful, sophisticated, even philosophical. The speaker, a courtier, has evidently urged an unsuccessful suit on a lady. Finding her reluctant, he is, as the poem opens, making use of his most eloquent "line." But it is a line that reveals him to be no common lover. It is couched in the form of an argument in three distinct parts, going something like this: (1) If we had all the time in the world, I could have no objection to even an indefinite postponement of your acceptance of my suit. (2) But the fact is we do not have much time at all; and once this phase of existence (that is, life) is gone, all our chances for love are gone. (3) Therefore the only conclusion that can logically follow is that we should love one another now, while we are young and passionate, and thus seize what pleasures we can in a world where time is all too short. After all, we know nothing about any future life and have only the grimmest observations of the effects of death.

This is, as a matter of fact, a specious argument, viewed from the rigorous standpoint of formal logic. The **fallacy** is called denying the antecedent, in this case the first part of the conditional statement beginning with "if." The argument goes like this: If we have all the time and space in the world, your coyness is innocent (not criminal). We do not have all the time and space in the world. Therefore, your coyness is not innocent. Both premises are true, and the conclusion is still false. The lady's coyness may not be innocent for other reasons besides the lovers' not having all the time and space in the world. The male arguer undoubtedly does not care whether his argument is valid or not as long as it achieves his purpose. As Pope so well expressed it in *The Rape of the Lock:*

> For when success a Lover's toil attends,
> Few ask, if fraud or force attained his ends. (2.33–34)

b. *Hamlet: Revenge Tragedy Par Excellence*

1. *The Genre*   The genre to which *Hamlet* belongs is the drama, surely among the very earliest literary forms; but it differs from all others in that it is created not primarily for readers but for beholders. It tells a story by means of characters who enact events on some kind of stage. Western drama has its sources in two places, both religious. The first is that of the ancient Greeks in their worship of Dionysus (ca. sixth century B.C.); the second, that of the liturgy in the medieval Christian church.

Scholars believe that the worship of Dionysus, god of wine and fertility, evolved into a rite wherein two lines of dancers moved rhythmically on each side of an altar (a permanent fixture on the Greek stage). These dancers chanted the praises of the god antiphonally until in the course of time one inspired dancer/chanter moved out of the chorus line and began intoning his own lines. From some such crude beginnings, it is thought that dialogue was born and worship developed into a dramatic presentation of the life of Dionysus. The word *drama* comes from the Greek: the verb means "to do" and the noun, "the deed." This etymology accords with Aristotle's description of drama as "imitated human action."

In similar fashion, medieval churchmen sought to portray Bible stories, including the life of Christ, to illiterate worshippers. These productions in the sanctuary eventually moved outdoors to become mystery plays (that is, those performed by a "myster" or trade guild), miracle plays, and morality plays.

Hamlet is a tragedy, a branch of drama that deals, according to Aristotle, with a "serious action," usually the downfall and resultant misery or death of a person of significance. (Since the late 1800s, high rank has not been a prerequisite for the tragic hero.) Prince Hamlet, the titular protagonist of Shakespeare's play, fulfills the requirements for so-called imperial tragedy, including the tragic flaw, which in an otherwise admirable disposition leads to **catastrophe**. More specifically, *Hamlet* is a revenge tragedy, a popular type in Elizabethan times. It derives from the work of Seneca, the classical Roman dramatist. The theme usually dealt with in Seneca was the revenge of a father for a son or vice versa, with the revenge being mandated by the ghost of the murdered man. The typical ingredients of the revenge tragedy that occur in *Hamlet* are hesitation of the hero, suicide, intrigue, real or pretended insanity, a scheming villain, philosophic soliloquies, sensational murders, and dead bodies on stage.

2. *A Summary of the Play*   The main lines of the plot of *Hamlet* are clear. Hamlet, Prince of Denmark and heir presumptive to the Danish throne, is grief-stricken and plunged into melancholy by the recent death of his father and the "o'erhasty" remarriage of his mother to her late husband's brother, who has succeeded to the throne. The ghost of the prince's father appears to him and reveals that he was murdered by his brother, who now occupies the throne and whom he describes as "incestuous" and "adulterate." Enjoining young Hamlet not to harm his mother, the ghost exhorts him to take revenge on the murderer. In order to ascertain beyond question the guilt of his uncle and subsequently to plot his revenge, Hamlet feigns madness. His sweetheart Ophelia and his former schoolfellows Rosencrantz and Guildenstern attempt to discover from him the secret of his "antic behavior" (Ophelia because her father, Polonius, has ordered her to do so, Rosencrantz and Guildenstern because the king has ordered them to do so). All are unsuccessful.

Before actually initiating his revenge, Hamlet wants to be sure it will hit the guilty person. To this end, he arranges for a company of traveling players to present a drama in the castle that will depict the murder of his father as the ghost has described it. When the king sees the crime reenacted, he cries out and rushes from the assembly. This action Hamlet takes to be positive proof of his uncle's guilt, and from this moment he awaits only the right opportunity to kill him. After the play, Hamlet visits his mother's apartment, where he mistakes Polonius for the king and kills him. The killing of Polonius drives Ophelia mad and also convinces the king that Hamlet is dangerous and should be gotten out of the way. He therefore sends Hamlet to England, accompanied by Rosencrantz and Guildenstern, ostensibly to collect tribute, but in reality to be murdered. However, Hamlet eludes this trap by substituting the names of his erstwhile schoolfellows on his own death warrant and escaping through the help of pirates. He reaches Denmark in time for the funeral of Ophelia, who has apparently drowned herself. Laertes, her brother, has returned from Paris vowing vengeance on Hamlet for the death of his father. The king helps Laertes by arranging a fencing match between the two young men and seeing to it that Laertes's weapon is naked and poisoned. To make doubly sure that Hamlet will not escape, the king also poisons a bowl of wine from which Hamlet will be sure to drink. During the match, Laertes wounds Hamlet, the rapiers change hands, and Hamlet wounds Laertes; the queen drinks the poisoned wine; and Laertes confesses his part in the treachery to Hamlet, who then stabs the king to death. All the principals are thus dead, and young Fortinbras of Norway becomes king of Denmark.

c. Huckleberry Finn *Huckleberry Finn* is a novel—that is, an extended prose narrative dealing with characters within the framework of a plot. Such a work is usually fictitious, but both characters and situations or events may be drawn from real life. It may emphasize action or adventure (for example, *Treasure Island* or mystery stories); or it may concentrate on character delineation (that is, the way people grow or deteriorate or remain static in the happenings of life—*The Rise of Silas Lapham* or *Pride and Prejudice*); or it may illustrate a theme either aesthetically or propagandistically (*Wuthering Heights* or *Uncle Tom's Cabin*). It can, of course, do all three of these, as *Huckleberry Finn* does, a fact that accounts for the multiple levels of interpretation.

Huckleberry Finn is not only a novel, it is also a direct descendant of an important subgenre: the Spanish **picaresque** tale that arose in the sixteenth century as a reaction against the chivalric romance. In the latter type, pure and noble knights customarily rescued virtuous and beautiful heroines from enchanted castles guarded by fire-breathing dragons or wicked knights. In an attempt to debunk the artificiality and insipidity of such tales, Spanish writers of the day (notably the anonymous author of *Lazarillo de Tormes*) introduced into fiction as a central figure a kind of **antihero**, the picaro—a rogue or rascal of low birth who lived by his wits and his cunning rather than by exalted chivalric ideals. Indeed, except for the fact that the picaro is *in* each of the multitude of adventures, all happening "on the road," the plot is negligible by modern standards. In these stories we simply move with this new type of hero from one wild and sensational experience to another, involving many pranks and much trenchant satire. (Although not a pure picaro, Cervantes's Don Quixote is involved in a plot more rambling and episodic than unified and coherent.) Later treatments of the picaro have occasionally minimized and frequently eliminated his roguish or rascally traits. Dickens's picaros, for example, are usually model poor but good-hearted boys. However, others followed with darker, more modern picaros—Jack Kerouac and Hunter S. Thompson, for example, in the 1950s and 1960s. In later decades, films such as *Thelma and Louise* (1991) and *Borat* (2006) convey both the more disturbing aspects of the picaresque and its playful nature.

Many of the classics of world literature are much indebted to the picaresque tradition, among them René Le Sage's *Gil Blas,* Henry Fielding's *Tom Jones,* and Charles Dickens's *David Copperfield,* to mention only a few. *Huckleberry Finn* is an obvious example of the type. The protagonist is a thirteen- or fourteen-year-old boy living in the American antebellum South. He is a member by birth of the next-to-the-lowest stratum of Southern society, white trash—one who has a drunkard father who alternately abandons him and then returns to persecute him, but who has no mother, no roots, and no background or breeding in the conventionally accepted sense. He is the town bad boy who smokes, chews, plays hooky, and stays dirty, and whom two good ladies of St. Petersburg, Missouri, have elected to civilize.

The narrative moves onto "the road" when Huck, partly to escape the death threats of his drunken father but also to evade the artificially imposed restrictions and demands of society, decides to accompany Jim, the slave of his benefactors, in his attempt to run for his freedom. The most immediate reason for Jim's deciding to run away is the fact that Miss Watson, his owner, has decided to sell him "down the river"—that is, into the Deep South, where instead of making a garden for nice old ladies or possibly being a house servant, he will surely become a field hand and work in the cane or cotton fields. These two, the teenaged urchin and the middle-aged slave, defy society, the law, and convention in a daring escape on a raft down the dangerous Mississippi River.

Continually in fear of being captured, Huck and Jim travel mostly at night. They board a steamboat that has run onto a snag in the river and has been abandoned; on it they find a gang of robbers and cutthroats, whom they manage to elude without detection. In a vacant house floating down the river they discover the body of a man shot in the back, who, Jim later reveals, is Huck's father. They become involved in a blood feud between two aristocratic pioneer families. They witness a cold-blooded murder and an attempted lynching on the streets of an Arkansas village. They acquire two disreputable traveling companions who force them to render menial service and to take part in burlesque Shakespearean performances, bogus revival meetings, and attempted swindles of orphans with newly inherited wealth. Finally, after some uneasy moments when Jim is captured, they learn that Jim has been freed by his owner, and Huck decides to head west—away from civilization.

d. **"Young Goodman Brown"** "Young Goodman Brown" is a short story; that is, it is a relatively brief narrative of prose fiction (ranging in length from five hundred to twenty thousand words) characterized by considerably more unity and compression in all its parts than the novel—in theme, plot, structure, character, setting, and **mood**. In the story we are considering, the situation is this: one evening near sunset sometime in the late seventeenth century, Goodman Brown, a young man who has been married only three months, prepares to leave his home in Salem, Massachusetts, and his pretty young bride, Faith, to go into the forest and spend the night on some mission that he will not disclose other than to say that it must be performed between sunset and sunrise. Although Faith has strong forebodings about his journey and pleads with him to postpone it, Brown is adamant and sets off. His business is evil by his own admission; he does not state what it is specifically, but it becomes apparent to the reader that it involves attending a witches' Sabbath in the forest, a remarkable action in view of the picture of Brown, drawn early in the story, as a professing Christian who admonishes his wife to pray and who intends to lead an exemplary life after this one night.

The rising action begins when Brown, having left the village, enters the dark, gloomy, and probably haunted forest. He has not gone far before he meets the Devil in the form of a middle-aged, respectable-looking man with whom Brown has made a bargain to accompany on his journey. Perhaps the full realization of who his companion is and what the night may hold in store for him now dawns on Brown, for he makes an effort to return to Salem. It is at best a feeble attempt, however, for, though the Devil does not try to detain him, Brown continues walking with him deeper into the forest.

As they go, the Devil shocks Goodman Brown by telling him that his (Brown's) ancestors were religious bigots, cruel exploiters, and practitioners of the black art—in short, full-fledged servants of the Devil. Further, the young man is told that the very pillars of New England society, church, and state are witches (creatures actually in league with the Devil), lechers, blasphemers, and collaborators with the Devil. Indeed, he sees his childhood Sunday School teacher, now a witch, and overhears the voices of his minister and a deacon of his church as they ride past conversing about the diabolical communion service to which both they and he are going.

Clinging to the notion that he may still save himself from this breakup of his world, Goodman Brown attempts to pray, but stops when a cloud suddenly darkens the sky. A babel of voices seems to issue from the cloud, many recognizable to Brown as belonging to godly persons, among them his wife. After the cloud has passed, a pink ribbon such as Faith wears in her cap flutters to the ground. Upon seeing it, Goodman Brown is plunged into despair and hastens toward the witches' assembly. Once there, he is confronted with a congregation made up of the wicked and those whom Brown had always assumed to be righteous. As he is led to the altar to be received into this fellowship of the lost, he is joined by Faith. The climax of the story comes just before they receive the sacrament of baptism: Brown cries to his wife to look heavenward and save herself. In the next moment he finds himself alone.

The dénouement (resolution, unraveling) of the plot comes quickly. Returning the next morning to Salem, Goodman Brown is a changed man. He now doubts that anyone is good—his wife, his neighbors, the officials of church and state—and he remains in this state of cynicism until he dies.

The supernaturalism and horror of "Young Goodman Brown" mark the story as one variant of the **Gothic tale**, a type of ghost story originating formally in late eighteenth-century England and characterized by spirit-haunted habitations, diabolical villains, secret doors and passageways, terrifying and mysterious sounds and happenings, and the like. Obviously, "Young Goodman Brown" bears some resemblance to these artificial creations, the aesthetic value of most of which is negligible. What is much more significant is that here is a variation of the Faust legend, the story of a man who makes a bargain with the Devil (frequently the sale of his soul) in exchange for some desirable thing. In this instance Goodman Brown did not go nearly so far in the original indenture, but it was not necessary from the Devil's point of view. One glimpse of evil unmasked was enough to wither the soul of Brown forever.

e. "Everyday Use"   "Everyday Use" is another short story such as we defined in the treatment of "Young Goodman Brown." This story by Alice Walker is one of her most frequently anthologized. It was published in 1973, some nine years before she won the Pulitzer Prize for *The Color Purple,* which was subsequently made into a highly popular and much-discussed film. Like most of her work, this story deals with the lives of black people and the issues that affect them; Walker is particularly interested in the problems of black women and has written and spoken extensively about them. Here are the plot elements in this story.

1. *Situation*   Two black women, a mother (who narrates the story, and whose name we infer is Johnson) and her daughter Maggie (who appears to be in her twenties) are sitting in the neatly swept front yard of the three-room, tin-roofed shack that is their home somewhere in the American South. It is sunny and hot, but they are in the shade of an elm tree waiting for the arrival of Dee, Maggie's brilliant and talented sister who left home for the freedom and opportunities of the city, possibly New York or Los Angeles. The time is in the 1970s, as suggested by the following facts: Dee has followed the example of some African Americans in adopting an African name to replace her original family name; she is traveling with a black man who has chosen an Arabic name, which the narrator is advised to pronounce "Hakim-a-barber"; and the narrator refers to a group of black Muslim cattle farmers in the neighborhood who have been harassed by local whites and have armed themselves for defense.

2. *Generating Circumstance*   The reader's curiosity is aroused when Wangero (Dee's new name) takes a condescending attitude toward her mother and sister because of their simple living conditions and their apparent satisfaction with their underprivileged and politically unenlightened lives. They, on the other hand, are amazed if not amused at the unconventional appearance and behavior of their visitors. Maggie—homely, introverted, and less gifted intellectually than her sister—is intimidated by the latter's achievements.

3. *Rising Action* While affecting to despise virtually everything in her old home, Wangero still wants to take things like the hand-carved churn and benches and the quilts as heirlooms or examples of "primitive" art, which can be shown to her acquaintances back in the city. Such artifacts could there become conversation pieces only; they would not have utility, and they might not generate significant feeling or emotion. In their proper humble setting, they are useful, revered, and considered beautiful. Because of her ingrained assertiveness and her formidable abilities, Wangero assumes she can bully her mother into giving her these "aesthetic creations," which are too good for "everyday use." Her mother allows her to confiscate the churn and its dasher but draws the line at the quilts, which she had promised to Maggie for a wedding present.

4. *Climax* The climactic moment comes when the narrator snatches the quilts away from Wangero, and "dumps" them into the astounded Maggie's lap.

5. *Dénouement* Wangero, followed by Hakim-a-barber, leaves in a huff, charging as she goes that her mother does not really understand their "heritage." The story closes with Maggie, happy in her newly discovered worth, and her mother, blissful with a dip of snuff, sitting in the yard quietly and contentedly, enjoying the end of the day.

f. Frankenstein Like *Huckleberry Finn*, *Frankenstein* is a novel, that is, a long story involving characters in actions usually pointing to some kind of resolution. But *Frankenstein* is in a special category, the Gothic novel (defined above), a genre that made its first appearance in eighteenth-century England. Its principal features are an atmosphere of terror and horror brought about by dark and foreboding settings, often in mysterious medieval castles with creaking doors, the unexplained sounds of chains being dragged across attic floors, and long, dank subterranean passages leading to graveyards. Stormy weather, punctuated by lightning in horrid forests and a host of similar examples of contrived effects, help create the mood of the story. Characters tend to be one-dimensional, cardboard figures like black-hearted villains, pure and helpless maidens, and handsome and virtuous heroes.

It is also, like Bram Stoker's *Dracula* (1897), an **epistolary novel,** that is, a novel in the form of letters. However, *Frankenstein* clearly demonstrates how a novelist attentive to psychological, feminist, and domestic concerns can rise above the stereotypes of the Gothic or the conventions of the epistolary novel to create a much more complex and multifaceted study of human nature, both in the modern figure of the scientist and in the Creature.

Frankenstein continues to appeal most of all to contemporary moviegoers. The Creature, although unnamed, will remain firmly fixed in the popular imagination. (It is interesting to note that most people think Frankenstein *is* the monster.)

Frankenstein is a story within a story, which begins in the frozen reaches of the polar North. Robert Walton, an English explorer, commands a ship trapped in a sea of ice. As he writes to his sister, Mrs. Margaret Saville, a sledge on a large segment of ice comes into view, carrying a half-frozen man and one dog. During his convalescence, the man, Victor Frankenstein, tells Walton the story of his life. According to the tradition of the epistolary novel, Walton writes down what Victor says in a (long) letter to his sister.

Victor describes himself as a brilliant young Swiss scientist, born into a well-to-do and happy family in Geneva. His adopted sister Elizabeth is the same age as he, and over the years they have always loved each other. He also has a much younger brother, William; their mother, Caroline, died in childbirth with William, prompting Victor's sense of the injustice of death. At his university in Ingolstadt, Frankenstein discovers the secret of creating life and becomes obsessed with the idea of actually doing so. Frequenting the butcher shops and dissecting rooms and always working in secret in his laboratory, he creates an eight-foot-tall male, hideously ugly, and, we later learn, uncommonly strong and agile. Frankenstein rejects the Creature, who runs away and hides in a lean-to at a cottage, where he manages to survive undetected and even learns to talk and read, and not just in an elementary way: he masters *Paradise Lost,* Plutarch's *Lives,* and Goethe's *The Sorrows of Young Werther!* He manages this by overhearing Felix De Lacey teach French to Safie. Eventually, he discovers Frankenstein's journal in his coat pocket and reads it, to his horror.

He surfaces again in Frankenstein's life by murdering William and framing Justine, a servant girl, for the crime; she is executed by the village mob. Depressed by these tragedies, Frankenstein goes hiking in nearby mountains and spots a strange, agile figure far ahead on the glacier. When he sits down to rest, the Creature suddenly appears before him and forces Frankenstein to listen to his story. He eloquently blames Frankenstein for creating him so physically repulsive that all people hate him: "'Oh, Frankenstein, be not equitable to every other, and trample upon me alone, to whom thy justice, and even thy clemency and affection is most due. Remember, that I am thy creature: I ought to be thy Adam; but I am rather the fallen angel, whom thou drivest from joy for no misdeed. Everywhere I see bliss, from which I alone am irrevocably excluded. I was benevolent and good; misery made me a fiend" (Shelley 66). Embittered against all men, the Creature seeks either redress or revenge. Unless Frankenstein agrees to create a mate, that is, a bride, for him so that he will have some companionship, the Creature vows more murders. The Creature promises he will take his mate to the wilds of South America, where they will nevermore be seen by human beings. Victor agrees and departs for the Orkney Islands, where he fashions a female, but his conscience compels him to destroy her. However, the Creature has followed Victor to the Orkneys and is watching him through a window as he destroys the female. Enraged, the Creature warns Victor that a terrible fate awaits him on his wedding night. The Creature then flees, later killing Victor's friend Henry Clerval, to further torment his creator.

Victor returns to Geneva and marries Elizabeth, his foster sister, whom he has grown to love. On their wedding night, the Creature manages to get into their bedchamber when Frankenstein foolishly leaves the room briefly to check the security of the house. While he is gone, the Creature strangles the bride, then escapes out the window by which he has entered. Victor returns just in time to fire one pistol shot at the monster, but he misses.

The Creature later returns to taunt Frankenstein, who pursues him to the polar regions. There, half-frozen, he is rescued by Walton, to whom he has told the foregoing story. But his physical condition is beyond help. He dies, as Walton attends him, powerless to save his life. Within a short space of time, the Creature boards the ship and forces his way to the cabin where Frankenstein's body lies. Vowing to do no more evil, the monster declares he will incinerate himself on a funeral pyre far away on the ice.

C. Source Study: Did Earlier Writings Help This Work Come into Being?

The kind of approach, or the set of related approaches, discussed in this section does not have a generally accepted name. It would be pleasant but not altogether helpful if we could settle upon what Kenneth Burke called it—a "high class kind of gossip"—for Burke was describing part of what we are interested in: the "inspection of successive drafts, notebooks, the author's literary habits in general" (Gibson 171).

We might call the approach *genetic,* because that is the word sometimes used when a work is considered in terms of its origins. We would find the term appropriate in studying the growth and development of the work, its genesis, as from its sources including other literary works. Some use the term in David Daiches's account for the "characteristics of the writer's work" by looking at the sociological and psychological phenomena out of which the work grew (358–75). Similarly, the *Princeton Encyclopedia of Poetry and Poetics* uses the term *genetic* in surveying the methods of criticism that treat how the work "came into being, and what influences were at work to give it exactly the qualities that it has. Characteristically, [genetic critics] try to suggest what is in the poem by showing what lies behind it" (Preminger 167). These phrases would come near to what we are calling "source study and related approaches," except for the fact that these statements tend to have a sociological or psychological context, where the work is seen as a piece of documentary evidence for the milieu that gave rise to it. (This sort of criticism is now the province of the new historicists; see the section entitled "New Historicism" in Chapter 4.)

More precisely, then, by "source study and related approaches" we mean the growth and development of a work as seen through a study of the author's manuscripts during the stages of composition of the work, of notebooks, of sources and analogues, and of various other influences (not necessarily sociological or psychological) that lie in the background of the work. In such study, our assumption is that from the background we can derive clues to a richer, more accurate appreciation of the work. Some authors, like Jack London, derived many story plots and themes from such diverse sources as newspapers, missionary books about the South Seas, philosophers, explorers, and indigenous mythologies. In

The Waste Land T. S. Eliot used so many **allusions** to earlier literatures that the poem has to have his extensive footnotes and annotations. In a more contemporary example, postmodernist film director Quentin Tarantino sprinkles his films with dozens of allusions to other films and to popular culture; for example, in *Kill Bill* (2003–04), he blends the genres of kung fu films and American westerns.

Well-suited as an introduction to this kind of criticism and a pleasant indication of both the advantages and the disadvantages of this approach to literature is the collection of pieces from which we took the Kenneth Burke quotation: Walker Gibson's *Poems in the Making.* Introducing the pieces he has gathered, Gibson calls attention to the problem of the "relevance of any or all of these accounts" in our gaining a "richer appreciation of poetry," but at the same time he clearly believes connecting them offers possibilities. Accordingly, he provides a variety of specific approaches—different kinds of manuscript study, essays by the original authors (for example, Edgar Allan Poe and Stephen Spender on their own works), the classic study (in part) of "Kubla Khan" by John Livingston Lowes, and T. S. Eliot's devastating attack on that kind of scholarship. Not in Gibson's compendium but of interest because of the popularity of the poem is a similar study of Robert Frost's "Stopping by Woods on a Snowy Evening." An analysis of the manuscript of the poem shows how Frost worked out his words and his rhyme scheme, crossing out words not conducive to the experience of the poem. At the same time, Frost's own (separate) comments on the writing of the poem help us to interpret what the marks in the manuscript suggest (for this study see Charles W. Cooper and John Holmes, *Preface to Poetry*). An excellent example of this kind of work is Robert Gittings's *Odes of Keats and Their Earliest Known Manuscripts,* a handsome volume that provides an essay on how five of Keats's greatest poems were written and numerous, clear facsimile pages of the manuscripts.

These examples come from poems of the nineteenth and twentieth centuries, but source and analogue study has long been a staple of traditional scholarship on literature of an earlier day, such as various works on Shakespeare's plays and *Sources and Analogues of Chaucer's Canterbury Tales,* edited by W. F. Bryan and Germaine Dempster. A work like this last, it should be noted, provides materials for the scholar or student to work with, whereas other works are applications of such materials. An example of application can be found in the study of Sir Thomas Malory's *Morte Darthur.* Study of Malory's French and English sources helps us greatly in evaluating the art of his romance and the establishment of his purposes and has contributed to the debate over whether he intended to write one book (see Lumiansky's *Malory's Originality: A Critical Study of* Le Morte Darthur) or a compendium of eight stories (see Vinaver's *The Works of Sir Thomas Malory*). Milton's notes and manuscripts over a long period of time show us how he gradually came to write *Paradise Lost* and something of his conception of what he was working toward. This and more can be seen, aided again by facsimile pages, in Allan H. Gilbert, *On the Composition of* Paradise Lost: *A Study of the Ordering and Insertion of Material.* More helpful to the beginning student is the somewhat broader view of a briefer work by Milton offered by Scott Elledge in *Milton's "Lycidas," Edited to Serve as an Introduction to Criticism.*

There Elledge provides not only manuscript facsimiles of the poem, but materials on the **pastoral** tradition, examples of the genre, passages on the theory of **monody**, and information both from Milton's life and from his times.

For an example of the application of this approach to fiction, the reader might look at Matthew J. Bruccoli, *The Composition of "Tender Is the Night": A Study of the Manuscripts.* Bruccoli worked from thirty-five hundred pages of **holograph manuscript** and typescript, plus **proof sheets**, which represented seventeen drafts and three versions of the novel (xv). Perhaps this is more than the beginning student cares to have in this critical approach to literature. It may be well to mention, therefore, that, like Gibson's and Elledge's works on poetry cited earlier, there are some books on pieces of fiction that are intended for the student and offer opportunities to approach a piece of fiction by means of source and influence study. Such are, for example, some of the novels (*The Scarlet Letter, Adventures of Huckleberry Finn, The Red Badge of Courage*) in the Norton Critical Editions, as in the Bedford Case Studies in Contemporary Criticism series, where the text of the novel is accompanied by source and interpretive materials.

III. HISTORICAL AND BIOGRAPHICAL APPROACHES

A. General Observations

Although the historical-biographical approach has been evolving over many years, its basic tenets are perhaps most clearly articulated in the writings of the nineteenth-century French critic Hippolyte A. Taine, whose phrase *race, milieu, et moment,* elaborated in his *History of English Literature,* bespeaks a hereditary and environmental determinism. Put simply, this approach sees a literary work chiefly, if not exclusively, as a reflection of its author's life and times or the life and times of the characters in the work.

A historical novel is likely to be more meaningful when either its milieu or that of its author is understood. James Fenimore Cooper's *Last of the Mohicans,* Sir Walter Scott's *Ivanhoe,* Charles Dickens's *Tale of Two Cities,* and John Steinbeck's *Grapes of Wrath* are certainly better understood by readers familiar with, respectively, the French and Indian War (and the American frontier experience generally), Anglo-Norman Britain, the French Revolution, and the American Depression. And, of course, there is a very real sense in which these books are *about* these great historical matters, so that the author is interested in the characters only to the extent that they are molded by these events.

What has just been said applies even more to ideological or propagandist novels. Harriet Beecher Stowe's *Uncle Tom's Cabin,* Frank Norris's *The Octopus,* and Upton Sinclair's *The Jungle* ring truer (or falser as the case may be) to those who know about the antebellum South, railroad expansion in the late nineteenth century, and scandals in the American meat-packing industry in the early twentieth century. Sinclair Lewis's satires take on added bite and fun for those who have lived in or observed the cultural aridity of *Main Street,* who have been treated by shallow and materialistic physicians like some of those in *Arrowsmith,* who have sat through the sermons and watched the shenanigans of religious charlatans like Elmer Gantry, or who have dealt with and been in service clubs with all-too-typical American businessmen like Babbitt. Novels may lend themselves somewhat more readily than lyric poems to this particular interpretive approach; they usually treat a broader range of experience than poems do and thus are affected more by extrinsic and especially political factors.

It is a mistake, however, to think that poets do not concern themselves with social themes or that good poetry cannot be written about such themes. Actually, poets have from earliest times been the historians, the interpreters of contemporary culture, and the prophets of their people. Take, for example, a poet as mystical and esoteric as William Blake. Many of his best poems can be read meaningfully only in terms of Blake's England. "London" is an outcry against the oppression of human beings by his society: he lashes out against child labor in his day and the church's indifference to it, against the government's indifference to the indigent soldier who has served his country faithfully, and against the horrible and unnatural consequences of a social code that represses sexuality. His "Preface" to *Milton* is at once a denunciation of the "dark Satanic Mills" of the Industrial Revolution and a joyous battle cry of determination to build "Jerusalem/In England's green and pleasant Land." It has been arranged as an anthem for church choirs, is widely used in a hymn setting, and was sung in London in the 1945 election by the victorious Labour party. The impact of the Sacco and Vanzetti case upon young poets of the 1920s or of the opposition to the war in Vietnam upon almost every important American poet in the 1960s resulted in numerous literary works on these subjects, such as the poetry of Allen Ginsburg. Obviously, then, even some lyric poems are susceptible to historical-biographical analysis. Similarly, political and religious verse satires like John Dryden's in the seventeenth century and personal satires like Alexander Pope's in the eighteenth century have as one of their primary purposes the ridiculing of contemporary situations and persons.

B. Historical and Biographical Approaches in Practice

1. "To His Coy Mistress"

We know several facts about Marvell and his times that may help to explain this framework of logical argument as well as the mixed tone and learned allusions that pervade the poem. First, Marvell was an educated man (Cambridge B.A., 1639), the son of an Anglican priest with Puritan leanings. Because both he and his father had received a classical education, the poet was undoubtedly steeped in classical modes of thought and literature. Moreover, the emphasis on classical logic and polemics in his education was probably kept strong in his mind by his political actions. (He was a Puritan, a Parliamentarian, an admirer of Oliver Cromwell, a writer of political satires, and an assistant to John Milton, who was Latin secretary to the government.) That it should occur, therefore, to Marvell to have the speaker plead his suit logically should surprise no one.

There is, however, nothing pedantic or heavy-handed in this disputatious technique. Rather, it is playful and urbane, as are the allusions to Greek mythology, courtly love, and the Bible. When the speaker begins his argument, he establishes himself in a particular tradition of love poetry, that of **courtly love**. It is based on the elevation of the beloved to the status of a virtually unattainable object, one to be idolized, almost like a goddess. This status notwithstanding, she is capable of cruelty, and in the first **couplet** the speaker accuses her of a crime, the crime of withholding her love from him. Moreover, because she is like a goddess, she is also capricious and whimsical, and the worshipper must humor her by following the conventions of courtly love. He will complain (of her cruelty and his subsequent pain and misery) by the River Humber. He will serve her through praise, adoration, and faithful devotion from the fourth millennium B.C. (the alleged time of Noah's flood) to the conversion of the Jews to Christianity, an event prophesied to take place just before the end of the world (and there's a bit of humor on specifying an exact date ten years before the Flood). Doubtless, this is calculated to make the lady smile and to put her off her guard against the ulterior motive of the speaker.

However pronounced courtly love may be in the opening portion of the poem (the first part of the argument), by the time the speaker has reached the conclusion, he has stripped the woman of all pretense of modesty or divinity by his accusation that her "willing soul" literally exudes or breathes forth ("transpires") urgent ("instant") passion and by his direct allusion to kinesthetic ecstasy: "sport us," "roll all our strength," "tear our pleasures with rough strife/Thorough the iron gates of life" (the virginal body). All of this is consistent with a speaker who might have been schooled as Marvell himself was.

Many allusions in the poem that have to do with the passage of time show Marvell's religious and classical background. Two have been mentioned: the Flood and the conversion of the Jews. But there are others that continue to impress the reader with the speaker's plea. "Time's wingèd chariot" is the traditional metaphor for the vehicle in which the sun, moon, night, and time are represented as pursuing their course. At this point, the speaker is still in the humorous vein, and the image is, despite its serious import, a pleasing one. The humor grows increasingly sardonic, however, and the images become in the second stanza crude and repulsive. The allusions in the last stanza (the conclusion to the argument or case) do not suggest playfulness or a Cavalier attitude at all. Time's "slow-chapped [slow-jawed] power" alludes to the cannibalism of Kronos, chief of the gods, who, to prevent ever being overthrown by his own children, devoured all of them as they were born except Zeus. Zeus was hidden, later grew up, and ultimately became chief of the gods himself. The last couplet,

> Thus, though we cannot make our sun
> Stand still, yet we will make him run,

suggests several possible sources, both biblical and classical. Joshua commanded the sun to stand still so that he could win a battle against the Amorites (Josh. 10:13). Phaeton took the place of his father, the sun, in a winged chariot and had a wild ride across the sky, culminating in his death (Ovid, *Metamorphoses*). Zeus bade the sun to stand still in order to lengthen his night of love with Alcmene, the last mortal woman he embraced. In this example it is, of course, easy to see the appropriateness of the figures to the theme of the poem. Marvell's speaker is saying to his mistress that they are human, hence mortal. They do not have the ear of God as Joshua had, so God will not intervene miraculously and stop time. Nor do they possess the power of the pagan deities of old. They must instead cause time to pass quickly by doing what is pleasurable.

In addition to Marvell's classical and biblical background, further influences on the poem are erotic literature and **Metaphysical poetry**. Erotic poetry is, broadly speaking, simply love poetry, but it must emphasize the sensual. In "Coy Mistress" this emphasis is evident in the speaker's references to his mistress's breasts and "the rest" of her charms and in the image of the lovers rolled up into "one ball." The poem is Metaphysical in its similarities to other seventeenth-century poems that deal with the psychology of love and religion and—to enforce their meaning— employ bizarre, grotesque, shocking, and often obscure figures (the Metaphysical **conceit**). Such lines as "My vegetable love should grow," the warning that worms may violate the mistress's virginity and that corpses do not make love, the liken- ing of the lovers to "amorous birds of prey," and the allusion to Time's devouring his offspring ("slow-chapped"—"chaps" being lips) all help identify the poem as a product of the seventeenth-century revolt against the saccharine conventions of Elizabethan love poetry. As for its relation to *vers de société*, "To His Coy Mistress" partakes more of the tone than the subject matter of such poetry, manifesting for the most part wit, gaiety, charm, polish, sophistication, and ease of expression—all of these despite some rough Metaphysical **imagery**.

2. Hamlet

Hamlet is viewed by some commentators to be topical and autobiographical. In view of Queen Elizabeth's advanced age and poor health—hence the precarious state of the succession to the British crown—Shakespeare's decision to mount a production of *Hamlet*, with its usurped throne and internally disordered state, comes as no surprise. (Edward Hubler has argued that *Hamlet* was probably writ- ten in 1600 [912, n.2].) There is some ground for thinking that Ophelia's famous description of Hamlet may be intended to suggest the Earl of Essex, formerly Elizabeth's favorite, who had incurred her severe displeasure and been tried for treason and executed:

> The courtier's, soldier's, scholar's, eye, tongue, sword
> The expectancy and rose of the fair state,
> The glass of fashion and the mould of form,
> The observed of all observers.... (III.i)

Also, something of Essex may be seen in Claudius's observation on Hamlet's madness and his popularity with the masses:

> How dangerous it is that this man goes loose!
> Yet must we not put the strong law on him:
> He's loved of the distracted multitude,
> Who like not in their judgment but their eyes;
> And where 'tis so, the offender's scourge is weighed,
> But never the offence. (IV.viii)

Yet another contemporary historical figure, the Lord Treasurer, Burghley, has been seen by some in the character of Polonius. Shakespeare may have heard his patron, the young Henry Wriothesley, Earl of Southampton, express contempt for Elizabeth's old Lord Treasurer; indeed, this was the way many of the gallants of Southampton's generation felt. Burghley possessed most of the shortcomings Shakespeare gave to Polonius; he was boring, meddling, and given to wise old adages and truisms. (He left a famous set of pious yet shrewd precepts for his son, Robert Cecil.) Moreover, he had an elaborate spy system that kept him informed about both friend and foe. One is reminded of Polonius's assigning Reynaldo to spy on Laertes in Paris (II.i). This side of Burghley's character was so well known that it might have been dangerous for Shakespeare to portray it on stage while the old man was alive (because Burghley had died in 1598, Shakespeare could with safety do so in 1600).

Other topical references include Shakespeare's opinion (II.ii) about the revival of the private theater, which would employ children and which would constitute a rival for the adult companies of the public theater, for which Shakespeare wrote. It is also reasonable to assume that Hamlet's instructions to the players (III.ii) contain Shakespeare's criticisms of contemporary acting, just as Polonius's description of the players' repertoire and abilities (II.ii) is Shakespeare's satire on dull people who profess preferences for rigidly classified genres. Scholars have also pointed out Shakespeare's treatment of other stock characters of the day: Osric, the Elizabethan dandy; Rosencrantz and Guildenstern, the boot-licking courtiers; Laertes and Fortinbras, the men of action; Horatio, the "true Roman" friend; and Ophelia, the courtly love heroine.

In looking at *Hamlet* the historical critic might be expected to ask, "What do we need to know about eleventh-century Danish court life or about Elizabethan England to understand this play?" Similar questions are more or less relevant to the traditional interpretive approach to any literary work, but they are particularly germane to analysis of *Hamlet*. For one thing, most contemporary American students, largely unacquainted with the conventions, let alone the subtleties, of monarchical succession, wonder (unless they are aided by notes) why Hamlet does not automatically succeed to the throne after the death of his father. He is not just the oldest son; he is the only son. Such students need to know that in Hamlet's day the Danish throne was an elective one. The royal council, composed of the most powerful nobles in the land, named the next king. The custom of the throne's descending to the oldest son of the late monarch had not yet crystallized into law.

As true as this may be in fact, however, J. Dover Wilson maintains that it is not necessary to know it for understanding *Hamlet,* because Shakespeare intended his audiences to think of the entire situation—characters, customs, and plot—as English, which he apparently did in most of his plays, even though they were set in other countries. Wilson's theory is based upon the assumption that an Elizabethan audience could have but little interest in the peculiarities of Danish government, whereas the problems of royal succession, usurpation, and potential revolution in a contemporary English context would be of paramount concern. He thus asserts that Shakespeare's audience conceived Hamlet to be the lawful heir to his father and Claudius to be a usurper and the usurpation to be one of the main factors in the play, important to both Hamlet and Claudius. Whether one accepts Wilson's theory or not, it is certain that Hamlet thought of Claudius as a usurper, for he describes him to Gertrude as

> A cutpurse of the empire and the rule,
> That from a shelf the precious diadem stole
> And put it in his pocket! (III.iv)

and to Horatio as one

> ...that hath killed my king and whored my mother,
> Popped in between th' election and my hopes.... (V.ii)

This last speech suggests strongly that Hamlet certainly expected to succeed his father by election if not by primogeniture.

Modern students are also likely to be confused by the charge of incest against the Queen. Although her second marriage to the brother of her deceased husband would not be considered incestuous today by many civil and religious codes, it was so considered in Shakespeare's day. Some dispensation or legal loophole must have accounted for the popular acceptance of Gertrude's marriage to Claudius. That Hamlet considered the union incestuous, however, cannot be emphasized too much, for it is this repugnant character of Gertrude's sin, perhaps more than any other factor, that plunges Hamlet into the melancholy of which he is victim.

And here it is necessary to know what "melancholy" was to Elizabethans and to what extent it is important in understanding the play. A. C. Bradley tells us that it meant to Elizabethans a condition of the mind characterized by nervous instability, rapid and extreme changes of feeling and mood, and the disposition to be for the time absorbed in a dominant feeling or mood, whether joyous or depressed. If Hamlet's actions and speeches are examined closely, they seem to indicate symptoms of this condition. He is by turns cynical, idealistic, hyperactive, lethargic, averse to evil, disgusted at his uncle's drunkenness and his mother's sensuality, and convinced that he is rotten with sin. To appreciate his apparent procrastination, his vacillating from action to contemplation, and the other superficially irreconcilable features in his conduct, readers need to realize that at least part of Hamlet's problem is that he is a victim of extreme melancholy. (For more detailed discussions of Hamlet's melancholy, see A. C. Bradley's *Shakespearean Tragedy,* J. Dover Wilson's *What Happens in "Hamlet,"* and Weston Babcock's *"Hamlet": A Tragedy of Errors.*)

One reason for the popularity of *Hamlet* with Elizabethan audiences was that it dealt with a theme they were familiar with and fascinated by—revenge. *Hamlet* is in the grand tradition of revenge tragedies and contains virtually every stock device observable in vastly inferior plays of this type. Thomas Kyd's *Spanish Tragedy* (ca. 1585) was the first successful English adaptation of the Latin tragedies of Seneca. The typical revenge tragedy began with a crime (or the recital of it); continued with an injunction by some agent (often a ghost) to the next of kin to avenge the crime; grew complicated by various impediments to the revenge, such as identifying the criminal and hitting upon the proper time, place, and mode of the revenge; and concluded with the death of the criminal, the avenger, and frequently all the principals in the drama.

One additional fact about revenge may be noted. When Claudius asks Laertes to what lengths he would go to avenge his father's death, Laertes answers that he would "cut [Hamlet's] throat i' th' church" (IV.vii). It is probably no accident that Laertes is so specific about the method by which he would willingly kill Hamlet. In Shakespeare's day it was popularly believed that repentance had to be vocal to be effective. By cutting Hamlet's throat, presumably before he could confess his sins, Laertes would deprive Hamlet of this technical channel of grace. Thus Laertes would destroy both Hamlet's soul and his body and would risk his own soul, a horrifying illustration of the measure of his hatred. Claudius's rejoinder

> No place indeed should murder sanctuarize;
> Revenge should have no bounds

indicates the desperate state of the king's soul. He is condoning murder in a church, traditionally a haven of refuge, protection, and legal immunity for murderers.

Elizabethan audiences were well acquainted with these conventions. They thought there was an etiquette, almost a ritual, about revenge; they believed that it was in fact a fine art and that it required a consummate artist to execute it.

3. *Huckleberry Finn*

At the surface level of the narrative, *Huckleberry Finn* is something of a thriller. The sensationalism may seem to make the story improbable, if not incredible, but we should consider its historical and cultural context. This was part of frontier America in the 1840s and 1850s, a violent and bloody time. It was the era of Jim Bowie and his murderous knife, of gunslingers like Jack Slade, of Indian fighters like Davy Crockett and Sam Houston. Certainly there is a touch of the frontier, of the South or the West, in the roughness, the cruelty, the lawlessness, and even the humor of *Huckleberry Finn*. Indeed, Mark Twain was very much in the tradition of such humorists of the Southwest as Thomas Bangs Thorpe and such professional comedians as Artemus Ward and Josh Billings; in various writings he employed dialect for comedy, burlesque, the tall tale, bombast, the frontier brag. *Huckleberry Finn,* of course, far transcends the examples of early American humor.

Furthermore, we know from Mark Twain's autobiographical writings and from scholarly studies of him, principally those of Bernard De Voto, A. B. Paine, and Dixon Wecter, that the most sensational happenings and colorful characters in *Huckleberry Finn* are based on actual events and persons Twain saw in Hannibal, Missouri, where he grew up, and in other towns up and down the Mississippi. For example, the shooting of Old Boggs by Colonel Sherburn is drawn from the killing of one "Uncle Sam" Smarr by William Owsley on the streets of Hannibal on January 24, 1845. The attempted lynching of Sherburn is also an echo of something that Mark Twain saw as a boy, for he declared in later life that he once "saw a brave gentleman deride and insult a [lynch] mob and drive it away." During the summer of 1847 Benson Blankenship, older brother of the prototype Huck, secretly aided a runaway slave by taking food to him at his hideout on an island across the river from Hannibal. Benson did this for several weeks and resolutely refused to be enticed into betraying the man for the reward offered for his capture. This is undoubtedly the historical source of Huck's loyalty to Jim that finally resulted in his electing to "go to Hell" in defiance of law, society, and religion rather than turn in his friend.

A point about Jim's escape that needs clarification is his attempt to attain his freedom by heading *south*. Actually, Cairo, Illinois, free territory and Jim's destination, is farther south on the river than St. Petersburg, Missouri, from which he is escaping. Thus when the fugitives miss Cairo in the fog and dark, they have lost their only opportunity to free Jim by escaping southward. Still another point is that if it had been Jim's object simply to get to *any* free territory, he might as easily have crossed the river to Illinois right at St. Petersburg, his home. But this was not his aim. Although a free state, Illinois had a law requiring its citizens to return runaway slaves. Jim therefore wanted particularly to get to Cairo, Illinois, a junction of the underground railroad system where he could have been helped on his way north and east on the Ohio River by abolitionists.

The obscene performance of the "Royal Nonesuch" in Bricksville, Arkansas, where the King prances about the stage on all fours as the "cameleopard," naked except for rings of paint, was based on some of the bawdier male entertainments of the old Southwest. This particular type featured a mythical phallic beast called the "Gyascutus." There were variations, of course, in the manner of presentation, but the antics of the King illustrate a common version. (Both Mark Twain and his brother Orion Clemens recorded performances of this type, Orion in an 1852 newspaper account of a Hannibal showing, Mark in a notebook entry made in 1865 while he was in Nevada.)

The detailed description of the Grangerford house with its implied yet hilarious assessment of the pretensions of nineteenth-century culture may be traced to a chapter from *Life on the Mississippi* entitled "The House Beautiful." Here may be observed the conformity to the vogue of sentimentalism, patriotism, and piousness in literature and painting and the general garishness in furniture and knickknacks.

One pronounced theme in *Huckleberry Finn* that has its origin in Twain's personality is his almost fanatical hatred of aristocrats. Indeed, aristocracy was one of his chief targets. *A Connecticut Yankee in King Arthur's Court* is less veiled than *Huckleberry Finn* in its attack on the concept. But it was not only British aristocracy that Twain condemned; elsewhere he made his most vitriolic denunciations of the American Southern aristocrat. Though more subtle, *Huckleberry Finn* nevertheless is the more searching criticism of aristocracy. For one thing, aristocracy is hypocritical. Aristocrats are not paragons of true gentleness, graciousness, courtliness, and selflessness. They are trigger-happy, inordinately proud, implacable bullies. But perhaps Twain's antipathy to aristocracy, expressed in virtually all his works, came from the obvious misery caused to all involved, perpetrators as well as victims. The most significant expression of this in *Huckleberry Finn* is, of course, in the notion of race superiority. Clinging as they did to this myth, aristocrats could justify any kind of treatment of blacks. They could separate families, as in the case of Jim and the Wilks slaves; they could load them with chains, forget to feed them, hunt them like animals, curse and cuff them, exploit their labor, even think of them as subhuman, and then rationalize the whole sordid history by affirming that the slaves ought to be grateful for any contact with civilization and Christianity.

Moreover, not only aristocrats but every section of white society subscribed to this fiction; thus a degenerate wretch like pap Finn could shoulder a free Negro college professor off the sidewalk and later deliver an antigovernment, racist tirade to Huck replete with the party line of the Know-Nothings, a semisecret, reactionary political group that flourished for a brief period in the 1850s. (Its chief tenet was hostility to foreign-born Americans and the Roman Catholic Church. It derived its name from the answer its oath-bound members made to any question about it, "I know nothing about it.") We thus sense the contempt Twain felt for Know-Nothingism when we hear its chief doctrines mouthed by a reprobate like pap Finn. (Indeed, it may be more than coincidental that Twain never capitalizes the word *pap* when Huck is referring to his father.)

Closely related to this indictment of aristocracy and racism and their concomitant evils are Twain's strictures on romanticism, which he thought largely responsible for the harmful myths and cultural horrors that beset the American South of his day. In particular, he blamed the novels of Sir Walter Scott and their idealization of a feudal society. In real life this becomes on the adult level the blood feud of the Grangerfords and Shepherdsons and on the juvenile level the imaginative high jinks of Tom Sawyer and his "robber gang" and his "rescue" of Jim.

There are many other examples of historical and biographical influences on the novel. Years spent as a steamboat pilot familiarized Mark Twain with every snag, sandbar, bend, or other landmark on the Mississippi, as well as with the more technical aspects of navigation—all of which add vivid authenticity to the novel. His vast knowledge of Negro superstitions was acquired from slaves in Hannibal, Missouri, and on the farm of his beloved uncle, John Quarles, prototype of Silas Phelps. Jim himself is modeled after Uncle Dan'l, a slave on the Quarles place. These superstitions and examples of folklore are not mere local color, devoid of rhyme or reason; but, as Daniel Hoffman has pointed out, they are "of signal importance in the thematic development of the book and in the growth toward maturity of its principal characters" (321). Huck was in real life Tom Blankenship, a boyhood chum of Twain's who possessed most of the traits Twain gave him as a fictional character. Although young Blankenship's real-life father was ornery enough, Twain modeled Huck's father on another Hannibal citizen, Jimmy Finn, the town drunk.

Like *The Canterbury Tales,* where Dryden found "God's plenty," *Huckleberry Finn* gives its readers a portrait gallery of the times. Scarcely a class is omitted. The aristocracy is represented by the Grangerfords, the Shepherdsons, and Colonel Sherburn. They are hardly Randolphs and Lees of tidewater Virginia, and their homes reveal that. The Grangerford parlor, for example, shows more of philistinism and puritanism than of genuine culture. These people are, nevertheless, portrayed as recognizable specimens of the traditional aristocrat. Colonel Sherburn in particular illustrates another aspect of the traditional aristocrat—his contempt for the common man, which is reflected in his cold-blooded shooting of Old Boggs, his cavalier gesture of tossing the pistol on the ground afterward, and his single-handedly facing down the lynch mob.

Towns of any size in *Huckleberry Finn* contain the industrious, respectable, conforming bourgeoisie. In this class are the Widow Douglas and her old-maid sister Miss Watson, the Peter Wilks family, and Judge Thatcher. The Phelpses too, although they own slaves and operate a "one-horse cotton plantation," belong to this middle class. Mrs. Judith Loftus, whose canniness undoes Huck when he is disguised as a girl, is, according to De Voto, the best-drawn pioneer wife in any of the contemporary records. The host of anonymous but vivid minor characters reflects and improves upon the many eyewitness accounts. These minor characters include the ferryboat owner, the boatmen who fear smallpox as they hunt Jim, the raftsmen heard from a distance joking in the stillness of the night. The Bible Belt poor white, whether whittling and chewing and drawling on the storefront benches of an Arkansas village or caught up in the fervor of a camp meeting or joining his betters in some sort of mob action, is described with undeniable authenticity.

Criminals like the robbers and cutthroats on the *Walter Scott* and those inimitable confidence men, the King and the Duke, play their part. Pap Finn is surely among the earliest instances of Faulkner's Snopes types—filthy, impoverished, ignorant, disreputable, bigoted, thieving, drunks, sure of only one thing, his superiority as a white man. Then we observe the slaves themselves, convincing because they include not just stereotyped minstrel characters but interesting human beings.

4. *"Young Goodman Brown"*

What kind of historical or biographical information do we need in order to feel the full impact of this story, aesthetically and intellectually? Obviously, some knowledge of Puritan New England is necessary. We can place the story in time easily, because Hawthorne mentions that it takes place in the days of King William (that is, William III, who reigned from 1688 to 1702). Other evidences of the time of the story are the references to persecution of the Quakers by Brown's grandfather (the 1660s) and King Philip's War (primarily a massacre of Indians by colonists [1675–1676]), in which Brown's father participated. Specific locales like Salem, Boston, Connecticut, and Rhode Island are mentioned, as are terms used in Puritan church organization and government, such as ministers, elders, meetinghouses, communion tables, saints (in the Protestant sense of *any* Christian), selectmen, and lecture days.

But it is not enough for us to visualize a sort of first Thanksgiving picture of Pilgrims with steeple-crowned hats, Bibles, and blunderbusses. For one thing, we need to know something of Puritan religion and theology. This means at least a slight knowledge of Calvinism, a main source of Puritan religious doctrine. A theology as extensive and complex as Calvinism and one that has been the subject of so many misconceptions cannot be described adequately in a handbook of this type. But at the risk of perpetuating some of these misconceptions, let us mention three or four tenets of Calvinism that will illuminate to some degree the story of Goodman Brown. Calvinism stresses the sovereignty of God—in goodness, power, and knowledge. Correspondingly, it emphasizes the helplessness and sinfulness of human beings, who have been since the Fall of Adam innately and totally depraved. Their only hope is in the grace of God, for God alone is powerful enough (sovereign enough) to save them. And the most notorious, if not the chief, doctrine is predestination, which includes the belief that God has, before their creation, selected certain people for eternal salvation, others for eternal damnation. Appearances are therefore misleading; an outwardly godly person might not be one of the elect. Thus it is paradoxical that Goodman Brown is so shocked to learn that there is evil among the apparently righteous, for this was one of the most strongly implied teachings of his church.

In making human beings conscious of their absolute reliance on God alone for salvation, Puritan clergymen dwelt long and hard on the pains of hell and the powerlessness of mere mortals to escape them. Brown mentions to the Devil that the voice of his pastor "would make me tremble both Sabbath day and lecture day." This was a typical reaction. In Calvinism, nobody could be sure of sinlessness. Introspection was mandatory. Christians had to search their hearts and minds constantly to purge themselves of sin. Goodman Brown is hardly expressing a Calvinistic concept when he speaks of clinging to his wife's skirts and following her to Heaven. Calvinists had to work out their own salvation in fear and trembling, and they were often in considerable doubt about the outcome. The conviction that sin was an ever-present reality that destroyed the unregenerate kept it before them all the time and made its existence an undoubted, well-nigh tangible fact. We must realize that aspects of the story like belief in witches and an incarnate Devil, were entirely credible to New Englanders of this period.

It is a matter of historical record that a belief in witchcraft and the old pagan gods existed in Europe side by side with Christianity well into the modern era. There was an analogous belief prevalent in Puritan New England. Clergymen, jurists, statesmen—educated people generally, as well as uneducated folk—were convinced that witches and witchcraft were realities. Cotton Mather, one of the most learned men of the period, attests eloquently to his own belief in these phenomena in *The Wonders of the Invisible World*, his account of the trials of several people executed for witchcraft.

Hawthorne's great-grandfather, John Hathorne (Nathaniel added the "w"), was one of the judges in the infamous Salem witch trials of 1692, during which many people were tortured, and nineteen hanged, and one crushed to death (a legal technicality was responsible for this special form of execution). Commentators have long pointed to "Young Goodman Brown," *The Scarlet Letter*, and many other Hawthorne stories to illustrate his obsession with the guilt of his Puritan forebears for their part in these crimes. In "The Custom House," his introduction to *The Scarlet Letter*, Hawthorne wrote of these ancestors who were persecutors of Quakers and witches and of his feeling that he was tainted by their crimes. The Devil says that he helped young Goodman Brown's grandfather, a constable, lash a "Quaker woman.... smartly through the streets of Salem," an episode undoubtedly related to Hawthorne's "Custom House" reference to his great-grandfather's "hard severity towards a woman of [the Quaker] sect."

Hawthorne's notebooks shed light on his preoccupation with the "unpardonable sin" and his particular definition of that sin. It is usually defined as blasphemy against the Holy Ghost, or continued conscious sin without repentance, or refusing to acknowledge the existence of God even though the Holy Spirit has made Him known. The notebooks, however, and works of fiction like "Ethan Brand," "Young Goodman Brown," and *The Scarlet Letter* make it clear that for Hawthorne the Unpardonable Sin was to probe, intellectually and rationally, the human heart for depravity without tempering the search by a "human" or "democratic" sympathy. Specifically in the case of "Young Goodman Brown," Brown's obduracy of heart cuts him off from all, so that "his dying hour [is] gloom."

5. "Everyday Use"

Alice Walker was born in Eatonton, Georgia, in 1944, ten years before the Supreme Court's landmark decision in *Brown v. Board of Education*, striking down segregation in schools. Because the South was slow to implement this decision, Walker and her five brothers and two sisters grew up in much the same racial environment as their parents, black sharecroppers, but not altogether typical. Her father, Willie Lee, and her mother, Minnie, were ambitious for their children, coveting education for them and wanting them to leave the South, where opportunities were limited. Despite the hard lot of blacks in the South of that day, Willie Lee had faith in much of the American system. He was among the very first black men to vote in his county in the 1930s after organizing a group of his fellow sharecroppers to seek their rights. He later became frustrated and disillusioned with the slowness of any real progress. These feelings and his poor health often resulted in his venting his anger and bitterness by beating his children. Alice, the youngest, seems to have received her full share of this harsh treatment.

Minnie, Walker's mother, was particularly outstanding as a role model for her children. Physically strong and strong-willed, she was a hard worker who managed to create beauty out of her limited surroundings by growing flowers, decorating the family cabin with flowers, quilting, and telling stories, at which she is reputed to have excelled.

Alice lost the sight of her right eye when she was only eight. A shot from a BB gun fired by one of her brothers accidentally hit her in this eye, blinding it and causing an unsightly white scar. Convinced that she was ugly by the way people stared at her face, she became shy and withdrawn. Six years later, when she was spending the summer in Boston with one of her brothers and his family—eventually all five brothers moved there—the scar was removed by a simple surgical procedure, which her brother and his wife paid for.

She returned home to Georgia, subsequently finished first in her high school class, and entered Spelman College in Atlanta, the nation's oldest college for black women. After two years at Spelman, she transferred to Sarah Lawrence College in New York, impelled undoubtedly by her increasing involvement with the civil rights movement and by Spelman's conservative educational and political philosophy. Her writing, which had started when she was still a child, increased in volume and quality under the tutelage of the distinguished poet Muriel Rukeyser and began to be recognized by prestigious prizes and fellowships.

Walker was deeply committed to the civil rights movement, working in voter registration and teaching black history in Mississippi in the 1970s. Other teaching appointments include Jackson (Mississippi) State, Tougaloo, the University of Massachusetts at Boston, the University of California at Berkeley in the 1980s, and Brandeis. When she left the South in 1974, she moved to Brooklyn and joined the editorial staff of the magazine *Ms.* Her controversial 1982 novel *The Color Purple* deals with the black experience as Walker has perceived and experienced it, especially the black woman's experience, wherein she finds black women to have been essentially victims, not only of racists but of men in general and black men in particular. They have, of course, been physically brutalized, but equally important has been the attempt to stifle all aesthetic creativity in them. The ways in which this attempt has failed are depicted in *The Color Purple* and, less sensationally, in *In Search of Our Mothers' Gardens,* a collection of autobiographical and critical essays, some of which describe the folk art that black women created in their limited leisure and environment.

And, indeed, "Everyday Use" has pronounced biographical elements. The **narrator** is like Minnie Walker, Alice's mother, who, according to Janet Gray, was strong and hardworking and "did not regard gender as a barrier to any kind of labor" (521). The narrator describes herself in ruggedly masculine terms: "large, big-boned.... rough man-working hands." She can perform typically male chores such as slaughtering, butchering, and dressing out hogs and calves. She boasts that she can work outdoors all day in subfreezing or scorching temperatures. She also has a refined and active aesthetic sensibility. She appreciates the material, the color, the artistry, and the history of the family quilts, which she regards as virtually sacred—but still to be used every day. Minnie Walker seems to have possessed similar characteristics. She worked all day in the fields with Alice's father, did her traditional female tasks in the evening, then exercised her widely recognized talents as a flower gardener and decorator with a strong sense of family history.

It was in this way that Minnie made creativity an important part of everyday life and demonstrated that no form or material or setting was too humble for its exhibition. Black women like her of an earlier day chose these outlets for their artistic urges and passed them down to their daughters, as Walker describes in *In Search of Our Mother's Gardens*.

Other features of the story that contain biographical elements include the character Maggie, who in several ways reflects the young Alice Walker. For example, Maggie has "burn scars down her arms and legs" which she suffered in the fire that destroyed the family home some ten years before the time of the story. Her inordinate shyness and pitiful lack of self-esteem, manifested by her shuffling gait, downcast eyes, and nondescript figure, have their counterpart in Walker's embarrassment at her disfigurement from the injury to her eye and its negative impact on her schoolwork. Another but different side of Walker is discernible in Dee's sophistication and educational achievements. Like Walker, Dee delights in the beautiful handmade objects in her mother's home though, unlike Walker's, Dee's appreciation also reflects the trendy and superficial.

The exact historical setting of the story is not indicated, but a number of details point to a period covering part of the 1970s in the American South. For example, the narrator mentions a television show that unites aged parents long separated from children who have attained a high degree of success. She also refers to Johnny Carson, long-time host of the "Tonight Show." Dee and her traveling companion have chosen to use African or Muslim names rather than their birth names, which to them represent the names of their oppressors. They are also wearing hairstyles which they believe to be African. The narrator also speaks of a group of industrious black stock farmers down the road, who have been the victims of harassment by their white racist neighbors. Many black entrepreneurs of this period converted to Islam and embarked on an austere course of economic and social self-determination. Another clue that the time is later than the 1960s is that the black stock farmers armed themselves with rifles to defend their property and lives, rather than calling upon local white law enforcement officers. That kind of action would have been uncommon even in the 1970s, so much so that the narrator said she "walked a mile and a half just to see the sight." It would have gratified her because she was a woman of an earlier generation, more apt to be intimidated by racial bullying (witness her rhetorical question and answer, "Who can even imagine me looking a strange white man in the eye? It seems to me I have always talked to them with one foot raised in flight"). This characteristic of the narrator, we might note, was decidedly not found in Minnie Walker, who according to Janet Gray "would explode at landlords" who pressured her to take her children out of school to work in the fields (521–22).

"Everyday Use" may profitably be read as a historical statement even though no specific years are actually mentioned. It describes, in addition to the human conflict which is its central business, a period and place where dramatic changes in racial relationships have taken place during the civil rights movement, within which one young Southern black woman has rebelled against racism and chosen to express that rebellion by leaving her homeland and rejecting traditional and conventional standards and values. Her **antagonists** are her mother and sister, who have not rebelled and who, indeed, have found their own peace and satisfaction in the same locale of their historical oppression. It is not likely that Alice Walker, a strong civil rights activist, is advocating passivity in the face of racial injustice, but she does in this story pay a beautiful tribute to those like the narrator and Maggie who remained in their homes and prevailed by enduring and affirming the best in their troubled heritage.

6. Frankenstein

Frankenstein was written in 1818, in the last years of the reign of George III. Its author, Mary Shelley, was born in 1797. Both the American and the French Revolutions were things of the past, but Mary grew up in a home where these principles were alive and well and were being carried to new heights, at least philosophically. Her parents were the brilliant, notorious, radical freethinkers, William Godwin, author of *Political Justice* (1793), and Mary Wollstonecraft, author of *A Vindication of the Rights of Women* (1792). These two had for some time been members of a group of radicals that included the poet William Blake and the American patriot Thomas Paine. Such people were regular visitors to Mary's home, and though her mother died when she was barely eleven days old, the influence of both parents on Mary can hardly be exaggerated. In this context her feeling for the poor is understandably one of the strongest beliefs she inherited, along with her rejection of conventional sexual morality. Between the ages of fifteen and seventeen, she made long visits to the home of her Scottish girlfriends, Isabel and Christy Baxter, who lived in Dundee. The Baxters' middle-class comfort and happy family life seem to have formed for Mary a pleasant contrast to the polar opposite of her normal milieu. Mary used the Frankenstein and Clerval families in her novel to hearken back to the Baxters (Rieger xiii).

It must be admitted that the social and political picture in England during Mary's formative years would have been enough to drive many sensitive and idealistic young people into radical thinking and action. For example, "dark satanic mills," as William Blake put it, were proliferating all over England; enclosure acts were driving small landowners, tenant farmers, and agricultural workers off their lands and into the slums of industrial cities; laborers everywhere endured horrible working conditions with no job security and faced the indifference and hostility of a new and growing capitalist class. The 300,000 discharged soldiers home from the Napoleonic Wars only aggravated these problems.

The radicalism of the times had its domestic counterpart, and Mary was also exposed to other forms of unconventionality. Although ardent believers in free love, her father and mother married five months before she was born. Her mother had borne another daughter out of wedlock; many of the freethinkers who frequented Godwin's famous salon were in unlawful relationships. This group soon included the poet Percy Bysshe Shelley accompanied by his sixteen-year-old wife, Harriet Westbrook. The young Shelley, already a radical himself—he had been expelled from Oxford in 1811 for writing *The Necessity of Atheism*—was attracted to Godwin's political, social, and economic thought. The Shelleys first called on Godwin in 1812 and soon began dining there regularly. Two years later, Shelley fell in love with the pretty, blonde Mary, by that time seventeen; the two eloped to the Continent in July 1814, leaving Harriet with Shelley's daughter Ianthe and pregnant. Mary then found herself scandalized—along with her husband—and soon very much at home in this freethinking circle that would soon number among its members Byron, his twenty-year-old physician Polidori, and Mary's stepsister Claire, to name perhaps the most notorious.

The Shelleys and Claire settled in a cottage on Lake Leman, outside Geneva, in 1816. Lord Byron was a neighbor. Between May and August of that year, Mary wrote *Frankenstein* as her contribution to a suggestion of Byron's during a period of bad weather that each of the group—Byron himself, Mary, Shelley, and Polidori—write a ghost story to while away the time during the frequently inclement weather. Only Mary ever completed the original assignment. *Frankenstein* was a tour de force for a young woman of nineteen. She published the novel anonymously in 1818, and it was an instant success. She continued to write fiction and poetry but nothing of significance.

A number of biographical features of Mary's life are to be found in *Frankenstein*. One is found in the scientific and pseudoscientific passages. Already interested in science in her early years, Mary shared her husband's passionate fascination with the natural sciences and the alchemical and science fiction spin-offs of that branch of learning. Hence, the detailed laboratory accounts of the creation of the monster. This interest did not end with the death of Percy, who drowned in a boating accident in 1822. She wrote scientific biographies for an encyclopedia and had a flying machine in her futuristic novel *The Last Man*.

Of course, to some extent, Mary is employing certain features of contemporary Gothic romances. But she departs from the stock formulas of the genre. One notable biographical detail may be found in the geography, topography, and climate of the settings of the novel. Mary had not, of course, been to the Arctic wastes described in the beginning and end of the novel, but she was more interested in creating an "Arctic of the mind" (Small 43) than in registering the climate and in describing glaciers and ice floes scientifically. She was, however, intimately acquainted with both the terrain and climatic conditions in the Alpine regions where she and Percy lived.

Thunderstorms, flashes of lightning, "the black sides of [Mount] Jura," "the bright summit of Mont Blanc," dreary winter nights, dismal and incessant rain, glaciers, ice caves—all these Mary knew and included in her Gothic tale.

There were aspects of her real life that Mary did not include in the novel: the unconventional attitudes toward religion and sex. As noted earlier, the Frankenstein and Clerval families are models of love and devotion, as are the minor figures in the cottage where the monster learns to read. But Mary manages to include hints of the darker side of domestic life by paralleling her experiences with those in the novel: the loss of children, especially in childbirth, irresponsible husbands, abandonment by a father, the loss of her mother, "inappropriate" pregnancies and births, and the repeated sacrifice of women for men. Victor has tried to establish a male-centered domestic sphere, having children without a woman and refusing to marry or protect Elizabeth from the fruit of his own sins.

Practicing the textual, source study, and genre studies approaches in this chapter has not changed appreciably in recent years. However, as presented in later chapters, applying historical-biographical approaches has fundamentally changed in contemporary theory and criticism. The "old" historicism has been replaced by the "new" historicism and politicized with a Marxist emphasis. Not kings and their "periods" but social history is now primarily investigated, as demonstrated in Fernand Braudel's *The Structures of Everyday Life*. History is not seen as a grand scroll of Western progress, but as competing narratives by the poor, by postcolonial subjects, and by women and other marginalized groups. In the same way, the biographical approach has been questioned in multiple ways by critics concerned with addressing its limitations as well as possibilities.

IV. MORAL AND PHILOSOPHICAL APPROACHES

A. General Observations

The moral-philosophical approach is as old as classical Greek and Roman critics. Plato, for example, emphasized moralism and utilitarianism; Horace stressed that literature should be delightful and instructive. Among its most famous exemplars are the commentators of the age of neoclassicism in English literature (1660–1800), particularly Samuel Johnson. The basic position of such critics is that the larger function of literature is to teach morality and to probe philosophical issues. They would interpret literature within a context of the philosophical thought of a period or group. From their point of view Jean-Paul Sartre and Albert Camus can be read profitably only if one understands existentialism. Similarly, Pope's *Essay on Man* may be grasped only if one understands the meaning and the role of reason in eighteenth-century thought. Such teaching may also be religiously oriented. Henry Fielding's *Tom Jones*, for example, illustrates the moral superiority of a hot-blooded young man like Tom, whose sexual indulgences are decidedly atoned for by his humanitarianism, tenderheartedness, and instinctive honor (innate as opposed to acquired through training). Serving as **foils** to Tom are the real sinners in the novel—the vicious and the hypocritical. Hawthorne's *Scarlet Letter* is likewise seen essentially as a study of the effects of secret sin on a human soul—that is, sin unconfessed before both God and man, as the sin of Arthur Dimmesdale with Hester Prynne, or, even more, the sin of Roger Chillingworth. Robert Frost's "Stopping by Woods on a Snowy Evening" suggests that duty and responsibility take precedence over beauty and pleasure.

A related attitude is that of Matthew Arnold, the Victorian critic, who insisted that a great literary work must possess "high seriousness." (Because he felt that Chaucer lacked it, Arnold refused to rank him among the very greatest English poets.) In each instance critics working from a moral bent are not unaware of form, **figurative language**, and other purely aesthetic considerations, but they consider them to be secondary. The important thing is the moral or philosophical teaching. On its highest plane this is not superficially didactic, though it may at first seem so. In the larger sense, all great literature teaches. The critic who employs the moral-philosophical approach insists on ascertaining and stating *what* is taught. If the work is in any degree significant or intelligible, this meaning will be there. As Henry James famously stated in "The Art of Fiction," "no great novel will ever proceed from a superficial mind." It seems reasonable, then, to employ historical-biographical or moral-philosophical analyses among other methods (such as textual study and recognition of genre) in getting at the meaning of a literary work when the work seems to call for them. Such approaches are less likely to err on the side of overinterpretation than are more esoteric methods.

The enemies of the traditional approach to literary analysis have argued that it has tended to be somewhat deficient in imagination, has neglected the newer sciences such as psychology and anthropology, ignored the political, and has been too content with a commonsense interpretation of material. But it has nevertheless performed one valuable service: in avoiding cultism and faddism, it has preserved scholarly discipline and balance in literary criticism. Any knowledge or insight (with special reference to scholarly disciplines like history, philosophy, theology, sociology, art, and music) that can help to explain or clarify a literary work ought to be given the fullest possible chance to do so. Indeed, in some sense these approaches represent a necessary first step that precedes most other approaches.

One way to look at moral-philosophical approaches is as *theme* (see Chapter 1). What is the "moral," or theme of the story? We caution readers to arrive at a theme or themes for a literary work only *after* some background and analysis. That is, it is a mistake to try to jump to "the theme" of a work before it has been thoroughly analyzed. Sometimes themes or meanings are fairly clear, but the most intriguing themes take some unearthing before they are apparent. A theme of revenge runs fairly constant in the six literary works analyzed in this handbook, especially in *Hamlet, Frankenstein,* and "Everyday Use," though it is expressed in very different ways. Hamlet and Laertes seek revenge against each other instead of, until the end, the evil Claudius; Victor seeks a sort of vindication of his science after his mother dies, and the Creature seeks revenge upon Victor for doing so; Maggie, through no action of her own, gets her own quiet revenge on her domineering sister Dee. But there are subtler echoes in "To His Coy Mistress" (Does the speaker take revenge on Time by seducing women? Does the mistress get revenge on him by refusing him?), "Young Goodman Brown" (Is Brown's complacency avenged by the Devil? Is Faith's abandonment by her husband avenged for her?); and *Huckleberry Finn* (the Grangerford-Shepherdson feud and the revenge of Colonel Sherburn). In the past, moralistic authors such as Dickens, Thackeray, and Stowe made their messages plain. Since the advent of the modernists, some of the most moralistic writers have obscured their messages through elaborate narrative strategies designed to make the reader puzzle out his or her own answers: James Joyce, Henry James, and William Faulkner, to name some major examples.

B. Moral and Philosophical Approaches in Practice

1. *"To His Coy Mistress"*

An examination of what "Coy Mistress" propounds morally and philosophically reveals the common theme of *carpe diem*, "seize the day," an attitude of "eat and drink, for tomorrow we shall die." Many of Marvell's contemporaries treated this idea. This type of poetry naturally exhibits certain fundamental moral attitudes toward the main issue this poem treats—sex. These attitudes reflect an essentially pagan view. They depict sexual intercourse as strictly dalliance ("Now let us sport us while we may"), as solely a means of deriving physical sensations. Although not a **Cavalier poet**, Marvell is here letting his speaker express a more Cavalier (as opposed to Puritan) idea.

One more aspect of the historical background of the composition of the poem is helpful in understanding its paradoxically hedonistic and pessimistic stance. The seventeenth century, it should be remembered, was not only a period of intense religious and political struggle, but a period of revolutionary scientific and philosophical thought. It was the century when Francis Bacon's inductive method was establishing itself as the most reliable way of arriving at scientific truth; it was the century when the Copernican theory tended to minimize the uniqueness and importance of the earth, hence of humankind, in the universe; it was the century when Thomas Hobbes's materialism and degrading view of human nature tended to outrage the orthodox or reflective Christian. Given this kind of intellectual milieu, readers may easily see how the poem might be interpreted as the impassioned utterance of a man who has lost anything resembling a religious or philosophical view of life (excluding, of course, pessimism). The paradox of the poem consists in the question of whether the speaker is honestly reflecting his view of life—pessimism—and advocating sensuality as the only way to make the best of a bad situation or whether he is simply something of a cad—stereotypically male, conceited, and superior, employing eloquence, argument, and soaringly passionate poetry merely as a line, a devious means to a sensual end. If the former is the case, there is something poignant in the way the man must choose the most exquisite pleasure he knows, sensuality, as a way of spitting in the face of his grand tormentor and victorious foe, Time. If the latter, then his disturbing images of the female body directed at his lady only turn upon him to reveal his fears and expose his lust. A feminist reading, as in Chapter 8, sees the rhetoric of the poem very differently than does a traditional reading.

2. Hamlet

Any discussion of *Hamlet* should acknowledge the enormous body of excellent commentary that sees the play as valuable primarily for its moral and philosophical insights. Little more can be done here than to summarize the most famous of such interpretations. They naturally center on the character of Hamlet. Some explain Hamlet as an idealist temperamentally unsuited for life in a world peopled by fallible creatures. He is therefore shattered when he discovers that some humans are so ambitious for a crown that they are willing to murder for it and that others are so highly sexed that they will violate not only the laws of decorum (for example, by remarrying within a month of a spouse's death) but also the civil and ecclesiastical laws against incest. He is further crushed when he thinks that his beloved and his former schoolfellows are tools of his murderous uncle. Other critics see Hamlet's plight as that of the essentially moral and virtuous intellectual man, certainly aware of the gentlemanly code that demands satisfaction for a wrong, but too much the student of philosophy and the Christian religion to believe in the morality or the logic of revenge. Related to this is the view of Hamlet as a kind of transitional figure, torn between the demands and the values of the Middle Ages and those of the modern world. The opposed theory maintains that Hamlet *is* a man of action, thwarted by such practical obstacles as how to kill a king surrounded by bodyguards. Many modern critics emphasize what they term Hamlet's psychoneurotic state, a condition that obviously derives from the moral complexities with which he is faced.

Hamlet fulfills the technical requirements of the revenge play as well as the salient requirements of a classical tragedy; that is, it shows a person of heroic proportions going down to defeat under circumstances too powerful for him to cope with. For most readers and audiences the question of Hamlet's tragic flaw will remain a moot one. But this will not keep them from recognizing the play as one of the most searching artistic treatments of the problems and conflicts that form so large a part of the human condition, especially revenge.

3. Huckleberry Finn

Huckleberry Finn is a living panorama of a country at a given time in history. It also provides insights, and it makes judgments that are no less valid in the larger sense today than they are about the period Mark Twain chronicled. This fidelity to life in character, action, speech, and setting; this personal testament; this encyclopedia of human nature; this most eloquent of all homilies—all of these are what cause this book to be not only a supreme artistic creation but also, in the words of Lionel Trilling, "one of the central documents of American culture" (6).

Important as are its historical and biographical aspects, the chief impact of *Huckleberry Finn* derives from its morality. This is, indeed, the *meaning* of the novel. All other aspects are subservient to this one. Man's inhumanity to man, especially within slavery (as Huck says, "Human beings *can* be awful cruel to one another"), is the major theme of this work, and it is exemplified in both calm and impassioned denunciation and satire. Almost all the major events and most of the minor ones are variations on this theme. The cruelty may be manifested in attempts to swindle young orphans out of their inheritance, to con village yokels with burlesque shows, to fleece religion-hungry frontier folk with camp meetings, or to tar and feather malefactors extralegally. Pap Finn is the archetype of the cruel father. Cruelty can and often does have even more serious consequences: for example, the brutal and senseless slaughter of the aristocratic Grangerfords and Shepherdsons and the murder of a harmless old windbag by another arrogant aristocrat; everywhere in the novel one encounters the violence of racism and slavery.

The ray of hope that Mark Twain reveals is the relationship of Huck and Jim; Huck rejects the values of the society of his time (he has all along had misgivings about them) and decides to treat Jim as a fellow human being. The **irony** is that Huck has made the right decision by scrapping the "right" reasons (that is, the logic of conventional theology) and by following his own conscience. He is probably too young to have intellectualized his decision and applied it to black people as a whole. Doubtless it applies only to Jim as an individual. But this is a tremendous advance for a boy of Huck's years. It is a lesson that is stubbornly resisted, reluctantly learned. But it is *the* lesson of *Huckleberry Finn.*

How ironic, then, that Twain will not allow us to enjoy that lesson—in the Phelps Farm episodes at the end of the novel Twain has Huck forget his epiphany and join Tom in tormenting Jim while he is held prisoner. Unlike most "moral" heroes, Huck fails, and, instead of returning home, he flees. Huck's failure to live up to his heroic ideals and to return home to live them out is not to be blamed on him, however: Twain is indicting the society around Huck that so overpoweringly reinforces racist beliefs. And one wonders what will become of Jim as a free man; such people had many hurdles to clear and could end up at any moment back in slavery. Most importantly, the troubled conclusion of *Huckleberry Finn* reflects Twain's suspicions about justice and especially God's justice. Twain believed in God, to be sure, but he thought God was a cruel trickster at best and a malevolent cosmic force at worst. In the novel God is symbolized in the unlikely form of pap Finn, who, after all, is Huck's father figure, a proponent of the racist and antichild values of Huck's hometown—even as he also spouts the worst racial invective in the book.

4. *"Young Goodman Brown"*

The terror and suspense in the Hawthorne story function as integral parts of the allegory that defines the story's theme. In **allegory**—a narrative containing a meaning beneath the surface one—there is usually a one-to-one relationship; that is, one idea or object in the narrative stands for only one idea or object allegorically. A story from the Old Testament illustrates this. The pharaoh of Egypt dreamed that seven fat cows were devoured by seven lean cows. Joseph interpreted this dream as meaning that seven years of plenty (good crops) would be followed by seven years of famine. "Young Goodman Brown" clearly functions on this level of allegory (while at times becoming richly **symbolic**). Brown is not just one Salem citizen of the late seventeenth century, but rather seems to typify humankind, to be in a sense Everyman, in that what he does and the reason he does it appear very familiar to most people, based on their knowledge of others and on honest appraisal of their own behavior.

For example, Goodman Brown, like most people, wants to experience evil—not perpetually, of course, for he is by and large a decent chap, a respectably married man, a member of a church—but he desires to "taste the forbidden fruit" ("have one last fling") before settling down to the business of being a solid citizen and attaining the good life. He feels that he can do this because he means to retain his religious faith, personified in his wife, who, to reinforce the allegory, is even named Faith. But in order to encounter evil, he must part with his Faith at least temporarily, something he is either willing or compelled to do. It is here that he makes his fatal mistake, for evil turns out to be not some abstraction nor something that can be played with for a while and then put down, but the very pillars of Goodman Brown's world—his ancestors, his earthly rulers, his spiritual overseers, and finally his Faith. In short, so overpowering are the fact and universality of evil in the world that Goodman Brown comes to doubt the existence of any good. By looking upon the very face of evil, he is transformed into a cynic and a misanthrope whose "dying hour was gloom."

Thomas E. Connolly has remarked that Goodman Brown has not *lost* his faith; he has *found* it (370–75). That is, Goodman Brown believes that he understands the significance of the Calvinistic teaching of the depravity of humans; this realization makes him doubt and dislike his fellows, and in effect paralyzes his moral will so that he questions the motivation of every apparently virtuous act. But this is surely a strange conclusion for Brown to reach, for he has violated the cardinal tenets of Calvinism. If Calvinism stressed anything, it stressed the practical and spiritual folly of placing hope or reliance on human beings and their efforts, which by the very nature of things are bound to fail, whereas God alone never fails. Therefore all trust should be reposed in Him. It is just this teaching that Brown has not learned. On the practical plane, he cannot distinguish between appearance and reality. He takes things and people at face value. If a man *looks* respectable and godly, Brown assumes that he is. And if the man turns out to be a scoundrel, Brown's every standard crumbles. He is in a sense guilty of a kind of idolatry: human institutions in the forms of ministers, church officers, statesmen, and wives have been his god. When they are discredited, he has nothing else to place his trust in and thus becomes a cynic and a misanthrope.

Thus, rather than making a frontal attack on Calvinism, Hawthorne indicted certain reprehensible aspects of Puritanism: the widespread holier-than-thou attitude; the spiritual blindness that led many Puritans to mistake a pious front for genuine religion; the latent sensuality in the apparently austere and disciplined soul (the very capstone of hypocrisy, because sins of the flesh were particularly odious to Puritan orthodoxy).

It will perhaps be argued that Calvinism at its most intense, with its dim view of human nature, is quite likely to produce cynicism and misanthropy. But historically, if paradoxically, Calvinists have been dynamic and full of faith; they have been social and political reformers, educators, enterprisers in business, explorers, foes of tyranny. The religious furnace in which these souls were tempered, however, is too hot for Goodman Brown. He is of a weaker breed, and the sum of his experience with the hard realities of life is disillusion and defeat. He has lost his faith. Whether because his faith was false or because he wished for an objectively verifiable certainty that is the antithesis of faith, Hawthorne does not say. He does not even say whether the whole thing was a dream or reality, replacing a firm conclusion with ambiguity. Actually, it does not matter. The result remains: faith has been destroyed and supplanted by total despair because Brown is neither a good Calvinist, a good Christian, nor, in the larger sense, a good man.

5. *"Everyday Use"*

It is obvious that racism, perhaps society's most troubling moral issue, underlies the actions in this story. It has unjustly reduced the narrator and Maggie to a low socioeconomic position and kept them there; it has bred an innate fear and mistrust of whites in the narrator, an otherwise strong, upright, and intelligent woman; it has alienated Dee, a bright and talented young woman, from whites to a degree that makes reconciliation unlikely; and along with its handmaiden, religious bigotry, it has allowed whites to engage in illegal and threatening action against hardworking black cattle raisers. And yet it is not the main moral or didactic point of the story. That point is Dee's misjudgment and mistreatment of her mother and sister, actions traceable to her ideological attitude that blinds her to their beauty and quiet heroism and the way these qualities have allowed them to know and respect themselves and their history in a way that Dee cannot understand. Like most dogmatists of whatever stripe, Dee is frequently obtuse. She assumes that her mother and sister have "chosen" to live in poverty in a racist community. She is too ashamed to bring her friends to her family's home, but she snaps numerous Polaroid pictures of the dilapidated shack, her "backward" family, even the cow wandering through the yard. Such pictures will not demonstrate tender or nostalgic feelings for the subjects but will serve some sort of political agenda. Dee is so arrogant and callous that she wants to appropriate for her own use even the few artifacts her mother and sister do possess that are special and practically useful to them.

The narrator dominates the story, telling it from her point of view as both observer and participant. Though uneducated after the second grade and untraveled except in her dreams, she is a most remarkable woman, who demonstrates intelligence, sophistication, and a wry sense of humor in her narration. Her religion, a source of unalloyed joy to her as she worships, is also strength and guidance for tough living. Ideologues like Dee may think the church merely keeps her docile and uninvolved by its promises of "pie in the sky bye and bye." But it is an important part of black heritage, and it played a key role in the civil rights movement. It should also be noted here that it furnished part of the money for Dee's education. As far as the narrator is concerned, her religion has enabled her to rise above her oppressors without bitterness and without being obsessed by them. She feels no compulsion toward recrimination. In her dreams, Johnny Carson is "a smiling, gray, sporty man," who shakes her hand and compliments her on having a fine daughter like Dee. When thinking about the persons who poisoned some of the cattle belonging to her Black Muslim neighbors, the narrator simply calls them "white folks." They and the outrages of their kind, historic and contemporary, do not perpetually occupy her mind.

The narrator's dream of being reunited on the Johnny Carson show with Dee, the *Wunderkind* who has "made it" in the modern world, is an ironic inversion of what is about to take place. In her brief visit Dee does not find that her mother has shed a hundred pounds or used cosmetics to lighten the appearance of her skin or become a clever conversationalist. Nor does she pin an orchid on her and embrace her with tears of gratitude. After a generally unsatisfactory meeting, Dee leaves while lecturing her mother about not understanding her "heritage" and exhorting Maggie to reject her lifestyle—and, by implication, her mother—and to "make something" of herself.

The characters—the narrator and Maggie on one side, Dee and Hakim-a-barber on the other—represent two different points of view. The narrator depicts Dee and Hakim unsympathetically, satirically. To her, they look odd. Dee, who always had style, looks like a sideshow: colors too loud and garish, dress too long (though the narrator concedes she likes its loose flowing quality), and excessive jewelry, jangling and gauche. Hakim's hair is long, and his chin whiskers look like a "kinky mule tail." The names these two have chosen sound ridiculous to the narrator though she is willing to learn them. She dashes cold water on Dee's claim that her given name is an oppressive white name by pointing out that she was named for her aunt and her grandmother.

When Hakim announces that he accepts some of the doctrines of the narrator's Muslim neighbors but that "farming and raising cattle is not my style," he implicitly criticizes the narrator, who has brained a bull calf with a sledgehammer and had the meat dressed out before nightfall. Dee's trendy pretensions to folk arts and crafts—which would have cruelly robbed her mother and sister of their most treasured possessions—reveal an even uglier aspect of character, one which the narrator thwarts with righteous indignation. Finally, Dee's condescension, self-aggrandizement, and arrogance prevent her from having a clue about her mother's and sister's feelings.

What the narrator reveals about herself and Maggie makes them very sympathetic characters. Early in the story, we admire the towering, matriarchal strength and wisdom of the narrator, her natural and keen ability to size up people, her dry wit, her refusal to become cynical and disillusioned about Dee or her own hard lot in life, her tenderness for the pitiful Maggie. Our hearts go out to Maggie, homely and less gifted than Dee, and thus cowed by her, scarred by the house fire in her childhood, and yet willing to relinquish her birthright of the family quilts to Dee, who could "appreciate" them. The moralist would maintain that readers may learn valuable lessons from both groups of characters, but the lessons are far from simple and clear-cut. It is too easy to reject Dee's militant individualism and pride with its implicit reverse racism and too easy to accept unquestioningly the narrator and Maggie's Christian stoicism and its suggested "Uncle Tom" attitude. It may be possible to reconcile these conflicting views of life. There is certainly nothing in the traditional moral approach that insists on an all-or-nothing interpretive position.

6. Frankenstein

If one studies even in a cursory way the years of Mary Shelley's life when she was first the mistress to Percy Bysshe Shelley and then his wife, and notes the characteristics of the ménage in which she lived during those years, one would hardly expect to find in her novel any extended endorsement of conventional sexual morality and family relationships. But indeed the novel is heavily imbued with notions of familial piety, with love of one's siblings, and with the expectation of a conventional marriage between Frankenstein and his cousin Elizabeth (that they were in fact cousins was not a bar in the society of the day). This familial bonding extends also to Frankenstein's friend Clerval, who is as close in a fraternal way as a blood brother might be. In short, to the traditional critic, the contrast between the reality of Mary's relationships and the ones depicted in the family of the Frankensteins is evident.

The novel's moral and philosophical considerations are interesting and challenging to an age when cloning, fertility techniques, end-of-life issues, and stem cell research are the latest headlines. Frankenstein is akin to some scientists of our own day, against whom ethicists bring charges that the scientists attempt and achieve developments more because they have the technical ability to make those developments than because they have the ethical clarity to direct their studies. Frankenstein stoked his ambition by the self-deluding thought that he would discover the secret of life and create a living being that in turn would be the flower of humanity. In Chapter 3 of the first volume, he says,

> Although I possessed the capacity of bestowing animation, yet to prepare a frame for the reception of it, with all its intricacies of fibres, muscles, and veins, still remained a work of inconceivable difficulty and labour. I doubted at first whether I should attempt the creation of a being like myself or one of simpler organization; but my imagination was too much exalted by my first success to permit me to doubt of my ability to give life to an animal as complex and wonderful as man.

Moved, however, by the awareness of "the improvement which every day takes place in science and mechanics," he resolves upon "the creation of a human being." Arrogating to himself the power conventionally attributed only to the Almighty, Frankenstein is moved by a **hubris** akin to that of the tragic heroes of classic Greek drama. He does not think through the full range of possibilities, including the possibility of disastrous failure in the midst of his seeming success.

In our own day, those who express great caution about such issues as stem cell research on human cloning need not base that caution on religious grounds alone, for there is another dimension in Mary Shelley's novel besides the creation of another life, momentous as that is. That dimension is the later responsibility for the created being as that being enters the world and society, responsibility for one's own children. For clearly Frankenstein is self-deluding and morally culpable for his failure to accept responsibility, a charge that ironically the Creature, who—in some of his actions an immoral murderer—cogently lodges. In fact, Frankenstein projects his own failure (inadequate paternity, we might say) onto the Creature. To Frankenstein, it is the Creature who is the epitome of evil, a murderer, a vengeance-seeking beast. Frankenstein refuses to accept responsibility for his progeny and to society for the horrors he himself has inflicted upon it.

Even in pursuing the Creature into the frozen wastes of the North to wreak his revenge—possibly symbolic of the absence of love, as it is in Dante's *Inferno* and in Frost's "Fire and Ice"—Frankenstein's monomania is that of a person who has totally lost his moral compass. Something like Melville's Captain Ahab as he attacks the white whale, Frankenstein is challenging a moral universe in which he himself has become the worst of sinners.

And if Frankenstein the character challenges a moral universe, *Frankenstein* the nineteenth-century novel challenges the twenty-first century, for as Sharon Begley wrote in an article for the *Wall Street Journal*,

> If researchers manage to create living cells from scratch, their mastery of the machinery of life could blur the line between alive and not-alive....Scientists are close enough to creating life in the lab that it is time to start a public debate about what that would mean—for traditional views of the sanctity of life as well as for whether the creators will be able to control their creations (B-1).

V. SUMMARY OF KEY POINTS

- The "old" historicism gave way to formalism, or New Criticism, and then this in turn was followed by a return to historicizing, called "new historicism."
- All critical approaches influence each other and have more in common than may at first appear. For example, deconstruction is partly built upon formalism.
- *Textual Study*: Different versions of many texts exist, and textual critics try to research and edit a work in order to establish an accurate, authentic text for the reader, or "what the writer intended." Textual critics not only

prepare a reliable text but also provide information on the genesis of the text. Textual critics use the terms "accidentals" (spelling, punctuation, capitalization) and "substantives" (the actual reading of the text, e.g. which word is meant or which passage should be restered).

- *Genre Study*: Genre critics, inspired by Aristotle's *Poetics*, determine the type of text and identify that genre's special features in its form as a short story, poem, novel, or drama. Aristotle specified the features of drama, especially tragedy, such as mimēsis, the tragic hero, hubris, and catharsis. The elements of any drama he identified as action (plot), character, thought (theme), diction (language), melody, and spectacle (special effects). Modern critics such as Northrop Frye, E. D. Hirsch, and Robert Scholes expanded the study of genre.

- *Source Study*: Scholars of source study identify the other texts that influenced the creation of a given text, especially as shown through the use of allusion.

- *Historical-Biographical Approaches*: For these traditional critics the focus is upon the life, times, and environment of the author and/or the literary characters.

- *Moral-Philosophical Approaches*: These approaches examine the moral and philosophical issues in a text, focusing mostly on what it says, what is being taught in the text, not on its technique.

VI. LIMITATIONS OF TRADITIONAL APPROACHES

The traditional approaches—textual studies, genre studies, source study, historical and biographical approaches, and moral and philosophical approaches—are sometimes lumped together as merely "traditional" in the sense of "old," but remain fundamental to literary study of any kind and inform many of the more contemporary approaches. They are also quite diverse. Thus they present different kinds of limitations.

To be sure, after the New Critics the text became central to literary criticism in a way that it had rarely been before (though we must remember that a focus on the formal features of the text goes back to Aristotle's *Poetics*). Of these approaches, textual studies, genre studies, and source study have not been diminished by subsequent literary theory, as they address the basics of establishing *what* the text is and *how* it is related to other texts. Genre studies actually anticipates the New Critics' emphasis upon form and, later, deconstruction and related approaches. Traditional historical approaches, once seen as hopelessly outdated, have newly informed such later movements as new historicism and postcolonialism. The danger in any historical approach is that it can tend to reduce a work of art to an "example" of a certain historical period, eliding its unique features and the artist's craft. Biographical studies have come in for the most criticism—structuralists and poststructuralists announced the "death" of the author and, like the New Critics, focused only on the text, in their case its linguistic features. Moral and philosophical approaches also have their limitations—mainly, as Henry James argued in "The Art of Fiction," drawing *only* the "moral of the story" as a sort of life-lesson, without really encountering the text as art—but have reemerged in areas as diverse as Marxism, feminism, and postcolonial studies, in which the message is privileged over the form. Historical/biographical and moral/philosophical approaches, like the more contemporary content-based theories, can become a Procrustean bed in which the "theme" of the work is addressed prematurely or even exclusively. Too often students are asked about themes when they should begin with form.

The more one learns about critical approaches to literature, the more one is struck not so much by the differences between approaches or by the limitations of any one approach, but by their ongoing interrelatedness. As we shall see in the chapters to come in this handbook, what is new is often old, and what is old persists in informing readers.

QUICK REFERENCE

Altick, Richard D. *The Art of Literary Research*, Rev. ed. New York: Norton, 1975.

Babcock, Weston. *"Hamlet": A Tragedy of Errors*. Lafayette, IN: Purdue University Press, 1961.

Begley, Sharon. "Researchers Exploring 'What Is Life?' Seek to Create a Living Cell." *Wall Street Journal* (Friday 2 April 2004): B-1.

Beyer, Art. *From the New Criticism to Deconstruction: The Reception of Structuralism and Post-Structuralism*. Champaign-Urbana: University of Illinois Press, 1988.

Bradley, A. C. *Shakespearean Tragedy*. London: Macmillan, 1914.

Brandel, Fernand. *The Structures of Everyday Life: Civilization and Capitalism, 15ᵗʰ–18ᵗʰ Century*. Vol. I. New York: Harper and Row, 1982.

Bruccoli, Matthew J. *The Composition of "Tender Is the Night": A Study of the Manuscripts*. Pittsburgh: University of Pittsburgh Press, 1963.

Bryan, W. F., and Germaine Dempster, eds. *Sources and Analogues of Chaucer's Canterbury Tales*. 1941. Reprint, New York: Humanities Press International, 1958.

Cargill, Oscar. *Toward a Pluralistic Criticism*. Carbondale: Southern Illinois University Press, 1965.

Chandler, Daniel. "An Introduction to Genre Theory" (1977). http://www.aber.ac.uk/media/Documents/intgenre/intgenre.html

Christian, Barbara T. "Everyday Use." In *Women Writers: Texts and Contexts*. New Brunswick, NJ: Rutgers University Press, 1994.

Connolly, Thomas E. "Hawthorne's 'Young Goodman Brown': An Attack on Puritanic Calvinism." *American Literature* 28 (Nov. 1956): 370–75.

Cooper, Charles W., and John Holmes. *Preface to Poetry*. New York: Harcourt, 1946.

Crane, Ronald S. *A Collection of English Poems, 1660–1800*. New York: Harper, 1932.

Crane, Ronald S. *Critics and Criticism: Ancient and Modern*. Chicago: University of Chicago Press, 1952.

Daiches, David. *Critical Approaches to Literature*. Englewood Cliffs, NJ: Prentice Hall, 1956.

Derrida, Jacques. "The Law of Genre." *Critical Inquiry,* 7, 1 (Autumn 1980): 55–81.

Devitt, Amy J. *"Writing Genres."* Carbondale: Southern Illinois University Press, 2004.

Eliot, T. S. Introduction to *The Adventures of Huckleberry Finn.* London: Cresset, 1950. Reprinted in *Adventures of Huckleberry Finn.* 2nd ed. Ed. Sculley Bradley, Richard Croom Beatty, E. Hudson Long, and Thomas Cooley. New York: W. W. Norton, 1977.

Elledge, Scott. *Milton's "Lycidas," Edited to Serve as an Introduction to Criticism.* New York: Harper, 1966.

Frye, Northrop. *Anatomy of Criticism: Four Essays.* Princeton: Princeton University Press, 1957.

Gibson, Walker, ed. *Poems in the Making.* Boston: Houghton Mifflin, 1963.

Gilbert, Allan H. *On the Composition of* Paradise Lost: *A Study of the Ordering and Insertion of Material.* 1947. Reprint, New York: Octagon Press, 1966.

Gittings, Robert. *Odes of Keats and Their Earliest Known Manuscripts.* Kent, OH: Kent State University Press, 1970.

Gray, Janet. "Alice Walker." In *American Writers: A Collection of Literary Biographies.* Supp. III, pt. 2. Ed. Lea Baechler and A. Walton Litz. New York: Scribner's, 1991.

Greetham, D. C. *Textual Scholarship: An Introduction.* Hamden, CT: Garland Publishing, 1994.

Hemingway, Ernest. *Green Hills of Africa.* New York: Scribner's, 1935.

Hill, Hamlin, and Walter Blair. *The Art of "Huckleberry Finn."* New York: Intext, 1962.

Hirsch, E. D. *Validity in Interpretation.* New Haven, CT: Yale University Press, 1967.

Hoffman, Daniel. *Form and Fable in American Fiction.* New York: Oxford University Press, 1961.

Holman, Hugh. "The Defense of Art: Criticism Since 1930." In *The Development of American Literary Criticism.* Ed. Floyd Stovall. Chapel Hill: University of North Carolina Press, 1955.

Housman, A. E. "The Application of Thought to Textual Criticism." In *Art and Error: Modern Textual Editing.* Ed. Ronald Gottesman and Scott Bennett. Bloomington: Indiana University Press, 1970.

Hoy, Cyrus, ed. *Hamlet.* New York: Norton (Critical Edition), 1963.

Hubler, Edward. Introduction to *Hamlet.* In *The Complete Signet Classic Shakespeare.* Ed. Sylvan Barnet. New York: Harcourt, 1972.

Hunter, J. Paul, ed., *Mary Shelley, Frankenstein.* New York: W. W. Norton and Co., 1996.

Hyman, Stanley Edgar. *The Armed Vision.* New York: Random House, 1955.

James, Henry. "The Art of Fiction." *Partial Portraits.* London: Macmillan, 1888.

Kennedy, Beverly. "Cambridge MS. Dd. 4.24: A Misogynist Scribal Revision of the *Wife of Bath's Prologue?*" *Chaucer Review* 30 (1996): 343–58.

Levin, David. "Shadows of Doubt: Specter Evidence in Hawthorne's 'Young Goodman Brown.'" *American Literature* 34 (Nov. 1962): 344–52.

Lord, George de F. *Andrew Marvell, Complete Poetry.* New York: Random House (Modern), 1968.

Lumiansky, R. M., ed. *Malory's Originality: A Critical Study of* Le Morte Darthur. Baltimore: Johns Hopkins University Press, 1964.

Martz, Louis L. *The Anchor Anthology of Seventeenth-Century Verse.* Vol. 1. Garden City, NY: Doubleday, 1969.

Preminger, Alex, ed. *Princeton Encyclopedia of Poetry and Poetics.* 3rd ed. Princeton, NJ: Princeton University Press, 1993.

Ransom, John Crowe. *The New Criticism.* Norfolk, CT: New Directions, 1941.

———. *The World's Body.* New York: Scribner's, 1938.

Rieger, James, ed. *Frankenstein, or the Modern Prometheus: The 1818 Text,* by Mary Wollstonecraft Shelley. Chicago: University of Chicago Press, 1982.

Robinson, Charles E., ed. *Frankenstein or the Modern Prometheus: The Original Two-Volume Novel of 1816-1817 from the Bodleian Library Manuscripts by Mary Wollstonecraft Shelley (with Percy Bysshe Shelley).* Oxford: Bodleian Library, 2008.

Rodway, Allan. "Generic Criticism: The Approach Through Type, Mode, and Kind." In *Contemporary Criticism.* Stratford-Upon-Avon Studies 12. Ed. Malcolm Bradbury and David Palmer. London: Edward Arnold, 1970.

Scholes, Robert. *Structuralism in Literature: An Introduction.* New Haven, CT: Yale University Press, 1974.

Small, Christopher. *Mary Shelley's* Frankenstein: *Tracing the Myth.* Pittsburgh, PA: University of Pittsburgh Press, 1972.

Thorpe, James. *Principles of Textual Criticism.* San Marino, CA: The Huntington Library, 1972.

Trilling, Lionel. "Introduction." *The Adventures of Huckleberry Finn.* New York: Holt, 1948.

Utley, Francis Lee, Lynn Z. Bloom, and Arthur F. Kinney, eds. *Bear, Man, and God: Eight Approaches to William Faulkner's "The Bear."* 2nd ed. New York: Random House, 1971.

Vinaver, Eugène, ed. *The Works of Sir Thomas Malory,* by Thomas Malory. 2nd ed. Oxford: Oxford University Press, 1967.

White, Hayden. "Anomalies of Genre: The Utility of Theory and History for the Study of Literary Genres." *New Literary History* 34, 3 (Summer 2003): 597–615.

Williams, Carolyn. "Genre Matters: Response. (Analysis of Literary Genres)." *Victorian Studies,* 48, 2 (Winter 2006): 295–304.

Wilson, J. Dover. *What Happens in "Hamlet."* London: Cambridge University Press, 1935.

Wonham, Henry B. "The Disembodied Yarn-Spinner and *Huckleberry Finn.*" In *Mark Twain and the Art of the Tall Tale.* New York: Oxford University Press, 1993.

3

Formalist Approaches

I. THE PROCESS OF FORMALIST ANALYSIS: MAKING THE CLOSE READER

The term *formalism* as a critical approach means that obviously we are to be alert to "form." But to say that is just as obviously to beg the question "What is form?" And we cannot say simply that form is structure, or that structure is form, for that is to go in circles. So what are the ways to appreciate form?

Intensive reading begins with a sensitivity to the words of the text and all their **denotative** and **connotative** values and implications. An awareness of multiple meanings, even the **etymologies** of words as traced in dictionaries, will offer significant guidelines to what the work says. Usually adequate for most readers is one of the standard collegiate dictionaries. But one should also be aware of the vastly larger resources in unabridged dictionaries and especially the details and examples of historical changes in word meanings as recorded in the most recent edition of *The Oxford English Dictionary.* So first let us look at the words and the sentences in which we find them.

But just as we begin to study closely the words and their meanings, almost simultaneously we must also begin to look for structural relationships and patterns—not just in the words and their relationships, but also in larger units. Form becomes much more than sentence patterns; it becomes the relationship of **stanzas** in a poem, or the interplay of an **octave** and a **sestet** in a **sonnet**. It becomes the **tone** or **mood** that the text builds, and possibly the shifting and alternating of moods. It becomes the sequence of plot elements, even episodes, in a narrative, or the juxtaposition of scenes in a play. It becomes the relationship between the teller of the narrative and the hearer, possibly the **ambiguity** of the teller's version of the story. Because the reader's response is in a very important sense part of the formal structure of a text, we also include in this chapter Reader-Response Theory, which was a reaction to the text-only centeredness of formalism.

So let us assume that now we have some degree of knowledge of the words of the text, at least in their denotative senses. Let us also assume that we can mentally plot out the sequence of actions, or of sequences and shifting of what the words seem to be telling us. Now we can note that some of these words are deeply connotative also, or perhaps they name objects that have symbolic value, and as we probe the connotations and **symbols** they take on associations, or develop patterns that somehow have relevance within themselves and to other patterns. Images emerge as more and more important, perhaps insistently forcing themselves to the fore. We note that certain images, or colors, or references to time—a host of possibilities in our human experience—keep coming up. Some of these may contribute to the setting of the work, its actual place and time, or more subtly, its ambience. Bit by formal bit, we think we begin to see a theme emerging from the work.

None of this is happening in any set sequence. It is more like when we walk into a room new to us, crowded with people, furniture, art works, a fire in the hearth. How do we see things? How do our eyes move across the scene? What do we see first, what next?

In the printed text perhaps the next thing is an **allusion** that has caught our attention, a reference to a bit of history or mythology, or to another work of literature. Maybe a word has taken on more than one meaning, causing us to read the text at more than one level; or we suspect that **irony** is developing in what we see, and we become suspicious that first impressions need modification. Or details of a narrative seem especially vivid or striking, but not yet clearly important as we move through the plot's complication—and then, suddenly perhaps, the narrative reaches a climactic point, and all details fall into place by the point in the narrative that we sometimes call the dénouement.

Then there is a sense of closure, a sense of fulfillment of the expectations that have been built up.

What did the author do by so arranging those words, those images and symbols, those details of plot and action? How did the author "achieve" this accomplishment? (We will return to the concept of "achieved content" later in this chapter.)

In retrospect, we can say that what the author did was to make us see that internal relationships gradually reveal a form, a principle by which all subordinate patterns can be accommodated and accounted for. When all the words, phrases, **metaphors**, images, and symbols are examined in terms of each other and of the whole, any literary text worth our efforts will display its own internal logic. When that logic has been established, the reader is close to identifying the overall form of the work.

So now, in review, what must we do to make ourselves close readers in a formalist way? Let this list remind us of what we shall look for in the works we will study in this chapter: structure, shape, interplay, interrelationships, denotations and connotations, contexts, images, symbols, repeated details, climax (rising action, falling action), dénouement, balances and tensions, **rhythms** and **rhymes** that catch our attention, sounds that do the same, the speaker's apparent voice, a

The idea of seeing beyond the text?

single line—or even a word—set off all by itself. Whatever, in other words, contributes to the uniqueness of the work.

II. A BRIEF HISTORY OF FORMALIST CRITICISM

A. The Course of Half a Century

Formalism, as we use the term in this book, emphasizes the manner of reading literature that was most significantly given its special dimensions by English and American critics in the first two-thirds of the twentieth century. To many, indeed to most, students of literature during that era, this approach was known as the New Criticism. However, though the New Critics held sway in literary criticism for a long time, today they have been critiqued by more contextual approaches and joined by new formalisms as well. In the last third of the century, the New Criticism came to be called by other names, not always favorable, especially in the face of more politically and culturally based approaches. Now the New Criticism is the "old" criticism, to be sure, but its emphasis on form and close reading still informs and underlies subsequent approaches. Being a good reader of literature and using any approach to understanding literature necessitates reading closely and reading well. Reading well is what the New Critics helped us learn to do—especially as they succeeded the traditional approaches such as historical criticism.

The New Critics taught us to look at the individual work of art as an **organic form**. They articulated the concept that in organic form there is a consistency and an internal validity that we should appreciate. In doing so, we would make the work part of our consciousness.

One of the most salient considerations of the New Critics was emphasis on form, on the work of art as an object. Can we imagine any art—whether literary, musical, plastic, or dramatic, and regardless of its era, even our own—when formlessness is sometimes important and that does not have some sense of form? The form need not be geometric or physical or otherwise perceptible to the eye, and indeed often it is not, but it is there. To be sure, it might be most easily perceived first at a physical level: the external and obvious shape of a statue, the geometric pattern of arches and of horizontal and vertical lines in a building, the four-line stanza of Sappho, or the careful physical shape of a sonnet or a haiku. The New Critics did not invent these forms, but they helped us read better by reminding us of what was there in the past and teaching us how to read the new—the new forms, new symbols, new ironies.

B. Backgrounds of Formalist Theory

Classical art and aesthetics amply testify to a preoccupation with form. Plato exploits dialectic and shapes the movement toward Socratic wisdom with his imagery, metaphor, dramatic scenes, characterization, setting, and tone. Aristotle's *Poetics* recommends an "orderly arrangement of parts" that form a beautiful whole or "organism." Horace admonishes the would-be poet: "In short, be your subject

developed by greek philosophers

what it will, let it be simple and unified." And some awareness of formalism is at least implicit in many other classical, medieval, and Renaissance treatises on art or poetics.

But the Romantic movement in Europe in the late eighteenth and nineteenth centuries intensified speculations about form in literature. Samuel Taylor Coleridge (1772–1834) brought to readers of English the conception of a dynamic *imagination* as the shaping power and unifier of vision—a conception he had acquired from his studies of the German philosophical idealists: Kant, Hegel, Fichte, and Schelling. Such a conception encouraged discrimination between a poem and other forms of discourse by stressing the poem's power to elicit delight as a "whole" and "distinctive gratification from each component *part*." In a "*legitimate* poem," Coleridge declared, the parts "mutually support and explain each other; all in their proportion harmonizing with, and supporting the purpose and known influences of metrical arrangement."

This interrelationship between the whole and the parts—**organic form**—was manifested in a consistently recurring image among the Romantics—the image of growth, particularly of vegetation. Perhaps because of the Romantics' infatuation with nature, the analogy usually likened the internal life of a painting or poem to the quintessential unity of parts within a tree, flower, or plant: as the seed determines, so the organism develops and lives. In a letter to John Taylor (February 27, 1818) Keats wrote that one of his "axioms" was "That if Poetry comes not as naturally as the Leaves to a tree it had better not come at all." Shelley uses imagery of growth and of vegetation several times in his "Defence of Poetry." In talking of the relationship of sounds in poetry, he counsels against "the vanity of translation; it were as wise to cast a violet into a crucible that you might discover the formal principle of its colour and odour, as to seek to transfuse from one language into another the creations of a poet. The plant must spring again from its seed, or it will bear no flower. ..." He calls the thoughts of the poet "the germs of the flower and the fruit of latest time," claiming, "All high poetry is infinite; it is as the first acorn, which contained all oaks potentially." And again of poetry,

> ...this power arises from within, like the colour of a flower which fades and changes as it is developed.... The instinct and intuition of the poetical faculty is still more observable in the plastic and pictorial arts; a great statue or picture grows under the power of the artist as a child in the mother's womb....

In America, Edgar Allan Poe (1809–1849), extending Coleridge's theory, asserted the excellence of short **lyric** poems and short tales because they can maintain and transmit a single, unitary effect more successfully than can long works like *Paradise Lost*. In "The Philosophy of Composition" Poe demonstrated how the parts of his "The Raven" allegedly developed from the single effect he desired. Poe also reprimanded certain contemporary poets like Henry Wadsworth Longfellow for committing what he called the "heresy of the didactic" by tacking on obtrusive (thus inorganic) moral lessons and accordingly violating the lyric effects of their poems.

Later in the nineteenth century and on into the twentieth, Henry James in "The Art of Fiction" and the prefaces to his tales and novels argued for fiction as a "fine art" and for the intricate, necessary interrelationships of parts and the whole:

> There are bad and good novels, as there are bad pictures and good pictures; but that is the only distinction in which I can see any meaning, and I can as little imagine speaking of a novel of character as I can imagine speaking of a picture of character. When one says picture one says of character, when one says novel one says of incident, and the terms seem to be transposed at will. What is character but the determination of incident? What is incident BUT the illustration of character? What is either a picture or a novel that is *not* of character? What else do we seek in it and find in it? It is an incident for a woman to stand up with her hand resting on a table and look at you in a certain way; or if it not be an incident, I think it will be hard to say what it is.

James implies the same interdependence and kinship for all other aspects of a work of fiction—setting, theme, scene and narrative, image and symbol. When the artist is attending to his or her craft, nothing that goes into the work will be wasted, and form will be present: "Form alone *takes,* and holds and preserves, substance—saves it from the welter of helpless verbiage that we swim in as in a sea of tasteless tepid pudding." When the work achieves "organic form," everything will count.

C. The New Criticism

Although there were antecedents from Plato through James, a systematic and methodological formalist approach to literary criticism appeared only with the rise in the 1930s of what came to be called the New Criticism. Coming together originally at Vanderbilt University in the years following World War I, the New Critics included a teacher-scholar-poet, John Crowe Ransom, and several bright students—Allen Tate, Robert Penn Warren, and Cleanth Brooks. Associated at first in an informal group that discussed literature, they in time adopted the name of Fugitives and published an elegant literary magazine called *The Fugitive* in Nashville from 1922 to 1925. When the poetry and critical essays of T. S. Eliot came to their attention, they found sturdy reinforcement for ideas that were emerging from their study and writing of lyric poetry. Ideas thus shared and promoted included literature viewed as an organic tradition, the importance of strict attention to form, a conservatism related to classical values, the ideal of a society that encourages order and tradition, a preference for ritual, and the rigorous and analytical reading of literary texts. Eliot was particularly influential in his formulation of the **objective correlative** ("a set of objects, a situation, a chain of events which shall be the formula of [a] *particular* emotion; such that when the external facts are given, the emotion is immediately invoked"). Eliot was also influential in his endorsement of the English **Metaphysical poets** of the seventeenth century for their success in blending "states of mind and feeling" in a single "verbal equivalent." Such developments strengthened the emergent New Criticism, which by the 1950s had become the dominant critical system in such influential journals as *Sewanee Review, The Kenyon Review, The Southern Review,* and *The Hudson Review* and in college and university English departments.

The New Critics sought precision and structural tightness in the literary work; they favored a style and tone that tended toward irony; they insisted on the presence within the work of everything necessary for its analysis; and they called for an end to a concern by critics and teachers of English with matters outside the work itself—the life of the author, the history of his or her times, or the social and economic implications of the literary work. In short, they turned the attention of teachers, students, critics, and readers to the essential matter: *what* the work says and *how* it says it as inseparable issues. In this they were quite radical.

Members and disciples of the group advanced their critical theory and techniques through a series of brilliant college textbooks on literary analysis: *Understanding Poetry* (1939) and *Understanding Fiction* (1943) by Brooks and Warren; *Understanding Drama* (1945) by Brooks and Robert B. Heilman; *The Art of Modern Fiction* by Ray B. West, Jr., and Robert W. Stallman; and *The House of Fiction* (1950) by Caroline Gordon and Allen Tate. After 1942, *The Explicator,* a monthly publication, published hundreds of short textual explications of great varieties of literary works; and prestigious literary journals and quarterlies still publish articles that show the continuing influence of the New Criticism.

But even as the formalist approach of the New Critics was influencing readers, teachers, and students throughout the universities of the United States, well into the second half of the century, others were pointing to what they perceived to be deficiencies or worse in that approach. Frank Lentricchia in *After the New Criticism* (1980) offers a helpful overview of what was happening. He uses 1957 and the publication of three books that year to give one benchmark for the turn to other approaches and emphases. The three are Northrop Frye's *Anatomy of Criticism,* Cleanth Brooks and W. K. Wimsatt's *Literary Criticism: A Short History,* and Frank Kermode's *Romantic Image.* Coming hard upon Murray Krieger's *New Apologists for Poetry* (1956), they seem to fulfill, Lentricchia says, Krieger's prediction "that the New Criticism had done all it could do for American literary critics.... By about 1957, the moribund condition of the New Criticism and the literary needs it left unfulfilled placed us in a critical void. Even in the late 1940s, however, those triumphant times of the New Criticism, a theoretical opposition was already gathering strength" (3–4).

D. Reader-Response Criticism: A Reaction

Reader-response theory arose in large measure as a reaction against the New Criticism. If formalism regards a piece of literature as an art object with an existence of its own, independent of or not necessarily related to its author, its readers, the historical time it depicts, or the historical period in which it was written, formalism finds all meaning and value in it and regards everything else as extraneous, including readers, whom formalist critics regard as downright dangerous as sources of interpretation. To such critics, relying on readers as a source of meaning—precisely what reader-response criticism does—is to fall victim to subjectivism, and relativism.

Reader-response critics take a radically different approach. They feel that readers have been ignored in discussions of the reading process, when they should have been the central concern. The argument goes something like this: a text does not even exist, in a sense, until it is read by some reader. Indeed, the reader has a part in creating or actually does create the text. It is somewhat like the old question posed in philosophy classes: if a tree falls in the forest and no one hears it, does it make a sound? Reader-response critics are saying that in effect, if a text does not have a reader, it does not exist—or at least, it has no meaning. It is readers, with whatever experience they bring to the text, who give it its meaning. Whatever meaning it may have inheres in the reader, and thus it is the reader who should say what a text means.

We should, perhaps, point out here that reader-response theory is by no means a monolithic critical position. Those who give an important place to *readers* and their *responses* in interpreting a work come from a number of different critical camps. Reader-response critics see formalist critics as narrow, dogmatic, elitist, and certainly wrong-headed in essentially refusing readers even a place in the reading-interpretive process. Conversely, reader-response critics see themselves, as Jane Tompkins has put it, "willing to share their critical authority with less tutored readers and at the same time to go into partnership with psychologists, linguists, philosophers, and other students of mental functioning" (223).

Although reader-response ideas were present in critical writing as long ago as the 1920s, most notably in that of I. A. Richards, and in the 1930s in D. W. Harding's and Louise Rosenblatt's work, it was not until the mid-twentieth-century that they began to gain currency. Walker Gibson, writing in *College English* in February 1950, talked about "mock readers," who enact roles that actual readers feel compelled to play because the author clearly expects them to by the way the text is presented (265–69). By the 1960s and continuing into the present as a more or less concerted movement, reader-response criticism had gained enough advocates to mount a frontal assault on the bastions of formalism.

Because the ideas underlying reader-response criticism are complex, and because their proponents frequently present them in technical language, it will be well to enumerate the forms that have received most attention and to attempt as clear a definition of them as possible.

Although individual reader-response theorists will differ on a given point, the following tenets reflect the main perspectives in the position as a whole. First, in literary interpretation, the text is not the most important component; the reader is. In fact, there is no text unless there is a reader. And the reader is the only one who can say what the text is; in a sense, the reader creates the text as much as the author does. This being the case, to arrive at meaning, critics should reject the autonomy of the text and concentrate on the reader and the reading process, the interaction that takes place between the reader and the text.

This premise perplexes people trained in some traditional methods of literary analysis. It declares that reader-response theory is subjective and relative, whereas earlier theories sought for as much objectivity as possible in a field of study that has a high degree of subjectivity by definition. Paradoxically, the ultimate source of this subjectivity is modern science itself, which has become increasingly skeptical that any objective knowledge is possible. Einstein's theory of relativity stands as the best known expression of that doubt. Also, the philosopher Thomas S. Kuhn's demonstration (in *The Structure of Scientific Revolutions*) that scientific fact is dependent on the observer's frame of reference reinforces the claims of subjectivity.

Another special feature of reader-response theory is that it is based on rhetoric, the art of persuasion, which has a long tradition in literature dating back to the Greeks, who originally employed it in oratory. Rhetoric, among other roles, now refers to the myriad devices or strategies used to get the reader to respond to a literary work in certain ways. Thus, by establishing the reader firmly in the literary equation, the ancients may be said to be precursors of modern reader-response theory. Admittedly, however, when Aristotle, Longinus, Horace, Cicero, and Quintilian applied rhetorical principles in judging a work, they concentrated on the presence of the formal elements within the work rather than on the effect they would produce on the reader.

In view, then, of the emphasis on the audience in reader-response criticism, its relationship to rhetoric is quite obvious. Wayne Booth in his *Rhetoric of Fiction* was among the earliest of modern critics to restore readers to consideration in the interpretive act. The New Criticism had actually proscribed readers, maintaining that it was a critical **fallacy**, the **affective fallacy**, to mention any effects that a piece of literature might have on them. And although Booth did not go as far as some critics in assigning readers the major role in interpretation, he certainly did give them prominence and called rhetoric "the author's means of controlling his reader" (Preface to *Rhetoric of Fiction*). For example, in a close reading of Jane Austen's *Emma*, Booth demonstrates the rhetorical strategies that Austen uses to ensure the reader's seeing things through the heroine's eyes.

In 1925 I. A. Richards, usually associated with the New Critics, published *Principles of Literary Criticism,* in which he constructed an affective system of interpretation, that is, one based on emotional responses. Unlike the New Critics who were to follow in the next two decades, Richards conceded that the scientific conception of truth is the correct one and that poetry provides only pseudostatements. These pseudostatements, however, are crucial to the psychic health of humans because they have now replaced religion as fulfilling our desire—*appetency* is Richards's term—for truth, that is, for some vision of the world that will satisfy our deepest needs. Matthew Arnold had in the nineteenth century predicted that literature would fulfill this function. Richards tested his theory by asking Cambridge students to write their responses to and assessments of a number of short unidentified poems of varying quality. He then analyzed and classified the responses and published them along with his own interpretations in *Practical Criticism*. Richards's methodology is decidedly reader-response, but the use he made of his data is new critical. He arranged the responses he had received into categories according to the degrees to which they differed from the "right" or "more adequate" interpretation, which he demonstrated by referring to "the poem itself."

Louise Rosenblatt, Walker Gibson, and Gerald Prince are critics who, like Richards, affirm the importance of the reader but are not willing to relegate the text to a secondary role. Rosenblatt feels that irrelevant responses finally have to be excluded in favor of relevant ones and that a text can exist independently of readers. However, she advances a transactional theory: a poem comes into being only when it receives a proper ("aesthetic") reading, that is, when readers interact with a given text (see, for example, Ch. 3, "Efferent and Aesthetic Reading"). Gibson, essentially a formalist, proposes a mock reader, a role that the real reader plays because the text asks him or her to play it "for the sake of the experience." Gibson posits a dialogue between a speaker (the author?) and the mock reader. The critic, overhearing this dialogue, paraphrases it, thereby revealing the author's strategies for getting readers to accept or reject whatever the author wishes them to. Gibson by no means abandons the text, but he injects the reader further into the interpretive operation as a way of gaining fresh critical insights. Using a different terminology, Prince adopts a perspective similar to Gibson's. Wondering why critics have paid such close attention to narrators (omniscient, first person, unreliable, etc.) and have virtually ignored readers, Prince too posits a reader, whom he calls the *narratee*, one of a number of hypothetical readers to whom the story is directed. These readers, actually produced by the narrative, include the real reader with book in hand; the virtual reader, for whom the author thinks he or she is writing; and the ideal reader of perfect understanding and sympathy; yet none of these is necessarily the narratee. Prince demonstrates the strategies by which the narrative creates the readers (7–25).

The critics mentioned so far—except Prince—were the advance guard of the reader-response movement. While continuing to insist on the importance of the text in the interpretive act, they equally insist that the reader be taken into account; not to do so will, they maintain, either impoverish the interpretation or render it defective. As the advance guard, they cleared the way for the principal theorists of reader-response criticism. Though there will be disagreement on who belongs in this latter group, most scholars would recognize Wolfgang Iser, Hans Robert Jauss, Norman Holland, and Stanley Fish as having major significance in the movement.

Wolfgang Iser applies the philosophy of *phenomenology* to the interpretation of literature. Phenomenology stresses the perceiver's (in this case, the reader's) role in any perception (in this case, the reading experience) and asserts the difficulty, if not the impossibility, of separating anything known from the mind that knows it. According to Iser, the critic should not explain the text *as an object* but its *effect on the reader*. Iser's espousal of this position, however, has not taken him away from the text as a central part of interpretation. He also has posited an implied reader, one with "roots firmly planted in the structure of the text" (34). Still, his phenomenological beliefs keep him from the formalist notion that there is one essential meaning of a text that all interpretations must try to agree on. Readers' experiences will govern the effects the text produces on them. Moreover, Iser says, a text does not tell readers everything; there are gaps or blanks, which he refers to as the "indeterminacy" of the text. Readers must fill these in and thereby assemble the meaning(s), thus becoming coauthors in a sense. Such meanings may go far beyond the single "best" meaning of the formalist because they are the products of such varied reader backgrounds. To be sure, Iser's implied readers are fairly sophisticated: they bring to the contemplation of the text a conversance with the conventions that enables them to decode the text. But the text can transcend any set of literary or critical conventions, and readers with widely different backgrounds may fill in those blanks and gaps with new and unconventional meanings. Iser's stance is that at the center of interpretation lies the reader's experience. Nor does this creation of text by the reader mean that the resultant text is subjective and no longer the author's. It is rather, says Iser, proof of the text's inexhaustibility.

Yet another kind of reader-oriented criticism, also rhetorically grounded, is *reception theory*, which documents reader responses to authors and/or their works in any given period. Such criticism depends heavily on reviews in newspapers, magazines, and journals and on personal letters for evidence of public reception. There are varieties of reception theory, one of the most important recent types promulgated by Hans Robert Jauss in his *Toward an Aesthetic of Reception*. Jauss seeks to bring about a compromise between that interpretation which ignores history and that which ignores the text in favor of social theories. To describe the criteria he would employ, Jauss proposes the term *horizons of expectations* of a reading public. These result from what the public already understands about a genre and its conventions. For example, Pope's poetry was judged highly by his contemporaries, who valued clarity, decorum, and wit. The next century had a different horizon of expectations and thus actually called into question Pope's claim to being considered a poet at all. Similarly, Flaubert's *Madame Bovary* was not well received by its mid-nineteenth-century readers, who objected to the impersonal, clinical, **naturalistic** style. Their horizon of expectations had conditioned them to appreciate an impassioned, lyrical, sentimental, and florid narrative method. Delayed hostile reader response to firmly established classics surfaced in the latter half of the twentieth century. *Huckleberry Finn* became the target of harsh criticism on the grounds that it contained racial slurs in the form of epithets like "nigger" and demeaning portraits of blacks. Schools have been in some instances required to remove the book from curriculums or reading lists of approved books and in extreme cases from library shelves.

Horizons of expectations do not establish the final meaning of a work. Thus, according to Jauss, we cannot say that a work is universal, that it will make the same appeal to or impact on readers of all eras. Is it possible, then, ever to reach a critical verdict about a piece of literature? Jauss thinks it is possible only to the extent that we regard our interpretations as stemming from a dialogue between past and present and thereby representing a fusion of horizons.

The importance of psychology in literary interpretation has long been recognized. Plato and Aristotle, for example, attributed strong psychological influence to literature. Plato saw this influence as essentially baneful: literature aroused people's emotions, especially those that ought to be stringently controlled. Conversely, Aristotle argued that literature exerted a good psychological influence; in particular, tragedy did, by effecting in audiences a **catharsis** or cleansing or purging of emotions. Spectators were thus calmed and satisfied, not excited or frenzied, after their emotional encounter.

As we note in our chapter on the psychological approach, one of the world's preeminent depth psychologists, Sigmund Freud, has had an incalculable influence on literary analysis with his theories about the unconscious and about the importance of sex in explaining much human behavior. Critics, then, have looked to Plato and Aristotle in examining the psychological relations between a literary work and its audience and to Freud in seeking to understand the unconscious psychological motivations of the characters in the literary work and of the author.

If, however, followers of Freud have been more concerned with the unconscious of literary characters and their creators, more recent psychological critics have focused on the *unconscious of readers*. Norman Holland, one such critic, argues that all people inherit from their mother an identity theme or fixed understanding of the kind of person they are. Whatever they read is processed to make it fit their identity theme, he asserts in "The Miller's Wife and the Professors: Questions about the Transactive Theory of Reading." In other words, readers interpret texts as expressions of their own personalities or psyches and thereby use their interpretations as a means of coping with life. Holland illustrates this thesis in an essay entitled "*Hamlet*—My Greatest Creation." This highly personal response to literature appears in another Holland article, "Recovering 'The Purloined Letter': Reading as a Personal Transaction." Here, Holland relates the story to his own attempt to hide an adolescent masturbatory experience.

Holland's theory, for all of its emphasis on readers and their psychology, does not deny or destroy the independence of the text. It exists as an object and as the expression of another mind, something different from readers themselves, something they can project onto. But David Bleich, in *Subjective Criticism,* denies that the text exists independent of readers. Bleich accepts the arguments of such contemporary philosophers of science as Thomas S. Kuhn who deny that objective facts exist. Such a position asserts that even what passes for scientific observation of something—of anything—is still merely individual and subjective perception occurring in a special context. Bleich claims that individuals everywhere classify things into three essential groups: objects, symbols, and people. Literature, a mental creation (as opposed to a concrete one), would thus be considered a symbol. A text may be an object in that it is paper (or other matter) and print, but its meaning depends on the symbolization in the minds of readers. Meaning is not found; it is developed. Better human relations will result from readers with widely differing views sharing and comparing their responses and thereby discovering more about motives and strategies for reading. The honesty and tolerance required in such operations are bound to help in self-knowledge, which, according to Bleich, is the most important goal for everyone.

The last of the theorists to be treated in this discussion is Stanley Fish, who calls his technique of interpretation *affective stylistics*. Like other reader-oriented critics, Fish rebels against the so-called rigidity and dogmatism of the New Critics and especially against the tenet that a poem is a single, static object, a whole that has to be understood in its entirety at once. Fish's pronouncements on reader-response theory have come in stages. In an early stage (*Surprised by Sin*), he argued that meaning in a literary work is not something to be extracted, as a dentist might pull a tooth; meaning must be negotiated by readers, a line at a time. Moreover, they will be surprised by rhetorical strategies as they proceed. Meaning is *what happens to readers during this negotiation*. A text, in Fish's view, could lead readers on, even set them up, to make certain interpretations, only to undercut them later and force readers into new and different readings. So, the focus is on the reader; the process of reading is dynamic and sequential. Fish does insist, however, on a high degree of sophistication in readers: they must be familiar with literary conventions and must be capable of changing when they perceive they have been tricked by the strategies of the text. His term for such readers is "informed."

Later, in *Is There a Text in This Class?*, Fish modified the method described above by attributing more initiative to the reader and less control by the text in the interpretive act. Fish's altered position holds that readers actually create a piece of literature as they read it. Fish concludes that every reading results in a new interpretation that comes about because of the different strategies that readers use. The text as an independent director of interpretation has in effect disappeared. For Fish, interpretation is a communal affair. The readers just mentioned are informed; they possess linguistic competence; they form interpretive communities that have common assumptions; and, to repeat, they create texts when they pool their common reading techniques. These characteristics mean that such readers are employing the same or similar interpretive strategies and are thus members of the same interpretive community.

It seems reasonable to say that there may be more than one response to or interpretation of a work of literature and that this is true because responders and interpreters see things differently. It seems equally accurate to observe that to claim the meaning of literature rests exclusively with individual readers, whose opinions are all equally valid, is to make literary analysis ultimately altogether relative. Somewhere within these two points of view most critics and interpreters will fall. Fish himself has re-adjusted his views as time has gone by.

To summarize, two distinguishing features characterize reader-response criticism. One is the effect of the literary work on the reader, hence the moral-philosophical-psychological-rhetorical emphases in reader-response analysis: how does the work *affect* the reader, and what strategies or devices have come into play in the production of those effects? The second feature is the relegation of the text to secondary importance: the reader is of primary importance. Thus, reader-response criticism attacks the authority of the text. This is where subjectivism comes in. If a text cannot have any existence except in the mind of the reader, then the text loses its authority. There is a shift from objective to subjective perspective. Texts mean what individual readers say they mean or what interpretive communities of readers say they mean. Thus, interpretation becomes the key to meaning—but without the ultimate authority of the text or the author.

When reader-response critics analyze the effect of the text on the reader, the analysis often resembles formalist criticism or rhetorical criticism or psychological criticism. The major distinction is the emphasis on the reader's response in the analysis. Meaning inheres in the reader and not in the text. This is where reception theory fits in. The same text can be interpreted by different readers or communities of readers in very different ways. A text's interpretive history may vary considerably, as with Freudian interpretations of *Hamlet* versus earlier interpretations. Readers bring their own cultural heritage along with them in their responses to literary texts, a fact that allows for the principle that texts speak to other texts only through the intervention of particular readers. Thus, reader-response criticism can appropriate other theories—as all theories attempt to do.

Reader-response theory is likely to strike many people as both esoteric and too subjective. Unquestionably, readers had been little considered in the New Criticism, but they may have been overemphasized by the theorists who seek to give them the final word in interpreting literature. Communication as a whole is predicated on the demonstrable claim that there are common, agreed-upon meanings in language, however rich, metaphorical, or symbolic. To contend that there are, even in theory, as many meanings in a poem as there are readers strongly calls into question the possibility of intelligible discourse. That some of the theorists themselves are not altogether comfortable with the logical implications of their position is evidenced by their positing of mock readers, informed readers, real readers, and implied readers—by which they mean readers of education, sensitivity, and sophistication.

Despite the potential dangers of subjectivism, reader-response criticism has been a corrective to literary dogmatism and a reminder of the richness, complexity, and diversity of viable literary interpretations, and it seems safe to predict that readers will never again be completely ignored in arriving at verbal meaning.

III. CONSTANTS OF THE FORMALIST APPROACH: SOME KEY CONCEPTS, TERMS, AND DEVICES

A. Form and Organic Form

We must, of course, begin with form. In systems of the past, the word *form* usually meant what we would call *external form*. Thus, when we identify a poem with fourteen lines of **iambic pentameter**, a conventional pattern of rhymes, and a conventional division into two parts as a sonnet, we are defining its external form. The same kind of description takes place when we talk about couplets, **tercets**, *ottava rima*, **quatrains**, **Spenserian stanzas**, **blank verse**, or even **free verse**. But the formalist critic is only moderately interested in external forms (in fact, only when external form is related to the work's total form, when stanzaic or metrical pattern is integral to internal relationships, reverberations, patterns, and systems). The process of formalist analysis is complete only when everything in the work has been accounted for in terms of overall form.

Organic form is a particular concept important to the New Critics, inherited, as we have noted, from the English Romantics. In the Romantics, we find the emphasis on organicism not just in literary forms but in a broader, philosophical context, where the world itself is organic; objects within it are organisms that interact with each other in a larger organic universe. This notion may go so far as to Wordsworthian pantheism, or what some thought to be pantheism, where a breeze in nature may awaken within the persona of the *Prelude* (in this case the poet himself) a "correspondent breeze" (1.35). Similarly there is the Romantic emphasis on the Aeolian lyre or harp, as in Coleridge's poem "The Eolian Harp," and the reference to the lyre in the imagery and symbolism of Shelley's "Ode to the West Wind," a notion that recurs in the second paragraph of Shelley's "Defence of Poetry." The vegetation imagery, mentioned earlier, is of course part of this organicism. Now the question for us is how this concept of organicism came into formalist criticism of the twentieth century, especially among critics many of whom expressed no fondness for English Romanticism. Also, in the context of "greening," what does it suggest today?

In the formalist approach, the assumption is that a given literary experience takes a shape proper to itself, or at the least that the shape and the experience are functions of each other. This may mean at a minimum that a precise metrical form couples with a complex of sounds in a line of verse to present one small bit of the experience. Or it may mean that a generic form, like that of the sonnet, is used repeatedly in a sonnet cycle to show the interrelationship of thoughts to images, or a problem to a comment or solution. In such a case, even though the overt structure of the sonnet is repetitive, still the experience in any one Italian sonnet is structured across the octave and sestet or in the English form across the three quatrains and the concluding couplet. In a larger work, a full-length play or a novel might adopt much more complex and subtle forms to communicate the experience, such as the interrelationships of plot and subplot in Shakespeare's *Hamlet, Henry IV, Part 1,* or *The Tempest;* or in the complex **stream of consciousness** of Joyce's *Ulysses* or Faulkner's *Sound and the Fury.* Indeed, the fragmentation of story line and of time line in modern fiction and in some **absurdist drama** is a major formalist device used not only to generate within the reader the sense of the immediacy and even the chaos of experience but also to present the philosophical notion of nonmeaning and nihilism. Thus we have the seeming **paradox** that in some cases the absence of form *is* the form, precisely.

Statements that follow discovery of form must embrace what Ransom called local texture and logical structure (*World's Body* 347). The logical structure refers to the argument or the concept within the work; local texture comprises the particular details and devices of the work (for example, specific metaphors and images). However, such a dualistic view of a literary work has its dangers, for it might encourage the reduction of logical structure to précis or summary—what Brooks has called the "heresy of paraphrase." In *Understanding Poetry*, Brooks and Warren simply include "idea," along with rhythm and imagery, as a component of form: "the form of a poem is the organization of the material.... for the creation of the total effect" (554). The emphasis, in any case, is upon accounting for all aspects of the work in seeking to name or define its form and effect. Mark Schorer pressed the distinction further between the critic's proper concentration on *form* and an improper total concern with *content only:* "Modern [i.e., formalist] criticism has shown that to speak of content as such is not to speak of art at all, but of experience; and that it is only when we speak of the *achieved* content, the form, the work of art as a work of art, that we speak as critics. The difference between content, or experience, and achieved content, or art, is technique" (67). He goes on to say that "technique is the only means [an author] has of discovering, exploring, developing his subject, of conveying its meaning, and, finally, of evaluating it."

B. Texture, Image, Symbol

As we turn more specifically to **texture**, we find that as with form and its potential to embody meaning, **imagery** and metaphor are an integral part of the work, especially in the poem. Once again, the formalist critics—obviously—did not invent metaphor: Aristotle, very much a formalist, discussed metaphor in his *Poetics*. But the New Critics delighted in close analysis of imagery and metaphor, and they laid stress on a careful working out of imagery. The consistency of imagery in a lyric, whether it be a single dominant image throughout the poem or a pattern of multiple but related images, became for some an index to the quality of a given poem. Such consistency of imagery helped to create what John Crowe Ransom among others called texture. It was for such reasons that there was much interest in Metaphysical poetry and in the Metaphysical **conceit**. The interest was aided by publication of Herbert Grierson's collection *Metaphysical Lyrics and Poems of the Seventeenth Century* (1921). It was furthered by the attention of T. S. Eliot, Ransom, and Allen Tate. Critics praised the Metaphysical conceit because of its carefully worked out ("wrought") images that were elaborated over a number of lines, richly textured and endowed with a complexity of meanings, as in John Donne's "The Flea" or in the "stiff twin compasses" of his "Valediction: Forbidding Mourning." Donne's image of the "well-wrought urn" in "The Canonization" gave Cleanth Brooks the title to *The Well-Wrought Urn* (1947).

When an image (or an incident or other discrete item) takes on meaning beyond its objective self, it moves into the realm of **symbol**. Here is a dilemma

for some formalist critics, those who espouse the autonomous and autotelic concept of a literary work so strenuously that anything outside it becomes a problem.
Symbols may sometimes remain within the work, as it were; but it is the nature of
symbols to have extensional possibilities, to open out to the world beyond the art
object itself. When meaning and value outside the work of literature are the real
purposes of the symbol, some formalist critics may find fault with the work. On
the other hand, symbol is a way of using something integral to the work to reach
beyond the work and engage the world of value outside the work and hence its
meaning, external or internal.

A symbol is different from a metaphor. Metaphors are comparisons between
two seemingly dissimilar things, while symbols associate two things. The symbol's
meaning is both literal and figurative and reaches out of the text to cultural and
artistic contexts. No symbols have absolute meanings, because for example, different cultures will interpret the same symbol differently. Rather than asking what
a given symbol means, we could ask what it *could* mean, or what it has meant.
How we interpret the dark woods and pink ribbons of "Young Goodman Brown"
will depend on how they are seen through the eyes of a given culture. Similarly,
the journey means completely different things when we compare the journeys of
Goodman Brown and Huckleberry Finn. Myth critics (see Chapter 7) tend to argue
that certain symbols are universal, such as the sea or the sun, but their claims are
disputed by critics more sensitive to cultural difference. Symbols are also distinct
from allegories; **allegory** implies a one-on-one correspondence between symbol
and referent, but a given work can contain symbols from so many different sources
that it avoids the restrictions of allegory: think of Melville's *Moby-Dick,* Eliot's *The
Waste Land,* or Whitman's *Leaves of Grass.*

C. Fallacies

Another formalist term is the **intentional fallacy**, along with its corollary the
affective fallacy. In the intentional fallacy, we are told, the critic or the reader
makes the mistake of not divorcing the literary work from any intention that the
author might have had for the work. Instead, say Wimsatt and Beardsley in *The
Verbal Icon* (1954), the work must give us from within itself any intention that
might be garnered, and we must not go to the author for his or her intention. At
the very least the author is not a reliable witness. Wimsatt and Beardsley review
the arguments of some of the intentionists, and there are legitimate considerations
on both sides of the question. For us a proper middle ground would be to take
note of external evidence when it seems worthy, but to accept the caution that
the work itself must first and always be seen as a work unto itself, having now left
the author's care. Wimsatt and Beardsley also warned against the affective fallacy,
wherein the work is judged by its effect on the reader or viewer, particularly its
emotional effect. Again, however, those avoiding the reductionist tendency of formalist criticism would note that no work of literary art can be divorced from the
reader and therefore from the reader's response. For that matter, no less a critic

than Aristotle gave us the concept of catharsis, the purging of the audience at a tragedy that cleanses the emotions.

D. Point of View

A formalist approach also heeds **point of view**, especially the **omniscient third-person** narrator, which, like consistency of imagery, is generally considered a virtue in the work of literary art, for it preserves the internal form, the organic quality of the work. Conversely, a nonexistent point of view (that is, one in which several points of view are not clearly demarcated from each other) can flaw the work, for the work then may go in several directions and therefore have no integrity: the center does not hold; yet numerous modern and postmodern works have done just this.

In more restricted points of view, such as the **limited third-person** point of view, or the **first-person** point of view, the very form of the work is conditioned by the point of view to which the author limits the narrator. As Wayne Booth has reminded us, narrators may be either **reliable** (if they support the explicit or implicit moral norms of the author) or **unreliable** (if they do not). Thus Jake Barnes in *The Sun Also Rises* is a completely reliable narrator, for he or she is the very embodiment of what is often called the "Hemingway code"; on the other hand, the narrator of Chuck Palahniuk's novel *Fight Club* (1996) is unreliable in the extreme because he is delusional. Whatever the point of view we encounter, it has to be recognized as a basic means of control over the area or scope of the action, the quality of the fictional world offered to the reader, and even the reactions of the reader.

In a first-person narration the author may condition the form even more. Thus a young boy named Huckleberry Finn, who narrates his own story, must not be allowed to know more than a young boy such as he would know. His view is also limited to what he sees and reports. Nor does he understand all that he reports, not—at least—as a mature person devoid of cultural bias and prejudice might understand. In this first-person point of view, the narration is limited to a person's telling. If the author wishes to communicate anything beyond that to the reader, that wish becomes a challenge in technique, for the information must be reported naively by Huck Finn and interpreted maturely by the reader on the basis of what the author has Huck Finn say. In this sense Huck Finn is honest on the one hand, but an unreliable narrator on the other. In some circumstances the author may choose to have a shifting point of view to achieve different effects at different times (possibly this is what Chaucer the author did to Chaucer the pilgrim). Or there may be multiple points of view, as in Faulkner's *Sound and the Fury* or Melville's *Moby-Dick*. Still another type is the point of view that would claim total objectivity—the scenic or dramatic: we read only the dialogue of characters, with no hints of a narrator to intrude any perspective other than what we get from the dialogue itself. All these points of view condition the form of literature, and a formalist approach must study them for the reader to appreciate the fullness of the work.

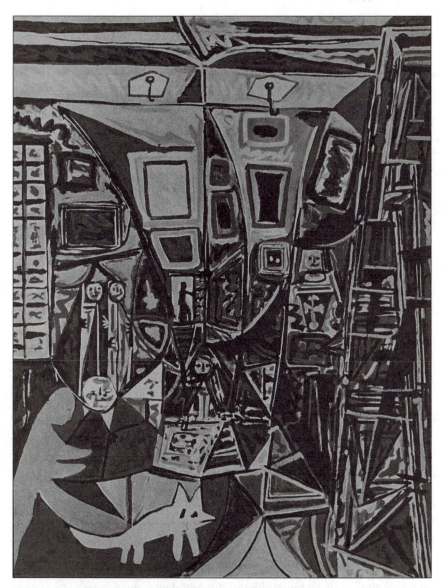

Figure 3.1. Pablo Picasso, *Las Meniñas conjunto sin Velázquez* (1957).
Museo Picasso, Barcelona, Spain/© DACS/The Bridgeman Art Library International/© 2009 Estate of Pablo Picasso/Artists Rights Society (ARS), New York.

E. The Speaker's Voice

Failure to note point of view as an aspect of form will result in a misreading or in an inadequate reading of the work. This challenge to the reader may be further illustrated by turning briefly to lyric poetry, where tone of voice is analogous to point of view. Although we do not usually think of point of view as an

---

**Pablo Picasso, *Las Meninas conjunto
sin Velázquez* (28), Cannes (1957)**

In this interpretation of Velázquez's painting Picasso breaks the composition down
into colors and geometric shapes in a style of modern painting called "Cubism,"
which he helped invent. Against a set of washes ranging from teal to green to light
green to yellow, Picasso overlays the rigid block-like bodies of the three young girls
in the foreground and the two chaperones on the right, who have been interpreted
as coffin-like vertical boxes with flipper-like hands and faces composed of an aster-
isk-like symbol. Added emphasis is placed on the windows in the room, which
become a structural element balancing the forms of the characters; the windows
seem to be heavily barred, adding a sense of tension. The mirror on the back wall is
enlarged, but the king and queen are not shown. Neither is the painter of the canvas. The focus is on the dress of the Infanta, since it is alone in displaying a vibrant
yellow. The entire focus is on the three maids: their hair, faces, and clothing stylized
into cubes with minimal expressions.

   Questions: How can we use formalist analysis of literature to help us read this
painting? What are the primary structural relationships portrayed? Why are the
dog and the man entering the back door so enlarged? What does it mean that the
two "centers" of the traditional painting, the king and queen as well as the painter,
are absent? The only character with any emotional register is the Infanta; why does
she have such an angry look on her face?

---

aspect of lyric poetry, the fact is that in a lyric there is a speaker—that is, a first-
person situation. This immediately sets a context and a set of circumstances,
for the speaker is doing something, somewhere. Possibly there is also a hearer,
a second person (we readers only *over*hear the speaker), so that the hearer also
conditions the experience. In Robert Browning's "Andrea del Sarto" it means
much to know that Andrea is addressing a woman and that they are among his
paintings at a certain time of day. Consequently it is even more important to
know what Andrea feels about his inadequacy as a painter and as a man: his
tone of voice, as much as details revealed to us, will largely reveal those feelings. Conversely, another painter, Fra Lippo Lippi in the poem of that name,
responds ebulliently to his world and his confidence about his ability to capture and interpret it in his painting: his colloquial, jovial tone communicates
this attitude. In Browning's "Porphyria's Lover" the reader will go totally astray
if he does not understand that the lover is a madman—and that the beloved
though present has been murdered by him. In a more traditional love lyric or
in one that describes a beautiful scene in nature, the speaker may reasonably
be trusted to speak the truth. But how does one interpret the speaker's voice in
Donne's "Song" ("Go and Catch a Falling Star")? What is the mixture of genial
satire, sardonicism, mere playfulness? The way the reader hears the speaker will
condition the poem, give it its form, indeed may make the poem into poems by

varying the voice. So the formalist critic ends up with a problem: one poem, or several? Perhaps, finally, there is only one, and that one is the resolution of all the possibilities in one reality, a kind of super-form that resolves and incorporates all the several forms.

F. Tension, Irony, Paradox

Plot resolution just mentioned is like the principle of the arch. In an arch the way down is the way up: the arch stands because the force of gravity pulls the several stones down while at the same time pushing them against the keystone. Gravity therefore counteracts itself to keep the entire arch standing; for that matter, the arch can carry great weight—just as a piece of literature might.

This aspect of formalist criticism might be called **tension**, the resolution of opposites, often in irony and paradox. Coleridge enunciated at least part of this notion early on; the New Critics laid great stress on the terminology. The basic terms—tension, irony, paradox—are often nearly indistinguishable, so closely do they work together. C. Hugh Holman and William Harmon summarize tension as "A term introduced by Allen Tate, meaning the integral unity that results from the successful resolution of the conflicts of abstraction and concreteness, of general and particular, of denotation and connotation." One could hardly find a better demonstration of the interrelationships of tension, irony, and paradox than what Robert Penn Warren provided in "Pure and Impure Poetry." In making a case for impure poetry—poetry of "inclusiveness"—Warren not only analyzed the arguments of purists but also provided excellent analyses of poems and passages that include the impure and thereby prove themselves as poetry. Regularly the ironies and paradoxes—the tensions—are at the heart of the success of the items he studies. Near the conclusion of the essay he says:

> Can we make any generalizations about the nature of the poetic structure? First, it involves resistances, at various levels. There is the tension between the rhythm of the poem and the rhythm of speech....; between the formality of the rhythm and the informality of the language; between the particular and the general, the concrete and the abstract; between the elements of even the simplest metaphor; between the beautiful and the ugly; between ideas....; between the elements involved in iron....; between the prosaisms and poeticisms. (27)

Let us practice close reading to analyze a brief but well-known poem. Here is the poem:

A slumber did my spirit seal;
    I had no human fears;
She seemed a thing that could not feel
    The touch of earthly years.

No motion has she now, no force;
    She neither hears nor sees;
Rolled round in earth's diurnal course,
    With rocks, and stones, and trees.

The poem seems quite simple, easy to grasp and to understand. The speaker—a **persona**, not necessarily the poet—recalls a frame of mind sometime in the past, when "she" (the female figure) was so active and alive that the speaker (mother? father? lover?) could hardly comprehend any earthly touch to the living female figure. Now, in the present, the speaker tells the reader or listener that the female is dead, but does so by circumlocution, or indirect statement. Only one word, "diurnal," should give even the mildest pause to most readers: it means "daily." Monosyllabic words dominate the poem. The **meter** is unvarying almost to the point of monotony—alternating soft and strong syllables, usually four of each in the first, third, fifth, and seventh lines; three of each in the other four lines. The rhymes are equally regular and predictable. There is classic restraint and regularity, a tight control.

There is also powerful emotional impact.

Whence comes that impact? Largely from the tightly stated irony and paradox of the poem. The speaker has both gotten what he or she desired and not gotten it: the expectations for the female figure have been realized—and incontrovertibly they have been demolished. Initially the speaker was confident in the eternal life of the female figure. What parent nurtures and enjoys a child while thinking thoughts of death rather than life? What lover thinks constantly if at all that the beloved will die, and prematurely at that? Life seems to ensure continued life. This female figure would somehow transcend earthly normalities, would not even age. The speaker was secure (slumbering) in that assumption. So we know from the first stanza.

But there is a huge gap, and at once a leap beyond that gap, between the first and second stanza. Something happened. Somehow the child or woman died. She already has been buried. The "slumber" of line one has become the eternal sleep of death. The "seal" of the "spirit" has become the coffin seal of the body. Even more poignantly, the life of the dynamic person in lines three and four, where sense perceptions of touching and feeling seem to be transmuted into ethereal or angelic dimensions, is now the unfeeling death of one who has no energy, no vitality, no sense of hearing or seeing. She is no more and no less than a rock or a stone or a tree fixed to the earth. The final irony, that paradox, is that the once motion-filled person is still in motion—but not the vital motion of a human person; she now moves daily a huge distance, a full turn of the earth itself, rotating with a motion not her own, but only that of rocks and stones—gravestones—and rooted trees.

The essential structure, or form, of the poem is the irony that the speaker got precisely what he or she wanted—but hardly in the way anticipated—a structure that at a fairly obvious level contrasts by means of the two stanzas and resolves the paradox by their interaction. A closer look takes the reader beyond this now-evident contrast of two stanzas. The texture of the poem is enriched by the sleep imagery, the sleep of life becoming the sleep of death. The "slumber" of line 1 connotes rest and quiet, even that of a baby or young child. The sibilant sounds of "s" at first suggest that quiet contentment, but the **alliteration** appears throughout the poem, taking on the irony of the second stanza almost like mournful echoes of the first. "Spirit" and "seal" not only continue the sibilant quality but also in retrospect are ambiguous terms, for "spirit" suggests death as well as life, and "seal" suggests not only security but finality: the coffin and the grave. In the third line the word "thing" at first seems to be a noncommittal, simply denotative word: perhaps the poet was not even able to think of a better word, and used a filler. But in retrospect the female figure now is indeed a "thing," like a rock or a stone, a mere thing—in truth, dust. Furthermore, "thing" contrasts with its bluntness of sound with the sibilant sounds of so much of the rest of the poem, and anticipates the alternating sounds of the last line, the "s" sounds alternating with the harder sounds of "r" and the consonant clusters "st" and "tr" in "rocks," "stones," and "trees."

Like the reference to sleep, the references to the senses ("feel," "touch") in the first stanza are expanded in the second: motion, or its lack, involves the muscles in kinetics and **kinesthesia**; hearing and seeing are explicitly mentioned. But in each of the three cases a negative word precedes the sense word—"no," "neither," "nor." Then in line 7, we meet the awesome reality of kinetic motion without kinesthesia. In "Rolled round" we have the forced motion of the inert body. In a striking change of **metrics**, we realize that the seeming monotony of the alternating soft and hard syllables is broken here by a spondee in place of the dominant iamb (see **foot**), and the spondee in turn is strengthened by the alliterating "r" and the consonance of the "d" at the end of each of the two words, echoed in the initial "d" of "diurnal." Once having noticed that pounding spondee, we might in retrospect reconsider the two uses of "no" in line 5, for they can be read almost as strongly as the stressed syllables of the line, giving still greater impact to the negative effect of the whole statement. Finally, the contrast between lines 7 and 8 is devastating. If we lift the line totally from its context, we can hear almost an ebullient sound in the seventh line, a glorious sweeping rhythm, aided by the vowels or assonance in the middle several words: "Rolled round in earth's diurnal course." But that sweeping, soaring quality comes up against the finality and slowed pace of the heavily impeded line 8, where the punctuation and the three accented monosyllabic words join to give the impact of three strong chords at the end of the symphony.

• • •

We have read a poem. Unless we know from other contexts, we still do not know the name of the author, the nationality, or the era of composition. We do not know who the speaker is, not even the sex of the speaker. We do not know if the poem concerns a real-life situation or a totally fictive one. We do not know whether the author took some similar real-life situation or incident that he or she then adapted and transmuted into a poem. We know only the poem itself, a short piece of richly textured literary art that bears up well under close analysis and resolves its tensions by means of irony and paradox, showing them not only in the contrast between two stanzas but also in seemingly minute details. We have read a poem and have analyzed it by using the formalist approach to literature.

P. S. For the curious, the poem is by William Wordsworth.

We may now turn to the formalist approach in practice.

IV. THE FORMALIST APPROACH IN PRACTICE

A. Word, Image, and Theme: Space-Time Metaphors
in "To His Coy Mistress"

August Strindberg, the Swedish novelist and playwright, said in the preface to *Miss Julie* that he "let people's minds work irregularly, as they do in real life." As a consequence, "The dialogue wanders, gathering in the opening scenes material which is later picked up, worked over, repeated, expounded and developed like the theme in a musical composition." Bit by bit as we notice instances of a pattern, we work our way into the experience of the story, poem, or play. As we follow the hints of thematic statement, recognize similar but new images, or identify related symbols, we gradually come to live the experience inherent in the work. The evocative power of steadily repeated images and symbols as **motifs** makes the experience a part of our own consciousness and sensibility. Thus the image satisfies our senses, the pattern our instinctive desire for order, and the thematic statement our intellect and our moral sensibility.

Andrew Marvell's poem "To His Coy Mistress" presents us with a clear instance of how a particular set of images can open out to themes in the way just described. The opening line of the poem—"Had we but world enough and time"—introduces us to the space-time continuum. Rich in possibilities of verbal patterns, the motif is much more, for the structure of the poem depends on the **subjunctive** concept, the condition contrary to fact, which gives the whole poem its meaning: "Had we," the speaker says, knowing that they do not. From that point on, the **hyperbole**, the playfulness, the grim fear of annihilation are all based on the feeling of the speaker that he is bound by the dimensions of space and time.

Clearly, this poem is a proposition made by the stereotypical male to the stereotypical female. Just as clearly, and in a wholly different realm, the motif of space and time shows this poem to be a philosophical consideration of time, of eternity, of pleasure (hedonism), and of salvation in an afterlife (traditional Christianity). In this way Marvell includes in one short poem the range between lust and philosophy.

On the other hand, we find that the words used to imply this range tend to be suggestive, to shift their meanings so as to demand that they be read on different levels at the same time. Let us begin with instances of the space motif. The space motif appears not only in obvious but also in veiled allusions. In the first section of the poem we find "world," "sit down," "which way/To walk," the suggested distance between "Indian Ganges" and the Humber, the distance implicit in the allusions to the Flood and to the widespread Jews of the Diaspora, "vaster than empires," the sense of spatial movement as the speaker's eyes move over the woman's body, and the hint of spatial relationship in "lower rate." The word "long" (line 4) refers to time, but has spatial meaning, too. Several other words ("before," "till," "go," "last") also have overlapping qualities, but perhaps we strain too far to consider them.

Space and time are clearly related in the magnificent image of the opening lines of the second stanza: "But at my back I always hear/Time's winged chariot hurrying near." The next couplet provides "yonder," "before," "deserts," and, again, a phrase that suggests both space and time: "vast eternity." In the third stanza the word "sits" echoes the earlier use of the word, and several words suggest movement or action in space: "transpires," "sport," "birds of prey," "devour," "languish in slow-chapped power," "roll," "tear. . . . /Thorough." The space motif climaxes in an image that again incorporates the time motif: the sun, by which the man measures time and which will not stand still in space, will be forced to run.

The time motif also appears in its own right, and not only by means of imagery. The word itself appears once in each stanza: near the beginning of stanzas 1 and 2 (lines 1 and 22), and in the third stanza as a central part of the lover's proposition (39). Clustering around this basic unifying motif are these phrases and allusions from the first stanza: the "long love's day," the specific time spans spent in adoring the woman's body and the vaster if less specific "before the Flood" and "Till the conversion of the Jews," and the slow growth of "vegetable love" and the two uses of "age" (lines 17 and 18). At the beginning of stanza 2, the powerful image of time's winged chariot as it moves across a desert includes the words "always" and "eternity." Other time words are "no more" and "long-preserved." There is also the sense of elapsed time in the allusions to the future decomposition of the lovers' bodies. The third stanza, although it delays the use of the word "time," has for its first syllable the forceful, imperative "now." The word appears twice more in the stanza (lines 37 and 38). It is strengthened by "instant," "at once," and "languish in [Time's] slow-chapped power." The phrase "thorough the iron gates of life," though it has more important meanings, also may suggest the passing from temporal life into the not so certain eternity mentioned earlier. The concluding couplet of the poem, as already shown, combines space and time. Further, it may extend time backward to suggest Old Testament days and classic mythology: Joshua stopped the sun so that the Israelites could win a battle, and, even more pertinently, Zeus lengthened the night he spent with Amphitryon's wife.

For the poem is also a love poem, both in its traditional context of the **courtly love** complaint and in the simple fact of its subject matter: fearing that the afterlife may be a vast space without time, the speaker looks for a means of enjoying whatever he can. This *carpe diem* theme is not uncommon, nor is the theme of seduction. What gives the poem unusual power, however, is the overbearing sense of a cold, calculated drive to use the pleasures of sex to counterbalance the threats of empty eternity. Thus a second major motif—after the space-time relationship— used to present the theme is the sexual motif.

We can follow this theme beginning with the title, which immediately sets up the situation. In the second line the word "coyness" leads us into the poem itself; even the word "crime" suggests the unconventional (though crime and conventional morality are reversed in the context of the lover's address). The motif gradually emerges, romantically at first, but more frankly, even brutally, as the speaker continues. In the first stanza the distant Ganges and the redness of rubies are romantic enough; the word "complain," in the sense of the courtly lover's song, echoes the whole courtly tradition. The word "love" appears twice before the courtly **catalogue** of the lady's beautiful body. The catalogue in turn builds to a climax with the increasing time spans and the veiled suggestiveness of "rest" and "part."

The second stanza, though it continues to be somewhat veiled, is less romantic, and becomes gruesome even while insisting upon sexual love. The lady's beauty will disappear in the marble vault. We may associate the word "marble" with the texture and loveliness of the living woman's skin, but here the lover stresses the time when that loveliness will be transferred to stone. The same type of transference of the lover's song, which finds no echoes in that vault, occurs in a veiled image of unrealized sexual union in life: worms will corrupt the woman in a way that the lover could not. "Quaint honor" is an ironic play on words to suggest the pudendum (*quaint* as in Middle English *queynte*; see Chaucer's "Miller's Tale"). The fires of lust will become ashes (with an implicit comparison to the coldness of marble), and the stanza closes with puns on "private" and "embrace."

The third stanza resumes the romantic imagery of the first ("youthful hue," "morning dew"), but it continues the bolder imagery of the second section. "Pore" is a somewhat unromantic allusion to the woman's body, and "instant fires" recalls the lust and ashes of the preceding stanza. "Sport" takes still a different tack, though it reminds us of the playfulness of the first stanza. After this line, the grimness of the second stanza is even more in evidence. The amorous birds are not turtle-doves, but birds of prey, devouring time—and each other. Although the romantic or sentimental is present in the speaker's suggestion that they "roll all our strength and all/Our sweetness up into one ball," the emphasis on the rough and violent continues in the paradoxical "tear our pleasures with rough strife." Once the coy lady's virginity is torn away, the lover will have passed not through the pearly gates of eternity, but through the iron gates of life. Thus the lover's affirmation of life, compounded of despair and defiance, is produced by his suggestion that the birth canal of life and procreation is preferable to the empty vault and deserts of vast eternity. On the one hand, the instances of the sexual motif point to a degeneration from romantic convention in the first section to scarcely veiled explicitness in the last. But on the other hand, the speaker has proceeded from a question about the nature of eternity and the meaning of the space-time relationship in this world to an affirmation of what he suspects is one of the few realities left him. The very concreteness, the physicality of the sexual motif, provides an answer to the philosophical speculation about space, time, and eternity. Obviously different, the motifs just as obviously fuse to embody the theme of the poem.

There are other, lesser motifs that we could trace had we ourselves space enough and time, such as wings and birds, roundness, and minerals and other things of earth (rubies, marble, iron, ashes, and dust). Each of these serves as a means to greater insights into the poem.

In sum, a formalist reading of "To His Coy Mistress" can originate in a study of images and metaphors—here, space-time images. It can then lead to complexes of other images—precious stones and marble vaults, chariots and rivers, worms and dust. Finally, it is the nature of a formalist approach to lead us to see how images and metaphors form, shape, confect a consideration of philosophical themes—in this case a speculation on whether love and even existence itself can extend beyond the time we know, and, if they cannot, whether instant gratification is a sufficient response to the question raised.

B. The Dark, the Light, and the Pink: Ambiguity as Form in "Young Goodman Brown"

In short fiction, as in a poem, we can look for the telling word or phrase, the recurring or patterned imagery, the symbolic object or character, the hint of or clue to meaning greater than that of the action or plot alone. Because we can no more justify stopping with a mere summary of what happens outwardly in the story than we can with a mere prose paraphrase of a lyric poem's content, we must look for the key to a story's form in one or more devices or images or motifs that offer a pattern that leads us to larger implications. In short, we seek a point at which the structure of the story coincides with and illuminates its meaning.

As we approach a formalist reading of Hawthorne's story, we should make another point or two of comparison and contrast. The lyric poem generally embraces a dramatic situation. That is, a speaker reacts to an experience, a feeling, an idea, or even a physical sensation. Only one voice is ordinarily present in the lyric poem, but in other literary genres there is usually a group of characters. In fiction the story is told by the author, by one of the characters in the story, or by someone who has heard of an episode. Unlike the novel, the other major fictional type, the short story is characteristically concerned with relatively few characters and with only one major situation, which achieves its climax and solution and thus quickly comes to an end. The short story is restricted in scope, like a news story, for example, but unlike the news story, the short story possesses balance and design—the polish and finish, the completeness that we associate with the work of art. A principle of unity operates throughout to give that single effect that Poe emphasized as necessary.

Though it may seem paradoxical, ambiguity is a formal device in "Young Goodman Brown," particularly in the relationships between light and dark in the story, the interplay of daylight and darkness, of town and dark forest. Richard Harter Fogle's classic study, *Hawthorne's Fiction: The Light and the Dark*, addresses this motif. Let us then look at an aspect of ambiguity not so well known.

In "To His Coy Mistress" the recurrent pattern of words, images, and metaphors of space and time is a means of seeing the form that embodies meaning in that poem. In "Young Goodman Brown" a clearly emphasized image almost immediately takes on symbolic qualities. That is the set of pink ribbons that belongs to Faith, young Brown's wife. The pink ribbons are her emblem as much as the scarlet letter is Hester Prynne's. They are mentioned three times in the first page or so of the story. Near the center of the story, a pink ribbon falls, or seems to fall, from a cloud that Goodman Brown sees, or thinks he sees, overhead. At the end of the story, when Faith eagerly greets her returning husband, she still wears her pink ribbons. Like the admixture of light and dark in the tale—as in much of Hawthorne—the ribbons are neither red nor white. They are somewhere between: they are ambiguity objectified. Clearly Hawthorne meant them to be suggestive, to be an index to one or more themes in the tale. But suggestive of what? Are they emblematic of love, of innocence, of good? Conversely, do they suggest evil, or hypocrisy, or the ambiguous and puzzling blend of good and evil? Are they symbolic of sex, of femininity, or of Christian faith? It is instructive to recall that brown is also a blended color—it teaches a lesson Brown never learns, that people are morally ambiguous.

1. Virtues and Vices

Of this we can be sure: to follow this motif as it guides us to related symbols and patterns of relationships is to probe the complex interweaving of ideas within the story. Specifically, in the interpretation that follows we suggest that the mysterious pink ribbons are—at least among other things—an index to elements of theology. To see that relationship let us first consider the theological matrix of the story.

Because the Puritan setting of "Young Goodman Brown" is basic to the story, we can expect that some of its thematic patterns derive from traditional Christian concepts. For example, readers generally assume that Goodman Brown loses his faith—in Christ, in human beings, or in both. But the story is rich in ambiguities, and it is therefore not surprising that at least one reader has arrived at the opposite conclusion. Thomas E. Connolly has argued that the story is an attack on Calvinism, and that Faith (that is, faith) is not lost in the story. On the contrary, he says, Goodman Brown is confirmed in his faith, made aware of "its full and terrible significance." Either way—loss of faith or still firmer belief—we see the story in a theological context. Although we do not have to accept either of these views, we do not have to deny them either. Instead, let us accept the theological matrix within which both views exist as the pattern of relationships of faith, hope, and love, and their opposed vices.

We can assume that Hawthorne was familiar with some of the numerous passages from the Bible that bear upon the present interpretation. Twice in the first epistle to the Thessalonians, St. Paul mentions the need for faith, hope, and love (1:3 and 5:8). In 1 Corinthians 13, after extolling love as the most abiding of the virtues, Paul concludes his eloquent description with this statement: "So there abide faith, hope, and love, these three; but the greatest of these is love." The author of the first epistle of Peter wrote, "But above all things have a constant mutual love among yourselves; for love covers a multitude of sins" (4:8). To these may be added the telling passages on love of God and neighbor (Matt. 22:36–40 and Rom. 13:9–10) and related passages on love (such as Col. 3:14 and 1 Tim. 1:5). Faith, hope, and love, we should note, have traditionally been called the theological virtues because they have God (*theos*) for their immediate object.

Quite possibly Hawthorne had some of these passages in mind, for it appears that he wove into the cloth of "Young Goodman Brown" a pattern of steady attention to these virtues often verging on ambiguity. Surely he provided a clue for us when he chose Faith as the name for Goodman Brown's wife. Hawthorne thereby gave faith first place in the story, not necessarily because faith is the story's dominant theme, but because it is traditionally listed as the first of the three Christian virtues. Allusions to faith could be made explicit in so many passages in the story and implicit in so many others that they would provide an evident pattern to suggest clearly the other two virtues. (Similarly, the epithet *goodman* could take on symbolic qualities and function almost as Brown's given name, not simply as something comparable to modern *mister*.)

The story reveals implicit allusions to the virtues of faith, hope, and love, and to their opposed vices, doubt, despair, and hatred.

2. Symbol or Allegory?

With these passages in mind, let us recall that there may be both symbolical and allegorical uses of the word "faith." Such ambivalence can complicate a reading of the story. If the tale is allegorical, for example, it may be that Goodman Brown gained his faith (that is, the belief that he is one of the elect) only three months before the action of the story, when he and Faith were married. The fall of the pink ribbon may be a sin or a fall, just as Adam's fall was the original sin, a lapse from grace. The allegory may further suggest that Goodman Brown shortly loses his new faith, for "he shrank from the bosom of Faith." But allegory is difficult to maintain, often requiring a rigid one-to-one equivalence between the surface meaning and a "higher" meaning. Thus if Faith is faith, and Goodman Brown loses the latter, how do we explain that Faith remains with him and even outlives him? Strict allegory would require that she disappear, perhaps even vanish in that dark cloud from which the pink ribbon apparently falls. On the other hand, a pattern of symbolism centering on Faith is easier to handle, and may even be more rewarding by offering us more pervasive, more subtly interweaving ideas that, through their very ambiguity, suggest the difficulties of the theological questions in the story. Such a symbolic view also frees the story from a strict adherence to the Calvinistic concept of election and conviction in the faith, so that the story becomes more universally concerned with Goodman Brown as Everyman Brown.

3. Loss upon Loss

Whether we emphasize symbol or allegory, however, Goodman Brown must remain a character in his own right, one who progressively loses faith in his ultimate salvation, in his forebears as members of the elect or at least as "good" people, and in his wife and fellow townspeople as holy Christians. At a literal level, he does not lose Faith, for she greets him when he returns from the forest, she still wears her pink ribbons, she follows his corpse to the grave. Furthermore, she keeps her pledge to him, for it is *he* who shrinks from her. In other words, Brown has not completely lost Faith; rather he has lost faith, a theological key to heaven.

But when faith is lost, not all is lost, though it may very nearly be. Total loss comes later and gradually as Brown commits other sins. We can follow this emerging pattern when we recall that the loss of faith is closely allied to the loss of hope. We find that, in the story, despair (the vice opposed to hope) can be easily associated with doubt (the vice opposed to faith). For example, the two vices are nearly allied when Goodman Brown recognizes the pink ribbon: "'My Faith is gone!' cried he, after one stupefied moment. 'There is no good on earth; and sin is but a name. Come, devil; for to thee is this world given.' And, maddened with *despair,* so that he laughed loud and long, did Goodman Brown grasp his staff and set forth again..." (our italics).

Doubt, although surely opposed to belief, here leads to despair as much as to infidelity. Similarly, many passages that point to faith also point to hope. When Goodman Brown says, "'I'll follow her to heaven,'" he expresses hope as well as belief. When he says, "'With heaven above and Faith below,'" he hopes to "'stand firm against the devil.'" When he cries, "'Faith, look up to heaven,'" he utters what may be his last hope for salvation. Once again we see how motifs function in a formal structure. It is easy to touch the web at any one point and make it vibrate elsewhere.

Thus Brown's hope is eroded by increasing doubt, the opposite of faith. When Goodman Brown reenters the town, he has gone far toward a complete failure to trust in God. His thoughts and his actions when he sees the child talking to Goody Cloyse border on the desperate, both in the sense of despair and in the sense of frenzy. Later, we know that he has fully despaired, "for his dying hour was gloom" and "no hopeful verse" appears on his gravestone."

"But the greatest of these is love," and "love covers a multitude of sins," the Scriptures insist. Goodman Brown sins against this virtue too, and as we follow these reiterations of the structural components we may well conclude that Hawthorne considered this sin the greatest sin in Brown's life. Sins against love of neighbor are important in other Hawthorne stories. It is a sin against love that Ethan Brand and Roger Chillingworth commit. It is a sin against love of which Rappaccini's daughter accuses her lover Guasconti: "Farewell, Giovanni! Thy words of hatred are like lead within my heart; but they, too, will fall away as I ascend. Oh, was there not, from the first, more poison in thy nature than in mine?" In *The House of the Seven Gables,* it is love that finally overcomes the hate-engendered curse of seven generations.

In "Young Goodman Brown" the motif of love-hate is first suggested in the opening scene, when Goodman Brown refuses his wife's request that he remain: "'My love and my Faith,' replied young Goodman Brown, 'of all nights in the year, this one night must I tarry away from thee....What, my sweet, pretty wife, dost thou doubt me already, and we but three months married?'" Note how Brown turns *his* lack of faith into hers with that question. Significantly, the words "love" and "Faith" are used almost as **synonyms**. When the pink ribbons are mentioned in the next paragraph almost as an epithet ("Faith, with the pink ribbons"), they are emblematic of one virtue as much as the other. Later, Goodman Brown's lack of love of others is further revealed when he learns that he is of a family that has hated enough to lash the "Quaker woman so smartly through the streets of Salem" and "to set fire to an Indian village." Instead of being concerned for his own neighbor, he turns against Goody Cloyse, resigning her to the powers of darkness: "What if a wretched old woman do choose to go to the devil....?" He turns against Faith and against God Himself when, after the pink ribbon has fallen from the cloud, he says, "'Come, devil; for to thee is this world given.'" To be sure, he still loves Faith enough at the forest conclave to call upon her yet to look to heaven; but next morning when she almost kisses her husband in front of the whole village, "Goodman Brown looked sternly and sadly into her face, and passed on without a greeting." He shrinks from the blessing of "the good old minister," he disparages the prayers of old Deacon Gookin, he snatches a child away from the catechizing of "Goody Cloyse, that excellent old Christian." Thenceforth he stubbornly isolates himself from his fellow men and from his own wife. On the Sabbath day he questions their hymns and their sermons, at midnight he shrinks from his wife, at morning or eventide he scowls at family prayers. Having given his allegiance to the devil, he cannot fulfill the injunction of the second great commandment any more than he can fulfill that of the first. Unable to love himself, he is unable to love his neighbor.

"Faith, hope, and love: these three" he has lost, replacing them with their opposed vices, and the pink ribbons in particular serve as emblems for them all and lead to a double pattern of virtues and vices. In "Young Goodman Brown" the motifs of faith, hope, and love, summed up in the pink ribbons, blend each into each. If the blend sometimes confuses us, like the alternating light and dark of the forest conclave, and more particularly like the mystery of the pink ribbons, it is perhaps no less than Hawthorne intended when he presented Goodman Brown's initiation into the knowledge of good and evil, a knowledge that rapidly becomes confusion.

C. Romance and Reality, Land and River:
The Journey as Repetitive Form in *Huckleberry Finn*

In the preceding section on formalist qualities in "Young Goodman Brown," we noted that the short story is generally concerned with relatively few characters and with only one major situation. The short story achieves its climax and solution, and quickly concludes. The novel, however, contains more characters, and its plot, a number of episodes or situations. Its ampler space provides opportunity for creation of a world, with the consequent opportunity for the reader to be immersed in that world. But because the novel is ample, in comparison with a lyric poem or a short story, it offers a further challenge to its creator to give it its form. In fact, historically the formalist approach in criticism has focused more on lyric poetry and short stories than on the novel. Nevertheless, the novel, too, is an art form, and a close reading will present one or more ways of seeing its form and how the author controls that form.

It will become clear as we approach the form of *Huckleberry Finn* that at one level its form can be simplistically diagrammed as a capital letter "I" lying on its side. At each end there is a block of chapters set on the land and in a world where Tom Sawyer can exist and even dominate. In the middle are chapters largely related to the river as Huck and Jim travel down that river; here **realism**, not a Tom Sawyer **romanticism**, dominates. Further, in the central portion there is a pattern of alternations between land and river. Taking the novel as a whole, then, there is a pattern of departures and returns.

But Twain was not limited to a pattern that can be charted, as it were, on graph paper. In a master stroke of the creative art, he chose Huck Finn himself as the narrator. In doing so, Twain abandoned the simpler omniscient (or authorial) point of view that he had very successfully used in *The Adventures of Tom Sawyer* for a relatively sophisticated technique. He allowed the central character to relate his adventures in his own way. T. S. Eliot refers to the difference in points of view as indicative of the major qualitative distinction between *Tom Sawyer* and *Huckleberry Finn*: Tom's story is told by an adult looking at a boy and his gang; Huck's narrative requires that "we see the world through his eyes." Granted that Twain sometimes allows us to see beyond Huck's relatively simple narrative manner some dimensions of meaning not apparent to Huck, the point of view has been so contrived (and controlled) that we do not see anything that is not at least implicit in Huck's straightforward narration.

But Twain is something of an antinarrator/author, a Trickster "god" in the shadows who, though he allows Huck to describe his moral transformation on the river ("I'll *go* to hell"), reveals Huck's limitations by bookending the novel with Tom Sawyer. In the conclusion Tom's influence causes Huck to forget or ignore his insight. It is finally Twain who is the hoaxer, and it is his perspective on meaning that dominates.

Several questions can be raised. What is the character of Huck like? How does his manner of telling his story control our responses to that story? Finally, how does this point of view assist us in perceiving the novel's form?

First, Huck is an objective narrator. He is objective about himself, even when that objectivity tends to reflect negatively upon himself. He is objective about the society he repeatedly confronts, even when, as he often fears, that society possesses virtues and sanctions to which he must ever remain a stranger. He is an outcast, he knows that he is an outcast, and he does not blame the society that has made and will keep him an outcast. He always assumes in his characteristic modesty that he must somehow be to blame for the estrangement. His deceptions, his evasions, his lapses from conventional respectability are always motivated by the requirements of a given situation; he is probably the first thoroughgoing, honest pragmatist in American fiction. When he lies or steals, he assumes that society is right and that he is simply depraved. He does not make excuses for himself, and his conscience is the stern voice of a pietistic, hypocritical backwoods society asserting itself within that sensitive and wistful psyche. We know that he is neither depraved nor dishonest, because we judge that society by the damning clues that emerge from the naive account of a boy about fourteen years old who has been forced to lie in order to get out of trouble but who never lies to himself or to his reader. In part, his lack of subtlety is a measure of his reliability as narrator: he has mastered neither the genteel speech of "respectable" folks nor their deceit, evasions of truth, and penchant for pious platitudes. He is always refreshingly himself, even when he is telling a tall tale or engaging in one of his ambitious masquerades to get out of a jam.

Thus the point of view Twain carefully establishes from the first words of the narrative offers a position from which the reader must consider the events of the narrative. That position never wavers from the trustworthy point of view of the hero-narrator's clear-eyed gaze. He becomes at once the medium and the norm for the story that unfolds. By him we can measure (although he never overtly does it himself) the hypocrisy of Miss Watson, perceive the cumulative contrast between Huck and the incorrigible Tom Sawyer, and finally judge the whole of society along the river. Eliot makes this important discrimination: "Huck has not imagination, in the sense in which Tom has it; he has, instead, vision. He sees the real world; and he does not judge it—he allows it to judge itself."

Huck's characteristic mode of speech is ironic and self-effacing. Although at times he can be proud of the success of his tall tales and masquerades, in the things that matter he is given to understatement. Of his return to "civilized" life with the Widow Douglas, he tersely confides, "Well, then, the old thing commenced again." Of the senseless horror with which the Grangerford-Shepherdson feud ends, Huck says with admirable restraint: "I ain't a-going to tell *all* that happened— it would make me sick again if I was to do that. I wished I hadn't ever come ashore that night to see such things. I ain't ever going to get shut of them—lots of times I dream about them." And in one of the most artfully conceived, understated, but eloquent endings in all fiction, Huck bids his reader and civilization goodbye simultaneously: "But I reckon I got to light out for the Territory ahead of the rest, because Aunt Sally she's going to adopt me and sivilize me, and I can't stand it. I been there before."

The movement of the novel likewise has an effect on the total shape of the work. The apparently aimless plot with its straightforward sequence—what happened, what happened next, and then what happened after that, to paraphrase Gertrude Stein—is admirably suited to the personality of Huck as narrator. In the conventional romantic novel, of course, we expect to find a more or less complex central situation, in which two lovers come together by various stratagems of the novelist, have their difficulties, resolve their problems, and are destined to live happily ever afterward. Even in such a classic novel as Jane Austen's *Pride and Prejudice,* the separate chapters and the pieces of the plot concern the manifestations, against the background of early nineteenth-century English provincial life, of the many facets of Mr. Darcy's insuperable pride and Elizabeth Bennet's equally tenacious prejudice, but everything works toward the happy union of two very attractive young people.

In *Huckleberry Finn,* however, there is no real center to the plot as such. Instead we have what Kenneth Burke has called repetitive form: "the consistent maintaining of a principle under new guises.... a restatement of the same thing in different ways.... A succession of images, each of them regiving the same lyric mood; a character repeating his identity, his 'number,' under changing situations; the sustaining of an attitude as in satire…" (125). The separate situations or episodes are loosely strung together by the presence of Huck and Jim as they make their way down the Mississippi River from St. Petersburg, while the river flows through all, becoming really a vast highway across backwoods America. In the separate episodes there are new characters who, after Huck moves on, usually do not reappear. There are new settings and always new situations. At the beginning, there are five chapters about the adventures of Huck and Tom and the gang in St. Petersburg; at the end, there are twelve chapters centering on the Phelps farm that chronicle the ridiculous high jinks Tom forces on Huck in trying to free Jim; in between, there are twenty-six chapters in which Huck and Jim pursue true freedom and in which Tom Sawyer does not appear. This large midsection of the book includes such revealing experiences as Jim and Huck's encounter with the "house of death" (Ch. 9); the dual masquerades before the perceptive Mrs. Judith Loftus (Ch. 11); Huck's life with the Grangerfords (Chs. 17 and 18); the performance of the Duke and Dauphin at Pokeville (Ch. 20); the Arkansas premiere of Shakespeare and the shooting of Boggs by Colonel Sherburn (Chs. 21 and 22); and, finally, the relatively lengthy involvement with the Wilks family (Chs. 24–29).

Despite changes in settings and **dramatis personae**, the separate episodes share a cumulative role (their repetitive form): Huck learns bit by bit about the depravity that hides beneath respectability and piety. He learns gradually and unwillingly that society or civilization is vicious and predatory and that the individual has small chance to assert himself against a monolithic mass. He witnesses slavery from a slave's point of view. Harmless as the sentimental tastes of the Grangerfords or their preference for the conventionally pretty may seem, Twain's superb sense for the objective correlative allows us to *realize* (without being *told*) that conventional piety and sentimentality hide depravity no more effectively than the high coloring of the chalk fruit compensates for the chips that expose the underlying chalk. Likewise, elaborate manners, love of tradition, and "cultivated" tastes for Graveyard School poetry and lugubrious drawings are merely genteel facades for barbarism and savagery. Mrs. Judith Loftus, probably the best-developed minor character in the entire novel, for all her sentimental response to the hackneyed story of a mistreated apprentice, sees the plight of the runaway slave merely in terms of the cash reward she and her husband may win. Even the Wilks girls, as charming as they seem to Huck, are easily taken in by the grossest sentimentality and pious clichés. A review of the several episodes discloses that, for all their apparent differences, they are really reenactments of the same insistent revelation: the mass of humanity is hopelessly depraved, and the genuinely honest individual is constantly being victimized, betrayed, and threatened.

The framework of the plot is, then, a journey—a journey from north to south, a journey from relative innocence to horrifying knowledge. Huck tends to see people for what they are, but he does not suspect the depths of evil and the pervasiveness of sheer meanness, of man's inhumanity to man, until he has completed his journey. The relative harmlessness of Miss Watson's lack of compassion and her devotion to the letter rather than the spirit of religious law or of Tom's incurable and sometimes dangerous romanticism does not become really sinister until Huck reenters the seemingly good world at the Phelps farm, a world that is really the same as the "good" world of St. Petersburg—a connection that is stressed by the kinship of Aunt Sally and Aunt Polly. Into that world the values of Tom Sawyer are once more injected, and Huck becomes Tom's **foil** again.

Only the great, flowing river defines the lineaments of otherwise elusive freedom; that mighty force of nature opposes and offers the only possible escape from the blighting tyranny of towns and farm communities. The Mississippi is the novel's major symbol. It is the one place where a person does not need to lie to himself or to others. Its ceaseless flow mocks the static, stultifying society on its banks. There are lyrical passages in which Huck communicates, even with all his **colloquial** limitations, his feelings about the river, its symbolic functions, as in the image-packed description that follows the horrors of the Grangerford-Shepherdson carnage (Ch. 19). In that memorable passage Huck extols the freedom and contemplation that the river encourages. In contrast to the oppressive places on land, the raft and the river promise release: "We said there warn't no home like a raft, after all. Other places do seem so cramped up and smothery, but a raft don't. You feel mighty free and easy and comfortable on a raft."

Like the river, Huck's narrative flows spontaneously and ever onward. Around each bend lies a possible new adventure; in the eddies, a lyrical interlude. But the river always carries Huck and Jim out of each adventure toward another uncertain try for freedom. That freedom is never really achieved is a major irony, but the book's structure parallels the river's flow. The separate adventures become infinite variations upon (and repetitive forms of) the quest for freedom. That the final thwarting of freedom is perpetrated by the forces of St. Petersburg, of course, is no fault of the river or its promise of freedom; that Huck is "free" to leave for the Territory does not mean that he is necessarily free. If Twain is right about human nature, Huck will encounter the same social sins wherever he goes. In the end, the reader senses the shadow narrator, Twain, in sardonic laughter at the very notion of human freedom or salvation.

D. Dialectic as Form: The Trap Metaphor in *Hamlet*

1. *The Trap Imagery*

> My stronger guilt defeats my strong intent;
> And like a man to double business bound,
> I stand in pause where I shall first begin,
> And both neglect. (III.iii)

The words are not those of Hamlet. They are spoken by Claudius, as he tries to pray for forgiveness, even as he knows that he cannot give up those things for which he murdered his brother—his crown, his fulfilled ambition, and his wife. But the words may easily have been Hamlet's, for he too is by "double business bound." Indeed, much of the play centers on doubleness. In that doubleness lies the essence of what we mean by "dialectic" here—a confrontation of polarities. A consequence of that doubleness for many of the characters is that they are apparently caught in a trap—a key metaphor in the play—or, in another image, "Hoist with [their] own petard[s]" (III.iv).

Let us examine that metaphor of the trap, for it leads clearly to our seeing how dialectic provides form in *Hamlet*. Several times in the play, but in varying images, we find allusions to different kinds of entanglement. Polonius injudiciously uses the metaphor to warn Ophelia away from Hamlet's "holy vows of heaven," vows that he says are "springes to catch woodcocks" (I.iii). More significant is Hamlet's deliberate misnaming of "The Murder of Gonzago"; he calls it "The Mousetrap" (III.ii) because it is, as he says elsewhere, "the thing/Wherein I'll catch the conscience of the King" (II.ii). Claudius feels that he is trapped: "O limed soul, that, struggling to be free,/Art more engag'd" (III.iii). Hamlet, in the hands of plotters, finds himself "thus be-netted round with villainies" and one for whom Claudius has "Thrown out his angle [fish hook] for my proper life" (V.ii). The dying Laertes echoes his father's metaphor when he tells Osric that he is "as a woodcock to mine own springe" (V.ii). Here we have a pattern of trap images—springes, lime, nets, mousetraps, and angles or hooks. Now traps are usually for animals, but we are dealing with human beings, people who are trapped in their own dilemmas, in their own questions, in the very questioning of the universe.

2. The Cosmological Trap

We need go no further than the first scene of act I to realize that it is a disturbed world, that a sense of mystery and deep anxiety preoccupies the soldiers of the watch. The ghost has appeared already and is expected to appear again. The guards instinctively assume that the apparition of the former king has more than passing import; and, in their troubled questions to Horatio about the mysterious preparations for war, the guards show how closely they regard the connection between the unnatural appearance of the dead king and the welfare of the state. The guards have no answers for the mystery, their uncertainty, or their premonitions; their quandary is mirrored in abundant questions and minimal answers—a rhetorical phenomenon that recurs throughout the play, even in the **soliloquies** of Hamlet; in other words, an instance of dialectic. The sense of cosmic implication in the special situation of Denmark emerges strongly in the exchange between Hamlet and his friends Rosencrantz and Guildenstern:

> HAMLET: Denmark's a prison.
>
> ROSENCRANTZ: Then is the world one.
>
> HAMLET: A goodly one; in which there are many confines, wards, and dungeons, Denmark being the one o' th' worst. (II.ii)

These remarks recall the assertion of Marcellus as Hamlet and the ghost go offstage: "Something is rotten in the state of Denmark" (I.iv). Indeed, Hamlet acknowledges that the rottenness of Denmark pervades all of nature: "... this goodly frame the earth seems to me a sterile promontory; this most excellent canopy, the air, look you, this brave o'erhanging firmament, this majestical roof fretted with golden fire—why, it appeareth nothing to me but a foul and pestilent congregation of vapors" (II.ii). Much earlier, before his encounter with the ghost, Hamlet expressed his extreme pessimism at man's having to endure earthly existence within nature's unwholesome realm:

> How weary, stale, flat and unprofitable
> Seem to me all the uses of this world!
> Fie on't, ah, fie, 'tis an unweeded garden
> That grows to seed. Things rank and gross in nature
> Possess it merely. (I.ii)

As he speaks these lines, Hamlet apparently has no idea of the truth of his father's death but is dismayed over his mother's hasty marriage to the new king. He has discovered a seeming paradox in the nature of existence: the fair, in nature and humanity, inevitably submits to the dominion of the foul. His obsession with the paradox focuses his attention on Denmark as the model of nature and human frailty. Thus a pattern of increasing parallels between Denmark and the cosmos and between humans and nature develops. Question and answer, dialogue and soliloquy, become a verbal unity of repeated words and phrases, looking forward to larger thematic assertion and backward to earlier adumbration.

The play constitutes a vast poem in which speculation about nature, human nature, the health of the state, and human destiny intensifies into a passionate dialectic. Mystery, riddle, enigma, and metaphysical questions complicate the dialogue. Particularly in his soliloquies Hamlet confronts questions that have obsessed protagonists from Sophocles's Oedipus to Tom Stoppard's Rosencrantz and Guildenstern. What begins with the relatively simple questions of the soldiers of the watch in act I is magnified and complicated as the play moves on. Increasingly tenuous and rarified probes of the maddening gulf between reality and appearance proliferate. Moreover, the contrast between what the simple man cheerfully accepts at face value and what the thoughtful man is driven to question calls into doubt every surface of utterance, act, or thing. In the world of *Hamlet* the cosmic implications of myriad distinctions between "seem" and "be" confront us at every hand.

3. "Seeming" and "Being"

An index to form looms in the crucial qualitative differences between Hamlet's mode of speech and that of the other inhabitants of his strange world. Because Hamlet's utterances and manners are characteristically unconventional, the other major characters (except Horatio, of course) assume that he is mad or at least temporarily deranged. Conversely, because they *do* speak the simple, relatively safe language of ordinary existence, he assumes that they are hiding or twisting the truth. No one who easily settles for *seeming* is quite trustworthy to the man obsessed with the pursuit of *being*. Even the Ghost's nature and origin (he may be a diabolical agent, after all) must be tentative for Hamlet until he can settle the validity of the ghost's revelations with the "play within the play." Even Ophelia must be treated as the possible tool of Claudius and Polonius. The presence of Rosencrantz and Guildenstern, not to mention their mission on the journey to England, arouses Hamlet's deepest suspicions. Only Horatio is exempt from distrust, and even to him Hamlet cannot divulge the full dimension of his subversion. Yet though Hamlet seems to speak only in riddle and to act solely with evasion, his utterances and acts always actually bespeak the full measure of his feelings and his increasingly single-minded absorption with his inevitable mission. The important qualification of his honesty lies in his full knowledge that others do not (or cannot) comprehend his real meanings and that others are hardly vitally concerned with deep truths about the state, mankind, or themselves.

For our purposes, of course, the important fact is that these contrasting levels of meaning and understanding achieve formal expression. When the king demands some explanation for his extraordinary melancholy, Hamlet replies, "I am too much in the sun" (I.ii). The reply thus establishes, although Claudius does not perceive it, Hamlet's judgment of and opposition to the easy acceptance of "things as they are." And when the queen tries to reconcile him to the inevitability of death in the natural scheme and asks, "Why seems it so particular with thee?" he responds with a revealing contrast between the seeming evidences of mourning and real woe—an unequivocal condemnation of the queen's apparently easy acceptance of his father's death as opposed to the vindication of his refusal to view that death as merely an occasion for ceremonial mourning duties. To the joint entreaty of Claudius and Gertrude that he remain in Denmark, he replies only to his mother: "I shall in all my best obey you, madam" (I.ii). But in thus disdaining to answer the king, he has promised really nothing to his mother, although she takes his reply for complete submission to the royal couple. Again we see that every statement of Hamlet is dialectic: that is, it tends toward double meaning— the superficial meaning of the world of Denmark and the subtler meaning for Hamlet and the audience.

As we have observed, Hamlet's overriding concern, even before he knows of the ghost's appearance, is the frustration of living in an imperfect world. He sees, wherever he looks, the pervasive blight in nature, especially human nature. Humanity, outwardly the acme of creation, is susceptible to "some vicious mole of nature," and no matter how virtuous a person otherwise may be, the "dram of evil" or the "stamp of one defect" adulterates nobility (I.iv). Hamlet finds that "one may smile and smile, and be a villain" (I.v). To the uncomprehending Guildenstern, Hamlet emphasizes his basic concern with the strange puzzle of corrupted and corrupting man:

> What a piece of work is a man, how noble in reason, how infinite in faculties, in form and moving how express and admirable, in action how like an angel, in apprehension how like a god: the beauty of the world, the paragon of animals! And yet to me what is this quintessence of dust? Man delights not me—no, nor woman either, though by your smiling you seem to say so. (II.ii)

Instead of the ideal world Hamlet seeks, the real world that he finds is his father's death, his mother's remarriage, the defection of his supposed friends, and the fallen state of humankind.

Reams have been written about Hamlet's reasons for the delay in carrying out his revenge; for our purpose, however, the delay is not particularly important, except insofar as it emphasizes Hamlet's greater obsession with the pervasive blight within the cosmos. From almost every bit of verbal evidence, he considers as paramount the larger role of investigator and punitive agent of all humankind: his verbal attack on the queen, his accidental murder of Polonius, his indignation about the state of the theater, his castigation of Ophelia, his delight in foiling Rosencrantz and Guildenstern and arranging their destruction, and his fight with Laertes over the grave of Ophelia. Hamlet, in living up to what he conceives to be a higher role than that of mere avenger, recurrently broods about his self-imposed mission, although he characteristically avoids naming it. In his warfare against bestiality, however, he asserts his allegiance to heaven-sent reason and its dictates:

What is a man,
If his chief good and market of his time
Be but to sleep and feed? A beast, no more.
Sure he that made us with such large discourse,
Looking before and after, gave us not
That capability and godlike reason
To fust in us unused. Now, whether it be
Bestial oblivion, or some craven scruple
Of thinking too precisely on th'event—
A thought which, quartered, hath but one part wisdom
And ever three parts coward—I do not know
Why yet I live to say, "This thing's to do,"
Sith I have cause, and will, and strength, and means
To do't. (IV.vi)

With some envy he regards the active competence of Fortinbras as opposed to his own "craven scruple/Of thinking too precisely on th'event" (that is, his obligation to act to avenge his father's death). In short, almost from his first appearance in the play, Hamlet, unlike Fortinbras, is overwhelmed that to him is given a vast and ambiguous task:

The time is out of joint. O cursed spite
That ever I was born to set it right! (I.v)

The time, like the place of Denmark, has been corrupted by men vulnerable to natural flaws. And once again Hamlet's statement offers formal reinforcement for the dialectic of the play—the opposition of two attitudes toward human experience that must achieve resolution or synthesis before the play's end.

To the ideal of setting things right, then, Hamlet gives his allegiance. The order he supports transcends the expediency of Polonius, the apostle of practicality, and of Claudius, the devotee of power and sexuality. Again and again we see Hamlet's visionary appraisal of an order so remote from the ken of most people that he appears at times inhuman in his refusal to be touched by the scales of ordinary joy or sorrow. He will set straight the political and social order by ferreting out bestiality, corruption (of state, marriage bed, or theater), trickery, and deceit. He is obsessed throughout the play by the "dusty death" to which all must come, and his speeches abound in images of sickness and death. But if he has finally gotten the king, along with his confederates, "Hoist with his own petard" (III.iv), Hamlet also brings himself, through his own trickery, deceit, perhaps even his own ambitions, to the fate of Yorick.

Thus does the play turn upon itself. It is no simple morality play. It begins in an atmosphere of mourning for the late king and apprehensions about the appearance of the ghost, and it ends in a scene littered with corpses. The noble prince, like his father before him, is, despite his best intentions, sullied by the "foul crimes done in my days of nature" (I.v). All men apparently are, as Laertes says of himself, "as a woodcock to mine own springe" (V.ii) (that is, like a fool caught in his own snare). And though all beauty and aspiration (a counterpoint theme) are reduced ultimately to a "quintessence of dust," it is in Hamlet's striving, however imperfectly and destructively, to bend the order of nature to a higher law that we must see the play's tragic assertion in the midst of an otherwise pervasive and unrelieved pessimism.

4. "Seeing" and "Knowing"

The design of the play can be perceived in part in the elaborate play upon the words "see" and "know" and their cognates. Whereas the deity can be understood as "Looking before and after" (IV.iv), the player king points out to his queen that there is a hiatus between what people intend and what they do: "Our thoughts are ours, their ends none of our own" (III.ii). Forced by Hamlet to consider the difference between her two husbands, Gertrude cries out in anguish against having to see into her own motivations:

> O Hamlet, speak no more.
> Thou turn'st mine eyes into my very soul,
> And there I see such black and grained spots
> As will not leave their tint. (III.iv)

But she does not see the ghost of her former husband, nor can she see the metaphysical implications of Hamlet's reason in madness. The blind eye sockets of Yorick's skull once saw their quota of experience, but most people in Denmark are quite content with the surface appearances of life and refuse even to consider the ends to which mortality brings everyone. The intricate weavings of images of sight thus become a kind of tragic algebra for the plight of a man who "seemed to find his way without his eyes" (II.i) and who found himself at last "placed to the view" of the "yet unknowing world" (V.ii). Formally, the play progresses from the relatively simple speculations of the soldiers of the watch to the sophisticated complexity of metaphysical inquiry. There may not be final answers to the questions Hamlet ponders, but the questions assume a formal order as their dimensions of "seeing" and "knowing" are structured by speech and action—in miniature, by the play within the play; in extension, by the tragedy itself.

Ophelia, in her madness, utters perhaps the key line of the play: "Lord, we know what we are, but we know not what we may be" (IV.v). Hamlet has earlier said that if the king reacts as expected to the play within the play, "I know my course" (II.ii); that is, he will spring the trap. But he is not sure of his course, nor does he even know himself—at least not until the final act. In the prison of the world and its myriad traps he can only pursue his destiny, which, as he realizes before the duel, inevitably leads to the grave. The contest between human aspiration and natural order in which Hamlet finds himself is all too unequal: idealism turns out to be a poor match for the prison walls of either Denmark or the grave. Hamlet's quest for revenge itself becomes his trap—and his tomb.

E. Irony and Narrative Voice:
A Formalist Approach to "Everyday Use"

The formalist critic deals with irony and paradox, with ambiguity, with the tensions that result from multiple interactions within the organic form of the literary piece.

Reminded of these principles, we find that they abound in Alice Walker's "Everyday Use: for your grandmama." Indeed, the very title sets us going. "Everyday Use" seems easy enough, at first: it is a phrase used by Dee, the educated and supposedly sophisticated of the two sisters. But for her it is a term of disparagement about the use of the quilts; for her sister Maggie and for her mother the phrase suggests a worthy, daily use of the quilts. The quilts have different meanings for the members of the family.

And what are we to make of the subtitle, "for your grandmama"? Is it a dedication to a "real" grandmother, an actual specific person, about whom the author tells us nothing more in the text? If so, to whom does "your" refer? Or perhaps it is a kind of generic grandmother, a typical figure that compares with many women in the rural, predominantly African American culture that provides the setting of the story? Or is the subtitle not a dedication, but a recollection of the quilts' association with Maggie and Dee's grandmother? Someone who was there in fact, an everyday, dependable matriarchal figure? And the early pieces of the quilts were hers, "every day."

But the title is just the beginning of the formal interplay throughout this story.

At a fairly obvious level, what we earlier called "external form" is evident in "Everyday Use." Consider the sequence of events. The scene is set with the mother of the two sisters reporting the events to an unidentified and nonspeaking listener, or maybe just remembering what has happened, speaking ruminatively to herself. But in that report or reminiscence, she moves sequentially from the initial setting to the description of Maggie to the central episode—the visit by

Dee and her friend, their meal and conversation together, the altercation between Dee and her mother about the quilts, the departure of the visitors, and the final lines about Maggie and her mother, just sitting there, "enjoying," as the day comes to a close. In this simple yet artfully structured way, the story has what Aristotle called for—an "orderly arrangement of parts." Neat, compact, controlled. A good external form.

However, there is an interesting discontinuity of sorts—a paradox—that might catch the reader's attention. Repeatedly, the mother notes her lack of sophistication and, specifically, her lack of education: "I never had an education myself. After second grade the school was closed down." She recalls that both her daughters have read to her—possibly a hint that she herself is illiterate, or almost so. On the other hand, the reader must soon note that the mother does not narrate as one without education would; nor does she speak in a less than standard dialect, although with a few colloquialisms, to be sure; nor is she at loss for words, whether as narrator or as speaker. In fact, she has a rich vocabulary, has a good sense of standard **syntax**, and is quite capable of turning a phrase or calling up a vivid image. Why, may we ask, is there this seeming discontinuity between what the narrator tells us about her lack of education and what she shows us? We have no reason to believe that she is an unreliable narrator. If she says that she has no education and if she may be illiterate, then quite possibly that is the factual truth.

But the actual telling of the episode, in the first person, seemingly belies the factual truth. Is it possible that she is telling herself the story, again, at some point in the time well beyond the original setting, when she is "free to sit here" (just as she said that she would be doing once Maggie was married and gone)? If so, then the telling is at the level not of monologue to an unidentified listener, but at the level of the mother's own mind, her own thought processes. And that is a significant point.

For the mother clearly is intelligent and rich in insight and understanding. She has a depth and wisdom (indeed even a sense of humor) that Dee cannot fathom.

That contrast between the lack of education and the real thought processes of the mother presents us with a remarkable "tension," not of a negative sort (though there is a psychological tension in the story that might be negative) but of the sort that the New Critics found important in the internal form of a piece of literary art. What the mother seems to be to daughter Dee is in fact belied by the thought processes, the articulate pattern of words and memories, that the mother in fact commands. Such a tension between narrator and an "appropriate" voice is also an interpretive issue in Faulkner's works, when poor and uneducated people narrate using elaborate vocabularies and diction.

Not surprisingly, this discontinuity compares with other tensions—which also resolve themselves into the organic form of the story—in "Everyday Use." For example, it is easy enough to see the overt conflict between the mother and Maggie on one side and Dee and Hakim-a-barber on the other. At a deeper level we see that there are cultural contrasts between them, richly shown in various symbolic details such as the butter churn, the furniture, and of course the quilts. But the contrast between the college-educated Dee and her mother and sister does resolve itself in what is a virtual thematic statement: the lived culture of the mother is richer and more vital than either Dee's college-oriented culture or what is represented by the "African" names assumed by Dee and her friend. That resolution comes in the forthright denial of the quilts to Dee and the giving of them to Maggie, just as in a less dramatic way the use of snuff amid a quiet setting concludes the story.

There are other contrasts also, filling out the form of the story and further adumbrating its themes. Names, for example, are clearly in this pattern. The mother's name—maiden or married is not clear—is Johnson, a simple, traditional name, appropriate enough for her sturdy personality. Her daughters' names and what they represent are a study in contrasts. "Maggie" is not much out of the ordinary and seemingly has no family "history," but it is Maggie who remembers some family name history: Dee says that Maggie has a "brain like an elephant's." On the other hand, "Dee" has been in the family for generations, with clear connections to individual forebears. But there is the rub, for Dee has rejected family history while claiming to want to preserve their "heritage." Rejecting her name, she has adopted a pseudotraditional name that her mother finds difficult to pronounce: "Ream it out again," she says. Of course, Dee's friend's name is even more difficult, and with a hint of disapproval the mother plays upon his initial greeting ("Asalamalakim") as if it were his name, and later she reduces his name to "the barber." Clearly, names are not just incidentals in this story.

More might be said of a few other details that seem significant in the story, details that have some symbolic force. Some of these are the house fire and the building of the second house much like the first, the apparent confusion between Maggie and Dee's friend about the handshake, the recurrent "uhnnnh" that the mother associates with snakes and implicitly then with Dee's friend, and the interplay of the mother's dream of something like Johnny Carson's program and Dee's virtual dream world of assuming a different culture while claiming to preserve her original "heritage." Ambiguity about the cause of the fire leads one to suspect that Dee, ashamed of her house, started it.

Finally a more positive word about Dee and her actions. Most of what has been said thus far about Dee seems satiric. But let us remember that we are seeing Dee through her mother's eyes. Earlier we noted that the mother is probably a reliable narrator at least insofar as she talks about her lack of education and other specific details of their family life. But is she totally reliable when she talks about Dee? After all, there is a contrast between two worlds here—one relatively unchanged from what it has been, one that reflects major changes in the society and economy. Dee is somewhat obtuse—but she has been to college, she has been in a different environment, she does suggest that Maggie "make something" of herself. And that is not wrong. Would most readers rather be Dee or Maggie? Just about anyone would answer Dee. Perhaps that is the final irony, the lasting ambiguity, of the story.

F. *Frankenstein*: A Thematic Reading

The outward form, almost the visual shape, of Mary Shelley's *Frankenstein* in the 1818 edition is obvious even to the casual reader because of two recognizable devices. One is the use of letters to structure the novel, a characteristic which appeared at the very beginning of what some critics consider the rise of the modern realistic novel in England in the eighteenth century, beginning with Samuel Richardson's *Pamela, or Virtue Rewarded*, published in 1740. The full-length work totally in the form of letters is called the **epistolary novel.**

In *Frankenstein,* letters are exchanged by various characters, but it is especially the letters of Captain Walton to his sister that form the epistolary structure, as the book is, technically, written in his letters. The book thus has a **frame structure** recorded by Walton: his letters at the beginning, his transcription of Victor's story, and within that Victor's version of the Creature's lengthy narrative. Such story-within-a-story frame devices also occur in Joseph Conrad's *Heart of Darkness* and Henry James's "The Turn of the Screw."

As a consequence of this structure, we encounter shifts of narrative point of view that compete with each other and raise questions about the veracity of any of the narrators. One may wonder to what extent the personality of Captain Walton is different from that of Frankenstein, or in other words what is the effect, if any, of different points of view. Both Walton and Frankenstein tell their versions of the story in what is called "first person point of view"—the use of the pronoun "I" by the teller. But is there really any difference in either personality? Does Walton think as Frankenstein does? Is there any stylistic difference in their (apparent) speech? Little difference, if any, is to be found. Indeed, they both have a quest for great scientific success under daunting circumstances. Only the specific quest and the circumstances differ. Is there any real difference between them in the last pages of the novel? Or may one believe that in Walton's listening to Frankenstein's tale, and his observation of Frankenstein's appearance and his appreciation of Frankenstein's mind, what we get is a melding of the two personalities into one? Finally, these questions—really left to the reader for answers—present the ultimate question of the believability of the narrator, what some have called the "unreliable narrator." We must also recall that the Creature's first-hand narrative is the longest single narrative in the book.

But let us now turn to a different aspect of a formalist reading of *Frankenstein*. In this aspect, the element of form is considerably more abstract than the obvious box-within-a-box structure alluded to above. The close reader of the novel must soon perceive that two opposing concepts, with related word and phrase patterns, give not a visual shape or form to the novel but a contrast that forms (informs) a major theme of the novel, even as the contrast provides an aesthetic appreciation of the novel. Let us repeat what was just suggested about the two quests of Walton and Frankenstein: they dream of great scientific successes that would win for them enduring respect from their fellow human beings. But they both fail stupendously, while sacrificing the lives of others (Frankenstein) or endangering lives (Walton). If we write large the nature of this contrast, we have the enduring hope of human beings to achieve what seems impossible side by side with the constant danger of failure, with sometimes disastrous circumstances. It is the dream of the *Star Wars* movies parallel with the explosion of the *Challenger* spacecraft off Cape Canaveral in 1986 as it carried several men toward space, along with the first woman to venture there—a failure made even more dramatic in 2003 with the *Columbia* explosion. It is the effort to clone human cells for therapeutic purposes along with the fear that some monstrous human beings may yet emerge from such efforts.

This pattern of dreams and disasters is clearly manifested in *Frankenstein,* particularly in recurrent words and phrases, the words *hope* and *despair* being the dominant ones. Once a reader begins watching for these words, or their synonyms, the sheer quantity of recurrences almost forces the reader to be aware of the thematic implications. As such they might be called **exponents**, in the sense that they are signs or symbols of patterns of meaning. The word *exponent,* in fact, derives from the Latin *exponere,* "to put forth," with the extended meaning of explaining (cf. "expound").

If we pursue this exponential approach to Shelley's novel, we begin quite at the beginning, for in Walton's first letter to his sister we already see his desire (his hope) to discover the "power" of "the needle," and he has "ardent curiosity" to pursue his study of what the magic of the compass may be. (It is worth noting that the motifs of magnetism and of electricity, specifically of lightning, run through the novel; they are related to the very creation of the monster, and the references to lightning are often indicative of these mysteries—"exponents" of them, we may say.) Once the theme of hope (and despair) is introduced, the reader can perceive the importance of a passage in Letter IV, where Walton quotes Frankenstein as saying, "You have *hope,* and the world before you, and have no cause for *despair.* But I—I have lost everything, and cannot begin life anew" (emphasis ours).

The pattern is set. It will be augmented detail by detail, by repetition of the more obvious exponential words, but by related words. One such example is "ardour" and "ardent," occurring three times in the first twenty-five lines or so of Chapter 3 and twice more two pages later, after Frankenstein tells the reader that he discovered how to bestow "animation upon lifeless matter." A few paragraphs later, Frankenstein tells how, "with unremitting ardour," he clung to the hope that "A new species would bless me as its creator and source"; sometimes he had some failures, "yet still I clung to the hope...." Such repetition points to Frankenstein's delusion that by making the Creature shows his love of humanity.

In Chapter 4, shortly after he has infused "life into an inanimate body," an action he had desired with an immoderate "ardour," "the beauty of the dream vanished, and breathless horror and disgust filled my heart." Words like "wretch" and "overthrow so complete" come to his mind. Only after this do we learn that his given name is "Victor," an irony that cannot be ignored.

Time passes, there is some recovery, and Chapter 5 ends with Frankenstein's spirits "high" and he "bounded" on "with feelings of unbridled joy and hilarity." But Chapter 6 begins with Victor's receiving his father's letter telling him that young William has been murdered. The pattern of point-counterpoint continues even in the juxtaposition of events at the ends of chapters with those at the beginnings of the following chapters. Not surprisingly, the word *despair* appears shortly after the close of the father's letter; it will be seen many times in the rest of the book—some four times, for example, in a few paragraphs reporting the aftermath of the trial of Justine, along with the equally exponential "no hope." The motif is inescapable as Volume One concludes.

The first sentence of Volume Two picks up the refrain: "deprives the soul.... of hope," and two lines later we read of "despair." Five times in the first two pages of Chapter 1 we find either "hope" or "despair." And "despair" occurs twice more before the end of the chapter. In Chapter 2, Victor leaves his family to go out on a glacier, a "sea of ice," where he is met by his monstrous creation. The imagery of ice, as noted in Chapter 4, reminds us of Dante's deepest part of hell in the *Inferno*, where there is no love, only despair, of Robert Frost's "Fire and Ice," where ice suffices to show the essence of hate, and of the physical and spiritual challenge of the northland in Jack London's story "The White Silence."

As the Creature tells Frankenstein the story of his life subsequent to his "creation" (Chs. 3 and 4), the Creature reports of his high hopes as he did good deeds for others, particularly for his "neighbours" outside of whose house he lived, unknown to them. Chapter 4 ends with his echoing *Paradise Lost:* "Happy, happy earth! Fit habitation for gods.... the present was tranquil [another word with exponential quality] and the future gilded by bright rays of hope, and anticipation of joy." But the reader knows from the opening sentence of Chapter 5 that evils will come.

As the Creature continues his tale (we recall the box-within-a-box framing devices), the reader learns more of his good fortune followed by bad. Chapter 7 is a rich system of contrasts. Suffice it to say that the system is summed up by what the blind father of the family says to the Creature, not knowing to whom he is speaking: "Do not *despair*. To be friendless is indeed to be unfortunate; but the hearts of men when unprejudiced by any obvious self-interest, are full of brotherly love and charity. Rely, therefore, on your *hopes;* and if these friends are good and amiable, do not *despair*" (emphasis ours). But almost immediately the rest of the family return, scream, flee, beat the Creature—and Chapter 7 ends on that note of despair.

And on that note Chapter 8 opens: "Cursed, cursed creator! Why did I live?" Why, asks the Creature, "...did I not extinguish the spark of existence" that Frankenstein "had so wantonly bestowed?.... [D]espair had not yet taken possession of me...." But two paragraphs later, he says that he "sank on the damp grass in the sick impotence of despair." About a page later, he continued "in my hovel in a state of utter and stupid despair." Still another page later, after quoting—probably with full ironic intent—the hopeful final lines of *Paradise Lost*, he tells Frankenstein, "but I did not despair. From you only could I hope for succour." This alternation between hope and despair continues, for shortly, alluding to the first day of spring during his subsequent journeying, the Creature "dared to be happy." At this time, he rescues a girl who has fallen into a swift stream—and is rewarded with a bullet wound. The Creature tells Frankenstein of how he came upon William, killing him as his "first victim." In his "exultation" at the murder, he says, "I, too, can create desolation; my enemy is not impregnable; this death will carry despair to him. . . ." Chapter 8 ends with the Creature's request that Frankenstein create a monster "of the same species" to be his companion.

In Chapter 9, the last of Volume Two, Frankenstein agrees to the request, upon which the Creature departs. The word *hope* does not occur here, but clearly it is a moment of hope for him. For Frankenstein, however, it is another low ebb, and "the gentle affection of my beloved Elizabeth was inadequate to draw me from the depth of my despair." Even so, the family ambience provides him with "at least some degree of tranquillity," as the chapter and volume end with that motif of something between hope and despair.

There is in the opening paragraph of Volume Three a hint of what some might call manic depression in Frankenstein, when he alludes to how his bouts of melancholy would "return by fits." That alternation between moods is much the same, of course, as the alternating uses of words like *hope* and *despair*. The reader by this time would not be surprised when, after the elder Frankenstein has broached the subject of marriage between Elizabeth and Victor, we find in a short passage three of the motif words, or exponents, that we are tracing: "my kindly father forbore to question me further concerning the cause of my *dejection*. He *hoped* that new scene. . . . would restore my *tranquillity*" (emphasis ours). Two paragraphs later, Elizabeth hopes that after his two-year sojourn away, Victor would "return happy and tranquil." Indeed, the trip through the Rhine valley does bring to Victor a "tranquillity."

In Chapter 2, Victor is now in England, "But a blight had come over my existence. . . . ," and the "joyous faces" around him serve only to bring back "despair to my heart." Amid what should have been pleasant in Oxford, Frankenstein is "a blasted tree," an image of lightning again strengthening his forlorn state. Having arrived at his island retreat in the Orkneys, he works in his laboratory to create a female monster, as he "looked towards its completion with a tremulous and eager hope. . . ."

In Chapter 3, after he has made some progress, he sees the Creature peering through a window at him, whereupon Victor destroys his female creature, and the Creature withdraws "with a howl of devilish despair. . . ." Shortly, however, the Creature returns and asks Frankenstein whether he "dare destroy my hopes?" In the course of that colloquy, the Creature promises that "soon the bolt will fall" on Frankenstein—possibly another hint of the motif of electricity. In succeeding paragraphs we find "the depths of despair," "gloomy despair," and "despairing."

In the following pages the obvious words are fewer, but Frankenstein's instances of momentary good fortune (his father's coming, his being released from jail) are hardly enough to balance a phrase like "paroxysms of anguish and despair." He experiences some "joy" when he anticipates return to Geneva (Ch. 4), and the aid of his father is tender and "unremitting," for the father "would not despair" in his assistance (Ch. 5). When Elizabeth writes to Victor, she "yet. . . hope[s] to see peace in [his] countenance," and "tranquillity" in his heart; late in the letter she uses the word *tranquillity* with reference to herself. However, the letter brings little relief to Victor, who—perhaps thinking of the last lines of *Paradise Lost* again—says "but the apple was already eaten, and the angel's arm bared to drive me from all hope." Back in Geneva, "The tranquillity which I now enjoyed did not endure." Victor alludes to his "real insanity." Ironically, in an effort to gain "a greater degree of tranquillity," he carries a dagger and pistols as he prepares for marriage. He even "hoped" for his marriage, when "the threat appeared more as a delusion...." And "Elizabeth seemed happy" because his "tranquil demeanour" calmed her mind. During their short ride by boat after the wedding, he alludes to his "despair," and she, to "hope."

If Chapter 5 ends with the placid and lovely boat ride, the first page of Chapter 6 is starkly countrapuntal, for within a few paragraphs Elizabeth is dead, she who had been "the best hope, and the purest creature of earth." Victor knows anew "the agony of despair." When he comes out of a fainting spell, he sees the monster at the window; the crowd pursues the monster, but failing to find him "we returned hopeless." The word *hope* recurs in passages like "A fiend had snatched from me every hope of future happiness. . . ."

But how deep is his despair? After Elizabeth's murder he laments only his own sense of loss—not once does he think, "Poor Elizabeth!" Throughout the novel he blames everyone—his father, Cornelius Agrippa, the Creature—everyone but himself. Thus some readers do not believe in his hopes and despairs because he is so self-deluded.

Victor finds himself in the cemetery where now lie the remains of William, Elizabeth, and his father, and his fresh grief "gave way to rage and despair" (Ch. 7). He calls upon the "spirits of the dead" to aid him in having the Creature "feel the despair that now torments me." Again, he feels only his despair, no one else's, and certainly does not feel a sense of responsibility at *causing* the near-universal despair of the characters.

Pursuing the Creature in the icy north, Victor learns that the monster has set out on the sea of ice, at which Victor "suffered a temporary access of despair." As Victor comes near to the end of his narrative as recorded by Captain Walton, the thematic words we are tracing come in a rush—"hope...despair...hope...hopes were suddenly extinguished....hopes of succour...."

At this point Walton resumes his letter, and he notes that sometimes Victor narrated his story "with a tranquil voice," which in turn would give vent to rage. About a page later, there is a fairly long paragraph in which Frankenstein contrasts for Walton's benefit the vast extremes of his hope when he was creating a "sensitive and rational animal" and the "despondency" to which he has fallen. This paragraph, perhaps as much as any other passage in the book, shows the thematic tension to which the exponential words and motifs have pointed for so many pages.

But the motifs continue to the end. In resuming his letter to his sister (the part dated September 2), Walton himself within three successive paragraphs preserves the sequence: "hopes...despair...hope...hope...despair...." There are more instances in the letter fragments that follow. Shortly we hear again from

Frankenstein, in another passage that is at the heart of the theme we are tracing. He tells Walton, "Farewell, Walton! Seek happiness in tranquillity, and avoid ambition, even if it be only the apparently innocent one of distinguishing yourself in science and discoveries. Yet why do I say this? I have myself been blasted in the hopes, yet another may succeed." Once again, tranquillity seems to be a balance point, a middle point between hope and despair.

The Creature now makes his appearance to Walton, and again the recurring words appear—"dared to hope," and "despair," and "excess of my despair," "loathing despair," "I falsely hoped." The final irony is his "For whilst I destroyed his hopes, I did not satisfy my own desires." As the novel comes to an end, the Creature plans to immolate himself on the fires of his "funeral pile." Those fires, we note, will be on the ice of the north, and these twin symbols of hell are the last images the book gives us.

In review, the form of the novel is largely shaped by the contrast between hubristic hopes and human despair. Vaulting ambition, the novel seems to say, will carry with it the potential of massive failure. The words *hope* and *despair* are clear exponents of this theme, along with synonyms and countrapuntal episodes that have much the same function. Along the way there are associated motifs, like electricity and lightning and "blasting," and perhaps even more tantalizing the recurrent word "tranquillity," for the subtheme of placidity plays off the two extremes like a melody in a symphony or opera that faintly suggests there might be another way, somewhere.

V. SUMMARY OF KEY POINTS

- The formalist critic abandons historical and biographical information and instead focuses on the text as a discrete object. This approach is sometimes characterized as "art for art's sake."
- Formalist critics examine the intrinsic factors of the work's structure. Is it presented in chapters, stanzas, or sections?
- Formalist critics came to be called the New Critics when several prominent critics adopted the name in the 1930s. Many of these, such as Robert Penn Warren, were members of an intellectual circle at Vanderbilt University who called themselves the Fugitives. Many were also poets themselves.
- Reader-Response Theory: This approach is inspired by but differs from formalism in that meaning is found not in the text but in the reader's imaginative interaction with what is presented by the author. Accordingly, not so much form but strategies and practices of reading are emphasized.
- Formalists distinguish between organic and merely external form.
- Formalists look for such textual features as texture, image, and symbol; fallacies; point of view; the speaker's voice; and tension, irony, and paradox.
- Other important formal concerns include denotative and connotative language, ambiguity, dialectic, objective correlative, and conceits.

VI. LIMITATIONS OF THE FORMALIST APPROACH

By the 1950s, dissent was in the air. Still outraged by the award of the Bollingen Prize for Poetry to Ezra Pound in 1949, some voices thought they detected a pronounced elitism, if not more sinister rightist tendencies, in the New Critics, their disciples, and the poets to whom they had granted the favor of their attention. By 1955, some doubters were pointing to the formalist critics' absorption with details, their greater success with intensive than with extensive criticism, their obvious preference for poets like Eliot and Yeats, and their lack of success with the novel and the drama (Holman, "The Defense of Art" 238–39).

Less general caveats have emphasized the restriction of formalist criticism to a certain kind of literature simply because that kind proved itself especially amenable—lyric poetry generally but especially English poetry of the seventeenth century and the "modernist" poetry that stems from Pound and Eliot, and some virtually self-selecting fiction that significantly displays poetic textures (for example, *Moby-Dick* and *Ulysses*). New Critics tended to ignore or undervalue some poetry and other genres that do not easily respond to formalist approaches. The problems increase whenever the language of the literary work tends to approach that of the polemicist. The formalist approach sometimes seems to lapse into a treasure hunt for objective correlatives, conceits, the image, or ironic turns of phrase. It has not seemed to work particularly well for most American poetry written since 1950; as students often point out, it tends to overlook feeling and appears cold in its absorption with form.

Robert Langbaum pronounced the New Criticism "dead—dead of its very success." For, said he, "We are all New Critics nowadays, whether we like it or not, in that we cannot avoid discerning and appreciating wit in poetry, or reading with close attention to words, images, ironies, and so on" (11). There is more to criticism than "understanding the text, [which] is where criticism begins, not where it ends" (14). Langbaum believed that the New Criticism took us for a time outside the "main stream of criticism" (represented by Aristotle, Coleridge, and Arnold), and that we should return, with the tools of explication and analysis given us by the New Critics, to that mainstream. That is, instead of insisting upon literature's autonomy, we must resume relating it to life and ideas, including political ideas, radical theories, and cultural context.

Still later, various charges were leveled against the New Critics, and a number of them will be noted in succeeding chapters.

QUICK REFERENCE

Bleich, David. *Subjective Criticism*. Baltimore: Johns Hopkins University Press, 1978.

Booth, Wayne. *The Rhetoric of Fiction*. Chicago: University of Chicago Press, 1961.

Brooks, Cleanth, and Robert Penn Warren. *Understanding Poetry*. 3rd ed. New York: Holt, 1960.

Burke, Kenneth. *Counter-Statement*. Los Altos, CA: Hermes, 1953.

Connolly, Thomas E. "Hawthorne's 'Young Goodman Brown': An Attack on Puritanic Calvinism." *American Literature* 28 (Nov. 1956): 370–75.

Crane, Ronald S. "Cleanth Brooks; or the Bankruptcy of Critical Monism." *Modern Philology* 45 (1948): 226–45.

Eco, Umberto. *The Role of the Reader: Explorations in the Semiotics of Texts.* Bloomington: Indiana University Press, 1978.

Eliot, T. S. Introduction to *The Adventures of Huckleberry Finn.* London: Cresset, 1950. Reprinted in *Adventures of Huckleberry Finn.* 2nd ed. Eds. Sculley Bradley, Richard Croom Beatty, E. Hudson Long, and Thomas Cooley. New York: W. W. Norton & Co., 1977.

Fetterley, Judith. *The Resisting Reader: A Feminist Approach to American Fiction.* Bloomington: Indiana University Press, 1978.

Fish, Stanley. *Surprised by Sin: The Reader in "Paradise Lost."* Berkeley: University of California Press, 1967.

——. *Is There a Text in This Class?* Cambridge, MA: Harvard University Press, 1980.

Fogle, Richard Harter. *Hawthorne's Fiction: The Light and the Dark.* Norman: University of Oklahoma Press, 1952.

Freund, Elizabeth. *The Return of the Reader: Reader-Response Criticism.* London: Methuen, 1987.

Gibson, Walker. "Authors, Speakers, Readers, and Mock Readers." *College English* 11, no. 5 (1950): 265–69.

Harding, D. W. "Regulated Hatred: An Aspect of the Work of Jane Austen." *Scrutiny* 8 (March 1940): 346–62.

Harmon, William. *A Handbook to Literature.* 9th ed. Upper Saddle River, NJ: Prentice-Hall, 2002.

Holland, Norman. "*Hamlet*—My Greatest Creation." *Journal of the American Academy of Psychoanalysis* 3 (1975): 419–27.

——. "Recovering 'The Purloined Letter': Reading as a Personal Transaction." In *The Reader in the Text.* Ed. Susan Suleiman and Inge Crosman. Princeton, NJ: Princeton University Press, 1980.

——. "The Miller's Wife and the Professors: Questions About the Transactive Theory of Reading." *New Literary History* 17 (1986): 423–47.

Holman, C. Hugh. "The Defense of Art: Criticism Since 1930." In *The Development of American Literary Criticism.* Ed. Floyd Stovall. Chapel Hill: University of North Carolina Press, 1955.

Holman, C. Hugh, and William Harmon. *A Handbook to Literature.* 6th ed. New York: Macmillan, 1992.

Iser, Wolfgang. *The Act of Reading.* Baltimore: Johns Hopkins University Press, 1978.

James, Henry. "The Art of Fiction." *Partial Portraits.* London: Macmillan, 1888.

Jauss, Hans Robert. *Toward an Aesthetic of Reception.* Trans. Timothy Bahti. Minneapolis: University of Minnesota Press, 1982.

Kuhn, Thomas S. *The Structure of Scientific Revolutions.* Chicago: University of Chicago Press, 1962.

Langbaum, Robert. *The Modern Spirit: Essays on the Continuity of Nineteenth- and Twentieth-Century Literature.* New York: Oxford University Press, 1970.

Lentricchia, Frank. *After the New Criticism.* Chicago: University of Chicago Press, 1980.

Mailloux, Steven. *Interpretive Conventions: The Reader in the Study of American Fiction.* Ithaca, NY, and London: Cornell University Press, 1984.

Mailloux, Steven. "Reading *Huckleberry Finn:* The Rhetoric of Performed Ideology." In *New Essays on Huckleberry Finn.* Ed. Louis Budd. Cambridge: Cambridge University Press, 1985.

Pottle, Frederick A. "The Case of Shelley." *PMLA* 67 (1952): 589–608.

Prince, Gerald. "Introduction to the Study of the Narratee." In Tompkins.

Ransom, John Crowe. *The World's Body.* New York: Scribner's, 1938.

———. *The New Criticism.* Norfolk, CT: New Directions, 1941.

Richards, I. A. *Principles of Literary Criticism.* New York: Harcourt, 1925.

———. *Practical Criticism.* New York: Harcourt, 1929.

Rosenblatt, Louise. *The Reader, the Text, the Poem.* Carbondale: Southern Illinois University Press, 1978.

Schorer, Mark. "Technique as Discovery." *The Hudson Review* 1 (Spring 1948): 67–87.

Tompkins, Jane, ed. *Reader-Response Criticism: From Formalism to Post-Structuralism.* Baltimore: Johns Hopkins University Press, 1980.

Warren, Robert Penn. *Selected Essays of Robert Penn Warren.* New York: Random House (Vintage), 1966.

Wimsatt, W. K., and Monroe Beardsley. *The Verbal Icon: Studies in the Meaning of Poetry.* Lexington: University of Kentucky Press, 1954.

4

~

Materialisms

I. MARXISM

Karl Marx (1818–1883), the chief theorist of modern socialism, believed that life is materialistic, beginning with the need for food and shelter; the physical facts of life may be said to shape human consciousness rather than the other way around. The material economic world he called the *base;* a *superstructure* is built upon that base, and its economics is the driving material force of society and of the class differences between the *bourgeoisie,* the capitalist upper class, and the *proletariat,* the working class that supplies the *capitalists,* or owners of wealth, with their labor. (Capital is not just money, but money used to make a profit.) Marx believed that history shows a **dialectic** between opposing economic forces, as classes battle each other, but he believed that a socialist future would arrive when the proletariat would revolt and defeat the bourgeoisie. Dialectic is how historical transformations occur: *thesis* and *antithesis* allow opposing historical forces to call each other into being and ultimately give rise to a third force, *synthesis,* which transcends the opposition. Because Marx saw life as having a materialist base, spiritual expressions he saw as a culture's **ideology**, and that ideology would support the needs of the dominant class.

Marx argued specifically that the development of the *division of labor* led to social inequalities, as different classes had different interests. Marx described the *alienation of labor*—the fact that we are quite distant from the products we consume, as we rarely make our own products today; factory workers assemble only pieces of a product. Marx distinguished between *use value* versus *exchange value:* use value is the actual purpose of the object; exchange value is market value. He defined what he called the *commodity fetish,* when exchange value takes on a power of its own that renders an object only abstractly, such as status clothing, cars, and homes. He saw art and literature as commodities as well, and this is why he is important to understanding literature. But contemporary Marxist theory and criticism are not really about revolution, but are used to interpret contemporary society.

How do these terms and concepts fit together? It is important to recognize that they are not concerns only of Marxists but are part of an overarching theory of human economy that Marx traces throughout history, especially postindustrial history. Georg Wilhelm Friedrich Hegel (1770–1831), a German philosopher, conceived a comprehensive philosophical framework to account for an integrated relation of mind and nature, subject and object, and psychology, the state, history, art, religion, and philosophy. Hegel's concept of mind or spirit, like Marx's, reveals itself in a set of contradictions and oppositions that it attempts to integrate and unite, such as nature and freedom, and immanence and transcendence, without eliminating either pole or reducing it to the other. His most influential conceptions for Marxism are of speculative logic or "dialectic," "absolute idealism," "the "Master/Slave" dialectic, "ethical life," and the importance of history. Thus, given that there is a division of labor in modern society between the proletariat and the bourgeoisie, between labor and capital, a dialectical analysis reveals the ultimate instabilities in the logic of capitalism and its inevitable (Marx believed) collapse in favor of a socialistic society. The proletariat would eventually rebel against its masters, throw off the slave mentality, and end the alienation of labor from the means and results of production. Within this vast economic, social, and historical framework, literature too has its place—especially as it either supports or challenges the hegemonic status of the society in which it is produced.

Marx's ideas were welcomed by many. In the United States of the 1930s, there was thriving socialism and interest in communism, but after World War II the cold war meant that his ideas were regarded as dangerous. However, a group of New York intellectuals and literary critics jettisoned "vulgar" Marxism and took up liberal political positions, describing literature as a way that liberal culture is expressed. This group included Lionel Trilling, Philip Rahv, Alfred Kazin, and Irving Howe. There were two main schools of thought influenced by Marxism about how literature reflects social reality. Leon Trotsky held that **mimesis** in literature should give us a "slice of life" without necessarily commenting on it. However, another school, represented by Hungarian philosopher and critic Georg Lukács, held that authors must take pains to portray not the slice of life but the *forces* that act on society and that bring about social change.

Lukács, who served under Hungary's Communist government, expanded Marx's notion of *reification,* the way that commodification reduces social relations, ideas, and people to things and thus accelerates alienation. He addressed commodity fetishism and its opposite, unseen labor (a major issue in globalization today). He faulted the **modernism** of William Faulkner, James Joyce, and Franz Kafka for its fragmentation, which for him sacrificed the content of what he preferred, social **realism**. To him, modernists seemed interested only in form and technique, such as **stream of consciousness**, which isolates the individual. He also sharply criticized **naturalists** such as Émile Zola and Theodore Dreiser for merely presenting characters trapped in the social order. In contrast, he admired Sir Walter Scott, Stendahl, Honoré Balzac, Leo Tolstoy, and Thomas Mann for representing not fragmentation but modern society within the history of the dialectical

Figure 4.1. Karl Marx (ca. 1870s–80s).
Getty Images/English School.

class conflict. German playwright Bertolt Brecht, like Lukács, believed that realism was embedded in even fanciful works; in his *Threepenny Opera,* for example, the thieves and beggars of London present the surface story, but underneath are its provocative themes directed at Brecht's contemporaries in Germany.

Antonio Gramsci was a leader of the Italian Communist Party and wrote most of his works while imprisoned by the Italian Fascist dictator Benito Mussolini. Accordingly, he had to phrase many of his key ideas in indirect ways, which means his readers have to struggle. His prison notebooks were smuggled to Moscow and published after his death; they have been very influential among Marxist critics. Gramsci criticized the central Marxist notion of *economic determinism.* He drew a distinction between what he called *state* (government and politics) and *civil society* (culture). He focused on the latter, emphasizing that many things can be explained by culture and not just economics. He analyzed why the proletariat had not revolted and had in fact supported the Right. He believed that **hegemony** (how dominant groups maintain their power) does not dominate through the exercise of violence or coercion, but more subtly wins the consent of the masses through capitalist cultural leadership. People are deceived by false choices to believe they are exercising autonomy, but what they want has been decided for them by marketing and advertising, or the delusion of consumer choice. Rather than revolution, Gramsci advocated for a practical plan (*praxis*) with which to move forward.

The Frankfurt School of Max Horkheimer, Theodor Adorno, Herbert Marcuse, and later Jürgen Habermas tried to reinterpret relations among philosophy, art, modernism, and public debate. They believed that there has been no revolution because the capitalist superstructure, through technology, reproduces capitalist ideology, a good example being the entertainment industry. Art thus becomes another commodity, discouraging revolutionary or critical thinking. Habermas proposed what he called the *public sphere* as a space between art and society that could be influenced by reason. Walter Benjamin, influenced by the Frankfurt School, granted that technology replaced the traditional aesthetic specialness of a work of art, but he also believed new technologies meant new ways of critical thinking.

After World War II and especially after the civil rights movement and feminism, a new wave of Marxist critics, mostly in academia, coalesced as contemporary Marxism, which disdained classical or what they called the "old" or "vulgar" Marxism. This Marxism returned to critiques of the base and superstructure and to the idea that economics decides everything, even art. French Marxist Louis Althusser saw ideology as "the imaginary relationship of individuals to their real conditions of existence" ("Ideology and Ideological State Apparatuses," 162). He borrows the term *imaginary* from Jacques Lacan to describe ideology as unconscious; his thought was an important influence on Jacques Derrida. The ruling system, he says, calls to us *(interpellation)* and when we answer we become its subjects. Althusser's Ideological State Apparatus (ISA) is much like Gramsci's "civil society" and includes all the institutions in society such as the media, schools, churches, and families. In contrast, there is the Repressive State Apparatuses (RSA) such as the police and the courts, which is similar to Gramsci's *state.* Althusser's key contribution is his idea that ISAs recruit subjects into ideological conformity better than RSAs, resulting in people's thinking becoming so interpellated that they act against their own interests. For Althusser, history is not primarily grounded in economic facts, but is itself a myth or text to be interpreted.

Lucien Goldmann tried to combine the mediation theories of the Frankfurt School and the structural Marxism of Althusser by practicing what he called "genetic Marxism," focusing on a work's genesis in the ideology of its times. He believed only the greatest works of an age, not the minor entertainments, contained its deeper consciousness. Goldman's British follower, Raymond Williams, brought what he had learned from his own proletarian background. Williams spoke of "complex forms of feeling" within which literature and ideology find what he called "correspondences." Williams sought "structures of feeling" in the arts instead of "ideology." Williams shifted his focus on Marxism throughout his long career. In his book *Culture and Society,* Williams announced himself as a "cultural materialist," influenced heavily by Gramsci's notion of hegemony. As Williams notes in *Marxism and Literary Criticism,*

> Hegemony is...a lived system of meanings and values—constitutive and constituting—which, as they are experienced as practices, appear as reciprocally confirming. It thus constitutes the sense of reality for most people in the

society...beyond which it is very difficult for most members of the society to move...It is...in the strongest sense a "culture" but a culture which has also to be seen as the lived dominance and subordination of particular classes. (110)

But Williams saw in the cultural productions of the working class alternative hegemonies that challenge the ruling class.

Terry Eagleton, one of the most prominent British Marxists, held that literary works are not merely determined by the economic base but are influenced by a large number of interrelated factors including the circumstances of their creation, marketing, and sales, as well as **genre**. Eagleton thus stressed the historical embeddedness of literature and the consequences of a literary theory or practice. He advocated a return to classical Marxism and that authors as well as critics keep in mind the radical and deconstructive possibilities for literature and literary criticism. His model for social transformation was feminism, and he called for a criticism that would do for class what feminism did for women. As he notes in his book *Walter Benjamin, or Towards a Revolutionary Criticism,* "Partly under the pressure of global capitalist crisis, partly under the influence of new themes and forces within socialism, the centre of such studies is shifting from narrowly textual or conceptual analysis to problems of cultural production and the political use of artefacts" (xii).

Pierre Bourdieu, though he criticized Marxism, extended the notion of false choices when he described *cultural capital,* including aesthetic choices people believe are their own but are dictated by the ruling class. In *Distinction: A Social Critique of the Judgment of Taste,* he argues that our tastes in everything from home decorating to opera are defined not by economic capital but by such factors as family and education. Working-class consumers favor realism and escapism. The elite favor forms they have learned to appreciate. This tends to make people remain in their class, as their aesthetic choices continue to define them. Art can thus reproduce and legitimize class.

Frederic Jameson, perhaps the leading American Marxist critic, wove many disciplines together: European Marxism, structuralism, and poststructuralism, Russian Formalism, psychoanalysis, popular culture studies, and American formalism into his notion of the *political unconscious.* He called for recognition of how psychology's social dimension points to the bourgeois culture's determination to repress its recognition of it own darker motives. His slogan was "Always historicize!" In his book *Marxism and Form,* he concluded that a genuine dialectical-materialist criticism can exist if it include what he called "metacommentary," or commentary on itself and its own orientation. **Point of view** in his mind was not the neutral tool Wayne Booth described in *A Rhetoric of Fiction.* Thus the critic must be self-conscious about his or her **subject-position.** In *The Political Unconscious: Narrative as a Socially Symbolic Act,* he criticizes the bourgeois belief that art is "pure" and separate from history and politics (cf. formalism). He called for the "return of the repressed" in literary texts, the revelation of the social conflicts in its society, including politics, history, and society as the three "horizons" of the text. He also criticizes **postmodernism** in his book *Postmodernism, or the Cultural*

Logic of Late Capitalism as a mere fragmenting of reality until it becomes merely **pastische,** not even **parody,** which could criticize the bourgeoisie. Modernism has degenerated in postmodernism to the merely allusive and playful, without a serious political orientation.

II. BRITISH CULTURAL MATERIALISM

Beginning in the 1950s, an influential group of British intellectuals adopted Marxist analysis to read literary texts; they called themselves "cultural materialists." However, their approach has a long tradition in England. In the later nineteenth century Matthew Arnold sought to redefine the "givens" of British culture. Edward Burnett Tylor's pioneering anthropological study *Primitive Culture* (1871) argued that "Culture or civilization, taken in its widest ethnographic sense, is a complex whole which includes knowledge, belief, art, morals, law, custom, and any other capabilities and habits acquired by man as a member of society" (1). Claude Lévi-Strauss's influence moved British thinkers to assign "culture" to primitive peoples, and then, with the work of British scholars such as Raymond Williams, to attribute culture to the working class as well as to the elite. As Williams memorably states: "There are no masses; there are only ways of seeing [other] people as masses" (300).

To appreciate the importance of this revision of "culture" we must situate it within the controlling myth of social and political reality of the British Empire upon which the sun never set, an ideology left over from the previous century. In modern Britain two trajectories for "culture" developed: one led back to the past and the feudal hierarchies that ordered community in the past; here, culture acted in its sacred function as preserver of the past. The other trajectory led toward a future, socialist utopia that would annul the distinction between labor and leisure classes and make transformation of status, not fixity, the norm. This cultural materialism furnished a leftist orientation "critical of the aestheticism, formalism, antihistoricism, and apoliticism common among the dominant postwar methods of academic literary criticism"; such was the description in the *Johns Hopkins Guide to Literary Theory and Criticism* (Groden and Kreiswirth 180).

Cultural materialism began in earnest in the 1950s with the work of F. R. Leavis, heavily influenced by Matthew Arnold's analyses of bourgeois culture. Leavis sought to use the educational system to distribute literary knowledge and appreciation more widely; Leavisites promoted the "great tradition" of Shakespeare and Milton to improve the moral sensibilities of a wider range of readers than just the elite.

However, British cultural materialist Stuart Hall agreed that the mass media reflect the interests of the ruling class, but that people's interpretive responses are the other part of the picture. In his essay "Cultural Studies: Two Paradigms," he advocates that historians learn from "breaks" in history and that critics attend to "breaks" in texts; by this he meant "where old lines of thought are disrupted, older constellations replaced, and elements, old and new, are regrouped around a different set of premises and themes" (in Richter 1404). His colleague at the Centre for Contemporary Cultural Studies at the University of Birmingham, Richard Hoggart, argued similarly in his book *Uses of Literacy*, and he also helped create the new discipline of cultural studies with a Marxist basis, along with Raymond Williams and E. P. Thompson somewhat later on. Like Leavis before them, cultural materialists advocated that "high" culture be made available to the masses and that working class culture be recognized as culture. Culture, states Hall, has been "democratized and socialized." No longer would it consist of Arnold's "the best that has been thought and said," but art would show its social context; as Williams put it, culture is "ordinary" (in Richter 1406). Hall summarizes: cultural studies "conceptualizes culture as interwoven with all social practices"; these practices, in turn, demonstrate the "sensuous human praxis, the activity through which men and women make history" (in Richter 1409). But culture will always emanate from all classes, not merely be imposed on one by another.

Ironically the threat to their project *was* mass culture. Williams applauded the richness of canonical texts such as Leavis promoted, but also found they could seem to erase certain communal forms of life. Inspired by Marx, British theorists were also influenced by Georg Lukács, Theodor Adorno, Louis Althusser, Max Horkheimer, Mikhail Bakhtin, and Antonio Gramsci. They were especially interested in problems of cultural hegemony and in the many systems of domination related to literature. From Gramsci, an Italian Marxist, for example, they got the concept of cultural "hegemony," referring to relations of domination not always visible as such. Williams noted that hegemony was "a sense of reality for most people...beyond which it is very difficult for most members of society to move" (*Marxism and Literature* 110). But the people are not always victims of hegemony; they sometimes possess the power to change it. As noted earlier, Althusser insisted that ideology was ultimately in control of the people, that "the main function of ideology is to reproduce the society's existing relations of production, and that that function is even carried out in literary texts." Ideology must maintain this state of affairs if the state and capitalism can continue to reproduce themselves without fear of revolution. As noted earlier, Althusser saw popular literature as merely "carrying the baggage of a culture's ideology," whereas "high" literature retained more autonomy and hence had more power (233). Walter Benjamin attacked fascism by questioning the value of what he called the "aura" of culture. Benjamin helps explain the frightening cultural context for a film such as Leni Riefenstahl's *Triumph of the Will* (1935). Lukács developed what he called a "reflection theory," in which he stressed literature's reflection, conscious or unconscious, of the social reality surrounding it—not just a flood of realistic detail but a reflection of the essence of a society. Fiction formed without a sense of such reflection can never fully show the meaning of a given society.

Cultural materialists also turned to the more humanistic and even spiritual insights of the great student of Rabelais and Dostoevsky, Russian Formalist Bakhtin, especially his amplification of the *dialogic* form of meaning within narrative and class struggle, at once conflictual and communal, individual and social.

Feminism was also important for cultural materialists in recognizing how seemingly "disinterested" thought is shaped by power structures such as patriarchy.

III. NEW HISTORICISM

Laputa—"the whore." What did Jonathan Swift mean when he gave that name to the flying island in the third voyage of *Gulliver's Travels?* It is a question that has tantalized readers since the eighteenth century. The science fiction aspect of that island still amuses us, but why "the whore?" There may be an answer, and as we will show later, new historicism is the right approach to answer this question.

"If the 1970s could be called the Age of Deconstruction," writes Joseph Litvak, "some hypothetical survey of late twentieth-century criticism might well characterize the 1980s as marking the Return to History, or perhaps the Recovery of the Referent" (120). Michael Warner phrases new historicism's motto as, "The text is historical, and history is textual" (5). Frederic Jameson insisted, "Always historicize!" (*The Political Unconscious* 9). As a return to historical scholarship, new historicism concerns itself with extraliterary matters—letters, diaries, films, paintings, medical treatises—looking to reveal opposing historical tensions in a text. New historicists seek "surprising coincidences" that may cross generic, historical, and cultural lines in borrowings of metaphor, ceremony, or popular culture (Veeser xii). New historians see such cross-cultural phenomena as texts in themselves. From Hayden White, cultural studies practitioners learned how figural relationships between present and past **tropes** are shaped by historical discourses. From Clifford Geertz, they derived the importance of immersion in a culture to understand its "deep" ways, as opposed to distanced observation. Carolyn Porter credits the emergence of American Studies, Women's Studies, and Afro-American Studies on college and university campuses for ushering in new historicism as a volatile new presence in literary criticism (743–49).

New historicists describe the old historicism (see Ch. 2) as simply background and context, seeing literature as reflecting only history. New historicists join the study of literature and history together primarily to observe how they influence *each other.* They caution that we cannot any longer make claims such as "during the reign of George III British people believed that" or speak of an "Elizabethan world view." For new historicists, history is as complex, nuanced, and unstable as literature—in other words, it is only a set of cultural discourses, just as interpretable as a literary text. And literary texts shape history in an ongoing cycle of mutual relationship. New historicists learned from deconstruction to study history with close attention to a multiplicity of meanings, contradictions, and omissions so as to question the "facts" of history—and the "facts" of literature.

New historicism versus *old historicism:* the latter, says Porter, saw history as "world views magisterially unfolding as a series of tableaux in a film called Progress," as though all Elizabethans, for example, held views in common. The new historicism rejects this periodization of history in favor of ordering history only through the interplay of forms of power (765).

Stephen Greenblatt, a Renaissance scholar and founding editor of the journal *Representations,* may be credited with the coining of the term "new historicism." Greenblatt identifies major influence on his thought from Frederic Jameson, Michel Foucault, and Jean-François Lyotard, all of whom raise the question of art and society as related to institutionalized practices. Jameson blames capitalism for perpetrating a false distinction between the public and the private, and Lyotard argues that capitalism has forced a false integration of these worlds. New historicism exists, H. Aram Veeser explains, between these two poles in an attempt to work with the "apparently contradictory historical effects of capitalism" without insisting upon an inflexible historical and economic theory (1–6). From Foucault, new historicists developed the idea of a broad "totalizing" function of culture observable in its literary texts, which Foucault called the *épistème.* For Foucault history was not the working out of "universal" ideas: because we cannot know the governing ideas of the past or the present, we should not imagine that "we" even have a "center" for mapping the "real." Furthermore, history itself is a form of social oppression, told in a series of ruptures with previous ages; it is more accurately described as discontinuous, riven by "fault lines" that must be integrated into succeeding cultures by the *épistèmes* of power and knowledge. Methods of expression can also be methods of oppression; even though the modern age is governed by a complex master narrative, it may still be seen as only a narrative to succeed those of earlier generations. A new *épistème* will render obsolete our ways of organizing knowledge and telling history.

Like Marxist critics, Foucault believed that our expectations arise from the surrounding culture; there is no "essence" of a human mind, but rather "outer" knowledge—or history—constructs the self as a *knowledge discourse* that produces what it seems only to describe. There is no pure truth, only ideologies, but unlike the Marxists Foucault did not believe all was economics; as he noted, patterns of gender are also constructed by repeated patterns of expectation and action. The dominant discourse can be interrupted by resistance, but resistance is rare. Foucault examined social institutions such as prisons, insane asylums, and hospitals; in *Discipline and Punish: The Birth of the Prison,* he shows how people are manipulated by discourses of criminality, madness, and illness. He analyzes a prison model advocated by eighteenth-century philosopher Jeremy Bentham called the Panopticon; though never built, it featured a central tower in which guards could watch inmates while undetected by them. Whether a guard was watching at any given time did not matter because the inmates would not know. For Foucault, modern society is a Panopticon in which the powers-that-be, whether of gender or other social "norms," can regulate, discipline, police, and surveil people's behavior and beliefs. Then people learn to surveil themselves for aberrant beliefs and practices. Such self-discipline works much better than coercion, as Gramsci argued. In *The History of Sexuality, Volume One: The Will to Knowledge,* Foucault sees the discourse of sexuality as the primary hegemonic regulation. Criticizing Freud's notion of repression, he argues that before modern times there were a variety of sexual practices not codified into discourses, but

DISCUSSION OF FOUCAULT

In the chapter "Las Meniñas" from his book *The Order of Things* (1966), Foucault analyzes the famous painting as representing the relationship between creators of art and viewers of art and emphasizes its conscious artifice as well as the complex network of visual relationships among painter, subject-model, and viewer: "We are looking at a picture in which the painter is in turn looking out at us. A mere confrontation, eyes catching one another's glance, direct looks superimposing themselves upon one another as they cross. And yet this slender line of reciprocal visibility embraces a whole complex network of uncertainties, exchanges, and feints. The painter is turning his eyes towards us only in so far as we happen to occupy the same position as his subject" (4–5). The artist himself is at work on a large canvas, only the back of which is visible. In the front center is the Infanta Margarita and her maids; at first glance, the painter seems to be painting the Infanta, but despite the fact that she is the center of the painting this is not spatially possible.

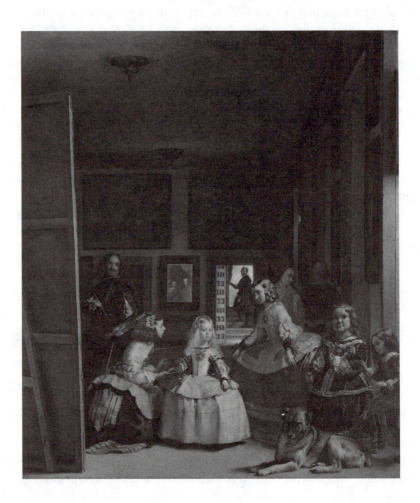

On a mirror hung in the background are the faces of the king and queen, who are being painted, looking straight back into their reflection, or possibly looking at us, the viewers, as are most of the people in the painting including the painter (a self-portrait of Velásquez). Aside from this "reflected" image, the king and queen are not visible to us.

According to Foucault, the painting evokes the reciprocity of vision: we look at the painting, and it looks back at us. It is looking at us because we are standing in the exact spot the king and queen are standing in and are reflected in the mirror on the opposite wall. The painting introduces uncertainties in visual representation, and Foucault describes it as an early critique of the supposed power of representation to confirm visually an objective order of reality (representations of power relationships). The painting is thus a sort of hoax on the usual "order of things." For Foucault, *Las Meniñas* contains the first signs of a new *épistème,* or way of thinking, in European art, a midpoint between the two "great discontinuities" in art history, the classical and the modern: "Perhaps there exists, in this painting by Velázquez, the representation as it were of Classical representation, and the definition of the space it opens up to us.…Representation, freed finally from the relation that was impeding it, can offer itself as representation in its pure form" (18).

In the painting, the painter glances at his model, his arm motionless; perhaps he has just painted a stroke or is just about to, displaying the temporality of the scene. Through what Foucault calls "a subtle system of feints" we cannot see the painting itself, and when the painter returns—in a moment—to his picture we will not see him either. The painter might be said to be at the threshold of representation. Foucault speaks of conflicts of visibility/invisibility, multiple "gazes," and "a vast cage projected backward" to describe the power relationships portrayed. Foucault concludes from his study of *Las Meniñas* that "no gaze is stable" and no point of view the "correct" one; thus no single meaning can be said to exist: "Invisibility is made visible to the painter and transposed into an image forever invisible to himself" (21). Thus the free play of competing points of view leaves the flat surface of the painting and converges into spaces around it.

---

today sexual behavior is converted into identity. New historicists are drawn to Foucault for his dramatic analyses of the discourses of hegemony and the possibilities in art for resistance. Roland Barthes, Jacques Derrida, and Jacques Lacan also helped inspire new historicism to address issues of knowledge and power.

Perhaps Michael Warner has summarized new historicism best:

While critics have realized on the one hand that language and the symbolic are never essential and timeless but always contingent on cultural politics, on the other hand they have realized that cultural politics is always symbolic. New Historicism has a motto: "The text is historical, and history is textual." The first part means that meaning does not transcend context but is produced within it; the second part means that human actions and institutions and relations, while certainly hard facts, are not hard facts as distinguished flora language. They are themselves symbolic representations, though this is not to say, as so many old historicists might conclude, that they are not real. (5)

Thus, ethnologist Clifford Geertz insists in *The Interpretation of Cultures* that to understand a culture an observer cannot stand apart from it, but must immerse himself in it, and he cannot give a credible report without doing so and without acknowledging his own position. This contribution Geertz calls "thick description." If anthropology cannot thus be an empirical science, then neither can history—or literature. There is no "objective" point of view.

New historicism frequently borrows terminology from the marketplace: *exchange, negotiation,* and *circulation* of ideas are described. Veeser calls "the moment of exchange" the most interesting to new historicists, since social *symbolic capital* may be found in literary texts: "the critic's role is to dismantle the dichotomy of the economic and the non-economic, to show that the most purportedly disinterested and self-sacrificing practices, including art, aim to maximize personal or symbolic profit" (xiv). Greenblatt adds that "contemporary theory must situate itself...in the hidden places of negotiation and exchange" ("Towards a Poetics of Culture" 13). Bourdieu's insights are again a resource, especially his definition of the *habitus,* a "system of dispositions" comparable to what linguists analyze as the sum of tacit knowledge one has to know to speak a given language.

What about Laputa? How can new historicism help us answer the question raised a few pages ago?

In "The Flying Island and Female Anatomy: Gynaecology and Power in *Gulliver's Travels,*" Susan Bruce offers a reading of Book III that makes some new historicist sense out of Swift's use of *Laputa.* Bruce ties together some seemingly disparate events of the year 1727, soon after the book was published, including relations between eighteenth-century midwives and physicians and a famous scandal involving a "monstrous birth" that rocked the Royal Court.

Bruce examines a four-volume commentary on *Gulliver's Travels* by one Corolini di Marco, in which the author gives a fairly dry account of his observations until he gets to the episode in Book IV, "A Voyage to the Houyhnhnms," in which Gulliver captures rabbits for food. At that point, di Marco launches into a tirade:

> But here I must observe to you, Mr. Dean, en passant, that Mr. Gulliver's Rabbits were wild Coneys, not tame Gutless ones, such as the consummate native effronterie of St. André has paulmed upon the publick to be generated in the Body of the Woman at Godalming in Surrey. St. André having, by I know not what kind of fatality, insinuated himself among the foreigners, obtained the post of Anatomist-Royal.

Di Marco was referring to a scandal involving the royal physician St. André and the so-called "rabbet-woman" of Surrey, Mary Toft, who managed to convince prominent members of the medical profession in 1727 that she had given birth to a number of rabbits, which she had actually inserted into her vagina and then "labored" to produce. Bruce asks why di Marco felt it necessary to allude to this event. By researching records of Toft's trial and the ultimate ruin of St. André, she illuminates the depiction of the female body as island in Book III of *Gulliver's Travels* and elsewhere.

Bruce describes the trend toward the education of midwives and the medical profession's desire to stamp them out. Examining books published for literate midwives during this period and testimony from Mary Toft's trial allows Bruce to describe the hostility not only toward the midwife who collaborated with Toft in the hoax but toward women in general. Bruce then connects the male establishment's outrage at the female power expressed in the hoax to Gulliver's observations on women, especially his nauseating description of the Queen of Brobdingnag at the table or his seeing another Brobdingnagian woman with a breast tumor with holes so large that he "could have easily crept" into one. The implication is that under the male gaze, the magnification of the female body leads not to enhanced appreciation but rather to horror and disgust. Bruce connects Gulliver's anxious fixation on the female body to the anxieties of his age involving the rise of science and the changing role of women.

Laputa is a gigantic trope of the female body: the circular island with a round chasm at the center, through which the astronomers of the island descend to a domelike structure of the "Flandona Gagnole," or "astronomer's cave." Laputa has at its center a giant lodestone on which the movement of the island depends. The floating physical structure of Laputa is like a uterus and vagina; Gulliver and the Laputians are able to enter this cavity at will and control not only the movements of the lodestone and island, but also the entire society. As Bruce remarks, "It is this which engenders the name of the island: in a paradigmatic instance of misogyny, the achievement of male control over female body itself renders that body the whore: *la puta*" (71).

But eventually the control over the feminine that drives Laputa becomes its own undoing, for the more the men of the island try to restrict their women from traveling below to Balnibarbi (where they engage in sexual adventures with Balnibarbian men), the more male impotence threatens Laputian society. Gulliver notes the men's ineffectuality in several ways, abstracted as they are in their foolish "science"; they are so absent-minded they must have an attendant called a "Flapper" who constantly must slap them out of their reveries. The women, on the other hand, have an "Abundance of Vivacity; they condemn their Husbands, and are exceedingly fond of Strangers.... Mistress and Lover may proceed to the greatest Familiarities before [the husband's] Face, if he be but provided with Paper and implements, and without his *Flapper* by his side." Bruce connects the men's "doomed attempt of various types of science to control the woman's body" to the debate about language in Book III. While the men invent the "Engine for Improving Speculative Knowledge" that produces only broken sentences, the women and other commoners clamor "to speak with their own Tongues, after the Manner of their Forefathers." Thus in "A Voyage to Laputa," control of women has to mean control of their discourse as well as their sexuality, reflecting the contemporary debates of Swift's day. One final historical note: a pamphlet published in 1727 was purportedly written by "Lemuel Gulliver, Surgeon and Anatomist to the Kings of Lilliput and Blefescu, and Fellow of the Academy of Sciences in Balnibarbi." It is entitled *The Anatomist Dissected: or the Man-Midwife finally brought to Bed*. Its subject is Mary Toft, the "rabbet-woman."

IV. ECOCRITICISM

William Rueckert first used the term *ecocriticism* in a 1978 essay, "Literature and Ecology: An Experiment in Ecocriticism," which addresses "the application of ecology and ecological concepts to the study of literature" (107). Rueckert describes poems as "stored energy" in the way that plants and animals store energy; they "are part of the energy pathways that sustain life," the "verbal equivalent of fossil fuel," and a "renewable source of energy, coming, as they do, from those ever-generative twin matrices, language and imagination" (109). In his essay "The Ecology of Victorian Fiction," Joseph Carroll describes ecological literary criticism as "criticism concentrating on the relationship between literature and the natural environment" and points out that it has become one of the fastest-growing areas in literary study. Ecocritics now have their own professional association, their own academic journal, and an impressive bibliography of scholarly studies. They sometimes identify as practicing "green cultural studies." Ecocritical scholars divide their attention between "nature writers" and ecological themes within literature. Thus, some scholars write on Henry David Thoreau, John Muir, or Annie Dillard; others write on topics such as the representation of nature in romantic poetry, the American West as a symbol, metaphors of landscape, or urban life as a polluted ecosystem. Ecocritics share in a certain broad set of attitudes, values, and public policy concerns in the absence of any overarching theory. As Carroll notes, ecocritics have usually sought to incorporate their ecological subject matter within other, already established, theoretical schools: Freudianism, Marxism, feminism, Bakhtin's dialogism, Lacanian psychoanalysis, new historicism, and Foucault's ideological theory. As Glen A. Love explains, "The most important function of literature today is to redirect human consciousness to a full consideration of its place in a threatened natural world. Why does nature writing, literature of place, regional writing, poetry of nature, flourish now—even as it is ignored or denigrated by most contemporary cultural criticism? Because of a widely shared sense—outside the literary establishment—that the current ideology which separates human beings from their environment is demonstrably and dangerously reductionist. Because the natural world is indubitably real and beautiful and significant" (237).

As Carroll also observes, ecocritics believe that they are not a sub-specialty but at the forefront of critical response to urgent practical problems of world-historical magnitude: global warming, pollution, misuse of ecological resources, and, finally, irreversible destruction of the Earth's environmental systems. Like feminist or postcolonialist critics, ecocritics thus have a strong sense of a political mission. They argue that the natural world claims a special status as the ultimate ground and frame of all existence. It is the primary experiential importance. Ecocritics thus propose a matrix for *all* literary study, much like Literary Darwinists. Carroll in fact believes ecocriticism should be integrated into Darwinian literary studies, especially considering E. O. Wilson's notion *of biophilia* or love of life. Carroll concludes that in analyzing literature, setting or physical place "is an elemental condition of human experience and that it is consequently an elemental component of literary meaning" (296–97). Similarly, in *The Future of Environmental Criticism: Environmental Crisis and Literary Imagination*, Lawrence Buell focuses on literary realism and representation in their relation to nature, the central role of place, space, and imagination for ecocritical thought, and a discussion of politics and ethics in ecocriticism that ranges from deep ecology to ecofeminism and environmental justice.

Ecocritics read well-known texts often quite differently from the way that other critics do. For example, many readers of Frank Norris's *The Octopus* (1901) are troubled by the "happy" ending Norris provides. His story of the oppression of California's independent wheat farmers by the Southern Pacific Railroad culminates in the massacre of the farmers. On the other hand, the ecocritic would support Norris's contention that the continuing life cycle of the wheat ameliorates the individual tragedies. They would not celebrate the tales of adventurers in the Northland such as Jack London wrote but would rather examine the Gold Rush's horrific impact upon the Natives and their environment. Through analyzing literature, ecocritics argue for social action to save the environment.

In their collection, *The Ecocriticism Reader: Landmarks in Literary Ecology*, Cheryll Glotfelty and Harold Fromm argue that the "world" addressed by other critical approaches is falsely limited to the social and ignores questions about the rest of the physical reality of the Earth. In addition to race, class, and gender, they propose "place" as a new location of meaning. They analyze how nature is represented in cultural works such as literary texts: "How is nature represented in this **sonnet**?... Are the values expressed in this play consistent with ecological wisdom? How do our **metaphors** of the land influence the way we treat it?... In what ways has literacy itself affected humankind's relationship with the natural world?... In what ways and to what effect is the environmental crisis seeping into contemporary literature and popular culture?" (xviii–xix). Thus ecocritics ask questions about the role of the landscape and the scenic in literature, about the ecological values of the author and text, how cultures are constructed by environments—or even, what is nature? And what do we mean by "wilderness?" They investigate how such related issues as gender affect the way a character or author perceives nature. And how do institutions such as business, government, and the media differ in their perceptions of and reactions to their views of nature? The environment is a continuously evolving process. In the introduction to their volume Glotfelty explains that literature should include the entire "ecosphere," since everything in human life is connected to everything else. Nature is not "just the stage upon which the human story is acted out, but [is] an actor in the drama" (xix–xxi). She compares the stages of ecocriticism's development to Elaine Showalter's three stages of feminist awareness, representations of women in male texts, women's literary traditions, and the theoretical phase (see Ch. 8). Her diverse set of ecocritical topics include the frontier, animals, cities, deserts, Natives, technology, and garbage, and such writers as Willa Cather, Robinson Jeffers, W. S. Merwin, Adrienne Rich, Wallace Stegner, Gary Snyder, Mary Oliver, Ursula Le Guin, and Alice Walker.

In this collection numerous perspectives on ecocritism are presented. Native American novelist Leslie Marmon Silko demonstrates the importance of the approach for reading contemporary Native American writers and understanding traditional, oral literatures of Indians, especially for folklore and cultural traditions. For her, understanding the environment informs how individuals view themselves and their histories, and how they set about living their lives. This includes recognition of animals and plants as well as physical terrain, and a perception of the living energy that exists in all beings, and even in mountains, stones, and rivers. She points out the value of the Pueblo Indians' oral traditions in emphasizing certain elements of nature depending upon the tribes' particular needs at the time. She describes the interdependency of all nature, including stories about human nature. Explaining the Indians' practice of thanking the animals they kill for food, Silko moves on to Indian arts, noting, for example, that "Pueblo potters, the creators of petroglyphs and oral narratives, never conceived of removing themselves from the earth and sky. So long as the human consciousness remains *within* the hills, canyons, cliffs, and the plants, clouds, and sky, the term *landscape*...is misleading." "A portion of territory the eye can comprehend in a single view" does not describe the relationship between humans and their surroundings. The Pueblo Indian is not outside his territory but is part of the landscape and participates in it as a thing in itself that needs no improvement or representation in traditional realistic ways (265–66). Ancient Pueblo Indians believed that all life, human, animal, and plant, emerged at the same moment from the netherworld. Silko thus distinguishes between history kept as a written, linear record and the way that knowledge is passed down through collective memory in oral form; each member of the tribe was expected to be able to tell stories about past harvests, wars, and relocations, so that when someone died another would remember a certain fact or an entire story, since all are interrelated in their creation. Place nearly always plays a central role in their stories, a geographical feature near which something happened, for example, or a special rock or plant that was found in a certain place and that effected some good. Thus, living as part of nature, "the ancient Pueblo people sought a communal truth, not an absolute" (269). She concludes:

> The effect of these interfamily or interclan exchanges is the reassurance for each person that she or he will never be separated or apart from the clan, no matter what might happen. Neither the worst blunders or disasters nor the greatest financial prosperity and joy will ever be permitted to isolate anyone from the rest of the group. In ancient times, cohesiveness was all that stood between extinction and survival. (274)

(See also Paula Gunn Allen's "The Sacred Hoop" in this collection for more on the role of "literature" within ceremony among Native Americans.)

Ecofeminisrn is an offshoot of ecocriticism, focusing specifically on women, literature, and "the world." It argues that the violence perpetrated on the Earth is a direct result of patriarchal forms of domination that have been espoused and enacted on throughout the world for over 2000 years. They see aggression against the earth as a parallel to male aggression against women. Thus Annette Kolodny writes of such long-standing metaphors in American literature as "back to nature" to reflect their feminine context: the idea that returning to nature is salvational—Eden, Paradise, the Golden Age, the New World—that it reflects a desire for "regression from the cares of adult life and a return to the primal warmth of the womb or breast in a feminine landscape" (173). Thinking of such iconic literary heroes as Huck Finn, she adds that "Our continuing fascination with the lone male in the wilderness, and our literary heritage of essentially adolescent, presexual pastoral heroes, suggest that we have yet to come up with a satisfying model for mature masculinity on this continent; while the images of abuse that have come to dominate the **pastoral** vocabulary suggest that we have been no more successful in our response to the feminine qualities of nature than we have to the human feminine" (177).

According to Cathleen McGuire and Colleen McGuire, "ecofeminism sprouted in the early 1970s as Western women became disillusioned with the ideologies of the day" but gained real momentum after the mid-1990s, when ecofeminists realized that by and large the Left had little interest in women, the environment, or animals. Ecofeminism was perceived as a "meta-feminism" to which individuals are drawn from a wide range of interests, including "environmentalism, alternative spirituality, animal rights, and other progressive affiliations." They argue for the synthesis of the political and the spiritual and reject dualism, or the view that "mind is separate from body, spirit from matter, male from female, and humans from nature" because "these dichotomies give rise to an 'other' which is then demonized and discriminated against." Because Western patriarchy places a high value on "linear, analytical, and rational qualities," they see "the intuitive, emotional, anarchic, and earthly [as] . . . passive, weak, irrational—and female. Nature is paradoxically considered inert, dead mass, *and* a wild, chaotic force." This is not just an intellectual problem: "men own 99% of the world's property while women perform two-thirds of the world's labor." Thus ecofeminist activists and critics "affirm qualities traditionally considered 'female' such as being cooperative, nurturing, supportive, nonviolent and sensual." In the anthology *Sisters of the Earth,* editor Lorraine Anders presents such authors as Emily Dickinson, Silko, Laura Ingalls Wilder, and Rita Dove as writers who address their connection to the earth, which is perceived as essentially feminine in its natural cycles and maternity ("Mother Earth").

V. LITERARY DARWINISM

Literary Darwinism furnishes theory and critical approaches to literature based on the application of the evolutionary theory of Charles Darwin, especially his idea of natural selection. It represents an emerging trend of neo-Darwinian thought in a number of intellectual disciplines including sociobiology and evolutionary psychology, as well as literary studies. Literary Darwinism is opposed to the prevailing poststructuralist and postmodernist theory, especially the argument that discourse

Figure 4.2. Cartoon drawing of Charles Darwin, "A Venerable Orang Outang, A Contribution to Unnatural History," from *The Hornet* (March 1871).
Getty Images/English School.

constructs reality. Literary Darwinists argue that evolution precedes, and to some extent, explains discourse. Literary Darwinism emphasizes that humans share a common nature that can be revealed through the scientific method and that this universal nature is the product of Darwinian selection over tens of thousands of years. All literary criticism and theory should therefore be based on evolutionary theories of human nature. Those theories and approaches that deny the biological basis of behavior are seen as unsound. Literature is not just representative of reality but is the product of living creatures who are both genetically determined and influenced by environment as well as culture. Literary Darwinists thus see their approach as more objective than such culturally based theories as poststructuralism.

Literary Darwinists explain the existence of literature according to several theories. Literature may be a reaction to the expansion of humans' mental life that took place around 40,000 years ago. By engaging in imaginative processes, people found life more manageable and less threatening; thus the story helps achieve order. Another theory posits that stories are attempts to elicit an audience reaction that will be of benefit later on when confronted with a dangerous situation. Writing may also be seen as a sex-display trait to attract a desirable mate. Or perhaps the main function of literature is to integrate humans into a unified culture, so that **myths** produce social cohesion, conferring survival advantage through cooperation. In another view, literature began as religion or wish fulfillment: humans enhanced their success in the next hunt by recounting the triumph of the last one.

Because the human mind—including the artistic impulse—exists within evolving organic structures such as the brain, researchers should be able to explain mental characteristics not only of cognitive systems such as language ability, but also of cultural systems such as art and literature, in large part in terms of the environmental factors, or selection pressures, that give rise to them. A chief goal of Darwinian literary studies is to show how the reading and writing of literature contributes to what Darwin called *evolutionary fitness*—the ability to survive and pass along one's genes. There are several factors of evolutionary Darwinism that can be usefully applied to understanding literature, especially characters' behavior: adaptability, kin preference, selection of superior mates, child bearing and rearing, competition for resources, and cooperation.

The founder of literary Darwinism was E. O. Wilson, whose concept of *consilience*, or the unity of knowledge, especially between the sciences and humanities, dates back to the ancient Greek sense of the unity of the cosmos and was widely discussed by philosophers of science during the Enlightenment. His book *Consilience: The Unity of Knowledge* attempts to bridge the culture gap between the sciences and the humanities that was also the subject of C. P. Snow's *The Two Cultures and the Scientific Revolution*. Wilson believes the sciences, humanities, and arts share the common goal of promoting human understanding. By applying evolutionary principles to explain the *social* behavior of insects to the understanding of the social behavior of other animals, including humans, Wilson founded the field of *sociobiology*, "the systematic study of the biological basis of all social behavior." All animal behavior, including that of humans, is the product of heredity, environmental stimuli, and past experiences; free will is an illusion, as we live on a "genetic leash" (127–28). Wilson argues that the human mind is shaped as much (if not more) by genetic inheritance as it is by culture. There are limits on just how much influence social and environmental factors can have in altering human behavior. Such a philosophical position is in complete opposition to the postmodernist and poststructuralist notion of identity as only socially constructed.

In the Introduction to *Madame Bovary's Ovaries: A Darwinian Look at Literature*, David P. Barash and Nanelle R. Barash describe the evolutionary reasons that classic works of literature continue to inspire modern readers: "The reason *Othello* is still being read and performed five hundred years [sic] after Shakespeare wrote it is because this play tells us something timeless and universal not so much about a fellow named Othello but about ourselves. It speaks to the Othello within everyone: our shared human nature.... [J]ealousy is a particularly potent and widespread human emotion, one to which *men* are especially vulnerable. That's precisely why it's okay to talk about Othello or Madame Bovary or Huckleberry Finn in the present tense; they live on, at least in part, because they have distinctly human characteristics that transcend the artistry by which they are depicted" (2). Barash and Barash argue that "much of human life is not socially constructed. In short, even though learning and cultural traditions exert a powerful influence, there also exists an underlying human nature, universally valid and characteristic of all *Homo sapiens*" (2). A cardinal principle all literary Darwinists agree on is "selfish genes," a force that influences nearly everything humans do, including telling stories. (6). As they note, "In his advice to the traveling players, Hamlet suggested that the role of the artist is to hold a mirror up to nature—not, as some theorists would have it, to hold a mirror up to another mirror and thereby reflect only the infinite emptiness of mirrors. The 'nature' here isn't wild animals, pretty landscapes, or magnificent wilderness, but *human* nature. And human nature isn't like a unicorn or some other mythical beast. It exists. It does so because human genes exist and have produced a different kind of creature than horse genes or hyacinth genes have" (3). Characters like Hamlet, Don Quixote, and Achilles are memorable because they display human vitality and weakness. Indeed, "fictional characters are believable when they reveal their human nature, which is to say, when they behave in concert with biological expectation" (7).

The greatest storytellers for thousands of years have perceived this human nature. As Barash and Barash also point out, "anyone wanting to get a sense of human nature in, say, the Bronze Age can do no better than to excavate among the works of Homer, or for the Elizabethan Age, Shakespeare. However, not until Darwin was the scientific basis for human nature revealed, when the genetic basis for natural selection was discovered and applied to human beings" (3). People are inclined to act in ways that enhance their evolutionary fitness; this does not mean everyone is constantly seeking to reproduce, but that the genes of those who did are part of us and account for certain behaviors (4–5). "'From the crooked timber of humanity,' wrote Kant, 'nothing straight was ever fashioned.' And from the squishy stuff of humanity, nothing nonbiological was ever fashioned. Even the loftiest products of human imagination are, first of all, emanations of that gooey, breathing, eating, sleeping, defecating, reproducing, evolving, and evolved creature known as *Homo sapiens*. We aren't idealized, ethereal essences but genuine biological beings, shaped by evolution and twisted and gnarled by life itself. This is why the most damning observation about a character in a novel (or play or movie) is that he or she isn't believable, which is another way of saying that for fiction to make sense, it must accord with a kind of evolutionary reality" (8).

Barash and Barash thus read *Othello* as a case of male sexual jealousy, Jane Austen's works as about proper mating, male mating preferences in Thomas Hardy's *Tess of the D'Urbervilles*, the "biology of adultery" in Gustave Flaubert's *Madame Bovary*, kin selection in Mario Puzo's *The Godfather*, parent-offspring conflict in Philip Roth's *Portnoy's Complaint* and J. D. Salinger's *The Catcher in the Rye*, the plight of stepchildren in Victor Hugo's *Les Miserables* and Charles Dickens's *David Copperfield*, and the many roles of friendship in Alexandre Dumas *pere's Three Musketeers* and John Steinbeck's *The Grapes of Wrath*.

Similarly, in their collection *The Literary Animal*, Jonathan Gottschall and David Sloan Wilson state in their introduction that the human mind is "constructed to think in terms of stories" (xxiv). Among the essays in their book, two stand out that best explain the new approach. Daniel Nettle points out that in 1999 the average Briton spent 369 hours "immersed in some kind of dramatic performance," such as the theater, television, or film, roughly six percent of all waking life. Why, he asks, do humans spend so much time at this? "Hard-nosed Darwinism seems to suggest people should be ceaselessly preoccupied with the perpetuation of their genes. So is **drama** helping them to do this?... [W]hat features do dramas have that are found compelling and ensure their survival and reenactment? Are there features that make some stories adept at survival in the pool of stories?" He identifies "remarkable continuity" in 2000 years of drama (56–57). Quoting Darwin's statement in his *Notebook* that "He who understands baboon would do more toward metaphysics than Locke," Nettle explains that by comparing simian grooming practices with modern relationships, literature may be seen as a kind of shortcut to maintaining relationships within a group: "Language binds us together as grooming binds monkeys and apes. Place a group of monkeys or apes in a room together, and if they do not fight or mate, they will groom each other. Repeat the same experiment with a group of people, and if they do not fight or mate they will talk." The dramatic mode is thus "a contrived conversation that simulates the mechanisms of reward that evolved for natural conversation," which is "prototypically concerned with exchanging information about the vicissitudes of relationships within a small social group" (65). They will concern the most vital parts of human life: Who mates with whom? Who wields power? Who betrayed whom? Since the viewers of drama do not really know the characters personally, the drama will need to generate interest through powerful conflicts. Interestingly, Nettle compares the usual number of important characters in a Shakespeare play to those in most cliques of apes within their larger group: they average about six apiece. He concludes, "The human mind is structured in such a way that domain-specific schemata about kinship, love, competition, and cooperation are easily evoked, sometimes by a single word or image. Thus, certain stories or situations richly and intrinsically *afford* possibilities for dramatic meaning, even if that meaning varies in one time and place" (73).

Similarly, in another essay, renowned British novelist Ian McEwan refers to Darwin's *The Expression of Emotions in Man and Animals,* which traces involuntary human facial and bodily expressions of emotion to their roots in animals. As Darwin demonstrated "a common descent for all races of mankind," he "opposed himself forcefully to the racist views of scientists like Louis Agassiz, who argued that Africans were inferior to Europeans because they were descended from a different and inferior stock." In applying these ideas to literature, McEwan argues that "It would not be possible to read and enjoy literature from a time remote from our own, or from a culture that was profoundly different from our own, unless we shared some common emotional ground, some deep reservoir of assumptions, with the writer....What we have in common with each other is just as extraordinary in its way as all our exotic differences." One might thus think of literature as "encoding both our cultural and genetic inheritance." This dissolves the oppositions of nature to nurture: "If one reads accounts of the systematic nonintrusive observation of troops of bonobo—bonobos and common chimps rather than baboons are our closest relatives—one sees rehearsed all the major themes of the English nineteenth-century novel: alliances made and broken, individuals rising while others fall, plots hatched, revenge, gratitude, injured pride, successful and unsuccessful courtship" (10–11). One thinks of *Hamlet*, to be sure, but also of "Young Goodman Brown." While Brown may be driven by a biological need to spread his genes by attending a witch-meeting in the woods (which, in the popular imagination of the time, involved orgies), he may be said to fail evolutionarily; not only does he fail to mate in the forest, but when he returns home he gives his wife the cold shoulder. Readers have wondered how he ever had children. Furthermore, his ideas have not evolved out of their religious lock-box, and such a lack of adaptability does not bode well for the future of men like him or his culture.

The most prominent literary Darwinist today is the prolific Joseph Carroll. In his book *Literary Darwinism,* among many other classic works he reads Jane Austen's *Pride and Prejudice* to show how the fundamental biological problem of choosing a mate narrates a social order in which males compete using money and rank and females compete using their youth and beauty. In this work and others he finds that the role of the arts is to "make sense of human needs and motives. They simulate subjective experience, map out social relations, evoke sexual and social interactions, depict the intimate relations of kin, and locate the whole complex and interactive array of behavioral systems within models of the total world order. Humans have a universal and irrepressible need to fabricate this sort of order, and satisfying that need provides a distinct form of pleasure and fulfillment" (198).

In reviewing Carroll's book, Tim Horvath remarks that unlike many theorists Carroll has great respect for the common reader. Literary writers "are conceived of as intuitive psychologists, who provided humanity with the most astute and searching 'data' and 'commentary' available until psychologists came along to hang up shingles and formalize a field; we can envision the cultural icon of Shakespeare, unschooled formally but somehow peering and tapping into humanity's deepest character, as representative of all writers in this regard." Carroll's most compelling arguments concern "the need to create cognitive order" as a universal human motive, and the notion of the "cognitive behavioral system" to respond to "concerns of survival, technology, mating, parenting, kin, and social existence. Literary works are created by, and about 'people seeking to perceive meaning in or impose meaning on the events of their own lives and the lives of every person they know'" (Carroll 202). There is a place for the individual in Carroll's scheme, not just for biologically determined behaviors. Horvath observes that "One of the surprising and somewhat refreshing benefits of buying into a Darwinian perspective on literature is that anything that can be said about authors can by definition also be related to characters in some way, and vice versa; how strange that it should often appear strange that one is reflecting on people and not only textual and cultural constructs."

Similarly, Robert Storey's *Mimesis and the Human Animal: On the Biogenetic Foundations of Literary Representation* analyzes sex differences, cognitive psychology, the neurosciences, the study of emotions, and evolutionary psychology, linguistics, epistemology, and anthropology as they can be applied to literary studies, including genre theory (particularly **tragedy** and **comedy**), narrative theory, and the theory of reading. Storey opposes what he sees as the glibness of postmodern cultural theory. As Carroll remarks in a review of this book, Storey "demonstrates that commonly held views of linguistic autonomy and the literary construction of reality will not stand up against even the most rudimentary appeal to empirical knowledge, and at the same time he shows how making this appeal to empirical knowledge opens up rich new possibilities for understanding basic literary problems."

Resistance to literary Darwinism has come not only come from constructivist theorists but from race theorists as well, since, as Gottschall and Wilson explain, when speaking of human behavior, psychology, and culture in evolutionary terms, many instantly think of " 'Hitler,' 'Galton,' 'Spencer,' 'IQ differences,' 'holocaust,' 'racial phrenology,' 'forced sterilization,' 'genetic determinism,' 'Darwinian fundamentalism,' and 'disciplinary imperialism' "(xx). However, most of its critics have misunderstood the claims of literary Darwinism as it echoes Darwin's sense of the relatedness of all human beings (and animals) and not their surface differences.

In 2005, D. T. Max, in "The Literary Darwinists," explained to readers of the *New York Times Sunday Magazine* the growing popularity of literary Darwinism and the concerns raised about it. As he observes,

> It is useful to know a bit about current literary criticism to understand how different the Darwinist approach to literature is. Current literary theory tends to look at a text as the product of particular social conditions or, less often, as a network of references to other texts. (Jacques Derrida, the father of deconstruction, famously observed that there was "nothing outside the text.") It often focuses on how the writer's and the reader's identities—straight, gay, female, male, black, white, colonizer or colonized—shape a particular narrative or its interpretation. Theorists sometimes regard science as simply another form of language or suspect that when scientists claim to speak for nature, they are disguising their own assertion of power.

As McEwan puts it, "Like Christian theologians, cultural relativists freed us from all biological constraints and set mankind apart from all other life on earth" (15). Literary Darwinism breaks with these tendencies. First, its goal is to study literature through biology—not politics or semiotics. Second, it takes as a given not that literature possesses its own truth or many truths but that it derives its truth from laws of nature. Much of what people believe is cultural is actually determined by genes, including literature itself. (However, for a sense of how the environment shapes gene expression and alters evolution, see Jared Diamond's Pulitzer Prize-winning book *Guns, Germs, and Steel.*)

As Frederick Crews summarizes, "Those of us who embrace Darwinian knowledge without cavil are convinced that all existence is unplanned and therefore quite pointless, leaving humanity with the task of *rendering* its life dignified in moral, intellectual, and aesthetic ways scrounged and adjusted from our evolved heritage of repertoires. When the gods have been shipped back to fairyland to rejoin the Easter bunny, we can direct our awe toward beings who actually deserve it—Shakespeare, Rembrandt, Beethoven, Einstein—without cheapening their achievements by ascribing them to mysterious infusions of spirit" (xiii). Or, as McEwan concludes, "Literature must be our anthropology" (18).

VI. MATERIALISMS IN PRACTICE

A. A New History of "To His Coy Mistress"

Because of his political life, Marvell was one of the first poets to be fully explored by new historicists. Marvell supported Oliver Cromwell during the interregnum (serving as a tutor to Cromwell's children) but sympathized with the executed King Charles I, as shown in his "Horatian Ode." Marvell reflects the ambivalence the English felt about the conflict between the divine right of kings, in which the king is answerable only to God, and the burgeoning desire for democratic freedoms. His speaker in "To His Coy Mistress" figuratively rebels against the monarch, represented by his beloved Mistress herself. As the author of "Andrew Marvell's 'To His Coy Mistress': A New Historicist Reading" points out, the speaker employs the **Petrarchan sonnet** form and language, including "excessive and hyperbolic reverence for an elusive woman," a style made famous in the medieval **sonnets** of the Italian poet Petrarch. Marvell's choice is significant because it would have evoked for his readers sixteenth-century **lyrics** in praising Queen Elizabeth. These **courtly love** poets "were courtiers who solicited the queen's support, ingratiated themselves by representing her as an intangible, ideal beloved." Yet by insisting on physical instead of spiritual devotion, "Marvell's speaker suggests that such promises of eternal devotion are inappropriate in a world that is governed by 'Time's wingèd chariot,' the universal experience of human mortality to which they are both vulnerable. While the Tudor monarchs had referred to the 'two bodies' of the king, the material body a correspondent to a divine form, here the speaker insists only on the former." The poem concludes with "an ominous and thickly symbolic challenge to the sun itself—a common pun for the 'son' of the monarch in contemporary literature." Perhaps Marvell is speaking directly to the " 'son,' Charles II, who became his father's successor with the restoration of the monarchy in 1660." Referring to the sun, "emblematic of the monarch's ostensible divinity, 'carpe diem' becomes as much a cry of lust as one of insurrection."

Let us take these insights about Marvell's attitudes toward monarchy and apply them closely to the poem. In the very first line the speaker suggests a world in flux, a world in which the traditional definitions of "world" and "time" were challenged by political and social change. The world of the poem is not stable, not after regicide, and though the speaker wishes for a stable time and space he realizes it is now only a limited and conditional zone of change. Whereas once English people may have thought of the order of heaven and earth as unchanging, after the execution of Charles I in 1649, the kingdom—and hence the "world"—were at the mercy of time and the changes it brings. "Ladies" such as the mistress may not always be able to enjoy their privileges, either. Key words such as "rubies," "empires," and the pun on "state" in the first **stanza** suggest a once wealthy and powerful "state" that is now only the plaything of time (England was constantly at war with other European nations in the seventeenth century). The way the speaker connects the humble English river Humber to the great Ganges figuratively suggests the broad reach of the British Empire. In the second stanza, "deserts" replace the happy landscape the speaker envisions for himself and his lady; many in England mourned the sight of the countryside decimated by the civil wars. There were desecrated Catholic churches, burned villages, mobs, intrigue, and murder at Court. As in Shakespeare's plays, especially *King Lear* and *Hamlet,* the sense that the heavens are out of order is applied to the situation on earth—we are no longer in paradise, but in a place of death and decay. The final allusion to the monarchy appears in stanza three, with the image of Time devouring his subjects. The reference to the first "king" in Western tradition is to the Titan Cronos, who devoured his children as they were born until their mother, Rhea, tricked him into sparing Zeus by substituting a large stone for the boy; Zeus would grow up to become king of the Olympian gods and defeat the Titans, ushering in the Greek Golden Age. The poem concludes that since this all-powerful monarch of time cannot be easily appeased, the lovers must make him, as the "sun," run, that is, make them unconscious of the passing time, as they pursue on a personal level what had become politically problematic in England, the normal relations of men and women in a peaceable kingdom on earth.

B. Hamlet's Evolution

Hamlet is an especially appropriate subject for Literary Darwinism. First of all, the play itself was a product of an evolving identity. There were many versions of the play before the *First Folio* was presented after Shakespeare's death, and it has remained one of the most difficult of Shakespeare's plays for which to identify an authentic version. But the action of the play itself is also inviting, including as it does mating, incest, kinship, territory, and the struggle for survival. That Hamlet himself (along with most of his family and friends) is dead at the end suggests a failed "evolutionary fitness" in the hero, as Darwin called it; that is, he does not gain power, a mate, and the passing along of his genes. In a Darwinian sense, Hamlet fails mainly at being a man.

Psychological critics have described Hamlet's Oedipus Complex, but what are the biological bases for Freud's definition of the failed Oedipus Complex: the inability of a young male to separate himself from his family and seek a mate on his own? The answer may lie in the overall tone of incest that pervades the play: Laertes and Polonius are too close to Ophelia, Hamlet is jealous of his mother, and Claudius marries in violation of incest taboos of the time. But Hamlet is not able successfully to adapt to the changes in his environment, grievous though they are. He is not able to evolve into a king himself, despite killing Claudius, because his lack of maturity (mainly his naiveté about Claudius) and his assumptions about his mother's guilt prevent him from attaining his "rightful" place in the kingdom. Indeed, in his most famous speech, "To be or not to be," Hamlet even questions his desire to live faced with the challenges he fears—he only continues to live because God has "fixed his canon 'gainst self-slaughter." Suicide would be the preferred way out, Hamlet reasons, and only out of fear of damnation does he desist. It is obvious that to a Darwinian, suicide would be the ultimate failure of an organism. That Hamlet does not kill himself is a significant adaptive choice. Elimination of one's rivals would also be an adaptive strategy, but not at the cost of one's own life and one's entire family. The evolutionary price of justice in *Hamlet* is too high a price to pay for revenge. In this futility lies the tragic heart of the play.

As one of Darwin's main interpreters, Thomas Henry Huxley, asserted, nature is not a role model for human life; humans are called upon to develop workable ethics and abide by them even in the face of the chaos of nature. Unfortunately, no one in *Hamlet* is able to do so, or to survive, except an outsider, the Norwegian invader-king Fortinbras, who seems to have no such shortcomings when it comes to his and his people's survival. In the end, he and he alone is able to assess the damage and move on with life and struggle. He is certain to leave his mark.

C. *Frankenstein*: The Creature as Proletarian

We recall from earlier chapters that Mary Shelley lived during times of great upheaval in Britain; not only was her own family full of radical thinkers, but she also met many others such as Thomas Paine and William Blake. Percy Shelley was thought of as a dangerous radical bent on labor reform and was spied upon by the government. In *Frankenstein,* what Johanna M. Smith calls the "alternation between fear of vengeful revolution and sympathy for the suffering poor" (14) illuminates Mary Shelley's own divisions between revolutionary ardor and fear of the masses. Like her father, who worried about the mob's "excess of a virtuous feeling," fearing its "sick destructiveness" (*Letters* 2.122; Smith 15), Mary Shelley's Creature is a political and moral paradox, both an innocent and a cold-blooded murderer.

Monsters like the Creature are indeed paradoxical. On the one hand, they transgress against "the establishment" (which is often blamed for their creation); if the monster survives he represents the defiance of death, an image of survival, however disfigured (Skal 278). On the other hand, we are reassured when we see that society can capture and destroy monsters. Such dualism would explain the great number of Frankenstein-as-mutant movies that appeared during the cold war. But the Creature's rebellious nature is rooted far in the past. In the De Laceys' shed he reads three books, beginning with *Paradise Lost*. Not only are the eternal questions about the ways of God and man in *Paradise Lost* relevant to the Creature's predicament, but in Shelley's time Milton's epic poem was seen, as Timothy Morton puts it, as "a seminal work of republicanism and the sublime that inspired many of the Romantics." The Creature next reads a volume from *Plutarch's Lives,* which in the early nineteenth century was read as "a classic republican text, admired in the Enlightenment by such writers as Rousseau." Goethe's *The Sorrows of Young Werther,* the Creature's third book, is the prototypical rebellious Romantic novel.

In short, says Morton, "The creature's literary education is radical" (151). But the Creature's idealistic education does him little good, and he has no chance of reforming society so that it will accept him. His self-education is his even more tragic second birth into an entire culture impossible for him to inhabit, however well he understands its great writings about freedom.

D. "The Lore of Fiends": Hawthorne and His Market

A materialist approach often concerns not only the work that is produced but also the means of production. Questions of how to support the author, of finding a publisher, and even of marketing the particular work are germane to the cultural milieu in which the work is produced.

In that context, under what conditions and in what frame of mind did the young Hawthorne handle the challenges of getting a work of fiction published? Our answer involves two seemingly disparate worlds: (1) Hawthorne's exploration of his own personal fears during the middle third of the nineteenth century and (2) the world of American publishing at the time. He was able to translate his fear of failure and his own unconscious demons into a classic story of good and evil, of hypocrisy in society and in the church.

"Young Goodman Brown" was one of Hawthorne's first publications, appearing in *The New England Magazine* in 1835, though he had begun it as early as 1829. Some indication of his early struggles with authorial identity can be gleaned from his "Custom House" preface to *The Scarlet Letter* (1850), the first and most successful of his four romances. There he meditates upon how the writer's Puritan forebears would have scorned his profession, which they would have called that of "an idler" instead of following in the footsteps of his "grave, bearded, sable-cloaked, and steeple-crowned progenitor," his Salem ancestor William Hathorne, who condemned Quaker women to death in the early colonial days:

> No aim, that I have ever cherished, would they recognize as laudable; no success of mine—if my life, beyond its domestic scope, had ever been brightened by success—would they deem otherwise than worthless, if not positively disgraceful. "What was he?" murmurs one gray shadow of my forefathers to the other. "A writer of story-books! What kind of business in life,—what mode of glorifying God, or being serviceable to mankind in his day and generation,—may that be? Why, the degenerate fellow might as well have been a fiddler!"

Perhaps Hawthorne takes up the position of "editor" in the preface to *The Scarlet Letter* rather than author so he may then protect his own "rights" to "keep the inmost Me behind its veil," as he says. Hawthorne also discusses the material conditions of this novel's production: if he had not been fired when the election of Zachary Taylor put him and other political appointees out of favor, he would not have been intellectually free enough to write the novel. Still, as a mark of his anxieties, he had to use the ruse of a "found" manuscript to publish the book.

Hawthorne published his first story, "The Hollow of the Three Hills," a witchcraft tale, in the *Salem Gazette,* his hometown newspaper, in 1830. For the next twenty years, he wrote brief fictions and published them anonymously, except for periods when he worked as an editor, a custom house clerk, or a member of the utopian colony at Brook Farm in 1841, and over that time nearly a hundred of his tales appeared in print. After *The Scarlet Letter* (1850), his production of short stories ceased, and he turned to his remaining three longer romances. He seemed to feel guilty about his early sketches, for as he wrote in his preface to *Mosses from an Old Manse* (1854), a collection of stories published a few years before he became a Custom House surveyor, they did not "evolve some deep lesson." They were "fitful sketches" only "half in earnest." But his construction of himself in the short fiction—the "Romantic solitary"—was emblematic of more than he realized, offering important insights not only into the psychology of the artist but also into the changing literary market of the 1830s and 1840s.

If Hawthorne had a sense of guilt about being the equivalent of a "fiddler" in 1850, what could his feelings have been so much earlier when any sort of success seemed entirely remote? Hawthorne's social milieu when he composed "Young Goodman Brown" and his evolving identity as a teller of tales are addressed in the story.

Hawthorne wrote "Young Goodman Brown" while living as a near recluse in his mother's house. Though a graduate of Bowdoin College, he had as yet no income; he was a young man longing for the way up and out. Hawthorne's father had died when Nathaniel was very young, and his mother had moved back in with her family, the Mannings, who seemed to have taken supporting the penurious but determined writer in stride (some readers surmise that Hester Prynne was a tribute to his mother, who had been treated badly by the socially more highly placed "Hathornes," as his father's family spelled the name). But the way out was also the way *into* something—in the Puritan sense, evil, but in Hawthorne's mind, the self, with its curse of writing. Hawthorne seems to have developed an equation between writing and the devil's work: "But authors are always poor devils, and therefore Satan may take them," he told his mother. In his early tale "The Devil in Manuscript" (1835), Oberon, a "damned author," confronts "the fiend." Burning his manuscripts, Oberon accidentally sets fire to his village, screaming into the conflagration, "I will cry out in the loudest spirit with the wildest of the confusion." Oberon, it is important to note, was a name Hawthorne used for himself in college and in journal entries. Readers of "Young Goodman Brown" note how the Devil seems like the smartest person in the story and has all the best lines; indeed, he furnishes a critique of Salem society that sounds right on the mark. More on him in a moment.

In addition to entertaining self-doubt and guilt at his chosen profession, Hawthorne found the publication market difficult. Because there were no international copyrights, publishers in America would pirate works by British writers and sell them cheaply, which made it hard for American writers to compete. In addition, Hawthorne's seriousness and complex prose style made him more difficult to read than the average popular author. Melville praised Hawthorne as a rebel in his classic review of *Mosses on an Old Manse*, recognizing a fellow explorer of the murkier haunts of human psychology and society who is willing to experiment, to "say NO in thunder" to those who wish to mask the darkness within. Melville thus identifies a reason for Hawthorne's greatness: his willingness to return, however ambivalently, again and again to the forbidden topics that drew him, whether they would sell or not. Almost a century later, D. H. Lawrence summed this up when he said, "You *must* look through the surface of American art, and see the inner diabolism of the symbolic meaning. Otherwise it is all mere childishness. That blue-eyed darling Nathaniel knew disagreeable things in his inner soul. He was careful to send them out in disguise" (83).

In light of his habit of elevating his female characters, we should note that Hawthorne's audience, like that of most novelists, was largely female, and so were many of his competitors. Such writers as Harriet Beecher Stowe and Catherine Sedgwick supplied the demand for sentimental, overtly moralistic themes in fiction. Hawthorne seemed to have embraced art itself as a feminine quality, and as we noted in Chapter 8 he addressed the feminine **archetype** in fruitful ways that helped him define his own identity. But how to compete in the sentimental marketplace and remain true to his romantic soul?

One means was to write **Gothic** fiction, to expose evil where it is commonly thought to exist, in obvious villains and sinners. But Hawthorne chose to expose evil in unlikely places, too; in *The Blithedale Romance* (1852) the lives of utopian reformers, so visible in mid-nineteenth-century intellectual life, are exposed. This choice brought into focus the dichotomy between his sunlit and sardonic sides. Hawthorne took aim at the social "perfectionism" formulated by the French socialist Charles Fourier, especially as it affected women. His writings about Puritan hypocrisies also demonstrate the toll on women, such as Faith in "Young Goodman Brown." The dark events of "Young Goodman Brown" are in keeping with the threats Hawthorne perceived in oppressive social systems of any kind; his linking of diabolism and reformism points to deep and often highly ironic divisions in Hawthorne's world.

A popular subgenre in fiction of the 1830s was the "dark reform" text. If we examine other texts in the 1835 issue of *The New England Magazine* that contained Hawthorne's "Young Goodman Brown," we can compare his assessment of such public concerns as social reform with popular dark reform writers. *Dark reform* writing may be described as "immoral didacticism." While supposedly communicating warnings against certain tabooed sexual practices like prostitution, it in fact deliberately aroused interest in them and was often quite lewd. David S. Reynolds has identified "an almost schizophrenic split" between the conventional and the subversive spirit: these works may "exemplify the post-Gothic,...obsessed by themes like fruitless quests, nagging guilt, crime, perversity, and so forth," but they would also employ conventional "simplified piety, patriotic history, comforting angelic visions, domestic bliss, and regenerating childhood purity" (114).

One of the most characteristic figures in dark reform writing was the secretly sinful churchgoer or the evil preacher, the "reverend rake" (Reynolds 253–54, 262). In "Young Goodman Brown" the reverend rake is the Devil, in his guise of

Goodman Brown's grandfather. He speaks smoothly, in fact almost exactly like an experienced pastor; he is at once chillingly diabolical and tantalizingly seductive. In that same issue of *New England Magazine,* the reverend rake appears in an essay called "Atheism in New England." The author takes a dim view of certain literary freedoms assumed by utopian reformers, and he urges the "good men" of New England to defend "the morals, the laws, and the order of society" against the devilish reform activities of "the Infidel Party." He associates the "Free Inquirers" with "licentious indulgence," misdirection of youth, and avoidance of the conventional warnings of consciences; they "strive to spread doctrines, so subversive to morality, and destructive of social order..." The essay takes especial note of the sexual freedoms advocated by the reformers and their "gratification of animal desire" contained in books "sold for filthy lucre" (54–56). Thus in exposing not only Satanic evil but also religion, sexuality, and politics, Hawthorne hit upon a sensational combination.

Sensationalism sells. In a publishing world that made it difficult for an American writer to be rewarded on the basis of his own efforts, in a time when women writers and women readers were dominant, in a time when Hawthorne was wrestling with being a writer at all and probing his own dark recesses of imagination, he was able to spin a tale of evil, of "the power of blackness," and demonstrate his fitness for both classic literature and his contemporary marketplace. The difference between the harping essayist of "Atheism in New England," decrying the reformers, and the complex, multilayered ironies of "Young Goodman Brown" (not the least of which is the Devil as New England minister, his flock as diverse, from highly born to lowly, as Heaven itself), demonstrates clearly not only the difference between popular trend and great literature but also their common roots in popular culture.

E. Fathers and Sons, Gods and Slaves: The Material versus the Spiritual in *Huckleberry Finn*

Generations of critics writing on *Adventures of Huckleberry Finn* have identified slavery and religion as the institutions most under attack in the novel. Twain once described Western slavery in general as a "Christian monopoly"; he went on to observe of Americans, "Our own conversion came at last. We began to stir against slavery. Hearts grew soft, here, there, and yonder. There was no place in the land where the seeker could not find some small budding sign of pity for the slave. No place in all the land but one—the pulpit. It yielded at last; it always does. It fought a strong and stubborn fight, and then did what it always does, joined the procession—at the tail end" (Twain, "Bible Teaching and Religious Practice," 108–09). Yet besides racism and religion there is a third social institution under attack in this novel, and that is parenting—specifically fathering. Bad fathering is deeply implicated in the failures of religion and slavery in the novel, whether the paternalism of the Old South or the religious lie that "equality" through salvation is available only for a few—or that it is available at all. Bad fathering provides a

heuristic to connect society's sin of slaveholding to God's own enslavement of the human race. In fact, in keeping with the novel's satiric shifts in values, one of the most memorable representatives not only of the Old South's racism but also its religion is none other than the worst character in the book, the alcoholic, abusive pap Finn. Pap is not only one of the most memorable bad fathers in literature, but, as we will see, in this novel at least, pap is God. Critics have seen Jim as Christ, Huck as Christ, even Tom as Moses, but none have suggested that pap is compared to the Deity Himself. Thus critics have followed a hopeful theme in the novel but have ignored its material facts. Twain does not separate the brutal materiality of Huck's world from its failed spiritual dimensions, but he clearly demonstrates that when it comes down to a choice, spirituality in the novel is actually based in such material realities as power, control, and exploitation—not to mention threats against Huck's very life.

The hairball tells Jim in Chapter 4 that pap, lately returning to collect Huck's money, has "'two angels hoverin' roun' 'bout him. One uv 'em is white en shiny en t'other one is black. De white one gits him to go right, a little while, den de black one sail in en bust it all up'" (21–22). Jim is also describing the two fathers on either side of Huck, a bad one and a good one—here pap, then later, Jim, with the color symbolism ironically reversed. Huck must run away from pap in order to save his life, but Huck also betrays Jim in the fog at Cairo and in the concluding chapters. By the end, Huck is a Son who refuses to serve any Father. If, at a key point in the novel, Huck says he'll *"go to hell"* for Jim, like Christ, and if, like Jim's parent, he would make a sacrifice such as this, Huck reverses his behavior in the end and abandons everyone. Throughout the novel parenting roles are exchanged among the men and boys of the book, with Huck and Jim debating and exchanging the roles of "father" and "son" as they travel downriver to meet all kinds of inappropriate fathers. This is because there is no reliable father figure in the book, and the position is up for grabs. To be sure, there are many surrogate mothers for Huck, but none provides him with a role model that can make up for the lack of a father, and Huck runs away from Aunt Sally too in the end.

Huck's rebellion against pap as a father sets in motion not only the entire plot, but also critiques pap's sense of privilege as a white Christian citizen. As pap voices his support for social institutions in his self-righteous verbal rampages, he and society appear more and more ridiculous. Pap's drunken speech in Chapter 6, which is the longest set-piece monologue by any main character in the book, represents him as a proponent of white racism but also of traditional—religiously derived—notions of parenting, especially the duties (including financial) a son owes his father from a (misconstrued) biblical model. Pap has not tended his fields, in the biblical or any other sense, but he has the idea that somehow he is owed the rights to this prodigal son to support him in his old age, when he has provided nothing of fatherhood.

In the end, Huck rejects all social and religious institutions, preferring to trust only the material facts of life, running for the undefined "Territory." In helping Jim flee slavery, Huck escapes his own slavery under pap and also the religious pieties of a false community which returned him to his abusive parent. In rejecting what the Widow Douglas and Miss Watson proffer as an alternative to pap, Huck rejects *religion* at the outset of the novel, but in the conclusion he also rejects *God* by refusing to be sacrificed. Comparing pap's behavior with the criticisms of God that Twain noted throughout his career creates an uneasy sense of recognition: pap's fecklessness, neglect, abuse, jealousy, self-aggrandizement (especially as a white man), and even murderousness all correspond to faults Twain found in God—hardly spiritual ideals. As Twain observed, "With a fine sarcasm we ennoble God with the title of Father—yet we know quite well that we should hang his style of father wherever we might catch him" (Twain, *The Devil's Race-Track*, 7). Huck as a failed Christ and apostate from an evil Father suggests a thematic apostasy from all "civilized" society and even from God Himself. Someone is saved in the concluding chapters of the novel, but it is not Huck. Perhaps Huck helps save Jim because Jim is the only real Christian in the story, but Huck refuses to sacrifice himself. He departs the scene, but not into Heaven. He is as aimless at the end of the book as he was at the beginning, and his departure saves only himself—for an uncertain fate. He is a failed son of pap, society, and God Himself, and he is left alone in the end to contemplate the physical challenges of the frontier, having given up on the "spiritual" qualities his society promotes.

Huck's parental figures include not only the ones he repeatedly makes up as his lost family, but pap, the Judge, the Widow Douglas, Miss Watson, Jim, Mrs. Judith Loftus, the Grangerfords, the King and the Duke, Mary Jane Wilks, Aunt Sally and Uncle Silas Phelps, and Tom Sawyer. Huck sometimes acts as "parent" to Jim, as when he tries to educate him according to Tom's literary and biblical ideas or when he defends him or says he'll go to hell for him. But as racism and religion prove to be poor parents, so the very idea of parenting is suspect in *Huckleberry Finn*, reflected most dramatically in pap's alcoholic abuse of his son. The crisis that precipitates Huck's flight from their home and the plot of the novel is of course pap's reappearance. Huck gives the Judge his money and asks Jim to consult his hairball, then plans his escape. Contrary to the views of critics who see Huck's journey as an idealistic search for freedom, he is motivated only by *material* concerns, for example, his very life. We first meet pap in chapter 5 in a bogey-man description:

> His hair was long and tangled and greasy, and hung down, and you could see his eyes shining through like he was behind vines. It was all black, no gray; so was his long, mixed-up whiskers. There warn't no color in his face, where his face showed; it was white; not like another man's white, but a white to make a body sick, a white to make a body's flesh crawl—a tree-toad white, a fish-belly white. As for his clothes—just rags, that was all. He had one ankle resting on t'other knee; the boot on that foot was busted, and two of his toes stuck through, and he worked them now and then. His hat was laying on the floor—an old black slouch with the top caved in, like a lid. (23)

The stomach-turning whiteness of pap echoes the horror of Melville's chapter in *Moby-Dick* "The Whiteness of the Whale," in that the supposed "good" color is

Figure 4.3. "Git up," from *The Adventures of Huckleberry Finn,* Chapter 7. Illustration by E. W. Kemble (1884).

here shown to be the color of disease and death. Pap wears his alcoholism, from his deathly pallor to his unkempt appearance, with both laziness and menace. He is furious that Huck has been going to school, typical of the alcoholic's vengeful desire that no one be healthier than he and typical of an abusive father toward a son he sees as bettering him:

> "I'll learn people to bring up a boy to put on airs over his own father and let on to be better'n what *he* is. You lemme catch you fooling around that school again, you hear? Your mother couldn't read, and she couldn't write, nuther, before she died. None of the family couldn't before *they* died. *I* can't; and here you're a-swelling yourself up like this. I ain't the man to stand it—you hear?...I'll lay for you, my smarty; and if I catch you about that school I'll tan you good. First you know you'll get religion, too. I never see such a son." (24)

Faced with pap, even the courts are unable to help Huck. When Judge Thatcher among all the townspeople tries to remove Huck from pap, a judge new to town takes pity on pap and tries to reform him, believing pap's "spiritual" conversion. Note the new judge's idealism contrasted with the material facts of Huck's home: "[T]he courts mustn't interfere and separate families if they could help it.... That pleased the old man till he couldn't rest. He said he'd cowhide me till I was black and blue if I didn't raise some money for him" (26). But pap disappoints; his spiritual conversion is only skin deep, and the new judge is left with a destroyed guest room and pap passed out in his front yard.

Pap appears only early in the novel, but he receives three full chapters. His rant in Chapter 6 reveals the elements in society and religion that repel Huck but also specifically suggest pap as Twain's God figure in the novel. Pap rages against the government for turning his son against him ("Call this a govment! why, just look at it and see what it's like. Here's the law a-standing ready to take a man's son away from him—a man's own son, which he has had all the trouble and all the anxiety and all the expense of raising. Yes, just as that man has got that son raised at last, and ready to go to work and begin to do suthin' for HIM and give him a rest, the law up and goes for him. And they call THAT govment!"). But he also blames his entire life on the government, much as some people blame their mistakes on God: "Here's what the law does: The law takes a man worth six thousand dollars and up'ards, and jams him into an old trap of a cabin like this, and lets him go round in clothes that ain't fitten for a hog." Pap threatens to leave the United States, as if anyone would care: "Yes, and I *told* 'em so; I told old Thatcher so to his face. Lots of 'em heard me, and can tell what I said. Says I, for two cents I'd leave the blamed country and never come a-near it agin. Them's the very words" (33–34). Not only does pap feel deprived of being one of St. Petersburg's foremost citizens, but his speech also expresses his outrage at a free Negro he has encountered, which caused him to decide that he will never vote again. Pap joins the themes of race and parenting to reveal traits in himself that are very similar to those Twain criticized in God, being venal, selfish, jealous, condemning, abusive, murderous, and unreliable in the extreme. He thinks he is a superior being when in fact he is a monster. His son—his "creation"—is only a means to glorify himself and can be disposed of if he fails. When Twain called God to task in his *Notebook,* the language could also have described pap: "The Book of Nature tells us distinctly that God cares not a rap for us—nor for any living creature. It tells us that His laws inflict pain and suffering and sorrow, but it does not say that this is done in order that He may get pleasure out of this misery. We do not know what the object is, for the Book is not able to tell us. It may be mere indifference" (Twain, *Notebook,* 362). This is, to put it mildly, a materialist point of view. Judging from pap's tirade against Huck and the free Negro, one concludes that if Twain did not believe in free will, pap does not believe in human freedom. He is trapped by himself and so everyone else must be trapped as well.

Upon providentially (?) reaching the Phelps farm, where it just so happens Tom Sawyer is expected, Huck assumes a middle-class identity, totally inappropriate now for his even more "onery" lack of an institutional self. Huck would seem to have reached a safe place, but his assuming Tom's identity is a bad sign. At the Phelps farm, the menace of evil drunks like the King and the Duke is replaced by Twain's renewed assault on racism and religion, as Huck seems to forget his decision to "*go to hell*" for Jim and instead in a distinctly un-Savior-like way goes along with Tom's ridiculous tricks on Jim. Perhaps this shows that Huck's religious resolve was a passing fantasy, as he is so demoralized he can no longer help Jim, or Tom represents the twinned malicious influences of racism and religion by reenacting sentimental romance clichés in his "saving" of Jim and acting as a surrogate father for Huck, someone he can boss around. Yet Tom is another capricious and unreliable father, but Huck looks up to him and seeks to imitate him. Again, this is about power and control instead of loftier values.

Uncle Silas Phelps is also used to satirize fatherhood and religion, demonstrating, as Victor Doyno points out, "that someone can read the Bible devotedly yet certainly not apply the information to his own situation." Though Uncle Silas mentions that he has been studying Acts 17, he seems unaware of its appropriateness (Doyno, *Writing Huck Finn*, 160). Acts 17 begins with the mob violence incited by the influential Jews of Thessaloniki against St. Paul and his companion Silas, who are chased out of the city as pariahs, and it ends with St. Paul's admonishment of the men of Athens who worship false gods, including a monument to "an unknown God" (Acts 17:23). It is ironic that Uncle Silas is reading this passage, first, because like all unreliable father-gods in this novel, he is proud and probably mostly interested in the mention of his namesake in the passage. Second, the passage presages the vigilante mob Uncle Silas himself suggests to catch Jim. Third, there is a distinction in the passage between false gods and real gods, that is, between whatever there is of God in Huck's love of Jim as against the false religion Huck has been taught by people exactly like preacher Silas. If God raised Jesus as "proof to all men," as the verses state, in Silas's universe this means only white men and only people who believe as he does. Huck again faces failed manhood. As David Cozy observes, "Where the Grangerfords were merely Christian, Silas Phelps is not just Christian but a Christian preacher. While the Grangerfords own slaves but are never depicted as being cruel to them (with the significant exception, of course, of enslaving them in the first place), the Phelpses are shown imprisoning a slave, putting him in chains and restricting him to a diet of bread and water (but not neglecting to pray with him)."

Further, when the slave escapes, the Phelpses organize a gang of armed vigilantes to pursue him. As Huck reports that "some of [this gang] wanted to hang Jim for an example to all the other niggers," it is clear that "the Phelpses' vigilantes could easily have become a lynch mob." In fact, it is only the timely reminder that the mob may have to reimburse his owner—not Christian ideals of charity or forgiveness—that saves Jim from a cruel death (Cozy n.p.). The Phelps farm provides Twain with a final opportunity to strengthen the connection between the wickedness of slavery and that of the Christian religion, both "ideals" of Huck's society. Fittingly, Huck's depression from Chapter 1 reappears in the Phelps farm episodes:

> When I got there it was all still and Sunday-like, and hot and sunshiny; the hands
> was gone to the fields; and there was them kind of faint dronings of bugs and

flies in the air that makes it seem so lonesome and like everybody's dead and gone; and if a breeze fans along and quivers the leaves it makes you feel mournful, because you feel like it's spirits whispering—spirits that's been dead ever so many years—and you always think they're talking about *you*. As a general thing it makes a body wish *he* was dead, too, and done with it all. (276)

In Chapter the Last, Tom suggests that now that it is all over he and Huck and Jim should "all three slide out of here one of these nights and get an outfit, and go for howling adventures amongst the Injuns, over in the Territory, for a couple of weeks or two." Huck wearily responds, "[A]ll right, that suits me, but I ain't got no money for to buy the outfit, and I reckon I couldn't get none from home, because it's likely pap's been back before now, and got it all away from Judge Thatcher and drunk it up" (361). Huck suspects all institutions of continued failure to protect his welfare, even the Judge and the courts, which were temporarily a (weak) refuge. This leads Jim to reveal the truth about Huck's father:

> "He ain't a-comin' back no mo', Huck." I says: "Why, Jim?" "Nemmine why, Huck—but he ain't comin' back no mo'." But I kept at him; so at last he says: "Doan' you 'member de house dat was float'n down de river, en dey wuz a man in dah, kivered up, en I went in en unkivered him and didn' let you come in? Well, den, you kin git yo' money when you wants it, kase dat wuz him." (361)

Now Huck is presumably "free" and able to return home or do whatever he likes. Jim has most likely withheld this information from Huck not only as a protective father but also as a controlling father: if Huck had known pap was dead he may not have accompanied Jim down the river. Jim's need of Huck is forgivable, given his enslavement, though it does place him in a different camp, father-wise, a less spiritual than material one. But as Huck's Father-God pap is dead, it falls upon Huck to sacrifice himself for the community by returning home to it (and spending his money there, the natural end of the *Bildungsroman Huckleberry Finn* is not), and he refuses to do it. It is Tom who returns home a hero to amaze the people with his adventures and "transformation": "Tom's most well now, and got his bullet around his neck on a watch guard for a watch, and is always seeing what time it is," says Huck. But he continues, claiming an alternate space for himself outside of Tom's respectability, outside of fathers and slaves and religion, "[A]nd so there ain't nothing more to write about, and I am rotten glad of it, because if I'd a knowed what a trouble it was to make a book I wouldn't a tackled it, and ain't a-going to no more. But I reckon I got to light out for the Territory ahead of the rest, because Aunt Sally she's going to adopt me and sivilize me, and I can't stand it. I been there before" (362). One thing neglected in readings of this famous conclusion is Huck's claim to authorship. Has he displaced pap as the father and society with its racism and found a place (a no-place outside the pale of the plot) to claim for himself, in effect to become his own father and creator in his own "spiritual" realm? If he allowed that Twain created him in the beginning and now he claims to have invented himself without a creator's agency, he is figuratively a man without a God. He is a failed Christ, but only according to the religious and social values of his society. For himself, he is enough; he does not reappear on earth (St. Petersburg) to spread a gospel. Instead, he disappears into the West, all on his own. Huck does not take anyone with him.

F. "'But they're priceless!'": Material versus Exchange Value in "Everyday Use"

We recall from the discussion of Marxism earlier in this chapter that Marx believed the *division of labor* led to social inequalities, and he described the *alienation of labor*—the fact that people rarely make their own products today, and factory workers assemble only pieces of a product. Marx also distinguished between *use value* versus *exchange value,* the actual purpose of the object versus its market value. The *commodity fetish* occurs when exchange value takes on a power of its own that abstracts an item's use into mere status value. Marxist analysis of "Everyday Use" reveals much about the situation in the Johnson family.

The first item Dee wants is the butter churn, which is symbolically rich, like the quilts, one a source of sustenance and one of shelter. As Timothy Sexton observes,

> The churn was made from a tree,... its identity was forged into something new based upon its labor value from something that was naturally formed.... The wood that was in and of itself something important and of value was fashioned into a butter churn, an instrument that takes one thing, milk, and transforms it into something else, butter.... Dee perhaps sees making the churn top into a centerpiece as an emancipation of sorts; the churn no longer has to do work, it can become merely ornamental. The churn turns one thing into another, just as slavery turned Africans into Americans.

Sexton points out that the quilts Dee wants were made out of parts of old dresses that her grandmother used to wear, thus, "the quilt, like the butter churn, is a utilitarian device. However, the quilt differs from the churn in that it is made out of pre-existing utilitarian devices—the dresses.... Once again, Dee wants to take something that has a use and turn it into an ornamental device." On the one hand, readers might view Dee's desire to take simple tools and transform them into something greater as art as a reflection of W.E.B. Du Bois's call to fight against prejudice that "engenders self-abasement in the black individual. The way to fight back against this self-abasement is by aspiring to culture." Dee considers herself cultured beyond the "abased quality of the lives" lived by her mother and sister. Maggie would merely use the quilts to keep warm, but Dee believes she recognizes the true quality and value of the quilts: "She will hang them on the wall. Taking something that has a use and a purpose and using it for something besides that purpose is the ultimate accomplishment in high culture. For Dee, the quilts and her ability to use them for decoration rather than for warmth represent her emancipation." Though Dee treats her mother and sister with contempt, her identity struggles, Sexton finds, suggest Du Bois's "double consciousness." She has not yet integrated her warring African and American selves into one: "The heritage inherent in the dresses was passed onto the quilt; everything was utilitarian because it had to be. Either you made a quilt from your old dresses or you froze. That is heritage. Taking a quilt and putting it up on a wall is American waste at its most obvious. Dee may have become Wangero, but she just as well could have changed her name to JC Penney. Dee has successfully conformed to the greater ideals of the American Republic at its worst, but she has done so specifically in opposition to and contempt of her own race."

Lois Tyson finds that Dee's economic success in escaping poverty invites a Marxist reading. As she notes, Dee is portrayed according to four Marxist principles: competition, commodification, the American Dream, and rugged individualism. Her competitive streak is obvious in the story, from her clothing to her plans for the quilt. The quilts have become commodified for her as status symbols, and will help her achieve the American Dream. Though Maggie and Mrs. Johnson have failed to get their slice of the Dream, Dee emerges as a strong individual, and thus the story could read as pro-capitalist. However, Dee is mistaken in behaving as if she accomplished everything on her own—as though she was able to succeed without the support of her family, church, and community—thus alienating herself from the labor that produced her (61–63). The story rejects such alienation in favor of the family.

From Maggie's point of view, the quilts have a very different value from that which Dee assigns them, the utilitarian (though this should not suggest that Maggie does not value the "history" sewn into the quilt). For her the use of the quilt is what is important; she doesn't even think in terms of a "market" but a family craft. However, there is an important moment of exchange value at the end of the story, when Mrs. Johnson snatches the quilts out of Dee's hands and gives them to Maggie; *she* has revalued the quilts and rejects their market value. Even though the story contains numerous false exchanges of names, of nationalities, of place and home, this transaction—off the market—is the climax of the story. Mrs. Johnson can fantasize about exchanging herself for a thin, light-skinned guest of Johnny Carson, but she knows fantasy from reality. She does not participate in the kinds of exchanges Marx wrote about, but she is able to transform the spaces and objects—and daughters—around her as an artist. The story in fact opens with her true abilities to transform: her "yard is not just a yard. It is like an extended living room. When the hard clay is swept clean as a floor and the fine sand around the edges lined with tiny, irregular grooves, anyone can come and sit and look up into the elm tree." She is a woman able to work like a man. Unlike Dee with her photographs of the house, Mrs. Johnson simply lives in the house and works her farm. It is appropriate that the closing paragraph is a testament to such "living": "Maggie smiled; maybe at the sunglasses. But a real smile, not scared. After we watched the car dust settle, I asked Maggie to bring me a dip of snuff. And then the two of us sat there just enjoying, until it was time to go in the house and go to bed."

VII. SUMMARY OF KEY POINTS

- *Marxism*: Holds that economics is the driving force in history. Capitalism creates class hierarchies and discord. Literary texts often critique society from a Marxist perspective, and Marxist critics approach all texts through Marxist theory. Marxists are less interested in form than in content or message.
- Important Marxist terms:
    bourgeoisie
    proletariat
    dialectic
    ideology
    exchange value
    commodity fetish
    reification
    determinism
    hegemony
    cultural capital
    subject-position
- Marxist key figures:
    Lionel Trilling
    Georg Lukács
    Antonio Gramsci
    Theodor Adorno
    Jürgen Habermas
    Louis Althusser
    Raymond Williams
    Terry Eagleton
    Pierre Bourdieu
    Frederic Jameson
- *British Cultural Materialism*: Argued that culture belongs to the working classes as well as to the elite. These critics used Marxism to reinterpret high and low culture. They argue that there is no stable cultural center in a society. Feminism was an important model for cultural materialists.
- British Cultural Materialism key figures:
    F. R. Leavis
    Raymond Williams
    Stuart Hall
    Walter Benjamin
- *New Historicism*: Looks for surprising coincidences and correspondences between literature and history and how literature and history resemble each other. New historicists' motto might be "The text is historical and history is a text." They see literature and history as narratives of power and exchange.

This approach differs from the "old" historicism by politicizing the historical context and its effects on the work.

- New Historicism key terms:
  symbolic capital
  circulation of ideas
  habitus
- New Historicism key figures:
  Stephen Greenblatt
  Michel Foucault
  Jean-François Lyotard
- *Ecocriticism*: A new field but one growing fast—applies ecology and ecological concepts to the study of literature. Ecocritics believe their field is fundamental and are often activists for the environment. An offshoot is ecofeminism, which argues that there are parallels between how women and the environment are treated in a patriarchy.
- Ecocriticism key figures:
  Joseph Carroll
  Lawrence Buell
  Leslie Marmon Silko
- *Literary Darwinism*: Based on Darwin's theory of natural selection, this approach argues that the human mind is constructed to think in stories and that literature, like human behavior, can be best interpreted by reference to its evolutionary features. Evolution precedes and explains literary discourse, which so often centers on selective mating, kin preference, adaptability, childrearing, competition for resources, cooperation, and other Darwinian concepts. Related to studies in sociobiology, evolutionary psychology, genetics and epigenetics, this is an instance in which the sciences and humanities can interact. Darwinist critics ask: Why does literature continue to exist?
- Key Darwinist terms:
  natural selection
  "the struggle for survival"
  evolutionary fitness
  adaptability
  consilience
  selfish genes
- Literary Darwinism key figures:
  Charles Darwin
  Thomas Henry Huxley
  Herbert Spencer
  E. O. Wilson
  Jonathan Gottschall
  Ian McEwan

VIII. LIMITATIONS OF MATERIALIST APPROACHES

Marx wrote during the mid-nineteenth-century Industrial Revolution, before a number of labor reforms were in place. In the 1930s, the rise of communism, the Great Depression, and the rise of an international Left, led to calls for socialist realism, a literature that would glorify the common man and woman. After World War II, the West turned against the Left during the cold war. Marxist criticism was attacked for being too prescriptive and especially for being deaf to the aesthetic value of a text. It still feels that way to readers more concerned about the aesthetic value of a work of art as a worthy object of study in itself. However, Marxist critics of many types continue working today, and Marxism certainly inspired basic features of such later approaches as new historicism and postcolonialism. Its critique of capitalist society has gained new depth with such postmodern developments as globalization.

QUICK REFERENCE

Adorno, Theodor W. *Aesthetic Theory*. 1970. Trans. Robert Hullot-Kentor. Eds. Gretel Adorno and Rolf Tiedemann. London: Athlone Press, 1997.

Allen, Paula Gunn. "The Sacred Hoop: A Contemporary Perspective." In *The Ecocriticism Reader: Landmarks in Literary Ecology*. Ed. Cheryll Glotfelty and Harold Fromm. Athens and London: University of Georgia, 1996. 241–263.

Althusser, Louis. "Ideology and Ideological State Apparatuses (Notes towards an investigation)." *Lenin and Philosophy and Other Essays*. Trans. Ben Brewster. New York: Monthly Review Press, 1971.

Anders, Lorraine, ed. *Sisters of the Earth*. 2nd edn. New York: Vintage, 2003.

"Andrew Marvell's 'To His Coy Mistress': A New Historicist Reading." Bedford/St. Martins VirtuaLit. http://bcs.bedfordstmartins.com/Virtualit/poetry/critical_define/newhistessay.pdf

Arnold, Matthew. *Culture and Anarchy*. 1869. Rpt. Yale University Press, 1994.

Barash, David P., and Nanelle R. Barash. *Madame Bovary's Ovaries: A Darwinian Look at Literature*. New York: Delacorte, 2005.

Benjamin, Walter. *Illuminations*. Ed. Hannah Arendt. Trans. Harry Zohn. New York: Harcourt, Brace & World, 1968.

Bourdieu, Pierre. *Distinction: A Social Critique of the Judgment of Taste*. Trans. Richard Nice. 1979. Cambridge, Mass.: Harvard University Press, 1984.

Bruce, Susan. "The Flying Island and Female Anatomy: Gynaecology and Power" in *Gulliver's Travels*. Genders 2 (July 1988): 60–76.

Buell, Lawrence. *The Environmental Imagination: Thoreau, Nature Writing, and the Formation of American Culture*. Cambridge, Mass.: Harvard University Press, 1995.

——. *The Future of Environmental Criticism: Environmental Crisis and Literary Imagination*. London: Wiley-Blackwell, 2005.

——. *Writing for an Endangered World: Literature, Culture, and Environment in the United States and Beyond*. Cambridge, Mass.: Harvard University Press, 2001.

Carroll, Joseph. "The Ecology of Victorian Fiction," *Philosophy and Literature*, 25 (2001): 295–313.

——. *Evolution and Literary Theory*. Columbia: University of Missouri Press, 1995.

Carroll, Joseph. *Literary Darwinism.* New York: Routledge, 2004.

———. Rev. of *Mimesis and the Human Animal: On the Biogenetic Foundations of Literary Representation* by Robert Storey. Evanston, Ill. Northwestern University Press, 1996. http://cogweb.ucla.edu/Abstracts/Carroll_S98.html

Crews, Frederick. "Foreword from the Literary Side." *The Literary Animal: Evolution and the Nature of Narrative.* Eds. Jonathan Gottschall and David Sloan Wilson. Evanston, Ill.: Northwestern University Press, 2005. xiii–xv.

Darwin, Charles. *Darwin.* Ed. Philip Appleman. 3rd edn. Rpt. New York: W. W. Norton & Co., 2001.

———. *The Descent of Man.* London: J. Murray, 1871. Rpt. Chicago: William Benton, 1952.

———. *The Origin of Species.* London: J. Murray, 1859. Rpt. as *On the Origin of Species: A Facsimile of the First Edition.* Cambridge, Mass.: Harvard University Press, 1964.

Diamond, Jared. *Guns, Germs, and Steel.* New York: Norton, 1999.

Victor A. Doyno, *Writing Huck Finn: Mark Twain's Creative Process.* Philadelphia: University of Pennsylvania Press, 1991.

Eagleton, Terry, *Criticism and Ideology: A Study in Marxist Literary Theory.* New York: New Left Books, 1976.

———. *Ideology: An Introduction.* London: Verso, 1991.

———. *Marxism and Literary Criticism.* Berkeley: University of California Press, 1976.

———. *Walter Benjamin, or Towards a Revolutionary Criticism.* London: Verso, 1981.

Foucault, Michel. *Discipline and Punish: The Birth of the Prison.* 1975. Rpt. and trans. New York: Vintage, 1995.

———. *The History of Sexuality, Volume One: The Will to Knowledge.* 1976. Rpt. New York: Random House, 1978. Rpt. 1990 Vintage Books.

———. *The Order of Things.* 1966. Rpt. New York: Random House, 1970.

Gallagher, Catherine, and Stephen Greenblatt. *Practicing New Historicism.* Chicago, Ill.: University of Chicago Perss, 2000.

Geertz, Clifford. *The Interpretation of Cultures: Selected Essays.* New York: Basic Books, 1973.

Glotfelty, Cheryll, and Harold Fromm, eds. *The Ecocriticism Reader: Landmarks in Literary Ecology.* Athens and London: University of Georgia, 1996.

Goldmann, Lucien. *Towards a Sociology of the Novel.* 1964. Trans. Alan Sheridan. Rpt. New York: Tavistock Publications, 1975.

Gottschall, Jonathan, and David Sloan Wilson, eds. *The Literary Animal: Evolution and the Nature of Narrative.* Northwestern University Press. 2005.

Grady, Hugh, and Terence Hawkes, eds. *Presentist Shakespeares.* London: Routledge, 2007.

Gramsci, Antonio. *Prison Notebooks.* Trans. Joseph A. Buttigieg. 2 vols. New York: Columbia University Press, 1991.

Greenblatt, Stephen. *Shakespearean Negotiations: The Circulation of Social Energy in Renaissance England.* Berkeley: University of California Press, 1988.

Groden, Michael and Martin Kreiswirth. *The John Hopkins Guide to Literary Theory and Criticism.* Baltimore. John Hopkins University Press. 1994.

Habermas, Jürgen. *The Structural Transformation of the Public Sphere: An Inquiry into a Category of Bourgeois Society.* 1968. Trans. Thomas Burger with Frederick Lawrence. Cambridge, Mass.: MIT Press, 1989.

Hall, Stuart. "Cultural Studies: Two Paradigms." 1980. Rpt. in David H. Richter.

Hegel, Georg Wilhelm Friedrich. *Phenomenology of Mind.* 1907. Trans. J. B. Baillie, 1910; 2nd ed. 1931. Rpt. New York: Harper/Torch Books, 1967.

Hoggart, Richard. *The Uses of Literacy: Changing Patterns in English Mass Culture.* Harmondsworth, England: Penguin, 1957.

Horkheimer, Max, and Theodor Adorno. *Dialectic of Enlightenment.* 1944. Trans. John Cumming. New York: Continuum, 1962.

Horvath, Tim. "Literary Darwinism and Literary Darwinisms: Let the Games Begin..." 1 January 2005. http://cogweb.ucla.edu/Culture/Horvath-on-Carroll-04.html.

Howard, John. *Darwin: A Very Short Introduction.* Oxford: Oxford University Press, 1982.

Huxley, Thomas H. *Evolution and Ethics and Other Essays.* New York: Appleton, 1915.

Jameson, Frederic. *Marxism and Form: Twentieth Century Dialectical Theories of Literature.* Princeton, NJ: Princeton University Press, 1971.

———. *The Political Unconscious: Narrative as a Socially Symbolic Act.* Ithaca, NY: Cornell University Press, 1981.

———. *Postmodernism, or, the Cultural Logic of Late Capitalism.* Durham, NC: Duke University press, 1991.

Kolodny, Annette. "Unearthing Herstory." In *The Ecocriticism Reader: Landmarks in Literary Ecology.* Ed. Cheryll Glotfelty and Harold Fromm. Athens and London: University of Georgia, 1996. 170–81.

Leavis, F. R. *The Great Tradition.* 1948. Rpt. New York: New York University Press, 1963.

Levi-Strauss, Claude. *Cultural Anthropology.* 1958. Trans. Clare Jacobson and Brooke Grundfrest Schoepf. New York: Basic Books, 1963.

Litvak, Joseph. *Strange Gourmets: Sophistication, Theory, and the Novel.* Durham, NC: Duke University Press, 1997.

Love, Glen A. "Revaluing Nature: Toward and Ecological Criticism." In *The Ecocriticism Reader: Landmarks in Literary Ecology.* Ed. Cheryll Glotfelty and Harold Fromm. Athens and London: University of Georgia, 1996. 225–40.

Lukács, Georg. *The Meaning of Contemporary Realism.* 1958. Trans John and Necke Mander. London: Merlin, 1963.

Lyotard, Jean-Francois. *The Postmodern Explained: Correspondence 1982–1985.* Minneapolis: University of Minnesota Press, 1992.

McEwan, Ian. "Literature, Science, and Human Nature." In *The Literary Animal: Evolution and the Nature of Narrative.* Eds. Jonathan Gottschall and David Sloan Wilson. Northwestern University Press. 2005. 5–19.

McGuire, Cathleen, and Colleen McGuire. "Ecofeminist Visions." *American Political Thought.* 5th edn. Eds. Kenneth Dolbear and Michael S. Cummings. *Congressional Quarterly*: 2003. <http://www.eve.enviroweb.org/about/index.html.>

Marx, Karl. *Das Kapital.* 1867; trans. English 1887. Rpt. Chicago, Illinois: Charles Kerr, 1909.

Max, D. T. "The Literary Darwinists." *New York Times Sunday Magazine,* November 6, 2005.

Nelson, Cary, and Lawrence Grossberg, eds. *Marxism and the Interpretation of Culture.* Urbana: University of Illinois Press, 1988.

Nettle, Daniel. "What Happens in *Hamlet*? Exploring the Psychological Foundations of Drama." In *The Literary Animal: Evolution and the Nature of Narrative.* Eds. Jonathan Gottschall and David Sloan Wilson. Northwestern University Press. 2005. 56–75.

Nordlund, Marcus. *Shakespeare and the Nature of Love: Literature, Culture, Evolution.* Evanston, Ill.: Northwestern University Press, 2007.

Phillips, Dana. *The Truth of Ecology: Nature, Culture, and Literature in America.* Oxford: Oxford University Press, 2003.

Pittenger, Mark. *American Socialists and Evolutionary Thought, 1870–1920*. Madison: University of Wisconsin Press, 1993.

Porter, Carolyn. "Are We Being Historical Yet?" In David Carroll, ed. *The States of Theory: History, Art, and Critical Discourse*. New York: Columbia University Press, 1990.

Rueckert, William. "Literature and Ecology: An Experiment in Ecocriticism." In *The Ecocriticism Reader: Landmarks in Literary Ecology*. Ed. Cheryll Glotfelty and Harold Fromm. Athens and London: University of Georgia, 1996. 105–23.

Richter, David H. *The Critical Tradition: Classic Texts and Contemporary Trends*. 3rd edn. New York: St Martin's, 2007.

Sarup, Madan. *An Introductory Guide to Post-Structuralism and Postmodernism*. 2nd edn. Athens: University of Georgia Press, 1993.

Sexton, Timothy. "Black America and Double Consciousness: W.E.B. Dubois and Alice Walker's 'Everyday Use,'" *Associated Content*. July 23, 2006. http://www.associatedcontent.com/article/45237/black america and double consciousn ess.html?cat=38

Silko, Leslie Marmon. "Landscape, History, and the Pueblo Imagination." In *The Ecocriticism Reader: Landmarks in Literary Ecology*. Ed. Cheryll Glotfelty and Harold Fromm. Athens and London: University of Georgia, 1996. 264–75.

Sinclair, Upton, ed. *The Cry for Justice: An Anthology of Literature of Social Protest*. Philadelphia, Penn.: John C. Winston Co., 1915.

Snow, C. P. *The Two Cultures and the Scientific Revolution*. Cambridge: Cambridge University Press, 1958.

Spencer, Herbert *First Principles*, 4th edn. New York: A.L. Burt, Pub., 1880.

———. *Social Statics: or, the Conditions Essential to Human Happiness specified, and the first of them developed*. London: J. Chapman, 1851. Rpt. New York: Robert Schalkenbach Foundation, 1995.

Storey, Robert. *Mimesis and the Human Animal: On the Biogenetic Foundations of Literary Representation*. Evanston, Ill.: Northwestern University Press, 1996.

Twain, Mark. "Bible Teaching and Religious Practice." *Mark Twain and the Three R's: Race, Religion, Revolution and Related Matters*, ed. Maxwell Geismar (New York: Bobbs-Merrill, 1973, 108–09.

———. Mark Twain, *The Devil's Race-Track: Mark Twain's Great Dark Writings*, ed. John Tuckey (Berkeley: University of California Press), 2005.

———. *Mark Twain's Notebook*, ed. Albert Bigelow Paine (New York: Harper, 1935).

Tyson, Lois. *Learning for a Diverse World: Using Critical Theory to Read and Write About Literature*. New York: Routledge, 2001.

Veeser, H. Aram, ed. *The New Historicism*. New York: Routledge, 1989.

Warner, Michael. "Literary Studies and the History of the Book." *The Book* 12 (1987): 3–9.

White, Hayden. "Anomalies of Genre: The Utility of Theory and History for the Study of Literary Genres." *New Literary History* 34, 3 (Summer 2003): 597–615.

Williams, Raymond. *The Country and the City*. New York: Oxford University Press, 1973.

———. *Culture and Society, 1780–1950*. London: Chatto, 1958.

———. *Marxism and Literature*. New York: Oxford University Press, 1977.

Wilson, E. O. *Consilience: The Unity of Knowledge*. New York: Knopf, 1998.

5

Literature and Linguistics

I. STRUCTURALISM AND POSTSTRUCTURALISM, INCLUDING DECONSTRUCTION

A. Structuralism: Context and Definition

Structuralism has been applied to linguistics, psychology, sociology, anthropology, folklore, mythology, and Biblical studies—in fact, to all social and cultural phenomena. Its attractions are considerable: structuralism is, at least seemingly, scientific and objective. It identifies *structures,* systems of relationships, which endow signs (e.g., words) or items (e.g., clothes, cars, table manners, rituals) with identities and meanings, and shows us *the ways in which we think.*

Structuralism claims intellectual linkage to the prestigious line of French rationalists stretching from Voltaire to Jean-Paul Sartre. Its representatives in Britain and the United States tend to retain French terminology. Structuralists emphasize that description of any phenomenon or artifact without placement in the broader systems that generate it is misleading if not impossible. Accordingly, they have developed analytical, systematic approaches to literary texts that avoid traditional categories like plot, character, setting, theme, tone, and the like. Even more significantly, however, structuralists tend to deny the text any inherent privilege, meaning, or authority; to them the text is only a system that poses the question of *how* such a construct of language can contain meaning for us.

Such a view denies any claim of privilege for any author, any school, any period, and any "correct" explication. The structuralists have encouraged us to reread, rethink, and restudy all literary works and to equate them with all other cultural and social phenomena—for example, language, landscaping, architecture, kinship, marriage customs, fashion, menus, furniture, and politics.

B. The Linguistic Model

Structuralism emerged from the structural linguistics developed by Ferdinand de Saussure, mainly in his lectures at the University of Geneva between 1906 and

1911. Not available in English until 1959, Saussure's *Course in General Linguistics* in French (1916) attracted thinkers far beyond Switzerland, linguistics, and universities: it became the model for Russian formalism, semiology or semiotics, French structuralism, and deconstruction, each of which we will treat briefly below. Saussure's model is acceptable as an analogy for the study of many systems other than language.

Saussure's theory of language systems distinguishes between *la langue* (language, the system possessed and used by all members of a particular language community—English, French, Urdu, etc.) and *la parole* (word; by extension, speech-event or any specific application of *la langue* in speech or writing). The *parole* is impossible without the support—the structural validity, generation, meaning—conferred upon it by the *langue*, the source of grammar, phonetics, morphology, syntax, and semantics. As Saussure explained, *paroles* appear as phonetic and semantic signs (*phonemes* and *semes*). A linguistic sign joins a *signifier* (a conventional sound construction) to a *signification* (semantic value, meaning). Such a sign does not join a thing and its name, but an allowable concept to a "sound image" (Pettit 6). The sign thus has meaning *only within its system*—a *langue* or some other context. An item is meaningful only within its originating system. Further, Saussure stressed the importance of considering each item in relationship to all other items within the system.

The approach to analyzing sentences is *syntagmatic*—word by word in the horizontal sequence of the parts or *syntagms* of the sentence. Saussure's "structural" linguistics furnishes a functional explanation of language according to its structural hierarchy—that is, structures within structures. He suggested that his system for studying language had profound implications for other disciplines. In the study of a literary work, Saussure's syntagmatic approach explains our usual, instinctive approach: we read the poem from its start to its finish, we see the narrative work in terms of the sequence of events or the scenes of the play, we inventory the details from the first to the last, from their start to their finish. This approach emphasizes the *surface structures* of the work, as it does for the sentence in Saussure's scheme, as opposed to the *deep structures*, those not on the surface—the understood but unexpressed signs. Saussurean linguistics applies, moreover, to *synchronic* features (i.e., language as it exists at a particular time) rather than to *diachronic* features (details of language considered in their historical process of development).

Roman Jakobson, a prominent linguist, did much to spread structuralism among theorists of literature. Jakobson defined communication as occurring when a *sender* makes *contact* with a *receiver* and sends a *message* using both *context* and *code;* these six factors are the six functions of communication. Most communication is *referential* to the context and content; the emotive function of communication privileges the sender, while the *conative* function emphasizes the receiver. The *phatic* function is merely establishing contact, but in contrast the *metalinguistic* function interrogates the code. The *poetic* function centers on the message itself. Jakobson's dissection of communication holds many possibilities for literary analysis.

C. Russian Formalism: Extending Saussure

A group of scholars in Moscow during World War I perceived the dynamic possibilities of using Saussure's work as a model for their investigations of phenomena other than language. Vladimir Propp studied Russian folktales as structural units that together contained a limited number of types of characters and actions; Propp called these *actants* and *functions*. The functions recur and thus constitute in their unity the grammar or rules for such tales. According to the Saussurean model, we can say that the entire group of functions is the *langue;* the individual tale is a *parole*. A number of these characters and functions are introduced in our Chapter 7 on mythological approaches; for example, Propp's theory identifies **hero**, rival or opponent, villain, helper, king, princess, and so on, and such actions as the arrival and the departure of the hero, the unmasking of the villain, sets of adventures, and the return and reward of the hero.

Victor Shklovsky pointed out literature's constant tendency toward *estrangement* and *defamiliarization,* away from habitual responses to ordinary experience and/or ordinary language. In **poetry**, for example, we see a particular drive toward the strange and away from the familiar in its lineation of words, its rhythmic patternings, and its choice of language. Its texture is typically packed with meanings and suggestions; it might be arcane or even ritualistic, and it calls attention to itself as different. This is true of the simplest nursery rhymes. At the opposite extreme, in English **Metaphysical poetry**, for example, it is the defamiliarization, the estrangement, that often takes the poems well beyond the usual and into the complex intellectual and emotional experience that we associate with those poems.

Shklovsky also emphasized that **narrative** has two aspects: *story,* the events or functions in normal chronological sequence, and *plot,* the artful, subversive rearrangement and thus defamiliarization of the parts of that sequence. Story is the elementary narrative that seeks relatively easy recognition, as in most nursery tales, whereas plot estranges, prolongs, or complicates perception as in, say, one of Henry James's fictions.

In general, the Russian formalists adapted Saussure's syntagmatic, linear approach—examining structures in the sequence of their appearance—but showed how to use Saussure's theory in disciplines far beyond linguistics. Propp and Shklovsky demonstrated that literature can be made the equivalent of *langue* and the individual literary work the equivalent of *parole*. Finally, we may note that the work of the Russian formalists reminds us to some extent of American New Criticism in its concern for linking form to its constituent devices or conventions.

D. Structuralism, Lévi-Strauss, and Semiotics

Structuralism attracted interest in the United States after the publication of Claude Lévi-Strauss's *Structural Anthropology* in the 1950s, even though an American edition did not appear until 1963. In contrast to Saussure and the Russian formalists, Lévi-Strauss concentrated on the *paradigmatic* approach—that is, on the *deep* or *imbedded structures* of discourse that seem to evade a conscious arrangement by the literary artist but are somehow embedded vertically, latently, within texts and can be represented sometimes as abstractions or as paired opposites (*binary oppositions*). Lévi-Strauss, an anthropologist who studied myths of aboriginal peoples in central Brazil, combined psychology and sociology in cross-cultural studies and found structures comparable to those discovered by Saussure in language— that is, systems reducible to structural features. He traced structural linkages of riddles, the Oedipus myth, American Indian myths, the Grail cycle, and anything else that might be found to structure codes of kinship (including codes of chastity and incest). He believed these linkages reached out to embrace the most profound mysteries of human experience and may very well remind us of the simultaneous layers of literary and mythic images in works like Eliot's *The Waste Land,* Joyce's *Ulysses* or *Finnegans Wake,* and Conrad's *Heart of Darkness.* But Lévi-Strauss warns that literary critic-scholars ought not to attempt structural studies solely from a literary fund of knowledge, for sufficient command of multidisciplinary knowledge is necessary to construct adequate models (*Structural Anthropology* 275). (cf. our Chapter 4, which treats Literary Darwinism.)

The myth studies of Lévi-Strauss suggest the kind of links we infer between, say, *Oedipus Rex* and *Hamlet* (the emphases on kingship, marriage, incest, gross sexuality; the sacrificial scapegoat; the health of the society vis-à-vis the throne; the uses of reason), or between *King Lear* and *Moby-Dick* (structures of sight, the tyranny of pride, or "reason in madness"), or between the *Divine Comedy* and *Leaves of Grass* (the poet's quest, the scope of vision, and the sequence of confrontations). Lévi-Strauss recommended the semiotic approach (semiotics being the study of *signs*) because the approach links *messages* in individual works to their respective codes, the larger system which permits individual expression—connects *parole* to *langue* (*The Raw and the Cooked* 147). Like studies by the Russian formalists, Lévi-Strauss's semiotics is important because it prepares for mainstream structuralism; indeed, most explanations of structuralism identify Lévi-Strauss as its founding father.

To Lévi-Strauss, the structures of myth point to the structures of the human mind common to all people—that is, to the way all human beings think (cf. our discussion in Chapter 7 on the universality of **myth**). Myth thus becomes a language—a narrative mode that transcends cultural or temporal barriers and speaks to all people, in the process tapping deep reservoirs of feeling and experience. To Lévi-Strauss, even though we have no knowledge of any entire mythology, such myths as we do uncover reveal the existence within any culture of a system of abstractions by which that culture structures its life. In his study of the Oedipus myth, Lévi-Strauss found a set of *mythemes*—units of myth analogous to linguistic terms like morphemes or phonemes, and like those linguistic counterparts based in *binary oppositions.* The structural patterns of these *mythemes* invest the myth with meaning. For example, Oedipus kills his father (a sign of the undervaluation of kinship) and marries his mother, Jocasta (an overvaluation of kinship). In either case, Oedipus has choices: what he does and what he does not do are significant binary oppositions within the myth. Although Lévi-Strauss was not interested in the *literariness* of myths, some of his contemporaries saw in his work promising implications for purely literary studies, particularly studies of narrative.

E. French Structuralism: Codes and Decoding

As a response to Lévi-Strauss, the "school of Paris," as it is often called, produced a French new criticism in the 1950s and 1960s. It included the work of Roland Barthes, Jacques Derrida, Michel Foucault, and Tzvetan Todorov. Mainly these writers were interested in relatively sophisticated narrative—the fiction of Proust or Balzac—and in some popular modes like mystery novels and humor, rather than in folk or native art. Yet they too accept the Saussurean linguistic model and thus an essentially syntagmatic (horizontal) approach to texts. They viewed narrative as a kind of analogy to the sentence: the text, like the sentence, expresses the writer's mind and is a whole composed of distinguishable parts. Instead of the Russian formalists' distinction between story and plot, the French structuralists use the terms *histoire* (essentially the sequence of events from the beginning to the end) and *discours* (discourse; the narrative rearranged and reconstructed for its own purposes and aesthetic effects, as in the artful, intricate rearrangements of time and events in Faulkner's "Rose for Emily," which conceals or withholds an essential fact until the very last sentence in the work). Discursive manipulation of the raw data is another instance of the defamiliarization we associate with and expect in literary art; other kinds of estrangement are flashbacks, unequal treatment of time, alternation of dramatic and expository passages, shifts of viewpoint or speaker, or even the absence of viewpoint (as in the French *nouveau roman* of Alain Robbe-Grillet and others; see Culler, *Structuralist Poetics* 190–92).

In such an approach, the text is a *message* that can be understood only by references to the *code* (the internalized formal structure consisting of certain semantic possibilities that explain and validate the content of a message). The reader gets the message (*parole*) only by knowing the code (*langue*) that lies behind it. Structuralist reading is essentially the quest for the code.

Todorov has assured us that structuralism cannot interpret any literary work: it can only show us how to identify a work's characteristic features and perhaps how to perceive their likenesses to or differences from structures in other works. Barthes, usually considered the preeminent structuralist (and later, a major French deconstructionist), and Todorov declared their indifference to authors, who after all cannot claim—they said—any originality, since authorship is merely the rearrangement of structures already present in the code. Any literary criticism inevitably will be totally subjective; even if a critic claims to be a Freudian or a Marxist, the artifact is irreducible to any such semiological, psychological, or political systems.

On the other hand, it is, or should be, according to Jonathan Culler, the object of a structuralist poetics "to specify the codes and conventions [i.e., the codes of art] which make...meanings possible" (Foreword to *The Poetics of Prose* 8). We can learn those codes and conventions, of course, only by experience. The author

Pablo Picasso, Las Meniñas, *Infanta Margarita Maria*, Cannes (1957)

In this interpretation, Picasso treats only the Infanta, who has grown to take over nearly the entire field. Only a pair of subservient hands to the left represent anyone else as they offer her a drink on a tray. Her white dress has become a yellow square, her torso a vertical box, and her arms triangular geometric shapes. The face is divided into fields of green, blue, black and white, and the whiteness of the dress has migrated to her hair. Nothing appears in the background. The painting is enlivened by a strategic use of red: her left eye, the center rosette on her chest, sleeve details. There is something mask-like about the Infanta's face, and the different eye suggests mystery about her vision and about vision at all. Yet she is at last the center of attention.

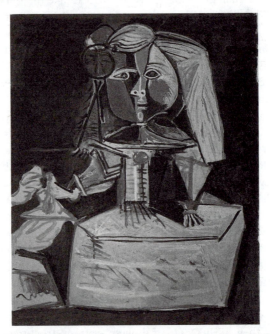

Figure 5.1. Pablo Picasso, *Las Meniñas, Infanta Margarita María* (1957).
Museo Picasso, Barcelona, Spain/© DACS/Index/The Bridgeman Art Library International/© 2009 Estate of Pablo Picasso/Artists Rights Society (ARS), New York.

Questions: What is suggested by the block-like shape of the skirt? It almost resembles a block of stone or concrete. How could we described her as "located" within this block? Does that suggest something ironic in her prominence in the painting, e.g., that she is really just a small part of a large institution, and not the most important part, either? Why does Picasso retain the serving hands of Isabel de Velasco? Does this heighten the Infanta's power? All serve the king and the state, no matter how well-dressed and well-attended. Students may wish to use Marxist or structuralist analysis to dig for some of these implications, referring back to Velázquez's original to analyze power relationships in it as parts of a structure.

encodes a work; the reader must try to *decode* it. For example, Todorov points out, Henry James's fictions typically encode an essential secret in the narrative machinery, so subtly that it can entrap the unwary or inexperienced reader. Examples of encoded mysteries, riddles, or **ambiguities** could be multiplied from many works (e.g., *Hamlet*) and authors (e.g., Hawthorne).

In his often-cited analysis of a story by Balzac, Barthes classifies five literary codes in fiction:

1. The code of actions (proairetic code) asks the reader to find meaning in the sequence of events.
2. The code of puzzles (hermeneutic code) raises the questions to be answered.
3. The cultural code refers to all the systems of "knowledge and values invoked by a text."
4. The connotative code expresses themes developed around the characters.
5. The symbolic code refers to the theme as we have generally considered it, that is, the meaning of the work.

(See Scholes 153–55 for a fuller explanation of the scheme that Barthes provided in *S/Z*.) The reader of a work need not use all codes at once, and in practice may blend codes. The awareness of the tendency of the codes to coalesce, and appear and disappear, may remind us of formalism's concentration on the theory of **organic form**.

In *S/Z*, Barthes also defined one other term, *lexie*, which is the basic unit of a narrative text—"the minimal unit of reading, a stretch of text which is isolated as having a specific effect or function different from that of the neighboring stretches of text" (in Culler, *Structuralist Poetics* 202). In size the *lexie* can be anything from a single word to a nexus of several sentences which will fit into and support one of the five narrative codes.

F. British and American Interpreters

Jonathan Culler is usually credited with the greatest success in mediating European structuralism to students of critical theory in Britain and the United States, mainly through his *Structuralist Poetics*; however, Robert Scholes's *Structuralism in Literature* may have done more to simplify and clarify the issues and the practical possibilities of structuralism for nonprofessional students of literature. Although both Culler and Scholes pass along the pervasive structuralist caveat that favors theory of literature in general over analysis of particular texts, in fact they repeatedly express regret that texts are neglected in structuralist studies.

However, Culler, by specifying a structuralist poetics based on the model of Saussurean linguistic theory, invites intelligent and unprejudiced readers to contribute to the expansion of that poetics, which he defines simply as the "procedures of reading" that ought to be found in any discourse *about* literature. Literature, Culler insists, can have no existence beyond a display of literary conventions that enable readers to identify the sign system that they already know and that is analogous to the way we read sentences by recognizing phonetic, semantic, and grammatical structures in them. Through experience, readers acquire degrees of literary competence (just as children gradually acquire degrees of syntactical and grammatical complexity) that permit degrees of textual penetration. Culler stresses that it is the reader's business to *find* contexts that make a text intelligible and to reduce the "strangeness" or defamiliarization achieved by the text. Learning literary conventions (the equal of Saussure's *langue*) and resisting any inclination to grant the text autonomy (to privilege the text) dispose the structuralist reader to search out and identify structures within the system of the text and, if possible, expand poetics rather than to explicate the organic form of a privileged text.

G. Poststructuralism: Deconstruction

Poststructuralism and deconstruction are virtually synonymous. Deconstruction arises out of the structuralism of Roland Barthes as a reaction against the certainties of structuralism. Like structuralism, deconstruction identifies textual features but, unlike structuralism, concentrates on the *rhetorical* rather than the *grammatical.*

Deconstruction accepts the analogy of text to **syntax** as presented by Ferdinand de Saussure and adapted by the structuralists. But whereas structuralism finds order and meaning in the text as in the sentence, deconstruction finds disorder and a constant tendency of the language to refute its apparent sense. Hence the name of the approach: texts are found to deconstruct themselves rather than to provide a stable identifiable meaning. Meaning may exist, but it is always deferred—it is what language cannot get at.

Deconstruction views texts as subversively undermining an apparent or surface meaning, and it denies any final explication or statement of meaning. It questions the presence of any objective structure or content in a text. Instead of alarm or dismay at their discoveries, the practitioners of deconstruction celebrate the text's self-destruction, that inevitable seed of its own internal contradiction, as a never-ending free play of language. Instead of discovering one ultimate meaning for the text, as formalism seems to promise, deconstruction describes the text as always in a state of change, furnishing only provisional meanings. All texts are thus open-ended constructs, and sign and signification are only arbitrary relationships. Meaning can only point to an indefinite number of other meanings.

The greatest interpreter of Derrida is Gayatri Chakravorty Spivak, who, through her process of translating Derrida, is able to give definitions of his key terms. *Différance* means "the setting ... as well as its continuation—the pushing away." The "track" or "trace" she defines as the evidence "of a previous differentiation." For Spivak and Derrida, "the origin of the possibility of language is the capacity to articulate differences among linguistic and verbal units rather than some internalized knowledge or reservoir of chunks of language." Derrida named such differentiation "(setting off) from, and deferment (pushing away)" as the trace of "all that is not being defined or posited." This "irreducible work of the trace not only produces an unrestricted economy of same and other, rather than a relatively restricted dialectic of negation and sublation,....It also places our selfhood (ipseity) in a relationship of *différance* with what can only be 'named' radical alterity (and thus necessarily effaced)" (423–24). For Derrida and Spivak, *différance* is what is usually and systematically effaced by language that is not a "call to the wholly other," or "that which must be differed-deferred so that we can post ourselves, as it were" (424–25).

Thus, deconstruction involves taking apart any "meaning" to reveal contradictory structures hidden within. Neither meaning nor the text that seeks to express it has any privilege over the other, and this extends to critical statements about the text.

The break with structuralism is profound. Structuralism claims kinship between systems of meaning in a text and structuralist theory itself: both would reveal the way human intelligence works. When deconstruction denies connections of mind, textual meaning, and methodological approach, it represents for structuralists only nihilism and anarchy.

For example, in her introductory guide to poststructuralism and postmodernism, Madan Sarup offers a set of four typical critiques posed by poststructuralism: the critique of the human subject (dismissing Descartes's self-knowability), the critique of historicism (the idea of an overall pattern in history), the critique of meaning (the notion that there is a one-to-one correspondence between signifier and signified), and the critique of philosophy (that philosophy, especially Marxist, is a science) (1–3).

Further, deconstruction opposes *logocentrism*, the notion that written language contains a self-evident meaning that points to an unchanging meaning authenticated by the whole of Western tradition. It would demythologize literature and thus remove the privilege it has enjoyed in academe. In deconstruction, knowledge is viewed as embedded in texts, not authenticated within some intellectual discipline. Since meaning in language shifts and remains indeterminate, deconstructionists argue that all forms of institutional authority shift in like manner. Since there is no possibility of absolute truth, deconstructionists seek to undermine all pretensions to authority, or power systems, in language. (Here they reveal the influence of Marxism.)

Derrida's philosophical skepticism became widely adopted when his work was translated in the early 1970s. Because of the academic location of many other deconstructionists at the time, deconstruction also came to be known by some as the Yale School of criticism.

Derrida claimed that the Western tradition of thought repressed meaning by repressing the limitless vitality of language and by moving thought to the margin. Yet while Derrida argued to subvert the dominant Western mindset, he also recognized that there is no privileged position outside the instabilities of language from which to attack. Thus, deconstruction deconstructs itself; in a self-contradictory effort, it manages to leave things the way they were, the only difference being our expanded consciousness of the inherent play of language-as-thought.

Derrida believed that all thought is inscribed in language, that it is expressed in paradoxes, but this does not mean that thought does not exist at all. Deconstruction leaves meaning open for the reader, in contrast to structuralism, with its claims of using language to synthesize knowledge into a system. Because most readers and critics today resist the idea of a single meaning for a literary work, they are still drawn to deconstruction and its freedoms. As Robert F. C. Young observes in *White Mythologies,* "deconstruction involves the decentralization and decolonization of European thought" (18). Furthermore, the deconstruction theory of Michel Foucault, a disciple of Nietzsche and opponent of structuralism, still privileges the author. As David H. Richter explains: "Foucault concentrates on the humanistic version of truth-power: authorship can be seen as a form of authority. Despite the apparent collapse of the **Romantic** conception of the author as incomprehensible genius and the advent of formalism and structuralism, which have successively substituted the central terms of work and of *écriture* (writing) for the romantic god-term of author, Foucault claims that authorship still retains its old power within advanced capitalism. While the author has been declared dead by some literary theorists, the author-function remains" (Richter 833). However, he would caution, like the Marxist critics, that *authority* also means the author exists with the text in a capitalist world of power and authority that shapes him or her.

Some recent explorations of the continuing relevance of deconstruction include Derek Attridge, who asks, "Who could have foreseen that Derrida's highly demanding engagements with his philosophical forebears and contemporaries, and occasionally with literary figures, would lead to a situation where it is almost impossible to enumerate exhaustively the fields that his work has touched?" One thinks of electronic media such as the internet. Derrida is widely translated, and his work is supplemented by his followers, among them Hélène Cixous, J. Hillis Miller, Hayden White, Jonathan Culler, Tzvetan Todorov, and Judith Butler. In his own day he greatly influenced Barthes, Foucault, Lacan, Bourdieu, Habermas, and de Man. Derrida also helped make possible the work of scholars Henry Louis Gates, Barbara Johnson, and Eve Kosofsky Sedgewick, and the general field of postcolonial studies (45–46). Attridge concludes with the claim for "Derrida's continuing engagement with the question of responsibility to the other" (49).

II. DIALOGICS

Dialogics is the key term used to describe the narrative theory of Mikhail Mikhailovich Bakhtin (1895–1975) and is specifically identified with his approach to questions of language in the **novel**. Dialogics (cf. "dialogue," "speaking across") refers to the inherent "addressivity" of all language; that is, all language is addressed to someone, never uttered without consciousness of a relationship between the speaker and the addressee. Though strongly influenced by linguistic approaches, in this humanistic emphasis, Bakhtin departed from purely linguistically based theories of literature and from other Russian formalists. He also felt suspicious of what was to become the psychological approach to literature, for he saw such an approach as a diminishment of the human soul and an attendant sacrifice of human freedom. It is safe to say that Bakhtin would have rejected *any* "ism" as an approach to the novel if it failed to recognize the essential indeterminacy of meaning outside the dialogic—and hence open—relationship between voices. Bakhtin would call such a closed view of meaning *monological* (single-voiced). For him, not only the interaction of characters but also the act of reading the novel in which they exist are living events. (In several ways, his ideas used reader-response criticism; see Chapter 3.)

The writings of Bakhtin go back to the 1920s and 1930s, but he remained largely unknown outside of the Soviet Union until translations in the 1970s brought him to world attention. His thought emphasizes language as an area of social conflict, particularly in the ways the discourse of characters in a literary work may disrupt and subvert the authority of ideology as expressed in a single voice of a narrator. He contrasts the monologic novels of writers such as Leo Tolstoy with the dialogic works of Fyodor Dostoyevsky. Instead of subordinating the voices of all characters to an overriding authorial voice, a writer such as Dostoyevsky creates a *polyphonic discourse* in which the author's voice is only one among many, and the characters are allowed free speech. Indeed, Bakhtin seems to believe that a writer such as Dostoyevsky actually thought in *voices* rather than in *ideas* and wrote novels that were thus primarily dialogical exchanges. What is important in them is not the presentation of facts about a character, but the significance of facts voiced by characters. Bakhtin identifies such polyphony as a special property of the novel, and he traces it back to its carnivalistic sources in classical, medieval, and Renaissance cultures (for "carnivalistic," see later discussion).

Bakhtin's focus is thus on the many voices in a novel, especially the way that some authors in particular, such as Dostoyevsky, allow characters' voices free play by actually placing them on the same plane as the voice of the author. In the 1970s, when his works were translated, Bakhtin became very important to critics of many literatures and has been found to be especially appropriate to the many-voiced, open-ended American novel.

In a sense there are multiple Bakhtins. He is read differently by Marxist critics, for example, than by more traditional humanistic critics. He himself partook of both Christianity and revolutionary Marxism. Marxist critics respond more to his notion of *chronotope*, or how time is encoded in fiction, and to his notion of the hidden *polemic* in all speech, whereas humanistic or moral critics address themselves more to his notion of *addressivity* because "addressing" someone promotes human connection and community. Since his emergence inside and outside the Soviet Union, his ideas have proved attractive to critics of all sorts of ideologies, including feminist critics.

Bakhtin's definition of the modern polyphonic, dialogic novel made up of a plurality of voices that avoids reduction to a single perspective indicates a concern on his part about the dangers of knowledge, whether inside or outside a text. That is, he points toward a parallel between issues of knowledge and power among the characters and those between the author and the reader. In both cases, knowledge is best thought of as dialogic rather than monologic, as open to the "other" rather than closed, as *addressing* rather than *defining*. Obviously Bakhtin's theory and criticism feature a powerful moral lesson about freedom.

Another of Bakhtin's key terms is *carnivalization*. Out of the primordial roots of the carnival tradition in folk culture, he argues, arises the many-voiced novel of the twentieth century. Dostoyevsky, for example, writes out of a rich tradition of seriocomic, dialogic, satiric literature that may be traced through Socratic dialogue and Menippian satire, Apuleius, Boethius, medieval mystery plays, Boccaccio, Rabelais, Shakespeare, Cervantes, Voltaire, Balzac, and Hugo. In the modern world this carnivalized antitradition appears most significantly in the novel. Just as the public ritual of carnival inverts values in order to question them, so may the novel call closed meanings into question. Of particular importance is the ritual crowning and decrowning of a mock king: in such actions, often through the medium of the **grotesque**, the people of a community express both their sense of being victims of power and their own power to subvert institutions. (One thinks of the Ugly King, El Rey Feo, of Latina\o tradition, as well as of the King of Comus in New Orleans' Mardi Gras.) As carnival concretizes the abstract in a culture, so Bakhtin claims that the novel carnivalizes through diversities of speech and voice reflected in its structure. Like carnival's presence in the public square, the novel takes place in the public sphere of the middle class. Carnival and the novel make power relative by *addressing* it. This makes the novel unique among other genres, many of which arose in the upper classes.

As Michael Holquist points out, rather than seeing the novel as a **genre** alongside others, such as **epic**, **ode**, or **lyric**, Bakhtin sees it as a supergenre that has always been present in Western culture, always breaking traditional assumptions about form. Holquist explains that " 'novel' is the name Bakhtin gives to whatever force is at work within a given literary system to reveal the limits, the artificial constraints of that system. Literary systems are comprised of **canons**, and 'novelization' is fundamentally anticanonical." The novel, Bakhtin argues, is "the only developing genre" (Bakhtin, *The Dialogic Imagination* 261–62, 291; Holquist, Introduction to *The Dialogic Imagination* xxxi). One can easily see the importance of such a transforming or relativizing function for Bakhtin, living as he did through the oppressions of the czars, the gloomy years of Stalin's purges, and the institution of official Soviet bureaucracy, even serving time in prison. Through carnivalization in the novel, opposites may come to know and understand one another in a way not otherwise possible. The key is the unfettered but clearly addressed human voice. Such a system is quite different from Marx's thesis, antithesis, and synthesis in that it does not offer a conclusion.

In his insistence on the novel's dynamism, Bakhtin provides an instructive perspective on its history and its future. As he observes, although the novel has existed since ancient times, its full potential was not developed until after the Renaissance. A major factor was the development of a sense of linear time, past, present, and especially future, moving away from the cyclical time of ancient epochs. Whereas the epic lives in cyclical time, the novel is oriented to contemporary reality. "From the very beginning, then," says Bakhtin, "the novel was structured...in the zone of direct contact with inconclusive present-day reality. At its core lay personal experience and free creative imagination." In its contemporaneity, the novel is "made of different clay [from] the other already completed genres," and "with it and in it is born the future of all literature." Bakhtin adds that the novel may absorb any other genre into itself and still remain a novel and that no other genre can do so. It is "ever-questing, ever examining itself and subjecting its established forms to review" (*The Dialogic Imagination* 38–40).

Bakhtin extends his ideas to *dialogicity*, which moves past genre to describe language. The person is always the "*subject of an address*" because one "cannot talk about him; one can only address oneself to him." One cannot understand another person as an object of neutral analysis or "master him through a merging with him, through empathy with him." The solution, dialogue, "is not the threshold to action, it is the action itself." Indeed, "to be means to communicate dialogically. When dialogue ends, everything ends." Bakhtin's principles of dialogue of the hero are by no means limited to actual dialogue in novels; they refer to a novelist's entire undertaking. Yet in a polyphonic novel, dialogues are unusually powerful (*The Dialogic Imagination* 338–39, 342).

Bakhtin's major principles include the freedom of the hero, special placement of the idea in the polyphonic design, and the principles of linkage that shape the novel into a whole—including multiple voices, **ambiguity**, multiple genres, stylization, **parody**, the use of negatives, and the function of the double address of the word both to another word and to another speaker of words. An author may build indeterminacies into his or her polyphonic design, introduce multiple voices, render ideas intersubjective, and leave novels seemingly unfinished—all to leave characters free. And no reader may "objectify an entire event according to some ordinary monologic category." The novel does not recognize any overriding monologic point of view outside the world of its dialogue, "but on the contrary, everything in the novel is structured to make dialogic opposition interminable. Not a single element of the work is structured from the point of view of a non-participating 'third person'" (*Problems of Dostoevsky's Poetics* 17).

Bakhtin describes how the novelist may voice a moral concern through narrative technique, particularly the power of knowledge to enact a design on that which is known. To think about other people "means to *talk with them; otherwise they immediately turn to us their objectivized side:* they fall silent, close up and congeal into finished, objectivized images." For this reason, the author of the polyphonic novel does not renounce his or her own consciousness but "to an extraordinary extent broaden[s], deepen[s] and rearrange[s] this consciousness...in order to accommodate the consciousness of others," and he or she does not turn other consciousnesses, whether character or reader, into objects of a single vision, but instead "re-creates them in their authentic *unfinalizability*" (*Problems of Dostoevsky's Poetics* 6–7, 59, 68). In "Author and Hero in Aesthetic Activity," an early essay, Bakhtin asks "What would I have to gain if another were to *fuse* with me? He would see and know only what I already see and know, he would only repeat in himself the inescapable closed circle of my own life; let him rather remain outside me" (quoted in Emerson 68–80).

By allowing characters their free speech, then, authors may thus ensure that they do not perpetrate a narrowing design by using their knowledge of the characters, a design that would violate them by restricting their freedom. To do this the author must create a "design for discourse" that allows the reader to interpret the characters' actions and words without the direct intervention of the author. Such "dialogic opposition" means that the greatest challenge for an author, "to create out of heterogeneous and profoundly disparate materials of varying worth a unified and integral artistic creation," cannot be realized by using a single "philosophical design" as the basis of artistic unity, just as musical polyphony cannot be reduced to a single accent. Contrasting this polyphony with novels in which the hero is the "voiceless object" of the "ideologue" author's "deduction," Bakhtin describes such intrusive narrators as those of many nineteenth-century British novelists. In the polyphonic novel, "there are only ... voice-viewpoints." Through characterization, Dostoyevsky structurally dramatizes "internal contradictions and internal stages in the development of a single person," allowing his characters "to converse with their own doubles, with the devil, with their alter egos, with caricatures of themselves."

Dialogicity in characterization also leads to particular structures. A polyphonic novel seeks to "*juxtapose* and *counterpose* [forms] dramatically," to "*guess at their interrelationships in the cross-section of a single moment.*" Not "evolution" but "*coexistence and interaction*" characterize such structures. "It cannot be otherwise," Bakhtin insists, for "only a dialogic and participatory orientation takes another person's discourse seriously, and is capable of approaching it as both a semantic position and another point of view." It is only through such orientation that one can come into "intimate contact with someone else's discourse" and yet not "fuse with it, not swallow it up, not dissolve in itself the other's power to mean" (*Problems of Dostoevsky's Poetics* 7–8, 18–20, 28–30, 63–64, 82–85).

Bakhtin's ideas are enjoying a resurgence of influence, especially among critics describing the voices of women of color. For example, Mae Gwendolyn Henderson, "Speaking in Tongues: Dialogics, Dialectics, and the Black Woman Writer's Literary Tradition," analyzes Sherley Anne Williams's novel *Dessa Rose* (1986) in terms of *heteroglossia* (discourse of different tongues) and *glossolalia* ("speaking in tongues"). Combining these two terms allows a model "that seeks to account for racial difference within gender identity and gender difference within racial identity" (117). Through heteroglossia, for characters like Williams's, "consciousness becomes a kind of 'inner speech' reflecting 'the outer word' in a process that links the psyche, language, and social interaction; if "the psyche functions as an internalization of heterogeneous social voices, black women's speech/writing becomes at once a dialogue between self and society and between self and psyche" (118–19). According to Henderson, such internal dialogues by black women authors of the late twentieth century have led the authors to privilege, rather than repress, "the other in ourselves" (119): While "glossolalia refers to the ability to 'utter the mysteries of the spirit,' heteroglossia describes the ability to speak in the multiple languages of public discourse" (122–23). Henderson describes how black women writers, "[i]n negotiating the discursive dilemma of their characters,… accomplish two objectives: the self-inscription of black womanhood, and the establishment of a dialogue of discourses with the other(s)" (131). By "others" she means hegemonic voices. She adds, "The self-inscription of black women requires disruption, rereading and rewriting the conventional and canonical stories, as well as revising the conventional generic forms that convey these stories" (131). This is a new black *Bildungsroman,* with its roots in the slave narrative. Other recent writers whose work can be analyzed this way include Ntozake Shange, especially her novel *Sassafrass, Cypress & Indigo* (1996); Sapphire, especially her novel *PUSH* (1996); and Tina McElroy Ansa, in *Ugly Ways* (1991) and its sequel *Taking After Mudear* (2007).

Bakhtinian literary theory continues to investigate new readings of literary texts. Lakshmi Bandlamudi sees Bakhtin's theory as concerning "collective consciousness, shared knowledge and meaning"; she also sees Bakhtin's literary analysis as expressing "moral judgments" (460). When we think about such stories as "Everyday Use," for example, her interpretation of Bakhtin that "meanings are constructed through a social intercourse" calling for "interdependence between the self and the other," becomes critical when we realize that "the other is crucial in accomplishing individual consciousness. Understanding comes not merely from the individual's own observation and knowledge construction but through human interactions." For Bakhtin, meanings are located not in the individual but "in between" the self and the other. While the former tradition states "'I own the meaning,' Bakhtin suggests 'We own the meaning.'" All individuals "experience and view the world from a unique position that they occupy in the world at a particular time in a particular place." It is this interconnectedness of time and space that Bakhtin calls the *chronotope.* The other, in Bakhtin's scheme, "does not necessarily complete the self's knowledge, but it certainly points out the incompleteness of the self's view" (462–63). In sum, she says "Bakhtin's theory of dialogics therefore suggests that deep meanings are revealed only when one comes in contact with the other. Such an encounter leads to a dialogue that transcends a one-sided view of particular meanings" (465).

III. LINGUISTIC APPROACHES IN PRACTICE

A. Deconstructing "To His Coy Mistress"

Marvell's poem may be said to "deconstruct" the speaker's object, love, even as he makes his suit. When he warns his Mistress that unless she makes love now, one day "worms shall try / That long-preserved virginity, / And your quaint honor turn to dust, / And into ashes all my lust," one wonders how this grotesquerie struck the Mistress.

The poem is a fantastic set of images moving over time and space at will, with no regard to **realism**. Thus it can be read as primarily a linguistic construction with little reference to the real world. From the Humber to the Ganges, from the Flood to the Conversion of the Jews, the poem takes liberties with what it will. Its goal seems to be to show the Mistress the speaker's erudition and wit and to amuse her, but his images are not always amusing. With deserts, the grave, vaults, gnawing time, fire, and birds of prey, Marvell deconstructs the **Petrarchan sonnet** into something altogether more modern and less certain about order in the world. Where Petrarch and the **courtly love** poets inspired by him would praise the mistress's body, Marvell disturbingly deconstructs her body, especially when he demands that she "show" her heart, which sounds quite literal given his dismemberment of her. The poem as a whole is full of plays on words, which Derrida saw as evidence of the deferral of meaning and of how language addresses only language. For example, the speaker puns on the word "quaint," which carries the pun on the common word for the pudendum, and her "quaint" is what will dry up after being penetrated by worms—hardly light-hearted play. Why would a lover use such shocking images? Do they perhaps indicate some doubt on his part, not whether he will be loved, but whether in the end it even matters?

The poem ends with neither a yes nor a refusal, and so it has no conclusion. We do not know what will happen or be said next. Whatever it is, it will be a response to the poem's words and, judging by the speaker's desperation, only words.

B. The Deep Structure of *Hamlet*

As structuralism views the literary text in regard to its connections to other systems at work, mainly other texts and the system of language itself, it looks for meaning in the units of the *signifier* (word/symbol) and the *signified,* the concept of the thing to be represented.

Unlike formalism, which still assumes a reality behind the matters of text, or the materialist approaches (such as Marxism) that see the extrinsic reality of author and thus the discourse as "real," structuralism sees the text as "virtual," containing within it a discourse among levels of what is "real." As Tzvetan Todorov claims: structuralists "can be satisfied neither by a pure description of the work nor by its interpretation in terms that are psychological or sociological or, indeed philosophical.... Its object is the literary discourse rather than works of literature" ("Structural Analysis of Narrative," 2100). That is, while formalism and structuralism both attend to the intricacies of the text, the structuralist is not interested in its meaning but only in *how* it achieves meaning. Todorov tends to focus on comparative plots in works looking at **motifs** and patterns, then he assigns the patterns the grammatological function of a sentence (subject, predicate, and adjective) to demarcate difference—thus *function* is born out of a discursive linguistic *experience.* Like Roland Barthes and Claude Lévi-Strauss, he believes that the role of structuralism is to chart how textual discourse reflects cultural discourses already at work. Structuralists thus look for motifs and patterns; for example, since Homer's ancient Greek epic, the journey and quest narrative has repeated up to the present time, as has ancient **drama** that first presented the plot of a **protagonist** who is high in power but who becomes too prideful and falls. Even when we divide literature up into genres—**comedy, tragedy, romance, satire** —we are being structuralists because we are describing an underlying structure that makes them identifiable.

Hamlet is an excellent text for structuralist analysis because its plot proceeds through a series of binaries, or oppositions, and these are played out in its language through powerful **images** and **metaphors**: male/female, life/death, madness/reason, sons/fathers, sons/mothers, mother/lover, father/murderer, reality and appearance (the Ghost), friendship and betrayal, and so on, making this motif of division the essential, or "deep," structure of the play and its language.

The motif of the theater stage itself questions appearance and reality. The Mousetrap Play at the center suggests that everything is both an illusion and a reality, as the players' words mimic the unspoken "word" Hamlet desires from Claudius. Hamlet's very first words in the play, "A little more than kin, and less than kind," addressed to the audience in an aside, is a sardonic response to Claudius's greeting and makes it clear that Hamlet sees and voices himself as separate from Claudius, who he condemns for his sinful act. However, the **alliteration** is a clue that these words actually mean the same thing (as their **etymologies** reveal, "a group of people united by common traits or interests"), or *should* mean the same thing, which in Denmark's court they do not. Hamlet is punning to say that his uncle is both too close to him now and also that he is anything but kindly disposed toward him, despite his false speechifying about his affection for his nephew. Neither "kin," "kind," nor "kingly," Hamlet views Claudius as a false value, especially because of his pompous (and self-contradictory) speech explaining his sudden marriage—"with mirth in funeral."

Shakespeare uses Hamlet's several **soliloquies** as interruptions in the "orderly" false narrative of the new king, disrupting the official line (or discourse) of the court with his own, and thus exposing its hypocrisy of false binaries. Like Hamlet's famous "To be, or not to be" soliloquy, his first one in Act I, Scene 2, begins immediately with a binary of life and death, of form and lack of form: "O, that this too too solid flesh would melt / Thaw and resolve itself into a dew!" Solidity opposes melting or thawing, and the motif of evaporating expresses his suicidal feelings. But the binary is not only personal and social; it suggests the overarching motif of the play, the distance between the physical and spiritual. Hamlet will not kill himself as he desires because of God's law against it. In the middle of the soliloquy, Hamlet cries out, "Heaven and earth!" Obviously, he is expressing a conflict he has with the demands of earthly things and his disgust with them and the mysterious demands of God. Another binary appears in Hamlet's comparison of his father and Claudius (it is interesting to note that in the play no one ever calls Claudius by name, as though he is merely negation). Hamlet also unfavorably compares his mother to his dead father, again stressing the need for the spiritual to control the bestial.

Structuralists have found the textual history of *Hamlet* another source for identifying parallel plots and sources. They refer to the revenge plays of Thomas Kyd, an older version of *Hamlet* called the *Ur-Hamlet,* and texts of medieval Danish law.

C. Language and Discourse in *Frankenstein*

Frankenstein is a very "talky" novel composed mainly of three competing discourses: Walton's, Victor's, and the Creature's. Students complain of the ornate Latinate style of **diction** from all three, though they are pleasantly surprised at the strong autonomous voice the Creature creates for himself. Scholars have contrasted Mary Shelley's discursive style, which privileges the concrete and concise, with her husband and editor Percy Shelley's highly formal and decorative style, which he employed when he edited the manuscript. Thus there are several competing discourses—to complicate things even more, there are several versions, Mary's manuscript, Percy's edited manuscript, the 1818 edition, and the 1831 edition, with the latter showing Mary's determination to restore some of her simpler language but at the same time to valorize her late husband. But what is revealed in *Frankenstein's* competing discourses is actually what is absent: there are very few dialogues in the novel, but in those which do appear, the interlocutors learn little about each other, preferring to stay within their own projections of "**Other.**" And in the **autobiographical** narratives, self-authorship fails or is subsumed by the narrative of an Other. Discourse in the novel is broken up not into an orderly system of signifier and signified, but a chaos of failed identities: creators who are not able to parent, men who create children without women, science and reason that lead to horror, Victor's "good" purpose to save the dead that brings about terrific destruction of human life, and a wholesale failure of social structure.

Such emphasis upon language and discourse and the presence of such binaries and structural problems opens up the novel to structuralist and poststructuralist analysis. Though the structuralist approach reveals much about discourse in *Frankenstein,* the novel's perverseness at every level makes it even more appealing to poststructuralists and deconstructionists. After all, it is *about* an unnatural construction that can speak and thus undermine his own construction *as* unnatural.

Let's begin with the overall structure of the novel. *Frankenstein* is often called a **"frame narrative,"** in this case having three frames. One might think the frame structure could neatly organize discourse into separate "boxes" and subordinate some to others, but this is not the case, as the competing narratives address one another in countless (and often disturbing) ways. The reader is not allowed to synthesize them but must continually respond to their differences and the ways discourses interpenetrate one another. For example, when Walton narrates Victor and Victor narrates the Creature, whose discourse is it? There is also an absent frame that disrupts the "order" or meaning of the three narratives, that of Mrs. Margaret Saville, whose response to these strange, disjointed narratives, unbelievable facts and stories, is not known. We assume that her rhetoric—if she is entirely absent from the story as a character—proved to be the most persuasive of all, if Walton indeed abandons his ambitions and returns home, but we do not know for sure. By extension, if she is a stand-in for the reader, the reader's response is deferred and hence ultimately invested with endless meanings, parallel to the many blanks and ellipses of the novel. Victor's ultimate goal—knowledge of life and death—is unattainable, just as a reader's "final" knowledge of the text is out of reach. All of the conflicting discourses of *Frankenstein* point to the failure of the kind of absolute knowledge Victor pursues and support a deconstructive philosophy.

Negation and binaries define each character. None of them is able to use words effectively to gain a desired outcome or overcome an unacceptable situation. For such a talky book, so many words fall on deaf ears: Elizabeth's and Clerval's heartfelt pleas to Victor, Margaret Saville's begging Walton to return home, Justine's protestations of innocence in the murder of William, the Creature's appeal for sympathy from Victor. Interestingly, despite his elision by his "author," Victor, and the world around him, the Creature is the most eloquent character in the book and the most intelligent and worth listening to. Amazingly, by merely eavesdropping on the De Laceys, he not only learns language but reads Milton, Goethe, and Plutarch. This is appropriate because he is also the only one who, through language, has to create himself as human. Yet the Creature is never named, and he is hardly physically described at all, as though words fail Victor in trying to understand what he has done. The Creature claims to be Victor's "Adam" but is described by his "father" as a devil. He wants only what any other human being would want, but his words draw no honest response from Victor; they completely miss their mark. Yet the Creature, in finding himself talking back to his "author," cannot be excluded so easily by the reader. Though Victor rejects the Creature's linguistic demand for his own signification, readers recognize that the Creature becomes himself through language and discourse; thus he most resembles an author.

Against monstrosity, which appears as "nature" time and time again in the novel, the Creature attempts to discover culture through language as an antidote to nature. This effort Peter Brooks calls "the pathos of a monsterism in doomed dialectic with nature" (205). His analysis of language in *Frankenstein* leads him to see it as a theme in itself: "There is, first of all, a criss-crossing of languages implicit in the text: with the arrival of Safie, we have a lesson in French being offered to a Turkish Arab, in a German-speaking region, the whole rendered for the reader in English. This well-ordered Babel calls attention to the fact and problem of transmission and communication, the motive for language" (210). Language is the Creature's only hope for a linkage with humankind, but it is an ambiguous gift; it helps him understand himself but does not provide a means to persuade Victor, or, in the case of his touching conversation with the elder De Lacey, a refuge from what Agatha and Felix see when they burst through the door and interrupt them. It ultimately fails to gain him entry into humankind though it has made him aware of his terrible origins and separation. But as Brooks points out, "[I]f language has failed to accomplish the Monster's desire, it has nonetheless provided the means for construction of a story within Frankenstein's story that will subvert the entire set of relations of which Frankenstein is a part. The Monster's use of language has contextualized desire itself as a systematic chain of signifiers whose rhetorical effect cannot be denied by the narratee" (211). Brooks also notes that it is Victor's fear of "the propagation of an aberrant signifier," that is, the possibility that the Creature will produce offspring (as another kind of "author") that leads him to break his word and destroy the female Creature. Another kind of deferral of meaning occurs as the Creature does not strike directly at his signifier, Victor, "but, by displacement, by **metonymy,** at closely related elements in Frankenstein's own chain of existence and events"—Clerval, William, Justine, Elizabeth. For creator and created, the other represents what is lacking in the self; thus the Creature's death will mean Victor's own (213–14). They cannot escape each other because they cannot adequately address each other as separate selves and so remain entwined in mutual failure to signify.

The novel is rampant with verbal misunderstandings and misinterpretations. For example, Victor misinterprets his father's rejection of Cornelius Agrippa; though his father calls it "sad trash," Victor doesn't seem to get the message and later blames his father for not dissuading him more thoroughly. Victor misinterprets the Creature's threat to be with him on his wedding night (though one wonders how he could miss this). But most importantly Victor fails to understand his *own* words; even at the end, when he warns Walton against similar endeavors, he still fails to display more pity for his victims than self-pity, as when he moans about how affected he is by Elizabeth's death but says nothing about her suffering. His words are obfuscation of his guilt. And of course, Victor entirely misunderstands the teachings of science and morality, and of life itself, despite his long-winded defense of himself and his lofty aims.

Had the Creature in the novel been inarticulate as he is so often portrayed in film and popular culture, Victor might have had the last word. In comparing Victor's and the Creature's discourses, however, one cannot help but recognize how the Creature's narrative—which Victor fails to appreciate—forms a powerful counter-discourse to "meaning" of any earthly kind, since it comes from the marginalized and negated space of a nonperson. But if the idealized romantic self is the cause of Victor's blindness to others, if in his **hubris** Victor wanted to find the secret of life, he seeks to avoid his own secrets. (For example, he seems inordinately attached to his mother, blames his father, refuses to marry his sweetheart, and betrays friends and family alike; because he just can't explain himself and what he did, he adds layer upon layer of deception to his discourse.) Like Hamlet, Victor fails at the most important kind of knowledge: self-knowledge, let alone the ability to articulate it clearly in a stable discourse. The attempt to deconstruct the binaries of *Frankenstein*—including life/death, men/women, children/parents, domestic/ professional, science/morality, nature/culture, indeed, right and wrong—results only in more contradictions, mirroring the Creature's own constructed/deconstructed body.

Such a deconstructed set of discourses in *Frankenstein* reflects its **Gothic** nature and demonstrates how deconstruction fits the text more than just structuralism. As David Punter notes, "in the 1990s in particular, we have found ourselves at a peculiar confluence between the major motifs of the Gothic and a set of ways of thinking increasingly current in contemporary criticism and theory"—poststructuralist concerns such as competing discourses or slips of the tongue, tricks of the eye, endless meaning and nonmeaning" (Punter, ix–x). Commenting on

Punter, Mark Hennelly notes that this means that "what we see is always haunted by something else, by that which has not quite been seen, in history or in text—just as Gothic itself, we might say, consists of a series of texts which are always dependent on other texts, texts which they are not, texts which are ceaselessly invoked while no less ceaselessly misread, models of reconnaissance in the form of lost manuscripts, of misheard messages in cyberspace, in the attempt to validate that which cannot be validated, the self-sufficiency, the autonomy of textuality that is already ruined beyond repair" (Hennelly 70). Such disorder, while clearly describing the world of *Frankenstein,* leaves readers with a seemingly endless array of failures to "order" the text or know its "nature." Who, after all, is speaking in *Frankenstein,* and to whom?

D. Huck and Jim: Dialogic Partners

In *Was Huck Black?* Shelley Fisher Fiskin argues that Twain drew Huck's voice from that of a young African American servant he knew, making the issue of (interracial) voices in dialogue in the novel an element of its very creation. As Twain's **vernacular** American narrator, Huck and his voice had enormous influence on later American fiction; indeed, some attribute the novel's greatness to Huck's unique and original voice. Twain claimed that he had carefully studied the **dialects** he uses in the novel, but it is probably more his own exquisite ear for voices that brought the world such memorable speakers as pap Finn, the King and the Duke, and the raftsmen, and Huck himself. Why is Huck's voice believable and "honest" and others merely the mere tricks of criminals and con men?

One answer is that Huck, unlike these pontificating fakes, does not deliver monologues but is always in dialogue with someone, beginning with the reader (if negatively, "You don't know me..."), but also including the various night watchmen and posses he encounters, to whom he lies with increasing skill, often based on whatever they say to him, as well as Tom Sawyer, Jim, Mrs. Judith Loftus, Buck Grangerford, Sophia Grangerford, "the Harelip," and Mary Ann Wilks. When he talks to someone but is not in dialogue with them, as Bakhtin would define it, he becomes a fool: with the "harelip," with lawyer Levi Bell, and, in the end, with Tom. Dialogic relationships of the kind Bakhtin described, in which *heteroglossia* uncovers the relationships between speakers, are the only safe ones in the novel. Church piety, pap's claims to own his son, bourgeois pretentions: all these are counteracted by the primary dialogic relationship between Huck and Jim.

As Jonathan Arac observes, *Huckleberry Finn* is seen by Bakhtinian critics as transforming "the materials of everyday life into the dignity of art through the power of its idiomatic, vernacular style, which in turn exercises a critical force against traditionally elevated notions of dignity." Bakhtin's emphasis upon "vernacular realism" is based on his analysis of Dostoyevsky's radical and atheistic characters, whose speeches make them appear as heroes and **antiheroes**. (Dostoyevsky himself was a Russian Orthodox Christian and a Marxist.) For Bakhtin, a novel's greatness arises from "antagonistic 'dialogue' among different ways of speaking—representing different social values" (37).

Bakhtin sees the novel as an ever-developing, multilayered genre that is full of dialogues, dialects, and parodies, the only literary genre able to accomplish full dialogicity because it is infinitely flexible in form and can include multiple voices. Through dialogicity, Twain thus invented a new kind of novel. If ever there was what Bakhtin envisioned as the polyphonic novel, *Huckleberry Finn* is it. Voices from all classes, races, ages, and genders mingle with varying regional dialects, the whole sprinkled with the rich and comically engaging lingo of the frontier, though spattered, to be sure, with the language of the sermon, oratory, Bible, Shakespeare, and romantic novels and poetry. In its linguistic texture alone *Huckleberry Finn* is unique.

Aileen Chris Shafer helps explain Bakhtin's relevance to reading *Huckleberry Finn*, beginning with Huck's own discourse, which vacillates to and from others that dominate him at various times from "the language and concepts of Tom's romantic discourse to the widow's religious discourse to Pap's [sic] larcenous discourse.... Additionally, Huck finds himself in a dilemma because 'racial' discourse, a discourse that dehumanizes slaves, does not jibe with what he learns about Jim." The novel demonstrates how slippery it is to engage multiple discourses, how easy it is to fall back into the prevailing discourse of racism of his world when Huck assumes Tom's identity. Paradoxically, Shafer points out, it is in Jim's "signifying" discourse of indirection and deception that an authentic voice is able to invert through parody dominant discourses; however, Jim also employs a "freeman's discourse" when he chastises Huck for putting "trash" on him after they are separated in the fog at Cairo. Jim's shifts, and not Huck's, are truly "dialogic." Jim speaks by signifying on others throughout the novel, "a technique that allows him to appear to keep within cultural expectations and prescriptions, but when he speaks directly, when he oversteps 'knowing his place,' his discourse astonishes, frightens, and disconcerts Huck—responses Twain satirizes" (150–52).

But Jim's free speech is what helps Huck recognize him as a person, so he can never go back to the Widow and Miss Watson. Jim's powers of interpretation distinguish him among the other slaves, with his five-cent piece and hairball. Two episodes Shafer singles out as demonstrating Jim's "system of signs" include the disputes between Huck and him over King Solomon's wisdom and another over the French language. In the first case "Jim recognizes the absolute power of one man over another" instead of the received interpretation of Solomon's decree, and in the second the issue is "speaking like a man," which Jim's society does not permit him to do (154–55). If Jim has once again to put on the voice of the subservient slave to please Tom and Huck in their games with him at the Phelps Farm, he ends up free, while Huck remains unable to adopt a single social discourse nor synthesize ("dialogize") the multiple discourses he encounters, and so disappears.

Let us further apply these perspectives from Bakhtin. From the very opening of the novel the question of who is speaking to whom is paramount. Twain as author threatens readers with death if they find a (unitary) plot, and the first paragraph raises troubling questions about a traditional speaker-audience rhetorical direction:

> You don't know about me without you have read a book by the name of The Adventures of Tom Sawyer; but that ain't no matter. That book was made by Mr. Mark Twain, and he told the truth, mainly. There was things which he stretched, but mainly he told the truth. That is nothing. I never seen anybody but lied one time or another, without it was Aunt Polly, or the widow, or maybe Mary. Aunt Polly—Tom's Aunt Polly, she is—and Mary, and the Widow Douglas is all told about in that book, which is mostly a true book, with some stretchers, as I said before. (1)

In this opening, which should draw in the reader, announce its subject, and, most importantly, introduce the authority of the narrator's voice, Huck's words undermine these intentions by casting doubt on who is the "author" of the text and who is merely a character, putting into dialogue elements of a text usually kept apart by convention. The dialogic must be the model for reading, since the authority of the author has been questioned. In addition, the number of times Huck mentions that *Tom Sawyer* was "mostly" true, with "stretchers," indicates Huck's own doubts about truth as he has been taught truth by adults, and how he learns truth can exist only contingent upon its interpreters. His later decision to tear up the letter to Miss Watson is a decision against definitive truth, so that going to hell is preferable to conformity with received ideas. Twain and his protégé Huck are thus the trickster-authors who disengage "truth" from monologic relationships.

It is really only in his dialogues with Jim that Huck develops new moral understanding, the two bonding in long conversations and debates as they drift downriver. In Chapter 16, the subject of language itself is debated, as Huck tries to explain to Jim that French people speak another language. Though one might feel drawn to laugh at Jim's ignorance, as usual he has the last word when he establishes that a cow and a cat could talk differently, but a man is a man and should speak the same language, leading Huck to abandon his lesson. As in many dialogues in the book, such as the one in the same chapter on King Solomon, Jim may appear to be ignorant, but he is right on the larger theme: King Solomon should not be so arrogant as to perform his experiment upon human nature, and men should talk straight-talk to men. Yet misunderstandings are not abated in the novel; when, for instance, the King and the Duke pose as the brothers of the deceased Peter Wilks, the King employs his fake English accent, and he says instead of "obsequies" "orgies." He furiously tries to explain "orgies" as the way people in England now pronounce the word, generating his own self-parody and a parody of discourse itself. Just talking will not save anyone in this novel, due to its theme of lies, unidirectional and hence destructive.

Through his self-voicing and dialogues with Jim, Huck should, like the **Bildungsroman** hero, be able to achieve selfhood. But Jim is going home, he has lost the sense of dialogue with Tom, and all that surrounds him is false rhetoric masking base actions. He recedes into silence by heading for the Territory, an eloquent if silent indictment of the world of false discourse he escapes. Huck silently "talks back" to civilization in the end and disappears, leaving interpretation of him up to the reader's responsibility in the dialogue.

Paul Lynch's Bakhtinian reading of *Huckleberry Finn* confirms a number of our observations and provides more. Lynch invokes Bakhtin's statement that "The prose writer does not purge words of intentions and tones that are alien to him, he does not destroy the seeds of social *heteroglossia* embedded in words, he does not eliminate those language characterizations and speech mannerisms (potential narrator-personalities) glimmering behind the words and forms, each at a different distance from the ultimate semantic nucleus of his work, that is, the center of his own personal intentions" (298). Lynch points out, "Whereas the narrator of *Tom Sawyer* is absolutely authoritative, Huck presents a rather uniliterary authority. In *Tom Sawyer*, Twain forces language to submit to his own intentions; however, by making Huck the narrator of *Huckleberry Finn*, Twain relinquishes control over heteroglossia"; while Tom is a "sanctioned rebel," Huck and Jim are beyond sanction. Because Twain allows Huck to tell his own tale, he can be seen by the reader to experience a Bakhtinian "ideological becoming," a successful struggle between the authoritative discourse that surrounds him and his own "internally persuasive" word, as when he tears up the letter to Miss Watson. He is an outcast from the authoritative discourse of St. Petersburg and everywhere else on the river. Back home, the Widow Douglas's attempts to "override Huck's own accents, gestures, and modifications by 'sivilizing' him" place these two "words" within him in conflict (173–74).

Today, the book's use of the word "nigger," often referred to as the "n-word," and even its use of dialect for Jim has kept it a subject of ongoing dialogue about its suitability for the classroom, as well as its appropriateness of being called the great American novel. Despite the historical accuracy, understanding and even hearing the "n-word" may be the biggest challenge of interpreters of *Huckleberry Finn* today, but it should not elide *all* the other dialogic discourse of what surely is one of the greatest works against slavery ever written. It is a tribute to Twain that the book remains in dialogue with its opponents, just what a satirist would desire.

E. "Speak of the Devil!": The Sermon in "Young Goodman Brown"

Earlier in this chapter we enumerated how poststructuralism and deconstruction engage in a critique of meaning: the stability or unity of signifier and signified is challenged, and instead emphasis is placed mostly on the free play of language. Poststructuralism also entails an antihumanistic criticism of the human subject itself—that is, the subject as a stable, unified source of consciousness and an autonomous agent. This critiques the concept of "author" too—especially with reference to Michel Foucault's definition of the "author" as a "discursive unit," splitting "subject" into the *subject of enunciation* and the *enunciated subject*. Finally, poststructuralism looks for texts that exhibit self-referentiality and hence question the act of textual representation of an **Other**.

Hawthorne was primarily concerned with issues of subjectivity and individual psychology, mainly in how these can fit a person for success in a social reality. His dilemma was to validate individual consciousness and subjectivity but do it within community. Joseph Alkana puts it this way: "How can the affirmation of individual consciousness and conscience authorize a commitment to social cohesion, a commitment that simultaneously would assure the possibility of individual experience?" (3). In "Young Goodman Brown," Hawthorne critiques the anti-individualistic religious authority of the day as well as the autonomy of the individual.

Puritanism is the **hegemony** that rules Young Goodman Brown, his wife, and his community. According to the Calvinism they practice, there is no room for "gray areas"; humans are either sinners or saved, though the saved are sinners who happen to be forgiven. Sin defines and wholly describes the human spirit. Against this essential category Hawthorne uses situations, settings, plot, character, and word-pairs to attack the binaries of good/evil, saved/damned, truth/dream, male/female, body/spirit. The human spirit in the reader rebels at the conclusion of the story, for Goodman Brown falls prey to the worst that his religious and social binaries can do to him.

There are so many linguistic oppositions that reveal binaries in this story that we give only a few representative ones from the opening of the story, beginning with the first lines:

> "Young Goodman Brown came forth at sunset into the street at Salem village; but put his head back, after crossing the threshold." (liminal time of day, indecision)
>
> "'What, my sweet, pretty wife, dost thou doubt me already, and we but three months married?'" (a rhetorical turning of the tables on his wife's protests)
>
> "'Then God bless you!' said Faith, with the pink ribbons; 'and may you find all well when you come back.'" (***double-entendre***)
>
> "'Well, she's a blessed angel on earth; and after this one night I'll cling to her skirts and follow her to heaven.'" (denial)
>
> "With this excellent resolve for the future, Goodman Brown felt himself justified in making more haste on his present evil purpose." (rationalization)

As many have noted, the story makes symbolic use of word *play*: "My poor little Faith"; "Faith kept me back a while"; "'My Faith is gone!' cried he, after one stupefied moment." There are several cases of mistaken identity: "'We are a people of prayer, and good works to boot, and abide no such wickedness,'" says Goodman Brown. And, from Goody Cloyse, "'Ah, forsooth, and is it your worship indeed?' cried the good dame. 'Yea, truly is it, and in the very image of my old gossip, Goodman Brown, the grandfather of the silly fellow that now is.'"

Binaries flourish between words and images in the story: "Whither, then, could these holy men be journeying so deep into the heathen wilderness?" "Once the listener fancied that he could distinguish the accents of townspeople of his own, men and women, both pious and ungodly, many of whom he had met at the communion table, and had seen others rioting at the tavern. The next moment, so indistinct were the sounds, he doubted whether he had heard aught but the murmur of the old forest, whispering without a wind." And "But, irreverently consorting with these grave, reputable, and pious people, these elders of the church, these chaste dames and dewy virgins, there were men of dissolute lives and women of spotted fame, wretches given over to all mean and filthy vice, and suspected even of horrid crimes." Dichotomies—not **dialectics**—of opposites only confuse Young Goodman Brown: holy men/evil journey, hearing/understanding, the pious/the godless.

When he arrives at the witch meeting, Young Goodman Brown initially describes the congregation as "a grave and dark-clad company," setting up the image of Puritan church-goers and describing them both from what he has been taught of heaven: all are equal at last. But it is not until the sermon of preacher/ devil that the target of Hawthorne's satire becomes clear: it is the church itself, and especially the Calvinist religion. Everything the devil says is demonstrably true, especially what he explains as the knowledge of good and evil. But unlike the church's management of good and evil, the devil seems to describe reality; all *are* sinners before God. However, neither Goodman Brown nor the rest of his audience, presumably, are quite ready for this message; if we are to understand the story at all realistically, then everyone in Salem is to some degree a hypocrite, even Faith herself. Hardly a shocking teaching in Christianity, but to this repressive Puritan it is blasphemy. Ironically, the devil spells out the awful truth of sin Calvinism taught.

In the devil's sermon, the deconstruction of Brown's received ideas about Calvinism and his community are eloquently challenged: "With reverence be it spoken, the figure bore no slight similitude, both in garb and manner, to some grave divine of the New England churches." He invites Brown and Faith, his ' "children' " to join "the communion" of their race. Pointing to the diverse assembly below, from savage Indians to "hoary" elders of the church: " 'Ye deemed them holier than yourselves, and shrank from your own sin, contrasting it with their lives of righteousness and prayerful aspirations heavenward. Yet here are they all in my worshipping assembly." Theirs will be the ability to sniff out sin in everyone, which, contrary to Calvinist teachings, damns them to misery. The devil concludes, " 'Evil must be your only happiness. Welcome again, my children, to the communion of your race.' " The key word is *communion,* for here it means anything but that. Rather it ironically foreshadows a lifeless isolation of the individual that drives everyone away from Goodman Brown. "Communion" is appropriately displaced by the last word of the story, "gloom."

F. "Asalamalakim!": Linguistic Distortion in "Everyday Use"

There is some confusion over names in "Everyday Use," just as there is conflict over identity itself. Hearing Dee's boyfriend's greeting, "Asalamalakim," Mrs. Johnson at first thinks this is his name, but it is actually an Arabic-Lugandan phrase meaning "peace be with you," like the Hebrew *shalom aleichem*. In both cases the person being greeted repeats the words in reverse order. Dee, who wants to hold to her African heritage, also greets her mother in Lugandan (Lugandan is the main language spoken in Uganda). Dee's adopted name "Wa-su-zo-Tean-o" means "Good Morning" in Lugandan. Perhaps she is not yet comfortable with it, as she pronounces it carefully by syllables as though she has merely memorized it. Hakim-a-Barber is the name of Dee's boyfriend, and this name too is contested: it is a corruption of the name Hakim al *Baba* (Barber is not an Arab name, but in Mrs. Johnson's mouth it would probably have been pronounced the same way). Walker is satirizing African Americans who try to shed their modern, American roots to take on African names without question. *Hakim* means (religious) ruler or leader; Walker therefore may be adding to the irony when Mrs. Johnson shows her respect for her Muslim neighbors when she says: "You must belong to those beef-cattle peoples down the road. They said Asalamalakim when they met you, too." But Hakim answers: "I accept some of their doctrines, but farming and raising cattle is not my style." He accepts what is suitable for him and leaves the rest, picking and choosing among interests.

The irony in "Asalamalakim" and "Wa-su-zo-Tean-o" is also evident in other linguistic conflicts within the story. Mrs. Johnson fantasizes about appearing with Dee on the Tonight Show, thinking how "Johnny Carson has much to do to keep up with my quick and witty tongue." But she reflects, "that is a mistake.... Who ever knew a Johnson with a quick tongue?" Yet Dee has just that. Dee subdued what friends she had as a girl—Furtive boys in pink shirts hanging about on washday after school. Nervous girls who never laughed. Impressed with her, they worshipped the well-turned phrase, the cute shape, the scalding humor that erupted like bubbles in lye. She read to them." Thus Dee uses the word as a form of power her mother lacks, but we must recognize that this description of Dee and her friends *is* her mother's. Mrs. Johnson underestimates her own linguistic power, as in her **metaphor** of a humor that feels like lye, a powerful and accurate simile for Dee. Dee rejects her name, not understanding that it was not imposed on her by whites but is her aunt's, grandmother's, and great-grandmother's, just in the way that she values the quilts for their form but not their substance, disrespecting the family history. Maggie, the quietest person in the room, is a source of family history; when Dee asks about who whittled the butter churn, Maggie informs her that it was Aunt Dee's first husband, Henry, called "Stash." Dee responds, "'Maggie's brain is like an elephant's.'" And then Maggie gets to speak the most generous words in the story: "'She can have them, Mama....I can 'member Grandma Dee without the quilts.'" In the structuralist sense, Maggie is drawn not to the signifier (the literal word, the quilt) but to the signified, her memory of family stories. Though Dee accuses her mother and sister of not understanding their "heritage," it is she who does not. Replacing all the old words with new ones will neither preserve the past nor elide it. In satisfied silence, the mother and daughter sit in the yard, until it is time for bed. Nothing else about the day's events need be said: Maggie's smile says it all.

IV. SUMMARY OF KEY POINTS

- *Structuralism*: Identifies structures in language, or systems of relationships, which endow *signs* (e.g., words) or items (fashion, automobiles, the mall) with identities and meanings that show how we think. Based in philosophy and linguistics.

- *The Linguistic Model*: Ferdinand de Saussure's *Course in General Linguistics* (1916) distinguishes between *la langue* (language possessed by the community) and *la parole* (a speech-event or application of *la langue* in writing). *La langue* is the source of grammar and syntax. In *la parole,* semantic signs occur which join the *signifier* (word) with the *signification* (meaning). These can be in the form of surface elements or comprise the "deep structure" of a text. Interpretation is thus a system like language itself.

- *Russian Formalism*: Figures such as Vladimir Propp and Victor Shklovsky used structuralism to study many phenomena, such as folk tales. Shklovsky defined literature's tendency to *estrangement* and *defamiliarzation* to move readers away from habitual responses to ordinary experience; he also distinguished between *story* (events in chronological sequence) and *plot* (artful rearrangement and thus defamiliarization).

- *Claude Lévi-Strauss and Semiotics*: Lévi-Strauss's *Structural Anthropology* appeared in the 1950s and used what he called the *paradigmatic* approach to analyze the *deep* or *embedded* structures in a text, especially those that seem to evade a conscious or rational arrangement by the literary artist; these he identified as *binary oppositions.* His work is closely related to structuralism and also to myth criticism.

- *French Structuralism*: Sometimes called the "school of Paris," these structuralists include Roland Barthes, Jacques Derrida, Michel Foucault, and Tzvetan Todorov. They followed Saussure and argued that narrative is a kind of analogy to the sentence: the text, like the sentence, expresses the writer's mind and is a whole composed of distinguishable parts. They use the terms *histoire* (sequence of events from beginning to end) and *discours* (discourse, that is, the narrative rearranged for aesthetic effects). The text is a *message* which requires a *code* to read it, such as the code of puzzles the text raises, symbolic codes, or cultural codes.

- *British and American Interpreters*: Jonathan Culler and Robert Scholes helped bring structuralism to the English language; Culler insists that literature has no existence beyond a display of literary conventions that enable readers to identify as a sign system they know and to find contexts that make the text less strange and defamiliarized.

- *Deconstruction*: Views texts as subversively undermining their surface meanings; as the slippages and deferrals of meaning between words in the text are dynamic, the text is always in a state of linguistic change and thus can furnish only provisional meanings. Analysis is uncovering the contradictions within a text. Jacques Derrida was the most important deconstructionist;

he especially emphasized the *"play"* of language as opposed to the idea of a single meaning, or *logocentrism*.

- *Dialogics*: The key term used in the narrative theory of Mikhail Bakhtin, who saw all language as *addressed* to someone, and hence meaning is to be found not in its structure as a system but in the relationship between partners in dialogue. The language of dialogue is often *polemic* but it is also *humanistic*. The novel best exemplifies the importance of language as dialogic. Bakhtin studied Fyodor Dostoyevsky as a master of such *polyphonic discourse* and the grotesque as a means of social rebellion. He privileges such forms as multiple genres, parody, and satire. Bakhtin's notion of *chronotope* describes how time is encoded in fiction.

V. LIMITATIONS OF LINGUISTIC APPROACHES

As David H. Richter has noted, the main problem with structuralism "was the irresponsible promise of a synthesis of all human knowledge," based on the assumption that literature always directly mirrors the linguistic features of the language in which it was written, a claim that has been hard to prove (Richter 826). In nature, he points out, second-order systems (literature) do not necessarily replicate first-order (language) systems. However, without the structuralists, there would have been no poststructuralism to question such linguistic order. Deconstruction, which followed, returned to close reading of individual texts rather than merely commenting on the process of interpretation as the critical goal.

Deconstruction certainly has its critics as well, but we should remember that it was as much inspired by the New Critics and their formalism (no deconstruction without close reading—*really* close reading) as it was a reaction against structuralism. The major attacks on deconstruction have responded to what is perceived as a seeming lack of seriousness about reading literature, and, more seriously, to refuse to privilege reading as an act at all. Its opponents feel that it threatens the stability of the literary academy, that it promotes philosophical and professional nihilism, that it is too dogmatic, that it is willfully obscure and clique-ridden, and that it is mostly responsible for the heavy emphasis on theory over practical criticism in recent decades. Various critiques of deconstruction have pointed out that the deconstructive readings all sound oddly similar, that it does not seem to matter if the author under study is Nietzsche or Wordsworth. Furthermore, deconstructive readings always seem to start out with a set conclusion, lacking any suspense about the outcome of the reading.

QUICK REFERENCE

Alkana, Joseph. *The Social Self: Hawthorne, Howells, William James, and Nineteenth-Century Psychology.* Lexington: University Press of Kentucky, 1997.
Arac, Jonathan. *Huckleberry Finn as Idol and Target: The Functions of Criticism in Our Time.* Madison: University of Wisconsin Press, 1997.

Attridge, Derek. "Deconstruction Today." *Etudes Anglaises* 58,1 (2005): 43–52.

Bakhtin, Mikhail. *The Dialogic Imagination*. Ed. Michael Holquist. Trans. Caryl Emerson and Michael Holquist. Austin: University of Texas Press, 1981.

———. *The Dialogic Imagination: Four Essays by M. M. Bakhtin*. Trans. Caryl Emerson and Michael Holquist. Austin: University of Texas Press, 1981.

———. *Problems of Doestoevsky's Poetics*. Ed. and trans. Caryl Emerson. Introduction by Wayne C. Booth. Minneapolis: University of Minnesota Press, 1984.

Bandlamudi, Lakshmi. *The History of Understanding and Understanding of History: A Dialogue with Epic Heroes and Heroines*. Diss. City University of New York, 1994.

Barthes, Roland. S/Z Paris: Seuil, 1970.

———. *The Pleasure of the Text*. 1973. Trans. Richard Miller. New York: Hill and Wang, 1975.

———. "The Death of the Author." *Image-Music-Text*. Selected and Trans. Stephen Heath. New York: Hill and Wang, 1977. 142–48.

Bauer, Dale M. *Feminist Dialogics: A Theory of Failed Community*. Albany: State University of New York Press, 1988.

Brooks, Peter. " 'Godlike Science/Unhallowed Arts': Language, Nature, and Monstrosity." In *The Endurance of Frankenstein: Essays on Mary Shelley's Novel*. Eds. George Levine and U. C. Knoepflmacher. Berkeley: University of California Press, 1979. 205–220.

Clark, Katerina, and Michael Holquist. *Mikhail Bakhtin*. Cambridge, MA: Harvard University Press, 1985.

Culler, Jonathan. *Structuralist Poetics: Structuralism, Linguistics, and the Study of Literature*. Ithaca, NY: Cornell University Press, 1975.

———. *On Deconstruction: Theory and Criticism After Structuralism*. Ithaca, NY: Cornell University Press, 1982.

———. Foreword to *The Poetics of Prose*, by Tzvetan Todorov, Trans. Richard Howard. Ithaca, NY: Cornell University Press, 1977.

de Man, Paul. *Blindness and Insight: Essays in the Rhetoric of Contemporary Criticism*. New York: Oxford University Press, 1971.

———. *Allegories of Reading: Figural Language in Rousseau, Nietzsche, Rilke, and Proust*. New Haven, CT: Yale University Press, 1979.

de Saussure, Ferdinand. *Course in General Linguistics*. 1916. Trans. Roy Harris. New York: McGraw–Hill, 1965.

Derrida, Jacques. *A Derrida Reader: Between the Blinds*. Ed. Peggy Kamuf. New York: Columbia University Press, 1991.

———. "Différence." *Margins of Philosophy*. Trans. Alan Bass. Chicago: University of Chicago Press, 1982.

———. *Of Grammatology*. Trans. Gayatri Chakravorty Spivak. Baltimore: Johns Hopkins University Press, 1976.

———. *Speech and Phenomena: And Other Essays on Husserl's Theory of Signs*. Trans. David B. Allison. Evanston, IL: Northwestern University Press, 1973.

———. *Writing and Difference*. 1967. Trans. Alan Bass. Chicago, Ill.: University of Chicago Press, 1978.

Eco, Umberto. *A Theory of Semiotics*. Bloomington: Indiana University Press, 1976.

Emerson, Caryl. "The Tolstoy Connection." *PMLA* 100 (1985): 68–80.

Erlich, Victor. *Russian Formalism: History, Doctrine*. 4th edn. The Hague: Mouton, 1980.

Fishkin, Shelley Fisher. *Was Huck Black?: Mark Twain and African-American Voices*. Stanford, Calif.: Stanford University Press, 1993.

Foucault, Michel, "What Is an Author?" 1969. Rpt. trans. Josué Harari. *The Critical Tradition: Classic Texts and Contemporary Trends*. Ed. David H. Richter. 3rd edn. New York: St. Martin's, 2007, 904–14.

Greimas, A. J. *On Meaning: Selected Writings in Semiotic Theory*. 1970–73. Trans. Paul J. Perron and Frank Collins. Minneapolis: University of Minnesota Press, 1987.

Hall, Stuart. "Cultural Studies: Two Paradigms." 1980. Rpt. in David H. Richter, *The Critical Tradition: Classic Texts and Contemporary Trends*. 3rd edn. New York: St. Martin's, 2007, 1404–18.

Hartman, Geoffrey. *Criticism in the Wilderness: The Study of Literature Today*. New Haven, Conn.: Yale University Press, 1980.

Hawkes, Terence. *Structuralism and Semiotics*. Berkeley: University of California Press, 1977.

Henderson, Mae Gwendolyn. "Speaking in Tongues: Dialogics and Dialectics and The Black Woman Writer's Literary Tradition." In *Changing Our Own Words*. Ed. Cheryl Wall. Rutgers University Press, 1989.

Hennelly, Mark M. "Framing the Gothic: From Pillar to Post-Structuralism." *College Literature* 28.3 (Fall 2001): 68–87.

Hoggart, Richard. *The Uses of Literacy: Changing Patterns in English Mass Culture*. Harmondsworth, England: Penguin, 1957.

Holquist, Michael. Introduction to *The Dialogic Imagination: Four Essays by M. M. Bakhtin*. Trans. Caryl Emerson and Michael Holquist. Austin: University of Texas Press, 1981.

———. *Dialogism: Bakhtin and His World*. New York: Routledge, 1990.

Jackson, Claire. Translator's Preface to *Structural Anthropology*, by Claude Lévi-Strauss. Vol. 1. New York: Basic Books, 1963.

Jakobson, Roman. "Closing Statement: Linguistics and Poetics." *Style in Language*. Ed. Thomas A. Sebeok. Cambridge, Mass.: MIT Press, 1960. 350–77.

Jameson, Frederic. *The Prison-House of Language: A Critical Account of Structuralism and Russian Formalism*. Princeton, NJ: Princeton University Press, 1972.

Johnson, Barbara. *A World of Difference*. Baltimore, MD: Johns Hopkins University Press, 1988.

Leitch, Vincent B. *Deconstructive Criticism: An Advanced Introduction*. New York: Columbia University Press, 1983.

———. "Structural Analysis of Narrative." *The Norton Anthology of Theory and Criticism*. Leitch, Vincent. et al. New York: Norton, 2001. 1099–2105.

Lévi-Strauss, Claude. *Structural Anthropology*. 1958. Trans. Claire Jacobson and Brooke Grundfest Schoepf. New York: Basic Books, 1963.

———. *The Raw and the Cooked*. London: Jonathan Cape, 1970.

———. *Structural Anthropology*. Vol. 2. Trans. Monique Layton. New York: Basic Books, 1976.

Lynch, Paul. "Not Trying to Talk Alike and Succeeding: The Authoritative Word and Internally-Persuasive Word in *Tom Sawyer* and *Huckleberry Finn*." *Studies in the Novel* 38, 2 (Summer 2006): 172–86.

Miller, J. Hillis. *Fiction and Repetition: Seven English Novels*. Cambridge, Mass.: Harvard University Press, 1982.

———. *Ariadne's Thread: Story Lines*. New Haven, Conn.: Yale University Press, 1992.

Morson, Gary Saul. "The Heresiarch of *Meta*." *PTL: A Journal for Descriptive Poetics and Theory of Literature* 3 (1978): 407–27.

———., ed. "Forum on Mikhail Bakhtin." *Critical Inquiry* 10 (Dec. 1983): 225–320.

————., ed. *Literature and History: Theoretical Problems and Russian Case Studies*. Stanford, CA: Stanford University Press, 1986.

Morson, Gary Saul, and Caryl Emerson, eds. *Rethinking Bakhtin: Extensions and Challenges*. Evanston, IL: Northwestern University Press, 1987.

Neel, Jasper. "Plot, Character, or Theme? *Lear* and the Teacher." In *Writing and Reading Differently: Deconstruction and the Teaching of Composition and Literature*. Ed. G. Douglas Atkins and Michael L. Johnson. Lawrence, KS: University Press of Kansas, 1985.

Norris, Christopher. *Deconstruction: Theory and Practice*. 3rd edn. London: Routledge, 2002.

Pettit, Philip. *The Concept of Structuralism: A Critical Analysis*. Berkeley: University of California Press, 1975.

Prince, Gerald. *A Dictionary of Narratology*. Rev. edn. Lincoln: University of Nebraska Press, 2003.

Propp, V. *Morphology of the Folktale*. 1928. Trans. Laurence Scott. 2nd edn. Austin: University of Texas Press, 1968.

————. *Theory and History of Folklore*. Minneapolis: University of Minnesota Press, 1984.

Reesman, Jeanne Campbell. *American Designs: The Late Novels of James and Faulkner*. Philadelphia: University of Pennsylvania Press, 1991.

Reising, Russell J. *The Unusable Past*. New York: Methuen, 1986.

Richter, David H., ed. *The Critical Tradition: Classic Texts and Contemporary Trends*. 3rl edn. New York: St. Martin's, 2007.

Ryan, Michael. *Marxism and Deconstruction: A Critical Articulation*. Baltimore, MD: Johns Hopkins University Press, 1982.

Sarup, Madan. *An Introductory Guide to Post-Structuralism and Postmodernism*. 2nd edn. Athens: University of Georgia Press, 1993.

Saussure, Ferdinand de. *Course in General Linguistics*. Ed. Charles Bally and Albert Reidinger. Trans Wade Baskin. New York: Philosophical Library, 1959.

Scholes, Robert. *Structuralism in Literature: An Introduction*. New Haven, CT: Yale University Press, 1975.

Shafer, Aileen Chris. "Jim's Discourses in *Huckleberry Finn*." *Southern Studies*. NS 1, 2 (Summer 1990): 149–63.

Shklovsky, Viktor. *Theory of Prose*. Normal, IL: Dalkey Archive Press, 1991.

Spivak, Gayatri Chakravorty. *A Critique of Postcolonial Reason: Towards a History of the Vanishing Present*. Cambridge, Mass.: Harvard University Press, 1992.

Todorov, Tzvetan. *The Poetics of Prose*. Trans. Richard Howard. Ithaca, NY: Cornell University Press, 1977.

Tompkins, Jane. "A Short Course in Post-Structuralism." *College English* 50 (1988): 733–47.

6

The Psychological Approach
Freud

I. AIMS AND PRINCIPLES

Of all the critical approaches to literature, the psychological has been one of the most controversial, the most abused, and—for many readers—the least appreciated. Yet, for all the difficulties involved in its proper application to interpretive analysis, the psychological approach can be fascinating and rewarding. Our purpose in this chapter is threefold: (1) to account briefly for the misunderstanding of psychological criticism; (2) to outline a psychological theory often used as an interpretive tool by modern critics; and (3) to show by examples how readers may apply this mode of interpretation to enhance their understanding and appreciation of literature.

The idea of *enhancement* must be understood as a preface to our discussion. It is axiomatic that no single approach can exhaust the manifold interpretive possibilities of a worthwhile literary work: each approach has its own peculiar limitations. For example, the limitations of the historical approach lie in its tendency to overlook the structural intricacies of the work. The formalist approach, on the other hand, often neglects historical and sociological contexts that may provide important insights into the meaning of the work. In turn, the crucial limitation of the psychological approach is its aesthetic inadequacy: psychological interpretation can afford many profound clues toward solving a work's thematic and symbolic mysteries, but it can seldom account for the beautiful symmetry of a well-wrought poem or of a fictional masterpiece. Though the psychological approach is an excellent tool for reading beneath the lines, the interpretive craftsperson must often use other tools for a proper rendering of the lines themselves.

A. Abuses and Misunderstandings of the Psychological Approach

In the general sense of the word, there is nothing new about the psychological approach. As early as the fourth century B.C., Aristotle used it in setting forth his classic definition of tragedy as combining the emotions of pity and terror to produce

Figure 6.1. Sigmund Freud (1920).
Getty Images/Stevie Taylor.

catharsis. The "compleat gentleman" of the English Renaissance, Sir Philip Sidney, with his statements about the moral effects of **poetry**, was psychologizing literature, as were such Romantic poets as Coleridge, Wordsworth, and Shelley with their theories of the imagination. In this sense, then, virtually every literary critic has been concerned at some time with the psychology of writing or responding to literature.

During the twentieth century, however, psychological criticism came to be associated primarily with a particular school of thought, the psychoanalytic theories of Sigmund Freud (1856–1939) and his followers. From this association have derived most of the abuses and misunderstandings of the modern psychological approach to literature. Abuses of the approach have resulted from an excess of enthusiasm, which has been manifested in several ways. First, the practitioners of the Freudian approach often push their critical theses too hard, forcing literature into a Procrustean bed of psychoanalytic theory at the expense of other relevant considerations (for example, the work's total thematic and aesthetic context). Second, psychoanalytic literary criticism has at times degenerated into a special occultism with its own mystique and jargon exclusively for the in-group. Third, many critics of the psychological school have been either literary scholars who have understood the principles of psychology imperfectly or professional psychologists who have had little feeling for literature as art: the former have abused Freudian insights through oversimplification and distortion; the latter have bruised our literary sensibilities.

Though such terms as *anal eroticism, phallic symbol,* and *Oedipal complex* no longer have shock value, some critics are puzzled by the clinical diagnoses of literary problems (for example, the interpretation of Hamlet's character as a "severe case of hysteria on a cyclothymic basis"—that is, a bipolar disorder) and have rejected all psychological criticism other than the commonsense type as pretentious nonsense. By explaining a few of the principles of Freudian psychology that have been applied to literary interpretation and by providing some cautionary remarks, we hope to introduce the reader to a balanced critical perspective that will enable him or her to appreciate the instructive possibilities of the psychological approach while avoiding the pitfalls of either extremist attitude.

B. Freud's Theories

The foundation of Freud's contribution to modern psychology is his emphasis on the unconscious aspects of the human psyche. A creative genius, Freud provided convincing evidence, through his many carefully recorded case studies, that most of our actions are motivated by psychological forces over which we have very limited control. He demonstrated that, like the iceberg, the human mind is structured so that its great weight and density lie beneath the surface (below the level of consciousness). In "The Anatomy of the Mental Personality," Freud discriminates between the levels of conscious and unconscious mental activity:

> The oldest and best meaning of the word "unconscious" is the descriptive one; we call "unconscious" any mental process the existence of which we are obligated to assume—because, for instance, we infer it in some way from its effects—but of which we are not directly aware.... If we want to be more accurate, we should modify the statement by saying that we call a process "unconscious" when we have to assume that it was active *at a certain time,* although *at that time* we knew nothing about it. (99–100)

Freud further emphasizes the importance of the unconscious by pointing out that even the "most conscious processes are conscious for only a short period; quite soon they become *latent,* though they can easily become conscious again" (100). In view of this, Freud defines two kinds of unconscious:

> one which is transformed into conscious material easily and under conditions which frequently arise, and another in the case of which such a transformation is difficult, can only come about with a considerable expenditure of energy, or may never occur at all.... We call the unconscious which is only latent, and so can easily become conscious, the "preconscious," and keep the name "unconscious" for the other. (101)

That most of the individual's mental processes are unconscious is thus Freud's first major premise. The second (which has been rejected by a great many professional psychologists, including some of Freud's own disciples—for example, Carl Jung and Alfred Adler) is that all human behavior is motivated ultimately by

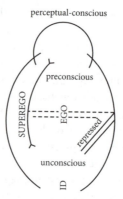

Figure 6.2. Freud's three psychic zones.

what we would call sexuality. Freud designates the prime psychic force as *libido*, or sexual energy. His third major premise is that because of the powerful social taboos attached to certain sexual impulses, many of our desires and memories are repressed (that is, actively excluded from conscious awareness).

Starting from these three premises, we may examine several corollaries of Freudian theory. Principal among these is Freud's assignment of the mental processes to three psychic zones: the *id*, the *ego*, and the *superego*. An explanation of these zones may be illustrated with a modification of Freud's own diagram (*New Introductory Lectures* 78).

The diagram reveals immediately the vast portion of the mental apparatus that is not conscious. Furthermore, it helps to clarify the relationship between ego, id, and superego, as well as their collective relationship to the conscious and the unconscious. We should note that the id is entirely unconscious and that only small portions of the ego and the superego are conscious. With this diagram as a guide, we may define the nature and functions of the three psychic zones.

1. The *id* is the reservoir of libido, the primary source of all psychic energy. It functions to fulfill the primordial life principle, which Freud considers to be the *pleasure principle*. Without consciousness or semblance of rational order, the id is characterized by a tremendous and amorphous vitality. Speaking metaphorically, Freud explains this "obscure inaccessible part of our personality" as "a chaos, a cauldron of seething excitement [with] no organization and no unified will, only an impulsion to obtain satisfaction for the instinctual needs, in accordance with the pleasure principle" (103–4). He further stresses that the "laws of logic—above all, the law of contradiction—do not hold for processes of the id. Contradictory impulses exist side by side without neutralizing each other or drawing apart.... Naturally, the id knows no values, no good and evil, no morality" (104–5).

The id is, in short, the source of all our aggressions and desires. It is lawless, asocial, and amoral. Its function is to gratify our instincts for pleasure without regard for social conventions, legal ethics, or moral restraint. Unchecked, it would lead us to any lengths—to destruction and even self-destruction—to satisfy its impulses for pleasure. Safety for the self and for others does not lie within the province of the id: its concern is purely for instinctual gratification, heedless of consequence. For centuries before Freud, this force was recognized in human nature but often attributed to supernatural and external rather than natural and internal forces: the id as defined by Freud is identical in many respects to the Devil as defined by theologians. Thus there is a certain psychological validity in the old saying that a rambunctious child (whose id has not yet been brought under control by ego and superego) is "full of the devil." We may also see in young children (and neurotic adults) certain uncontrolled impulses toward pleasure that often lead to excessive self-indulgence and even to self-injury.

2. In view of the id's dangerous potentialities, it is necessary that other psychic agencies protect the individual and society. The first of these regulating agencies, that which protects the individual, is the *ego*. This is the rational governing agent of the psyche. Though the ego lacks the strong vitality of the id, it regulates the instinctual drives of the id so that they may be released in nondestructive behavioral patterns. And though a large portion of the ego is unconscious, the ego nevertheless comprises what we ordinarily think of as the conscious mind. As Freud points out in "The Dissection of the Psychical Personality," "To adopt a popular mode of speaking, we might say that the ego stands for reason and good sense while the id stands for the untamed passions" (76). Whereas the id is governed solely by the pleasure principle, the ego is governed by the *reality principle*. Consequently, the ego serves as intermediary between the world within and the world without.

3. The other regulating agent, that which primarily functions to protect society, is the *superego*. Largely unconscious, the superego is the moral censoring agency, the repository of conscience and pride. It is, as Freud says in "The Anatomy of the Mental Personality," the "representative of all moral restrictions, the advocate of the impulse toward perfection, in short it is as much as we have been able to apprehend psychologically of what people call the 'higher' things in human life" (95). Acting either directly or through the ego, the superego serves to repress or inhibit the drives of the id, to block off and thrust back into the unconscious those impulses toward pleasure that society regards as unacceptable, such as overt aggression, sexual passions, and the Oedipal instinct. Freud attributes the development of the superego to the parental influence that manifests itself in terms of punishment for what society considers to be bad behavior and reward for what society considers good behavior. An overactive superego creates an unconscious sense of guilt (hence the familiar term *guilt complex* and the popular misconception that Freud advocated the relaxing of all moral inhibitions and social restraints). Whereas the id is dominated by the pleasure principle and the ego by the reality principle, the superego is dominated by the *morality principle*. We might say that the id would make us devils, that the superego would have us behave as angels (or, worse, as creatures of absolute social conformity), and that

it remains for the ego to keep us healthy human beings by maintaining a balance between these two opposing forces. It was this balance that Freud advocated—not a complete removal of inhibiting factors.

One of the most instructive applications of this Freudian tripartition to literary criticism is the well-known essay "In Nomine Diaboli" by Henry A. Murray, a knowledgeable psychoanalyst and a sensitive literary critic as well. In analyzing Herman Melville's masterpiece *Moby-Dick* with the tools provided by Freud, Murray explains the White Whale as a symbolic embodiment of the strict conscience of New England Puritanism (that is, as a projection of Melville's own superego). Captain Ahab, the monomaniac who leads the crew of the *Pequod* to destruction through his insane compulsion to pursue and strike back at the creature who has injured him, is interpreted as the symbol of a rapacious and uncontrollable id. Starbuck, the sane Christian and first mate who struggles to mediate between the forces embodied in Moby-Dick and Ahab, symbolizes a balanced and sensible rationalism (that is, the ego), as does, more importantly, Ishmael, who has to craft his own tenuous position among competing beliefs.

Though many scholars are reluctant to accept Freud's tripartition of the human psyche, they have not reacted against this aspect of psychoanalytic criticism so strongly as against the application of his sexual theories to the symbolic interpretation of literature. Perhaps the most controversial (and, to many, the most offensive) facet of psychoanalytic criticism is its tendency to interpret imagery in terms of sexuality. Following Freud's example in his interpretation of dreams, the psychoanalytic critic tends to see all concave images (ponds, flowers, cups or vases, caves, and hollows) as female or **yonic symbols**, and all images whose length exceeds their diameter (towers, mountain peaks, snakes, knives, lances, and swords) as male or **phallic symbols**. Perhaps even more objectionable to some is the interpretation of such activities as dancing, riding, and flying as symbols of sexual pleasure. For example, in *The Life and Works of Edgar Allan Poe: A Psycho-Analytic Interpretation*, Marie Bonaparte interprets the figure of Psyche in "Ulalume" as an ambivalent mother figure, both the longed-for mother and the mother as superego who shields her son from his incestuous instincts, concluding with the following startling observation: "Psyche's drooping, trailing wings in this poem symbolise in concrete form Poe's physical impotence. We know that flying, to all races, unconsciously symbolises the sex act, and that antiquity often presented the penis erect and winged." For the skeptical reader Bonaparte provides this explanation:

> Infinite are the symbols man has the capacity to create, as indeed, the dreams and religions of the savage and civilized well show. Every natural object may be utilised to this end yet, despite their multiple shapes, the objects and relations to which they attach are relatively few: these include the beings we loved first, such as mother, father, brothers or sisters and their bodies, but mainly our own bodies and genitals, and theirs. Almost all symbolism is sexual, in its widest sense, taking the word as the deeply-buried primal urge behind all expressions of love, from the cradle to the grave. (294)

Although such observations as these may have a sound psychoanalytic basis, their relevance to sound critical analysis has been questioned by many scholars. We may sympathize with their incredulousness when we encounter the Freudian essay that interprets even a seemingly innocent fairy tale like "Little Red Riding Hood" as an allegory of the age-old conflict between male and female in which the plucky young virgin, whose red cap is a menstrual symbol, outwits the ruthless, sex-hungry "wolf" (Fromm 235–41).

Perhaps even more controversial than Freudian dream symbolism are Freud's theories concerning child psychology. Contrary to traditional beliefs, Freud found infancy and childhood a period of intense sexual experience, sexual in a sense much broader than is commonly attached to the term. During the first five years of life, the child passes through a series of phases in erotic development, each phase being characterized by emphasis on a particular *erogenous zone* (that is, a portion of the body in which sexual pleasure becomes localized). Freud indicated three such zones: the *oral*, the *anal*, and the *genital*. (Note that the uninitiated layman, unfamiliar with the breadth of Freud's term, generally restricts the meaning of "sexuality" to "*genital* sexuality.") These zones are associated not only with pleasure in stimulation but also with the gratification of our vital needs: eating, elimination, and reproduction. If for some reason the individual is frustrated in gratifying these needs during childhood, the adult personality may be warped accordingly (that is, development may be arrested or *fixated*). For example, adults who are compulsively fastidious may suffer, according to the psychoanalyst, from an anal fixation traceable to overly strict toilet training during early childhood. Likewise, compulsive cigarette smoking may be interpreted as a symptom of oral fixation traceable to premature weaning. Even among "normal" adults, sublimated responses occur when the individual is vicariously stimulated by images associated with one of the major erogenous zones. In his *Fiction and the Unconscious,* Simon O. Lesser suggests that the anal-erotic quality in *Robinson Crusoe* (manifested in the hero's scrupulous record keeping and orderliness) accounts at least partially for the unconscious appeal of Defoe's masterpiece (306).

According to Freud, the child reaches the stage of genital primacy around age five, at which time the Oedipus complex manifests itself. In simple terms, the Oedipus complex derives from the boy's unconscious rivalry with his father for the love of his mother. Freud borrowed the term from the classic Sophoclean tragedy in which the hero unwittingly murders his father and marries his mother. In *The Ego and the Id,* Freud describes the complex as follows:

> . . . . the boy deals with his father by identifying himself with him. For a time these two relationships [the child's devotion to his mother and identification with his father] proceed side by side, until the boy's sexual wishes in regard to his mother become more intense and his father is perceived as an obstacle to them; from this the Oedipus complex originates. His identification with his father then takes on a hostile colouring and changes into a wish to get rid of his father in order to take his place with his mother. Henceforward his relation to his father is ambivalent; it seems as if the ambivalence inherent in the identification from the beginning had

become manifest. An ambivalent attitude to his father and an object-relation of a solely affectionate kind to his mother make up the content of the simple positive Oedipus complex in a boy. (21–22)

Further ramifications of the Oedipus complex are a fear of castration and an identification of the father with strict authority in all forms; subsequent hostility to authority is therefore associated with the Oedipal ambivalence to which Freud refers. A story like Nathaniel Hawthorne's "My Kinsman, Major Molineux," for instance, has been interpreted by Simon O. Lesser as essentially a symbolic rebellion against the father figure. And with this insight we may find meaning in the young hero's disturbing outburst of laughter as he watches the cruel tarring and feathering of his once-respected relative: the youth is expressing his unconscious joy in being released from parental authority. Now he is free, as the friendly stranger suggests, to make his own way in the adult world without the help (and restraint) of his kinsman.

C. Other Theories

Jacques Lacan's revisions to Freudian theory have been influential in literary theory since he presented them in France beginning in the 1960s; he has influenced Julia Kristeva, Michel Foucault, and Roland Barthes. Lacan was not so much interested in a therapeutic model as a philosophical one. Freud located the unconscious in the libido, or pleasure principle, while Lacan believed we feel the unconscious as an absence. Lacan replaces such Freudian stages as the child's oral stage with linguistic progressions away from the formlessness of what he called the prelinguistic *Realm of the Mother* and towards its eventual membership in adult society, the linguistic order of the *Law of the Father.* He described the *Mirror-Stage* of development as the moment when a child can identify himself as a separate subject. Since there is nothing to repress in the Realm of the Mother, Lacan calls it the *Imaginary,* which remains in adults and draws them to see reality as a set of images and desires rather than a logical system. When the child learns language, it also leaves the unconscious, which now has to be repressed. From now on desires will have to be sublimated; entering the field of the *Symbolic* means attaching to the rules of language and the subjugation by law. The unconscious remains submerged and has its own language of metaphor, but it is an alien tongue for the conscious mind, what Lacan called "the discourse of the Other." Lacan saw language as a unified and oppressive system that can squelch and silence the feminine primordial in every person, but literature and art and music are means of accessing that fountain of feeling and imagination.

To summarize psychological approaches, there are three stages of a literary work in which psychoanalysis can be employed: the author, the characters, and the reader. Later critics such as Ernest Jones and Norman N. Holland chose one or more of these to analyze. Analyzing the author has proven to be most attractive. Thus Frederick C. Crews investigates texts for the author's buried motives and hidden neurotic conflicts in his *The Sins of the Fathers: Hawthorne's Psychological Themes* (though he later rejected this approach). Peter Brooks, in his *Reading for the Plot,* applies Freud's

Pablo Picasso, *Las Meniñas, The Family of Philip IV*, Cannes (1957)

In this interpretation of Velázquez's painting, Picasso has chosen to limit the composition only to four characters in the painting, mainly one maid of honor, Isabel de Velasco; María Bárbola, a female dwarf; and the young boy Pertusato, also a dwarf. Instead of the subservient relationship these three occupy toward the Infanta in the original, the Infanta has been replaced with María Bárbola in the role of the child. The two figures on either side of her resemble doting parents, and her position in the painting is underplayed; instead of being white and blond like the Infanta, her face is grey and her dress blue, which harmonizes with the strong primary green, red, and yellow of other features of the painting. The dog, a mastiff in the original, appears throughout Picasso's interpretations as a small white dog that vaguely resembles a fox. Strong blocks of color—white, black, and grey—combine to create the visual logic of the painting.

Questions: How does Picasso imagine possible relationships among the three human figures in the painting? Characters have been pared down to symbolic parents and a child, even with a dog to complete the domestic scene. All adults have been banished. Instead of an Infanta, the center is occupied by a dwarf. How does

Figure 6.3. Pablo Picasso, *The Family of Philip IV, no. 42 from* Las Meniñas (1957).
Museo Picasso, Barcelona, Spain/© DACS/Giraudon/The Bridgeman Art Library International/© 2009 Estate of Pablo Picasso/Artists Rights Society (ARS), New York.

this "scene" contrast with the family group portrayed by Velázquez? One notes that Isabel de Velasco is not looking at María Bárbola, though she bends to look at the Infanta in the original. What does this suggest? How does the Psychological or Mythological Approach function for this painting with its family group? What does the substitution of one person for another mean? Freud and Lacan can be referenced to tease out some of the parent-child relationships and also the symbolic presence of the white dog. Students might note that the original catalogue referred to it as *La Familia* ("The Family").

Beyond the Pleasure Principle. This principle examines *repetition–compulsion,* a neurosis that supplants remembrance with repetition when a memory is too painful for repression to overcome, and it may result in literature. Harold Bloom theorizes that authorial literary influence is an issue of paternity that has to be overcome by the "son" by "killing" the "father"; he does so by creatively misreading the father in a way that makes his own labors necessary. Sandra Gilbert and Susan Gubar in *The Madwoman in the Attic* extend Bloom's observation to analyze how women writers also face a special struggle in rejecting prescriptive male influence.

II. THE PSYCHOLOGICAL APPROACH IN PRACTICE

A. *Hamlet*: The Oedipus Complex

Although Freud himself made some applications of his theories to art and literature, it remained for an English disciple, the psychoanalyst Ernest Jones, to provide the first full-scale psychoanalytic treatment of a major literary work. Jones's *Hamlet and Oedipus,* originally published as an essay in *The American Journal of Psychology* in 1910, was later revised and enlarged.

Jones bases his argument on the thesis that Hamlet's much-debated delay in killing his uncle, Claudius, is to be explained in terms of internal rather than external circumstances and that the "play is mainly concerned with a hero's unavailing fight against what can only be called a disordered mind." In his carefully documented essay Jones builds a highly persuasive case history of Hamlet as a psychoneurotic who suffers from manic-depressive hysteria combined with an *abulia* (an inability to exercise will power and come to decisions)—all of which may be traced to the hero's severely repressed Oedipal feelings. Jones points out that no really satisfying argument has ever been substantiated for the idea that Hamlet avenges his father's murder as quickly as practicable. Shakespeare makes Claudius's guilt as well as Hamlet's duty perfectly clear from the outset—if we are to trust the words of the Ghost and the gloomy insights of the hero himself. The fact is, however, that Hamlet does not fulfill this duty until absolutely forced to do so by physical circumstances—and even then only after Gertrude, his mother, is dead. Jones also elucidates the strong misogyny that Hamlet displays throughout the play, especially as it is directed against Ophelia, and his almost physical revulsion to sex. All of this adds up to a classic example of the neurotically repressed Oedipus complex.

The ambivalence that typifies the child's attitude toward his father is dramatized in the characters of the Ghost (the good, lovable father with whom the boy identifies) and Claudius (the hated father as tyrant and rival), both of whom are dramatic projections of the hero's own conscious-unconscious ambivalence toward the father figure. The Ghost represents the conscious ideal of fatherhood, the image that is socially acceptable:

> See, what a grace was seated on this brow:
> Hyperion's curls, the front of Jove himself,
> An eye like Mars, to threaten and command,
> A station like the herald Mercury
> New-lighted on a heaven-kissing hill,
> A combination and a form indeed,
> Where every god did seem to set his seal,
> To give the world assurance of a man:
> This was your husband. (III.iv)

His view of Claudius, on the other hand, represents Hamlet's repressed hostility toward his father as a rival for his mother's affection. This new king-father is the symbolic perpetrator of the very deeds toward which the son is impelled by his own unconscious motives: murder of his father and incest with his mother. Hamlet cannot bring himself to kill Claudius because to do so he must, in a psychological sense, kill himself. His delay and frustration in trying to fulfill the Ghost's demand for vengeance may therefore be explained by the fact that, as Jones puts it, the "thought of incest and parricide combined is too intolerable to be borne. One part of him tries to carry out the task, the other flinches inexorably from the thought of it" (78–79).

Norman N. Holland neatly summed up the reasons both for Hamlet's delay and his motives:

> Now what do critics mean when they say that Hamlet cannot act because of his Oedipus complex? The argument is very simple, very elegant. One, people over the centuries have been unable to say why Hamlet delays in killing the man who murdered his father and married his mother. Two, psychoanalytic experience shows that every child wants to do just exactly that. Three, Hamlet delays because he cannot punish Claudius for doing what he himself wished to do as a child and, unconsciously, still wishes to do: he would be punishing himself. Four, the fact that this wish is unconscious explains why people could not explain Hamlet's delay. (158)

A corollary to the Oedipal problem in *Hamlet* is the pronounced misogyny in Hamlet's character. Because of his mother's overblown affection for her son, an affection that would have deeply marked Hamlet as a child with an Oedipal neurosis, he has in the course of his psychic development repressed his incestuous impulses so severely that this repression colors his attitude toward all women: "The total reaction culminates in the bitter misogyny of his outburst against Ophelia, who is devastated at having to bear a reaction so wholly out of proportion to her own offense and has no idea that in reviling her Hamlet is really expressing his bitter resentment against his mother" (Jones 96). The famous "Get thee to a nunnery" speech has even more sinister overtones than are generally recognized, explains Jones, when we understand the pathological degree of Hamlet's conditions and read "nunnery" as Elizabethan slang for brothel.

> The underlying theme relates ultimately to the splitting of the mother image which the infantile unconscious effects into two opposite pictures: one of a virginal Madonna, an inaccessible saint towards whom all sensual approaches are unthinkable, and the other of a sensual creature accessible to everyone.... When sexual repression is highly pronounced, as with Hamlet, then both types of women are felt to be hostile: the pure one out of resentment at her repulses, the sensual one out of the temptation she offers to plunge into guiltiness. Misogyny, as in the play, is the inevitable result. (97–98)

Thus Hamlet rails against a mother and a father—no wonder he is tormented. Although it has been attacked by the anti-Freudians and occasionally disparaged as "obsolete" by the neo-Freudians, Jones's critical tour de force has nevertheless attained the status of a modern classic. "Both as an important seminal work which led to a considerable re-examination of *Hamlet,* and as an example of a thorough and intelligent application of psychoanalysis to drama," writes Claudia C. Morrison, "Jones's essay stands as the single most important Freudian study of literature to appear in America..." (175).

B. Rebellion Against the Father in *Huckleberry* Finn

Mark Twain's great **novel** has this in common with Shakespeare's masterpiece: both are concerned with the theme of rebellion—with a hostile treatment of the father figure. In both works the father figure is finally slain, and knowledge of his death brings a curious sense of relief—and release—for the audience. As we have seen, from the psychoanalytic viewpoint all rebellion is in essence a rejection of parental, especially paternal, authority. Sociologically speaking, Huck rebels against the unjust, inhumane restrictions of a society that condones slavery, hypocrisy, and cruelty. However, Mark Twain showed a remarkable pre-Freudian insight when he dramatized this theme of rebellion in the portrayal of Huck's detestable father as the lowest common denominator of social authority. The main plot of the novel is launched with Huck's escape from pap Finn ("pap," in keeping with the reductive treatment of this father figure, is not capitalized), a flight that coincides with Jim's escape from Miss Watson. Huck redefines family and takes a (silent) revenge against it.

Symbolically, Huck and Jim, in order to gain freedom, must escape Miss Watson and pap Finn (who reminds Huck of Adam all covered with mud—that is, Adam after the Fall). Despite their differences, Miss Watson and pap Finn have much in common. They represent extremes of authority: authority at its most respectable and at its most contemptible. What is more, they represent social and legal morality in the extremes of the social spectrum. Notwithstanding his

Figure 6.4. Mark Twain (ca. 1870).
Getty Images/American School.

obvious worthlessness, pap Finn is still Huck's sole guardian by law and holds near-absolute power over him, an authority condoned by society, just as Miss Watson has a similar power over Jim. In the light of such authority both Miss Watson and pap Finn may be said to represent the superego (for example, when Huck goes against his conscience by refusing to turn Jim in to the authorities, it is the letter to Miss Watson that he tears up). In this sense, then, it is to escape the oppressive tyranny and cruel restraints of the superego that Huck and Jim take flight on the river.

Huckleberry Finn cannot by any means be read as a psychological **allegory**, and it would be foolish to set up a strict one-to-one relationship of characters and events to ideas, particularly because Mark Twain wrote the book with no notion of Freudian concepts. But like most great writers, Twain knew human nature; and from the psychoanalytic perspective, a "linked analogy" can be seen between the structure of his novel and the Freudian structure of the human psyche. Water in any form is generally interpreted by the psychoanalysts as a female symbol, more specifically as a maternal symbol. From the superegoistic milieu of society Huck and Jim flee to the river, where they find freedom. Except when invaded by men, the river is characterized by a strange, fluid, dreamlike peacefulness; Huck's most lyrical comments are those describing the beauty of the river:

> Two or three days and nights went by; I reckon I might say they swum by, they slid along so quiet and smooth and lovely.... Not a sound anywheres—perfectly still—just like the whole world was asleep.... [Then] the nice breeze springs up,

and comes fanning you from over there, so cool and fresh and sweet to smell on account of the woods and flowers; but sometimes not that way, because they've left dead fish laying around, gars and such, and they do get pretty rank.... [And] we would watch the lonesomeness of the river, and kind of lazy along, and by and by lazy off to sleep.... It's lovely to live on a raft. We had the sky up there, all speckled with stars, and we used to lay on our backs and look up at them, and discuss about whether they was made or only just happened.... Jim said the moon could 'a' *laid* them; well, that looked kind of reasonable, so I didn't say nothing against it, because I've seen a frog lay most as many, so of course it could be done. (Ch. 19)

The foregoing passage is redolent with female-maternal imagery; it also suggests the dark, mysterious serenity associated with the prenatal state, as well as with death, in psychoanalytic interpretation. The tension between land and water may be seen as analogous to that between the conscious and the unconscious in Freudian theory. Lacking a real mother, Huck finds his symbolic mother in the river; in Freudian terms, he returns to the womb. From this matrix he undergoes a series of symbolic deaths and rebirths, punctuated structurally by the episodes on land. As James M. Cox has pointed out, Huck's fake murder in escaping from pap Finn is crucial to our understanding the central informing pattern of death and rebirth: "Having killed himself, Huck is 'dead' throughout the entire journey down the river. He is indeed the man without identity who is reborn at almost every river bend, not because he desires a new role, but because he must re-create himself to elude the forces which close in on him from every side. The rebirth theme which began with pap's reform becomes the driving idea behind the entire action." Enhancing this pattern is the androgynous figure of Jim, Huck's adopted friend and parent, whose blackness coincides with the darkness associated with death, the unconscious, and the maternal. Jim's qualities are more maternal than paternal. He possesses the gentleness, unquestioning loyalty, and loving kindness that we traditionally ascribe to the mother, in sharp contrast to the brutal author-itarianism of pap.

Viewed from a slightly different psychological angle, *Huckleberry Finn* is a story of the child as victim, embodying the betrayal-of-innocence theme that has become one of the chief motifs in American fiction. Philip Young has detected similarities between Huck's plight and that of the Hemingway hero. Young sees Huck as the wounded child, permanently scarred by traumas of death and vio-lence; he counts thirteen corpses in the novel and observes that virtually every major episode in the book ends with violence or death. Young makes explicit the causal relationship between the traumatic experiences suffered by Huck (and later by Hemingway's protagonists) and the growing preoccupation with death that dominates much modern literature:

[Huck] is a wounded and damaged boy. He will never get over the terror he has seen and been through, is guilt-ridden and can't sleep at night for his thoughts. When he is able to sleep he is tortured with bad dreams.... This is a boy who has undergone an unhappy process of growing up, and has grown clean out of his creator's grasp.... Precisely as Clemens could never solve his own complications, save in the unmitigated but sophomoric pessimism of his last books, so he could not solve them for Huck, who had got too hot to handle and was dropped. What the man never realized was that in his journey by water he had been hinting at a solution all along: an excessive exposure to violence and death produced first a compulsive fascination with dying, and finally an ideal symbol for it. (200–201)

This ideal symbol is the dark river itself, which is suggestive of the Freudian death instinct, the unconscious instinct in all living things to return to nonliving, fluid state and thereby achieve permanent surcease from the pain of living.

Our recognition of these symbolic implications does not, by any means, exhaust the interpretive potential of Twain's novel, nor does it preclude insights gained from other critical approaches. Such recognition should *enhance* our appreciation of the greatness of *Huckleberry Finn* by revealing that Mark Twain produced a master-work that, intentionally or not, has appealed in a profound psychological way to many generations of readers. The Freudian reading—particularly in its focus on the death of the Father and the search for the Feminine—has enjoyed renewed attention from feminist psychoanalytic critics (see Chapter 8 on feminist approaches).

C. Prometheus Manqué: The Monster Unbound

Although we cannot be sure of the extent to which the irony in Mary Shelley's subtitle for her famous novel—*Frankenstein; or, The Modern Prometheus*—was intentional, that subtitle is nonetheless wonderfully ironic. The qualifying term *modern* certainly indicates irony on the author's part. In any event, the fire that her modern-day Prometheus brings to humankind—unlike that so dearly stolen from the gods—is hellish and—like the more enormities of modern science—holocaustal.

At the very outset, Shelley's subtitle provides a strong psychoanalytic clue. As we have noted, according to Freud, all forms of rebellion are essentially rebellions against the restrictions of patriarchal authority—that is, the controlling powers of the Father. To be released from these bonds, the son must dispatch the Father; indeed, the Father must die, either symbolically or literally (and, in many cases, both). Early in the novel, Victor rejects the elder Frankenstein's advice against reading the "sad trash" of Cornelius Agrippa. Later on, of course, the Father must die literally of "an apoplectic fit" in the arms of his guilty son, whose own rebellion (not only against paternal authority but also against the higher laws of God and Nature) has created the monstrous instrument of death. **Irony** upon irony (all that goes around must come around): that same diabolical monster likewise rebels against his father/creator, ultimately effecting his demise as well as a half dozen others in his own tale of revenge against his "family."

Viewed from the Freudian perspective, Frankenstein's phallic creation (note his enormous height and his symbolic affinity to tall mountains) may be seen as a projection of his creator's own id, unbound and rampant. Such are the monstrous consequences of libidinous obsession, unchecked by ego and ungoverned by superego. If at the end of the novel the Creature is "lost in darkness and distance," the dire psychological significance of his fate—and that of his creator (and family and friends)—should not be lost upon his modern audience.

D. "Young Goodman Brown": Id Versus Superego

The theme of innocence betrayed is also central to Nathaniel Hawthorne's "Young Goodman Brown," the tale of the young bridegroom who leaves his wife Faith to spend a night with Satan in the forest. The events of that terrifying night are a traumatic experience for the youth. At the center of the dark wilderness he discovers a witches' Sabbath involving all the honored teachers, preachers, and friends of his village. The climax is reached when his own immaculate bride is brought forth to stand by his side and pledge eternal allegiance to the Fiend of Hell. Following this climactic moment in which the hero resists the diabolical urge to join the fraternity of evil, he wakes to find himself in the deserted forest wondering if what has happened was dream or reality. Regardless of the answer, he is a changed man. He returns in the morning to the village and to his Faith, but he is never at peace with himself again. Henceforth he can never hear the singing of a holy hymn without also hearing echoes of the anthem of sin from that terrible night in the forest. He shrinks even from the side of Faith. His dying hour is gloom, and no hopeful epitaph is engraved upon his tombstone.

Aside from the clearly intended allegorical meanings discussed elsewhere in this book, it is the story's underlying psychological implications that concern us here. We start with the assumption that, through **symbolism** and technique, "Young Goodman Brown" means more than it says. In this respect our task is one of extrapolation, an inferring of the unknown from the known. Our first premise is that Brown's journey is more than a physical one: it is a psychological one as well. To see what this journey means in psychological terms, we need to examine the setting, the time, and the place. Impelled by unmistakably libidinal force, the hero moves from the village of Salem into the forest. The village is a place of light and order, both social and spiritual order. Brown leaves Faith behind in the town at sunset and returns to Faith in the morning. The journey into the wilderness is taken in the night: "My journey... forth and back again," explains the young man to his wife, "must needs be done 'twixt now and sunrise." It is in the forest, a place of darkness and unknown terrors, that Brown meets the Devil. On one level, then, the village may be equated with consciousness, the forest with the dark recesses of the unconscious. But, more precisely, the village, as a place of social and moral order (and inhibition) is analogous to Freud's superego, conscience, the morally inhibiting agent of the psyche; the forest, as a place of wild, untamed passions and terrors, has the attributes of the Freudian id. As a would-be mediator between these opposing forces, Brown himself resembles the poor ego, which tries to effect a healthy balance and is shattered because it is unable to do so.

Why can't he reconcile these forces? Is his predicament that of all human beings, as is indicated by his common, nondistinctive surname? If so, are we all destined to die in gloom? Certainly, Hawthorne implies, we cannot remain always in the village, away from the forest. Sooner or later, we must all confront Satan. Let us examine this diabolical figure for a moment. When we first see him (after being prepared by Brown's expressed fear, "What if the devil himself should be at my very elbow!"), he is "seated at the foot of an old tree"—an allusion to the "old tree" of forbidden fruit and the knowledge of sin. He is described as "bearing a considerable resemblance" to the hero himself. He is, in short, Brown's own alter ego, the dramatic projection of a part of Brown's psyche, just as Faith is the projection of another part of his psyche. The staff Satan is carrying, similar to the maple stick he later gives to Brown, is like a "great black snake...a living serpent"—a standard Freudian symbol for the uncontrollable phallus. As he moves on through the forest, Brown encounters other figures, the most respected of his moral tutors: old Goody Cloyse, Deacon Gookin, and, at last, even Faith herself, her pink ribbon reflecting the **ambiguity** that Brown is unable to resolve, for pink is the mixture of white (for purity) and red (for passion). Thoroughly unnerved—then maddened—by disillusionment, Brown capitulates to the wild evil in this heart of darkness and becomes "himself the chief horror of the scene, [shrinking] not from its other horrors." That the whole lurid scene may be interpreted as the projection of Brown's formerly repressed impulses is indicated in Hawthorne's description of the transformed protagonist:

> In truth, all through the haunted forest there could be nothing more frightful than the figure of Goodman Brown. On he flew among the black pines, brandishing his staff with frenzied gestures, now giving vent to an inspiration of horrid blasphemy, and now shouting forth such laughter as set all the echoes of the forest laughing like demons around him. *The fiend in his own shape is less hideous than when he rages in the breast of man.* (our italics)

Though Hawthorne implies that Brown's problem is that of Everyman, he does not suggest that all humans share Brown's gloomy destiny. Like Freud, Hawthorne saw the dangers of an overactive suppression of libido and the consequent development of a tyrannous superego, though he thought of the problem in his own terms as an imbalance of head versus heart. Goodman Brown is the tragic victim of a society that has shut its eyes to the inevitable "naturalness" of sex as a part of humankind's physical and mental constitution, a society whose moral system would suppress too severely natural human impulses.

Among Puritans the word "nature" was virtually synonymous with "sin." In Hawthorne's *The Scarlet Letter*, little Pearl, illegitimate daughter of Hester Prynne and the Reverend Mr. Arthur Dimmesdale, is identified throughout as the "child of nature." In his speech to the General Court in 1645, Governor John Winthrop defined "natural liberty"—as distinguished from "civil liberty"—as a "liberty to do evil as well as good...the exercise and maintaining of [which] makes men grow more evil, and in time to be worse than brute beasts...." Hawthorne, himself a descendant of Puritan witch hunters and a member of New England society, the moral standards of which had been strongly conditioned by its Puritan heritage, was obsessed with the nature of sin and with the psychological results of violating

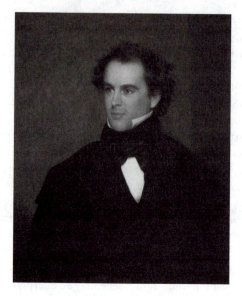

Figure 6.5. Nathaniel Hawthorne (1840).
Portrait by Charles Osgood. Courtesy Peabody Essex Museum.

the taboos imposed by this system. "Young Goodman Brown" dramatizes the neurosis resulting from such a violation.

After his night in the forest Brown becomes a walking guilt complex, burdened with anxiety and doubt. Why? Because he has not been properly educated to confront the realities of the external world or of the inner world, because from the cradle on he has been indoctrinated with admonitions against tasting the forbidden fruit, and because sin and Satan have been inadvertently glamorized by prohibition, he has developed a morbid compulsion to taste of them. He is not necessarily evil; he is, like most young people, curious. But because of the severity of Puritan taboos about natural impulses, his curiosity has become an obsession. His dramatic reactions in the forest are typical of what happens in actual cases of extreme repression. Furthermore, the very nature of his wilderness fantasy substantiates Freud's theory that our repressed desires express themselves in our dreams, that dreams are symbolic forms of wish fulfillment. Hawthorne, writing more than a generation before Freud, was a keen enough psychologist to be aware of many of the same phenomena Freud was to systematize through clinical evidence.

One final note: Hawthorne appears to be the first American author to use the word "unconscious" in its present psychological connotation—before Freud himself.

E. Sexual Imagery in "To His Coy Mistress"

In Andrew Marvell's "To His Coy Mistress" the speaker begins his proposition of love by stating an impossible condition: "Had we but world enough, and time,/

This coyness, Lady, were no crime." Flattering his prospective mistress as "Lady," he proceeds to outline the "ideal" relationship of the two lovers:

> We would sit down and think which way
> To walk and pass our long love's day.
>
> . . . .
>
> For, Lady, you deserve this state,
> Nor would I love at lower rate.

The speaker's argument in this first **stanza** achieves a fine sublimation. He has managed to refine his seductive motive of all its grossness, yet, ever so subtly, he has not swerved from his main purpose. His objective despite the contradictory deceptiveness of "vegetable love" (a passion whose burning is so slow as to be imperceptible), is nevertheless the same: it is only a matter of time before the woman must capitulate to his blandishments.

But this "only" makes all the difference in the world, as he demonstrates in his second stanza, shifting dramatically from the allusive persuasion of the first stanza to the overt pressure of the second. The flying chariot of Time (again we find the subtle implication of sexual union in the image of flying) is juxtaposed against an eternity of oblivion, just as the slow but sure fecundity of a vegetable love growing to the vastness of empires is contrasted with the barren deserts of death. After setting forth this prospect, the speaker dares to reveal precisely what all this means in terms of love. The "marble vault" is a thinly disguised vaginal metaphor suggesting both rigor mortis and the fleshless pelvis of the skeleton. This statement, in even sharper contrast with the gentle cajolery of the first stanza, is brutal in its explicitness. "My echoing song" and the sensual meanings of the lines following are extremely coarse ("quaint" is a **yonic** pun). From the vegetable passion, in the face of reality, we see that all love must at last end in ashes—just as all chastity must end, the same as sexual profligacy, in dust.

In the final stanza the speaker relaxes his harsh irony and appeals passionately to his reluctant sweetheart to seize the moment. Again, in contrast with both the vegetable metaphor of the first stanza and the frightening directness of the second stanza, he achieves a sublimation of sensual statement through the bold sincerity of his passion and through the brilliance of his **imagery**. Here, too, the sexual imagery is overt. The fire image, which smolders in stanza 1 and turns to ashes in stanza 2, explodes into passion in the concluding stanza. Here love-as-destruction is set forth rapturously. The poet conveys, instead of sinister corruption, a sense of desperate ecstasy. The eating-biting metaphor (oral eroticism in its primal form) is fused with the flying symbol in "amorous birds of prey" and set with metaphysical brilliance against the alternative of a slow, cannibalistic dissolution within the horrible maw of Time. In his last four lines the lover drives his message home with an orgastic force through the use of harshly rhythmic spondees ("Thus, though" and "Stand still") and strongly suggestive puns ("make our sun" and "Make him run").

To read Marvell's great poem as nothing more than a glorification of sexual activity is, of course, a gross oversimplification. We agree with the formalist critic

Figure 6.6. Andrew Marvell (ca. 1660).
Getty Images/English School.

that literature is autonomous, but we must also concur with critic Wayne Shumaker that it is "continuous with nonaesthetic life" (263). As Simon O. Lesser has said, "Among [literary works] whose artistic authenticity cannot be questioned we give the highest place precisely to those works which ignore no aspect of man's nature, which confront the most disagreeable aspects of life deliberately and unflinchingly…." (55). Great literature has always dealt not merely with those aspects of the human mind that are pleasant and conscious but with the total human psyche and the body. The enduring appeal of Marvell's poem derives from this kind of artistic and honest confrontation.

F. Morality Principle over the Pleasure Principle in "Everyday Use"

"I will wait for her in the yard that Maggie and I made so clean and wavy yesterday afternoon," the **narrator** tells us in the opening sentence of Alice Walker's story. The "her" refers, of course, to the prodigal daughter who is about to make her first visit home since her transformation from old-fashioned "Dee" into the newly liberated "Wangero Leewanika Kemanjo."

We are told in the second paragraph of the story that Maggie is "ashamed of the burn scars down her arms and legs" and—even more revealingly—that "'no' is a word the world never learned" to say to her sister.

In the next two paragraphs the narrator reveals her recurrent dream of being featured along with Dee on a major TV talk show like Johnny Carson's: "On TV mother and child embrace and smile into each other's faces. Sometimes the mother and father weep, the child wraps them in her arms and leans across the table to tell how she would not have made it without their help."

Thus far, we may see two symbolic components of Freudian theory at work in Walker's story: the superego and the id. At this point Maggie is clearly associated with two basic characteristics of the superego: order (the clean, neat yard) and guilt (shame over her appearance in social situations). As the story progresses, we will see an even more important identification of Maggie with the superego—but before that see Dee's affinity with the Freudian id.

As we pointed out earlier in this chapter, the id knows no moral or social restraints, being driven solely by the pleasure principle. Dee's entire life has been governed by the pleasure principle: "Dee wanted nice things. A yellow organdy dress to wear to her graduation from high school; black pumps to match a green suit she'd made from an old suit somebody gave me. She was determined to stare down any disaster in her efforts.... Hesitation was no part of her nature." Still further, the id is not only amoral but totally self-centered and asocial: "Mama, when did Dee ever *have* any friends?" Maggie remarks.

And what is the mother's role in our Freudian reading of this fine little **drama**? Early in her TV fantasy, as the narrator sees herself emerging from "a dark and soft-seated limousine" and being greeted by a famous "smiling, gray, sporty man like Johnny Carson" before an applauding audience, she is clearly associating herself with Dee's pleasure principle: "Then we are on the stage and Dee is embracing me with tears in her eyes." But the pleasurable vision begins to grow dim in the next sentence: "She pins on my dress a large orchid, even though she has told me once that she thinks orchids are tacky flowers."

And she wakes from her tinsel dream of glory in the next paragraph: "In real life I am a large big-boned woman with rough, man-working hands" that can brain a bull-calf with one blow of a sledgehammer. In the fantasy, like Dee she dazzles the audience with her "quick and witty tongue"; in real life, she is slow, deliberate, and inarticulate. But she is not dim-witted; she is, in fact associated with the reality principle. In brief, she is representative of the ego, caught momentarily in precarious tension between the pleasure principle and the morality principle.

Naturally attracted to her pleasure-driven daughter, the narrator eagerly anticipates Dee's arrival—despite Maggie's open aversion to the meeting (" 'Come back here,' I say. And she stops and tries to dig a well in the sand with her toe"). But her bright expectancy fades at the first glimpse of Dee's unctuously phallic companion, Hakim-a-barber. Her morally perceptive younger daughter sees him at once for what he is: "I hear Maggie suck in her breath. 'Uhnnnh,' is what it sounds like. Like when you see the wriggling end of a snake just in front of your foot on the road."

And with the fading of her false pleasure-vision comes the increasing clarity of Mrs. Johnson's moral vision. Dee (a.k.a. Wangero) wants it all and, given her own way, will have it all: " 'This churn top is what I need.... And I want the dasher, too.' " (She will " 'think of something artistic to do with the dasher' "!) Finally, uninhibited by ethical restraint or consideration for others, she will have the quilts made by Grandma Dee and promised to Maggie for her marriage to John Thomas. Lacking the aggressive intensity of the id, once-burned and still-scarred Maggie would acquiesce to her sister's libidinous will. But the mother, no longer dazzled by her false pleasure-dome, now turning her full attention from Dee to Maggie, has another vision more real as well as more moral: "Just like when I'm in church and the spirit of God touches me and I get happy and shout. I did something I never had done before: hugged Maggie to me, then dragged her on into the room, snatched the quilts out of Miss Wangero's hands and dumped them into Maggie's lap.... 'Take one or two of the others,' I said to Dee." For once, at least in Walker's well-wrought morality play, sweet reasonableness has prevailed over rampant self-interest—or, as a Freudian critic might put it, "Ego, bolstered by superego, has regulated the id."

III. SUMMARY OF KEY POINTS

- *Psychological Approaches*: Provide insight into the thematic and symbolic mysteries of a work of literature and enhance other readings. These critics seek the possible motives behind the literary work, reading "between the lines" for author's and characters' psychological conflicts.
- Abuses and misunderstandings of psychological approaches include its tendency to limit interpretation, ignoring the aesthetic value of the text in favor of psychoanalyzing author and characters.
- *Freud's theories*: Most of our actions are motivated by psychological forces over which we have limited control. The mind is divided into the conscious and unconscious; most of an individual's mental processes are driven by the unconscious and ultimately by sexuality. Due to social taboos and pressure, sexual impulses, desires, and memories are repressed.
- Freud's map of the mind: Freud divided the mind into the *id* (libido or unconscious, the pleasure principle), the *ego* (the conscious sense of self, the reality principle), and *superego* (learned rules and customs, the morality principle).
- Phallic and yonic symbols, male and female genital symbols.
- Oedipus Complex: The son's strong feelings for an attachment to the mother and subsequent struggle with the father.
- Jacques Lacan: A follower of Freud's who is very influential in poststructuralist literary theory. Lacan identified the Realm of the Mother as the Imaginary—the source of inspiration and creativity—and the Realm of the Father as symbolic order, the source of language.

IV. OTHER POSSIBILITIES AND LIMITATIONS OF THE PSYCHOLOGICAL APPROACH

This brings us to a final recapitulation and a few words of defense as well as of caution about the Freudian approach. First, in defense: incredibly far-fetched as some psychoanalytic interpretations seem to many readers, such interpretations, handled by qualified critics, are not unsubstantiated in fact; they are based upon psychological insights often derived from and supported by actual case histories, and they are set forth in such works as those of Ernest Jones and Marie Bonaparte with remarkable cogency. They are—if we accept the basic premises of psychoanalysis—very difficult to refute. Furthermore, regardless of their factual validity, such theories have had a tremendous impact upon modern writing (in the works of such creative artists as James Joyce, Eugene O'Neill, Tennessee Williams, Philip Roth, and Edward Albee, to mention only a few) and upon modern literary criticism (for example, in the essays of such major and diverse critics as Edmund Wilson, Lionel Trilling, F. L. Lucas, Frederick Hoffman, Sandra Gilbert, Hélène Cixous, and Julia Kristeva). It is therefore important that the serious student of literature be acquainted with psychoanalytic theory.

The danger is that the serious student may become theory-ridden, forgetting that Freud's is not the only approach to literary analysis. To see a great work of fiction or a great poem primarily as a psychological case study is often to miss its wider significance and perhaps even the essential aesthetic experience it should provide. A number of great works, despite the claims of the more zealous Freudians and post-Freudians, do not lend themselves readily, if at all, to the psychoanalytic approach, and even those that do cannot be studied exclusively from the psychological perspective. Literary interpretation and psychoanalysis are two distinct fields, and though they may be closely associated, they can in no sense be regarded as parts of one discipline. The literary critic who views the masterpiece solely through the lens of Freud is liable to see art through a glass darkly. However, those readers who reject psychoanalysis as neurotic nonsense deprive themselves of a valuable tool in understanding not only literature but human nature and their individual selves as well.

QUICK REFERENCE

Appignanesi, Richard. *Freud for Beginners*. New York: Pantheon, 1979.

Bloom, Harold. *The Anxiety of Influence*. New York: Oxford University Press, 1975.

Bonaparte, Marie. *The Life and Works of Edgar Allan Poe: A Psycho-Analytic Interpretation*. London: Imago, 1949.

Cox, James M. "Remarks on the Sad Initiation of Huckleberry Finn." *Sewanee Review* 62 (1954): 389–405.

Crews, Frederick. *The Sins of the Fathers: Hawthorne's Psychological Themes*. New York: Oxford, 1966.

Freud, Sigmund. *The Ego and the Id*. New York: W. W. Norton, 1962.

———. "The Anatomy of the Mental Personality." *New Introductory Lectures on Psychoanalysis*. New York: W. W. Norton, 1964.

———. "The Dissection of the Psychical Personality." *New Introductory Lectures on Psychoanalysis*. Trans. and ed. James Strachey. New York: W. W. Norton, 1965.

Fromm, Erich. *The Forgotten Language*. New York: Grove, 1957.

Gallop, Jane. *Reading Lacan*. Ithaca, NY: Cornell University Press, 1985.

Gilbert, Sandra, and Susan Gubar. *The Madwoman in the Attic: The Woman Writer and the Nineteenth-Century Literary Imagination.* New Haven, Conn.: Yale University Press, 1979.

Grosz, Elizabeth. *Jacques Lacan: A Feminist Introduction.* London: Routledge, 1990.

Hill, Philip. *Lacan for Beginners.* New York: Writers & Readers, 1997, 1999.

Holland, Norman N. *The Shakespearean Imagination.* Bloomington: Indiana University Press, 1968.

Jones, Ernest. *Hamlet and Oedipus.* Garden City, NY: Doubleday (Anchor), 1949.

Jung, Carl Gustav. *Psychology of the Unconscious: A Study of the Transformations and Symbolisms of the Libido—A Contribution to the History of the Evolution of Thought.* Ed. and Trans. Beatrice Hinkle. New York: 1916. Rpt. ed. William McGuire. Princeton, N.J.: Princeton University Press, 2001.

Lacan, Jacqus. *Ecrits: A Selection.* Trans. Alan Sheridan. New York: Norton, 1977.

Lesser, Simon O. *Fiction and the Unconscious.* Boston: Beacon Press, 1957.

Mellard, James. *Using Lacan, Reading Fiction.* Urbana: University of Illinois Press, 1991.

Mitchell, Juliet. *Psychoanalysis and Feminism: A Radical Reassessment of Freudian Psychoanalysis.* 2nd edn. New York: Basic Books, 2000.

Morrison, Claudia C. *Freud and the Critic.* Chapel Hill: University of North Carolina Press, 1968.

Muller, John P., and William J. Richardson, eds. *The Purloined Poe: Lacan, Derrida, and Psychoanalytic Reading.* Baltimore, MD: Johns Hopkins University Press, 1988.

Murray, Henry A. "In Nomine Diaboli." *New England Quarterly* 24 (1951): 435–52.

Shumaker, Wayne. *Literature and the Irrational.* Englewood Cliffs, NJ: Prentice Hall, 1960.

Smith, Joseph H., and William Kerrigan, eds. *Taking Chances: Derrida, Psychoanalysis, and Literature.* Baltimore: Johns Hopkins University Press, 1988.

Wright, Elizabeth. *Psychoanalytic Criticism: A Reappraisal.* 2nd edn. London: Routledge, 1998.

Young, Phillip. *Ernest Hemingway.* New York: Holt, 1952.

Young, Robert F. C. *White Mythologies: Writing History and the West.* London: Routledge, 1990.

Zizek, Slavoj. *Looking Awry: An Introduction to Jacques Lacan Through Popular Culture.* Cambridge, Mass.: MIT Press, 1991.

Mythological and Archetypal
Approaches

I. DEFINITIONS AND MISCONCEPTIONS

In *The Masks of God,* Joseph Campbell recounts a curious phenomenon of animal behavior. Newly hatched chickens, bits of eggshells still clinging to their tails, will dart for cover when a hawk flies overhead; yet they remain unaffected by other birds. Furthermore, a wooden model of a hawk, drawn forward along a wire above their coop, will send them scurrying (if the model is pulled backward, however, there is no response). "Whence," Campbell asks, "this abrupt seizure by an image to which there is no counterpart in the chicken's world? Living gulls and ducks, herons and pigeons, leave it cold; but *the work of art strikes some very deep chord!*" (31; our italics).

Campbell's hinted analogy, though only roughly approximate, will serve none-theless as an instructive introduction to the mythological approach to literature. For it is with the relationship of literary art to "some very deep chord" in human nature that mythological criticism deals. The myth critic is concerned to seek out those mysterious elements that inform certain literary works and that elicit, with almost uncanny force, dramatic and near-universal human reactions. The myth critic wishes to discover how certain works of literature, usually those that have become, or promise to become, "classics," image a kind of reality to which readers respond—while other works, seemingly as well constructed, and even some forms of reality, leave them cold. Speaking figuratively, the myth critic studies in depth the "wooden hawks" of great literature: the so-called *archetypes* or archetypal patterns that the writer has drawn forward along the tensed structural wires of his or her masterpiece and that vibrate in such a way that a sympathetic resonance is set off deep within the reader.

An obviously close connection exists between mythological criticism and the psychological approach discussed in Chapter 6: both are concerned with the motives that underlie human behavior. (See Chapter 4 for our discussion of Literary Darwinism—how humans respond to certain images in an evolutionary sense.) Between the two approaches are differences of degree and of affinities. Psychology tends to be experimental and diagnostic; it is closely related to biological science. Mythology tends to be speculative and philosophical; its affinities are with religion, anthropology, and cultural history. Such generalizations, of course, risk oversimplification; for instance, a great psychologist like Sigmund Freud ranged far beyond experimental and clinical study into the realms of myth, and his distinguished sometime protégé, Carl Gustav Jung, became one of the foremost mythologists of our time. Even so, the two approaches are distinct, and mythology is wider in its scope than psychology. For example, what psychoanalysis attempts to disclose about the individual personality, the study of myths reveals about the mind and character of a people. And just as dreams reflect the unconscious desires and anxieties of the individual, so myths are the symbolic projections of a people's hopes, values, fears, and aspirations.

According to the common misconception and misuse of the term, myths are merely primitive fictions, illusions, or opinions based upon false reasoning. Actually, mythology encompasses more than stories about the Greek and Roman deities or clever fables invented for the amusement of children. It may be true that myths do not meet standards of factual reality. Instead, they both reflect a more profound reality. As Mark Schorer says in *William Blake: The Politics of Vision*, "Myth is fundamental, the dramatic representation of our deepest instinctual life, of a primary awareness of man in the universe, capable of many configurations, upon which all particular opinions and attitudes depend" (29). According to Alan W. Watts, "Myth is to be defined as a complex of stories—some no doubt fact, and some fantasy—which, for various reasons, human beings regard as demonstrations of the inner meaning of the universe and of human life" (7).

Myths are by nature collective and communal; they bind a tribe or a nation together in common psychological and spiritual activities. Myth is a dynamic factor everywhere in human society; it transcends time, uniting the past (traditional modes of belief) with the present (current values) and reaching toward the future (spiritual and cultural aspirations).

II. SOME EXAMPLES OF ARCHETYPES

Having established the significance of **myth**, we need to examine its relationship to **archetypes** and archetypal patterns. Although every people has its own distinctive mythology that may be reflected in legend, folklore, and **ideology**—although, in other words, myths take their specific shapes from the cultural environments in which they grow—that myth exists is, in the general sense, universal. But even though similar **motifs** or themes may be found among many different mythologies, and certain images recur in the myths of peoples widely separated in time and place and tend to have a common meaning or, more accurately, tend to elicit comparable psychological responses and to serve similar cultural functions, there are no individual universal archetypes. As Philip Wheelwright explains in *Metaphor and Reality,* such **symbols** are

> those which carry the same or very similar meanings for a large portion, if not all, of mankind. It is a discoverable fact that certain symbols, such as the sky father and earth mother, light, blood, up-down, the axis of a wheel, and others, recur again and again in cultures so remote from one another in space and time that there is no likelihood of any historical influence and causal connection among them. (111)

Examples of some of the most widely recognized archetypes and the symbolic meanings with which they tend to be widely associated follow (again, it should be noted that these meanings may vary significantly from one context to another).

A. Images

1. Water: the mystery of creation; birth-death-resurrection; purification and redemption; fertility and growth. According to Jung, water is also the commonest symbol for the unconscious.
    a. The sea: the mother of all life; spiritual mystery and infinity; death and rebirth; timelessness and eternity; the unconscious.
    b. Rivers: death and rebirth (baptism); the flowing of time into eternity; transitional phases of the life cycle; incarnations of deities.
2. Sun (fire and sky are closely related): creative energy; law in nature; consciousness (thinking, enlightenment, wisdom, spiritual vision); father principle (moon and earth tend to be associated with female or mother principle); passage of time and life.
    a. Rising sun: birth; creation; enlightenment.
    b. Setting sun: death.
3. Colors
    a. Red: blood, sacrifice, violent passion; disorder.
    b. Green: growth; sensation; hope; fertility; in negative context may be associated with death and decay.
    c. Blue: usually highly positive, associated with truth, religious feeling, security, spiritual purity (the color of the Great Mother or Holy Mother).
    d. Black (darkness): chaos, mystery, the unknown; death; primal wisdom; the unconscious; evil; melancholy.
    e. White: highly multivalent, signifying, in its positive aspects, light, purity, innocence, and timelessness; in its negative aspects, death, terror, the supernatural, and the blinding truth of an inscrutable cosmic mystery (see, for instance, Herman Melville's chapter "The Whiteness of the Whale" in *Moby-Dick*).
4. Circle (sphere): wholeness, unity.
    a. Mandala (a geometric figure based upon the squaring of a circle around a unifying center; see the accompanying illustration of the classic Shri-Yantra mandala): the desire for spiritual unity and psychic integration.

Note that in its classic Asian forms the mandala juxtaposes the triangle, the square, and the circle with their numerical equivalents of three, four, and seven.

   b. Egg (oval): the mystery of life and the forces of generation.

   c. Yang-yin: a Chinese symbol (below) representing the union of the opposite forces of the yang (masculine principle, light, activity, the conscious mind) and the yin (female principle, darkness, passivity, the unconscious).

   d. Ouroboros: the ancient symbol of the snake biting its own tail, signifying the eternal cycle of life, primordial unconsciousness, the unity of opposing forces (cf. yang-yin).

5. Serpent (snake, worm): symbol of energy and pure force (cf. libido); evil, corruption, sensuality; destruction; mystery; wisdom; the unconscious.

6. Numbers:

   a. Three: light; spiritual awareness and unity (cf. the Holy Trinity); the male principle.

   b. Four: associated with the circle, life cycle, four seasons; female principle, earth, nature; four elements (earth, air, fire, water).

   c. Five: signifying integration, the four limbs and the head that controls them; the four cardinal points plus the center.

   d. Seven: among the most potent of all symbolic numbers—signifying the union of *three* and *four*, the completion of a cycle, perfect order.

7. The archetypal woman (Great Mother—the mysteries of life, death, transformation); the female principle associated with the moon):

   a. The Good Mother (positive aspects of the Earth Mother): associated with the life principle, birth, warmth, nourishment, protection, fertility, growth, abundance (for example, Demeter, Ceres).

   b. The Terrible Mother (including the negative aspects of the Earth Mother): the witch, sorceress, siren, whore, lamia, femme fatale—associated with sensuality, sexual orgies, fear, danger, darkness, dismemberment, emasculation, death; the unconscious in its terrifying aspects.

   c. The Soul Mate: the Sophia figure, Holy Mother, the princess or "beautiful lady"—incarnation of inspiration and spiritual fulfillment (cf. the Jungian anima).

8. The demon lover (the male counterpart of the Terrible Mother): the devil, Satan, Dracula (cf. Blake's "The Sick Rose" and the Jungian animus).

9. The Wise Old Man (savior, redeemer, guru): personification of the spiritual principle, representing "knowledge, reflection, insight, wisdom, cleverness, and intuition on the one hand, and on the other, moral qualities such as goodwill and readiness to help, which make his 'spiritual' character sufficiently plain.... Apart from his cleverness, wisdom, and insight, the old man ... is also notable for his moral qualities; what is more, he even tests the moral qualities of others and makes gifts dependent on this test.... The old man always appears when the hero is in a hopeless and desperate situation from which only profound reflection or a lucky idea ... can extricate him. But since, for internal and external reasons, the hero cannot accomplish this himself, the knowledge needed to compensate the deficiency comes in the form of a personified thought, i.e., in the shape of this sagacious and helpful old man" (Jung, *Archetypes* 217ff.). Merlin, Gandalf, Yoda, and Dumbledore are all wise old men.

10. The Trickster (joker, jester, clown, fool, fraud, prankster, picaro [rogue], poltergeist, confidence man ["con man"], medicine man [shaman], magician [sleight-of-hand artist], "Spirit Mercurius" [shape-shifter], *simia dei* ["the ape of God"], witch). The trickster appears to be the opposite of the wise old man because of his close affinity with the shadow archetype (for "shadow," see III.B.1); however, he has a positive side and serves a healing function through his transformative influence. Jung remarks that "He is a forerunner of the saviour, and, like him, God, man, and animal at once. He is both subhuman and superhuman, a bestial and divine being..." (*Archetypes* 263). Jane Wheelwright's definition is particularly instructive: "Image of the archetype of mischievousness, unexpectedness, disorder, amorality, the trickster is an archetypal shadow figure that represents a primordial, dawning consciousness. Compensating for rigid or overly righteous collective attitudes, it functions collectively as a cathartic safety valve for pent-up social pressures, a reminder of humankind's primitive origins and the fallibility of its institutions" (286). Jeanne Rosier Smith points out that myths, "as they appear in literature, can be read as part of an effort for human and cultural survival. The trickster's role as survivor and transformer, creating order from chaos, accounts for the figure's universal appeal and its centrality to the mythology and folklore of so many cultures" (3). While the trickster archetype has appeared in cultures throughout the world from time immemorial, beginning with examples like Prometheus, he (or, in some cases, she) is particularly notable in African American and American Indian cultures (see our discussion of *Huckleberry Finn* in Chapter 9).

11. Garden: paradise; innocence; unspoiled beauty (especially feminine); fertility.

12. Tree: "In its most general sense, the symbolism of the tree denotes life of the cosmos: its consistence, growth, proliferation, generative and regenerative processes. It stands for inexhaustible life, and is therefore equivalent to a symbol of immortality" (Cirlot 328; cf. the depiction of the cross of redemption as the tree of life in Christian iconography).

13. Desert: spiritual aridity; death; nihilism, hopelessness.

14. Mountain: aspiration and inspiration; meditation and spiritual elevation. "The mountain stands for the goal of the pilgrimage and ascent, hence it often has the psychological meaning of the self" (Jung, *Archetypes* 219n).

These examples are by no means exhaustive, but represent some of the more common archetypal images that the reader is likely to encounter in literature. The images we have listed do not necessarily function as archetypes every time they appear in a literary work. The discreet critic interprets them as such only if the total context of the work logically supports an archetypal reading.

B. Archetypal Motifs or Patterns

1. Creation: perhaps the most fundamental of all archetypal motifs—virtually every mythology is built on some account of how the cosmos, nature, and humankind were brought into existence by some supernatural Being or beings.

2. Immortality: another fundamental archetype, generally taking one of two basic narrative forms:

   a. Escape from time: "return to paradise," the state of perfect, timeless bliss enjoyed by man and woman before their tragic Fall into corruption and mortality.

   b. Mystical submersion into cyclical time: the theme of endless death and regeneration—human beings achieve a kind of immortality by submitting to the vast, mysterious rhythm of Nature's eternal cycle, particularly the cycle of the seasons.

3. Hero/Heroine archetypes (archetypes of transformation and redemption):

   a. The **quest**: the hero (savior, deliverer) undertakes some long journey during which he or she must perform impossible tasks, battle with monsters, solve unanswerable riddles, and overcome insurmountable obstacles in order to save the kingdom.

   b. **Initiation**: the hero undergoes a series of excruciating ordeals in passing from ignorance and immaturity to social and spiritual adulthood, that is, in achieving maturity and becoming a full-fledged member of his or her social group. The initiation most commonly consists of three distinct phases: (1) separation, (2) transformation, and (3) return. Like the quest, this is a variation of the death-and-rebirth archetype.

   c. The sacrificial **scapegoat**: the hero, with whom the welfare of the tribe or nation is identified, must die to atone for the people's sins and restore the land to fruitfulness.

C. Archetypes as Genres

Finally, in addition to appearing as images and motifs, archetypes may be found in even more complex combinations as genres or types of literature that conform with the major phases of the seasonal cycle. Northrop Frye, in his *Anatomy of Criticism,* indicates the correspondent genres for the four seasons as follows:

1. The mythos of spring: **comedy**
2. The mythos of summer: **romance**
3. The mythos of fall: **tragedy**
4. The mythos of winter: **irony**

Frye identifies myth with literature, asserting that myth is a "structural organizing principle of literary form" (341) and that an archetype is essentially an "element of one's literary experience" (365). And in *The Stubborn Structure* he claims that "mythology as a whole provides a kind of diagram or blueprint of what literature as a whole is all about, an imaginative survey of the human situation from the beginning to the end, from the height to the depth, of what is imaginatively conceivable" (102).

III. MYTH CRITICISM IN PRACTICE

Unlike the critic who relies heavily on history and the biography of the writer, the myth critic is interested more in prehistory and the biographies of the gods. Unlike the critic who concentrates on the shape and symmetry of the work itself, the myth critic probes for the inner spirit which gives that form its vitality and its enduring appeal. And unlike the critic who is prone to look on the artifact as the product of some sexual neurosis, the myth critic sees the work holistically, as the manifestation of vitalizing, integrative forces arising from the depths of humankind's collective psyche. Yet only during the past century did the proper interpretive tools become available through the development of such disciplines as anthropology, psychology, and cultural history.

A. Anthropology and Its Uses

The rapid advancement of modern anthropology since the end of the nineteenth century has been the most important single influence on the growth of myth criticism. Shortly after the turn of the century this influence was revealed in a series of important studies published by the Cambridge Hellenists, a group of British scholars who applied recent anthropological discoveries to the understanding of Greek classics in terms of mythic and ritualistic origins. Noteworthy contributions by members of this group include *Anthropology and the Classics,* a symposium edited by R. R. Marett; Jane Harrison's *Themis;* Gilbert Murray's *Euripides and His Age;* and F. M. Cornford's *Origin of Attic Comedy.* But by far the most significant member of the British school was Sir James G. Frazer, whose monumental *The Golden Bough* has exerted an enormous influence on twentieth-century literature, not merely on the critics but also on such creative writers as James Joyce, Thomas Mann, Joseph Conrad, and T. S. Eliot. Frazer's work, a comparative study of the primitive origins of religion in magic, ritual, and myth, was first published in two volumes in 1890, later expanded to twelve volumes, and then published in a one-volume abridged edition in 1922. Frazer's main contribution was to demonstrate the "essential similarity of man's chief wants everywhere and at all times," particularly as these wants were reflected throughout ancient mythologies. He explains, for example, in the abridged edition, that

> [u]nder the names of Osiris, Tammuz, Adonis, and Attis, the peoples of Egypt and Western Asia represented the yearly decay and revival of life, especially vegetable life, which they personified as a god who annually died and rose again from the dead. In name and detail the rites varied from place to place: in substance they were the same. (325)

The central motif with which Frazer deals is the archetype of crucifixion and resurrection, specifically the myths describing the "killing of the divine king." Among many primitive peoples it was believed that the ruler was a divine or semidivine being whose life was identified with the life cycle in nature and in human existence. Because of this identification, the safety of the people and even of the world was felt to depend upon the life of the god-king. A vigorous, healthy ruler would ensure natural and human productivity; on the other hand, a sick or maimed king would bring blight and disease to the land and its people. Frazer points out that if

> the course of nature is dependent on the man-god's life, what catastrophes may not be expected from the gradual enfeeblement of his powers and their final extinction in death? There is only one way of averting these dangers. The man-god must be killed as soon as he shows symptoms that his powers are beginning to fail, and his soul must be transferred to a vigorous successor before it has been seriously impaired by threatened decay. (265)

Among some peoples the kings were put to death at regular intervals to ensure the welfare of the tribe; later, however, substitute figures were killed in place of the kings themselves, or the sacrifices became purely symbolic rather than literal.

Corollary to the rite of sacrifice was the **scapegoat** archetype. This motif was centered in the belief that, by transferring the corruptions of the tribe to a sacred animal or person, then by killing (and in some instances eating) this scapegoat, the tribe could achieve the cleansing and atonement thought necessary for natural and spiritual rebirth. Pointing out that food and children are the primary needs for human survival, Frazer emphasizes that the rites of blood sacrifice and purification were considered by ancient peoples as a magical guarantee of rejuvenation, an assurance of life, both vegetable and human. If such customs strike us as incredibly primitive, we need only to recognize their vestiges in the civilized world—for example, the irrational satisfaction that some people gain by the persecution of such minority groups as blacks and Jews as scapegoats, or the more wholesome feelings of renewal derived from our New Year's festivities and resolutions, the homely tradition of spring cleaning, the celebration of Easter and the Eucharist. Modern writers themselves have employed the scapegoat motif with striking relevance—for example, Shirley Jackson's "The Lottery."

The insights of Frazer and the Cambridge Hellenists have been extremely helpful in myth criticism, especially in the mythological approach to **drama**. Many scholars theorize that **tragedy** originated from the primitive rites we have described. The tragedies of Sophocles and Aeschylus, for example, were written to be played during the festival of Dionysus, annual religious ceremonies during which the ancient Greeks celebrated the deaths of the winter-kings and the rebirths of the gods of spring and renewed life.

Sophocles's *Oedipus* is an excellent example of the fusion of myth and literature. Sophocles produced a great play, but the plot of *Oedipus* was not his invention. It was a well-known mythic narrative long before he immortalized it as tragic drama. Both the myth and the play contain a number of familiar archetypes, as a brief summary of the plot indicates. The king and queen of ancient Thebes, Laius and Jocasta, are told in a prophecy that their newborn son, after he has grown up, will murder his father and marry his mother. To prevent this catastrophe, the king orders one of his men to pierce the infant's heels and abandon him to die in the wilderness. But the child is saved by a shepherd and taken to Corinth, where he is reared as the son of King Polybus and Queen Merope, who lead the boy to believe that they are his real parents. After reaching maturity and hearing of a prophecy that he is destined to commit patricide and incest, Oedipus flees from Corinth to Thebes. On his journey he meets an old man and his servants, quarrels with them and kills them. Before entering Thebes he encounters the Sphinx (who holds the city under a spell), solves her riddle, and frees the city; his reward is the hand of the widowed Queen Jocasta. He then rules a prosperous Thebes for many years, fathering four children by Jocasta. At last, however, a blight falls upon his kingdom because Laius's slayer has gone unpunished. Oedipus starts an intensive investigation to find the culprit—only to discover ultimately that he himself is the guilty one, that the old man whom he had killed on his journey to Thebes was Laius, his real father. Overwhelmed by this revelation, Oedipus blinds himself with brooches taken from his dead mother-wife, who has hanged herself, and goes into exile. Following his sacrificial punishment, Thebes is restored to health and abundance.

Even in this bare summary we may discern at least two archetypal motifs: (1) In the quest motif, Oedipus, as the hero, undertakes a journey during which he encounters the Sphinx, a supernatural monster with the body of a lion and the head of a woman; by answering her riddle, he delivers the kingdom and marries the queen. (2) In the king-as-sacrificial-scapegoat motif, the welfare of the state, both human and natural (Thebes is stricken by both plague and drought), is bound up with the personal fate of the ruler; only after Oedipus has offered himself up as a scapegoat is the land redeemed.

Considering that Sophocles wrote his tragedy expressly for a ritual occasion, we are hardly surprised that *Oedipus* reflects certain facets of the fertility myths described by Frazer. More remarkable, and more instructive for the student interested in myth criticism, is the revelation of similar facets in the great tragedy written by Shakespeare two thousand years later.

1. The Sacrificial Hero: Hamlet

One of the first modern scholars to point out these similarities was Gilbert Murray. In his "Hamlet and Orestes," delivered as a lecture in 1914 and subsequently published in *The Classical Tradition in Poetry,* Murray indicated a number of parallels between the mythic elements of Shakespeare's play and those in *Oedipus* and in the *Agamemnon* of Aeschylus. The heroes of all three works derive from the *Golden Bough* kings; they are all haunted, sacrificial figures. Furthermore, as with the Greek tragedies, the story of Hamlet was not the playwright's invention but was drawn from legend. As literary historians tell us, the old Scandinavian story of Amlehtus or Amlet, Prince of Jutland, was recorded as early as the twelfth century by Saxo Grammaticus in his *History of the Danes.* Murray cites an even earlier passing reference to the prototypal Hamlet in a Scandinavian poem composed in about A.D. 980. Giorgio de Santillana and Hertha von Dechend in *Hamlet's Mill* have traced this archetypal character back through the legendary Icelandic Amlodhi to Oriental mythology. It is therefore evident that the core of Shakespeare's play is mythic. In Murray's words,

> The things that thrill and amaze us in *Hamlet*...are not any historical particulars about mediaeval Elsinore...but things belonging to the old stories and the old magic rites, which stirred and thrilled our forefathers five and six thousand years ago; set them dancing all night on the hills, tearing beasts and men in pieces, and giving up their own bodies to a ghastly death, in hope thereby to keep the green world from dying and to be the saviours of their own people. (236)

By the time Sophocles and Aeschylus were producing their tragedies for Athenian audiences, such sacrifices were no longer performed literally but were acted out symbolically on stage; yet their mythic significance was the same. Indeed, their significance was very similar in the case of Shakespeare's audiences. The Elizabethans were a myth-minded and symbol-receptive people. There was no need for Shakespeare to interpret for his audience: they *felt* the mythic content of his plays. And though myth may smolder only feebly in the present-day audience, we still respond, despite our intellectual sophistication, to the archetypes in *Hamlet.*

Such critics as Murray and Francis Fergusson have provided clues to many of Hamlet's archetypal mysteries. In *The Idea of Theater,* Fergusson discloses point by point how the scenes in Shakespeare's play follow the same ritual pattern as those in Greek tragedy, specifically in *Oedipus;* he indicates that

> in both plays a royal sufferer is associated with pollution, in its very sources, of an entire social order. Both plays open with an invocation for the well-being of the endangered body politic. In both, the destiny of the individual and of society are closely intertwined; and in both the suffering of the royal victim seems to be necessary before purgation and renewal can be achieved. (118)

To appreciate how closely the moral norms in Shakespeare's play are related to those of ancient vegetation myths, we need only to note how often images of disease and corruption are used to symbolize the evil that has blighted Hamlet's Denmark. The following statement from Philip Wheelwright's *The Burning Fountain,* explaining the organic source of good and evil, is directly relevant to the moral vision in *Hamlet,* particularly to the implications of Claudius's crime and its disastrous consequences. From the natural or organic standpoint,

> Good is life, vitality, propagation, health; evil is death, impotence, disease. Of these several terms *health* and *disease* are the most important and comprehensive. Death is but an interim evil; it occurs periodically, but there is the assurance of new life ever springing up to take its place. The normal cycle of life and death is a healthy cycle, and the purpose of the major seasonal festivals (for example, the Festival of Dionysus) was at least as much to celebrate joyfully the turning wheel of great creative Nature as to achieve magical effects. Disease and blight, however, interrupt the cycle; they are the real destroyers; and health is the good most highly to be prized. (197)

Wheelwright continues by pointing out that because murder (not to be confused with ritual sacrifice) does violence to both the natural cycle of life and the social organism, the murderer is symbolically diseased. Furthermore, when the victim is a member of the murderer's own family, an even more compact organism than the tribe or the political state, the disease is especially virulent.

We should mention one other myth that relates closely to the meaning of *Hamlet,* the myth of divine appointment. This was the belief, strongly fostered by such Tudor monarchs as Henry VII, Henry VIII, and Elizabeth I, that not only had the Tudors been divinely appointed to bring order and happiness out of civil strife but also any attempt to break this divine ordinance (for example, by insurrection or assassination) would result in social, political, and natural chaos. We see this Tudor revenge myth reflected in several of Shakespeare's plays (for example, in *Richard III, Macbeth,* and *King Lear*) where interference with the order of divine succession or appointment results in both political and natural chaos, and where a deformed, corrupt, or weak monarch epitomizes a diseased political state. This national myth is, quite obviously, central in *Hamlet.*

The relevance of myth to *Hamlet* should now be apparent. The play's thematic heart is the ancient, archetypal mystery of the life cycle itself. Its pulse is the same tragic rhythm that moved Sophocles's audience at the festival of Dionysus and moves us today through forces that transcend our conscious processes. Through the insights provided us by anthropological scholars, however, we may perceive the essential archetypal pattern of Shakespeare's tragedy. Hamlet's Denmark is a diseased and rotten state because Claudius's "foul and most unnatural murder" of his king-brother has subverted the divinely ordained laws of nature and of kingly succession. The disruption is intensified by the blood kinship between victim and murderer. Claudius, whom the Ghost identifies as "The Serpent," bears the primal blood curse of Cain. And because the state is identified with its ruler, Denmark shares and suffers also from his blood guilt. Its natural cycle interrupted, the nation is threatened by chaos: civil strife within and war without. As Hamlet exclaims, "The time is out of joint; O cursed spite,/That ever I was born to set it right!"

Hamlet's role in the drama is that of the prince-hero who, to deliver his nation from the blight that has fallen upon it, must not only avenge his father's murder but also offer himself up as a royal scapegoat. Hamlet's reluctance to accept the role of cathartic agent is a principal reason for his procrastination in killing Claudius, an act that may well involve his self-destruction. He is a reluctant but dutiful scapegoat, and he realizes ultimately that there can be no substitute victim in this sacrificial rite—hence his decision to accept Laertes's challenge to a dueling match that he suspects has been fixed by Claudius. The bloody **climax** of the tragedy is therefore not merely spectacular melodrama but an essential element in the archetypal pattern of sacrifice-atonement-**catharsis**. Not only must all those die who have been infected by the evil contagion (Claudius, Gertrude, Polonius, Rosencrantz and Guildenstern—even Ophelia and Laertes), but the prince-hero himself must suffer "crucifixion" before Denmark can be purged and reborn under the healthy new regime of Fortinbras.

Enhancing the motif of the sacrificial scapegoat is Hamlet's long and difficult spiritual journey—his initiation, as it were—from innocent, carefree youth (he has been a university student) through a series of painful ordeals to sadder, but wiser, maturity. His is a long night's journey of the soul, and Shakespeare employs archetypal imagery to convey this thematic motif: *Hamlet* is an autumnal, nighttime play dominated by images of darkness and blood, and the hero appropriately wears black, the archetypal color of melancholy. The superficial object of his dark quest is to solve the riddle of his father's death. On a deeper level, his quest leads him down the labyrinthine ways of the human mystery, the mystery of human life and destiny. (Observe how consistently his soliloquies turn toward the puzzles of life and of self.) As with the riddle of the Sphinx, the enigmatic answer is "man," the clue to which is given in Polonius's glib admonition, "To thine own self be true." In this sense, then, Hamlet's quest is the quest undertaken by all of us who would gain that rare and elusive philosopher's stone, self-knowledge.

2. Archetypes of Time and Immortality: "To His Coy Mistress"

Mythopoeic poets William Blake, William Butler Yeats, and T. S. Eliot carefully structured many of their works on myth. Even those poets who are not self-appointed myth-makers often employ images and motifs that, intentionally or not, function as archetypes. Andrew Marvell's "To His Coy Mistress" seems to fit into this latter category.

Because of its strongly suggestive (and suggested) sensuality and its apparently cynical theme, "To His Coy Mistress" is sometimes dismissed as an immature if not immoral love poem. But to see the poem as little more than a clever proposition is to miss its greatness. No literary work survives because it is merely clever, or merely well written. It must partake somehow of the archetypal.

Superficially a love poem, "To His Coy Mistress" is, in a deeper sense, a poem about time. As such, it is concerned with immortality, a fundamental motif in myth. In the first two stanzas we encounter an inversion or rejection of traditional conceptions of human immortality. Stanza 1 is an ironic presentation of the "escape from time" to some paradisal state in which lovers may dally for an eternity. But such a state of perfect, eternal bliss is a foolish delusion, as the speaker suggests in his **subjunctive** "Had we…." and in his description of love as some kind of monstrous vegetable growing slowly to an infinite size in the archetypal garden. Stanza 2 presents, in dramatic contrast, the desert archetype in terms of another kind of time, naturalistic time. This is the time governed by the inexorable laws of nature (note the sun archetype imaged in "Time's wingèd chariot"), the laws of decay, death, and physical extinction. Stanza 2 is as extreme in its philosophical **realism** as the first **stanza** is in its impracticable idealization.

The concluding stanza, radically altered in tone, presents a third kind of time, an escape into cyclical time and thereby a chance for immortality. Again we encounter the sun archetype, but this is the sun of "soul" and of "instant fires"—images not of death but of life and creative energy, which are fused with the sphere ("Let us roll all our strength and all/Our sweetness up into one ball"), the archetype of primal wholeness and fulfillment. In *Myth and Reality*, Mircea Eliade indicates that one of the most widespread motifs in immortality myths is the *regressus ad uterum* (a "return to the origin" of creation or to the symbolic womb of life) and that this return is considered to be symbolically feasible by some philosophers (for example, the Chinese Taoists) through alchemical fire:

> During the fusion of metals the Taoist alchemist tries to bring about in his own body the union of the two cosmological principles, Heaven and Earth, in order to reproduce the primordial chaotic situation that existed before the Creation. This primordial situation…corresponds both to the egg (that is, the archetypal sphere) or the embryo and to the paradisal and innocent state of the uncreated World. (83–84)

We are not suggesting that Marvell was familiar with Taoist philosophy or that he was consciously aware of immortality archetypes. However, in representing the age-old dilemma of time and immortality, Marvell employed a cluster of images charged with mythic significance. His poet-lover seems to offer the alchemy of love as a way of defeating the laws of naturalistic time; love is a means of participating in, even intensifying, the mysterious rhythms of nature's eternal cycle. If life is to be judged, as some philosophers have suggested, not by duration but by intensity, then Marvell's lovers, at least during the act of love, will achieve a kind of immortality by "devouring" time or by transcending the laws of clock time ("Time's wingèd chariot"). And if this alchemical transmutation requires a fire hot enough to melt them into one primordial ball, then it is perhaps also hot enough to melt the sun itself and "make him run." Thus we see that the overt sexuality of Marvell's poem is, in a mythic sense, suggestive of a profound metaphysical quest, an insight that continues to fascinate those philosophers and scientists who would penetrate the mysteries of time and eternity.

Figure 7.1. Carl Jung, cover of *TIME Magazine* (February 14, 1955).
Courtesy Wrights Reprints.

B. Jungian Psychology and Its Archetypal Insights

The second major influence on mythological criticism is the work of C. G. Jung, the great psychologist-philosopher and onetime student of Freud who broke with the master because of what he regarded as a too-narrow approach to psychoanalysis. Jung believed libido (psychic energy) to be more psychic than sexual; also, he considered Freudian theories too negative because of Freud's emphasis on the neurotic rather than the healthy aspects of the psyche.

Jung's primary contribution to myth criticism is his theory of racial memory and archetypes. In developing this concept, Jung expanded Freud's theories of the personal unconscious, asserting that beneath this is a primeval, *collective unconscious* shared in the psychic inheritance of all members of the human family. As Jung explains in *The Structure and Dynamics of the Psyche*,

> If it were possible to personify the unconscious, we might think of it as a collective human being combining the characteristics of both sexes, transcending youth and age, birth and death, and, from having at its command a human experience of one or two million years, practically immortal. If such a being existed, it would be exalted over all temporal change; the present would mean neither more nor less to it than any year in the hundredth millennium before Christ; it would be a dreamer of age-old dreams and, owing to its immeasurable experience, an incomparable prognosticator. It would have lived countless times over again the life of the individual, the family, the tribe, and the nation, and it would possess a living sense of the rhythm of growth, flowering, and decay. (349–50)

Just as certain instincts are inherited by the lower animals (for example, the instinct of the baby chicken to run from a hawk's shadow), so more complex psychic predispositions are inherited by human beings. Jung believed, contrary to eighteenth-century Lockean psychology, that "Mind is not born as a *tabula rasa* [a clean slate]. Like the body, it has its pre-established individual definiteness; namely, forms of behaviour. They become manifest in the ever-recurring patterns of psychic functioning" (*Psyche and Symbol* xv). Therefore what Jung called "myth-forming" structural elements are ever present in the unconscious psyche; again, his ideas are interestingly compared to the insights of Literary Darwinism (Chapter 4).

Jung was also careful to explain that archetypes are not inherited ideas or patterns of thought, but rather that they are predispositions to respond in similar ways to certain stimuli: "In reality they belong to the realm of activities of the instincts and in that sense they represent inherited forms of psychic behaviour" (xvi). In *Psychological Reflections*, he maintained that these psychic instincts "are older than historical man,...have been ingrained in him from earliest times, and, eternally living, outlasting all generations, still make up the groundwork of the human psyche. It is only possible to live the fullest life when we are in harmony with these symbols; wisdom is a return to them" (42).

In stressing that archetypes are actually "inherited forms," Jung also went further than most of the anthropologists, who tended to see these forms as social phenomena passed down from one generation to the next through various sacred rites rather than through the structure of the psyche itself. Furthermore, in *The Archetypes and the Collective Unconscious*, he theorized that myths do not derive from external factors such as the seasonal or solar cycle but are, in truth, the projections of innate psychic phenomena:

> All the mythologized processes of nature, such as summer and winter, the phases of the moon, the rainy seasons, and so forth, are in no sense allegories of these

objective occurrences; rather they are symbolic expressions of the inner, unconscious drama of the psyche which becomes accessible to man's consciousness by
way of projection—that is, mirrored in the events of nature. (6)

In other words, myths are the means by which archetypes, essentially unconscious
forms, become manifest and articulate to the conscious mind. Jung indicated further that archetypes reveal themselves in the dreams of individuals, so that we
might say that dreams are "personalized myths," and myths are "depersonalized
dreams."

Jung detected an intimate relationship between dreams, myths, and art in that
all three serve as media through which archetypes become accessible to consciousness. The great artist, as Jung observes in *Modern Man in Search of a Soul*, is a
person who possesses the "primordial vision," a special sensitivity to archetypal
patterns and a gift for speaking in primordial images that enable him or her to
transmit experiences of the "inner world" through art. Considering the nature of
the artist's raw materials, Jung suggests it is only logical that the artist "will resort
to mythology in order to give his experience its most fitting expression." This is not
to say that the artist gets materials secondhand: "The primordial experience is the
source of his creativeness; it cannot be fathomed, and therefore requires mythological imagery to give it form" (164).

Although Jung himself wrote relatively little that could be called literary criticism, what he did write leaves no doubt that he believed literature, and art in general, to be a vital ingredient in human civilization. Most important, his theories
have expanded the horizons of literary interpretation for those critics concerned
to use the tools of the mythological approach and for psychological critics who
have felt too tightly constricted by Freudian theory.

1. *Some Special Archetypes: Shadow, Persona, and Anima*

In *The Archetypes and the Collective Unconscious,* Jung discusses at length many of
the archetypal patterns that we have already examined (for example, water, colors,
rebirth). In this way, although his emphasis is psychological rather than anthropological, a good deal of his work overlaps that of Frazer and the others. But, as we
have already indicated, Jung is not merely a derivative or secondary figure; he is a
major influence in the growth of myth criticism. For one thing, he provided some
of the favorite terminology now current among myth critics. The term "archetype"
itself, though not coined by Jung, enjoys its present widespread usage among the
myth critics primarily because of his influence. Also, like Freud, he was a pioneer
whose brilliant flashes of insight have helped to light our way in exploring the
darker recesses of the human mind.

One major contribution is Jung's theory of *individuation* as related to those
archetypes designated as the *shadow,* the *persona,* and the *anima.* Individuation
is a psychological growing up, the process of discovering those aspects of one's
self that make one an individual different from other members of the species. It is
essentially a process of recognition—that is, as one matures, the individual must
consciously recognize the various aspects, unfavorable as well as favorable, of one's

total self. This self-recognition requires extraordinary courage and honesty but is absolutely essential if one is to become a well-balanced individual. Jung theorizes that neuroses are the results of the person's failure to confront and accept some archetypal component of the unconscious. Instead of assimilating this unconscious element into their consciousness, neurotic individuals persist in projecting it upon some other person or object. In Jung's words, projection is an "unconscious, automatic process whereby a content that is unconscious to the subject transfers itself to an object, so that it seems to belong to that object. The projection ceases the moment it becomes conscious, that is to say when it is seen as belonging to the subject" (*Archetypes* 60). In layman's terms, the habit of projection is reflected in the attitude that "everybody is out of step but me" or "I'm the only honest person in the crowd." It is commonplace that we can project our own unconscious faults and weaknesses on others much more easily than we can accept them as part of our own nature.

The shadow, the persona, and the anima are structural components of the psyche that Jung believed human beings have inherited, just as the chicken has inherited his built-in response to the hawk. In melodrama, such as the traditional western or cop story, the persona, the anima, and the shadow are projected, respectively, in the characters of the hero, the heroine, and the villain. The shadow is the darker side of our unconscious self, the inferior and less pleasing aspects of the personality, which we wish to suppress. "Taking it in its deepest sense," writes Jung in *Psychological Reflections,* "the shadow is the invisible saurian [reptilian] tail that man still drags behind him" (217). The most common variant of this archetype, when projected, is the Devil, who, in Jung's words, represents the "dangerous aspect of the unrecognized dark half of the personality" (*Two Essays* 94). In literature we see symbolic representations of this archetype in such figures as Shakespeare's Iago, Milton's Satan, Goethe's Mephistopheles, and Conrad's Kurtz.

The anima is perhaps the most complex of Jung's archetypes. It is the "soul-image," the spirit of a man's *élan vital,* his life force or vital energy. In the sense of "soul," says Jung, anima is the "living thing in man, that which lives of itself and causes life.... Were it not for the leaping and twinkling of the soul, man would rot away in his greatest passion, idleness" (*Archetypes* 26–27). Jung gives the anima a feminine designation in the male psyche, pointing out that the "anima-image is usually projected upon women" (in the female psyche this archetype is called the *animus*). In this sense, anima is the contrasexual part of a man's psyche, the image of the opposite sex that he carries in both his personal and his collective unconscious. As an old German proverb puts it, "Every man has his own Eve within him"—in other words, the human psyche is bisexual, though the psychological characteristics of the opposite sex in each of us are generally unconscious, revealing themselves only in dreams or in projections on someone in our environment. The phenomenon of love, especially love at first sight, may be explained at least in part by Jung's theory of the anima: we tend to be attracted to members of the opposite sex who mirror the characteristics of our own inner selves. In literature, Jung regards such figures as Helen of Troy, Dante's Beatrice, Milton's Eve, and H. Rider Haggard's She as personifications of the anima. Perhaps more recognizable today as anima figures are Pinocchio's Blue Fairy, the title character on television's *I Dream of Jeannie*, J. R.R. Tolkien's Galadriel, or even the somewhat coarser version in the character of Marla in Chuck Palahniuk's *Fight Club*. Following Jung's theory, we might say that any female figure who is invested with unusual significance or power is likely to be a symbol of the anima. (Examples for the animus came less readily to Jung; like Freud, he tended to describe features of the male psyche more than those of the female, even though both analysts' patients were nearly all women. But examples of animus figures would include the Tin Man, Cowardly Lion, and Scarecrow of L. Frank Baum's *The Wizard of Oz* books.) One other function of the anima is noteworthy here. The anima is a kind of mediator between the ego (the conscious will or thinking self) and the unconscious (or inner world) of the male individual. This function will be somewhat clearer if we compare the anima with the persona.

The persona is the obverse of the anima in that it mediates between our ego and the external world. Speaking metaphorically, let us say that the ego is a coin. The image on one side is the anima; on the other side, the persona. The personal is the actor's mask that we show to the world—it is our social personality, a personality that is sometimes quite different from our true self. The word derives from Greek and literally means "mask." Jung, in discussing this social mask, explains that, to achieve psychological maturity, the individual must have a flexible, viable persona that can be brought into harmony with the other components of his or her psychic makeup. He states, furthermore, that a personal that is too artificial or rigid results in such symptoms of neurotic disturbance as irritability and melancholy.

2. "Young Goodman Brown": A Failure of Individuation

The literary relevance of Jung's theory of shadow, anima, and persona may be seen in an analysis of Hawthorne's story "Young Goodman Brown." In the first place, Brown's persona is both false and inflexible. It is the social mask of a God-fearing, prayerful, self-righteous Puritan—the persona of a good man with all its pietistic connotations. Brown considers himself both the good Christian and the good husband married to a "blessed angel on earth." In truth, however, he is much less the good man than the bad boy. His behavior from start to finish is that of the adolescent male. His desertion of his wife, for example, is motivated by his juvenile compulsion to have one last fling as a moral Peeping Tom. His failure to recognize himself (and his own base motives) when he confronts Satan—his shadow—is merely another indication of his spiritual immaturity.

Just as his persona has proved inadequate in mediating between Brown's ego and the external world, so his anima fails in relating to his inner world. It is only fitting that his soul-image or anima should be named Faith. His trouble is that he sees Faith not as a true wifely companion but as a mother (Jung points out that, during childhood, anima is usually projected on the mother), as is revealed when he thinks that he will "cling to her skirts and follow her to heaven." In other words, if a young man's Faith has the qualities of the Good Mother, then he might expect to be occasionally indulged in his juvenile escapades. But mature faith, like marriage, is a covenant that binds both parties mutually to uphold its sacred vows. If one party breaks this covenant, as Goodman Brown does, he must face the unpleasant consequences: at worst, separation and divorce; at best, suspicion (perhaps Faith herself has been unfaithful), loss of harmony, trust, and peace of mind. It is the latter consequences that Brown has to face. Even then, he still behaves like a child. Instead of admitting to his error and working maturely for a reconciliation, he sulks.

In clinical terms, young Goodman Brown suffers from a failure of personality integration. He has been stunted in his psychological growth (individuation) because he is unable to confront his shadow, recognize it as a part of his own psyche, and assimilate it into his consciousness. He persists, instead, in projecting the shadow image: first, in the form of the Devil; then on the members of his community (Goody Cloyse, Deacon Gookin, and others); and, finally on Faith herself (his anima), so that ultimately, in his eyes, the whole world is one of shadow, or gloom. As Jung explains in *Psyche and Symbol*, the results of such projections are often disastrous for the individual:

> The effect of projection is to isolate the subject from his environment, since instead of a real relation to it there is now only an illusory one. Projections change the world into the replica of one's own unknown face....The resultant [malaise is in] turn explained by projection as the malevolence of the environment, and by means of this vicious circle the isolation is intensified. The more projections interpose themselves between the subject and the environment, the harder it becomes for the ego to see through its illusions. [Note Goodman Brown's inability to distinguish between reality and his illusory dream in the forest.]
>
> It is often tragic to see how blatantly a man bungles his own life and the lives of others yet remains totally incapable of seeing how much the whole tragedy originates in himself, and how he continually feeds it and keeps it going. Not *consciously*, of course—for consciously he is engaged in bewailing and cursing a *faithless* [our italics] world that recedes further and further into the distance. Rather, it is an unconscious factor which spins the illusions that veil his world. And what is being spun is a cocoon, which in the end will completely envelop him. (9)

Jung could hardly have diagnosed Goodman Brown's malady more accurately had he been directing these comments squarely at Hawthorne's story. That he was generalizing adds impact to his theory as well as to Hawthorne's moral insight.

3. *Creature or Creator: Who Is the Real Monster in* Frankenstein?

Speaking archetypally, we may say of Frankenstein, just as we have said of Brown, that he suffers from a failure of individuation. He seems to be constitutionally unable to come to terms with his shadow, blindly projecting it—wonderful irony!—upon the monster he himself has conjured up and manufactured from his own immature ego. Victor's selfish enthusiasm divides him from the salubrious influences both of nature and of society. While self-absorbed in his "workshop of filthy creation," he confesses that "my eyes were insensible to the charms of nature [and that] the same feelings which made me neglect the scenes around me caused me also to forget those friends who were so many miles absent, and whom I had not seen for so long a time." Moreover, his unholy quest, like Brown's, leads him to reject his anima (portrayed in the figure of Elizabeth). This rejection ultimately proves fatal not only to the anima-figure but also to the persona-figure portrayed by Henry Clerval, whom he characterizes as "the image of my former [better] self." Even in his dying moments Victor insists upon projecting his shadow-image upon the Creature, calling him "my adversary" and persisting in the sad delusion that his own past conduct is not "blameable." In the end, because of his failure of personality integration, just like Brown's, Victor Frankenstein's "dying hour was gloom."

In sum, Jung's words are once again relevant: "It is often tragic to see how blatantly a man bungles his own life and the lives of others yet remains totally incapable of seeing how much of the whole tragedy originates in himself, and how he continually feeds it and keeps it going."

4. Syntheses of Jung and Anthropology

Most of the myth critics who use Jung's insights also use the materials of anthropology. A classic example of this kind of mythological eclecticism is Maud Bodkin's *Archetypal Patterns in Poetry*, first published in 1934 and now recognized as the pioneer work of archetypal criticism. Bodkin acknowledges her debt to Gilbert Murray and the anthropological scholars, as well as to Jung. She then proceeds to trace several major archetypal patterns through the literature of Western civilization; for example, rebirth in Coleridge's "Rime of the Ancient Mariner"; heaven-hell in Coleridge's "Kubla Khan," Dante's *Divine Comedy*, and Milton's *Paradise Lost*; the image of woman as reflected in Homer's Thetis, Euripides's Phaedra, and Milton's Eve.

James Baird's *Ishmael: A Study of the Symbolic Mode in Primitivism* derives not only from Jung and the anthropologists but also from such philosophers as Susanne Langer and Mircea Eliade. Though he ranges far beyond the works of Herman Melville, Baird's primary objective is to find an archetypal key to the multilayered meanings of *Moby-Dick* (which, incidentally, Jung considered "the greatest American novel"). He finds this key in primitive mythology, specifically in the myths of Polynesia to which young Melville had been exposed during his two years of sea duty in the South Pacific. (Melville's early success as a writer was largely due to his notoriety as the man who had lived for a month among the cannibals of Typee.) Melville's literary primitivism is authentic, unlike the sentimental primitivism of such writers as Rousseau, says Baird, because he had absorbed certain Asian archetypes or "life symbols" and then transformed these creatively into "autotypes" (that is, individualized personal symbols).

The most instructive illustration of this creative fusion of archetype and autotype is Moby-Dick, Melville's infamous white whale. Baird points out that, throughout Asian mythology, the "great fish" recurs as a symbol of divine creation and life; in Hinduism, for example, the whale is an avatar (divine incarnation) of Vishnu, the "Preserver contained in the all being of Brahma." (Of course Christ was associated with fish and fishermen in Christian tradition.) Furthermore, Baird explains that *whiteness* is the archetype of the all-encompassing, inscrutable deity, the "white sign of the God of all being who has borne such Oriental names as Bhagavat, Brahma—the God of endless contradiction." Melville combined these two archetypes, the great fish or whale and whiteness, in fashioning his own unique symbol (autotype), Moby-Dick. Baird's reading of this symbol is substantiated by Melville's remarks about the contrarieties of the color white (terror, mystery, purity) in his chapter "The Whiteness of the Whale," as well as by the mysterious elusiveness and awesome power with which he invests Moby-Dick. Moby-Dick is therefore, in Baird's words, a "nonambiguous ambiguity." Ahab, the monster of intellect, destroys himself and his crew because he would "strike through the mask" in his insane compulsion to understand the eternal and unfathomable mystery of creation. Ishmael alone is saved because, through the wholesome influence of Queequeg, a Polynesian prince, he has acquired the primitive mode of accepting this divine mystery without question or hostility. Two generations later, Jack London also absorbed Polynesian mythology in his works, most effectively in his Hawaiian short fiction.

C. Myth Criticism and the American Dream: Huckleberry Finn as the American Adam

In addition to anthropology and Jungian psychology, a third influence has been prominent in myth criticism, especially in the interpretation of American literature. This influence derives not only from those already mentioned but also from a historical focus upon the informing myths of American culture. It is apparent in that cluster of myths called "the American Dream." The results of such analysis indicate that many works produced by American writers possess a certain distinctiveness largely attributed to the influence, both positive and negative, of the American Dream, as it has been traditionally perceived.

The central facet of the Euro-American myth cluster is the Myth of Edenic Possibilities, which reflects the hope of creating a second paradise, not in the next world and not outside time, but in the bright New World of the American continent. Europeans saw America as a land of boundless opportunity, a place where they, after centuries of poverty, misery, and corruption, could have a second chance actually to fulfill their mythic yearnings for a return to paradise. According to Fredrick I. Carpenter, as early as 1654 Captain Edward Johnson announced to the Old World–weary people of England that America was "the place":

> All you the people of Christ that are here Oppressed, Imprisoned and scurrilously derided, gather yourselves together, your Wifes and little ones, and answer to your several Names as you shall be shipped for His service, in the Westerne World, and more especially for planting the united Colonies of new England.... Know this is the place where the Lord will create a new Heaven, and a new Earth in new Churches, and a new Commonwealth together.

Carpenter points out that although the Edenic dream itself was "as old as the mind of man," the idea that "this is the place" was uniquely American:

> Earlier versions had placed it in Eden or in Heaven, in Atlantis or in Utopia; but always in some country of the imagination. Then the discovery of the new

world gave substance to the old myth, and suggested the realization of it on actual earth. America became "the place" where the religious prophecies of Isaiah and the Republican ideals of Plato [and even the mythic longings of primitive man, we might add] might be realized. (6)

The themes of moral regeneration and bright expectations, which derive from this Edenic myth, form a major thread in the fabric of American literature, from J. Hector St. John Crèvecoeur's *Letters from an American Farmer* through the works of Emerson, Thoreau, and Whitman to such later writers as Hart Crane, Thomas Wolfe, and Jim Harrison. (Today, however, the idea that "America" was "discovered" as a promised land for Europeans is viewed quite differently by the descendants of its indigenous peoples, to whom it has been an American nightmare.)

Competing theories of national destiny were hotly debated at the turn of the century; Herbert Baxter Adams's idea that national destiny was bound up with the northern European "germ" of race was contested by Frederick Jackson Turner's notion that what made Americans was not blood but the experience of the frontier, later called "frontier theory." Of course both were celebrated, along with such imperialist ideas as "manifest destiny" and "social evolution." Again, all of these ideas were from a Euro-American point of view. Native American writers obviously have a different view of what happened when the "New World" was "discovered." They were displaced, cheated of land, murdered, and in some cases were the victims of genocide. Native writers from the turn of the century on, including Zitkala Ša, John Oskison, Louise Erdrich, and Sherman Alexie, expressed their opposition and marginalization, while the historic speeches of such tribal leaders as Charlot and Cochise condemned the greedy and wasteful white man in eloquent terms.

The concept of the American Adam was for Europeans the mythic New World hero. In *The American Adam*, R. W. B. Lewis describes the type: "a radically new personality, the hero of the new adventure: an individual emancipated from history, happily bereft of ancestry, untouched and undefiled by the usual inheritances of family and race; an individual standing alone, self-reliant and self-propelling, ready to confront whatever awaited him with the aid of his own unique and inherent resources" (5). One of the early literary characterizations of this Adamic hero is James Fenimore Cooper's Natty Bumppo, the central figure of the Leatherstocking saga. With his moral purity and social innocence, Natty is an explicit version of Adam before the Fall. He is a child of the wilderness, forever in flight before the corrupting influence of civilization—and from the moral compromises of Eve (Cooper never allows his hero to marry). He is also, as we might guess, the literary great-grandfather of the Western hero. Like the hero of Owen Wister's *The Virginian* and Matt Dillon of television's long-running *Gunsmoke,* he is clean-living, straight-shooting, and celibate. In his civilized version, the American Adam is the central figure of another corollary myth of the American Dream: the dream of success. The hero in the dream of success is that popular figure epitomized in Horatio Alger's stories and subsequently treated by novelists as different as William Dean

Howells and Jack London: the self-made man who, through luck, pluck, and all the Ben Franklin virtues, rises from abject poverty to high social estate.

More complex, and therefore more interesting, than this uncorrupted Adam is the American hero during and after the Fall. It is with this aspect of the dream rather than with the Adamic innocence of a Leatherstocking that major writers have most often concerned themselves. The symbolic loss of Edenic innocence and the painful initiation into an awareness of evil constitutes a second major pattern in American literature from the works of Hawthorne and Melville through Mark Twain and Henry James to Theodore Dreiser, Ernest Hemingway, and William Faulkner, to Stephen King. This is the darker thread in our literary fabric, which, contrasting as it does with the myth of bright expectancy, lends depth and richness to the overall design; it also reminds us of the disturbing proximity of dream and nightmare. From this standpoint, then, we may recall Hawthorne's young Goodman Brown as a representative figure—the prototypical American hero haunted by the obsession with guilt and original sin that is a somber but essential part of America's Puritan heritage, as well as its postcolonial legacy.

We might observe that Brown is also oppressed by certain postcolonial pressures; in responding to this he becomes an extreme **antihero** and outcast. He and his mindset in particular do not fit into anyone's notion of an American Dream; they are perhaps a warning that to enter a far country one must be adaptable.

Huck Finn epitomizes the archetype of the American Adam, even as he also undercuts it. (We'll return to this point shortly.) Certainly *Huckleberry Finn* is one of the half-dozen most significant works in American literature, and not a few consider it to be the Great American Novel. The reasons for this high esteem may be traced directly to the mythological implications of Twain's book: More than any other novel in American literature, it embodies myth that is national. The book was believed by an earlier generation—to which most myth critics have belonged—to embody a quest for American freedom, a backwoods ***Bildungsroman***. It is still generally taught this way, and we present this traditional reading below. But in chapters 4, 9, and 10, we present some other, less hopeful interpretations of Twain's purpose.

First, *Huckleberry Finn* is informed by several archetypal patterns encountered throughout much of world literature:

1. *The Quest*: Like Don Quixote, Huck is a wanderer, separated from his culture, seemingly idealistically in search of one more substantial than that embraced by the hypocritical, materialistic society he has rejected. But is he a traditional quest hero?

2. *Water Symbolism*: The great Mississippi River, like the Nile and the Ganges, is invested with sacred attributes. As T. S. Eliot has written in "The Dry Salvages," the river is a "strong brown god" (line 2); it is an archetypal symbol of the mystery of life and creation—birth, the flowing of time into eternity, and rebirth. (Note, for example, Huck's several symbolic deaths, his various disguises and new identities as he returns to the shore from the

river; also note the mystical lyricism with which he describes the river's majestic beauty.) The river is also a kind of paradise, the "Great Good Place," as opposed to the shore, where Huck encounters hellish corruption and cruelty. It is, finally, an agent of purification and of divine justice.

3. *Shadow Archetype:* Huck's pap, with his sinister repulsiveness, is a classic representation of the devil figure designated by Jung as the shadow.

4. *Trickster:* Huck—as well as those notorious "con men," the King and the Duke—exemplifies this archetypal figure. Also see chapter 9.

5. *Wise Old Man:* In contrast to pap Finn, the terrible father, Jim exemplifies the Jungian concept of the wise old man who provides spiritual guidance and moral wisdom for the young hero.

6. *Archetypal Women:*
   a. The Good Mother: the Widow Douglas, Mrs. Loftus, Aunt Sally Phelps.
   b. The Terrible Mother: Miss Watson, who becomes the Good Mother at the end of the novel.
   c. The Soul-Mate: Sophia Grangerford, Mary Jane Wilks.

7. *Initiation:* Huck undergoes a series of painful experiences in passing from ignorance and innocence into spiritual maturity; he comes of age—is morally reborn—when he decides to go to hell rather than turn Jim in to the authorities, although he later fails in this epiphany.

In addition to these Western archetypes, *Huckleberry Finn* suggests its hero as the symbolic American hero; he epitomizes the paradoxes that make up the American character. He has all the glibness and practical acuity of businesspeople and politicians; he is free from the materialism and morality-by-formula of the Horatio Alger hero. He possesses the simple modesty, the quickness, the daring and the guts, the stamina and the physical skill Americans idolize in athletes. He is both ingenious and ingenuous. He is mentally sharp, but not intellectual. He also displays the ingratiating capacity for buffoonery that Americans so dearly love in public entertainers. Yet, with all these extraverted virtues, Huck is also a sensitive, conscience-burdened loner troubled by man's inhumanity to man and by his own occasional callousness to Jim's feelings. Notwithstanding his generally realistic outlook and his practical bent, he is a moral idealist, far ahead of his age in his sense of human decency, and at times, a mystic and a daydreamer (or, more accurately, a nightdreamer) who is uncommonly sensitive to the presence of a divine beauty in nature. He is, finally, the good bad boy whom Americans have always idolized in one form or another. And, though he is exposed to as much evil in human nature as young Goodman Brown had seen, Huck is saved from Brown's pessimistic gloom by his sense of humor and, what is more crucial, by his sense of humanity.

D. "Everyday Use": The Great [Grand]Mother

Alice Walker's brilliant tour de force clearly dramatizes the Great Mother, which is a major reason that this little gem has achieved classic status in less than a generation since its original publication.

If Walker's theme is only hinted at in her title, it is made explicit in her dedication: *"for your grandmama."* In brief, "Everyday Use" and all that title connotes is not simply a tribute to the author's—or any *one* person's—grandmama: it is a celebration for *your*—indeed, for all humanity's—Great (or, if you prefer, *Grand*) Mother.

In this story, the archetypal woman manifests herself as both Good Mother and Earth Mother. As she informs us at the outset, her *earthen* yard is "not just a yard...but an extended *living* room" (our italics). True to her nature, the Good Mother is appropriately associated with the life principle. She is also an androgynous figure, combining the natural strengths of female and male. "In real life," she says, "I am a large, big-boned woman with rough, man-working hands. In the winter I wear flannel nightgowns to bed and overalls during the day. I can kill and clean a hog as mercilessly as a man."

Further in keeping with her archetypal nature, the Good Mother is associated with such life-enhancing virtues as warmth, nourishment, growth, and protection. With a modicum of formal education (she can scarcely read), she has maintained her farm and brought two children into maturity—even despite such catastrophes as the burning of her old house and the scarring of her younger daughter. Now, as the story opens, it is her function to preserve the natural order of things, including tradition and her family heritage. The central symbol in the story is a nice combination of **metonymy** and symbol—the quilts, associated with warmth and signifying the family heritage:

> They had been pieced by Grandma Dee and then Big Dee and me had hung them on the quilt frames on the front porch and quilted them.... In both of them were scraps of dresses Grandma Dee had worn fifty and more years ago. Bits and pieces of Grandpa Jarrell's paisley shirts. And one teeny faded blue piece, about the size of a penny matchbox, that was from Great Grandpa Ezra's uniform that he wore in the Civil War.

For the Good Mother, hers is always a living heritage, a vital tradition of "everyday use." Dee, the daughter and antagonist, has broken that tradition.

"What happened to 'Dee'?" I wanted to know.

"She's dead," Wangero said. "I couldn't bear it any longer, being named after the people who oppress me."

For Wangero Leewanika Kemanjo (a.k.a. "Dee"), on the contrary, tradition is an essentially *useless* thing, heritage something inert to be framed and hung on the wall as mere ornament, as artificial and pretentious as her new name and her new prince consort "Hakim-a-barber."

But, touched by "the spirit of God," this mother righteously defends the natural order, protecting her precious "everyday" from the specious order of the "new day." Maggie, with scarred hands but unscarred spirit, will marry John Thomas, with mossy teeth and earnest face. The family myth will be hers to maintain. The quilts, emblems of this heritage—like Nature and the Good Mother herself—will endure. "This was Maggie's portion. This was the way she knew God to work."

Figure 7.2. Alice Walker (1989).
Getty Images/Harcourt Brace.

IV. SUMMARY OF KEY POINTS

- *Mythological Approaches*: Seeks out the mysterious elements informing certain works that elicit dramatic and near-universal human reactions. Myth critics try to discover how certain works become "classics" and works that are similar are forgotten. While the psychological approach examines underlying motives of behavior in the individual, myth criticism seeks to define symbols that help make possible cultural behavior.
- Misconceptions of Myth Criticism: these include the idea that myths are fictions or falsehoods, or are only derived from classical Greek and Roman sources.
- Archetypes: Similar motifs and themes found in multiple mythologies and recurrent patterns of imagery. Common archetypes are the sun, water, colors, the circle, the serpent, numbers, trees, gardens, deserts.
- The Archetypal Woman: Can be great mother or terrible mother, or anima (soul mate).
- The Wise Old Man: Helps the hero achieve his goal.
- Demon lover: Figure of the devil.
- Trickster figure.
- Common Archetypal Patterns or Motifs: the Creation myth, Immortality, the Hero.
- Hero: goes on quest and leaves home, faces dangers in an initiation into manhood, often returns home as sacrifice/king.
- Archetypes as Genres (Northrop Frye): genres have seasons, such as spring/comedy, summer/romance, fall/tragedy, winter/irony.

V. LIMITATIONS OF MYTH CRITICISM

It should be apparent from the foregoing illustrations that myth criticism offers some unusual opportunities for the enhancement of literary appreciation and understanding. An application of myth criticism takes us far beyond the historical and aesthetic realms of literary study—back to the beginning of humankind's oldest rituals and beliefs and deep into our own individual hearts. Because of the vastness and complexity of mythology, a field of study whose mysteries anthropologists and psychologists are still working to discover, our brief introduction can give only the most superficial and fragmentary overview. Many scholars and teachers of literature have remained skeptical of myth criticism because of its tendencies toward the cultic and the occult. There has been a discouraging confusion over concepts and definitions among the myth critics, causing them to turn their energies to more clearly defined approaches.

Another limitation of the mythological approach is that although myth critics have posited that certain archetypal and mythic patterns are "universal," today many critics disagree with the entire concept of universals. Jung's work, they point out, was Euro-centric and based primarily on Western mythology. There are so many obvious examples of archetypes that are culture-specific and not universal: for example, the evil dragon of *Beowulf is* not the same as the good luck dragon of the Chinese New Year, nor is the wise serpent of Pueblo Indian stories the same evil serpent as in Genesis.

Furthermore, as with the psychological approach, the reader must take care that enthusiasm for a new-found interpretive key does not tempt him or her to discard other valuable critical instruments or to try to open all literary doors with this single key. Just as Freudian critics sometimes lose sight of a great work's aesthetic values in sexual symbolism, so myth critics tend to forget that literature is more than a vehicle for archetypes and ritual patterns. They run the risk of being distracted from the aesthetic experience of the work itself. They forget that literature is, above all else, art. As we have indicated before, the discreet critic will apply such extrinsic perspectives as the mythological and psychological only as far as they enhance the experience of the art form, and only as far as the structure and potential meaning of the work consistently support such approaches.

QUICK REFERENCE

Baird, James. *Ishmael: A Study of the Symbolic Mode in Primitivism.* New York: Harper, 1960.

Baumlin, James S., Tita French Baumlin, and George H. Jensen, eds. *Post-Jungian Criticism, Theory and Practice.* Albany: State University of New York, 2004.

Bodkin, Maud. *Archetypal Patterns in Poetry: Psychological Studies of Imagination.* New York: Vintage, 1958.

Campbell, Joseph. *The Masks of God: Primitive Mythology.* New York: Viking, 1959.

Carpenter, Fredric I. *American Literature and the Dream.* New York: Philosophical Library, 1955.

Cirlot, J. E. *A Dictionary of Symbols*. Trans. Jack Sage. New York: Philosophical Library, 1962.

Cornford, F. M. *Origin of Attic Comedy*. London: Arnold, 1914.

Eliade, Mircea. *Myth and Reality*. New York: Harper, 1963.

Fergusson, Francis. *The Idea of Theater*. Princeton, NJ: Princeton University Press, 1949.

Fiedler, Leslie. *End to Innocence*. Boston: Beacon Press, 1955.

——. *Love and Death in the American Novel*. New York: Criterion, 1960.

——. *No! in Thunder*. Boston: Beacon Press, 1960.

Frazer, James G. *The Golden Bough*. Abridged ed. New York: Macmillan, 1922.

Frye, Northrop. *Anatomy of Criticism*. Princeton, NJ: Princeton University Press, 1957.

——. *The Stubborn Structure*. Ithaca, NY: Cornell University Press, 1970.

Harrison, Jane. *Themis*. London: Cambridge University Press, 1912.

Jung, C. G. *Modern Man in Search of a Soul*. New York: Harcourt, n.d.; first published in 1933.

——. *Psyche and Symbol*. Garden City, NY: Doubleday, 1958.

——. *Psychological Reflections*. New York: Harper, 1961.

——. *Two Essays on Analytical Psychology*. 2nd ed. Princeton, NJ: Princeton University Press, 1966.

——. *The Archetypes and the Collective Unconscious*. 2nd ed. Princeton, NJ: Princeton University Press, 1968.

——. *The Structure and Dynamics of the Psyche*. 2nd ed. Princeton, NJ: Princeton University Press, 1969.

Lawrence, D. H. *Studies in Classic American Literature*. New York: Viking, 1964.

Lewis, R. W. B. *The American Adam*. Chicago: University of Chicago Press, 1955.

Marett, R. R., ed. *Anthropology and the Classics*. New York: Oxford University Press, 1908.

Morrison, Toni. *Playing in the Dark: Whiteness in the American Literary Imagination*. New York: Random House, 1992.

Murray, Gilbert. *Euripides and His Age*. New York: Holt, 1913.

——. *The Classical Tradition in Poetry*. Cambridge, MA: Harvard University Press, 1927.

Pratt, Anis, et al., *Archetypal Patterns in Women's Fiction*. Bloomington: Indiana University Press, 1981.

de Santillana, Giorgio, and Hertha von Dechend. *Hamlet's Mill*. Boston: Gambit, 1969.

Smith, Jeanne Rosier. *Writing Tricksters: Mythic Gambols in American Ethnic Literature*. Berkeley: University of California Press, 1997.

Sugg, Richard P., ed. *Jungian Literary Criticism*. Evanston, IL: Northwestern University Press, 1992.

Tate, Allen, ed. *The Language of Poetry*. New York: Russell, 1960.

Vickery, John B., ed. *Myth & Literature: Contemporary Theory & Practice*. Lincoln: University of Nebraska Press, 1966.

Watts, Alan W. *Myth and Ritual in Christianity*. New York: Vanguard Press, 1954.

Wheelwright, Jane. *Death of a Woman*. New York: St. Martin's Press, 1981.

Wheelwright, Philip. *The Burning Fountain*. Bloomington: Indiana University Press, 1954.

——. *Metaphor and Reality*. Bloomington: Indiana University Press, 1962.

Feminisms and Gender Studies

I. FEMINISMS AND FEMINIST
LITERARY CRITICISM: DEFINITIONS

"I myself have never been able to find out precisely what feminism is," British author and critic Rebecca West remarks; "I only know that other people call me a feminist whenever I express sentiments that differentiate me from a doormat or prostitute" (219). Indeed, feminism has often focused upon what is absent rather than what is present, reflecting concern with the silencing and marginalization of women in a *patriarchal culture,* a culture organized in favor of men. Unlike many other critical approaches, but like Marxist approaches, feminism is an overtly *political* approach that criticizes false assumptions about women. As Judith Fetterly has bluntly pointed out, "Literature is political," and its politics "is male." When we read "the canon of what is currently considered classic American litera-ture," we "perforce...identify as male" (in Rivkin and Ryan 561). In recent decades this tendency has changed, in part because of the efforts of feminist critics and also because of social changes such as mass education, the civil rights movement, reactions to ongoing war, increasing urbanization, and the growing liberalization of sexual mores.

Though it once seemed fairly homogeneous, feminism is no longer presumed to have a single set of assumptions, and it is definitely no longer merely the "ism" of white, educated, bourgeois, heterosexual Anglo-American women. As Ross C. Murfin has noted, the "evolution of feminism into feminisms has fostered a more inclusive, global perspective" (301–2). The era of recovering women's texts has been succeeded by a new era in which the goal is to recover entire cultures of women. The historical phases of feminism are called first-, second-, and third-wave feminism.

No other cultural and intellectual movement has been more influential in changing literary criticism and theory than feminism, which paved the way for such later movements as ethnic studies, queer theory, and postcolonial studies, inaugurating the pursuit of what is called "identity politics" in literary analysis. Some would say that feminism is not a literary method in the sense of formalism, psychoanalytic criticism, or structuralism; they would say that it is a political commitment to the equality of women. Feminist critics employ a variety of methods in their analyses. Their concerns are especially relevant to women's struggles throughout much of the developing world.

II. FIRST-, SECOND-, AND THIRD-WAVE FEMINISMS

Feminism as we know it today began in Britain in the late eighteenth century with the stirrings of reform in women's rights, among the many reform movements that arose at that time—aid to the poor, abolition of slavery in the British Empire, labor reforms such as legislation against child labor, and so on. Indeed, feminism has always been at the forefront of social reform movements in the modern era. The primary gains of first-wave feminists were the right to vote and the right to practice birth control. Thus first-wave feminism was mainly concerned with establishing the legal policy that women are human beings and cannot be treated like property. This step held enormous promise for later generations.

British intellectual Mary Wollstonecraft's *Vindication of the Rights of Woman* (1792) is the first major written treatise on feminism; her daughter, Mary Shelley, extended feminine and domestic issues into the realm of science and challenged her male-dominated society through her fiction. Later authors such as George Eliot, Charlotte Perkins Gilman, and Virginia Woolf penned their own feminist works. Though Gilman is better known today for her shocking short story of post-partum depression and patriarchal oppression, "The Yellow Wall-Paper," in her own day she was best known for her breakthrough analysis of gender and economics, *Women and Economics* (1897), which argued that economic prosperity would not be attained in the United States until women were allowed to work. In the United States, with writers such as Gilman, Lydia Maria Child, Margaret Fuller, Sojourner Truth, Fanny Fern, and Kate Chopin, first-wave feminism began around 1848 and lasted roughly until the 1960s, though many felt its greatest moment was the passage of the Twentieth Amendment to the U. S. Constitution, which in 1920 gave women the right to vote.

In 1848, Elizabeth Cady Stanton organized the Seneca Convention. Her plan was "to discuss the social, civil, and religious condition and rights of woman." At that convention a Declaration of Sentiments was issued, objecting to the lack of women's vote. This affected law-making, ownership of property, legal rights for married women, divorce laws, employment opportunities including the professions of medicine and the law, admission to colleges and universities, and roles in churches. For the next 40 years, first-wave feminists campaigned for their rights. In addition, the birth control movement was begun by Margaret Sanger, a public health nurse, around 1919, and continues today. It was not until 1965, the year before the first edition of this handbook appeared, that married couples in all states could obtain legal contraceptives.

The second wave of feminism began after World War II; since many women had gone to work during the war, they expected—as did African-American soldiers—to be full citizens back home. As epitomized by the failed Equal Rights Amendment, the goal of second-wave feminists—like that of the first wave—was gender equality in social, political, legal, and economic rights. Second-wave feminism can be said to have lasted until the 1970s. In addition to legal rights, second-wave feminism addressed additional inequalities. As the postwar boom brought economic growth, the baby boom, the expansion of suburbs, and further entrenchment of capitalism, middle-class women found themselves faced with new challenges, especially the seeming national desire to return to prewar patriarchy. In the media of the day it would seem as though the nineteenth century "Cult of True Womanhood," which put women on a pedestal but also in a cage, had returned. Television showed idealized families such as those of *Father Knows Best*, in which the mothers would be in high heels, dresses, and pearls to cook dinner and never had outside employment. Second-wave feminism sought not only to overturn such conventions, but to celebrate the unique contributions of women, their distinctiveness, and alternate views of their world. Some pushed what is called *cultural feminism*, or the idea that a women's culture would be more positive and nurturing than patriarchy; others aligned themselves behind what is called *difference feminism*, or the aim not just of equal rights but of establishing women's difference from men, even their superiority. In general, when feminism is portrayed in the popular press it is second-wave feminism, especially when it is caricatured as a separatist "man-hating" philosophy.

The second-wave movement included the writings of Simone de Beauvoir, Kate Millett, and Betty Friedan, who examined a female "self" constructed in literature by male authors to embody various male fears and anxieties. They saw literary texts as models and agents of power. In her book *The Second Sex* (1949), de Beauvoir asked what is woman, and how is she constructed differently from men? Answer: she is constructed differently *by* men. The thesis that men write about women to find out more about men has had long-lasting implications, especially the idea that *man* defines the human, not woman.

In *The Feminine Mystique* (1963) Friedan demystified the dominant image of the happy American suburban housewife and mother. Her book appeared amidst new women's organizations, manifestos, protests, and publications that called for enforcement of equal rights and an end to sex discrimination. An author of essays in *Good Housekeeping*, Friedan also analyzed reductive images of women in American magazines.

Millett's *Sexual Politics* (1970) was the first widely read modern work of feminist literary criticism. Millett's focus was upon the twin poles of gender as biology and culture. In her analyses of D. H. Lawrence, Norman Mailer, Henry Miller, and Jean Genet she reads literature as a record of male dominance. As a "resisting reader," Millett included critiques of capitalism, male power, crude sexuality, and violence against women. She argued that male writers distort women by associating them with (male) deviance. She aptly concludes that the "interior colonization" of women by men is "sturdier than any form of segregation" such as class, "more uniform, and certainly more enduring" (24–25).

At the same time as women have been re-read in works by male writers, feminists have promoted the underappreciated work of women authors, and the writings of many women have been rediscovered, reconsidered, and collected in large anthologies such as *The Norton Anthology of Literature by Women*, including women who had never been considered seriously or had been elided over time. For example, Harriett E. Wilson, author of the first novel by an African American woman, *Our Nig, Sketches from the Life of a Free Black in a Two-Story White House, North* (1859), was "discovered" one hundred and fifty years later in a rare book store by Yale scholar Henry Louis Gates, Jr. However, merely unearthing women's literature did not ensure its prominence; in order to assess women's writings, the preconceptions inherent in a literary **canon** dominated by male beliefs and male writers have been reevaluated. Along with Fetterly, other critics such as Elaine Showalter, Annette Kolodny, Sandra Gilbert, and Susan Gubar questioned cultural, sexual, intellectual, and/or psychological stereotypes about women and their literatures using both essentialist and constructivist models, which we discuss below. The focus upon the silencing and oppressing of women gave way to deeper interrogations of what a history of women's oppression meant. As Julie Rivkin and Michael Ryan ask, "Was 'woman' something to be escaped from or into?" (528). Though much of the early "sisterhood" solidarity of the women's movement was lost as the field diversified, a good deal of philosophical and political depth was attained as these interrogations became more complex.

Third-wave feminism began in the early 1990s, challenging the second wave's essentialist definitions of femininity as a universal female identity while privileging upper-middle-class white women. Influenced by poststructuralism, third-wave feminists expand the interests of feminists—and, as well, center them—in the concerns of women of color, lower-class women, lesbians, transgendered women, "Third World" women, all previously marginalized. The separation is also an intergenerational issue between feminists who came to adulthood in the 1960s and those who in 2000 were only in their twenties. It is not so much an approach to criticism as a set of claims to identities and a set of arguments involving antiracism and women-of-color consciousness, postcolonial theory, transnationalism, queer and transgender studies, and spatial studies.

Second-wave feminists have criticized third-wave feminists for what they see as promoting casual sex, but third-wave feminists respond that their empowerment of their bodies and their sexuality is part of their politics and was attained for them by second-wave feminism. The criticism has been especially strong as regards their reanalyses of sex workers and pornography as "empowered." At issue too has been "girlie culture": is it permissible to be a feminist and be "girlie?" Third-wavers would not separate sexual self-esteem and equality from a choice to be "girlie." While second-wave feminists worked collectively, third-wave feminism allows women to define feminism individualistically. For example, though many third-wavers are social activists, they are still faulted by second-wavers as not working collectively.

Several second-wave feminists—such as Gloria Anzaldúa, bell hooks, Chela Sandoval, Cherrie Moraga, Eve Ensler, Audre Lorde, Judith Butler, Maxine Hong Kingston, and Rebecca Walker—a young southern bisexual African-American writer who first used the term "third-wave feminist" in a 1992 essay on the Thomas/Hill hearings called "Becoming the Third Wave"—have seen the women's movement as constantly transforming itself. As Rebecca Walker notes, the civil rights movement benefited black men, and the women's movement benefited white women, but black women were left out. Similarly, lesbians felt that the second-wave movement had little interest in them. At the same time, new voices represented working-class women and women in the developing world. As Rebecca Walker states, "To be a feminist is to integrate an ideology of equality and female empowerment into the very fiber of my life. It is to search for personal clarity in the midst of systemic destruction, to join in sisterhood with women when often we are divided, to understand the power structures with the intention of challenging them....Let Thomas's confirmation serve to remind you, as it did me, that the fight is far from over....Turn that outrage into political power" (41). If in a more "me-oriented" culture, women are not as politically organized, and if "family values" of the right have turned off some women, and the spectacle of career women foregoing motherhood has turned off others, feminists today consider that they have more power because they have more choices. In addition, AIDS, high divorce rates, gay and lesbian rights, and debates over abortion complicate many young women's definitions of feminism. Young women struggle with feminism only partly because they lack historical consciousness. Do all feminists somehow need to be the same, they wonder? Thus, third-wavers tend to work more outside academia and more in the public sphere, and often against a preconceived image of feminism projected by the media. Third-wavers especially ask: Do women always have to be portrayed as victims?

Third-wave feminism challenges the first and second waves' "essentialist" definitions of femininity (more on *essentialism* in a moment). Important to the interests of those women previously marginalized by feminism are poststructuralist and postmodern interrogations of binaries such as male and female, queer and straight, black and white, "first world" and "third." "Third-space" women find themselves triply oppressed by class, gender, and race. (However, not all women of color are third-space women, as they may have privilege, but no white woman is a third-space woman, as they retain what is termed "white privilege." However, there is no unified or essential third-space definition.) Thus third-wave theory usually concerns itself with subjectivities of women of color, transgender politics and a rejection of gender binaries—what Alice Walker and others define as "womanism"—postcolonial theory, transnationalism, and ecofeminism. Third-wave feminists work for battered women's shelters, daycare services, renewed attention to child protective services, attention to the stories of abuse survivors, availability of contraception and reproductive services including the legalization of abortion, upholding sexual harassment policies in the workplace, and women's studies programs designed to create feminist awareness for a greater diversity of women.

Anzaldúa, hooks, Sandoval, Moraga, Lorde, Kingston, and many other feminists of color seek to claim previously unexamined female spaces, whether of class, race, or gender. What, they wonder, does the day laborer in a border sweatshop have in common with an accountant who wants a raise? These feminists also deconstruct their postcolonial selves and strive to imagine new transcolonial selves to reclaim bodies, histories, and identities and to arrive at new voices and new visions (Pérez, Sandoval, Anzaldúa). They use their personal lives to remap identity as in Anzaldúa's "new mestizo" consciousness of class, race, sexuality or Emma Pérez's "decolonial imaginary" that exists between colonialism and postcolonialism. They seek transcolonial agency and a change in subaltern consciousness, what Sandoval calls a "differential oppositional consciousness" that seeks to reimagine **"Otherness"** outside of the **hegemony** of postcolonial discourse, thus reconfiguring the center.

A text that particularly lends itself to third-wave feminist analysis is Sapphire's novel PUSH (1996), in which the girl Precious, the protagonist, is an obese, illiterate teenage black mother with an abusive family and AIDS. Her mother *and* father abuse her mentally, physically, and spiritually; thus the subject of motherhood is complicated by her mother and her status as AIDS mother and the mother of a child with Down syndrome. Through education Precious finds her voice, herself, and her hope. The book's discourse changes from virtually illiterate to linguistically powerful by the conclusion, and it ends with several other survivor-girls' personal narratives. (The film *Precious* based an the novel premiered in 2009.)

A corollary to third-wave feminism is the emerging field of maternalist studies. Adrienne Rich in *Of Woman Born: Motherhood as Experience and Institution* describes motherhood as an institution dictated by patriarchy and thus historically constructed. Rich seeks to redefine motherhood as something that does not maintain the division between men and women based on biological function. She turns to prepatriarchal religions as well as to her own experiences as a mother, as well as antifeminist historical ideas such as the Cult of True Womanhood. Other prominent thinkers on maternal theory include Hazel Carby, Barbara Christian, Sara Ruddick, Hortense Spillers, James Phelan, and Linda Tate. Later theorists such as Kathryn Allen Rabuzzi and Azizah al-Hibri have continued to investigate the mythic sources of the mother's power. Prominent authors Toni Morrison, Anne Tyler, and Alice Walker and emerging authors Kaye Gibbons, Ellen Douglas, Sherley Anne Williams, Tina McElroy Ansa, Terry MacMillan, Gloria Naylor, Sue Monk Kidd, and Alice Randall address black and white mothering. For example, in her novel *Dessa Rose* Williams recovers the silenced voice of the black mother but also voices the white mother Ruth as a complement to the protagonist. Kidd interrogates the Mammy figure from a position of power rather than subservience. Randall rewrites Margaret Mitchell's *Gone With the Wind* from the perspective of a new character, Cynara, Scarlett's mulatto half-sister by Mammy; Cynara must find strength in her "Otherness" and so only calls Scarlett "Other," a renaming that inspires her recovery process from slave to woman.

III. WOMAN: CREATED OR CONSTRUCTED?

Parallel to the first-, second-, and third-wave feminisms Elaine Showalter identified three phases of modern women's literary development: the *feminine* phase (1840–80), during which women writers imitated the dominant male traditions; the *feminist* phase (1880–1920), when women advocated for their rights; and the *female* phase (1920–present), when dependency upon opposition—that is, on uncovering misogyny in male texts—is replaced by the rediscovery of women's texts and women. Women's literature is "an imaginative continuum [of] certain patterns, themes, problems, and images, from generation to generation" ("Feminist Criticism" 11). Within the present or "female" phase, Showalter describes four current *models of difference* taken up by many feminists around the world: biological, linguistic, psychoanalytic, and cultural.

Showalter's *biological model* is the most problematic: if the text can be said in some way to mirror the body, then does that reduce women writers merely to bodies? Yet Showalter praises the often shocking frankness of women writers who relate the intimacies of the female experience of the female body.

Showalter's *linguistic model* asserts that women are speaking men's language as a foreign tongue; purging language of "sexism" is not going far enough. Still, feminist critics see the very act of speaking—and of having a language—as a victory for women within a silencing patriarchal culture. Tillie Olsen demands to hear women's voices despite impediments to creativity encountered by women; in her 1978 work *Silences* she cites "those mute inglorious Miltons: those whose working hours are all struggle for existence; the barely educated; the illiterate; women. Their silence is the silence of the centuries as to how life was, is, for most of humanity" (327). Silences arise from "circumstances" of being born "into the wrong class, race or sex, being denied education, becoming numbed by economic struggle, muzzled by censorship or distracted or impeded by the demands of nurturing." But women's deployment of silence can also be "resistance to the dominant discourse," Olsen notes, such as Emily Dickinson's "slant truths" or the inner dialogues of such "quiet" characters as Charlotte Brontë's Jane Eyre or Virginia Woolf's Lily Briscoe (quoted in Fishkin and Hedges 5). A film treatment of this theme is *The Hours* (2002), starring Nicole Kidman, Meryl Streep, and Julianne Moore. This movie relates with unnerving clarity the inner lives of three women connected through their experiences with Woolf's novel *Mrs. Dalloway,* itself a study of female subjectivity.

Though women writers may have to use "male" language, feminist critics have identified sex-related writing strategies such as the use of associational rather than linear logic, other "feminine" artistic choices such as free play of meaning and a lack of closure, as well as genre preference such as letters, journals, confessional, domestic narratives, and body-centered discourse. As Showalter has observed, "English feminist criticism, essentially Marxist, stresses opposition; French feminist criticism, essentially psychoanalytic, stresses repression; American feminist criticism, essentially textual, stresses expression." All three, however, being woman-centered or *gynocentric,* must search for terminology to rescue themselves from becoming a synonym for inferiority ("Feminist Criticism" 186).

Showalter's *psychoanalytic model* identifies gender difference in the psyche and also in the artistic process. Her *cultural model* places feminist concerns in social contexts, acknowledging class, racial, national, and historical differences and determinants among women. It also offers a collective experience that unites women over time and space—a "binding force" ("Feminist Criticism" 186–88, 193, 196–202). These have been Showalter's most influential models. Showalter issued another important book, a general survey of American women writers called *A Jury of Her Peers: American Women Writers from Anne Bradstreet to Annie Proulx,* in 2009.

Today it seems that two general tendencies, one emphasizing Showalter's biological, linguistic, and psychoanalytic models, and the other emphasizing Showalter's cultural model, account for most feminist theories. On the one hand, certain theories may be said to have an *essentialist* argument for inherent feminine traits—whether from biology, language, or psychology—that have been undervalued, misunderstood, or exploited by a patriarchal culture because the genders are quite different. These theories focus on sexual difference and sexual politics and are often aimed at defining or establishing a feminist literary canon or re-interpreting and re-visioning literature (and culture and history and so forth) from a less patriarchal slant.

Opposed to this notion that gender confers certain essential feminine and masculine traits is *constructivist* feminism, which asks women (and men) to consider what it means to be gendered, to consider how much of what society has often deemed to be inherently male and female traits are in fact culturally and socially constructed. For the constructivist feminists the feminine and gender itself are made by culture in history and are not eternal norms. It is easy to see how constructivist feminism helped give rise to gender studies, the framing of all gender categories as cultural instead of biological. It is also clear that such fluidity of definition has links in poststructuralist and postmodernist thinking in general.

A. Feminism and Psychoanalysis

Many essentialist feminists have been attracted to the psychoanalytic approach, to which they have given their own stamp. Sandra Gilbert and Susan Gubar examine female images in the works of Jane Austen, Mary Shelley, Charlotte and Emily Brontë, and George Eliot, addressing such topics as mothering, living within enclosures, doubling of characters and of aspects of the self, women's diseases and their treatments, and feminized landscapes. They make the argument that female writers often identify themselves with the literary characters they detest through such types as the monster/madwoman figure counterposed against an angel/heroine figure. Despite this tendency, they describe a feminine utopia for which women authors yearn and where wholeness rather than "otherness" would prevail as a means of identity.

In the 1980s, French feminism developed as one of the most exciting of new feminist practices in the use of psychoanalytic tools for literary analysis. Essentialists found that psychoanalytic theory as espoused by Sigmund Freud, Carl G. Jung, Jacques Lacan, and Julia Kristeva, and the French Feminists Hélène Cixous and Luce Irigaray explained some of their biologically based assumptions about femininity; readers found original and compelling new psychic models for feminine identity, open to flexibility and change by their very "nature" as feminine (see Irigaray, "When Our Lips Speak Together").

Yet Freud has long been on feminism's Enemies List, the charge being that he misunderstood women and was interested only in what they meant for male psychology. Freud practiced upon his devoted daughter Anna and Marie Bonaparte, both of whom carried on his work. These and other women whom he diagnosed as "hysterics" were the cornerstone of psychoanalysis. In Freud's defense, the narratives given by his female patients represented radically new acceptance of their voices in their first-person accounts of fantasies, fears, injuries, and diseases. Before such maladies as Freud addressed could be treated medically, they first had to be voiced subjectively. Today such common (but often terrifying) complaints of women including postpartum depression, major depression, chronic fatigue syndrome, and fibromyalgia are responded to as real health crises with a combination of medical and psychological help; but in Freud's day they were dismissed as ordinary "female trouble." Particularly troublesome women in those days could even face hysterectomies (the uterus was considered the font of *hysteria,* from the same Greek word), or merely isolation and shock treatments. Freud's contribution was not only to identify and "medicalize" women's psychiatric obstacles but also to emphasize the textual nature of his cases; indeed, he seemed to read his patients like texts or languages. Freud also argued that art, whether by men or women, had a pathological origin; following Freud, maneuvers such as bringing a "repressed" subtext to light are similar moves in psychoanalysis and literary criticism, for the goal of both is deeper understanding (see Young-Bruehl, *Freud on Women: A Reader* for selections on women).

As noted in Chapter 6, from the Freudian revisionist Jacques Lacan comes the notion of the *Imaginary,* a pre-Oedipal stage in which the child has not yet differentiated her- or himself from the mother and as a consequence has not learned language, which is the *Symbolic Order* to be taught by the father. The Imaginary is the vital source of language later tamed by the Laws of the Father. The Oedipal crisis marks the entrance of the child into a world of language as Symbolic Order in which everything is separate, conscious and unconscious, self and other, male and female, word and feeling. In the realm of the *Law of the Father* we are confined by "isms" or rules; Lacan calls this the "phallogocentric" universe (phallus + logos) in which men are in control of "the word." French feminists practice what they call *l'écriture féminine* as a psychically freeing form of feminine discourse: the actual sex of the author, for them, is not always important (as it too is an expression of binary Laws of the Father).

The relevance of Freud and Lacan to feminism has mainly to do with the intersections of language and the psyche (combining Showalter's linguistic and psychoanalytic models). Like Freud, Lacan describes the unconscious as structured like a language; like language its power often arises from the sense of openness and play of meaning. When we "read" language, we may identify gaps in what is signified as evidence of the unconscious; for language is a mixture of fixed meaning (conscious) and **metaphor** (in part unconscious). The feminine "language" of the unconscious destabilizes sexual categories in the Symbolic Order of the Father, disrupting the unities of discourse and indicating its silencings. French feminists speak of "exploding" rather than interpreting a sign. Hélène Cixous proposes a utopian place, a primeval female space free of symbolic order, sex roles, otherness, and the Law of the Father. Here the self is still linked to the voice of the mother, source of all feminine expression; to gain access to this place is to find an immeasurable source of creativity.

However, as in the case of Luce Irigaray, no matter how theoretical and abstract French feminists' prose becomes or how complicated their psychoanalytic analyses, French feminists do not stray far from the body. As Rivkin and Ryan explain, "Luce Irigaray distinguishes between blood and shame, between the direct link to material nature in women's bodies and the flight from such contact that is the driving force of male abstraction, its pretense to be above matter and outside of nature (in civilization)." Irigaray etymologically links the word "matter" to "maternity" and "matrix," the latter being the space for male philosophizing and thinking. Matter is irreducible to "male western conceptuality.... [O]utside and making possible, yet impossible to assimilate to male reason, matter is what makes women women, an identity and an experience of their own, forever apart from male power and male concepts" (*Speculum* 529). As Rivkin and Ryan further note, essentialists like Irigaray see women as "innately capable of offering a different ethics from men, one more attuned to preserving the earth from destruction by weapons devised by men." It is because men "abstract themselves" from the material world as they separate from their mothers and enter the patriarchate that they adopt a "violent and aggressive posture' toward the world left behind, which is now construed as an 'object.'" For them the mother represents "the tie to nature that must be overcome... to inaugurate civilization as men understand it (a set of abstract rules for assigning identities, appropriate social roles and the like that favor male power over women)." Because women are not required to separate from the mother, "no cut is required, no separation that launches a precarious journey towards a fragile 'identity' predicated on separation that simply denies its links to the physical world." Irigaray would point out by way of example that when confronted with ethical issues, men think in terms of rights, "while women think in terms of responsibilities to others" (Rivkin and Ryan 529–30). A quotation from Jung seems apposite here: "When one has slain the father, one can obtain possession of his wife, and when one has conquered the mother, one can free one's self" (432).

(We anticipate here a comment on the novel *Frankenstein,* which we treat later. Victor Frankenstein certainly springs to mind as a man who must "cut" his ties with the material domestic world around him by abstracting life itself, then being repelled by its materiality, especially when he sets about making his female Creature. What a price he pays, and how awful the sacrifices of everyone around him, for his obsession with the Law of the Father.)

Julia Kristeva furnishes a more specifically therapeutic sort of psychoanalysis of women in works such as her *Desire in Language,* in which she presents a mother-centered realm of the *semiotic* as opposed to the *symbolic.* Echoing Lacanian theory, she argues that the semiotic realm of the mother is present in symbolic discourse as absence or contradiction, and that great writers are those who offer their readers the greatest amount of disruption of the nameable. (One thinks of Sethe's horrific memories in Toni Morrison's *Beloved.*) Like Cixous and Irigaray, Kristeva opposes phallogocentrism with images derived from women's corporeal experiences, connecting, like Marxist theory, the personal with the political and artistic. Kristeva's later work moves away from strictly psychoanalytic theorizing toward a more direct embrace of motherhood as the model for psychic female health. "Stabat Mater," her prose poem meditation on her own experience with maternity accompanied by a hypertext essay on the veneration of the Virgin Mary, understands motherhood as, like language, a separation accompanied by a joining of signification, the loss being the marker of the infant's embrace of identity (178). Many feminists follow Kristeva's privileging of motherhood, arguing that, as Rivkin and Ryan put it, "In the mother-child relationship might be found more of the constituents of identity…than are given during the later Oedipal stage" (531).

One other type of psychological approach, **myth** criticism (treated at length in Chapter 7), has its adherents in feminist studies. Feminist myth critics tend to center their discussions on such archetypal figures as the Great Mother and other early female images and goddesses, viewing such women as Medusa, Cassandra, Arachne, Isis, and others as radical "others" who were worshipped by women and men as alternatives to the more often dominant male deities such as Zeus or Apollo. Adrienne Rich and others have defined myth as the key critical approach for women. Criticizing Jung and such later myth critics as Northop Frye for privileging hegemonic Greco-Roman mythologies and consequently downplaying the role of the feminine from the pre-Greek past, as well as in diverse myths from other societies, Rich praises the mythic powers of motherhood even as she critiques the larger culture's ignorance and stereotyping of motherhood.

Because it manages to bring together the personal and the cultural, feminist myth criticism also holds promise for scholars interested in how various ethnic groups, especially minorities, can maintain their own rooted traditions and at the same time interact with other mythologies. Even the most negative images in mythology, such as Medusa from ancient Greece, retain attraction for modern women, for anthropology teaches us that when many formerly matriarchal societies in the "Western" tradition were supplanted by patriarchal societies that venerated male gods instead of the older "Earth Mothers," many goddesses were metamorphosed as witches, seductresses, or fools. Studying these ancient transformations alerts us to the plasticity of all sexual categories and the ongoing revisions of the power of "the feminine."

B. Feminists of Color

Among the most prominent of feminist minorities are women of color and lesbians. These feminists practice *identity politics,* based upon essential differences from white, heterosexual, "mainstream" society, hence they could be termed essentialists. Although many nonwhite feminists include each other in shared analyses of oppression, and while feminism has largely aligned itself with arguments against racism, xenophobia, and homophobia, third-wave feminists protest being lumped together as though their fundamental concerns are the same. Here we review some of the major concerns specific to these feminists, especially the largest "minority," black feminists, and later in our section on gender studies we note some important lesbian feminists. But feminists of many different groups, including Latina and Chicana feminists, Asian American feminists, and Native American feminists, all have their own particular sets of cultural issues: these are referenced at greater length in Chapter 9, "Cultural Studies." We must point out that "minority" feminisms share in both essentialist and constructivist views; that is, whereas ethnic difference is a fact to be celebrated, feminists of color recognize the ways women and race are both constructs in society.

Like lesbian feminists, feminists of color argue that they face additional layers of the patriarchy that discourage their "coming out"; not only do they reject the traditional Western literary **canon** as lopsided in favor of men and Euro-Americans, but they also specifically target its exclusion of black women. Black feminists in particular have accused their white sisters of wishing merely to become rewarded members of the patriarchy at the expense of nonwhite women. That is, they say that the majority of feminists want to become members of the power structure, counted as men and sharing in the bounties of contemporary capitalist culture, equal wages, child care, or other accepted social "rights." A black or lesbian feminist might see a heterosexual white woman as having more in common with men than with other women of different ethnicities and classes. Maggie Humm has suggested that "the central motifs of black and lesbian criticism need to become pivotal to feminist criticism rather than the other way around" (106). Michael Awkward makes black feminists' concerns clearer when he distinguishes between how they influence each other as opposed to traditional white male models of influence. In *Inspiriting Influences: Tradition, Revision, and Afro-American Women's Novels,* he claims that black women writers carry out relationships as mothers, daughters, sisters, and aunts as very different from the patriarchally enforced relationships of fatherhood and sonship, with their traditional Oedipal conflicts. Contemporary novelists who demonstrate this idea include not only Morrison and Walker, but also Sherley Anne Williams, Gloria Naylor, and Tina McElroy Ansa.

Black women writers were previously elided from critical history or included merely as tokens. Since the 1960s interest in black culture, especially

African-American culture, has grown dramatically in American literary criticism. In fact criticism, theory, conferences, and book publishing have barely been able to keep up with the flood of academic and popular interest in black feminism. The term *black feminist,* however, is problematic. Alice Walker, author of *The Color Purple* (1982), disputes the term *feminist* as applied to black women; she writes that she has replaced *feminist* with *womanist,* remarking that a womanist does not turn her back upon the men of her community. That charge was made against her by black male critics responding to the portrayal of African-American men in *The Color Purple* especially after the Steven Spielberg film version appeared in 1985 (see *In Search of Our Mothers' Gardens: Womanist Prose*). As in "Everyday Use," Walker identifies black female creativity from earlier generations in such folk arts as quilting, music, and gardening. Walker looks to her own literary mothers such as Zora Neale Hurston, Harlem Renaissance figure and folklorist, who insisted upon using authentic black dialect and folklore in her folktale book *Mules and Men* (1935) and her novel *Their Eyes Were Watching God* (1937) without apology or emendation. This tendency to privilege the black language and folkways she grew up with alienated Hurston from some of the male leaders of the Harlem Renaissance, including Langston Hughes, who preferred a more (mainstream) intellectual approach, which he saw as more activist in nature, like the protest novels of writers like Ralph Ellison and especially Richard Wright.

Seeking out other autobiographical voices, black feminists have often turned to the slave narrative and the captivity narrative, both old American forms of discourse. Challenges to the traditional canon have also included new **bibliographies** of neglected or suppressed works and the recovery and rehabilitation of such figures as the tragic mulatta or Mammy figure by such leading critics as bell hooks and Maya Angelou.

Related to the rise of feminisms among women of color is the area of postcolonial studies, which we treat in Chapter 10. Among its most prominent feminist voices is that of Gayatri Chakravorty Spivak, who examines the effects of political independence upon *subaltern,* or subproletarian women, in Third World countries. In such works as the essays of *In Other Worlds,* Spivak has made clearer both the worldwide nature of the feminist movement, as well as the great differences among feminisms, depending upon class, political structure, and "race."

The issues that black feminist critics raise are far from academic or confined to literary criticism. On September 28, 2005, former U.S. Secretary of Education and Officer of Drug Policy William Bennett, then host of Salem Radio Networks's Bill Bennett's Morning in America Show, allegedly stated that aborting black babies would decrease crime (quoted in Gumbs). Such a violent verbal assault on black families and children spurred black feminist critics to renew their arguments against racism and sexism—not to mention assaults upon their children—as central to debates on democracy and freedom in America.

With roots in the antislavery and women's rights movements of the nineteenth century, through the black and women's rights movements of the 1960s and 1970s, black American feminism of the twenty-first century looks back on three hundred years of liberation struggles. As Sherri L. Barnes points out, "Whether one chooses to use the term black feminism, African American feminism, womanism, or black American feminism, to articulate the complexity of black American women's demand for social, economic and political equality, understood is the desire for a compatible and progressive vision of social justice based on the historical and ongoing struggles against the race and gender (at least) oppression black American women have experienced at home, at work, in their communities and, moreover, within the dominant culture as a whole." Crucial themes in contemporary black feminism include the hope for "an alternative social construct for now and the future based on African-American women's lived experiences; a commitment to fighting against race and gender inequality across differences of class, age, sexual orientation, and ethnicity; recognition of Black women's legacy of struggle; the promotion of black female empowerment through voice, visibility and self definition; and a belief in the interdependence of thought and action." The liberation of black women entails freedom for all people, since it would require the end of racism, sexism, and class oppression.

Black feminists were disappointed by the civil rights movement in that black men took over and black women felt excluded as "merely" women. Black women had to face sexism as well as racism, and with their own men. Even today black women are largely unwilling to jeopardize their racial credibility by attacking black men. Yet as Stephen Henderson notes, black women writers increasingly expressed their sense of betrayal by their male contemporaries, whose ideas of the black community were divorced from what emerging women writers knew to be realistic images of black men, marriage, and, particularly, motherhood. He states:

> [T]he contradictions between knowledge and action that surfaced in the Civil Rights and Black Power movements forced sensitive and intelligent women to reexamine their own positions vis-à-vis the men and to conclude that they were the victims not only of racial injustice but of a sexual arrogance tantamount to dual colonialism—one from without, the other from within, the Black community. (xxiii)

As a consequence, black women writers began "free[ing] themselves from the roles assigned to them in the writings of their male counterparts where, depicted as queens and princesses, or as earth mothers and idealized Black Mommas of superhuman wisdom and strength, they were unrecognizable as individuals" (Henderson xxiv). Michele Wallace counterargues that the superwoman stereotype remains a strong tradition from which very few black female authors have strayed; consequently, it continues to mislead adolescent girls:

> From the intricate web of mythology which surrounds the black woman, a fundamental image emerges. It is of a woman of inordinate strength, with an ability for tolerating an unusual amount of misery and heavy, distasteful work. This woman does not have the same fears, weaknesses, and insecurities as other women, but believes herself to be and is, in fact, stronger emotionally than most men. Less of

a woman in that she is less "feminine" and helpless, she is really *more* of a woman in that she is the embodiment of Mother Earth, the quintessential mother with infinite sexual, life-giving, and nurturing reserves. In other words, she is a super-woman. Through the years this image has remained basically intact, unques-tioned even by the occasional black woman writer or politician. (107)

Alice Walker quotes Wallace in *In Search of Our Mothers' Gardens* (1984), but takes exception to Wallace's final sentence. "It's a lie," Walker maintains. "I've been hacking away at that stereotype for years, and so have many other black women writers" (*Mothers' Gardens* 324). She lists Zora Neale Hurston, one of her literary mentors, as another example.

Patricia Hill Collins, in *Black Feminist Thought: Knowledge, Consciousness, and the Politics of Empowerment*, observes that black women have been easily compartmentalized by white Western thinkers: "Knowledge is a vitally important part of the social relations of domination and resistance. By objectifying African-American women and recasting our experiences to serve the interests of elite white men, much of the Eurocentric masculinist worldview fosters Black women's subordination." But, she points out, if we place black women's experiences at the center of analysis we attain fresh insights into "the prevailing concepts, paradigms, and epistemologies of this worldview and on its feminist and Afrocentric cri-tiques. Viewing the world through a both/and conceptual lens of the simultaneity of race, class, and gender oppression and of the need for a humanist vision of com-munity creates new possibilities for an empowering Afrocentric feminist knowl-edge. Many Black feminist intellectuals have long thought about the world in this way because this is the way we experience the world" (222–23). She thus argues that "Afrocentric feminist notions of family reflect [a] reconceptualization pro-cess." As an alternative to Western family structures, black women's experiences as "bloodmothers, othermothers, and community othermothers" reveal that the mythical norm of a heterosexual, married couple and nuclear family is far from being natural and universal, "but instead is deeply embedded in specific race and class formations. Placing African-American women in the center of analysis not only reveals much-needed information about Black women's experiences but also questions Eurocentric masculinist perspectives on family" (225). As Walker notes, black women are called, "the *mule* of the world," because they have been handed the burdens that everyone else—*everyone* else—refused to carry (Walker, *In Search of Our Mothers' Gardens*, 237).

Thus black feminism and the feminism of women of color in general can pro-vide in place of this position of subservience, Collins observes, "a place where we feel ownership and accountability." There is always choice, and power to act, no matter how bleak the situation may appear to be; "Viewing the world as one in the making raises the issue of individual responsibility for bringing about change. It also shows that while individual empowerment is key, only collective action can effectively generate lasting social transformation of political and economic institutions" (Collins 238). Collins also writes extensively on black versus white motherhood. In order to analyze this dichotomy she argues for a theory that can differentiate motherhood as experience and institution; dismantle motherhood as an institution; and examine differences in real mothers. In West Africa, for example, childcare is a collective responsibility of an "age-stratified, woman-centered 'mothering' network" to make the daughters strong ("othermothers"). Nineteenth-century accounts often represented black motherhood as one of many roles for slave women.

In comparison, African-American authors Paule Marshall and Jewelle Gomez, science fiction writer Octavia Butler, filmmaker Julie Dash, and poet Lucille Clifton trace the invention and subsequent development of the "magic black daughter." Two key factors define her mother-daughter separation and reunion along with the mother as history. The second is the adoption of magic. In some texts, a daughter's return to the past results in the construction of an essentialist myth of black womanhood, while in others, the possibilities of/in historical return are examined more cautiously (e.g., Morrison's *Beloved*, 81). Other writers and critics who focus on black mothers and daughters include (some we have not previously mentioned) Nella Larsen, June Jordan, Andrea O'Reilly, and Phyllis Perry. Cynthia Dobbs has described in "Mother-Hunger: A Review of *Toni Morrison and Motherhood: A Politics of the Heart* by Andrea O'Reilly," the idea of mothering as essential to survival. As O'Reilly notes, "The challenge for Morrison's mothers...is not how to combine motherhood and work, but rather how, in the face of racism and sexism, to best provide the motherwork—both in and outside the home—necessary for the empowerment of children." Particularly for African-American women, Morrison and O'Reilly argue, motherhood is seamlessly interwoven with public and communal work. As Morrison described it in a 1981 interview in *Essence*:

> Black women [need to] pay...attention to the ancient properties—which for me means the ability to be "the ship" and the "safe harbor." Our history as Black women is the history of women who could build a house and have some children and there was no problem.... What we have known is how to be complete human beings, so that we did not let education keep us from our nurturing abilities...
> [T]o lose that is to diminish ourselves unnecessarily. It is not a question, it's not a conflict. You don't have to give up anything. You choose your responsibilities.
> (Morrison)

According to Dobbs, O'Reilly builds her theory of African-American motherhood on the "ancient properties" passed on by African-American women. Morrison's works, despite their representations of an often violent, fraught mother-child experience, demonstrate the crucial importance of African-American mothers as both "ship and safe harbor" to the survival of the African-American community as a whole. As O'Reilly outlines it, motherhood in Morrison is at heart about personal and political empowerment.

In "Mama's Baby, Papa's Maybe: A New American Grammar Book," Hortense Spillers emphasizes the difference between "motherhood" as the role of white women through the violent exclusion of the bodies of black women from the definition of the human, and second "the reproduction of 'mothering' which is the labor that black women have still been compelled to perform despite their exclusion from the domain of proper 'motherhood.'" This was an important point for Spillers to make in 1987, when both black nationalist invocations of motherhood as the role for the reproduction of a patriarchal black nation and white feminist views of black women's sexuality and subjectivity unspeakable.

Beginning in the 1970s, the black mother is "queered" with figures such as lesbian and bisexual radicals Audre Lorde and June Jordan. Cherríe Moraga, for example, has called black lesbian feminists such as Lorde, Jordan, and Pat Parker instances of bodies that could not be domesticized by middle-class American aspirations. The invocation of black maternity includes the production of a queer time and space within which black women can operate with a future radically different from their present.

In her book *Feminism on the Border*, Sonia Saldívar-Hull points out that far from being merely a subgroup of feminists, Chicana feminists, who largely feel they have little in common with second-wave white feminists, are in solidarity with other women of color "who share similarities in our histories under racism, class exploitation, and cultural domination in the United States—a kinship that extends beyond sharing a national language." She notes how Chicanas feel kinship with women in Third World countries who search for a feminist critical discourse; Chicana feminism thus "deconstructs the borders erected by Eurocentric feminism as it extends the borders of what is considered legitimately political." Through their shared *testimonios*, Latinas around the world—what Saldívar-Hull calls a "cultural diaspora"—can "contextualize themselves within a global literary history" (46–47). For Saldívar-Hull the two most important figures in Chicana feminism are Moraga and Anzaldúa. In her *Loving in the War Years* Moraga developed a Chicana feminist theory by linking "the genesis of Chicana and Third World feminisms to the Civil Rights movements and to Black feminist theory." She argues that "sexuality, specifically lesbian sexuality,...[is] a legitimate site of political struggle" (51–52). In her book *Borderlands/La Frontera: The New Mestizo* Gloria Anzaldúa articulates her border feminist theory of "Mestiza consciousness," centering her feminism in "the concrete, material locations of working-class identified women whose ethnicity and sexuality further dislocate and displace them." For Anzaldúa, the "New Mestiza," who challenges restrictions placed upon her, can emerge only "after she develops an oppositional consciousness" (59). Combining song, autobiography, historical analysis, literary theory, political theory, prose, and poetry, male and female symbols, Mexican and U.S. cultures, and First and Third Worlds, Indian gods with Catholic ones, Anzaldúa advocates consciousnesses with "tolerance for ambiguity": as Saldívar-Hull sees it, "mestiza consciousness breaks down dualisms that keep fronteristas from praxis. The border consciousness she ultimately develops produces a new, revolutionary theory of politics,...a new culture, a new way of being that will entail a global healing and freedom from violence" (62). Saldívar-Hull describes this foundational book as itself a *mestizaje*: "a postmodernist mixture"

Figure 8.1. Gloria Anzaldúa (2004).
Courtesy Annie Valva.

that "resists genre boundaries as well as geopolitical borders" (70). Saldívar-Hull examines many other important Chicana writers and theorists, including Alma Gómez, Mariana Romo Cardona, Sandra Cisneros, Helena María Viramontes, Rosaura Sánchez, Yvonne Yarbro Bejarano, and Norma Alarcón.

C. Marxist and Materialist Feminisms

Perhaps the most significant source of constructivist feminism is Marxism, especially its focus upon the relations between reading and other social constructions. The establishment of so many women's studies programs, cooperatives, bookstores, libraries, film boards, political caucuses, and community groups attests to the activist orientation of feminism. As Karl Marx argued that all historical and social developments are determined by the forms of economic production (see Chapter 4), Marxist feminists have attacked the "classist" values of the prevailing capitalist society of the patriarchal West as the world also gradually becomes "globalized." Marxist feminists do not separate "personal" identity from class identity, and they direct attention to the often nameless underpinnings of cultural productions, including the conditions of production of texts, such as the economics of the publishing industry.

As we learned in Chapter 4, according to Marxist theory, in capitalist societies the individual is shaped by class relations; that is, interests are determined by the mode of production that characterizes their society. Materialist, and, especially

Marxist feminists see gender inequality as determined ultimately by the capitalist mode of production and the major social divisions as class-related. Women's subordination is a form of oppression maintained because it serves the interests of capital and the ruling class. And, as Marx himself wrote, female prostitution "is only a specific expression of the general prostitution of the laborer" (Marx, quoted in Pateman, *Sexual Contract* 201).

However, there is debate between materialist and Marxist feminists. Donna Landry and Gerald McLean point out that while "Marxist feminism holds class contradictions and class analysis central, and has tried various ways of working an analysis of gender oppression around this central contradiction," a broader materialist feminism examines "class contradictions and contradictions within gender ideology... we are arguing that *materialist feminism* should recognize as material other contradictions as well.... including ideologies of race, sexuality, imperialism and colonialism and anthropocentrism, with their accompanying radical critiques" (229). Rosemary Hennessy traces the origins of materialist feminism to the work of British and French feminists who preferred the term to Marxist feminism because, in their view, Marxism had to be transformed to be able to explain the sexual division of labor. In the 1970s, Hennessy argues, Marxism was inadequate to the task because of its class bias and focus on production, while feminism was also problematic due to its essentialist and idealist concept of woman; this is why materialist feminism emerged as a positive alternative both to Marxism and mainstream feminism (*Materialist Feminisms*, xii).

Martha E. Gimenez notes that materialist feminism is a "way of reading" that rejects "the dominant pluralist paradigms and logics of contingency and seeks to establish the connections between the discursively constructed differentiated subjectivities that have replaced the generic 'woman' in feminist theorizing, and the hierarchies of inequality that exploit and oppress women." Subjectivities cannot be understood in isolation from systemically organized totalities." Materialist feminism, as a reading practice, is also a way of rewriting the world and, as such, "can influence reality through the knowledge it produces about the subject and her social context." This subject is "traversed by differences grounded in hierarchies of inequality which are not local or contingent but historical and systemic, such as patriarchy and capitalism. Difference, consequently, is not mere plurality but inequality. The problem of the material relationship between language, discourse, and the social or between the discursive (feminist theory) and the non-discursive (women's lives divided by exploitative and oppressive social relations) can be resolved through the conceptualization of discourse as ideology." Gimenez finds the materialist feminists more akin to cultural feminists because they do not set out to change the material realities of women's oppression to class (Gimenez, n.p.)

Yet in her essay, "What Is Socialist Feminism?" Barbara Ehrenreich sets out some of the correspondences and differences Marxist feminism has with classical Marxism. She argues that "Socialist feminists are in a very different camp from what I am calling 'mechanical Marxists.' We (along with many, many Marxists who are not feminists) see capitalism as a social and cultural totality. We understand that, in its search for markets, capitalism is driven to penetrate every nook and cranny of social existence. Especially in the phase of monopoly capitalism, the realm of consumption is every bit as important, just from an economic point of view, as the realm of production. So we cannot understand class struggle as something confined to issues of wages and hours, or confined only to workplace issues." Class struggle, she notes, occurs everywhere when the interests of classes conflict, in art, education, and health, for example. She points out that because Marxist feminists "see monopoly capitalism as a political/economic/cultural totality, we have room within our Marxist framework for feminist issues which have nothing ostensibly to do with production or 'politics,' issues that have to do with the family, health care, 'private' life." She is concerned with all working women including "housewives" as members of the working class with "a social existence quite apart from the capitalist-dominated realm of production. When we think of class in this way, then we see that in fact the women who seemed most peripheral, the housewives, are at the very heart of their class—raising children, holding together families, maintaining the cultural and social networks of the community." As she observes, in many instances, women's skills (productive skills, healing, midwifery) have been discredited or banned to make way for commodities. As she adds, "women are the culture-bearers of their class" (and culture). Thus there is a fundamental interconnection between women's struggle and the class struggle: "Not all women's struggles have an inherently anti-capitalist thrust (particularly not those which seek only to advance the power and wealth of special groups of women), but all those which build collectivity and collective confidence among women are vitally important to the building of class consciousness" (66–67).

Marxist feminists, like other Marxists, are attacked for misunderstanding the nature of quality in art. For them, literary value is not a transcendent property (just as sex roles are not inherent) but rather something conditioned by social beliefs and needs. What is "good" art for a Marxist critic often seems to be merely what a given group of people decide is good, and it is sometimes hard to differentiate that process from one which Formalists would endorse. Yet Lillian Robinson, a prominent Marxist feminist, has pointed out that even a seemingly innocuous approach such as Formalism is encoded with class interests, connecting it to the systematic exclusion of women, nonwhites, and the working class. Feminist criticism, in contrast, should be "criticism with a cause, engaged criticism.... It must be ideological and moral criticism; it must be revolutionary" (3).

D. Feminist Film Studies

Most significant among critical cultural theories in shaping film studies from the 1970s on was feminism. Feminist film critics address a pervasive set of issues such as cinematic representations of women, spectatorship by men, and sexual difference. As Patricia White notes,

> the female image—the female as image—has been a central feature of film and related visual media; in film criticism and theory, making gender the axis of

analysis has entailed a thoroughgoing reconsideration of films for, by, and about women, and a consequent transformation of the canons of film studies.... A concern with representation, in both a political sense (of giving voice to or speaking on behalf of women) and an aesthetic sense, has also united the activist and theoretical projects of women's film culture. (115)

The first book–length studies of women and film appeared in the United States in the early 1970s, both from those who analyzed women in films in terms of realism and those who saw women as co-opted by the medium. Molly Haskell and Marjorie Rosen proposed "reflection theory," or the idea that film reflects social reality for women but distorts their lives according to the conventions of mainstream media, advertising, pornography, and so on, what White describes as "an array of virgins, vamps, victims, suffering mothers, child women, and sex kittens" (116). Haskell relates the history of women in film as an arc from the "reverence" of the silent era to the "rape" of women by Hollywood in the 1970s. For Haskell the high point of powerful women in film was in the 1940s, with such heroines as Katharine Hepburn. But other critics such as Claire Johnston have felt that such an approach detaches women from their psychic structures and historical circumstances. Johnson sees film as a language and its women as a sign, "not simply a transparent rendering of the real" (White 116). Johnston analyzes the films of Howard Hawks and John Ford as well as those of women directors such as Ida Lupino or Dorothy Arzner. According to White, this analysis in turn set a pattern for subsequent feminist studies of Hollywood genres such as film noir, the musical, and the Western, which show how women as signifier performed precise iconographic and ideological functions, either constituting a genre's structural dimensions (woman = home in the Western) or exposing its ideological contradictions (the femme fatale figure in film noir)" (White 116–17).

Contemporary constructivist positions such as those by such scholars as Teresa de Lauretis and Laura Mulvey are inspired by the Marxist notion of the social construction of individual subjectivity (especially as outlined by Louis Althusser) and by the poststructuralist idea that languages write identities, and do not merely reflect them. "Gender identity is no less a construction of patriarchal culture than the idea that men are somehow superior to women; both are born at the same time and with the same stroke of the pen," as Rivkin and Ryan put it. Constructivists worry that essentialists are interpreting the subordination of women as women's nature: "At its most radical, the constructivist counter-paradigm embraces such categories as performativity, masquerade, and imitation, which are seen as cultural processes that generate gender identities that only appear to possess a pre-existing natural or material substance. Of more importance than physical or biological difference might be psychological identity." Following the thinking of Judith Butler, these theorists see gender as "performative," an imitation of a "code" that refers to no natural substance. Indeed, "Masculine means not feminine as much as it means anything natural" (Rivkin and Ryan 530).

Laura Mulvey's insight that films can compel the female viewer to participate in her own humiliation by watching the film as a man is borne out in her
analysis of the technical and psychological organization of the classic Hollywood
film, and her analysis has been eagerly embraced by literary critics, who transfer her insights on film to the printed page. The "male gaze" she describes (like
the Lacanian Symbolic Order) is based upon voyeurism and fetishism, the only
available pleasure (usually) being the male one of looking at women's bodies for
sexual cues. Mulvey uses examples from Alfred Hitchcock films to show how male
ambivalence toward the overall image of woman causes viewers to choose amongst
devaluing, punishing, or saving a guilty female, or turning her into a pedestal figure, a fetish. These extremes leave little place for the female viewer: according to
Mulvey, woman is the image, and man the bearer of the look, the voyeur: "In a
world ordered by sexual imbalance pleasure in looking has been split. . . . [and] the
male gaze projects its phantasy onto the female figure, which is styled accordingly"
(304–9).

White praises Mulvey for "[t]he most thorough-going and explicit introduction of neo-Freudian psychoanalytic theory to feminist film studies." As Mulvey
argued for a break with dominant cinema and the rejection of "visual pleasure,"
she found the "gendered processes of spectatorial desire and identification orches-
trated by classical narrative cinema" to mean that "woman" was merely the image
or "bearer of the look." Thus for Mulvey and her followers, "the institution of
cinema is characterized by a sexual imbalance of power"; Lacan's notion of
"pleasure in looking" addresses how films deploy unconscious mechanisms to
portray the woman as the signifier of sexual difference and the man as the subject and hence maker of meaning; Mulvey codifies these in cinema through the
manipulation of the gaze and narrative itself in terms of time and space, point of
view, editing, framing. Cinema thus affords "identificatory pleasure with one's
on-screen likeness, or ego ideal (understood in terms of the Lacanian mirror
state), and libidinal gratification from the object of the gaze." The male spectator is "doubly supported by these mechanisms of visual gratification as the gaze
is relayed from the male surrogate within the diegesis to the male spectator in
the audience. The woman, on the other hand, is defined in terms of spectacle,
or what Mulvey described as 'to-be looked-at-ness.'" This gaze, however, raises
the male spectator's anxieties about castration, and so he masters this by voyeurism (White 117). In her later work, Mulvey speculates on the results of this male
detour into voyeurism.

In the end, feminist film studies have taught viewers to "gaze" at women in
film differently. At the same time, women directors and film characters have also
challenged the "male gaze." Such diverse films as *Rebecca, All About Eve, Whatever
Happened to Baby Jane?, Thelma and Louise, The Color Purple, Steel Magnolias,
Mr. and Mrs. Smith, and The Secret Life of Bees* have all been described as feminist
films. How so? That is, how do these films portray women in the various environments they exist within? How do the women protagonists struggle to survive and
prevail in their environments?

Students can easily call to mind examples from other current films to corroborate Mulvey's insights: think about how differently women's bodies are portrayed in films like *Monster* (2003) and *Vicky Cristina Barcelona* (2007), or how both male and female gazes are engaged by the whirling assassins and viewpoints of *Kill Bill* (2003, 2004).

• • •

Despite their divergences and different goals, feminisms still seek to integrate competing worlds: Rich describes feminism as "the place where in the most natural, organic way subjectivity and politics have to come together" (in Gelpi and Gelpi 114). Such movement toward integration allows feminisms to do many different sorts of things: protest the exclusion of women from the literary canon, focus upon the personal (such as diary literature), make political arguments, align itself with other movements, and redefine literary theory and even language itself. Maggie Humm reminds us that male critics in the past were generally perceived to be "unaligned" and "a feminist [was] seen as a case for special pleading," but that today it is clear that masculinism rather than feminism tends to be blind to the implications of gender (12–13). Feminist criticism is not, as Toril Moi has observed, "just another interesting critical approach" like "a concern for sea-imagery or metaphors of war in medieval poetry" (204). It represents one of the most important social, economic, and aesthetic revolutions of modern times.

IV. GENDER STUDIES

As a constructivist endeavor, gender studies examines how gender is less determined by *nature* than it is by *culture,* and as we noted with Showalter's cultural model, a cultural analysis is at the center of the most complex and vital critical enterprises. Rivkin and Ryan name their introduction to their essays on gender studies "Contingencies of Gender," which aptly suggests the fluid nature of all gender categories. Since the late 1960s and early 1970s feminists and gender critics, especially those in Gay and Lesbian Studies, have experienced and articulated common ground in oppression and struggle. In the past, descriptions of prose in masculine terms (a "virile" style or "seminal" argument) were taken as the norm; today, a piece of writing might be criticized as limited by its masculine point of view. Myra Jehlen claims that traditional critics wish to reduce the complexities of sexuality to a false common denominator. With authors who seem unconscious of gender as an issue we must make an effort to read *for* it instead: "…literary criticism involves action as much as reflection, and reading for gender makes the deed explicit." As "heterosexual" and "homosexual" men and women escape the masculine norms of society, everyone benefits (263–65, 273). One recalls Huck's escape from gender (with Mrs. Judith Loftus) and race (with Jim) as key components of his ever-evolving identity.

For both feminists and gender critics, society portrays binary oppositions like masculine and feminine or straight and gay as natural categories, but as David

Richter notes, "the rules have little to do with nature and everything to do with culture." The word *homosexual* has only a short history of one hundred years or so (it was new at the time of Oscar Wilde's trial), and *heterosexual* is even newer. In any given culture, many theorists point out that what is "normal" sexually depends upon when and where one lives; for instance, pederasty was practiced by nobles of Periclean Athens, who also had sexual relationships with women, and both sorts of relationships were socially accepted. Homosexuality and heterosexuality today may thus be seen as not two forms of identity but rather a range of overlapping behaviors. Masculinity and femininity are constantly changing, of course. Ross C. Murfin sees gender as a construct, "an effect of language, a culture, and its institutions." Gender, not sex, makes an older man open the door for a young woman, and gender makes her expect it, resent it, or experience mixed feelings. Additionally, "Sexuality is a continuum not a fixed and static set of binary oppositions" (339). Similarly, Teresa de Lauretis has described the "technologies of gender," the forces in modern technological society that create sex roles in response to ideology and marketplace needs, specifically, "the product of various social technologies, such as cinema." Following Michel Foucault's theory of sexuality, she means by "technology" that "sexuality, commonly thought to be a natural as well as a private matter, is in fact completely constructed in culture according to the political aims of the society's dominant class." She concludes: "There is nothing outside or before culture, no nature that is not always and already enculturated" (2, 12).

In the 1970s and 1980s, after the famous Stonewall riots in New York that brought new focus upon gay, lesbian, and transvestite resistance to police harassment, gender critics studied more and more the history of gay and lesbian writing and how gay and lesbian life is distorted in cultural history. For example, Adrienne Rich's work focuses upon liberation from what she calls "compulsory heterosexuality," a "beachhead of male dominance" that "needs to be recognized and studied as a political institution" (143, 145). Sharon O'Brien writes on Willa Cather's problematic attitude toward her own lesbianism, Terry Castle analyzes "things not fit to be mentioned" in eighteenth-century literature, and Lillian Faderman explores love between women in the Renaissance.

Lesbian critics counter their marginalization by considering lesbianism a privileged stance testifying to the primacy of women. Terms such as *alterity, woman-centered,* and *difference* take on new and more sharply defined meanings when used by lesbian critics. Lesbianism has been a stumbling block for other feminists, and lesbian feminists have at times excluded heterosexual feminists. Some lesbians define lesbianism as the "normal" relations of women to women, seeing heterosexuality as "abnormal." This has led some heterosexual feminists to reject lesbian perspectives, but on the whole, lesbian feminists have guided other feminists into new appreciation of certain female traits in writing. They have also brought to the forefront the works of lesbian authors.

Lesbian critics reject the notion of a unified text, finding corroboration in poststructuralist and postmodernist criticism as well as among the French feminists. They investigate such textual features as mirror images, secret codes, dreams, and narratives of identity; they are drawn to neologisms, unconventional grammar, and other experimental techniques. One has only to think of the poetry and criticism of Gertrude Stein to see the difference such a self-consciously lesbian point of view entails. Like other feminists, they stress **ambiguity** and open-endedness of narratives and seek double meanings. Lesbian critics suggest new **genres** for study such as the female **Gothic** or female utopia. They are often drawn to such experimental women writers as Woolf, Stein, Radclyffe Hall, Colette, and Djuna Barnes, and to such popular genres as science fiction, especially involving created bodies such as cyborgs.

In 1978 the first volume of Foucault's *History of Sexuality* was translated. It argued that homosexuality is a social, medical, and ontological category invented in the late nineteenth century and then imposed on sexual practices that prior to that time discouraged and punished nonreproductive sexual alternatives (Rivkin and Ryan 676–77). In the late 1980s after the outbreak of the AIDS epidemic, the work of Eve Kosofsky Sedgwick, Michael Warner, and others in "Queer Theory" emerged as a way of providing gays and lesbians with a common term around which to unite and a more radical way of critiquing stigmatization, choosing the formerly derogatory name *queer* and transforming it into a slogan with pride (Rivkin and Ryan 677–78). Following Foucault, Queer Theorists view sexuality as disengaged from gender altogether and from the **binary** opposition of male/female.

Queer Theory relies on such postmodern concepts as gender ambivalence, ambiguity, and multiplicity of identities, which have replaced the more clearly defined sexual values of earlier generations. The controversy over the photographs of Robert Mapplethorpe in the early 1990s illustrates the intensity of conflicts that once arose when a gay male aesthetic is deployed.

In *Epistemology of the Closet,* Eve Kosofsky Sedgwick deconstructs the pathology of the homosexual and argues that sexuality is "an array of acts, expectations, narratives, pleasures, identity-formations, and knowledges…" (22–27). Using Sedgwick as a starting point, Queer Theorists have sought to create publics that "can afford sex and intimacy in sustained, unchastening ways," as Lauren Berlant and Michael Warner write in a special issue of *PMLA* devoted to Queer Theory. A "queer public" includes self-identified gays, lesbians, bisexuals, and the transgendered. At the same time, this public has "different understandings of membership at different times." The word *queer* was chosen both because of its shock value and because of its playfulness, its "wrenching sense of recontextualization" (343–45).

With a commitment only to pleasure, "queer" rejects the conventions of Western sexual mores. This rejection resembles the late nineteenth-century aesthete's embrace of the notion of "art for art's sake." (Indeed late nineteenth-century figures such as Oscar Wilde are important sources for Queer Theory.) Instead, the queer celebrates desire, what Donald Morton calls "the unruly and uncontainable excess that accompanies the production of meaning.… The excess produced at the moment of the human subject's entry into the codes and conventions of culture." Desire is an autonomous entity outside history, "uncapturable" and "inexpressible" (such formulations recall Freudian theory—see Chapter 6.) Morton identifies Queer Theory's roots in the anarchic skepticism of Friedrich Nietzsche (370–71). Queer commentary has produced analyses of such narrative features as "the pleasure of unruly subplots; **vernacular** idioms and private knowledge; voicing strategies; gossip; elision and euphemism; jokes; identification and other readerly reactions to texts and discourse" (Berlant and Warner 345–49). They read the normless Internet as "queer" because it is unpredictable and endlessly transformative. Critics such as Alan Sinfield have offered startling new readings of Shakespeare, while others have returned to such homosexual writers as Walt Whitman with better clues as to embedded sexual meanings and the role of desire in reading the text. Increasingly in the last few years, gay characters, themes, and programs now appear on all mainstream major television channels and are the subjects of Hollywood films. Gay marriage remains in the headlines as a controversial issue, but the queer or gay aesthetic has fully entered American culture. Widespread critical praise for such films as *Milk* (2008) attest to this.

V. FEMINISMS AND GENDER STUDIES IN PRACTICE

A. The Marble Vault: The Mistress in "To His Coy Mistress"

Addressing himself to a coy or putatively unwilling woman, the speaker in Andrew Marvell's poem pleads for sex using the logical argument that since they have not "world enough, and time" to delay pleasure, the couple should proceed with haste. But the poem's supposed logic and its borrowing from traditional love poetry only thinly veil darker psychosexual matters. What is most arresting about the address is its shocking attack upon the female body.

The woman in "To His Coy Mistress" not only is unwilling to accept the speaker but also is obviously quite intelligent; otherwise, he would not bother with such high-flown metaphysics. Yet the speaker seeks to frighten her into sexual compliance when his fancy philosophy does not seem persuasive enough. His use of such force is clearest in his violent and **grotesque** descriptions of her body.

Her body is indeed the focus, not his nor theirs together. Following a series of exotic settings and references to times past and present, the speaker offers the traditional adoration of the female body derived from the **Petrarchan sonnet**, but he effectively dismembers her identity into discrete sexual objects, including her eyes, her forehead, her breasts, "the rest" and "every part," culminating in a wish for her to "show" her heart. (Such maneuvers remind us of Freud's and Lacan's discussions of the Oedipal male's objectification of the mother.) This last image, showing the heart, moves in the direction of more invasive probings of her body and soul.

In the center of the poem the lady's body is next compared to a "marble vault." The speaker's problem is that despite the woman's charms, her vault is closed to him. He deftly uses this refusal as a means to advance his assault, however, since the word vault (a tomb) points toward her death (not his, however). He clinches the attack with the next image, the most horrifying one in the poem. If she refuses him, "then worms shall try/That long preserved virginity."

Returning to more traditional overtures, the speaker praises her "youthful hue" and dewy skin, from which, through "every pore," he urges her "willing soul" to catch fire. These pores though minute are more openings into her body; the connection with penetrating worms from the lines before is in the wish to penetrate and ignite her very soul. Attack upon the woman as fortress and the use of fire to suggest arousal were common **tropes** in sixteenth-century love **sonnets**, but Marvell's adaptation of them has a grotesque, literal feel more aligned with seventeenth-century Metaphysical poems, with their strange juxtapositions. The speaker's violence at the woman is, however, expanded to include himself, when he envisions the two of them as "amorous birds of prey" who may "devour" time, not "languish in his slow-chapped power" ("to chap" meaning "to chew"). It is significant that he does not foresee his own body moldering in the tomb, like hers, invaded by worms; he does admit that one day his lust will be turned to ashes, but that is a very different image from worms. He does not seem to see himself paying the same penalties that she will. The closing vision of how they will "tear our pleasures with rough strife/Thorough the iron gates of life" returns to the language of assault on her body. All in all, the lady of the poem is subject to being torn, opened up, or devoured by her admirer. A deep irony resides in the fact that he is absolutely right in suggesting she will pay more penalties for sex than he will.

It would be a mistake to see "To His Coy Mistress" as belittling women, however. If there were no power in the feminine, especially the mother, there would be no male identity crisis; the woman's silencing in such a text as this emphasizes not her helplessness but her power. The woman addressed is goddess-like: capricious and possibly cruel, she is one who must be complained to and served. Both the speaker's flattery and his verbal attacks mask his fear of her. To him the feminine is enclosed and unattainable—tomblike as well as womblike. The speaker's gracefulness of proposition, through the **courtly love** tradition, gives way to his crude **imagery** as his exasperation builds; her power lies in her continued refusal (it is evident that she has *already* said no to him). The feminine is portrayed here as a *negative* state: that is, she does not assent; she is not in the poem; and the final decision is not stated. It is a poem about power, and the power lies with the silent female, with the vault or womb—the negative space of the feminine. However, as the speaker's logic makes clear, her reserve has a price: she will not live as fully as she might, especially as a sexual being.

As distinct from his speaker, Marvell offers a portrayal of male and female roles of his day that celebrates their various positions while sharply indicating their limitations. It is a positive and negative evaluation. On the one hand, it is a poem about youth and passion for life, both intellectual and physical. It gives us a picture of the lives of sophisticated men and women during the time, people who enjoy sex for pleasure and who are not above making witty jokes and having fun arguing. No mention is made of procreation in the poem, nor marriage, nor even love. It is about sex. The poem is so sophisticated that instead of merely restating the courtly love tradition, it parodies it. Yet on the other hand as the male speaker satirizes his lady's coyness, he is also satirizing himself in his outrageous imagistic attempts to scare her into sex with him. The repellent quality of his images of women, like a bad dream, haunts us long after his artful invention and his own coy sense of humor fade.

B. Frailty, Thy Name Is Hamlet: Hamlet and Women

The hero of *Hamlet* is afflicted, as we pointed out in Chapter 6, with the world's most famous Oedipus complex, next to that of its namesake. The death of his father and the "o'erhasty marriage" of his mother to his uncle so threaten Hamlet's ego that he finds himself splintered, driven to action even as he resists action with doubts and delays. Unfortunately, he is a son who must act against both his "parents," Gertrude and Claudius, in order to avenge his real father and alleviate his own psychic injury, a symbolic castration. But because his conflict is driven by two irreconcilable father-images, Hamlet directs his fury toward his mother—and, to a lesser degree, toward his beloved Ophelia—even as he fails in his attempts to engage the father(s). A Freudian critic would point out that the two fathers in the play represent the two images of the father any boy has: one powerful and good and one powerful and bad, that is, sleeping with the adored mother. Hamlet's irresolvable polarity of father images creates a male-female tension that is likewise unannealed. The question of how to account for Hamlet's delay in avenging his father has occupied generations of critics. A feminist reading indicates a solution: for Hamlet, delaying and attacking the feminine is a handy substitute for avoiding Claudius. Several times Hamlet's speech signals his unconscious thought that everything is his mother's fault for being an object of competing male desires, whether she actually had a hand in the elder Hamlet's murder or not. The feminist reading that follows is based upon Hamlet's loathing of his mother and of all feminine subjects as well, including at times his own (feminized) self. His fear and hatred of woman turn inwardly and destroy him; Claudius's death at the end is accompanied by the deaths of Hamlet, Gertrude, Laertes—all of whom join Ophelia, who has died earlier.

Hamlet contends with a woman's body, his mother's, and he finds its sexual proclivities disgusting, as he rails at her in her chamber. He loathes himself for being born out of the female body; his own sexual conflicts and confused desires threaten him from the unconscious. He condemns his mother's incestuous union with Claudius but mirrors the incest in his own Oedipal desire for her. The world of *Hamlet* is riven by such struggles, and the play's psychological themes are made more powerful by their contact with the other major thematic pattern in the play, politics. As Shakespeare was writing his play, perhaps the advancing age of Queen Elizabeth I and the precariousness of the succession—always with the accompanying danger of war at home and abroad—were elements in the dramatist's conjoining a man's relations with women to his relations with political power. The play gives us a picture of the role of women in Elizabethan society, from the way Ophelia must obey her father without question, to the dangers maidens face from young male courtiers, to the inappropriateness of Queen Gertrude's sexual desires. But although cultural roles of such women of the court are not applicable to women of all classes in Elizabethan times or our own, what women stand for psychologically and sexually in *Hamlet* is more universal than not.

The emphasis upon family relationships and specifically the politics of sex from the beginning of the play is accompanied by an emphasis upon political matters of the realm at large. In this sense, it is about the politics of masculinity and femininity in addition to the politics of Elsinore Castle, Denmark, and the larger world. The night from which the Ghost initially emerges is described in female terms, compounding the fear of unrest in general with fear of the feminine: the Ghost lies in the "womb of earth" and walks in an unwholesome night in which a "witch has power to charm," banished only by a male figure, the crowing "cock" (I.i).

Claudius has taken as his wife "our sometime sister, now our queen... With mirth in funeral, and with dirge in marriage" (I.ii). The father-son images in Claudius's description of matters between Denmark and Norway are followed by Claudius's fatherly behavior to young Laertes and then by the first appearance of Hamlet, whose first words are directed to his mother in response to Claudius's greeting; when Claudius goes so far as to call Hamlet "my son," Hamlet mutters, "A little more than kin, and less than kind" (I.ii). Gertrude pleads with Hamlet to stop mourning his father, and Claudius asks him to think of him as a new father.

What follows is the first of his many soul-searching monologues. When Hamlet thinks of himself, he thinks first of "this too too solid flesh" (for which alternate readings have suggested "sullied" and "sallied" for "solid"), which he would destroy had "the Everlasting not fix'd/His canon 'gainst self-slaughter." If his flesh is sullied, his mother's is polluted: in the monologue he blames his mother's "frailty" for exchanging "Hyperion" for a "satyr." She is "unrighteous" in her lust (I.ii).

Hamlet's meditation upon his mother's faults and his later assault upon her are keys to understanding his torment, but while many critics have been content to move through the play seeing Gertrude only through her son's angry eyes, Carolyn Heilbrun has provided an important feminist revision of Gertrude. Instead of a "well-meaning but shallow" Gertrude, Heilbrun finds her queen-like in her pointed speech "and a little courageous." Gertrude expresses herself well throughout the play. She is solicitous of Hamlet, asking him to sit near her to give him a sense of belonging to the new court, and her speech to Laertes upon Ophelia's death is a model of decorum and sensitivity, one instance in which her usual directness would not be appropriate. If there is one quality that characterizes her speeches, it is her "ability to see reality clearly, and to express it," even when turned upon herself. As Hamlet rails against his mother and even violently seizes her in Act III (she cries out in fear, "Thou wilt not murder me?"), she betrays no knowledge of the murder. "What have I done, that thou dar'st wag thy tongue/In noise so rude against me?" she asks. Hamlet denounces her sexual passion, and she responds: "O Hamlet, speak no more!/Thou turn'st mine eyes into my very soul,/And there I see such black and grained spots/As will not leave their tinct" (III.iv). She admits her lust and sees it as sinful, but this is different from being an accomplice to murder. She thinks Hamlet mad and promises she will not betray him, and she does not. In the end, Heilbrun sums up Gertrude: "... if she is lustful, [she] is also intelligent, penetrating, and gifted" (1–17). We do not know her motives for marrying Claudius—perhaps she feared for her life and really did not have a choice—but she is honest enough to admit that sex had something to do with it. Hamlet is not able to face such a thing honestly. It is interesting that he assumes she had a choice in marrying Claudius; perhaps he sees her as much more powerful than she really is in the situation.

Let us contrast the distorted image of the mother Hamlet projects upon Gertrude with these evident dimensions of her character. Their relationship is most significant for a feminist reading, since Gertrude's body is the literal and symbolic ground of all the conflicts in the play; her body and soul are contested by her son, husbands, and courtiers.

When the Ghost of Hamlet's father addresses Gertrude's sin—"O Hamlet, what a falling-off was there"—he falls short of condemning her, but condemns her choice (I.v). He identifies his own body with the temple and the city ("And in the porches of my ears did pour/The leprous distilment"), while connecting Claudius with leprosy and filth and Gertrude with thorny vegetation. Though the Ghost's narrative of what happened to him leaves ambiguous the exact order of events (did Claudius seduce her before or after the murder?), he warns Hamlet against taking revenge upon his mother: "Leave her to Heaven" (I.v). The elder Hamlet's willingness to do that and not to cry for his son to take revenge for the perceived unfaithfulness of his spouse is a sign of his true nobility and perhaps Gertrude's innocence. But it is also a marker of how women were to be managed by men from the cradle and beyond—that she is his (Hamlet the Elder's) responsibility.

The Ghost's desire for leniency with his wife is not matched by similar sentiments of other male characters in the play. For example, there are the crude sex jokes of Rosencrantz and Guildenstern, who characterize first the earth and then fortune as whores. And when Laertes warns Ophelia about Hamlet's intentions, she jibes him about his own sexual escapades with women, and Polonius pays Reynaldo to spy on Laertes and see whether he is whoring. Ophelia is a more sympathetic—and more reliable—character compared to her hypocritical brother and scheming father. She also seems to be a better judge of Hamlet's strange behavior. Polonius puts it down merely to lovesickness.

When a troupe of players comes to the castle, Hamlet asks one of them to repeat Aeneas's speech to Dido on the death of King Priam, a doubly appropriate scenario in that Aeneas abandons Dido in order to pursue political greatness. Hamlet and the players speak of the "strumpet" Fortune, but Hamlet also mentions Hecuba, the wife of Priam, who mourns for her lost children (the opposite of Hamlet's mother, whose child mourns for her). Hamlet thinks of his own genuine grief in contrast to the players' pretended grief, and he calls himself "whore" and "drab" who must only "unpack" his heart with words instead of actions (II.ii), interestingly, continuing to relate making believe to "whoring." Claudius too uses the whore image, as he calls himself in an aside, a "harlot's cheek, beautied with plast'ring art" (III.i). ("Plast'ring" refers to the practice of covering syphilitic facial scars with paint, alluding again to the disease metaphor used for Claudius). The Queen's half-hearted questions to Hamlet evince her growing despair at his behavior, and *she* appears not whorish in the least, but merely sad and resigned. We must contrast her behavior with that of her husband, as he drinks and carouses loudly into the night.

Hamlet's famous "To be or not to be" speech (III.i) follows these shifting scenes of falsehood and betrayal. Ophelia interrupts him and is greeted as "nymph"; Hamlet asks her to pray for him, but then begins to berate her savagely, the first time he has really let his emotions go in front of someone else. He demands to know whether she is "honest" as well as "fair," and his demands escalate into his shouting, "Get thee to a nunnery" (*nunnery* being Elizabethan slang for *brothel*). His words recall the advice about young men she has heard from her father and brother. Hamlet ends by accusing her and all women of making monsters of men. In a case of repression and projection, he takes out his anger on her instead of its real object, Claudius. "Heavenly powers, restore him!" Ophelia prays after he leaves, adding: "O, what a noble mind is here o'erthrown," echoing Gertrude's fears for his sanity. Hamlet was the model for young manhood, "Th' expectation and rose of the fair state,/The glass of fashion and the mould of form" (III.i). Calling Hamlet a "rose" feminizes him to some degree (and recalls the Ghost's mention of "those thorns" that lie in Gertrude's "bosomy lodge to prick and sting her" [I.v]). The metaphor perhaps points toward his denial of unconscious drives and aspects, and her speech emphasizes his "feminine" traits of gentleness, a forgiving heart, stability, caught as he is in the throes of his male-gendered ego struggle. She pities and loves him but is herself much "o'erthrown" by his poisonous words.

Later, in the play-within-the-play, the poison used to kill the king is described as "Hecat's ban thrice blasted, thrice infected" (III.ii). The witch Hecate is a dark feminine image from early Greek mythology; the words "blasted" and "infected" invoke venereal disease again. The disease metaphors attached to the murderous Claudius and to "whores" point both toward his incestuous sin and to his own "whoredom": he marries to gain the kingdom. Everything points to the "sins" of sexuality, but also toward Gertrude and Ophelia, who inhabit a space outside the politics. Arguably, the destruction of their worlds leads to the wholesale royal and national defeat of Denmark.

We sense that the scene between Hamlet and his mother has been put off as long as it can when he bursts into her chamber and attacks her verbally and physically. But typical of the misdirected passions of Hamlet, he accidentally kills Polonius, who is hiding behind the curtains. (We must pause to note a certain voyeuristic quality to Polonius that would make an interesting analysis in the context of sexuality in *Hamlet*.) Again another person has stood in for Hamlet's real opponent, himself. Fittingly, when Laertes hears of his father's murder, he expresses himself in images derived from adultery: "That drop of blood that's calm proclaims me bastard,/Cries cuckold to my father, brands the harlot/Even here between the chaste unsmirched brow/Of my true mother" (IV.v), lines which seem to mean that if Laertes does not avenge his father, he is the son of a whore. (Compare this to Hamlet's dilemma.) Ophelia, now mad with grief at her father's death, sings a mock dirge for all women and perhaps for their sons too: "Good night, ladies, good night. Sweet ladies, good night, good night" (IV.v).

The final act begins with Hamlet and Laertes fighting in Ophelia's newly dug grave (a sexualized metaphor), after which Hamlet confesses his love for her, a question that has been left hanging until now. Perhaps her death has awakened in him his true nature as a lover of women instead of a victim of them, but we must remember it was his habit of misdirected anger that led to her despair and suicide. Laertes—as a **foil** or double of Hamlet and now the gentleman's model instead of Hamlet—has also taken Hamlet's aggressive, provoking, revenge-seeking place. When they fight in the last act, each is wounded with the poisoned sword. Laertes had provided the poison (IV.vii), but it was the father-king, Claudius, who had suggested the fencing match with one sword "unbated," a fittingly diseased **phallic** weapon to use against two sons. The queen drinks a poisoned cup, saying she "carouses" to Hamlet's "fortune." She calls, "Here, Hamlet, take my napkin, and rub thy brows," just as any proud and loving mother would (V.ii). Dying, Hamlet forces Claudius to drink from the cup he poisoned for Hamlet, but it is all too late, too late, even for revenge, and it is left for Horatio to tell Hamlet's tale. Hamlet and the two women he loved join his two fathers and Laertes in death. Political stability is restored by Fortinbras of Norway with a manly flourish, but at the price of Denmark's independence. The crisis of fathers and sons and sons and mothers is over, and the world of male political power is restored. Thus revenge destroys family.

C. "The Workshop of Filthy Creation": Men and Women in *Frankenstein*

As they sift through the artifacts of the early twenty-first century, surely archaeologists in the distant future will speculate on what sorts of gods were most widely worshipped around the world in our times, and they may very well conclude that one god had the face of Boris Karloff as the Creature in the Hammer Studios films of the 1930s, later portrayed in every conceivable medium from coffee mugs to billboards to T-shirts, consigning Batman and Elvis and Jacko to the footnotes. Considering the deterrents nineteenth-century women authors faced, it is a surprising fact that the world's most widely recognized fictional character, *Frankenstein*'s Creature, was created by a teenaged girl nearly two hundred years ago. But as many critics have noted, despite its huge popular success and mass commercialization, Mary Shelley's 1818 novel presents a startling array of interpretive questions, including especially questions concerning the women of Shelley's generation.

Understanding *Frankenstein* means understanding the gendered psychology of its creator. In *Frankenstein* femininity embraces life and regeneration, whereas masculinity murders and turns suicidally upon itself. Victor is alienated from the domestic sphere in his masculine quest for scientific glory, and as Mary Poovey observes, "the monster he creates completes his alienation by virtually wiping out his family" (16). Kate Ellis finds that *Frankenstein* critiques "a bifurcated social order" that separates "the masculine sphere of discovery and the feminine sphere of domesticity" (124). Victor's sin of expropriating the function of the female by giving "birth" to a child would seem to be a bridging of the two spheres. But though he sees himself as promoting social good in his supposedly unselfish desire to right the wrongs of material life (including its usual means of reproduction), the unnaturalness of his ambition to attain immortality is related to his forswearing normal relations with women, with his family and friends, and with his own "child." How fitting that people have confused Frankenstein with his creature, calling both

"Frankenstein": Victor, the creator who erases others' identities, has been partially erased by his Creature. Again, revenge destroys the family.

1. Mary and Percy, Author and Editor

Death and birth were "hideously mixed" in the life of Mary Shelley, notes Ellen Moers, just as they were in Victor's "workshop of filthy creation" (221). Mary experienced not only the untimely deaths of three children, two as infants, but also other violent deaths in her family. Her journal describes the loss of her first baby at age seventeen and the dreams she had in which she was able to bring it back to life. Mary's bereavements help one understand the otherwise puzzling compulsion that drives Victor to restore life.

Mary Shelley's experience, Moers points out, was highly unusual: "The harum-scarum circumstances surrounding her maternity have no parallel until our own time.... Mary Godwin sailed into teenage motherhood without any of the financial or social or family supports that made bearing and rearing children a relaxed experience for the normal middle-class woman of her day (as Jane Austen, for example, described her)." Mary was an unwed mother, partly responsible for breaking up the marriage of another young mother. Her adored father, philosopher William Godwin (1756–1836), cut her off (for a time) when she eloped, and of course her own mother, Mary Wollstonecraft (1759–97), whose memory she cherished and whose books she reread throughout her youth, died after giving birth to Mary herself. Thus it is not difficult to explain her "fantasy of the newborn as at once monstrous agent of destruction and piteous victim of parental abandonment." In having her Creature cry, " 'I, the miserable and the abandoned, I am an abortion to be spurned and kicked, and trampled on.... I have murdered the lovely and the helpless.... I have devoted my creator to misery; I have pursued him even to that irremediable ruin,' " she transformed the "standard Romantic matter of incest, infanticide, and patricide" into a "phantasmagoria of the nursery" (221–24). Of course many of these facts would also be noted by the historical-biographical approach (see Chapter 2) or the new historicist (Chapter 4).

At the time she began writing *Frankenstein*, Mary had been living with Percy Bysshe Shelley (1792–1822) for two years; they married halfway through the year that she spent writing the novel (from June 1816 to May 1817), just weeks after his first wife Harriett Shelley's suicide and two months after the suicide of Mary's half-sister, Fanny Imlay. As J. Paul Hunter observes, "Her mind was full of powerful (and conflicting) hopes and anxieties; and she often saw in traditional opposites—birth and death, pleasure and pain, masculinity and femininity, power and fear, writing and silence, innovation and tradition, competitiveness and compliance, ambition and suppression—things that overlapped and resisted easy borders and definitions" (viii).

Feminists argue that *Frankenstein* was written as an act of political and artistic resistance by a woman burdened by her parents' failures toward her, her husband's Promethean self-absorption, and the patriarchal oppressions of society at large. Percy Shelley plays the largest role in their analyses. Among other things, the name "Victor" was one Percy took for himself at times. His mother and sister were named Elizabeth. Like Victor, Christopher Small points out, Percy Shelley was an "ardent and high-spirited youth, of early promise and 'vehement passions'" (206–7). At the birth of ideas Victor is a poetic genius; at the living of life he is a hopeless failure.

Mary Shelley's name did not appear on the title page of the first publication of *Frankenstein* in 1818; rumors were that it had been authored by Percy Shelley, who did sign the preface. It was not unusual in that time for female writers to use male pseudonyms for publication or to omit their names. But in the 1831 revision of *Frankenstein,* Mary not only signed her name but wrote an introduction that provides commentary on the genesis and evolution of the book. For a time, family cares and her sense of being too "common-place" to live up to Percy's "far more cultivated mind" held her back, she recalls. But, as Betty T. Bennett notes, Mary also had a clear sense that "Percy had helped her to fulfill the promise of her literary heritage: Wollstonecraft's 'greatness of soul' and Godwin's 'high talents,' Mary told a friend in 1827, 'perpetually reminded me that I ought to degenerate as little as I could' from them, and Percy had 'fostered this ambition'" (Vol. 2, Ch. 4). Yet as she notes her husband's encouragement, she also remarks that "I certainly did not owe the suggestion of one incident, nor scarcely yet of one train of feeling, to my husband" (in Smith, "Introduction" 21–25).

According to feminist critics, Percy Shelley's role in the preparation of *Frankenstein* for publication has been overstated in the past. "Mary undoubtedly received more than she gave," according to a patronizing entry in the *Dictionary of*

Figure 8.2. Mary Shelley (ca. 1820).
Getty Images/Hulton Archive.

National Biography (1897): "Nothing but an absolute magnetising of her brain by [Percy] Shelley's can account for her having risen so far above her usual self as in 'Frankenstein'" (52:29). Feminist critics have sought to reclaim the genius of the novel for its author.

Just how much did Percy edit and revise, and what effect have his emendations had upon subsequent versions? In her important essay "Choosing a Text of *Frankenstein* to Teach," Anne Mellor reports her close examination of fragments of Mary's manuscript, noting an "eerie appropriateness" in the fact that the story has been so overtaken by adaptations that "Mary Shelley has seldom gotten full credit for her originality and creativity.... [S]he has remained in the shadow of what she created." Percy's contributions were in the end fairly minor, though they do reveal that he misunderstood Mary's intentions, especially as he made the Creature more horrific and less human and Victor less to blame for his transgressions. He also changed Mary's simpler Anglo-Saxon vocabulary into a "stilted, ornate, putatively Ciceronian prose style about which so many students complain," says Mellor, with its learned, polysyllabic terms instead of her more sentimental descriptions: "I want to claim not that Mary Shelley is a great prose stylist but only that her language, despite its tendency toward the abstract, sentimental, and even banal, is more direct and forceful than her husband's" (in Hunter 162–64). This is an example of how textual scholarship and feminist approaches find themselves aligned.

Among feminist critics, Mellor finds the earlier version truer to the author's feelings and ideas when she wrote it because it has a "greater philosophical coherence" clearly related to its historical context in the years just after the French Revolution. It portrays how male egotism can destroy families. It is also closer to the biographical facts of the death of Mary's first baby and her knowledge of scientific breakthroughs such as galvanism (in Hunter 160, 164–65).

2. Masculinity and Femininity in the Frankenstein Family

All three **narrators** are male, Walton, Victor, and the Creature, and all are **autobiographical**. Barbara Johnson describes them as attempts at "masculine persuasion": "The teller in each case is speaking into a mirror of his own transgression" (2–3). Indeed within the Frankenstein family, gender and parental roles are ambiguous and transgressive. Alphonse Frankenstein is a rather feminine patriarch. His wife Caroline, who is of a noble family, dies early on, a great loss, however, right away a substitute mother is conveniently available in Elizabeth, a cousin raised in the family. Henry Clerval furnishes further gender blending as "a model of internalized complementarity, of conjoined masculine and feminine traits," as Jeanne Rosier Smith describes him. With all of these androgynous domestic forces around him, Victor strays at his first opportunity. Victor's straying is a man's prerogative. As we see in Elizabeth's substituting for Caroline, and later in Justine's imitations of Caroline and in her death as Elizabeth's precursor, the Frankenstein family tends to reproduce itself incestuously, Smith observes, in an "insistent replication of the domestic icon," causing a destructive pattern of indebtedness that characterizes "the Frankenstein definition of femininity" ("'Cooped Up'" 317–18, 321). George Levine stresses the claustrophobic nature of the Frankenstein family: "Within the novel, almost all relations have the texture of blood kin," in contrast to the Creature, who has no kin. As the story and its characters are doubled and redoubled, Levine notes the appearance of the incest theme, one of Percy Shelley's favorites (212–13).

Walton's first letter to his sister begins: "You will rejoice to hear that no disaster has accompanied the commencement of an enterprise which you have regarded with such evil forebodings," a passage that might be read as an attempt to acknowledge feminine concerns about his safety, but is in fact a denial, setting the tone for the kinds of denials Victor will utter. Just before he discovers Victor on the Arctic ice, Walton's second letter confides his deep desire for a friend. When his "friend" appears, he seems to understand what Walton is about: "You seek for knowledge and wisdom, as I once did: and I ardently hope that the gratification of your wishes may not be a serpent to sting you, as mine has been." Nevertheless, Victor casts the blame for his own miseducation upon Cornelius Agrippa, Paracelsus, and Albertus Magnus (all favorites with Percy Shelley), but even more upon his father, who only "looked carelessly at the title-page" of Agrippa, and said, "'Ah! Cornelius Agrippa! My dear Victor, do not waste your time upon this; it is sad trash.' If, instead of this remark, my father had taken the pains to explain to me, that the principles of Agrippa had been entirely exploded, and that a modern system of science had been introduced, which possessed much greater powers than the ancient, because the powers of the latter were chimerical, while those of the former were real and practical; under such circumstances, I should certainly have thrown Agrippa aside and turned to modern chemistry." Not Agrippa but his father's cursoriness was the "fatal impulse." Victor's blaming behavior parallels Walton's excuses to his sister, and the two men bond.

In his attempt to circumvent his Oedipal drama, Victor says he wanted to create a "new species [that] would bless me as its creator and source.... No father could claim the gratitude of his child so completely as I should deserve their's." Reflecting his aspiration to be the ideal parent, he describes his labors in terms of giving birth:

> My cheek had grown *pale* with study, and my person had become emaciated with *confinement*. Sometimes, *on the very brink of certainty, I failed*; yet still I clung to the hope which the next day or the next hour might realise. One secret which I alone possessed was the hope to which I had dedicated myself; and the moon gazed on *my midnight labours,* while, with *unrelaxed and breathless eagerness,* I pursued nature to her hiding-places....My limbs now tremble and my eyes swim with the remembrance; but then *a resistless, and almost frantic, impulse urged me forward;* I seemed to have lost all soul or sensation but for this one pursuit.... [M]y *eye-balls were starting from their sockets* in attending to the details of my employment....whilst, still urged on by *an eagerness which perpetually increased,* I brought my work near to a conclusion. [emphases ours]

But though he next compares himself with the world's great conquerors, the reality of what he has produced panics him:

> Great God! His yellow skin scarcely covered the work of muscles and arteries beneath; his hair was of lustrous black, and flowing; his teeth of a pearly

whiteness; but these luxuriances only formed a more horrid contrast with his watery eyes, that seemed almost of the same colour as the dun white sockets in which they were set, his shriveled complexion, and straight black lips.... [N]ow that I had finished, the beauty of the dream vanished, and breathless horror and disgust filled my heart. Unable to endure the aspect of the being I had created, I rushed out of the room....

The Creature is conveniently nowhere to be found upon his return. In a panic Victor regresses to his bed and dreams of embracing Elizabeth, but embraces instead the worm-ridden corpse of his mother. As he awakens, he sees the terrible image of his own self: "...by the dim and yellow light of the moon,...I beheld the wretch—the miserable monster whom I had created," a monstrous baby who mutters "some inarticulate sounds, while a grin wrinkled his cheeks."

3. "I Am Thy Creature..."
Feminist readers lay more blame upon Victor for his abandonment of his creation than for his **hubris** in having first created him: the Creature demands, "How dare you sport thus with life? Oh, Frankenstein, be not equitable to every other, and trample upon me alone, to whom thy justice, and even thy clemency and affection, is most due. Remember that I am thy creature: I ought to be thy Adam; but I am rather the fallen angel, whom thou drivest from joy for no misdeed." Victor's response is an angry shout: "Begone! I will not hear you. There can be no community between you and me; we are enemies."

But the Creature's story is *the* story, the story of a community, and the novel's longest single section is narrated by the Creature, who tells of his education hiding in the De Laceys' cottage storeroom, observing them as "a vision of a social group based on justice, equality, and mutual affection," as Mellor notes in "Possessing Nature" (in Hunter 277). The De Laceys and Safie challenge the Frankenstein family's artificial reproduction of domesticity as well as Victor's refusal to parent. The Creature learns eagerly from Safie: "Safie was always gay and happy; she and I improved rapidly in the knowledge of language, so that in two months I began to comprehend most of the words uttered by my protectors." Safie's Christian-Arab mother had been enslaved by the Turks but escaped: "She instructed her daughter in the tenets of her religion, and taught her to aspire to higher powers of intellect, and an independence of spirit, forbidden to the female followers of Mahomet." Safie is an "incarnation of Mary Wollstonecraft," Mellor notes (in Hunter 286).

Typically, Victor procrastinates over making a bride for the Creature. What if she has desires and opinions that he cannot control, what if she procreates, what if she is so ugly the Creature rejects her, what if she rejects the Creature and seeks a human mate? The most fearful risks to him are her possible reproductive powers. He passionately tears her to pieces. One wonders whether Victor fears his own bride's sexuality, since he sends her into their wedding chamber alone. Victor's carelessness towards friends, family, and bride is repeatedly shown.

When Victor finds the murdered Elizabeth in their wedding chamber, only he could be shocked, and only he could respond, "no creature had ever been so miserable as I was," forgetting Elizabeth, just as he had forgotten the Creature's threat to her. As Johanna Smith observes, "Like Elizabeth's, the monsterette's creation and destruction dramatize how women function not in their own right but rather as signs of and conduits for men's relations with other men, simply 'counters' in the struggle between Victor and the monster in himself" ("Introduction" 100–102).

Yet there must also have been a great deal of Mary Shelley in Victor Frankenstein: she endows him with a fine mind, an inquiring spirit, and the urge to create. She gives him voice to explain himself, and he is in certain ways honest with himself. Why does Victor turn upon all that he loves? Perhaps articulating her conflicting ideas of her own identity, Mary Shelley speaks both through Victor's struggles and the words of his Creature, an articulate if abandoned child.

The last words of the text, in which the Creature is "lost in darkness and distance," are not necessarily the ending: we do not know what becomes of the Creature, and there is someone whose response has not yet been heard. The ending takes us into a realm that may be read as a feminine use of ambiguity, what Gayatri Chakravorty Spivak calls "an existential temporality." Margaret Saville, Walton's sister and the recipient of his letters, is, Spivak says, "the occasion, if not the protagonist of the novel. She is the feminine *subject*," an imagined female reader who must "intercept" the text and read its letters so that it may exist. The reader is thus encouraged to read the text *as* the skeptical Margaret: "Within the allegory of our reading, the place of both the English lady and the unnamable monster are left open"…("Three Women's Texts" 267–68).

D. Men, Women, and the Loss of Faith in "Young Goodman Brown"

Nathaniel Hawthorne's portraits of women go against the literary conventions of his day. Despite his remark that he was tired of competing with the "mob of scribbling women" novelists, he generally portrayed women not just as symbols of goodness (but more deeply than the "Cult of True Womanhood" tradition), as possessing knowledge that surpasses that of the male characters and approaches that of the author and narrator. Hawthorne treated women with more **realism** and depth than did most other writers, especially male writers, paving the way for the development of realism and **naturalism** at the close of the century in the works of Henry James, William Dean Howells, Edith Wharton, and Theodore Dreiser; all of these writers portray women as powerful moral *agents* rather than one-dimensional moral *objects*.

Hawthorne's most interesting women characters include Hester of *The Scarlet Letter*, Zenobia of *The Blithedale Romance*, Hepzibah of *The House of the Seven Gables*, Miriam of *The Marble Faun*, and such short story characters as Beatrice in "Rappaccini's Daughter" and Georgiana of "The Birthmark." All of these women engage in conflict with the men in their lives, and all of them have the sympathy of the author. Hester is Hawthorne's greatest character, male or female, and from the lips of the magnificent Zenobia, modeled in part on the feminist and author

Margaret Fuller, Hawthorne gives us as eloquent a speech on women's rights as any he may have heard in his time.

However, Faith Brown of "Young Goodman Brown" is not a heroic or even three-dimensional character. With her allegorical name and small role in the action of the story, readers might be likely to overlook her significance. But in fact, the story centers specifically on her husband's rejection of her; the tale may be read as a psychosexual parable of the rejection of the feminine in favor of a father-figure symbolized by the Devil. Good and evil are thus gendered qualities in this story.

Hawthorne's sympathies are with the woman and not the misconstrued masculinity of her rigid husband, whose failure is his rejection of his wife's sexuality for some unstated but sexually appalling ritual in the forest. Brown gives up his adult sexuality and regresses to the infantile fear of his father in his pre-Oedipal period.

Turning for a moment to a motion picture that readers might recall, we might compare Brown's vacillating desires with the behavior of Tom Cruise's character, Bill Hartford (note his task: to "ford," or get through, the "heart") in Stanley Kubrick's *Eyes Wide Shut* (1999). Bill's wife, Alice, played by Nicole Kidman, hears his horrified story of his night of debauchery at a Satanic orgy, where he went because of his fears of what *her* fantasies might be. She is at last able to respond to his question, "What should we do?" by saying, "Maybe I think we should be grateful that we've managed to survive through all of our adventures, real or only a dream." When Bill responds, "Are you sure of that?" Alice continues, "Am I sure? Only as sure as I am that the reality of one night—let alone that of a whole lifetime—can ever be the whole truth." Bill cannot seem to let go of his fears and fantasies, while his wife, shopping for children's clothes in this scene at the end, is more pragmatic; she is willing to live with ambiguities, and in that respect is a much healthier adult than her husband.

The sexuality inherent in Goodman Brown's forest meeting is reinforced by the repeated mention of the women who will be there, from Goody Cloyse and the governor's wife to the most spent of prostitutes. Brown learned his catechism from Goody Cloyse; when he wonders whether his journey will end up hurting his Faith, the Devil produces Goody Cloyse at that moment to make Brown suspect all women. Goody Cloyse says she is attending the ceremony to see a man, while the men on horseback whom Brown overhears say they are there for the women. The Devil's snaky staff is an appropriate **phallic** symbol, and the **symbols** included at the altar of unholy communion include a bloody basin. The tone is hardly celebratory of sexuality; it is more directed toward cruelty and especially the victimization of women. The Devil refers to Brown's grandfather, whom he helped to persecute Quaker women.

At the end, Brown, having himself become the most "frightful" figure in the forest, returns home not to repent of his ways but to rebuke his wife. We are told that at the end of his life his "hoary corpse" is carried to the grave followed by his wife, children, and grandchildren; and instead of shuddering at his gloomy death, one shudders instead to think that Faith and her children have had to live all those empty years with his blighted self, a failed husband, father, and human being.

E. Women and "Sivilization" in *Huckleberry Finn*

For a supposed boy's book, *Adventures of Huckleberry Finn* is oddly full of women; for a book primarily about race in America, it is also often about gender. The over-all theme of freedom, of the individual against the oppressive society around him, is connected to the feminine in important ways. On the one hand, the feminine appears to be what Huck is running away from—"sivilization" as defined by the Widow Douglas and Aunt Sally. But on the other hand, the novel satirizes rigid gender lines just as it does racial divisions. And **satire** of gender roles is typical of Twain, as also appears in such characters as Eve in *Letters from the Earth,* Roxy in *Pudd'nhead Wilson,* and perhaps most of all in his beloved Joan of Arc.

There have been several important studies of Twain and women, including that of Shelley Fisher Fishkin, who notes how Twain scholars have assumed that women were "bad" for Twain, and Twain "bad" for women. Biographers such as Van Wyck Brooks and Justin Kaplan seem to feel that Twain's wife, Olivia Langdon Clemens, sometimes emasculated his authorial power with her pious Presbyterian conventionality, and even Twain's early admirers, such as the influ-ential editor of the *Atlantic Monthly,* William Dean Howells, complained of the thinness of his female characters. Fishkin urges a "more nuanced" perspective on the subject, for she sees women as essential to Twain's creative process, includ-ing Olivia, and points out that his audience was largely female ("Mark Twain and Women," 53–54, 67–69). A more extreme stance is that of Laura Skandera-Trombley, who argues that Twain existed in a sort of "charmed circle" of women who read drafts, heard him read passages aloud, offered commentary, and even acted as editors. Skandera-Trombley's notion that Olivia and Twain's daughters were his "collaborators" (59, 131, 168) has been criticized by other scholars as overstating the feminine influence. Still, femininity in Twain is probably neglected by most of his critics.

The most positive figure in the story, the runaway slave Jim, is a happily mar-ried man who in the end is to be reunited with his family. Jim's tenderness and care of Huck are the book's most positive feminine traits, almost entirely absent from any of the other men Huck encounters. Jim makes fires, washes pots, shows hos-pitality to guests, and generally mothers and protects—and advises—Huck, whose father Jim knows to have been murdered. But most importantly, Jim is the moral touchstone of the book. Through him, Nancy Walker has noted, Huck begins to develop the virtues of "honesty, compassion, a sense of duty," which are defined in the novel as "female virtues" about which the Widow and Miss Watson lecture Huck without much effect, for in the end Huck must identify with a man instead of a woman (488).

The novel could be viewed as a **quest** for contact with the feminine in some abstract sense even as it is a flight from the conventional feminine. *Huckleberry Finn* may be better understood not merely as a flight from "sivilization" and all it represents (including the feminine proprieties the Widow, Miss Watson, and later Aunt Sally Phelps would administer), but rather as a flight from masculine author-ity to seek out alternatives particularly the authority of pap Finn, his drunken, violent father. In Huck's frequent lies, his "family" usually contains a dead mother and a threatened sister or female family friend (such as "Miss Hooker," the name of one of Olivia's friends, Alice Hooker Day, a niece of Henry Ward Beecher).

The Judith Loftus scene early in the novel, in which Huck poses as a girl, "Sarah Mary Williams," in order to glean information about his "death" and Jim's flight, calls the fixity of gender roles into question. Mrs. Loftus is quite schooled in the *appearance* of gender; after she finds Huck out, she gives him a list of how he ought to do things if he poses again as a girl. Her list points not to the inalterability of male and female behavior, but to the fact that behavior is just behavior, and sexes can be put on or taken off through behavior. For example, she tells him, "When you set out to thread a needle, don't hold the thread and fetch the needle up to it; hold the needle still and poke the thread at it—that's the way a woman most always does; but a man always does it t'other way." (In Chapter 13 of *The Prince and the Pauper*, Twain has Miles Hendon do it exactly opposite: "He did as men have always done, and probably always will do, to the end of time—held the needle still, and tried to thrust the thread through the eye, which is the opposite of a woman's way." That Twain seems unsure of women's and men's true ways heightens ambivalence about fixed gender roles in his work.) The notion that femininity is a role is important to Huck's growing awareness of many social conventions; if it is only a role, then perhaps racial roles are only just roles. As Quentin Compson in Faulkner's *The Sound and the Fury* observes, "A nigger is not a person so much as a form of behaviour; a sort of obverse reflection of the white people he lives among." And Mrs. Loftus is no ordinary housewife: one gets the feeling that she is somewhat bored and likes the diversion Huck provides. She is far from the arid disciplinarian Miss Watson. Her sagacity, kindness, and willingness to playact with Huck set the stage for Huck's own lies and performances throughout the novel in the various disguises he dons to protect himself and Jim.

The Judith Loftus episode is the most important interrogation of sex roles in the novel, but women's roles continue to be important throughout. Though women, like the men Huck and Jim encounter, are frequently satirized, and though they often seem reduced to their titles ("Widow" Douglas or "Sis" Hotchkiss), they also promote the values of nurturing and moral stability, especially as mothers. Huck's own mother is barely mentioned; but when she is, it is to oppose pap Finn's lawlessness and degeneration. Pap insists that Huck stop going to school because "Your mother couldn't read, and she couldn't write, nuther, before she died. None of the family could before they died. I can't; and you're a-swelling yourself up like this." Huck notes that he didn't want to go to school before, "But I reckoned I'd go now to spite pap," even though he is "thrashed" by pap for doing so.

The Widow Douglas, kind and motherly but ultimately ineffectual, is both the one from whom Huck runs and the one whom he consistently reveres. She seems, like Aunt Sally, to understand and love children, and she encourages him to develop a conscience: "She said she warn't ashamed of me." Huck thus finds himself torn between his desire to draw near to the Widow and his rebellion against the enforced identity she and Miss Watson propose for him. As Nancy Walker points out, it was the Widow who taught Huck to care about others, as is later evidenced in his concern for Jim's "essential humanity" (496). Miss Watson is the worst of feminized "sivilization": hypocritical, self-righteous, repressed. And yet it is she who frees Jim in the end. One wonders if she too comes to protest the proslavery male authority figures she has formerly revered, or at least to feel guilty about her dominion over Jim.

At the Phelps farm, gender roles along with racial roles return to the conventional, after the long idyll on the river. Huck says he feels "mean" and ashamed of his bad behavior at Aunt Sally's place; but at the same time the comedy of the last chapters hinges upon her overreactions to the boys' pranks. But when she voices her plan to adopt and civilize Huck, he heads for the Territory. A final mother figure is Aunt Polly, who appears like a *dea ex machina* in the conclusion; she is severe to the boys, but tender to a fault in her concern for Tom.

Younger women generally represent greater possibilities than the older women; the exception is Emmeline Grangerford, whose poetry evinces the worst of ignorant sentimentality that underlies slavery and other social ills along the journey. Her shallow, anemic romanticism is wasted on Huck, yet she also references important feminine characterizations of the times that Twain satirizes, especially the idea that well-bred women should be idle and even hysterical. She may be overly sentimental, but on the other hand, she also reveals in her gloomy paintings a realistic sense of the climate of darkness around her as the murderous feuds are enacted year after year. Sophia Grangerford is a welcome contrast, a beautiful and courageous young woman, the eternal bride. Through her friendship with Huck she is able to escape her fear-ridden world. The "Harelip," whom Huck meets at the Wilks home, is a humorous diversion between dangers: she wryly sees through Huck's ridiculous lies about life in England, made to impress her. Sober, serious-minded, and shrewd, she unveils Huck, just as Mrs. Loftus did, but also like her she does not tell on him. Mary Jane Wilks is like Sophia, but wiser and calmer, and like the Harelip, only more attractive. Mary Jane appeals to Huck because, as Mark Altschuler notes, she "embodies mother, victim, and orphan—the three most powerful images for Huck." Her "unearned nurturing" is a key to his ultimate moral development for she is the only mother figure in the text he does not reject. Her friendship allows Huck to save her and her family from the evil machinations of the King and the Duke. Huck respects this down-to-earth woman, and though one continues naively to follow his "betters," including Tom, one wishes he had been able to substitute his blind faith in Tom for a relationship with Mary Jane. Perhaps she will grow up to be a woman like the Widow, only with a little more of Huck's flexibility and pragmatism. As he helps her become a bride, she brings out Huck's masculinity in a positive way that allows both himself and others to grow and maintain human dignity. That he does not ultimately mature in the novel is not her fault; perhaps it is a larger statement about the "ineffectuality of women in his society," as Walker surmises (499).

Although *Huckleberry Finn* does seem to want to turn women into mothers, keep sex out of the picture, use women for the most part as symbols of undesirable cultural conventionality, and defeat the realm of women in the end, its variety of female characters offers an enriching dimension to the novel and continually emphasizes the importance of nurturing.

And let us remember: not only Huck and Jim journey downriver all the way to Arkansas. The redoubtable Aunt Polly also travels the same hundreds of miles to see to the safety of her Tom, and by chance, also to that of America's most famous orphan.

F. "In Real Life": Recovering the Feminine Past in "Everyday Use"

Whose story is this? "For your grandmama." For your mama, sister, daughter, friend. For you, girl, no matter where you are or who you are—for *you*. Are you like scarred and scared Maggie, afraid to be anything more? Or are you like Dee, with your grandiose design for your future and your college-educated contempt of your family heritage? Are you like the mother of these two sisters, whose rough work "does not show on television," but who knows when an insight hits her on top of her head "just like when I'm in church"? Are your hands quick with the needle,

Figure 8.3. Georgia woman sweeping her yard (ca. 1940).
Courtesy Georgia Archives, Vanishing Georgia Collection, 155.

piecing Lone Star and Walk Around the Mountain with scraps of old dresses? Or maybe Afroed and art-historied and aware? Or perhaps you live in "real life," living your heritage in the here and now, sitting sometimes "just enjoying"?

"Everyday Use" is about the everyday lives of women past and present, encircled by family and culture, and especially about the contemporary experiences of different generations of African-American women. Its quilt is an emblem of American women's culture, as it is an object of communal construction and female harmony. The quilt warms and protects our bodies; it is passed down like mother's wisdom from generation to generation; its designs mirror the most everyday but profound concerns of all women—marriage, family, children, love. Like much of women's art it is nonlinear, nonhierarchical, intimate. The story itself reserves judgment as something not needed, though it does not shy away from conflict. It is about bonding—daughter-mother, woman-woman, domestic-aesthetic, and so on, recalling the psychoanalytic notion of the feminine as the nonbinary described by Lacan, Cixous, and Irigaray. As Barbara Christian notes, Alice Walker "is drawn to the integral and economical process of quilt making as a model for her own craft," for it helps her answer the writer's eternal question, "From whence do I come?" (*Black Feminist Criticism* 85).

Walker identifies the quilt as one of the traditional art forms of African-American women, along with gospel singing and gardening, that "kept alive" the creativity of black women "century after century." African-American women slaves were "the mule[s] of the world," but also "creators...rich in spirituality" (*In Search* 233). Like Virginia Woolf in *A Room of One's Own*, Walker searches for her artistic foremothers, noting how "we have constantly looked high, when we should have looked low." In her poem "Women," Walker praises the "Headragged Generals" of her mother's generation, who, through manual labor, "battered down/Doors" for their children "To discover books" while "...they knew what we/Must know/ Without knowing a page/Of it/Themselves" (*Revolutionary Petunias* 5).

In "Everyday Use" Walker poses problems of heritage in response to the black power movements of the 1960s in which she grew up, especially the kind of cultural nationalism that demanded imitation of features of the African past. Walker critiques the short-sightedness of radicals who would have seen the narrator, the mother, as what Barbara Christian calls "that supposedly backward Southern ancestor the cultural nationalists of the North probably visited during the summers of their youth and probably considered behind the times." Walker "gives voice to an entire maternal history often silenced by the political rhetoric of the period," her way of "breaking silences and stereotypes about her grandmothers', mothers', sisters' lives" (*"Everyday Use": Alice Walker* 10–11).

In a 1973 interview with Mary Helen Washington, as reported by Christian, Walker identifies three cycles of historical black women characters who she feels are missing from contemporary writing. First are those "who were cruelly exploited, spirits and bodies mutilated, relegated to the most narrow and confining lives, sometimes driven to madness," shown in her novel *The Third Life of Grange Copeland* (1970) and in the short stories of *In Love and Trouble* (1973), including "Everyday Use." The women in Walker's second cycle are those who are not so much physically as psychically abused, a result of wanting desperately to participate in mainstream American life. In the third cycle are those black women who have gained a new consciousness and pride, what Christian calls "their right to be themselves and to shape the world," as in Walker's heroines of *Meridian* (1976), *The Color Purple*, and *You Can't Keep a Good Woman Down* (1981) (*"Everyday Use": Alice Walker* 3–7). By the end of the century, other African-American writers, most notably Toni Morrison, filled in many characters Walker only sketches. Walker and Morrison in turn inspired such third-wave African-American feminist writers as Sherley Ann Williams, Nzotake Shange, Gloria Naylor, Cheryl Glenn, and Sapphire.

"Everyday Use" contains women of all three cycles of history. Maggie does not know her worth; her mother says she walks like "a lame animal, perhaps a dog run over by some careless person rich enough to own a car." Dee inhabits the second cycle: though she seems to reject white society, she fails to appreciate her own heritage until it becomes fashionable to do so. Though her mother applauds Dee's personal strength, she is saddened by her embarrassment at Maggie, at herself, and at her home. The mother, though ironically the oldest person in the story, prefigures the women of Walker's third cycle in her self-reliance and firm sense of connectedness to her past. As an older woman, she is in a position within her little community to pass along her wisdom to Maggie and Dee, women of the first and second cycles, and in being such a person she seems fresh, modern, and believable. When she suddenly snatches the disputed quilt away from Dee and gives it to Maggie, she rejects Dee's stereotypes and reaffirms her own identity (Christian, *"Everyday Use": Alice Walker* 9, 12).

Walker has made a conscious choice in this story to use only women; all the men are dead, absent, unnamed (we never do find out what Dee's boyfriend is really named). Houston A. Baker, Jr., and Charlotte Pierce-Baker see Maggie as the "arisen goddess of Walker's story; she is the sacred figure who bears the scarifications of experience and knows how to convert patches into robustly patterned and beautifully quilted wholes" (162), connecting Maggie's understated feminine power with that of African goddesses of creativity and regeneration. Maggie's humility and sense of beauty ("just enjoying") make her the innocent in the story; her quiet femininity is upheld in the end when her mother takes her side. She will marry John Thomas and live with him, her quilts, and presumably the children begotten in their bed, and she will become an adult woman with her own life and traditions; but she would not have passed the point of fearing life if her mother had not helped her. Walker, herself scarred in a childhood accident to one of her eyes, presents Maggie with great tenderness and hope.

But Walker is part of Dee, too. Dee tells her mother that she just "doesn't understand," but she comes off to most readers as the one who fails to understand. Dee is very bossy, a fact which helps reveal her hypocrisy, and there is a hint that she may have been the one who set the house on fire when Maggie was burned. At the least, Dee is selfish and pretentious. But we must also recognize her as an example of what most of the girls who grew up with her could only dream of: she is the black feminist's ideal—a woman who makes a success of herself despite enormous odds. She has managed to move to the city, get an education, and get a good job. She is politically involved. She has many friends. She is the future. Walker's feelings toward Dee are mixed, as they were with Maggie. Dee is based not only upon Walker but also upon her older sister, Molly, who is also the subject of the bittersweet poem, "For My Sister Molly Who In the Fifties." In an interview Walker confided that when her sister, who had gone away to be educated, came back home to visit the family in Georgia,

> ...it was—at first—like having Christmas with us all during her vacation. She
> loved to read and tell stories; she taught me African songs and dances; she cooked
> fanciful dishes that looked like anything but plain old sharecropper food. I loved
> her so much it came as a great shock—and a shock I don't expect to recover
> from—to learn that she was ashamed of us. We were so poor, dusty, and sunburnt.
> We talked wrong. We didn't know how to dress, or use the right eating utensils.
> And so, she drifted away, and I did not understand it. ("Interview with Alice
> Walker," in Christian *"Everyday Use": Alice Walker* 79–80)

At the end of "Everyday Use," Dee has accepted the *things* but not the *spirit* of heritage. She has allowed heritage to become, as Christian points out, an "abstraction rather than a living idea," has subordinated people to artifacts, and has elevated culture above community *("Everyday Use": Alice Walker* 130). Dee is defeated, but to assert only that would be to miss the deeper point of the story, which is to redefine black feminism in terms that will reconcile Dee's aspiration with Maggie's traditionalism: their mother is the bridge that connects past and future, and they must both enter and emerge from what the psychoanalytic critics call the Realm of the Mother to become fully themselves.

The **narrator** of the story is the sort of woman who brings to mind what Walker has elsewhere called *Womanism* as opposed to *Feminism*. In an epigraph to *In Search of Our Mothers' Gardens,* Walker offers four definitions of *Womanist.* First, it is "a black feminist or feminist of color." She explains the derivation from *womanish,* a black folk expression mothers might use to warn female children who are "outrageous, audacious, or willful," who want to know more than what is good for them or want to grow up too soon. Second, the term refers to "a woman who loves other women, sexually and/or nonsexually," who "appreciates and prefers women's culture,...women's emotional flexibility,...and women's strength." Third, the Womanist "Loves music. Loves dance. Loves the moon. *Loves* the Spirit. Loves love and food and roundness. Loves struggle. *Loves* the Folk. Loves herself. *Regardless.*" And, finally, "Womanist is to feminist as purple is to lavender."

VI. SUMMARY OF KEY POINTS

- Feminism is concerned with the marginalization of women in a patriarchal culture.
- Feminist critics explain how the subordination of women is reflected or challenged by literary texts. They examine the experiences of women of all

races, classes, sexual preferences, and cultures.

- Feminist critics' goals: to expose patriarchal premises and resulting preju-dices, to promote the discovery and reevaluation of literature by women, and to examine social, cultural, and psychosexual contexts of literature and literary criticism.
- Feminism is divided up historically into first-, second-, and third-wave feminisms, roughly corresponding to the periods of the nineteenth century, the first three-quarters of the twentieth century, and the late twentieth- and early twenty-first centuries.
- Elaine Showalter similarly identifies three phases of feminism, the "feminine" in which women writers imitate men, the "feminist" in which they advocated minority rights and protested, and the "female" in which the focus is now on women's texts as opposed to merely uncovering misogyny in men's texts.
- Showalter also defines four models of sexual difference: biological, linguis-tic, psychoanalytic, and cultural.
- Gender studies examines how sexual identity influences the creation and reception of literary works.
- Writing styles are described by gender critics as sex-related; e.g., the novel as a female genre.
- Male and female discursive logic: sequential versus associational.
- Current practices of feminism include Marxist feminism, French femi-nism (*l'ecriture feminine*), feminist myth critics, feminist film theory, and "minority" feminism such as black and lesbian subgenres.
- Alice Walker prefers "womanism" to "feminism."

VII. THE FUTURE OF FEMINIST LITERARY STUDIES AND GENDER STUDIES: SOME PROBLEMS AND LIMITATIONS

Given the proliferation of the many feminisms and areas of gender studies we have been discussing in this chapter, it is hard to imagine limits. By way of illustration, we note that when the second edition came out in 1979, in our classes we taught very few women writers. In American literature, for example, we might teach only Dickinson, Wharton, and perhaps Chopin, who was arriving on the scene just then. The evolution of this book and of our teaching now reflects the massive changes brought to literary criticism by feminism and related fields.

Many ongoing issues generated in the various feminisms and gender studies are yet to be resolved. Opponents to Showalter's linguistic model of difference, for example, argue that there is not and never will be a separate women's language. Feminisms and gender studies will continue to challenge long-held beliefs and practices in Western culture and around the world, but they will also continue to draw fire for their tendency (shared with Marxism and certain cultural stud-ies approaches) to politicize the art right out of literature. Myra Jehlen asks us to remember that art can contain good ideas as well as bad ones, but that these do not determine literary value. The reductiveness of some feminist theory indicates the radical's dislike of compromise; this tendency has both attracted and alienated potential followers. "Where is beauty?" one might ask. Surely somewhere other than in "political correctness." And, in turn, feminists such as Showalter and Kolodny criticize each other for overly theorizing feminism to the point of losing sight of its social roots and practical applications.

Helen Vendler's criticisms of feminism's political biases, especially those of Gilbert and Gubar, promoted lively debate in the academy. Vendler finds feminist critics' versions of female characters in male-authored novels naïve, in seeing them as "real" people who should be treated accordingly. She disputes the idea of a "female" language or way of writing. She does not believe special virtue should be ascribed to women. Such a view is merely sentimental, "that men, as a class, are base and women are moral." If feminism is to succeed it must de-idealize women (19–22).

What to do with male feminists? Unlike male practitioners of other approaches, male feminist critics have a hard time of it. Some feminists believe that they are impostors; no man can possibly speak, write, or teach as a woman, because he can escape, as Maggie Humm notes, into the patriarchy at any point (13–14). Toril Moi even advises the would-be male feminist critic to ask himself "whether he as a male is really doing feminism a service in our present situation by muscling in on the one cultural and intellectual space women have created for themselves within 'his' male-dominated discipline" (208). But as many influential male feminist critics, including Houston A. Baker, Jr., and Paul Lauter, demonstrate, male critics have brilliantly explicated women's issues in the critical and artistic discourse of our times.

Today one hears that young women who have benefited from the dramatic struggles and sacrifices of their foremothers decline to use the term *feminist* to describe themselves. We read of a backlash against feminism, particularly on the political Right. But surely the self-consciousness about gender roles generated by feminism from its earliest days will continue to inspire new adaptations by women and men entering the new millennium of literary investigations in feminisms, gender studies, and elsewhere.

QUICK REFERENCE

Althusser, Louis. *For Marx*. Trans. Ben Brewster. New York: Pantheon Books, 1969.

Altschuler, Mark. "Motherless Child: Huck Finn and a Theory of Moral Development." *American Literary Realism* 22, no. 1 (Fall 1989): 31–41.

Andermahr, Sonya, Terry Lovell, and Carol Wolkowitz, eds. *A Glossary of Feminist Theory*. New York: Edward Arnold, 2000.

Angelou, Maya. *I Know Why the Caged Bird Sings*. New York: Random House, 1969.

Awkward, Michael. *Inspiriting Influences: Tradition, Revision, and Afro-American Women's Novels*. New York: Columbia University Press, 1989.

Baker, Houston A., Jr., and Charlotte Pierce-Baker. "Patches: Quilts and Community in Alice Walker's 'Everyday Use.'" In Christian, 1994.

Barnes, Sherri L. "Black American Feminisms, Multidisciplinary Biography." http://www.library.ucsb.edu/subjects/blackfeminism/introduction.html

Baym, Nina. *Feminism and American Literary History: Essays.* New Brunswick, NJ: Rutgers University Press, 1992.

Bederman, Gail. *Manliness and Civilization: A Cultural History of Gender and Race in the United States, 1880–1917.* Chicago: University of Chicago Press, 1995.

Bennett, Betty T., ed. *The Letters of Mary Wollstonecraft Shelley.* 3 vols. Baltimore: Johns Hopkins University Press, 1980–88.

Berlant, Lauren, and Michael Warner, eds. Introduction to Special Issue: Queer Theory. *PMLA* 110 (May 1995): 343–49.

Butler, Judith. *Bodies That Matter: On the Discursive Limits of "Sex."* New York: Routledge, 1993.

———. *Gender Trouble: Feminism and the Subversion of Identity.* New York: Routledge, 1990.

———. *The Judith Butler Reader.* Ed. Judith Butler and Sara Salih. London: Blackwell, 2004.

Carson, James B. "Bringing the Author Forward: *Frankenstein* through Mary Shelley's Letters," *Criticism* 30, no. 4 (Fall 1988): 431–53.

Castle, Terry. "Sylvia Townsend Warner and the Counterplot of Lesbian Fiction." In *Sexual Sameness: Textual Difference in Lesbian and Gay Writing.* Ed. Joseph Bristow. New York: Routledge, 1992.

Célestin, Roger, Eliane DalMolin, and Isabelle de Courtivron, eds. *Beyond French Feminisms: Debates on Women, Politics, and Culture in France, 1981–2001.* New York: Palgrave Macmillan, 2003.

Christian, Barbara. *Black Feminist Criticism.* New York: Pergamon Press, 1985.

———, ed. *"Everyday Use": Alice Walker.* New Brunswick, NJ: Rutgers University Press, 1994.

Cixous, Hélène. "The Laugh of the Medusa." *Signs* 1, no. 4 (1976): 875–93.

Collins, Patricia Hill, ed. *Black Feminist Though: Knowledge, Consciousness, and the Politics of Empowerment.* Boston, Mass.: Unwin Hyman, 1990.

de Beauvoir, Simone. *The Second Sex.* 1949. Reprint. Harmondsworth, England: Penguin, 1972.

de Lauretis, Teresa. *Technologies of Gender: Essays on Theory, Film, and Fiction.* Bloomington: Indiana University Press, 1987.

Dobbs, Cynthia. "Mother-Hunger: A Review of *Toni Morrison and Motherhood: A Politics of the Heart* by Andrea O'Reilly. New York: SUNY Press: 2004. *Literary Mama; A Literary Magazine for the Maternally Inclined.* http://www.literarymama.com/reviews/archives/00699.html

Ehrenreich, Barbara. "What is Socialist Feminism?" *Materialist Feminism: a Reader in Class, Difference, and Women's Lives.* Ed. Rosemary Hennessy and Chrys Ingraham. London: Routledge, 1997. 65–70.

Ellis, Kate. "Monsters in the Garden: Mary Shelley and the Bourgeois Family." In *The Endurance of* Frankenstein: *Essays on Mary Shelley's Novel.* Ed. George Levine and U. C. Knopelmacher. Berkeley: University of California Press, 1979.

Faderman, Lillian. *Surpassing the Love of Men: Romantic Friendship and Love Between Women from the Renaissance to the Present.* New York: Morrow, 1981.

Felski, Rita. *Literature After Feminism.* Chicago, Ill.: University of Chicago Press, 2003.

Fetterley, Judith. "On the Politics of Literature." In Rivkin and Ryan, 561–69. Excerpt from her *The Resisting Reader.* Bloomington: Indiana University Press, 1978.

Fishkin, Shelley Fisher, and Elaine Hedges, eds. *Listening to Silences: New Essays in Feminist Criticism.* Oxford: Oxford University Press, 1994.

———. "Mark Twain and Women." In *The Cambridge Companion to Mark Twain.* Ed. Forrest G. Robinson. Cambridge: Cambridge University Press, 1995.

Foucault, Michel. *The History of Sexuality, Volume One: The Will to Knowledge.* 1976. Trans. Robert Hurley. New York: Pantheon Books, 1978.

Foucault, Michel. *The History of Sexuality.* Vol. 1. Trans. Robert Hurley. New York: Random House, 1978.

——. *The Foucault Reader.* Ed. Paul Rabinow. New York: Pantheon Books, 1984.

Friedan, Betty. *The Feminine Mystique.* 1963. Reprint. Harmondsworth, England: Penguin, 1982.

Gelpi, Barbara C., and Albert Gelpi, eds. *Adrienne Rich's Poetry.* New York: W. W. Norton, 1975.

Gilbert, Sandra M., and Susan Gubar. *The Madwoman in the Attic.* New Haven, CT: Yale University Press, 1979.

Gimenez, Martha E. "Marxist Feminism / Materialist Feminism." 1998. Feminist Theory Website: Marxist / Materialist Feminism. http://www.cddc.vt.edu/feminism/mar.html. Center for Digital Discourse and Culture, Virginia Tech University.

Gumbs, Alexis Pauline. " 'We Can Learn to Mother Ourselves': A Dialogically Produced Audience and Black Feminist Publishing 1979 to the Present." *Gender Forum: Black Women's Writing Revisited* 22 (2008). http://www.genderforum.unikoeln.de/blackwo-menswriting/article gumbs. html.

Halberstam, Judith. *Female Masculinity.* Durham, NC: Duke University Press, 1998.

—— *In A Queer Time and Place: Transgender Bodies, Subcultural Lives.* New York: New York University Press, 2005.

Haskell, Molly. "Ideological Criticism: The Uses and Abuses of a Feminist Approach to Film." In Peter Ruppert, Eugene Crook, and Walter Forehand, eds. *Ideas of Order in Literature and Film.* Tallahassee: University Press of Florida,1980.

Henderson, Stephen E. Introduction. *Black Women Writers (1950–1980): A Critical Evaluation.* Ed. Mari Evans. New York: Anchor, 1984.

Heilbrun, Carolyn. *Hamlet's Mother and Other Women.* New York: Columbia University Press, 1990.

Hennessy, Rosemary. *Materialist Feminism and the Politics of Difference.* London: Routledge, 1993.

Hennessy, Rosemary, and Chrys Ingraham, eds. *Materialist Feminism: A Reader in Class, Difference, and Women's Lives.* 1997.

hooks, bell. *Ain't I a Woman: Black Women and Feminism.* Boston: South End Press, 1981.

——. *Feminist Theory from Margin to Center.* Boston: South End Press, 1984.

Humm, Maggie. *Feminist Criticism: Women as Contemporary Critics.* Brighton, England: Harvester, 1986.

Hunter, J. Paul, ed. *Mary Shelley, Frankenstein.* New York: W. W. Norton, 1996.

Irigaray, Luce. "When Our Lips Speak Together." *Signs* 6, no. 1 (1980): 69–79.

——. *Speculum of the Other Woman.* Trans. Gillian C. Gill. Ithaca, NY: Cornell University Press, 1985.

Jacobus, Mary. "Is There a Woman in This Text?" *New Literary History* 14 (1982): 117–41.

Jehlen, Myra. "Gender." In *Critical Terms for Literary Study.* Ed. Frank Lentricchia and Thomas McLaughlin. Chicago: University of Chicago Press, 1990.

Johnson, Barbara. "My Monster/My Self." *Diacritics* 12, no. 2 (1982): 2–10.

Johnson, E. Patrick, and Mae G. Henderson, eds. *Black Queer Studies: A Critical Anthology.* Durham, NC: Duke University Press, 2005.

Jung, C. G. *Psychology of the Unconscious: A Study of the Transformations and Symbolisms of the Libido.* Trans. Beatrice M. Hinkle. New York: Moffat, Yard and Co., 1916.

Kaplan, E. Ann, ed. *Feminism and Film.*Oxford: Oxford University Press, 2000.

Kolodny, Annette. "Dancing Through the Minefield: Some Observations on the Theory, Practice, and Politics of a Feminist Literary Criticism." In *The New Feminist Criticism: Essays on Women, Literature and Theory.* Ed. Elaine Showalter. New York: Pantheon Books, 1985.

Kristeva, Julia. *Desire in Language.* New York: Columbia University Press, 1980.

———. *The Kristeva Reader.* Ed. Toril Moi. New York: Columbia University Press, 1986.

Kuhn, Annette and Ann Marie Wolpe, eds., *Feminism and Materialism. Women and Modes of Production.* New York: Routledge and Kegan Paul, 1978.

Lacan, Jacques. *Écrits: A Selection.* 1966. Trans. Alan Sheridan. New York: W. W. Norton, 1977. Revised version reprinted 2002. Trans. Bruce Fink.

Landry, Donna and Gerald Maclean, *Materialist Feminism.* London: Blackwell, 1993.

Laqueur, Thomas. *Making Sex: Body and Gender from the Greeks to Freud.* Cambridge, Mass.: Harvard University Press, 1990.

Levine, George. "*Frankenstein* and the Tradition of Realism." In *Novel: A Forum on Fiction,* 7, no. 1 (Fall 1973): 17–23. Reprinted in Hunter.

Lorde, Audre. "Age, Race, Class, and Sex: Women Redefining Difference." In Rivkin and Ryan.

Mellor, Anne K. "Possessing Nature: The Female in *Frankenstein.*" In *From Romanticism and Feminism.* Ed. Anne K. Mellor. Bloomington: Indiana University Press, 1988. 220–32. Reprinted in Hunter.

———. "Choosing a Text of *Frankenstein* to Teach." In *Approaches to Teaching Shelley's Frankenstein.* New York: MLA, 1990, 31–37. Reprinted in Hunter.

Millet, Kate. *Sexual Politics.* 1970. Reprint. London: Virago, 1977.

Moers, Ellen. "Female Gothic: The Monster's Mother." In *Literary Women.* Garden City, NJ: Doubleday, 1976. Reprinted in Hunter.

Mohanty, Chandra Talpade. *Feminism Without Borders: Decolonizing Theory, Practicing Solidarity.* Durham, NC: Duke University Press, 2003.

Moi, Toril. "Feminist Literary Criticism." In *Modern Literary Theory: A Comparative Introduction.* 2nd ed. Ed. Ann Jefferson. Lanham, MD: Barnes Imports, 1987.

Morrison, Toni. *Playing in the Dark: Whiteness and the Literary Imagination.* New York: Vintage Press, 1993.

Morton, Donald. "Birth of the Cyberqueer." *PMLA* 110 (May 1995): 369–81.

Mulvey, Laura. *Movies and Methods: An Anthology.* Vol. 2. Ed. Bill Nichols. Berkeley: University of California Press, 1985.

Murfin, Ross C. "What Is Feminist Criticism?" In *Frankenstein* by Mary Shelley. Ed. Johanna M. Smith. 2nd ed. Boston: Bedford/St. Martin's, 2000.

Olsen, Tillie. *Silences.* New York: Delacorte Press/Seymour Lawrence, 1978.

O'Reilly, Andrea. *Maternal Theory: Essential Readings.* York, England: Demeter Press, 2007.

Pateman, Carole. *The Sexual Contract.* Stanford, Calif.: Stanford University Press, 1988.

Pérez, Emma. *The Decolonial Imaginary: Writing Chicanas into History.* Indianapolis: Indiana University Press, 1999.

Poovey, Mary. *The Proper Lady and the Woman Writer: Ideology as Style in the Works of Mary Wollstonecraft, Mary Shelley, and Jane Austen.* Chicago: University of Chicago Press, 1984.

Rich, Adrienne. "Compulsory Heterosexuality and Lesbian Existence." *Signs* 5, 4 (Summer 1980): 631–60 Rpt. *The* Signs *Reader: Women, Gender, and Scholarship.* Ed. Elizabeth Abel and Emily K. Abel. Chicago: University of Chicago Press, 1983.

Richter, David H., ed. *The Critical Tradition: Classic Texts and Contemporary Trends.* Boston: Bedford/St. Martin's, 1998.

Rivkin, Julie, and Michael Ryan, eds. *Literary Theory: An Anthology.* Rev. ed. Oxford: Blackwell, 1998.

Robinson, Lillian. *Sex, Class, and Culture.* Bloomington: Indiana University Press, 1978.

Rosen, Marjorie. "Truffaut's Trifle in Day for Night." *Jump Cut: A Review of Contemporary Media* 1(May 1974): 13.

Saldívar-Hull, Sonia. *Feminism on the Border: Chicana Gender Politics and Literature.* Berkeley: University of California Press, 2000.

Sandoval, Chela. *Methodology of the Oppressed.* Minneapolis: University of Minnesota Press, 2000.

Sedgwick, Eve Kosofsky. *Epistemology of the Closet.* Berkeley: University of California Press, 1990.

Showalter, Elaine. "Feminist Criticism in the Wilderness." *Critical Inquiry* 8 (1981): 181–205.

Sinfeld, Alan. *Cultural Politics: Queer Reading.* Philadelphia: University of Pennsylvania Press, 1994.

Skandera-Trombley, Laura. *Mark Twain in the Company of Women.* Philadelphia: University of Pennsylvania Press, 1994.

Small, Christopher, "[Percy] Shelley and *Frankenstein*." In *Ariel Like a Harpy: Shelley, Mary and Frankenstein.* London: Victor Gollancz, 1972. Reprinted in Hunter.

Smith, Johanna M. "'Cooped Up' with 'Sad Trash': Domesticity and the Sciences in *Frankenstein*." In Smith.

———. ed. "Introduction." *Frankenstein* by Mary Shelley. 1831 text. 2nd ed. Boston: Bedford/St. Martin's, 2000.

Spark, Muriel. *Mary Shelley.* Rev. ed. London: Sphere-Penguin, 1987.

Spillers, Hortense. *Black, White, and in Color: Essays on American Literature and Culture.* Chicago, Ill.: University of Chicago Press, 2003.

Spivak, Gayatri Chakravorty. "Three Women's Texts and a Critique of Imperialism." *Critical Inquiry* 12 (Autumn 1985): 243–61. Reprinted as "*Frankenstein* and a Critique of Imperialism." In Hunter.

———. *In Other Worlds: Essays in Cultural Politics.* New York: Methuen, 1987.

Stryker, Susan, ed.*The Transgender Studies Reader* New York: Routledge, 2006.

Vendler, Helen. "Feminism and Literature." *New York Review of Books,* 31 May 1990.

Walker, Alice. *In Search of Our Mothers' Gardens: Womanist Prose.* London: Women's Press, 1984.

———. *Revolutionary Petunias and Other Poems.* San Diego: Harcourt, 1973.

Walker, Nancy. "Reformers and Young Maidens: Women and Virtue in *Adventures of Huckleberry Finn*." In *One Hundred Years of* Huckleberry Finn*: The Boy, His Book, and American Culture.* Ed. Robert Sattlemeyer and J. Donald Crowley. Columbia: University of Missouri Press, 1985.

Wallace, Michele. *Black Macho and the Myth of the Superwoman.* 1979. Rpt New York: Verso, 1990.

Warner, Michael. *Fear of a Queer Planet: Queer Politics and Social Theory.* Minneapolis: University of Minnesota Press, 1993.

West, Rebecca. *The Young Rebecca.* Ed. Jane Marcus. London: Virago, 1982.

Woolf, Virginia. *A Room of One's* Own London: Hogarth Press, 1929.

White, Patricia. "Feminism and Film." In *Film Studies: Critical Approaches.* Eds. John Hill and Pamela Church Gibson. New York: Oxford University Press, 2000.

Young-Bruehl, Elisabeth, ed. *Freud on Women: A Reader.* New York: W. W. Norton, 1992.

Cultural Studies

I. DEFINING CULTURAL STUDIES

Because the word "**culture**" itself is so difficult to pin down, "cultural studies" is hard to define. As was also the case in Chapter 8 with Elaine Showalter's "cultural" model of feminine difference, "cultural studies" is not so much a discrete approach at all, but rather a set of practices. As Patrick Brantlinger has pointed out, cultural studies is not "a tightly coherent, unified movement with a fixed agenda," but a "loosely coherent group of tendencies, issues, and questions" (ix). Arising from the social turmoil of the 1960s, cultural studies is composed of elements of Marxism, poststructuralism and postmodernism, feminism, gender studies, anthropology, sociology, race and ethnic studies, film theory, urban studies, public policy, popular culture studies, and postcolonial studies: those fields that concentrate on social and cultural forces that either create community or cause division and alienation. For example, drawing from Roland Barthes on the nature of literary language and Claude Lévi-Strauss on anthropology, cultural studies was influenced by structuralism and poststructuralism. Jacques Derrida's "deconstruction" of the world/ text distinction, like all his deconstructions of hierarchical oppositions, has urged cultural critics to erase boundaries between high and low culture, classic and popular literary texts, and literature and other cultural **discourses.**

The discipline of psychology has also entered the field of cultural studies. For example, Jacques Lacan's psychoanalytic theory of the unconscious structured as a language promoted emphasis upon language and power as symbolic systems. From Michel Foucault came the notion that power is a whole complex of forces; it is that which produces what happens. A tyrannical aristocrat does not just independently wield power but is empowered by discourses—accepted ways of thinking, writing, and speaking—and practices that embody, exercise, and amount to power. From punishment to sexual mores, Foucault's "genealogy" of topics includes many things excluded by traditional historians, from architectural blueprints for prisons to memoirs of "deviants." Marxist, new historicist, psychoanalytic, structuralist, poststructuralist, and postcolonial approaches are treated elsewhere in this handbook; in the present chapter, we review cultural studies' connections with U.S. ethnic studies, postmodernism, and popular culture, since these areas are where cultural studies, especially in its beginnings, attracted so many American critics.

• • •

Cultural studies approaches generally share four goals.

First, cultural studies transcends the confines of a particular discipline such as literary criticism or history. Practiced in such journals as *Critical Inquiry, Representations,* and *boundary 2,* cultural studies involves scrutinizing the cultural phenomenon of a text—for example, Italian opera, a Mexican *telenovela, Robinson Crusoe,* body piercing—and drawing conclusions about the changes in textual phenomena over time. Cultural studies is not necessarily about literature in the traditional sense or even about "art." In their introduction to *Cultural Studies,* editors Lawrence Grossberg, Cary Nelson, and Paula Treichler emphasize that the intellectual promise of cultural studies lies in its attempts to "cut across diverse social and political interests and address many of the struggles within the current scene" (1–3). Intellectual works are not limited by their own "borders" as single texts, historical problems, or disciplines, and the critic's own personal connections to what is being analyzed may also be described. Henry Giroux and others write in their *Dalhousie Review* manifesto that cultural studies practitioners are "resisting intellectuals" who see what they do as "an emancipatory project" because it erodes the traditional disciplinary divisions in most institutions of higher education (478–80). For students, this sometimes means that a professor might make his or her own political views part of the instruction, which, of course, can lead to problems. But this kind of criticism, like feminism, is an engaged rather than a detached activity.

Second, cultural studies is politically engaged. Cultural critics see themselves as "oppositional," not only within their own disciplines but to many of the power structures of society at large. They question inequalities within power structures and seek to discover models for restructuring relationships among dominant and "minority" or "subaltern" discourses. Because they think meaning and individual subjectivity are culturally *constructed,* they can thus be *reconstructed.* Such a notion, taken to a philosophical extreme, denies the autonomy of the individual, whether an actual person or a character in literature, a rebuttal of the traditional humanistic "Great Man" or "Great Book" theory, and a relocation of aesthetics and culture from the ideal realms of taste and sensibility, into the arena of a whole society's everyday life as it is constructed.

Third, cultural studies denies the separation of "high" and "low" or elite and popular culture. You might hear someone remark at the symphony or at an art museum: "I came here to get a little culture." Being a "cultured" person used to mean being acquainted with "highbrow" art and intellectual pursuits. But isn't *culture* also to be found with a pair of tickets to a rock concert? How about in graffiti?

Cultural critics today work to transfer the term *culture* to include *mass culture,* whether popular, folk, or urban. Following theorists Jean Baudrillard and Andreas Huyssen, cultural critics argue that after World War II the distinctions among high, low, and mass culture collapsed, and they cite other theorists such as Pierre Bourdieu and Dick Hebdige on how "good taste" often only reflects prevailing social, economic, and political power bases. For example, the images of India that were circulated during the colonial rule of the British raj by writers like Rudyard Kipling seem innocent, but reveal an entrenched imperialist argument for white superiority and worldwide domination of other races, especially Asians. But race alone was not the issue for the British raj: money was also a deciding factor. Thus, drawing also upon the ideas of French historian Michel de Certeau, cultural critics examine "the practice of everyday life," studying literature as an anthropologist would, as a *phenomenon* of culture, including a culture's economy. Rather than determining which are the "best" works produced, cultural critics describe *what* is produced and how various productions relate to one another. They aim to reveal the political, economic reasons *why* a certain cultural product is more valued at certain times than others.

To explain this, Pierre Bourdieu's "The Market in Symbolic Goods" begins with his notion of "goods of restricted production" (objects reflecting highly skilled art or craft); these were once the property of the aristocracy or the church, but with the development of commercial capitalism cultural production was regulated by the market. This "cultural market" operates not only on contemporary production but that of the past; Shakespeare's plays, for example, which require some education to read today, were once the property of the masses. However, today they are symbolic goods that circulate in the market and come with a high "price." Bourdieu believed taste was not universal but was a means by which social distinctions are enforced in a capitalist power system. Speaking of American Studies, Paul Lauter famously put the question this way: "Why this thing, in this way, at this time?"

Transgressing of boundaries among disciplines high and low can make cultural studies just plain fun. Think, for example, of a possible cultural studies research paper with the following title: "The Origins of Captain Jack Sparrow." For sources of Johnny Depp's funky performance in Disney's *Pirates of the Caribbean* movies, you could research cultural topics ranging from the trade economies of the sea two hundred years ago, to real pirates of the Caribbean such as Blackbeard and Henry Morgan, then on to Robert Louis Stevenson's Long John Silver in *Treasure Island* (1881), Errol Flynn's and Robert Morgan's memorable screen pirates, John Cleese's rendition of Long John Silver on *Monty Python's Flying Circus,* and, of course, Keith Richards's eye makeup. You'd read interviews with Depp on his view of the character and, of course, check out the extra features on the DVD for background (did you know Depp is a book collector?). And you wouldn't want to neglect the galaxy of web sites devoted to the movie and to all topics *Pirate.*

Finally, cultural studies analyzes not only the cultural work, but also the means of production. Marxist critics have long recognized the importance of such paraliterary questions as these: Who supports a given artist? Who publishes his or her books, and how are these books distributed? Who buys books? For that matter, who is literate and who is not? A well-known analysis of literary production is Janice Radway's study of the American romance novel and its readers, *Reading the Romance: Women, Patriarchy and Popular Literature,* which demonstrates the textual effects of the publishing industry's decisions about books that will minimize its financial risks. Another contribution is the collection *Reading in America,* edited by Cathy N. Davidson, which includes essays on literacy and gender in colonial New England; urban magazine audiences in eighteenth-century New York City; the impact upon reading of such technical innovations as cheaper eyeglasses, electric lights, and trains; the Book-of-the-Month Club; and how writers and texts go through fluctuations of popularity and canonicity. These studies help us recognize that literature does not occur in a space separate from other concerns of our lives.

Cultural studies thus joins *subjectivity*—that is, culture in relation to individual lives—with *engagement,* a direct approach to attacking social ills. Though cultural studies practitioners deny "humanism" or "the humanities" as universal categories, they strive for what they might call "social reason," which often (closely) resembles the goals and values of humanistic and democratic ideals.

What difference does a cultural studies approach make for the student? First of all, it is increasingly clear that soon the United States will be what demographers call a "majority-minority" population; that is, the present numerical majority of "white," "Caucasian," and "Anglo"-Americans will be the minority, particularly with the dramatically increasing numbers of Latina/o residents, mostly Mexican Americans. As Gerald Graff and James Phelan observe, "It is a common prediction that the culture of the next century will put a premium on people's ability to deal productively with conflict and cultural difference. Learning by controversy is sound training for citizenship in that future" (v). To the question "Why teach the controversy?" they note that today a student can go from one class in which the values of Western culture are never questioned to the next class where Western culture is portrayed as hopelessly compromised by racism, sexism, and homophobia: professors can acknowledge these differences and encourage students to construct a conversation for themselves as "the most exciting part of [their] education" (8).

II. U.S. ETHNIC STUDIES

In 1965, when this book was first begun, the Watts race riots drew worldwide attention. The Civil Rights Act had passed in 1964, and the backlash was well under way in 1965: murders and other atrocities against blacks attended the civil rights march from Selma to Montgomery. President Lyndon Johnson signed the Voting Rights Act. The "long, hot summer" of 1966 saw violent insurrections in Newark, Detroit, Cleveland, Chicago, Milwaukee, Atlanta, San Francisco—the very television seemed ablaze. The Black Panther Party was founded. James Meredith, the first African-American student to enroll at the University of Mississippi, was wounded by a white segregationist. Julian Bond, duly elected State Representative, was denied his seat in the Georgia House. Nearly all African-American students in the South attended segregated schools, and discrimination was still unquestioned in most industries. Interracial marriage was still illegal in many states.

Nearly a half century later, in 2008 an African-American was elected president. Evolving identities of racial and ethnic groups have not only claimed a place in the mainstream of American life, but have challenged the very notion of "race," now seen by many social scientists as a construct invented by whites to assign social status and privilege, without scientific relevance. Unlike sex, for which there are X and Y chromosomes, race has no genetic markers. In fact, a 1972 Harvard University study by the geneticist Richard Lewontin found that most genetic differences were within racial groups, not between them (*New York Times,* 20 July 1996, A1, A7). In the new century, if interracial trends continue, Americans will be puzzled by race distinctions from the past since children of multiracial backgrounds may be the norm rather than the exception. And given the huge influx of Mexican Americans in particular into the United States over the last fifty years, immigration patterns indicate that soon English will not necessarily be the most widely spoken language. Administrators of the 2000 Census faced multiple problems with its assignment of racial categories, for many biracial or multiracial people did not identify with any of them.

Henry Louis Gates, Jr., suggests using the word "race" *only* in quotation marks, for it "pretends to be an objective term of classification," but it is a "dangerous trope ... of ultimate, irreducible difference between cultures, linguistic groups, or adherents of specific belief systems which—more often than not—also have fundamentally opposed economic interests." Without biological criteria "race" is arbitrary: "Yet we carelessly use language in such a way as to *will* this sense of *natural* difference into our formulations. To do so is a pernicious act of language, one which exacerbates the complex problem of cultural or ethnic difference, rather than to assuage or redress it" ("*Race*" 4–5). "Race" is still a critical feature of American life, full of contradictions and ambiguities; it is at once the greatest source of social conflict and the richest source of cultural development in America. Ironically, in the summer of 2009, Gates himself was allegedly a target of racial profiling by the Cambridge, Massachusetts police.

Questions of ethnicity and race pervade the current interest in multicultural literary studies: Which cultures should be canonized? Who decides? What constitutes a *culture?* Is culture only "ethnic," or can gays or lesbians or the disabled make up a separate culture? Is it good to celebrate "**the Other**" and bring others into the mainstream, or should the goal be the preservation of difference rather than continued marginalization? These questions are debated in America, particularly which books should be taught in colleges and universities. Leon Botstein believes a combination of traditional and newer perspectives offers the best alternative: students must read Aeschylus, Dante, Shakespeare "because what Shakespeare and Dante and the so-called Great Books are all about is penetrating through details to what's really essential about the common experience of being a member of this species." But at the same time that one reads Thucydides on the subject of being a member of a seafaring, global power, one should also read Bernal Diaz's account of the conquest of Mexico. "Every American should understand Mexico from the point of view of the observers of the conquest and of the history before the conquest.... No American should graduate from college without a framework of knowledge that includes at least some construct of Asian history, of Latin-American history, of African history" (in Sill 35).

The broad field of ethnic studies, like postcolonial studies (see Chapter 10) explores Euro-American imperialism and colonization in the last four centuries directed at ethnic groups such as African and African-American, Latina/o, Asian and Asian-American, and all "subaltern" or oppressed peoples of the postcolonial world. Ethnic studies generally is concerned with art and literature produced by ethnic groups marginalized or in a subordinate position to a dominant culture. It emphasizes the relationship of cultural identity to individual identity within this historical framework of overt racial oppression. Though, as we will see in this chapter, each group has its own history, culture, and aesthetics, ethnic studies in general seeks to find commonality among all oppressed ethnic groups in describing common patterns of oppression. How does the overall experience of living with what W. E. B. DuBois defined as a "double-consciousness" of racial identity find expression in literary and cultural identity? Examples of some overarching or pan-ethnic questions critics might address across different groups could include What is the comparative status of women? What roles do the same religion (e.g. Islam) play across different ethnic cultures? What is the relative importance of common literary **genres—drama**, for instance—in different ethnic settings? Ethnic studies thus explores traditions, sometimes suppressed, of ethnic literary activity while providing a critique of representations of ethnic identity as found within the majority culture. It argues that it is improper to apply theoretical models from Euro-American paradigms to the works of other writers because they do not take into account the ethnically derived ways of understanding ethnic speech and writing on their own terms. Among the earliest ethnic theorists was W. E. B. Du Bois, who theorized the position of African Americans within dominant white culture through his concept of "double-consciousness," a dual identity including both "American" and "Negro." Later Afro-Caribbean and African writers—Aime Cesaire, Frantz Fanon, Chinua Achebe—made significant contributions to the theory and practice of ethnic studies. Ethnic theorists of particular note today include Gates, Werner Sollors, Toni Morrison, and Kwame Anthony Appiah.

In Sollors's important collection, *An Anthology of Interracial Literature: Black-White Contacts in the Old World and the New,* the literary theme of black-white encounters throughout literature blends African-American studies with a newer field of "whiteness studies," and it covers literature from ancient Greece, the Middle Ages, the Italian Renaissance **novellas**, and plays from Spain, Denmark, England, and the United States, as well as essays, autobiographical sketches, and numerous **poems**. Sollors primarily explores themes of interracial love and family relations, passing, and the figure of the tragic mulatto. Some contemporary writers included are Gwendolyn Brooks, Rita Dove, and Adrienne Kennedy. A Ghanian writer and philosopher, Appiah is best known for his book *In My Father's House* (1992), in which he explores the role of African and African-American intellectuals in shaping contemporary African cultural life. But he is widely referenced by scholars and students of American literature. In 1996, he published *Color Conscious: The Political Morality of Race* with Amy Gutmann; in 1997 the *Dictionary of Global Culture,* coedited with Gates. He has been critical of the notion of "Afrocentrism," however, rejecting a search for Africa's "true" identity in the Egyptian past and instead focusing on contemporary issues of African and African-American identities.

A. African-American Writers

African-American studies is widely pursued in American literary criticism, from the recovery of eighteenth-century poets such as Phillis Wheatley to the experimental novels of Toni Morrison. In *Shadow and Act* (1964) novelist Ralph Ellison argued that any "viable theory of Negro American culture obligates us to fashion a more adequate theory of American culture as a whole" (253). This seems too obvious even to mention today, when American arts, fashion, music, and so much besides is based upon African-American culture, from Oprah to Lil Wayne. But in Ellison's day, the 1950s, such an argument was considered radical.

African-American writing often displays a folkloric conception of humankind; a "double consciousness," as Du Bois called it, arising from bicultural identity; **irony**, **parody**, **tragedy**, and bitter **comedy** in negotiating this ambivalence; attacks upon presumed white cultural superiority; a **naturalistic** focus on survival; and inventive reframings of language itself, as in language games like "jiving," "sounding," "signifying," "playing the dozens" (all involving playful insult-trading), and rapping. These practices symbolically characterize "the group's attempt to humanize the world," as Ellison puts it (in Bell xvi, 19). Ellison urged black writers to trust their own experiences and definitions of reality. He also upheld folklore as a source of creativity. This elevation of black folk culture to art is important, and it led to divisions among black artists: for example, Zora Neale Hurston's reliance upon folklore and **dialect** annoyed some of her fellow artists of the Harlem Renaissance, such as Langston Hughes, who wished to distance themselves from such "roots" and embrace the new international forms available in literary **modernism**.

Bernard Bell reviews some primary features of African-American writing and compares value systems:

> Traditional white American values emanate from a providential vision of history and of Euro-Americans as a chosen people, a vision that sanctions their individual and collective freedom in the pursuit of property, profit, and happiness. Radical Protestantism, Constitutional democracy, and industrial capitalism are the white American trinity of values. In contrast, black American values emanate from a cyclical, Judeo-Christian vision of history and of African-Americans as

a disinherited, colonized people, a vision that sanctions their resilience of spirit and pursuit of social justice. (5)

A Chosen People. It is a great historical **irony** that black Americans adopted the same metaphor of the Hebrew people being led into a Promised Land of freedom that was earlier employed by the first white settlers in Virginia and New England, especially the Puritans who were fleeing religious intolerance. It is a further irony that Puritan descendants turned to black slavery and other exploitative economic systems to make their Promise come even truer. As Bell correctly stresses, no other ethnic or social group in America has shared anything like the experience of American blacks: kidnapping, the Middle Passage, slavery, Southern plantation life, emancipation, Reconstruction and post-Reconstruction, Northern migration, urbanization, and ongoing racism (5).

Out of such painful cultural origins evolved African-American literature, which may be divided into several major periods, comprising Colonial, Antebellum, Reconstruction, Pre–World War I, Harlem Renaissance, Naturalism and Modernism, and Contemporary. Some of the most widely taught writers of the earlier periods include Harriet E. Wilson, whose *Our Nig: or Sketches from the Life of a Free Black, in a Two–Story White House, North* (1859) was the first novel published by an African American woman; Linda Brent, author of *Incidents in the Life of a Slave Girl* (1860); and Frances Ellen Watkins Harper, author of *Iola Leroy; or, Shadows Uplifted* (1892). Wilson's and Brent's heroines must fight merely to survive; Harper's confronts the dilemma of a light-skinned mulatta "passing" as white. At the turn of the century the novels of Charles Waddell Chesnutt heralded a turn toward naturalism but also made use of traditional folk elements; his novel of the Wilmington race riots, *The Marrow of Tradition* (1901), indicts white hypocrisy and cowardice. Chesnutt was remarkable in his incisive understandings of the troubled intersections of race and gender in the South.

The Harlem Renaissance (1918–1937) signaled a tremendous upsurge in black culture, with an especial interest in primitivist art. The so-called New Negroes, whom Zora Neale Hurston sarcastically dubbed the "Niggerati," celebrated black culture. Nathan Eugene "Jean" Toomer combined African spiritualism and Christianity with modern experimental prose in his novel *Cane* (1923). Hurston, Langston Hughes, and others including Countee Cullen were the center of literary life and black culture in the New York of the Roaring Twenties.

African-American writing turned to protest novels in the 1940s. Spurred by the Depression and the failures of Jim Crow in the South, naturalist author Richard Wright furiously attacked white American society at the start of the civil rights movement in works such as *Native Son* (1938) and *Black Boy* (1945). Bigger Thomas, the antihero of *Native Son,* is the archetypal "Bad Nigger" feared by whites: a murderous rebel in a mindless, exploitative society. Ralph Ellison was influenced by naturalism but even more by African-American traditions such as the **Trickster**, jazz, blues, "signifying," and political activism. He also sought to connect his reading in the European and American traditions of Conrad, Joyce, Eliot, Dostoyevsky, James, and Faulkner, as he discusses at length in the preface to *Invisible Man* (1949). This novel of a physical and spiritual odyssey by a black man who moves forward in time and north in direction, then finally underground for enlightenment, is a journey to reclaim himself and his culture. *Invisible Man* seemed to speak for his generation of young black intellectuals.

The 1960s brought Black Power and the Black Arts Movement, proposing a separate identification and symbology. Major figures were Amiri Baraka (previously known as LeRoi Jones), Gwendolyn Brooks, Margaret Abigail Walker, Ernest Gaines, John Edgar Wideman, and Ishmael Reed; in related arts, for example, music, the big names were Chuck Berry, B. B. King, Aretha Franklin, Stevie Wonder, and Jimi Hendrix. "Black" culture had "crossed over." Today, Toni Morrison shows irritation when she is constantly discussed as a "Black Writer" instead of merely a writer. Nevertheless, Morrison's works such as *The Bluest Eye* (1970), *Song of Solomon* (1977), and *Beloved* (1987) give readers riveting insights into the painful lives of her black protagonists as they confront racism in all its forms in American society. (See Chapter 8 for more on black feminist writers of the past three decades.)

B. Latina/o Writers

Latina/o. Hispanic. Mexican American. Puerto Rican. Nuyorican. Chicano. Or maybe Huichol or Maya. Which names to use? The choice often has political implications.

We will use the term "Latina/o" to indicate a broad sense of ethnicity among Spanish-speaking people in the United States. Mexican Americans are the largest and most influential group of Latina/o ethnicities in the United States.

Though there is of course no one culture that can accurately be described as Latina/o, the diversity of Spanish-speaking peoples—with different origins, nationalities, religions, skin colors, class identifications, politics, and varying names for themselves—has had an enormous impact upon "American" culture since its beginnings. These characteristics are now rapidly entering the mainstream of everyday life, so that "American Literature" and "American Studies" are now often referred to as "Literatures of the Americas" or "Studies of the Americas." Republicans and Democrats vigorously court the "Hispanic vote" like never before, and Latina/os are reflected at an unprecedented rate in government, business, the arts, broadcasting, and entertainment. This is also true of literature and film, as the careers of Sandra Cisneros and Robert Rodriguez show. Cisneros, of San Antonio, rose to national fame with her first book, *The House on Mango Street* (1984), the story of a young girl growing up in a Chicago barrio. *Mango Street* was published by a then relatively obscure press in Houston called Arte Público, now a major publisher of Latina/o books. Rodriguez, an Austin, Texas, resident, has made award-winning films such as *El Mariachi*, *Spy Kids*, and with Quentin Tarantino, *Grindhouse*.

The history of the indigenous cultures of the New World is punctuated by conquests of Indian nations; by European countries, especially Spain, Portugal, France, and England; then by the United States. Over time, there emerged in former Spanish possessions a *mestizo* (mixed blood) literary culture in addition to the colonial and native cultures.

What would become Mexican American literatures developed through combinations of Spanish with indigenous art forms to create new folk expressions. The political turning point came in 1848 when the Treaty of Guadalupe Hidalgo ended two years of warfare between Mexico and the United States and ratified the relinquishment of nearly half of Mexico's territory, including the present states of California, New Mexico, and Arizona, and parts of several others. The majority of Mexican residents stayed in place, transformed into Mexican Americans with a stroke of the pen. The trajectory of Mexican culture in the southwest shifted toward the newly expanded United States. Not surprisingly, one of the primary tropes in Latina/o studies has to do with the entire concept of borders—borders between nations, between cultures, and within cultures. As we noted in Chapter 8, in *Borderlands/La Frontera: The New Mestiza,* Gloria Anzaldúa demonstrates how Latinas live *between*—between two countries, between two languages, between two cultures; she describes this another way in her poem, "To Live in the Borderlands Means You." As a lesbian Latina critic, Anzaldúa calls her own *liminal,* or border space, a challenge to live "on the borders and in margins, [where] keeping intact one's shifting and multiple identity and integrity is like trying to swim in a new element, an 'alien' element" (1).

Anzaldúa evokes the liminality of Chicana culture when she expresses how her discourse crosses several borderlands of identity. She calls herself a *nahual,* a trickster shape-shifter who transforms herself; as a *mestiza* she exists on several borders: language, nationality, and race. She includes her Indian, Spanish, Mexican, African, Caucasian selves. Such consciousness, she argues, is richer and more fruitful than a single identity; as a lesbian she also embraces cross-gender discourse. Though such a person experiences inner conflicts and conversations, she is aiming at inclusiveness and balance in her own identity and in her cultural identity.

"Code-switching" is a border phenomenon studied by linguists. Speakers who code-switch move back and forth between Spanish and English, for instance, or resort to the "Spanglish" of border towns; linguists note why and when certain words are uttered in one language or another. They note that among code-switchers words that have to do with home or family or church are always in Spanish, whereas more institutional terms especially relating to authority are in English. Liminality, or "between-ness," is characteristic of postmodern experience but also has special connotations for the discourse of Latina/os.

Juan Flores and George Yudice write that since the "discovery" of America transformed the ocean into a frontier that Europeans might cross to get to a New World, today the map for Latina/os is a "cultural map which is all border." They define "America" as a "living border," a site of "continual crossover" of languages, identities, space, and political boundaries, a "trans-creation" that allows us to understand "the ultimate arbitrariness of the border itself, of forced separations and inferiorizations." For them, "the search for 'America,' the inclusive, multicultural society of the continent, has to do with nothing less than the imaginative ethos of remapping and renaming in the service not only of Latinos but of all claimants" (80). Thus, in many "immigrant" literatures one notes the frequency of autobiographical **tropes** of crossing over, of being in cultural hiding, of alienation within mainstream culture, of creating new identities. A new more inclusive "America" was also envisioned by Cuban writer and activist Jose Martí in his famous essay "Our America."

The Chicano Movement of the 1960s and 1970s meant renewed Mexican American political awareness and artistic production. World War II had greatly accelerated the process of Mexican-American acculturation. Rudolfo Anaya's *Bless Me, Ultima* (1973), perhaps the best-known Latino novel, focuses on the impact of World War II on a small community in New Mexico. With their academic training in Spanish and Latin American literatures, Rolando Hinojosa-Smith, Americo Paredes, and Tomás Rivera wrote in Spanish and frequently in *estampas*, or sketches, sometimes only a few paragraphs in length. Two other key contributors to Latino fiction of the period are Oscar Zeta Acosta, author of *The Revolt of the Cockroach People* (1973), and Richard Rodriguez, author of the memoir *Hunger of Memory* (1981) a commentator on PBS's *News Hour with Jim Lehrer*.

Some Latinas, such as María Amparo Ruiz de Burton, author of the 1885 novel of California, *The Squatter and the Don,* were among the early writers; Josephina Niggli's 1945 novel *Mexican Village* was the first literary work by a Mexican American to reach a general American audience. Yet until the 1970s only male authors were usually recognized. Today, Latinas have the task of redefining not only ethnicity but also gender roles and histories different from their men. They provide insight into the *machismo* of Mexican culture, call for liberation of women from abusive and exploitative relationships, and celebrate the newly heard voices of Mexican American women writers.

Three cultural archetypes have been central to Latina identity: La Malinche, La Virgen de Guadalupe, and La Llorona, but these are being newly interrogated today. Together they offer a range of Latina themes and concerns. *Malinche* is the name given to an Aztec woman sold into slavery by her parents, who eventually became the aide and lover of Hernan de Cortés following his conquest of Mexico and his settlement in Veracruz. She bore him a son, but he later married a Spanish noblewoman. Malinche's name has been synonymous with betrayal, but her son was the first *mestizo*. Latina critics have sought to revise the prevailing view of Malinche by dramatizing her victimization and her mothering of the new *mestizo* race. The Virgin of Guadalupe is the patron saint of Mexico, appearing everywhere, from churches to charms dangling from taxicab mirrors. She was originally a Spanish saint of seafarers, but when transferred to the Americas she also took on the role of the indigenous brown mother goddess, mother, protector, nurturer; she may be seen as a descendant of Tonantzin, an Aztec goddess of fertility, on whose horned moon she is portrayed. Guadalupe is another mother of the *mestizo* race, symbolizing the essence of virtue, self-sacrifice, and humility before God. La Llorona originates in native folklore. She is said to have been a woman who murdered her children after discovering her husband was unfaithful, and according to legend she was condemned to an eternal penance of sorrow. She wanders the roads at night crying for her lost children. Like the other female figures, she stands for a combination of the extremes of purity and guilt. "Chicanas are Malinches all," write Tey Diana Rebolledo and Eliana S. Rivera, "for they, too, are translators" (33). And there are of course more: Latina writers are some of the most energetically studied writers today.

C. Native American Literatures

In predominantly oral cultures, storytelling passes on religious beliefs, moral values, political codes, and practical lessons of everyday life. For Native Americans, stories are a source of strength in the face of centuries of silencing by Euro-Americans.

Again, a word on names: *Native American* seems to be the term preferred by most academics and many tribal members, who find the term *Indian* a misnomer and stereotype—as in "cowboys and Indians" or "Indian giver"—that helped whites wrest the continent away from indigenous peoples. And yet "American Indian" is often preferred by Indians over "Native American," as demonstrated in the names of such organizations as the American Indian Movement (AIM) or the Association for the Study of American Indian Literatures (ASAIL), as Alan R. Velie notes (3). The best names to use would be those of the hundreds of tribes, with an awareness of their differing languages, beliefs, and customs, confusingly lumped together as "Indian." Just as most Europeans identify themselves as French or Dutch or Basque rather than "European," so too American Indian identities are tribal.

Two types of Native literature have evolved as fields of U.S. study. *Traditional Native literature* includes tales, songs, and oratory that have existed on the North American continent for centuries, composed in tribal languages and performed for tribal audiences, such as the widely studied Winnebago Trickster Cycle. Today, traditional literatures are composed in English as well. *Mainstream Native literature* refers to works written by Natives in English in the traditional genres of fiction, poetry, and **autobiography**. Traditional literature was and is oral; because tribes did not have written languages, European newcomers assumed they had no literature, but as Velie observes, this would be like assuming that the Greeks of the *Iliad* and the *Odyssey* had no literature either. Far from the stereotype of the mute Indian, Natives created the first American literatures (9).

Traditional Native literature is not especially accessible for the average reader, as it is not easy to translate from Cherokee into English. Contextual frames do not translate well, nor does the oral/performative/sacred function of traditional literature. Furthermore, Natives do not separate literature from everyday life as a special category to be enjoyed in leisure time. All members of the tribe listen to songs and chants with no distinction between high and low culture. A tribe's myths and stories are designed to perpetuate their heritage and instruct the young, cure illnesses, ensure victory in battle, or secure fertile fields. It is a literature that is *practical.*

The earliest mainstream Native author in the anthologies is Samson Occom, a Mohegan schoolmaster, who published as early as 1772. Later writers of the nineteenth and early twentieth centuries, such as William Apess, Yellow Bird (John Rollin Ridge), Simon Pokagnon, Sara Winnemucca Hopkins, D'Arcy McNickle, and Mourning Dove (Humishuma), dealt with Native rights, the duplicities of U.S. government and military leaders, racial ambivalence, creation myths, trickster humor, and tribal constancy in the face of repeated assaults. Of particular interest to later generations was early twentieth-century writer Gertrude Bonnin, better known by her Dakota Sioux name Zitkala-Ša, who compiled a collection of trickster tales from her girlhood and wrote movingly of the experience of being sent to a white boarding school off the reservation.

Yet it was not until the 1960s that the American reading public at large became aware of works by Native writers, especially after the publication of Kiowa writer M. Scott Momaday's *House Made of Dawn* (1968), which won the Pulitzer Prize, and his memoir, *The Way to Rainy Mountain* (1969), beginning a renaissance of Native fiction and poetry. Louise Erdrich, Joy Harjo, and others became major literary figures, making little-known but historically rich sections of the country speak of their Native past and present. Erdrich's novels *Love Medicine* (1984), *The Beet Queen* (1986), and *Tracks* (1988) follow the fortunes of several North Dakota Native families in an epic unsparing in its satiric revelations of their venality, libidinousness, and grotesquerie. From her competing narrators emerges a unified story of a community under siege by the outside world. Creek Native Joy Harjo transforms traditional Indian poetic cadences into the hypnotic poetry of *She Had Some Horses* (1983), where her lyrics tell "the fantastic and terrible story of our survival" through **metaphors** of landscape and the body.

Patricia Clark Smith and Paula Gunn Allen describe the landscape available to native writers as "the land in its largest sense." For Native writers, "... the land is not only landscape as Anglo writers often think of it—arrangements of butte and bosque, mountain and river valley, light and cloud shadow. For natives the land encompasses butterfly and ant, man and woman, adobe wall and gourd vine, trout beneath the river water, rattler deep in his winter den, the North Star and the constellations, the flock of sandhill cranes flying too high to be seen against the sun. The land...is the whole cosmos." Thus Natives live and must be understood in the context of "both the land and the rituals through which they affirm their relationship to it." At the center of many of these reaffirming rituals are women and female sexuality: "The wilderness, American Indian women, ritual, and American Indian women's writing are inextricably woven together" (117). For tribal people, the land is "something mysterious, certainly beyond human domination." Neither is it a setting to do things in or to act upon, "a stage-set for human action." Instead, "it is a multitude of entities who possess intelligence and personality. These entities are active participants with human beings in life processes, in thoughts and acts simultaneously mundane and spiritual. People and the land hold dialogue within the structure of ritual, in order to ensure balance and harmony. Ritual is the means by which the people, spirits, rocks, animals, and other beings enter into conversation with each other. One major part of people's ritual responsibility is to speak with these nonhuman entities and to report the conversation; American Indian literature records echoes of that ongoing dialogue" (118).

D. Asian-American Writers

Asian-American literature is written by people of Asian descent in the United States, addressing the experience of living in a society that sometimes views them as alien. Asian immigrants were denied citizenship as late as the 1950s. Edward Said has written of *orientalism,* or the tendency to objectify and exoticize Asians, and their work has sought to respond to such stereotyping. Asian-American writers include Chinese, Japanese, Korean, Filipino, Vietnamese, Malaysian, Polynesian, and many other peoples of Asia, the Indian subcontinent, and the Pacific. These cultures present a bewildering array of languages, religions, social structures, and skin colors, and so the category is even more broad and artificial than Latina/o or American Indian. Furthermore, some Asian-American writers are relatively new arrivals in the United States, while others trace their American forebears for generations, as many Mexican Americans do. Names can get tricky here too: people with the same record of residence and family in the United States might call themselves Chinese, Chinese American, Amer-Asian, or none of the above. In Hawa'ii the important distinction is not so much ethnicity as being "local" versus *haole* (white).

Asian-American literature can be said to have begun around the turn of the twentieth century, primarily with autobiographical "paper son" stories and "confessions." Paper son stories were carefully fabricated for Chinese immigrant men to make the authorities believe that their New World sponsors were really their fathers. Each tale had to provide consistent information on details of their fictitious village life together. Confessions were elicited from Chinese women rescued by missionaries from prostitution in California's booming mining towns and migrant labor camps. A later form of this was the "picture bride" story, written by Asian women seeking American husbands.

Asian-American autobiography inherited these descriptive strategies, as Maxine Hong Kingston's *The Woman Warrior: Memoirs of a Girlhood Among Ghosts* (1976) illustrates. This book at first caused confusion in the Chinese-American literary community: was it a subtle critique of its narrator, or an unapologetic description of what it feels like for her to grow up a Chinese-American woman? The fact that it was sold as nonfiction supported the latter notion. The liminality of genre here is significant. Identity may be individually known within but is not always at home in the outward community.

Chinese-American women make up the largest and most influential group of Asian-American writers. Ironically, given the frequent cultural silencing of Asian women, they have produced an astonishing array of literary works, far outdistancing Asian-American men. The first to become known in the West tended to be daughters of diplomats or scholars or those educated in Western mission schools; two Eurasian sisters, Edith and Winnifred Eaton, were typical. They immigrated with their parents to the United States, and while Edith published stories of realistic Chinese people in *Mrs. Spring Fragrance* (1912) under the name Sui Sin Far, Winnifred, who adopted the Japanese pen name "Onoto Watanna," was the author of "Japanese" novels of a highly sentimentalized nature, full of moonlit bamboo groves, cherry blossoms, and doll-like heroines in delicate kimonos. A second family of sisters became popular just before World War II: Adet, Anor, and Meimei Lin, whose best-known work was their reminiscence *Dawn over Chunking* (1941), a firsthand experience of war written by a seventeen-year-old, a fourteen-year-old, and a ten-year-old, an unflinching portrayal of the horrifying sights of rotting corpses, burning houses, abandoned children. Anor Lin later took the name Lin Tay-yi and published a second novel, *War Tide* (1943), about the Japanese invasion of Hangchow.

Jade Snow Wong's female *Bildungsroman* was called *Fifth Chinese Daughter*. A story of growing up in San Francisco's Chinatown, it strikes a different note than the war novels. The heroine is tormented by a white child in a schoolyard who calls her "Chinky, Chinky, Chinaman." She does not react to him because she is astonished by his behavior:

> Jade Snow thought that he was tiresome and ignorant. Everybody knew that the Chinese people had a superior culture. Her ancestors had created a great art heritage and made inventions important to world civilization. . . . She had often heard Chinese people discuss the foreigners and their strange ways, but she would never have thought of running after one of them and screaming with pointed finger, "Hair on your chest!" (68)

Jade Snow and her family pursue the American Dream but remain proudly Chinese.

Amy Tan's *Joy Luck Club* (1989) was made into a successful film. Tan traces the lives of four Chinese women immigrants starting in 1949, when they form their mah-jongg club and swap stories of life in China; these mothers' vignettes alternate with their daughters' stories.

Increasing attention in Asian-American studies has been focused on writers from Hawai'i, Guam, and the Philippines, including Hawaiian writers Carolyn Lei-lanilau, author of *Ono Ono Girl's Hula* (1997), and Lois-Ann Yamanaka, author of *Wild Meat and the Bully Burgers* (1997). Works written about the Pacific by Anglo-American authors such as Herman Melville's *Typee* (1846), Robert Louis Stevenson's *Treasure Island* (1883), Jack London's *The House of Pride* (1912), and James Michener's *Hawaii* (1959) are now read in opposition to works by "local" writers. For example, London's story "Koolau the Leper" (1908), Piilani Kaluaikoolau's *The True Story of Kaluaikoolau: As Told by His Wife, Piilani* (1906, translated by Frances N. Frazier in 2001), and W. S. Merwin's epic poem *The Folding Cliffs: A Narrative* (2000) provide three different versions of Kauai's most celebrated hero.

III. POSTMODERNISM AND POPULAR CULTURE

A. Postmodernism

Richard Hebdige has memorably listed the ways postmodernism is applied. Among its features he includes "texts" from fiction and nonfiction to room décor, building design, film analysis, video productions, television commercials, or fashion lay-outs; he observes in postmodern creations "an anti-teleological tendency within epistemology, the attack on the 'metaphysics of presence' a general attenuation of feeling, the collective chagrin and morbid projections of a post-War generation of baby boomers confronting disillusioned middle age," and also the "predicament of reflexivity, a group of rhetorical tropes, a proliferation of surfaces, a new phase in commodity fetishism, a fascination for images, codes and styles, a process of cultural, political, or existential fragmentation and/or crisis, the 'de-centering' of the subject." Postmodern texts, he emphasizes, express an "incredulity towards metanarratives," as "unitary power axes" are replaced by a plurality of power/dis-course formations, causing an "implosion of meaning" and the collapse of cultural hierarchies (quoted in Storey 140).

Daryl B. Harris describes Western postmodernism as an approach that tends to "reject all notions of epistemological, ontological, and methodological certainty as expressed in the varied discourses of European modernity ranging from the arts to the sciences. Postmodernism sees designs that look for certitude as circumspect because of their possible use—especially in tyrannical hands, for example—for interposing a not so good rigidity, orthodoxy, and finality" (212). This tendency he sees as "the core European ethos of individualism" (213). It is "a consciousness of variability" (214). Thus postmodernism, like poststructural-ism and deconstruction, is a critique of the aesthetics of the preceding age, but besides mere critique, postmodernism celebrates the very act of dismembering tradition. Postmodernism questions everything rationalist European philosophy held to be true, arguing that it is *all* contingent and that most cultural construc-tions have served the function of empowering members of a dominant social group at the expense of "others." Beginning in the mid-1950s, postmodernism emerged in many fields.

Modernist literature rejected the Victorian aesthetic of prescriptive morality (famously argued by Henry James in "The Art of Fiction") and, using new tech-niques drawn from psychology, experimented with **point of view**, time, space, and **stream-of-consciousness** writing. Major figures of "high modernism" who radically redefined poetry and fiction include Virginia Woolf, James Joyce, Ezra Pound, T. S. Eliot, Wallace Stevens, Marcel Proust, Franz Kafka, and William Faulkner. Modernism typically displayed an emphasis on impressionism and subjectivity, on how subjectivity takes place, rather than on what is perceived. Modernists deployed fragmented forms, discontinuous **narratives**, and **pastiche** as in Faulkner's *The Sound and the Fury* (1929). Often narratives were sparse, even minimal, as in Stevens's poetry. Modernist novels sought to be **metafictive**, or self-referential about their status as texts, their production as art, and their reception.

Postmodernism borrows from modernism disillusionment with the givens of society; a penchant for irony; the self-conscious "play" within the work of art; frag-mentation and **ambiguity**; and a destructured, decentered, dehumanized subject. But while modernism presented a fragmented view of human history (as in Eliot's

The Waste Land [1925]), this fragmentation was seen as tragic. Despite their pessimism, modernist works still hope, following Matthew Arnold a generation before, that art may be able to provide the unity, coherence, and meaning that has been lost in most of modern life, as church and nation have failed to fullfill. One can locate this hope, faint as it sometimes is, in such memorable passages as the Molly Bloom section that closes Joyce's *Ulysses* (1922). In contrast, postmodernism not only does not mourn the loss of meaning, but celebrates the activity of fragmentation. Whereas modernism still seeks meaning in a work of art, postmodernism explores the provisionality and irrationality of art.

Aaron Schutz finds that "One way to think about postmodernism…is as an ultimately tragic commitment to respond ethically to contingency, and to live and act…amidst unresolveable tensions" (227). Michel Foucault believed that constructing knowledge about people or communities was a means of exercising power over them. Certainly the oldest writing in history, from ancient Sumeria and China, consisted of lists of commodities and the debts that would be paid for them, invented and maintained by the cultural elite. Schutz comments on Foucault by noting that "In the context of education,…postmodernists tend to argue that what we are led to believe about ourselves, what we learn about how we are supposed to act, the ways we are taught to frame 'problems,' and even the tools of reason that we use to solve these problems, do not simply represent neutral skills but are in fact ways of forming us into particular kinds of subjects. 'Power' in this vision does not merely suppress or restrict, but actually produced actions and desires" (216).

Ihab Hassan sees the origins of postmodernism as the fruit of a subversive strain in modernism, in such writers as Arthur Rimbaud, the Dadaists, Franz Kafka, and Samuel Beckett, which led to the literary avant-garde of the 1960s and such French experimenters as Alain Robbe-Grillet. Leslie Fiedler's criticism on American literature describes it as "post-white" and "post-male" and praised the youth culture that turned against modernism. He also praises literatures of parody such as those of John Barth, Thomas Pynchon, and Kurt Vonnegut, as well as their popular culture sources in crime fiction, mysteries, and science fiction. Thus the diversity and irreverence of popular art arrived at the same time as the new postmodernist sensibility.

Terry Eagleton defines postmodernism as "style of thought which is suspicious of classical notions of truth, reason, identity, and objectivity, of the idea of universal progress or emancipation, of single frameworks, grand narratives or ultimate grounds of explanations. Against these Enlightenment norms, it sees the world as contingent, ungrounded, diverse, unstable, indeterminate, a set of disunified cultures or interpretations which breed a degree of skepticism about the objectivity of truth, history and norms, the givenness of natures and the coherence of identities." Thus postmodernism is a "style of culture" that offers a "depthless, decentered, ungrounded, self-reflexive, playful, derivative, eclectic, pluralistic art which blurs the boundaries between 'high' culture and 'popular' cultures, as well as between art and everyday experience" (*Illusions of*

Postmodernism vii). Similarly, Umberto Eco sees in the postmodern sensibility an awareness of what he calls "the already said." Thus, a lover might not be able to say, 'I love you madly,' " but might say, "As Barbara Cartland would put it, 'I love you madly" ' (39). In the same way cable channels seem increasingly to recycle television's accumulated past. As John Storey observes, postmodernism is always a question not of substance but of "articulation" (144), its two most salient characteristics the reflection of the "collapse of absolute standards of value and the culture of globalization"(140). As Kristine M. Baber and Colleen I. Murphy note, "Postmodernism is also deconstructive. The deconstructive aspect of a postmodern approach serves as a tool to examine the way language operates to create oppositions and hierarchies, Deconstructing involves a critical analysis of concepts, categories, and metaphors; the process includes challenging taken-for-granted assumptions, examining how power functions as a regulatory mechanism, and considering what is included in traditional presentations of information as well as what is left out" (24).

Frederic Jameson defines artistic movements like modernism and postmodernism as cultural formations that accompany particular stages of capitalism and are to some extent constructed by it. **Realism** was the predominant style within eighteenth- and nineteenth-century market capitalism, with its new technologies such as the steam engine that transformed everyday life. From the late nineteenth century through World War II, modernism ruled the arts within monopoly capitalism, associated with electricity and internal combustion. The third phase is dominated by global consumer capitalism, the emphasis placed on advertising and selling goods, fueled by ever-expanding digital communication innovations and reflecting a postmodern point of view.

Yet societies must have order. Jean-François Lyotard argues that stability is maintained through "grand narratives" or "master narratives," stories a culture tells itself about its practices and beliefs in order to keep going. A grand narrative in American culture might be the story that democracy is the most enlightened or rational form of government, and that democracy will lead to universal human happiness. But postmodernism, Lyotard adds, is characterized by "incredulity toward metanarratives" that serve to mask the contradictions and instabilities inherent in any social organization. Postmodernism prefers "mini-narratives" of local events. As Lytotard states, the postmodern generates "that which in the modern invokes the unpresentable in presentation itself, that which refuses the consolation of correct forms, refuses the consensus of taste permitting a common experience of nostalgia for the impossible, and inquires into new presentations—not to take pleasure in them, but to better produce the feeling that there is something unpresentable" (15). Similarly, Jean Baudrillard describes the "simulacra" of postmodern life which have taken the place of "real" objects. For example, Iphones and virtual reality games add another dimension to the artificiality of postmodern life. As Madan Sarup observes, Baudrillard's thought reflects a widespread drift toward relativist thinking; he sees no difference between "fictive and other, truth-telling forms of discourses.... Truth and critique are hopelessly outmoded concepts....and appeal[s] to obsolete 'Enlightenment' habits of thought" (163). Perhaps postmodernism is best compared to the emergence of computer technology. In the future, anything not digitizable may cease to be knowledge. For Baudrillard, postmodernism marks a culture composed "of disparate fragmentary experiences and images that constantly bombard the individual in music, video, television, advertising and other forms of electronic media. The speed and ease of reproduction of these images mean that they exist only as image, devoid of depth, coherence, or originality" (in Childers and Hentzi 235). Postmodernism thus reflects both the energy and diversity of contemporary life as well as its frequent lack of coherence and depth. The lines between reality and artifice can become so blurred that virtual reality is now hard to distinguish from reality, and Baudrillard wrote this before Facebook and Twitter.

Henry Giroux argues that the writing practice of postmoderns does not try to describe the world the way it *is,* but rather it foregrounds the ways of intervening in and changing the world, creating "new spaces, practices, and values" (221). Accordingly, postmodernism is used and redefined by a number of critics in several approaches. For example, Chela Sandoval articulates a Lacanian approach to postmodernism in her book *Methodology of the Oppressed.* She defines "differential consciousness" as a postmodern feature not expressible in words but "accessed through poetic modes of expression: gestures, music, images, sounds, words that plummet or rise through signification to find some void—some no-place—to claim their due" (139). She lists third-world writers including Franz Fanon, Gloria Anzaldúa, Emma Pérez, Trinh Minh-ha, and Cherríe Moraga as writers who seek a differential consciousness.

As Rawwida Baksh-Soodeen has noted, postmodernism has also had "a profound impact" upon feminist theory. The critical theory and "standpoint epistemology" identified by the Frankfurt School influenced feminist politics in that critical theory challenged the use of the scientific method for cultural theory, rejecting the entire notion of "objective reality." As to epistemology, or the idea that certain points of view—especially those of the oppressed—are more reliable than those of the dominators, she notes that "In order to survive, they have a 'double vision,' a knowledge or awareness of and sensitivity to both the dominant world view and their own minority perspective." The focus is upon "the specificity of women's oppression, linking this to women being able to see the viewpoints of both women and men (the dominant group), and hence having an understanding that is potentially more complete, deeper, and sensitive than men's. She references the work of Joyce McCarl Nielsen as support. Nielsen and Baksh-Soodeen emphasize the power Third World women have in claiming such a "superior" point of view, and explain "the present movement of Third World feminism's standpoints of race, class, and nation from the periphery to the centre, the so-called cutting edge of the discourse" (77).

For Kristine M. Baber and Colleen I. Murray, "A postmodern approach stresses the importance of historical context, variations among people, and the expectation of change over time. Postmodernism provides a sophisticated and persuasive critique of essentialism—rejecting the reductionism and naïve dualism that result in dichotomous, either-or thinking and embracing ambivalence, paradox, and heterogeneity. Feminism, with its focus on gender and attention to power, adds to a postmodern perspective the social critique and the imperative for action" (24). A postmodern feminist approach sees sexuality as complex and fluid: "Unitary, monolithic theories of sexuality are rejected, and contradictory representations of experiences and desire are accommodated." Sexuality is not a fixed phenomenon fueled by biological drives but "constructed in relation to, and in interaction with, historically and culturally variable social practices like religion, education, and medicine." Constructions of sexuality reflect social relations of gender, ethnicity, and class; e.g., some sexual experiences are seen as legitimate and others are not. "The postmodern feminist push to acknowledge within-group diversity and to consider the experiences of those whose sexuality has been ignored or misrepresented leads us to seek out more inclusive information and to bring in the voices of those in marginal groups whenever possible" (24).

B. Popular Culture

There was a time before the 1960s when popular culture was not studied by academics—when it was, well, just popular culture. But within American Studies programs at first and then later in many disciplines, including semiotics, rhetoric, literary criticism, film studies, anthropology, history, women's studies, ethnic studies, and psychoanalytic approaches, critics examine such cultural media as pulp fiction, comic books, television, film, advertising, popular music, and computer cyberculture. They assess how such factors as ethnicity, race, gender, class, age, region, and sexuality are shaped by and reshaped in popular culture.

There are four main types of popular culture analyses: *production analysis, textual analysis, audience analysis,* and *historical analysis*. These analyses seek to get beneath the surface (**denotative**) meanings and examine more implicit (**connotative**) social meanings. These approaches view culture as a narrative or story-telling process in which particular texts or cultural artifacts (i.e., a film or television program) consciously or unconsciously link themselves to larger stories at play in the society. A key here is how texts create ***subject positions*** or identities for those who use them. Postmodernists tend to speak more of subject positions rather than the humanist notion of independent individuals. Production analysis asks the following kinds of questions: Who owns the media? Who creates texts and why? Under what constraints? How democratic or elitist is the production of popular culture? What about works written only for money? Textual analysis examines how specific works of popular culture create meanings. Audience analysis asks how different groups of popular culture consumers, or users, make similar or different sense of the same texts. Historical analysis investigates how these other three dimensions change over time.

As we will demonstrate in our discussion of *Frankenstein*, sometimes popular culture can so overtake and repackage a literary work that it is impossible to read the original text without reference to the many layers of popular culture that have developed around it. As we will also point out, the popular culture reconstructions of a work like *Frankenstein* can also open it to unforeseen new interpretations.

IV. CULTURAL STUDIES IN PRACTICE

A. Two Characters in *Hamlet*: Marginalization with a Vengeance

In Chapter 4 we noted emphases on power relationships in *Hamlet*. For example, we noted that cultural critics assume "oppositional" roles in terms of power structures, wherever they might be found. Aram Veeser, we pointed out, credited the new historicists with dealing with "questions of politics, power, indeed on all matters that deeply affect people's practical lives" (ix).

Let us now approach Shakespeare's *Hamlet* with a view to seeing power in its cultural context.

Shortly after the "mouse trap" play within the play, Claudius is talking privately with Rosencrantz and Guildenstern, Hamlet's fellow students from Wittenberg (III.iii). In response to Claudius's plan to send Hamlet to England, Rosencrantz delivers a speech that—if read out of context—is both an excellent set of metaphors (almost in the shape of a **sonnet**) and a summation of the Elizabethan concept of the role and power of kingship:

> The singular and peculiar life is bound
> With all the strength and armor of the mind
> To keep itself from noyance, but much more
> That spirit upon whose weal depends and rests
> The lives of many. The cease of majesty
> Dies not alone, but like a gulf doth draw
> What's near it with it. It is a massy wheel
> Fixed on the summit of the highest mount,
> To whose huge spokes ten thousand lesser things
> Are mortised and adjoined; which, when it falls,
> Each small annexment, petty consequence,
> Attends the boisterous ruin. Never alone
> Did the King sigh but with a general groan.
>
> (III.iii)

Taken alone, the passage is a thoughtful and imagistically successful passage, worthy of a wise and accomplished statesman.

But how many readers and viewers of the play would rank this passage among the best-known lines of the play—with Hamlet's **soliloquies**, for instance, or with the king's effort to pray, or even with the aphorisms addressed by Polonius to his son Laertes? We venture to say that the passage, intrinsically good if one looks at it alone, is simply not well known.

Why?

Attention to the context and to the speaker gives the answer. Guildenstern had just agreed that he and Rosencrantz would do the king's bidding. The agreement is only a reaffirmation of what they had told the king when he first received them at court (II.ii). Both speeches are wholly in character, for Rosencrantz and Guildenstern are among the jellyfish of Shakespeare's characters. Easy it is to forget which of the two speaks which lines—indeed easy it is to forget most of their lines altogether. The two are distinctly plot-driven: empty of personality, sycophantic in a sniveling way, eager to curry favor with power even if it means spying on their erstwhile friend. Weakly they admit, without much skill at denial, that they "were sent for" (II.ii). Even less successfully they try to play on Hamlet's metaphorical "pipe," to know his "stops," when they are forced to admit that they could not even handle the literal musical instrument that Hamlet shows them (III.ii). Still later these nonentities meet their destined "non-beingness," as it were, when Hamlet, who can play the pipe so much more efficiently, substitutes their names in the death warrant intended for him.

If ever we wished to study two characters who are marginalized, then let us look upon Rosencrantz and Guildenstern, but of course they marginalize themselves as much as do their betters into mere puppets in the game of politics.

The meanings of their names hardly match what seems to be the essence of their characters. Murray J. Levith, for example, has written that "Rosencrantz and Guildenstern are from the Dutch-German: literally, 'garland of roses' and 'golden star.' Although of religious origin, both names together sound singsong and odd to English ears. Their jingling gives them a lightness, and blurs the individuality of the characters they label" (50).

Lightness to be sure. Harley Granville-Barker once wrote in an offhand way of the reaction these two roles call up for actors. Commenting on Solanio and Salarino from *The Merchant of Venice*, he noted that their roles are "cursed by actors as the two worst bores in the whole Shakespearean canon; not excepting, even those other twin brethren in nonentity, Rosencrantz and Guildenstern" (1:345).

Obvious too is the fact that the two would not fit the social level or have the level of influence of those whom Harold Jenkins reports as historical persons bearing these names: "These splendidly resounding names, by contrast with the unlocalized classical ones, are evidently chosen as particularly Danish. Both were common among the most influential Danish families, and they are often found together" (422). He cites various appearances of the names among Danish nobles, and even notes the appearance of the names as Wittenberg students around 1590 (422).

No, these details do not seem to fit the personalities and general vacuity of Shakespeare's two incompetents. So let us look elsewhere for what these two characters tell us. From Wittenberg, they return to Denmark, apparently at the direct request of Claudius (II.ii). They try to pry from Hamlet some of his inner thoughts, especially of ambition and frustration about the crown (II.ii). Hamlet foils them. They crumble before his being students at questioning. Yet as noted above, Claudius later sends them on an embassy with Hamlet, carrying a letter to the King of England that would have Hamlet summarily executed. Though they may not have known the contents of that "grand commission," Hamlet's suspicion of them is enough for him to contemplate their future—and to "trust them as adders fanged":

> They must sweep my way,
> And marshal me to knavery. Let it work,
> For 'tis the sport to have the engineer
> Hoist with his own petard. And 't shall go hard
> But I will delve one yard below their mines
> And blow them to the moon: Oh, 'tis most sweet
> When in one line two crafts directly meet.
>
> (III.iv)

In a moment of utmost trickery on his own part, Hamlet blithely substitutes a forged document bearing their names rather than his as the ones to be "put to sudden death,/Not shriving time allowed" (V.ii). When Horatio responds laconically with "So Guildenstern and Rosencrantz go to 't," Hamlet is unmoved:

> Why, man, they did make love to this employment.
> They are not near my conscience. Their defeat
> Does by their own insinuation grow.
> 'Tis dangerous when the baser nature comes
> Between the pass and fell incensèd points
> Of mighty opposites.

And with that Shakespeare—as well as Hamlet—is done with these two characters. "They are not near [Hamlet's] conscience."

Again, why? For one thing, Hamlet may well see himself as righting the moral order, not as a murderer, and much has been said on that matter. But let us take note of another dimension: the implications for power. Clearly Hamlet makes reference in the lines just noted to the "mighty opposites" represented by himself and Claudius. Clearly, too, the ones of "baser nature" who "[made] love to this employment" do not matter much in this struggle between powerful **antagonists**. They are pawns for Claudius first, for Hamlet second. It is almost as if Hamlet had tried before the sea voyage to warn them of their insignificant state; he calls Rosencrantz a sponge, provoking this exchange:

HAMLET: ...Besides, to be demanded of a sponge! What replication should be made by the son of a king?

ROSENCRANTZ: Take you me for a sponge, my lord?

HAMLET: Aye, sir, that soaks up the King's countenance, his rewards, his authorities. But such officers do the King best service in the end. He keeps
them, like an ape, in the corner of his jaw, first mouthed, to be last swallowed. When he needs what you have gleaned, it is but squeezing you and,
sponge, you shall be dry again.

So they are pawns, or sponges, or monkey food: the message of power keeps coming through. Thus, they do not merit a pang of conscience. True, there may be
some room for believing that at first they intended only good for their erstwhile
schoolfellow (see, for example, Bertram Joseph 76). But their more constant motive
is to please the king, the power that has brought them here. Their fate, however, is
to displease mightily the prince, who will undermine them and "hoist [them] with
[their] own petard."

For such is power in the world of kings and princes. Nor is it merely a literary
construct. England had known the effects of such power off and on for centuries. Whether it was the deposing and later execution of Richard II, or the crimes
alleged of Richard III, or the beheading of a Thomas More or of a wife or two, or
the much more recent actions in and around the court of Elizabeth: in all these
cases, power served policy. Witness especially the fate of the second Earl of Essex,
whose attempt at rebellion led to his own execution in 1601, and even more especially the execution of Elizabeth's relative, Mary Queen of Scots, who had been
imprisoned by Elizabeth for years before Elizabeth signed the death warrant. A
generation later, another king, Charles I, would also be beheaded. With historical
actions such as these, we can understand why Shakespeare's work incorporates
royal power struggles.

Claudius was aware of power, clearly, when he observed of Hamlet's apparent
madness that "Madness in great ones must not unwatched go" (III.i). With equal
truth Rosencrantz and Guildenstern should have observed that power in great
ones also must not unwatched go.

To say, then, that the mighty struggle between powerful antagonists is the
stuff of this play is hardly original. But our emphasis is that one can gain a further insight into the play, and indeed into Shakespeare's culture, by thinking not
about kings and princes but about the lesser persons caught up in the massive
oppositions.

It is instructive to note that the reality of power reflective of Shakespeare's
time might in another time and in another culture reflect a radically different
worldview. In the twentieth century the dead, or never-living, Rosencrantz and
Guildenstern were resuscitated by Tom Stoppard in a fascinating re-seeing of
their existence, or its lack. In Stoppard's version, they are even more obviously two
ineffectual pawns, seeking constantly to know who they are, why they are here,
where they are going. Whether they "are" at all may be the ultimate question of this
modern play. In *Rosencrantz and Guildenstern Are Dead,* Stoppard has given the
contemporary audience a play that examines existential questions in the context

of a whole world that may have no meaning at all. The essence of marginalization is here: in this view, Rosencrantz and Guildenstern are **archetypal** human
beings caught up on a ship—spaceship Earth for the twentieth or the twenty-first
century—that leads nowhere, except to death, a death for persons who are already
dead. If these two characters were marginalized in *Hamlet,* they are even more so
in Stoppard's handling. If Shakespeare marginalized the powerless in his own version of Rosencrantz and Guildenstern, Stoppard has marginalized us all in an era
when—in the eyes of some—all of us are caught up in forces beyond our control.
In other words, a cultural and historical view that was Shakespeare's is radically
reworked to reflect a cultural and philosophical view of another time—our own.

B. "To His Coy Mistress": Implied Culture

As noted earlier, Andrew Marvell's "To His Coy Mistress" tells the reader a good
deal about the speaker of the poem. Among other things, we know that the speaker
is knowledgeable about poems and conventions of classic Greek and Roman literature, about other conventions of love poetry, such as the **courtly love** conventions
of medieval Europe, and about Biblical passages.

Indeed, if one accepts the close reading of Jules Brody, the speaker shows
possible awareness of the Provençal *amor de lohn,* neo-**Petrarchan** "complaints," St. Thomas Aquinas's concept of the triple-leveled soul, Biblical echoes,
a "Platonico-Christian corporeal economy" (59), and the convention of the **blazon**. The first stanza, says Brody, shows "its insistent, exaggerated literariness"
(60). In the second stanza Brody sees not only the conventional *carpe diem* theme
from Horace but also echoes from Ovid, joined by other echoes from the *Book of
Common Prayer,* from the *Greek Anthology,* and from "Renaissance vernacular and
neo-Latin poets" (61–64).

Brody posits the "implied reader"—as distinct from the fictive lady—who
would "be able to summon up a certain number of earlier or contemporaneous
examples of this kind of love poem and who [could] be counted on, in short, to
supply the models which Marvell may variously have been evoking, imitating, dis-
torting, subverting or transcending" (64). (The concept of the "implied reader," we
may note, bulks large in reader-response criticism; see Chapter 10.)

The speaker knows all of these things well enough to parody or at least to
echo them, for in making his proposition to the coy lady, he hardly expects to be
taken seriously in his detailing. He knows that he is echoing the conventions only
in order to satirize them and to make light of the real proposal at hand. He knows
that she knows, for she comes from the same cultural milieu that he does.

In other words, the speaker—like Marvell—is a highly educated person, one
who is well read, one whose natural flow of associated images moves lightly over
details and **allusions** that reflect who he is, and he expects his hearer or reader to
respond in a kind of harmonic vibration. He thinks in terms of precious stones, of
exotic and distant places, of a milieu where eating, drinking, and making merry
seem to be an achievable way of life. His thinking reflects his broader culture as

well: compare, for example, Renaissance "discovery" narratives by explorers and colonizers with his proposed possession of her body.

Beyond what we know of the speaker from his own words, we are justified in speculating that his coy lady is like the implied reader, equally well educated, and therefore knowledgeable of the conventions he uses in parody. He seems to assume that she understands the parodic nature of his comments, for by taking her in on the jests he appeals to her intellect, thus trying to throw her off guard against his very physical requests. After all, if the two of them can be on the same cultural plane in their thoughts and allusions, their smiles and jests, then perhaps they can shortly be together on a different—and literal—plane: literally bedded.

Thus might appear to be the culture and the era of the speaker, his lady—and his implied reader.

But what does he not show? As he selects these rich and multifarious allusions, what does he ignore from his culture? He clearly does not think of poverty, the demographics and socioeconomic details of which would show how fortunate his circumstances are. For example, it has been estimated that during this era at least one quarter of the European population was below the poverty line. Nor does the speaker think of disease as a daily reality that he might face. To be sure, in the second and especially in the third stanza he alludes to *future* death and dissolution. But wealth and leisure and sexual activity are his currency, his coin for present bliss. Worms and marble vaults and ashes are not present, hence not yet real.

Now let us consider historical reality, a dimension that the poem ignores. Consider disease—real and present disease—what has been called the "chronic morbidity" of the population. Although the speaker thrusts disease and death into the future, we know that syphilis and other sexually transmitted diseases were just as real a phenomenon in Marvell's day as in our era. What was the reality that the speaker chooses not to think about, as he pushes off death and the "vault" to some distant time?

Similarly, one might turn to a different disease that was even more ominous, more wrenching, in its grasp of the mind and body of the general population. Move ahead a few years, beyond the probable time of composition of the poem in the early 1650s: move to 1664–65. That was when the London populace was faced with an old horror, one that had ravaged Europe as early as A.D. 542. It did it again in its most thoroughgoing way in the middle of the fourteenth century (especially 1348), killing millions, perhaps 25 million in Europe alone. It was ready to strike again. It was, of course, a recurrence of the Black Death, in the Great Plague of London. From July to October, it killed some 68,000 persons, and a total of 75,000 in the course of the epidemic. Had we world enough and time, we could present the details of the plague here, its physical manifestations, its rapid spread, the quickness of death: but the gruesome horrors are available elsewhere. For example, the curious can get a sense of the lived experience by reading Daniel Defoe's *Journal of the Plague Year* (1722), an imaginative creation of what it was like.

So disease was real in the middle of the seventeenth century. There needed no ghost to come from the world of the dead to tell Marvell's speaker about the real world. Perhaps the speaker—and his lady—knew it after all. Maybe too well. Maybe that is why that real world is so thoroughly absent from the poem.

C. From *Paradise Lost* to Frank-N-Furter: The Creature Lives!

Mary Shelley's novel has morphed into countless forms in both highbrow and popular culture, including the visual arts, fiction and nonfiction, stage plays, film, television, advertising, clothing, jewelry, toys, key chains, coffee mugs, games, Halloween costumes, comic books, jokes, cartoons, pornography, academic study, fan clubs, web sites, and even food. (Remember "Frankenberry" and "Count Chocula" cereals?) Shelley's creation teaches us not to underestimate the power of youth culture.

1. Revolutionary Births

Born like its creator in an age of revolution, *Frankenstein* challenged accepted ideas of its day. As it has become increasingly commodified by modern consumer culture, one wonders whether its original revolutionary spirit and its critique of scientific, philosophical, political, and gender issues have become obscured, or whether instead its continuing transformation attests to its essential oppositional nature. Today, as George Levine remarks, *Frankenstein* is "a vital metaphor, peculiarly appropriate to a culture dominated by a consumer technology, neurotically obsessed with 'getting in touch' with its authentic self and frightened at what it is discovering" (Levine and Knopelmacher 3–4). Hardly a day goes by without our seeing an image or allusion to Frankenstein, such as magazine articles that warn of genetically engineered "Frankenfoods," test-tube babies, and cloning. Below we examine the political and scientific issues of the novel, then survey its amazing career in popular adaptations in fiction, drama, film, and television. Perhaps no other novel addresses such critical contemporary scientific and political concerns while at the same time providing Saturday afternoon entertainment to generations.

2. "A Race of Devils"

In Chapter 4 we noted the elements of this novel that reflect its author's sense of the proletarian (and her class fears), and in Chapter 8 we examined its maternal, domestic, and feminist messages. *Frankenstein* may also be analyzed in its portrayal of different "races." Though the Creature's skin is only described as yellow, it has been constructed "out of a cultural tradition of the threatening 'Other'— whether troll or giant, gypsy or Negro—from the dark inner recesses of xenophobic fear and loathing," as H. L. Malchow remarks (103). Antislavery discourse had a powerful effect on the depiction of Africans in Shelley's day, from gaudily dressed exotics to naked objects of pity.

Though the abolitionists wished to portray the black man or woman as brother or sister, they also created an image of the African as a childlike, suffering, and degraded being. In this vein, Victor could be read as guilty slave master. Interestingly, one of Mary Shelley's letters mentions an allusion to *Frankenstein* made on the floor of Parliament by Foreign Secretary George Canning (1770–1827), speaking on March 16, 1824, on the subject of proposed ameliorations of slave conditions in the West Indies: "To turn him [the slave] loose in the manhood of his physical strength, in the maturity of his physical passion, but in the infancy of his uninstructed reason, would be to raise up a creature resembling the splendid fiction of a recent romance" (in Malchow 30). *Frankenstein's* Creature also recalls theories of *polygeny* and *autogenesis* (the idea that the races were created separately) from German race theorists of the day. But Gayatri Chakravorty Spivak describes the novel as a critique of empire and racism, pointing out that "social engineering should not be based upon pure, theoretical, or natural-scientific reason alone...." *Frankenstein's* "language of racism—the dark side of imperialism understood as social mission—combines with the hysteria of masculism into the idiom of (the withdrawal of) sexual reproduction rather than subject-constitution." The novel is "written from the perspective of a narrator 'from below' " ("Three Women's Texts" 265–66).

Written in an age that saw tremendous divisions within industrialization, *Frankenstein* remains more relevant than ever. Developments in science were increasingly critical to society during the Romantic period, when a paradigm shift occurred from science as natural philosophy to science as biology, a crucial (and troubled) distinction in *Frankenstein,* as described in *Frankenstein: Penetrating the Secrets of Nature,* an exhibit mounted in 2002 by the National Library of Medicine. Mary Shelley attended public demonstrations of the effect of electricity on animal and human bodies, living and dead. At an 1802 show in London, electricity was applied to the ears of a freshly severed ox head, and to the amazement of the crowd (which included the Prince of Wales) the eyes opened and both tongue and head shook. The experiments of Luigi Galvani (1737–98), an Italian physicist and physician who discovered that he could use electricity to induce muscle contractions, were among the scientific topics discussed in the Geneva villa by Percy and Mary Shelley, Byron, and Polidori. Also discussed were the two different views of life represented by the *vitalism* of Scottish anatomist and surgeon John Abernathy (1764–1831), which implied a soul, and the *materialism* of William Lawrence (1783–1867), Percy Shelley's doctor from autumn 1815 on (Lederer 14, 18). Many of these ideas were feared as leading to unnatural results—even devilish ones.

Today we are constantly confronted with new developments in fertility science and new philosophical conundrums that result from genetic engineering, *in vitro* fertilization, cloning, and the prolongation of life by artificial means. Couples taking fertility treatments sometimes have to face the difficult choice of "selective reduction" or the possible adverse results of multiple, premature births. People wonder, Has science gone too far? According to cultural critic Laura Kranzler, Victor's creation of life and modern sperm banks and artificial wombs show a "masculine desire to claim female (re)productivity" (Kranzler 45). *Frankenstein* and its warnings about the hubris of science will be with us in the future as science continues to question the borders between life and death, between "viability" and "selective reduction," between living and life support. Such disciplines as bioengineering and such practices as stem-cell harvesting push the bounds of accepted medical practice.

3. The Frankenpheme in Popular Culture: Fiction, Drama, Film, Television

In the *Routledge Literary Sourcebook* on *Frankenstein,* Timothy Morton uses the term *Frankenphemes,* drawn from *phonemes* (sonic elements of language, as used in structural linguistics) and *graphemes* (visual elements), as "elements of culture that are derived from *Frankenstein.*" Either a separate work of art is inspired, or some kernel is derived from Shelley's novel and repeated in another medium. Broadly defined, Frankenphemes demonstrate the extent of the novel's presence in world cultures, as the encoding of race and class in the 1824 Canning speech in Parliament, in today's global debates about such things as genetically engineered foods, and of course in fiction and other media. We end this section with a quick look at some of the thousands of retellings, parodies, and other selected Frankenphemes as they have appeared in popular fiction, drama, film, and television.

Start thinking about this now: Who made the first film version of *Frankenstein?* Answer coming up. (But be warned: if you type "Frankenstein" into your Web browser, your computer may explode!)

a. "The Greatest Horror Story Novel Ever Written": Frankenstein's Fictions Peter Haining, editor of the indispensable *Frankenstein Omnibus,* has called *Frankenstein* "*the* single greatest horror story novel ever written and the most widely influential in its genre" (3). Apparently the first writer to attempt a straightforward short tale inspired by *Frankenstein* was Herman Melville, whose story "The Bell-Tower" was published in *Putnam's Monthly Magazine* in 1855. (This and many of the following entries are collected in the *Omnibus;* see also Florescu.) In Renaissance Italy, a scientist constructs a mechanical man to ring the hours on a bell in a tall tower, but it turns instead upon its creator.

The first story about a female monster is French author Villiers de L'Isle Adam's "The Future Eve" (*l'Eve future*), an 1886 novelette not translated into English until fifty years later, in which an American inventor modeled on Thomas Edison makes an artificial woman for his friend and benefactor, a handsome young lord who has despaired of finding a mate.

American writer W. C. Morrow published "The Surgeon's Experiment" in *The Argonaut* in 1887, in which an experimenter revives a headless corpse by attaching a metal head; there was a large cancellation of subscriptions in response. Two years later, a British journalist published a tale in reverse in *Cornhill Magazine:* a disembodied head is kept alive with electricity. Jack London's early story, "A Thousand Deaths" (1897), is a gruesome science fiction tale of a scientist who stays at sea on his laboratory ship, repeatedly killing then reviving his son, until the son has enough and kills his father. *Frankenstein* inspired the set of tales published in *Home*

Brew magazine called "The Reanimator" (1921–22) by H. P. Lovecraft, which later became a cult classic movie, "Herbert West: Reanimator" (1986), the saga of a young experimenter, barred from medical school, who practices unholy arts on the corpses of human beings and reptiles. "The Reanimator" helped initiate the "splatter film" genre. There have been numerous illustrated editions of *Frankenstein* for children, from full-scale reprintings to comic books, as well as politicized versions, such as Mikhail Bulgakov's satire on Stalinist Russia, *The Master and Margarita* (1940), and Theodore Roszak's ecofeminist novel *The Memoirs of Elizabeth Frankenstein* (1995). There is a surprising amount of Frankenstein-inspired erotica, especially gay- and lesbian-oriented. Finally, there are the unclassifiables, such as Theodore Leberthon's "Demons of the Film Colony," a strange reminiscence of an afternoon the Hollywood journalist spent with Boris Karloff and Bela Lugosi, published in *Weird Tales* in 1932.

b. Frankenstein on the Stage   From his debut on the stage, the Creature has generally been made more horrific, and Victor has been assigned less blame. Most stage and screen versions are quite melodramatic, tending to eliminate minor characters and the entire frame structure in order to focus upon murder and mayhem. No dramatist would want to try for all of the complexities of the novel. In stage versions, only a few key scenes—the creation scene, the bridal night, and the destruction of the Creature—are used. On the nineteenth-century stage, the Creature was a composite of frightening makeup and human qualities. He could even appear clownish, recalling Shakespeare's Caliban.

The first theatrical presentation based on *Frankenstein* was *Presumption, or, The Fate of Frankenstein* by Richard Brinsley Peake, performed at the English Opera House (the Lyceum) in London in the summer of 1823 and subsequently revived many times. Mary Shelley herself attended the play and pronounced it authentic. But this "serious" drama immediately inspired parodies, first with *Frankenstitch* in 1823, a burlesque featuring a tailor, who as the "Needle Prometheus," sews a body out of nine corpses. Later that year opened *Franke-n-steam,* in which a student foolishly revives the corpse of a bailiff. *The Devil Among the Players* opened at the Opera Glass in London in October of 1826, with a line-up featuring Frankenstein, Faust, and the Vampire. A play called *The Man in the Moon* (its title a foretaste of science fiction) was very popular in London during 1847; its script was *Hamlet* with the addition of a new act in which the Creature arises from Hell through a trap door and sings and drinks with the Ghost.

In more modern times *Frankenstein* has been a staple of many stages. *Frankenstein and His Bride* was performed at a club called Strip City in Los Angeles in the late 1950s. It included songs such as "Oh, What a Beautiful Mourning" and "Ghoul of My Dreams." The children's production *H. R. Pufnstuf* toured the United States in 1972 and featured Witchiepoo the Witch creating a Frankenstein monster. And who can forget *The Rocky Horror Show* with Richard O'Brien, first performed at the Royal Court Theatre Upstairs in London in 1973, then revived and filmed as *The Rocky Horror Picture Show,* directed by Jim Sharman (1975). In it Brad and Janet have pledged their love but must encounter the rapacious Frank-N-Furter, a transvestite from the planet Transsexual in the galaxy Transylvania, who has created a perfect male lover, Rocky Horror, to replace his former lover Eddie. After numerous seductions, Frank-N-Furter is eventually killed when the servants revolt, led by the hunchback Riff Raff.

c. Film Adaptations   In the *Frankenstein Omnibus,* readers can study the screenplay for the 1931 James Whale film *Frankenstein,* the most famous of all adaptations. It was loosely based on the novel with the addition of new elements, including the placing of a criminal brain into the monster's body. The first film version of *Frankenstein,* however, was produced by Thomas Edison in 1910, a one-reel tinted silent. The early films, including this one, were able to move away from the melodrama and clumsy moralism of the stage productions and focus on more dreamlike and bizarre episodes that have more to do with the novel's themes of creation. Early German films that were influenced by this *Frankenstein* were *The Cabinet of Dr. Caligari* (1920), *The Golem* (1920), and *Metropolis* (1927).

Whale's *Frankenstein* and especially Boris Karloff's performance have had the greatest influence on subsequent portrayals, and the changes Whale made to the story have also stuck: his grunting Creature has been dumbed down from Shelley's novel; Victor is called "Henry" Frankenstein—noble though a bit mad; an assistant named Fritz is added, who is responsible for getting the criminal brain; and there is a happy ending, with "Henry" saved. The criminal brain reflects the biological determinism popular in the early decades of the twentieth century. Many people considered heredity rather than environment, economic systems, or education to be the critical factor in problems of social unrest, immigration, unemployment, and crime, and they looked to such pseudosciences as eugenics to promote the reproduction of groups judged to have sound genetic backgrounds and to prevent those who did not. According to Lederer, "Fearing that the 'wrong people' would reproduce, a number of American states adopted compulsory sterilization laws for criminals, mentally retarded adults, epileptics, and other institutionalized individuals to insure that these populations would not breed" (45–46).

In Whale's *Bride of Frankenstein* (1935), there is a return to the frame structure, but this time we begin with Mary Shelley discussing her novel with Percy and Byron. She is played by Elsa Lanchester, who also plays the female creature, with her electric black eyes and silver-streaked hair. Unlike the first Whale film, this one tends toward comedy, parody, and **satire** rather than pure horror. Some viewers note its attacks on sacred institutions like marriage and its gay subtext. There are new characters such as Dr. Pretorius, another mad scientist, who grows people like little seedlings in his lab and who blackmails Henry Frankenstein into making the female (Morton 67). *Bride of Frankenstein* construes the Creature more as an innocent victim, showing that he kills only when provoked. The dramatic focus is on the posse that is after him; as Albert Lavalley explains, "The blindness of the rage expressed toward the Monster and his half-human incomprehension of it thus recaptures much of the bleak horror of the book, its indictment of society, and its picture of man's troubled consciousness" (265). The last days of James Whale as well as some of what inspired him are portrayed in Bill Condon's *Gods and Monsters* (1998), in which Whale's vision of the electrified Creature begins in the gruesome sights of the World War I trenches in which he served.

The *Frankenstein* film that billed itself as most true to the novel is Kenneth Branagh's 1994 *Mary Shelley's "Frankenstein,"* starring Branagh as Victor, Robert De Niro as the Creature, and Helena Bonham-Carter as Elizabeth. Though Branagh tries to stick to Mary Shelley's plot, three-fourths of the way through, the film diverges wildly from the novel and seems most interested in the love affair between Victor and Elizabeth.

And now, just for fun, we offer a quick survey of a few other film versions of Mary Shelley's classic:

- *Torticola contre Frankensburg* (Twisted Neck vs. Frankensburg). France, directed by Paul Paviot. 1952. Lorelei, a girl forced by poverty to live with her uncle at Todenwald ("Forest of Death") Castle, meets a talking cat, a man with a cat's brain, and a monster called Torticola whom the doctor has made from corpses.

- *Frankenstein, el Vampiro y Compañía* (Frankenstein, the Vampire and Company). Mexico, directed by Benito Alazraki. 1962. Loosely based on *Abbott and Costello Meet Frankenstein* (1948). Frankenstein's Creature and Dracula have it out, which is fitting, since they were born on the same night, Shelley with her Creature, and Polidori with the first vampire story.

- *Furankenshutain tai chitei kaijû Baragon* (Frankenstein vs. the Giant Devil Fish). Japan, directed by Ishirô Honda. 1965. Near the end of World War II, the Creature's heart, undying and self-regenerating, is stolen from a lab in Germany and taken to Japan, to be lost in the Hiroshima holocaust. A boy finds it and eats it. He grows into an ugly monster who ravages the mountainsides attacking humans and livestock. During an earthquake an ancient giant lizard, Baragon, is awakened and also commits havoc, but the blame is put upon the Creature. They battle, and Frankenstein's monster is victorious; however, he is swallowed up in an earthquake.

- *The Curse of Frankenstein.* England, directed by Terence Fisher. 1957. Christopher Lee as the Creature and Peter Cushing as Dr. Frankenstein. Gore and sexual suggestion earned it the equivalent of an X rating when it came out. This film inaugurated the endless *Frankenstein* films of the Hammer Studios "House of Horror" that went on to give the world *Frankenstein and the Monster from Hell, Frankenstein Must Be Destroyed, The Revenge of Frankenstein,* and so on.

- *I Was a Teenage Frankenstein.* U.S.A., directed by Herbert L. Strock. 1957. A British doctor descended from Frankenstein visits the United States as a university lecturer and lives in a house with labs and alligators for organ disposal; he uses young men for parts. His creature kills the doctor's mistress and others on campus.

- *Young Frankenstein.* U.S.A., directed by Mel Brooks. 1974. This parody is most people's favorite: Young Frederick Frankenstein (to be pronounced "Fronkensteen") unwillingly confronts his destiny as the descendant of Victor Frankenstein and creates a monster (it helps that his ancestor left behind a book called *How I Did It*). Brooks playfully invokes the Frankensteinian/Freudian opposition between the conscious and unconscious, so that young Frederick stabs himself in the leg with a scalpel during a medical school classroom lecture, just as he is in the act of insisting that he only wishes to preserve life, unlike his evil forebear. The cast includes Gene Wilder as Victor, Peter Boyle as the Creature, and Marty Feldman as the doctor's assistant, Igor (pronounced "Eye-gore," of course), along with such other film notables as Teri Garr, Cloris Leachman, Madeline Kahn, and Gene Hackman. Filming in black and white, Brooks re-created the *Frankenstein* laboratory using the same equipment from the original Whale *Frankenstein.*
- *Fanny Hill Meets Dr. Erotico.* U.S.A., directed by Barry Mahon. 1967. Hoping to find Lady Chatterly, Fanny Hill encounters Dr. Erotico at a castle where he has created a Frankenstein monster. She accidentally throws the switch; the monster awakens and falls in love with her. He kills the master's lesbian maid who also tries to make love to Fanny. The monster dies in a shack set ablaze by villagers.
- *Andy Warhol's Frankenstein.* U.S.A./Italy, directed by Antonio Margheriti and Paul Morrissey. 1974. 3D Color. Baron Frankenstein believes sex is dirty and gets his thrills disemboweling female corpses. He makes two zombies, one male and one female, and wants to mate them to make a superrace. Cult classic.
- *Blade Runner.* U.S.A., directed by Ridley Scott. 1982. One of the most successful films of the 1980s and the forerunner of the *Terminator, Alien,* and the *Matrix* films, *Blade Runner* was an adaptation of Philip K. Dick's *Do Androids Dream of Electric Sheep?* (1968). The film portrays the struggle between bosses and workers as do the themes of *Frankenstein.* "Replicants" are adult workers whose bodies have been manufactured by the "Corporation" to work at dangerous jobs in colony worlds far from civilization, their false memories of an entire life are wired in. They are "retired" (killed) at four years old. Stars Harrison Ford, Rutger Hauer, Daryl Hannah.
- *Blackenstein.* U.S.A., directed by William A. Levey. 1973. Doctor Stein grows new limbs for a Vietnam vet, Eddie, but his assistant Malcolm falls in love with Eddie's fiancée, Winifred, and turns Eddie into a murderous monster. Eddie kills Malcolm, who has tried to rape Winifred, among others. Vintage blaxploitation.
- *Frankenstein Unbound.* U.S.A., directed by Roger Corman, 1990. Based on a novel by Brian Aldiss, the film features John Hurt as Dr. Joe Buchanan, a scientist in the year 2031 who is working on a new secret weapon for the government that dispatches enemies by sending them into another

time. Buchanan ends up being randomly dispatched by his machine and going back two hundred years to find himself in the part of Shelley's novel where the younger brother of Dr. Victor Frankenstein (Raul Julia) has been killed by the creature (Nick Brimble). Buchanan runs into Mary Shelley (Bridget Fonda), Lord Byron (Jason Patric), and Percy Shelley (Michael Hutchence).

- *The 6th Day.* U.S.A., directed by Roger Spottiswoode, 2000. Arnold Schwarzenegger, who starred as a terrifying Frankensteinian robot in his first *Terminator* film (1984), plays a more sympathetic role in *The 6th Day*, battling to save humankind from a megalomaniacal tycoon (Robert Duvall) who plots to rule the world with human clones, including one of our hero.

d. Television Adaptations   *Frankenstein* has surfaced in hundreds of television adaptations, including *Night Gallery, The Addams Family, The Munsters, Star Trek: The Next Generation, Scooby-Doo, Frankenstein Jr. and the Impossibles, Alvin and the Chipmunks, The Simpsons, Wishbone,* and so on. Notable television Creatures have

Figure 9.1. Engraving in Luigi Galvani (1737–1798), *De Viribus Electricitatis in Motu Musculari*, 1742. Artist Unknown. Physicians like Galvani excited wonder in the 18th century with experiments upon animals and humans that used electricity to create movements by dead bodies.
Courtesy National Library of Medicine.

included Bo Svenson, Randy Quaid, David Warner, and Ian Holm. Perhaps the most authentic television version was *Frankenstein: The True Story* (NBC 1972), with script writing by Christopher Isherwood.

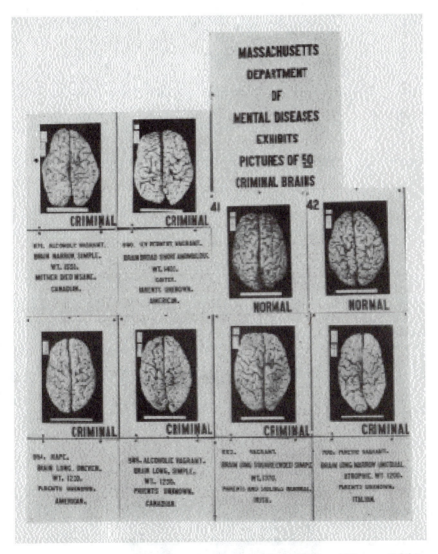

Figure 9.2. Harry H. Laughlin, *Massachusetts Department of Mental Diseases Exhibits: Pictures of 50 Criminal Brains.* Second International Exhibition of Eugenics, 1921. Baltimore, MD: Williams & Wilkins Co., 1923. Just as the "abnormal" brain is blamed in many *Frankenstein* films that followed *Bride of Frankenstein* (1935), U.S. eugenicists had been seeking to explain criminal behavior as inherent in certain "types" of brains, including racial types.
Courtesy of Pennsylvania State University Libraries.

Figure 9.3. *The Edison Kinelogram* advertised the first film of *Frankenstein* made by Thomas Edison in 1910. It starred Charles Stanton Ogle as the Creature, a grotesque performance surrounded with psychologically suggestive visual images.
Edison National Historic Park, New Jersey. Courtesy Billy Rose Collection, New York Public Library.

Figure 9.4. The best-known monster (and literary character) in the world? Boris Karloff as the Creature in James Whale's *Frankenstein* (1931).
Courtesy Photofest.

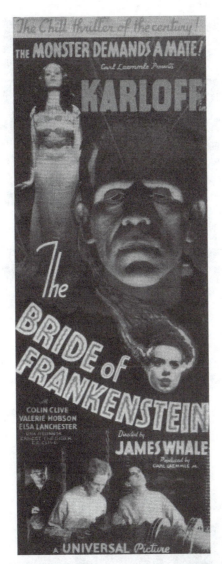

Figure 9.5. Poster for *The Bride of Frankenstein* (1935), directed by James Whale. Elsa Lanchester played both Mary Shelley and the Creature's Bride. Whale explored the story further, especially psychologically and sexually, though he also came up with the "abnormal brain" idea to ameliorate the blame upon Victor.
Courtesy Photofest.

Figure 9.6. Victor Frankenstein (Kenneth Branagh) embraces Elizabeth (Helena Bonham-Carter) on their ill-fated wedding night in Branagh's romantic film version *Mary Shelley's "Frankenstein"* (1994).
Courtesy Photofest.

Figure 9.7. Robert De Niro as the Creature in Kenneth Branagh's *Mary Shelley's "Frankenstein"* (1994). De Niro was an exceptionally articulate Creature, a departure from most film characterizations.
Courtesy Photofest.

D. Postmodern Goodman Brown

Postmodernist critics search out multivalence, ambiguity, epistemological uncertainties, self-referentiality, and indeterminacy. "Young Goodman Brown" has them all. The story concerns an attempt at a complete knowledge of humanity by a man who seems to achieve it, only to have it blight his soul. Like other hubristic strivers in Hawthorne's works—Aylmer, Rappaccini, Chillingworth—Brown's drive to use his knowledge leads only to darkness and death.

Writing of Brown's dilemma, critic Joseph Alkana asks, "When social judgments are themselves suspect, on what bases are individual insights to be validated?" (58). Certainly the lack of a coherent social structure contributes to Brown's weakness of mind. Hawthorne suggests that the kind of knowledge Brown wins cannot be successful without a sense of the knowledge of others, and such a communal verification of truth might seem unavailable to him. This is because the Puritan mindset forbade questions that did not have clear answers, questions that reflect doubt (or "otherness"). But in this tale, refusing to have doubts creates only the deepest suspicion about the human race without providing any kind of answer at all.

All of Hawthorne's stories are about telling and reading stories, for he saw the role of the author as the creator of the tale but not its interpreter. His narrators repeatedly say things like "one might think" or "it might have been." He uses the ruse of Surveyor Pue's manuscript in *The Scarlet Letter* to disparage his own talent. In the Preface to *The Blithedale Romance* he also casts doubt on his veracity as a narrator—but this is by design. The narrator of "Young Goodman Brown" will not even tell the reader whether Brown's experience was real or a dream. Hawthorne's ambiguity and other seemingly postmodern techniques mesh well with his sense of the **Gothic** and supernatural. How much of life, or of oneself, can one really know? Interestingly, he is the first American writer to use the term "unconscious" in its psychological sense. In his book *Hawthorne*, Henry James compliments Hawthorne when he observes that he "was not a man with a literary theory; he was guiltless of a system." Hawthorne is "silent, diffident, more inclined to hesitate—to watch, and wait, and meditate—than to produce himself, and fonder, on almost any occasion, of being absent more than of being present" (3–4, 22–23).

Before 1800, most American thinkers approached the problem of knowledge like other human problems, as a theological one; later, however, with writers such as Emerson, Thoreau, Melville, and Hawthorne, the question of how to know God broadens into the question of how to know oneself. Theology is then accompanied and to some sense replaced by psychology. Hawthorne secularizes such theological issues as the "Unforgivable Sin" (blasphemy against the Holy Spirit) into what he called the "Sin of Objectiflcation," or looking at another human being as an object of one's own interests. Knowledge is traditionally seen as objective and unidirectional (*epistemology*), but with the nineteenth-century "higher criticism" of the Bible— that is, interpretation of the Bible instead of literalism—the term *hermeneutics*

Figure 9.8. Dolly, the sheep cloned in 1996 by the Roslin Institute in Edinburgh, Scotland, was the first animal cloned from a cell taken from an adult animal. Until Dolly, most biologists thought the cells in our bodies were fixed in their roles: Dolly's creation showed this was not the case.
Courtesy Roslin Institute.

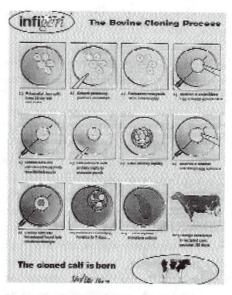

Figure 9.9. "The Bovine Cloning Process." Cloning has its own ethical issues and paved the way for debate on such questions as stem cell research.
Courtesy Roslin Institute.

described a different kind of knowledge, one of communal assent with no final answer, a contingent, interpretive knowledge that leaves knowledge open. There are limits to knowledge, Hawthorne suggests, and the penalty for crossing those limits is dire. When one says one "knows" someone, in Hawthorne's world this is a sign of sin.

Let us note some especially postmodern moments of doubt in "Young Goodman Brown." The story opens with Faith's doubts (and Brown's) about her husband's mission to the forest. The forest itself is an image of darkness and unknowable dangers. Faith brings up the possibility that Brown's journey was all a dream by mentioning that it is bedtime and that she may have bad dreams. As he progresses on his journey, everyone he sees makes him question his senses. The devil looks like an elegant older man, in fact, like Brown's father and grandfather. Goody Cloyse and Deacon Gookin, who taught him religion, are rank devil-worshippers. He worries " 'there may be a devilish Indian behind every tree.... What if the devil himself should be at my very elbow!' " But the irony of the story is that the devil is even closer than that: "In truth, all through the haunted forest there could be nothing more frightful than the figure of Goodman Brown.... The fiend in his own shape is less hideous than when he rages in the breast of man." However, he does not heed the (ironic) lesson in the devil's sermon, that they are all part of the "communion of the human race." Brown returns home not just with a taste of evil but with the terrible evil within of his harsh judgments of one and all. The reader is prevented from doing so, however, by the narrator's ambiguity. Was it all a dream? "Be it so, if you will." Was it a joke? If so, is it the author's hoax or his reader's? Why would he do this?

E. "Telling the Truth, Mainly": Tricksterism in *Huckleberry Finn*

The issue that has worried readers of *Huckleberry Finn* most is race, and how it is presented in the closing chapters at the Phelps Farm. After Jim has been presented as a fully realized human being, after Huck has sworn to go to hell rather than desert his friend, after all the comradeship and narrow escapes on the river, Twain again turns on the slapstick and allows Huck and Tom to torment Jim at the Phelps Farm and make him appear foolish. Furthermore, in a book often described as the greatest American novel and one of literature's most eloquent indictments of racism, one finds racist jokes and epithets throughout, as well as Edward Windsor Kemble's 1885 illustrations of Jim as a shabby, servile simpleton.

The problems of race and the Phelps Farm episodes have been addressed by such distinguished American critics as T. S. Eliot, Lionel Trilling, Leo Marx, James M. Cox, and Roy Harvey Pearce. Some see the ending as "fatal" to the book, a cop-out by the author. Perhaps he quit writing *Huckleberry Finn* for two years because he got Huck and Jim south of Cairo, Illinois, in Chapter 15. Perhaps Twain was just in a hurry to get it finished when he did return to it, and "forgot" about the themes of the first half. On the other hand, other critics find the ending a brilliant indictment of racism and also of Tom Sawyer's brand of **romanticism**, thus true to the book's overall satire. Still others add that it is the only appropriate ending, given Twain's rejection of romanticism; it is an antiheroic and anticlimactic conclusion that preserves Huck's essential freedom.

The controversies over race and the ending have increased. *Huckleberry Finn* has been banned in certain school districts, and numerous high school teachers who would be allowed to teach it do not because it is very difficult to deal with race as presented by the book, especially the word *nigger*. Of course, it was banned when it came out too, but then it was thought that it would encourage juvenile delinquency, smoking, and irreligion. It was and is a radical book; Twain would be delighted to know that it is still causing trouble.

Julius Lester calls it a "dangerous" book, arguing that Twain does not take Jim or black people seriously at all; Jim is the typical "good nigger," a plaything for the boys. He finds it incredible that Jim would be so naïve. For him, even the "lighting out for the territory" is a wrongful idealization of a white male fantasy of escaping responsibility, reflecting Twain's "contempt for humanity" (344, 347–48). But Justin Kaplan sees it quite differently: it is a "bitter irony" that the book has been called racist; it is instead a "savage indictment of a society that accepted slavery as a way of life." Huck and Jim are both moral, loyal, truthful, and Jim is "unquestionably the best person in the book." As to slavery, he finds Twain's portrait much more realistic and less stereotyped than Harriett Beecher Stowe's: "One has to be deliberately dense to miss the point Mark Twain is making..." (355–57). Toni Morrison urges that we *teach the controversy,* to release the novel from its "clutch of sentimental nostrums about lighting out to the territory, river gods, and the fundamental innocence of Americanness" and instead "incorporate its contestatory, combative critique of antebellum America" (54–57).

One of the most hotly debated contributions to scholarship on *Huckleberry Finn* has been Shelley Fisher Fishkin's *Was Huck Black? Mark Twain and African-American Voices.* Fishkin argues that Twain based Huck's voice on a ten-year-old black boy named Jimmy, whom he met two years before he published *The Adventures of Tom Sawyer.* Twain himself described Jimmy as a "bright, simple, guileless little darkey boy...ten years old—a wide-eyed, observant little chap,...the most exhaustless talker I ever came across" ("Sociable Jimmy," *New York Times,* 29 November 1874). This was the first item Twain published dominated by the voice of a child. So perhaps in addition to Tom Blankenship, a poor boy with a drunken father in Hannibal who has been described as a source for Huck, "Sociable Jimmy" should take his place as a contributor to "a measure of racial alchemy unparalleled in American literature" (Fishkin 14–15, 80).

In any case Huck's and Jim's voices are *culturally constructed* voices with many sources in Twain's milieu, including both whites and African Americans from such sources as minstrel shows, slave narratives, and African oral traditions, especially the trickster tale and the tall tale. Growing up in the South and listening to the tales of older slaves such as Henry, whom he knew from visits to an uncle's farm, Twain absorbed much of African and African-American culture, as did many other white children around him, and Jim's ideas engage Huck just as he joins him as a conversational partner. Huck does not look beneath the surface: for example, Jim's apparent gullibility about night-riders with witches might be laughed at as an example of his simple-mindedness. However, the tale of being "ridden by witches" has been recorded repeatedly by folklorists, and it may also relate to his fear of night-riders, the avenging ancestors of the Ku Klux Klan, who would ride at night committing violence against blacks whom they mistrusted. Similarly, when Jim says he has always been good to dead people, this may be read as foolish superstition; however, on the west coast of Africa there is a large range of burial practices and spiritual beliefs involving communication with the departed, long enshrined in cultural practice (Fishkin 85).

Was Huck "black"? We find it an intriguing question. Perhaps he was not "black" in the sense of being mostly inspired by "Sociable Jimmy," but he was a Southerner and an American, absorbing not only black voices and folktales, but also American native folklore, journalism, and frontier characters like those created by Johnson Jones Hooper and George Washington Harris, and a long list of Old World sources, including the Bible, Shakespeare, Calvinism, and traditions of satire, in short, Twain's many cultures as well.

For us, the most obvious way to assess the influences and currents of these characters is to look at what they have in common. Huck's voice is clearly the voice of a Trickster. Not surprisingly, as in Jim's story in the beginning, Trickster stories dominate the various streams of literary tradition to which Twain was most drawn.

Huckleberry Finn is full of evasions, impersonations, false leads, and unexpected reversals. Huck acts as Trickster, but the figure appears in many incarnations throughout the book, in Tom, Jim, and the King and the Duke, primarily. Known mainly to white Americans in Twain's day and ours through the Uncle Remus stories of Brer Rabbit, written by Joel Chandler Harris, the Trickster is important to African-American and Native American literatures, as well as Western American literatures in the tall tale, the hillbilly tale, and other forms of frontier humor. As a voice from outside middle-class culture, the Trickster helps construct Huck's honest, unsparing assessment of society around him. Paradoxically, the lying Trickster is ultimately a redemptive figure; his uncorrupted critique of social mores and prejudices may just "tell the truth," as Huck says Twain "mainly" does in the first paragraph of the novel.

As Elizabeth Ammons notes, the Trickster is one of the most ancient of mythic characters and one of the most unruly. Trickster's transgressions, whether stealing fire from Heaven or outwitting rivals, are an integral part of communal life in many cultures: disruptive though Trickster is, "the dynamic is one of interaction" (in Ammons and Parks vii, ix). The basic pattern or "tale type," as folklorists say, of the Trickster in Native American literatures is that "Trickster the Overreacher," prompted by his appetites, fixes on a goal, but to get it he will have to transform himself radically or change society's norms. He attempts his goal but fails; sometimes he is punished or killed, but he always returns again to engage in other forbidden activities. Native American

Trickster stories, often in long "cycles," tell of a discrete cultural scene—hosting customs or religious rituals—disrupted by Trickster. Trickster spoofs and exposes institutionalized powers but also addresses the limitations of human endeavor, especially the attempt to impose order on human nature (Wiget 91, 94). (Think of Huck and Tom raiding the Sunday School picnic to attack "Spaniards and A-rabs.")

In contrast, according to John Roberts, the African-American Trickster is in control of his situation; he manipulates people at will. He is indifferent to everything but making fools out of people or animals; yet his is somehow also a normative, even heroic action. African-American Trickster tales emphasize the importance of creativity and inventiveness in dealing with situations peculiar to slavery. The focus on obtaining food in the stories of clever slaves is a historical record of the fact that food was often scanty or even absent because of shortages imposed by uncaring masters or chiefs. Tricksterism was thus a justifiable response to oppression, a mode of survival. Trickster tales assert the right of the individual to contest the irrational authority of religious ritual that benefited those at the top of the social scale while those at the bottom survived only on their own wits (see "The African American Trickster" 97–106, 111; *From Trickster to Badman* 35–37). One thinks of Huck's lies of survival along the river.

"The Signifying Monkey" is an important trope of the African-American Trickster, described by Henry Louis Gates, Jr., as one who "dwells at the margins of discourse, ever punning, ever troping, ever embodying the ambiguities of language." "Signifying" may consist of such black vernacular practices as "testifying," playing with someone's name, rapping, playing the dozens, and giving back-handed compliments. The person signifying may goad, taunt, cajole, needle, or lie to his interlocutor, using what Roger D. Abrahams calls a "language of implication," the technique of "indirect argument." He may ask for a piece of cake by saying that "my brother wants a piece of cake," or make fun of a policeman by copying his speech or gestures behind his back (Gates, *The Signifying Monkey* 51–52; Abrahams 12).

Tom and Huck partake of the various satiric features of these Trickster traditions, including upsetting cultural norms, escaping punishment, and challenging religious authority, so that at times Huck is like the socially conscious Native Trickster, while Tom more resembles the manipulative African trickster, but at other times they trade roles. The boys know the value of never *seeming* to be a Trickster, of playing dumb and retaining control over a situation that seems on the surface to have them at its mercy.

Pranks, disguises, superstitions, prayers and spells, the hair-ball, con games, playacting, faked death, cross-dressing, outright rebellion, social humbuggery, hypocrisy, and delusion: from Tom Sawyer's gang in Chapter 2 to old Sis Hotchkiss's imagined cabin full of forty "niggers crazy's Nebokoodneezer" in Chapter 41, the folk Trickster shows himself in *Huckleberry Finn*. And he is there even before the story begins. On the back of the title page, along with the tongue-in-cheek "Explanatory" concerning dialects, we find the following "Notice":

Persons attempting to find a motive in this narrative will be prosecuted; persons attempting to find a moral in it will be banished; persons attempting to find a plot in it will be shot.

BY ORDER OF THE AUTHOR
Per G.G., CHIEF OF ORDNANCE

Even for an avowed satirist, this is a risky way to win over readers. The "Explanatory" is a warning to readers that what appears to be "true" may not be; an "authentic" voice may be a fake. And then the reader is threatened with extreme sanctions against finding a moral. Do we take this as encouragement to find a moral, or should we leave it at face value and credit Twain with something more than a simple moral? The "Explanatory" doesn't explain, and the "Notice" doesn't really tell us what to watch for, since it dismisses plot, motive, and moral altogether.

The first paragraph of the text also displays interesting (and tricky) ambiguities:

You don't know about me without you have read a book by the name of "The Adventures of Tom Sawyer," but that ain't no matter. That book was made by Mr. Mark Twain, and he told the truth, mainly. There was things which he stretched, but mainly he told the truth. That is nothing. I never seen anybody but lied, one time or another, without it was Aunt Polly, or the widow, or maybe Mary. Aunt Polly—Tom's Aunt Polly, she is—and Mary, and the Widow Douglas, is all told about in that book—which is mostly a true book; with some stretchers, as I said before.

Here is a character speaking as though he is writing the present book (and he later complains of how hard it was to do), but who confesses that his existence arises from another book by Mark Twain, who "mainly" told the truth (but also lied) about events which he, Huck, knows as facts. Several layers of narrative reality are present. What might "truth" be in such an environment?

Lying forms the basis for most episodes in the novel, and obviously the lies point downriver to the one huge lie of slavery. Huck's pattern of lying poses his fictions against the lies of society—white superiority, self-righteousness, social snobbery, confidence games, and a hundred others. Huck's lying leaves a negative space for readers to fill in the "truth" as they see it.

Huck's lies are generally about personal identity, and they are directed at survival for himself and Jim. They create alternate worlds in which he (and sometimes Jim) has a more stable identity and a family. Huck's lies thus express his desire for community, but at other times his lies preserve a sense of freedom beyond communal confines. This is most apparent when he lies for the fun of it, and occasionally he goes too far and gets caught. But he knows when that is happening, unlike Tom, who lies purely for fun and doesn't seem to know the difference between truth and fiction. Huck's lies are also unlike those of the King and the Duke, who lie only for profit. Typical of the novel's satiric reversals, Huck's essential goodness is confirmed when lawyer Levi Bell examines Huck and finds him too inexperienced a liar to be blamed. Unlike the Duke and the King, Huck is also capable of lying for altruistic reasons, as when he saves the robbers trapped aboard the *Sir Walter Scott.*

But then there is the bad lie. In Chapter 15 Huck fools Jim into thinking that their separation in the fog was only a dream, and he then lets Jim "'terpret" it. "Oh well, that's all interpreted well enough," Huck laughs, "but what does *these* things stand for?" Huck gestures at the leaves and rubbish on the raft and the smashed oar: "Jim looked at the trash, and then looked at me, and back at the trash again.... He looked at me steady, without ever smiling, and says: 'What do dey stan' for? I's gwyne to tell you.... Dat truck dah is trash; en trash is what people is dat puts dirt on the head er dey fren's en makes 'em ashamed.'" Huck says that he has to "work himself up to go and apologize to a nigger," but that "I warn't ever sorry for it afterwards, neither. I didn't do him no more mean tricks, and I wouldn't done that one if I'd a knowed it would make him feel that way."

This moment is as morally significant to Huck as his later famous decision not to "pray a lie" and to go to hell rather than betray Jim, and it leads directly to this second episode of moral growth. Huck learns the difference between tricks that are good and tricks that are harmful; when he says he will play no more mean tricks on Jim, he changes, but the world around him does not. When he does play mean tricks later on, including not telling Jim at first that the King and the Duke are frauds, or acquiescing in their binding Jim and dressing him as King Lear, and finally going along with Tom's imprisonment of Jim at the Phelps Farm, we may wonder at his promise and at Twain's narrative "tricks." Huck's ridiculous lies to the "Harelip" about his living in England and going to church with "William the Fourth" betray his corruption at the hands of the King and the Duke and his resulting absurdity. Mary Jane Wilks prevents him from sharing the fate of the King and Duke, but he is more fragile than we want him to be when again assaulted by the lies of bourgeois society. Even so, despite all the layers of trickiness, the reader is certain of Huck's essential innocence and basic honesty. The greatest trick, or irony, of course, is that Huck fails to realize that—contrary to what he has been taught by society—he is a profoundly moral being.

F. Cultures in Conflict: A Story Looks at Cultural Change

Alice Walker's "Everyday Use": represents an array of cultures and subcultures— some dominant, some lost or denied, all in some sort of conflict.

In an earlier period of American literature—the late nineteenth century, for example—Walker's depiction of the rural area with a predominantly black population might have been written as **local color**: the image of the house without real windows, the cow, the swept yard that is a kind of extension of the house, the conventional items found in such a house (the quilts, the benches used in place of chairs, the churn, the snuff). Alternatively, one can imagine these details as part of photographs taken for some WPA project, and now lodged in an archival collection, shown occasionally in some museum display. The timing would be about right: the mother in "Everyday Use" apparently was in the second grade in 1927, a couple of years before the crash that led to the Great Depression of the 1930s.

But this is not a local color story. Photographs are in fact being taken in the story, but they are only Polaroids to be part of the collection of one of the daughters, possibly just for her own use. She carefully snaps pictures that show her mother in front of the house, at one point managing to get mother, house, and cow all in the same shot. This daughter, Dee, has come back to visit her mother and her sister, but now Dee represents a culture quite different from what she left behind when she went to college. Her Polaroid and the automobile in which she has returned are distinctly different from what her mother and sister Maggie have as their conveniences and luxuries—a cool spot in the yard, some quilts, some snuff. Local color there is, but not simply as a variant of early realism. Rather, it serves to contrast a traditional culture with an emerging consciousness.

Dee has been sent to college where she has gotten an education. Her opportunity has come from her mother and her mother's church, which had the foresight to send her away so that she could better reach her potential. The traditional culture that she has left behind is the very culture that has enabled her to be part of a different world, a fact about which she seems to be at best dimly aware. But the culture of college is not the only new culture with which she has allied herself. Somewhat to the dismay of her mother and her sister, Dee has also attached herself to a subculture within a new world of African Americans who desire not only to break with the past of economic, social, and psychological hardship (and legalized slavery before that), but also to seek to reconnect with African roots. The phenomenon of seeking one's roots is of course not unique to late-twentieth-century American life (genealogical study has been around a long time), but the particular kind of seeking that is evident in this story is a late-twentieth-century phenomenon that manifested itself especially in the use of words and names, and sometimes of hair styles and clothing, indigenous not to America but to Africa.

So we watch Dee and her friend drive up to visit the mother and Maggie. Dee's hair "stands straight up like the wool on a sheep." She says "Wa-su-zo-Tean-o!" Her friend has "hair to his navel" and says, "Asalamalakim, my mother and sister." Dee denies her earlier name: "No, Mama. Not 'Dee,' Wangero Leewanika Kemanjo!" The mother asks what happened to "Dee," and her daughter answers, "She's dead. I couldn't bear it any longer being named after the people who oppress me." Clearly, for Dee her earlier name (in spite of her mother's effort to show its family history) represents the past, the oppressive culture of the dominant majority, from which she now seeks to separate herself so as to build on her roots as she now sees them.

Beginning in the 1960s some African Americans adopted African names to replace their given names. The names chosen reflected either an African pattern or a Muslim one, or both. The phenomenon became widespread, and various public figures adopted such names. Among them were major athletes like Muhammad Ali, who began his career as Cassius Clay, and Kareem Abdul-Jabbar, who was Lew Alcindor when he played college basketball in the sixties. Among literary figures we have Amiri Baraka, who earlier had published dramas as LeRoi Jones.

Another cultural item to be noted in Dee's rejoinder to her mother is the oppressiveness of the socioeconomics of their world. Dee, in urging a new name for herself upon her mother, says, "[Dee's] dead. I couldn't bear it any longer being named after the people who oppress me." "Oppression" is the operative concept here, clearly tied to the name Dee associates with her past. And with oppression we can see a connection that a Marxist or a new historical critical approach can bring to bear on the story (see Chapter 4). We need only recall the economic details of slavery, of the Jim Crow era that followed, or of the continuing disparity between income levels of white Americans and African Americans. The house that Dee's mother and sister live in is obviously the antithesis of the antebellum homes nearby.

In review, the collocation of the name that Dee asserts and the word "oppress" invites specific insights in a cultural studies approach to the story. But the story is not necessarily—or not only—a Marxist story. It is a story of cultures in conflict.

As such, it raises questions beyond oppression and economics, important though they may be. It raises a question of how one finds one's culture, one's roots. Dee has adopted a name that shows her resistance to the socioeconomic culture that she calls oppressive. Still, is a newly adopted culture with a claim on a world half a world away truly a "culture"? Rather, some would argue that a culture is something lived, part and parcel of one's everyday existence; it is almost as if one's lived culture must be below the level of consciousness if it is to be authentic. It must be natural; it must simply "be." When Dee and her friend use strange words to greet the mother and Maggie and when they announce their names (apparently recently adopted, at least by Dee), this is not the culture of the mother—nor perhaps of Africa either. But it does seem to be akin to a movement about which we hear within the story. The mother alludes to "those beef-cattle peoples down the road," who also "said 'Asalamalakim' when they met you, too." Dee's friend apparently knows of these Black Muslims who represent another post-1960s subculture and of some kind of movement associated with them, for he says, "I accept some of their doctrines, but farming and raising cattle is not my style." So even here we have a further complication of cultures or subcultures. Do they represent a more authentic Africanist past than Dee? Does Dee's mother see the new ideas as foreign to her? Is she more attuned to what she has known than to Dee's efforts to take on a new identity? It would seem so.

Because the story is told from the point of view of the mother, with her somewhat jaundiced view of what Dee has done and has become, we must be cautious about assuming an authorial favoritism toward any one view of which culture or subculture is "right." Rather, it seems more appropriate to say that what we have is an insight into late-twentieth-century shifts in America.

Much earlier in the century, the shift from an agrarian to an industrial-commercial base was an obvious phenomenon of American society. But for black Americans specifically, the shift had come at a markedly slower pace, with less successful results. The mother in "Everyday Use" seems not too eager to participate in that shift, even though she and her church furthered Dee's participation. Dee, on the other hand, is clearly eager for it. The Polaroid camera is an objective symbol of the shift, just as much as keeping the quilts for Maggie suggests the mother's reticence to make the change. The situation is complex, however, because Dee is also trying to hold on to a bit of the old culture, even as she converts its objective symbols to "something artistic," thus depriving them of their original vitality as "useful" objects.

There is no person in the story who directly or indirectly represents the dominant or majority white culture, but allusions to the dominant culture form an obvious and major subtext for the story. The most extended passage comes early in the story—the dream that the mother reports about seeing herself as part of a television show, something like what she associates with Johnny Carson. In that dream she would take on characteristics that daughter Dee would want her to have—"a hundred pounds lighter, my skin like an uncooked barley pancake. My hair glistens in the hot bright lights. Johnny Carson has much to do to keep up with my quick and witty tongue." But she knows that this is a dream, an entry into another culture that will not happen for her. "Who can even imagine me looking a strange white man in the eye?" There is some indication that the dominant culture was little interested in educating the blacks: "After second grade," the mother says, "the school was closed down. Don't ask me why: in 1927 colored asked fewer questions than they do now." Later, Dee directly mentions "the people who oppress me," as we have already noted.

In summary, "Everyday Use" represents a variety of cultures and subcultures, in varying degrees of tension among them: the dominant, white majority, not directly represented in the story, but important throughout; a black culture that is somewhat typical of the agrarian South; the changing and more assertive subgroup that is entering (or creating) a different culture from that earlier tradition; and a subset of this subgroup that associates itself with a different continent—but which is not even then homogeneous, as Dee's friend indicates about not accepting all of "their doctrines." This story may not be as oriented toward action or a political agenda as some pieces of literature might be because it seems to have a certain degree of ambiguity: neither Dee nor her mother is wholly right or wholly wrong. Nevertheless, the close reader must be aware of the social, economic, and political forces at work during the latter part of the twentieth century if the full impact of the story is to be appreciated.

V. SUMMARY OF KEY POINTS

- Cultural studies is not a discrete approach but a set of practices, and it transcends the limits of disciplines, as it is made up of elements of Marxism, poststructuralism, postmodernism, gender studies, anthropology, race and ethnic studies, popular culture and postcolonialist studies.
- Cultural studies is politically engaged.
- Cultural studies denies the separation of high and popular culture.
- Critics analyze not just the text but its modes of literary production and circulation.

- U. S. Ethnic Studies includes primarily African-American, Latina/o, Native American, and Asian American authors.
- Postmodernism celebrates the act of dismembering traditions of modernism and all previous periods; in literature postmodernism appears in such forms as stream-of-consciousness writing, pastische, and metafiction, among others.
- Important postmodernist critics include Frederic Jameson, Jean-François Lyotard, Jean Baudrillard, Ihab Hassan, Terry Eagleton, and others.
- Popular culture studies carry out production, textual, audience, and historical analyses.

VI. LIMITATIONS OF CULTURAL STUDIES

The weaknesses of cultural studies lie in its very strengths, particularly its emphasis upon diversity of approach and subject matter. Cultural studies can at times seem merely an intellectual smorgasbord in which the critic blithely combines artful helpings of texts and objects and then "finds" deep connections between them, without adequately researching what a culture means or how cultures have interacted. To put it bluntly, cultural studies is not always fueled by the kind of hard research (including scientifically collected data) that historians have traditionally practiced to analyze "culture." Cultural studies practitioners often know a lot of interesting things and possess the intellectual ability to play them off interestingly against each other, but they sometimes lack adequate knowledge of the "deep play" of meanings or "thick description" of a culture that ethnographer Clifford Geertz identified in his studies of the Balinese. Sometimes students complain that professors who overemphasize cultural studies tend to downplay the necessity of reading the classics, and that they sometimes coerce students into "politically correct" views.

David Richter describes cultural studies as "about whatever is happening at the moment, rather than about a body of texts created in the past. 'Happening' topics, generally speaking, are the mass media themselves, which, in a postmodern culture, dominate the cultural lives of its inhabitants, or topics that have been valorized by the mass media." But he goes on to observe that if this seems trivial, the strength of cultural studies is its "relentlessly critical attitude toward journalism, publishing, cinema, television, and other forms of mass media, whose seemingly transparent windows through which we view 'reality' probably constitute the most blatant and pervasive mode of false consciousness of our era" (Richter 1218). If we are tempted to dismiss popular culture, it is also worth remembering that when works like *Hamlet* or *Huckleberry Finn* were written, they were not intended for elite discussions in English classrooms, but exactly for popular consumption.

Defenders of tradition and advocates of cultural studies are waging what is sometimes called the "culture wars" of academia. On the one hand are offered impassioned defenses of humanism as the foundation, since the time of the ancient Greeks, of Western civilization and modern democracy. On the other hand, as

Marxist theorist Terry Eagleton has written, the current "crisis" in the humanities can be seen as a failure of the humanities; this "body of discourses" about "imperishable" values has demonstrably negated those very values in its practices.

Whatever the emphasis, cultural studies makes available one more approach—and several methodologies—to address these questions.

QUICK REFERENCE

Abrahams, Roger D., ed. *Afro-American Folktales: Stories from Black Traditions in the New World*. New York: Pantheon, 1985.

Adorno, Theodor. *The Adorno Reader*. Ed. Brian O'Connor. London: Blackwell, 2000.

Althusser, Louis. *For Marx*. Trans. Ben Brewster. New York: Pantheon, 1969.

Alkana, Joseph. *The Social Self: Hawthorne, Howells, William James, and Nineteenth-Century Psychology*. Lexington: University Press of Kentucky, 1997.

Allen, Paula Gunn. "The Sacred Hoop: A Contemporary Perspective." In *The Ecocriticism Reader: Landmarks in Literary Ecology*. Ed. Cheryll Glotfelty and Harold Fromm. Athens and London: University of Georgia, 1996.

Ammons, Elizabeth, and Annette White Parks, eds. *Tricksterism in Turn-of-the-Century American Literature: A Multicultural Perspective*. Hanover, MA: Tufts University Press, 1994.

An Anthology of Interracial Literature: Black-White Contacts in the Old World and the New. New York: New York University Press, 2004.

Andrews, William. "The Representation of Slavery and Afro-American Literary Realism." In *African American Autobiography: A Collection of Critical Essays*. Ed. William L. Andrews. Englewood Cliffs, N. J: Prentice Hall, 1993.

Anzaldúa, Gloria. *Borderlands/La Frontera: The New Mestiza*. 1987 Rpt. 2nd edn. San Francisco: Aunt Lute Books, 1999.

Appiah, Kwame Anthony. *In My Father's House*. New York: Oxford University Press, 1992.

———. "The State and the Shaping of Identity." In *The Tanner Lectures on Human Values*. Vol. 23. Ed. Grethe B. Peterson. Salt Lake City: University of Utah Press, 2002, 234–99.

Ashcroft, Bill, Gareth Griffiths, Helen Tiffin, and Sarah Menin, eds. *The Empire Writes Back: Theory and Practice in Post-Colonial Literatures*. New York: Routledge, 2000.

Baber, Kristine M., and Colleen I. Murray. "A Postmodern Feminist Approach to Teaching Human Sexuality." *Family Relations* 50, 1 (January 2001): 23–33.

Baker, Houston A., Jr. *Blues, Ideology, and Afro-American Literature: A Vernacular Theory*. Chicago, Ill.: University of Chicago Press, 1984.

Bakhtin, Mikhail. *The Dialogic Imagination: Four Essays*. Ed. Michael Holquist. Trans. Caryl Emerson. Austin: University of Texas Press, 1981.

Baksh-Soodeen, Rawwida. "Issues of Difference in Contemporary Caribbean Feminism." *Feminist Review*. Special Issue on Rethinking the Caribbean Difference 59 (Summer 1998): 74–85.

Barthes, Roland. *Mythologies*. Trans. Annette Lavers. New York: Hill and Wang, 1972.

Baudrillard, Jean. *Simulations*. Trans. Paul Foss, Paul Patton, and Philip Beitchnan. New York: Semiotext (e), 1981.

Bell, Bernard. *The Afro-American Novel and Its Tradition*. Amherst: University of Massachusetts Press, 1987.

Benjamin, Walter. *Illuminations.* Ed. Hannah Arendt. Trans. H. Zohn. New York: Harcourt, 1968.

Bérubé, Michael. *Public Access: Literary Theory and American Cultural Politics.* London: Verso, 1994.

Bhabha, Homi. *The Location of Culture.* New York: Routledge, 1994.

Botstein, Leon. "The De-Europeanization of American Culture." In Sill et al.

Bourdieu, Pierre. *Outline of a Theory of Practice.* Trans. Richard Nice. Cambridge Studies in Social Anthropology, no. 16. Cambridge: Cambridge University Press, 1977.

Brantlinger, Patrick. *Crusoe's Footprints: Cultural Studies in Britain and America.* New York: Routledge, 1990.

Brody, Jules. "The Resurrection of the Body: A New Reading of Marvell's 'To His Coy Mistress.'" *ELH* 56, no. 1 (1986): 53–80.

Bruce, Susan. "The Flying Island and Female Anatomy: Gynaecology and Power in *Gulliver's Travels.*" *Genders* 2 (July 1988): 60–76.

Cain, William E. "Why English Departments Should Focus on Close Reading, Not Cultural Studies." In *Chronicle of Higher Education* (13 Dec. 1996): B4.

Cantú, Norma. *Canícula: Snapshots of a Girlhood en la frontera.* Albuquerque: University of New Mexico Press, 1994.

Carby, Hazel. *Race Men, The W.E.B. Du Bois Lectures.* Cambridge, Mass.: Harvard University Press, 1998.

Childers, Joseph, and Gary Hentzi, eds. *The Columbia Dictionary of Modern Literary and Cultural Criticism.* New York: Columbia University Press, 1995.

Clifford, James. *The Predicament of Culture: Twentieth-Century Ethnography, Literature, and Art.* Cambridge, Mass.: Harvard University Press, 1988.

Crenshaw, Kimberté, et al., eds. *Critical Race Theory: The Key Writings that Formed the Movement.* New York: New Press, 1995.

Davidson, Cathy N., ed. *Reading in America: Literature and Social History.* Baltimore: Johns Hopkins University Press, 1989.

de Certeau, Michel. *The Practice of Everyday Life.* Trans. Steven F. Rendall. Berkeley: University of California Press, 1984.

Derrida, Jacques. *Of Grammatology.* Trans. Gayatri Chakravorty Spivak. Baltimore: Johns Hopkins University Press, 1974.

———. *Writing and Difference.* Chicago: University of Chicago Press, 1980.

Desmond, Jane C. *Staging Tourism: Bodies on Display from Waikiki to Sea World.* Chicago, IL: University of Chicago Press, 1999.

Du Bois, W. E. Burghardt. *The Souls of Black Folk.* 1903. Reprint. New York: St. Martin's Press, 1997.

Dyer, Richard. *White.* New York: Routledge, 1997.

Eagleton, Terry. "Foreword." In Daniel Cottom, ed. *Social Figures: George Eliot, Social History, and Literary Representation.* Minneapolis: University of Minnesota Press, 1987.

———. *The Illusions of Postmodernism.* Cambridge, Eng.: Blackwell, 1996.

Eco, Umberto. *The Role of the Reader: Explorations in the Semiotics of Texts.* Bloomington: Indiana University Press, 1978.

———. *A Theory of Semotics.* Bloomington: Indiana University Press, 1976.

Edmond, Rod. *Representing the South Pacific: Colonial Discourse from Cook to Gauguin.* Cambridge: Cambridge University Press, 1997.

Ellison, Ralph. *Shadow and Act.* New York: Random House, 1964.

Epstein, Marcus. "Black Libertarian: The Story of Zora Neale Thurston. http://www.lewrockwell.com/orig/epstein2.html.

Fanon, Frantz. *The Wretched of the Earth.* 1961. Reprint. Trans. Constance Farrington. New York: Grove Press, 1986.

Fiedler, Leslie. "Cross the Border—Close that Gap: Post-modernism." In *American Literature Since 1900.* Ed. Marcus Cunliffe. London: Sphere, 344–66.

Fishkin, Shelley Fisher. *Was Huck Black? Mark Twain and African American Voices.* New York: Oxford University Press, 1993.

Fiske, John. *Reading the Popular.* Boston: Unwin, Hyman, 1989.

Flores, Juan, and George Yudice. "Living Borders/Buscando America: Languages of Latino Self-Formation." *Social Text* 24 (1990): 57–84.

Florescu, Radu. *In Search of Frankenstein.* Boston: New York Graphic Society, 1975.

Foster, Frances Smith. *Witnessing Slavery: The Development of Ante-bellum Slave Narratives,* 2d. Ed. Madison: University of Wisconsin Press: 1994.

Foucault, Michel. "What Is an Author?" From *Discipline and Punish;* from *The History of Sexuality* (Vol. 1); and from *Truth and Power.* Reprinted in Leitch.

———. *The Foucault Reader.* Ed. Paul Rabinow. New York: Pantheon Books, 1984.

Gates, Henry Louis, Jr. *"Race," Writing and Difference.* Chicago: University of Chicago Press, 1986.

Gates, Henry Louis, Jr. *The Signifying Monkey.* New York: Oxford University Press, 1988.

Geertz, Clifford. *The Interpretation of Cultures.* New York: Basic Books, 1972.

Gilroy, Paul. *"There Ain't No Black in the Union Jack": The Cultural Politics of Race and Nation.* 2nd edn. Chicago, Ill.: University of Chicago Press, 1991.

———. *The Black Atlantic: Modernity and Double Consciousness.* Cambridge, MA: Harvard University Press, 1995.

Giroux, Henry, David Shumway, Paul Smith, and James Sosnoski. "The Need for Cultural Studies: Resisting Intellectuals and Oppositional Public Spheres." *Dalhousie Review* 64, no. 2 (1984): 472–86.

Graff, Gerald, and James Phelan, eds. Adventures of Huckleberry Finn: *A Case Study in Critical Controversy.* Boston: St. Martin's Press/Bedford Books, 1995.

Gramsci, Antonio. *Selections from the Prison Notebooks.* Ed. Quintin Hoare and Geoffrey Nowell Smith. New York: International, 1971.

Granville-Barker, Harley. *Prefaces to Shakespeare.* 2 Vols. Princeton: Princeton University Press, 1946.

Greenblatt, Stephen. "Towards a Poetics of Culture." In Veeser.

Groden, Michael, and Martin Krieswirth, eds. *The Johns Hopkins Guide to Literary Theory and Criticism.* Baltimore: Johns Hopkins University Press, 1994.

Grossberg, Lawrence. *We Gotta Get Out of This Place: Popular Conservatism and Postmodern Culture.* New York: Routledge, 1992.

Grossberg, Lawrence, Cary Nelson, and Paula Treicher, eds. *Cultural Studies.* New York: Routledge, 1992.

Haining, Peter, ed. *The Frankenstein Omnibus.* London: Orion, 1994. Reprint. Edison, NJ: Chartwell Books, 1994.

Hall, Stuart. "Cultural Identity and Cinematic Representation." *Framework* 36 (1989): 68–81.

Hall, Stuart, and Tony Jefferson, eds. *Resistance through Rituals: Youth Subcultures in Post-War Britain.* 2nd edn. London: Routledge, 2006.

Harris, Daryl B. "Postmodernist Diversions in African-American Thought." *Journal of Black Studies* 36, 2 (November 2005): 209–28.

Hassan, Ihab Habib. *The Postmodern Turn: Essays in Postmodern Theory and Culture.* Columbus: Ohio State University Press, 1987.

Hebdige, Dick. *Hiding the Light: On Images and Things.* New York: Routledge, 1988.

———. *Subculture: The Meaning of Style.* Rev. edn. London: Routledge, 2003.

Hill, Mike. *Whiteness: A Critical Reader.* New York: New York University Press, 1997.

Honour, Hugh, and John Fleming. *A World History of Art.* London: Macmillan, 1982.

hooks, bell. *Yearning: Race, Gender, and Cultural Politics.* Boston: South End Press, 1990.

———. *Outlaw Culture: Resisting Representations.* New York: Routledge, 1994.

———. *Black Looks: Race and Representation.* Boston: South End Press, 1997.

Horsman, Reginald. "Race and Manifest Destiny." In *Critical Whiteness Studies.* Ed. Richard Delgado and Jean Stefancic. Philadelphia: Temple University Press, 1997.

Hunter, J. Paul ed. *Mary Shelley, Frankenstein.* 1818 New York: W. W. Norton, 1996.

Huyssen, Andreas. *After the Great Divide: Modernism, Mass Culture, Postmodernism.* Bloomington: Indiana University Press, 1986.

Jacobson, Matthew Frye. *Whiteness of a Different Color: European Immigrants and the Alchemy of Race.* Cambridge, MA: Harvard University Press, 1999.

Jameson, Frederic. *The Political Unconscious: Studies in the Ideology of Form.* Ithaca, NY: Cornell University Press, 1979.

———. *Postmodernism, or the Cultural Logic of Late Capitalism.* Durham, NC: Duke University Press, 1991.

Jenkins, Harold, ed. *The Arden Shakespeare: Hamlet.* New York and London: Routledge, 1982. Reprint, 1989–90.

Joseph, Bertram. *Conscience and the King: A Study of Hamlet.* London: Chatto and Windus, 1953.

Kaplan, Justin. "Born to Trouble: One Hundred Years of *Huckleberry Finn.*" In Graff and Phelan.

Kranzler, Laura. "*Frankenstein* and the Technological Future." *Foundation* 44 (Winter 1988–89): 42–49.

Lacan, Jacques. *Ecrits: A Selection.* 1966. Trans. Alan Sheridan. New York: W. W. Norton, 1977. Revised version reprinted 2002. Trans. Bruce Fink.

"Las Meniñas." *The Order of Things: An Archaeology of the Human Sciences.* 1966. Trans. 1970. Rpt. New York: Vintage/Random House, 1994. 3–16.

Lawrence, D. H. *Studies in Classical American Fiction.* 1923. Reprint. New York: Viking/Compass, 1964.

Leavis, F. R. *Revaluation: Tradition and Development in English Poetry.* 1936. Reprint. New York: Ivan R. Dee, 1998.

Lederer, Susan E. Visiting Curator. *Frankenstein: Penetrating the Secrets of Nature.* Exhibition by the National Library of Medicine. New Brunswick, NJ: Rutgers University Press, 2002.

Leitch, Vincent, ed. *Norton Anthology of Theory Criticism.* New York: W. W. Norton, 2001.

Lester, Julius. "Morality and *Adventures of Huckleberry Finn.*" In Graff and Phelan.

Levine, George. "The Ambiguous Heritage of *Frankenstein.*" In Levine and Knopelmacher.

Levine, George, and U. C. Knopelmacher, eds. *The Endurance of* Frankenstein: *Essays on Mary Shelley's Novel.* Berkeley: University of California Press, 1979.

Levine, Lawrence. *Black Culture and Black Consciousness: Afro-American Folk Thought from Slavery to Freedom.* Oxford: University of Mississippi Press, 1977.

Lévi-Strauss, Claude. *The Raw and the Cooked.* Trans. John and Doreen Weightman. New York: Harper, 1975.

Levith, Murray J. *What's in Shakespeare's Names.* Hamden, CT: Shoe String Press/Archon, 1978.

Lipsitz, George. *The Possessive Investment in Whiteness: How White People Profit From Identity Politics.* Philadelphia: Temple University Press, 1988.

Litvak, Joseph. "Back to the Future: A Review-Article on the New Historicism, Deconstruction, and Nineteenth-Century Fiction." *Texas Studies in Literature and Language* 30 (1988): 120–49.

Lott, Eric. *Love and Theft: The Blackface Minstrelsy and the American Working Class.* New York: Oxford University Press, 1993.

Lowe, Lisa. *Immigrant Acts: On Asian American Cultural Politics.* Durham, NC: Duke University Press, 1996.

Lukács, Georg. *The Theory of the Novel.* 1920. Reprint. Cambridge, MA: Massachusetts Institute of Technology Press, 1971.

Lyotard, Jean-François. *The Postmodern Condition: A Report on Knowledge.* 1979. Rpt. Manchester: Manchester University Press, 1984.

Malchow, H. L. "Was Frankenstein's Monster 'a Man and a Brother'?" *Gothic Images of Race in Nineteenth-Century Britain.* Stanford: Stanford University Press, 1996.

Morrison, Toni. *Playing in the Dark: Whiteness and Literary Imagination.* New York: Vintage Press, 1993.

Morton, Timothy, ed. *A Routledge Literary Sourcebook on Mary Shelley's* Frankenstein. London and New York: Routledge, 2002.

Mullaney, Steven. "Brothers and Others, or the Art of Alienation." In *Cannibals, Witches, and Divorce: Estranging the Renaissance.* Ed. Marjorie Garber. Baltimore: Johns Hopkins University Press, 1987.

Napier, Winston, ed. *African American Literary Theory: A Reader.* New York: New York University Press, 2000.

Pechter, Edward. "The New Historicism and Its Discontents: Politicizing Renaissance Drama." *PMLA* 102 (May 1987): 292–303.

Porter, Carolyn. "Are We Being Historical Yet?" *South Atlantic Quarterly* 87 (Fall 1988): 743–86.

Radway, Janice. *Reading the Romance: Women, Patriarchy, and Popular Literature.* Chapel Hill: University of North Carolina Press, 1984.

Rebolledo, Diana, and Eliana S. Rivera, eds. *Infinite Divisions: An Anthology of Chicana Literature.* Tucson: University of Arizona Press, 1993.

Reynolds, David S. *Beneath the American Renaissance: The Subversive Imagination in the Age of Emerson and Melville.* New York: Alfred A. Knopf, 1988.

Richter, David, ed. *The Critical Tradition.* New York: St. Martin's, 1998.

Roberts, John. *From Trickster to Badman: The Black Folk Hero in Slavery and Freedom.* Philadelphia: University of Pennsylvania Press, 1989.

———. "The African American Animal Trickster as Hero." In *Redefining American Literary History.* Ed. A. LaVonne Ruoff and Jerry W. Ward. New York: MLA, 1990.

Roediger, David. *Towards the Abolition of Whiteness: Essays on Race, Politics, and Working-Class History.* London: Verso, 1994.

Said, Edward. *Orientalism.* New York: Pantheon, 1978.

Saldivar, José David. *Border Matters: Remapping American Cultural Studies.* Berkeley: University of California Press, 1997.

Sandoval, Chela. *Methodology of the Oppressed.* Minneapolis: University of Minnesota Press, 2000.

Sarup, Madan. *An Introductory Guide to Post-Structuralism and Postmodernism.* 2nd edn. Athens: University of Georgia Press, 1993.

Saxton, Alexander, *The Indispensable Enemy: Labor and the Anti-Chinese Movement in California.* Berkeley: University of California Press, 1971.

Schutz, Aaron. "Teaching Freedom? Postmodern Perspectives." *Review of Educational Research* 70, 2 (Summer 2000): 215–51.

Shelley, Mary. *The Letters of Mary Wollstonecraft Shelley.* Ed. Betty T. Bennett. 3 vols. Baltimore: Johns Hopkins University Press, 1980–88.

Shen Wu, Jean Yu-wen, and Min Song, eds. *Asian American Studies: A Reader.* New Brunswick, NJ: Rutgers University Press, 2000.

Sill, Geoffrey M., Miriam T. Chaplin, Jean Ritzke, and David Wilson, eds. *Opening the American Mind: Race, Ethnicity, and Gender in Higher Education.* Newark: University of Delaware Press, 1993.

Skal, David J. *The Monster Show: A Cultural History of Horror.* New York: Norton, 1993.

Smith, Johanna M., ed. Frankenstein *by Mary Shelley.* 1831 Text. 2nd ed. Boston: Bedford/St. Martin's, 2000.

Smith, Patricia Clark. "Coyote's Sons, Spider's Daughters: Western American Indian Poetry, 1968–1983." In *A Literary History of the American West.* Ed. Max Westbrook and James H. Maguire. Fort Worth: Texas Christian University Press, 1987.

Sollors, Werner. *Beyond Ethnicity: Consent and Descent in American Culture.* New York: Oxford University Press, 1986.

——. *Where We Stand: Class Matters.* New York: Routledge, 2000.

Spillers, Hortense J. *Black, White, and in Color: Essays on American Literature and Culture.* Chicago, Ill.: University of Chicago Press, 2003.

Spivak, Gayatri Chakravorty. "From *A Critique of Postcolonial Reason.*" In Leitch.

——. "Three Women's Texts and a Critique of Imperialism." *Critical Inquiry* 12 (Autumn 1985): 243–61. Reprinted as "*Frankenstein* and a Critique of Imperialism." In Hunter.

Storey, John. *Cultural Theory and Popular Culture: An Introduction.* Athens: University of Georgia Press, 2006.

Todorov, Tzvetan. "'Race,' Writing, and Culture." Trans. Loulou Mack. *Critical Inquiry* 13,1 (Autumn 1986): 171–82.

Tylor, Edward Burnett. *Primitive Culture.* New York: Holt, 1877.

Veeser, H. Aram, ed. *The New Historicism.* New York: Routledge, 1989.

Velie, Alan R., ed. *American Indian Literature: A Brief Introduction and Anthology.* New York: HarperCollins, 1995.

Warner, Michael. "Literary Studies and the History of the Book." *Book* 12 (1987): 3–9.

White, Hayden. *Metahistory: The Historical Imagination in Nineteenth-Century Europe.* Baltimore: Johns Hopkins University Press, 1973.

Wiget, Andrew. "His Life in His Tale: The Native American Trickster and the Literature of Possibility." In *Redefining American Literary History.* Ed. A. LaVonne Ruoff and Jerry W. Ward. New York: MLA, 1990.

Williams, Raymond. *Culture and Society: 1780–1950.* London: Chatto, 1958.

——. *Marxism and Literature.* New York: Oxford University Press, 1973.

Wong, Jade Snow. *Fifth Chinese Daughter.* 1945. Reprint. Seattle: University of Washington Press, 1978.

10

*

Postcolonial Studies

I. POSTCOLONIALISM: DEFINITIONS

Postcolonialism refers to a historical phase undergone by Third World countries after the decline of colonialism: for example, when countries in Asia, Africa, Latin America, and the Caribbean separated from the European empires and were left to rebuild themselves. Many Third World writers focus on both colonialism and the changes created in a postcolonial culture. Among the many challenges facing postcolonial writers are the attempts both to resurrect their culture and to combat the preconceptions about their culture.

It is impossible to return to a precolonial state of mind. Hence, as Bill Ashcroft notes, "Post-colonial critics and theorists should consider the full implications of restricting the meaning of the term to 'after-colonialism' or after-independence. All postcolonial societies are still subject in one way or another to overt or subtle forms of neocolonial domination, and independence has not solved this problem" (2). As Zilla Eisenstein observes, "Colonization allows the colonizers to view the world from their standpoint. From this site false universals are concocted and the colonizers' positions of power allow this deception, and enforce the falsity as truth. The colonized not only know themselves, but also are forced to know those who have done the colonizing. Native Americans were already here; their culture comes before Columbus. Those Blacks who were slaves knew themselves within their particular African origins before they became captives, of other Africans, or whites. To survive, they had to come to know the white slavemasters and slavemistresses. This 'deep' way of viewing is not necessary for the powerful." As she concludes, "Both victim and violator are locked together in discovering the truths that can allow them to be set free" (28–29, 57).

Postcolonial critics and theorists are speaking mainly about European colonization of the Americas, Africa, Asia, and the South Pacific mostly carried out in the seventeenth through twentieth centuries. Colonialism is generally viewed as a phenomenon of whites colonizing lands of peoples of color, not peoples of

Figure 10.1. Eighteenth-Century Map of the New World (1780).
Getty Images/Charles Marie Rigobert Bonne.

color colonizing others. Colonization was not so much a state of political and historical affairs, but an entire system of thought that accompanied other, more sal-
utary social developments, especially in the eighteenth and nineteenth centuries:
exploration, the expansion of science, the discovery of new sources of wealth and
employment, and the fruit of the Age of Reason. All were movements of reform,
of labor laws, of women's and children's rights, of social justice for the poor. The
status of women is of special concern to postcolonial critics.

In the last two centuries, the world changed dramatically: lands that had been
colonized mainly by Euro-American nations "became" free, often through pro-
tracted, bloody revolutions, but sometimes through relatively peaceful transfers
of sovereignty. India, Latin America, Africa, the Caribbean, South Asia, and the
South Pacific emerged from colonialism with a multitude of conflicting social,
cultural, and economic issues. The British Empire once ruled one-fourth of the
earth, but until the last few decades little attention was paid by literary critics to the
lasting and continuously evolving state of postcolonial peoples and their writers.
Beginning with Edward Said's enormously influential *Orientalism* (1978), and followed by the studies of Homi K. Bhabha, Frantz Fanon, Kwame Anthony Appiah,
and Gayatri Chakravorty Spivak, critics came to look at English as a postcolonial
language and the realities of postcolonialism—race, ethnicity, international and
national politics, diasporas—as the true nature of global society today. Fanon's
work also includes psychoanalytic theory. Postcolonial studies also sparked new
developments in ethnic studies, particularly in the United States. Postcolonial

studies also gave rise to such recent theoretical interests as spatial/geographical studies and ecofeminism, a cosmopolitanism as reflected in Appiah, Pheng Cheung, and Bruce Robbins. Postcolonialism thus celebrates and recovers writings of postcolonial and colonial subjects, but it distinguishes between "settler" colonies and "occupier" colonies and how this difference shapes writers.

Thus at first glance postcolonial studies would seem to be a matter of history and political science, rather than literary criticism. However, we must remember that English, as in "English Department" or "English Literature," has been since the age of the British Empire a global language (it is today, for example, almost exclusively the language of the internet). Britain seemed to foster in its political institutions as well as in literature universal ideals for proper living, while at the same time perpetuating the violent enslavement of Africans and other imperialist cruelties around the world, causing untold misery and destroying millions of lives. Postcolonial literary theorists study the English language within this politicized context, especially those writings that developed at the colonial "front," such as works by Rudyard Kipling, E. M. Forster, Jean Rhys, or Jamaica Kincaid. Earlier figures such as Shakespeare's Caliban are re-read today in their New World contexts. Works such as *The Empire Writes Back,* edited by Bill Ashcroft and others, and *The Black Atlantic* by Paul Gilroy have radically remapped cultural criticism.

II. SOME KEY FIGURES AND EMPHASES

Said's concept of *orientalism* was an important touchstone for postcolonial studies, as he described the stereotypical discourse about the East as constructed by the West. This discouse, rather than realistically portraying Eastern "others," *constructs* them based upon Western anxieties and preoccupations. Said sharply critiques the Western image of the Oriental as "irrational, depraved (fallen), childlike, 'different,' " which has allowed the West to define itself as "rational, virtuous, mature, 'normal' " (40).

Said drew on Foucault for his sense of the binaries constructed by the West for the East as Other: the East is lazy, sensual, inscrutable, treacherous, while the West is hard-working, rational, democratic, benevolent. Where the East is exotic and trapped in time, the West is modern and progressive. The West is seen as masculine and the East as feminine.

Fanon, a French Caribbean Marxist, drew upon his own horrific experiences in French Algeria and World War II to deconstruct emerging national regimes that are based on inheritances from the imperial powers, warning that class, not race, is a greater factor in worldwide oppression, and that if new nations are built in the molds of their former oppressors, then they will perpetuate the bourgeois inequalities from the past. His book *The Wretched of the Earth* (1961) has been an inspiration for postcolonial cultural critics and literary critics who seek to understand the decolonizing project of Third World writers, especially those interested in African and African-American texts.

Fanon addressed the psychologized or internalized racism that would lead to "neocolonialism." Though many colonized peoples romanticize their Edenic precolonial state, Fanon believed that that state was romantic and unattainable because cultures change continuously. He asked for revolutionary practice to lead to the future, not nostalgia for the past, and he advocated armed revolution.

Homi Bhabha's postcolonial theory involves analysis of nationality, ethnicity, and politics with poststructuralist ideas of identity and indeterminacy, defining postcolonial identities as shifting, hybrid constructions. Bhabha critiques the presumed dichotomies between center and periphery, colonized and colonizer, self and other, borrowing from deconstruction the argument that these are false binaries. He proposes instead a dialogic model of nationalities, ethnicities, and identities characterized by what he calls *hybridity;* that is, they are something new, emerging from a "Third Space" to interrogate the givens of the past. Perhaps his most important contribution has been to stress that colonialism is not a one-way street, that because it involves an interaction between colonizer and colonized, the colonizer is as much affected by its systems as the colonized. The old distinction between "industrialized" and "developing" nations does not hold true today, when so many industrial jobs have been moved overseas from countries like the United States to countries like India and the Philippines.

Bhabha stresses the psychological ambivalence of the colonized in postcolonial discourse. He defines mimicry as the way in which colonized people sometimes address their oppressors, adopting their language, clothes, religions, etc., but in their mimicry Bhabha describes their ambivalence; their performance alienates the colonizers from their essence, thus destabilizing colonialism.

Postcolonial critics accordingly study diasporic texts outside the usual Western genres, especially productions by aboriginal authors, marginalized ethnicities, immigrants, and refugees. Postcolonial literatures by such writers as Chinua Achebe and Salman Rushdie are read alongside European responses to colonialism by writers such as George Orwell and Albert Camus. We can see some powerful conflicts arising from the colonial past in Rushdie's *Midnight's Children* (1980), for example, which deconstructs from a postcolonial viewpoint the history of modern India.

Among the most important figures in postcolonial feminism is Spivak, who examines the effects of political independence upon "subaltern" or subproletarian women in the Third World. Spivak's subaltern studies reveal how female subjects are silenced by the dialogue between the male-dominated West and the male-dominated East, offering little hope for the subaltern woman's voice to rise up amidst the global social institutions that oppress her.

Spivak wishes to make plain what she calls the "worlding" of the Third World; its writing is not on the periphery of "metropolitan" culture but because of hybridity they are partly each other. Spivak criticizes Anglo-American feminists for privileging their heroines' achievements of independent subjectivity as "strong women" unlimited by imperialism and colonialism. Bourgeois feminists are slaves to colonialism whether they know it or not, and this should not be celebrated. There is a false freedom and false economy, exploiting the lives and labors of Third World women, who pay for their privilege. In her article "Can the Subaltern Speak?" (she borrows the term from Antonio Gramsci) Spivak asks: When Indian women told British authorities they did not wish to be immolated at their husbands' funerals, who was speaking? Can women (subalterns) speak for themselves at all? In this Spivak displays a Derridean skepticism on the existence of an automonous individual self. (More on the changing role of feminism in postcolonial studies in a moment.)

More recent postcolonial critics continue to redefine this emerging field. For example, Robert J. C. Young has defined postcolonialism as "turning the world upside down,...looking at the world from the other side of the photograph, experiencing how differently things look when you live in Baghdad or Benin rather than Berlin or Boston, and understanding why." Westerners see only mirror images of themselves when they look at the nonwestern subject. He continues: "If you are someone who does not identify yourself as western, or as somehow not completely western even though you live in a western country, or someone who is part of a culture and yet excluded by its dominant voices, inside yet outside, then postcolonialism offers you a way of seeing things differently, a language and a politics in which your interests come first, not last" (2). The aims of postcolonialism today, he argues, are to claim the rights of all people on earth to "the same material and cultural well-being." While this may be an unattainable goal for now, because "the west non-west relation was thought of in terms of whites versus the non-white races," white culture remained the basis for government and law—and culture. At the same time, increasing immigration has challenged "the clear division between the west and the rest in ethnic terms.... [W]hite Protestant America is being hispanicized. Hispanic and black America have become the dynamic motors of much live western culture" (3–4).

Postcolonialism today tends to look less for blame and influence and more for economic realities that continue to subordinate the emerging nations of the world, disputing the disparity between developed and developing nations. It also increasingly asserts the power of nonwhite cultures, as Young explains: "cultures that are now intervening in and transforming the societies of the west" (4). Drawing from increasingly many disciplines, including feminism, ecology, social justice, socialism, resource development, and national interests, it seeks to explore power structures that repress nonwestern, nonwhite peoples. Instead of a single technique, Young asserts, it uses the approach of "montage" to juxtapose sets of cultural values against each other, placing relations among peoples and their culture into dialectics rather than hegemonies. In sum, postcolonialism is not so much about static ideas or practices as about "relations of harmony, relations of conflict, generative relations between different peoples and their cultures." It is about "a changing world that has been changed by struggle and which its practitioners intend to change further" (*Postcolonialism* 6–7).

As noted earlier postcolonialism has been important to feminism, especially, most recently, Third World feminism. Chandra Mohanty identifies four main commonalities among Third World feminists: first, the "simultaneity of oppression" as both women and Third World inhabitants, the "grounding of feminist politics in the histories of racism and imperialism; second, the role of the hegemonic state "in circumscribing Third World women's daily lives and struggle"; third, "the significance of memory and writing in the creation of oppositional agency"; and fourth, "the differences, conflicts, and contradictions to Third World women's organizations and communities" (10). Similarly, Amrita Chhachhi addresses the question of whether feminist theory is "white" or "black." As Rawwida Baksh-Soodeen puts it, "From Chhachhi's point of view, the rejection of all feminist theory as 'western,' 'Eurocentric,' or 'Ethnocentric,' results from a failure to distinguish between the application of feminist theories to the historical, political, and socio-cultural specificities of black/Third World women, and the notion of all theory as 'white' " (76).

As Patricia Mohammed similarly observes, "In studying the colonized subject, the tendency has been to perceive the problem of reconfiguring gender identities as primarily that of the exploited group. It is, also, a problem which confronts the colonizers. Women, whether born in Europe or creole born, were themselves ill at ease with the situation. This is best illustrated by Jean Rhys, whose novel *Wide Sargasso Sea* (1966) and subsequent writings describe, with more pathos than historical writings can achieve, the insecurity and fears which also underlie the perceived 'privileged' spaces" (8). Ketu H. Katrak notes that "It is regrettable when any discussion of women's issues is dismissed as 'feminism equals westernism equals not relevant for third world women.'" Even as feminism in western locales must contend with attacks on its perceived power, it has a vocabulary and a system of ideas to contend with, and: "This academic engagement is more recent in postcolonial societies, not to imply that indigenous women whom we would describe as feminists are also a recent social phenomenon.... The need then is highly significant for postcolonial women writers to define feminism for their own purposes, and to identify issues that demonstrate how relevant feminism is for their societies" (16). She also points out that there is often a preexisting feminism before colonialist times: "The fact that women's resistances in pre-colonial times may not have been named as feminist does not mean that they did not exist. This is a misconception similar to the racist claim that since African cultures existed orally, and were invisible to a narrow print-oriented European bias, they did not exist at all! I distinguish between what is identified today as feminist models from what might have been recognized previously as female traditions of courage and resistance" (57).

Finally, postcolonialism has helped create the new field of spatial studies, which analyzes the importance of human constructions of physical with mental spaces, especially in political contexts. It explores such issues in literature as territorial competition, ownership, nation-building, conflicts with indigenous peoples, cartography, the perception of certain lands as available for conquest and colonialization, borders, versions of nature, the postcolonial body as a space, social linguistics, and especially human transformations of landscapes and other spaces, transformations which Benedict Anderson, in his book *Imagined Communities*, describes as a nation mapping itself onto a physical terrain. Spatial studies is thus connected with such diverse literary approaches as Marxism, new historicism, poststructuralisrn, ecocriticism, and feminism, and it maintains interdisciplinary connections with such fields as sociology, international relations, history, and of course geography.

Among the main preoccupations of spatial theorists of literature is how in colonial times the West viewed certain spaces ("Darkest Africa") as *empty* because they had no meaning outside of Western worldviews. However, Edward Soja's studies of "spatial ontology" argue not only that such spaces are not devoid of human significance but that they "not only are the spaces of nature and cognition used and incorporated into the social production of spatiality, [but] they are significantly transformed in the process" ("Spatiality of Social Life" 93). Soja quotes Henri Lefebvre's idea that "space has been shaped and moulded from historical and natural elements, but this has been a political process. Space is political and ideological. It is a product literally filled with ideology" ("Spatiality of Social Life" 101). The "space of physical nature is thus appropriated in the social production of spatiality—it is literally made social" ("Spatiality of Social Life" 92–93). Soja describes "a specifically capitalist spatiality: in the eighteenth-century British destruction of feudal property relations and the turbulent creation of a proletariat 'freed' from its former means of subsistence," the workplace was separated from the personal space and work from personal consumption of it, and this distance from means to production, as Marxists would put it, has been alienating ("Spatiality of Social Life," 97). Soja argues that modern academic study has privileged time and history over space as means of addressing the modem era: "Space still tends to be treated as fixed, dead, undialectical; time as richness, life, dialectic." Though geography has not replaced history in contemporary theory, "there is a new animating polemic on the theoretical and political agenda, one which rings with significantly different ways of seeing time and space together, the interplay of history and geography, the 'vertical' and 'horizontal' dimensions of being in the world." There are new possibilities for "a simultaneously historical and geographical materialism," what he calls a "postmodern critical human geography" ("History: geography: modernity" 137, 141). Turning to Foucault's attacks on historicism, he quotes Foucault's "ecumenical project": "A whole history remains to be written of *spaces*—which would at the same time be the history of *powers* (both of these terms in the plural)—from the great strategies of geopolitics to the little tactics of the habitat" (Foucault, "The Eye of Power" 149).

Similarly, in *Imperial Eyes*, Mary Louise Pratt writes that to the conqueror "the landscape is written as uninhabited, unpossessed, unhistoricized, unoccupied"; she refers to early travel narratives by Europeans, who viewed the mapping of these regions as "the moment of their 'birth' " (51). As an example, Richard Phillips argues that in the case of Daniel Defoe's *Robinson Crusoe*, by "transforming the island, Crusoe maps a specifically nineteenth-century brand of colonialism associated with emigration and settlement" (124). Later, the post-World-War-II idea of the first, second, and third worlds divided the nations of the world into states of industrial development, further inscribing meaning onto landscapes as dictated by the perceptions of the West. These "worlds" create barriers by defining by what they lack. As Mary Pat Brady has observed, this means "national borders utilize the fantasy that one side of the border a nation exists in one phase of temporal development while the nation on the other side functions in a different stage of temporality," yet the border can move as a "marker between the shifting periods of poverty and plenty" (178, 184). To illustrate these phenomena in literature Brady analyzes the girlhood memoirs of Gina Valdes's *There are No Madmen Here* and Norma Elia Cantú's *Canicula*, both powerful narratives of crossing childhood, adulthood, sexuality, and the border. Once again, the space is made representative of the ideas of the dominant gaze, and the power of this vision supersedes the relative neutrality of the physical terrain. Yet in Valdes and Cantú, "the border emerges not as a stable line, river, bridge, but as a shifting locus of identity and displacement" (185), which these authors are able to transform through their memories, development, and modern voices.

Literature addresses not only the individual "crossing" but also those of entire peoples. *Diasporic* communities are those in which individuals have moved within groups from one land to another while trying to maintain their original national or cultural identity and traditions. As Stanley Tambiah has noted, "diasporic nationalism" describes "the situation of those immigrant communities that are intact in the countries to which they have migrated but have lost or are losing connection with their homelands, although they are involved in the 'imaginings' of their countries of origin" (175). Tambiah describes some of the reasons for transnational movements. They are undertaken

> ...in search of employment in the more prosperous industrialized or industrializing countries as guest workers or as immigrants, and as a result of forced displacements of people owing to civil wars and the pogroms of ethnic cleansing and genocide. There is an intensification in the creation of diverse diaspora populations in many locations, who are engaged in complex interpersonal and intercultural relationships with both the host societies and their societies of origin. Rather than being deterritorialized, they in fact experience and live in dual locations and manifest dual consciousness. (163)

The spatial factors include "the flow of people through transnational migrations; the flow of capital in our present time of multinational capitalism; and the flow of information over vast distances in the context of modern developments in communication" (163). Immigrants face assimilation, exclusion, and integration as possible identities, and have written about all of these. Tambiah praises Salman Rushdie's *Satanic Verses* for displaying the most sophisticated "hybridization" of peoples. In commenting on his book Rushdie notes its "hybridity, impurity, intermingling, the transformation, that comes of new and unexpected combinations of human beings, cultures, ideas, politics, movies, songs. It rejoices in mongrelization and fears the absolutism of the pure. Mélange, hotchpotch, a bit of this and a bit of that is how newness enters the world" (Rushdie, "Imaginary Homelands" 394; quoted in Tambiah 178).

Jonathan Murdoch's *Post-Structuralist Geography* examines how such "play" of ideas as offered by poststructuralism would apply to books like Rushdie's. For him, poststructuralism informs a new sense of multiple geographies in competition for meaning, especially in its emphasis upon the relational nature of space and those who occupy it; spaces are not "containers" but active presences in social practice. Resistance to hegemonic spaces plays an important role. As Murdoch summarizes, "Spaces and places should not be seen as closed and contained but as open and engaged with other spaces and places." They are "multiplicities" with different "readings" from dominant and subaltern interpreters. Struggles can "lead to the need for spatial 'openings,' new forms of spatial identity." Space is "performed" just as social practice, and it is not fixed but mutable. Both performer and space are "entangled in the heterogeneous processes of spatial 'becoming'" (18). The significance of Murdoch's insights goes beyond poststructuralism to point out subtle but important contradictions in how space is portrayed in literature; for example, Joseph Conrad's *Heart of Darkness* posits the space of the Congo as unrelieved savagery and fantastic evil, while one hardly believes a native of that land would see it that way. In fact, in a well-known essay, Chinua Achebe takes issue with Conrad's appropriation of Africa.

Achebe describes "the desire—one might indeed say the need—in Western psychology to set Africa up as a foil to Europe, as a place of negations at once remote and vaguely familiar, in comparison with which Europe's own state of spiritual grace will be manifest.... Africa as 'the other world,' the antithesis of Europe and therefore of civilization, a place where man's vaunted intelligence and refinement are finally mocked by triumphant bestiality." The worry Conrad has, he adds, is not the Africans' remoteness but "the lurking sense of kinship, of common ancestry" (251–52). He calls Conrad "a thoroughgoing racist" and believes the novel fails accordingly: "Can nobody see the preposterous and perverse arrogance in thus reducing Africa to the role of props for the break-up of one petty European mind?" (256).

Thus social maps overlay all the lands of the earth and all people live within them, shifting though they may be. While maps change with nations over time, at any given moment the "authoritative" map of a land determines the impression, whether physical, social, religious, or literary. As Walter Mignolo observes in *Local Histories/Global Designs*, for example, "In Latin America different manifestations of the tensions between linguistic maps, literary geographies, and cultural landscapes can be linked with the dismissal of Amerindian languages under colonial rule and Western expansion" (225). Language thus plays a key role in spatial studies and in the literatures of the Americas. Mignolo defines "transculturalism" as the most important category needed for border studies, migrations, bi- or multilingualism. His conception of "border thinking" also invokes the borders between disciplines, especially the "human sciences" and "literature," and argues for literature's place in the "politics of language" that interprets spaces in which people live and move (223). Such intellectual crossings mean "moving away from the idea that language is a fact (e.g., a system of syntactic, semantic, and phonetic rules), and moving toward the idea that speech and writing are strategies for orienting and manipulating social domains of literature" (226). He concludes with the question, "What are national languages good for in a transnational world?" (248).

In their collection *Transcultural Localisms: Responding to Ethnicity in a Globalized World*, editors Yiorgos Kalogeras, Eleftheria Arapoglou, and Linda Manney bring together from many nations ideas on transculturalism and how it can preserve the "local." As they note, "[T]he centrifugal force of globalization is counteracted by the centripetal pull to an ethnic identity that can be defined by either a common origin, or a common structure of experience, or both." More and more authors are emerging from such transcultural/local situations. Though some "global spaces" sever "locals" from their home, others provide new means of bonding together, and especially for artists critical of the forces around them (xiii). Thus "transcultural localism" describes the *local* as challenging rather than being appropriated by the *global*, "a discourse that caters to the interests of institutional control[,]...a turning away from national canons and nationalisms and argues for a more inclusive...approach to literary production" (viii-ix). They note Kaeko Mochizuki's argument that "in the nuclear age, obsolete nationalism and arrogant unilateralism, approving of and even producing wars, neither protect 'home' nor control 'the Other,' but bring about the simultaneous destruction of both." They also include in the volume Sophia Emmanouilidou's examination of how Rudolfo Anaya's works describe a "Chicano collective unconscious" as a "writer who asserts his position as a social agent in order to expedite a collective mobilization." They see Pirjo Ahokas's essay on Bharati Mukherjee and Monica Ali as probing "into processes through which transnational, post-modern female identities are constructed and enacted"; their protagonists "employ cultural hybridity to challenge gender as well as racial oppression." Another of their essays, by Ilana Xinos, explores how the Greek writer Christophorus Castinis creates "an imagined community between himself, Greece, and America—one that is not territorially grounded, but culturally induced and ideologically determined" (x-xi). Theodore Schatski summarizes the contribution of spatial studies: "Social reality is interrelated individual lives. This conception differs from previous forms of individualism by expanding the 'individualist level' beyond actions and mental states to include a wider range of items constitutive of human life: objects, places, settings, a range of transactions" (667).

But of all these sources, perhaps Gloria Anzaldúa is the best-known recent writer and theorist of transculturalism and especially borders, an area of spatial studies that is especially suited to the conflicts along the United States-Mexico border today. In *Borderlands/La Frontera*, Anzaldúa combines poetry, memoir, history, cultural theory, and other discourses to create a body of text that reflects its border origins; as a lesbian, Chicana, and working-class woman she identifies and addresses the many borders she confronts and embodies. She recalls that as a child:

> I press my hand to the steel curtain—
> chainlink fence crowned with rolled barbed wire—
> rippling from the sea where Tijuana touches San Diego
>   unrollingoveer mountains
>   and plains
>   and deserts,
> this "Tortilla Curtain" turning into *el río Grande*
>   flowing down to the flatlands
>   of the Magic Valley of South Texas
>   its mouth emptying into the Gulf.
>
> 1,950 miles long open wound
>   dividing a *pueblo*, a culture,
>   running down the length of my body,
>   staking fence rods in my flesh,
>   splits me splits me
>   *me raja me raja*
>   This is my home
>   This thin edge of
>   Barbwire. (25)

Anzaldúa follows this excerpt of her poem with the observation that

> The U.S.-Mexican border *es una herida abierta* where the Third World grates against the first and bleeds. And before a scab forms it hemorrhages again, the lifeblood of two worlds merging to form a third country—a border culture. Borders are set up to define the places that are safe and unsafe, to distinguish *us* from *them*. A border is a dividing line, a narrow strip along a steep edge. A borderland is a vague and undetermined place created by the emotional residue of an unnatural boundary. It is in a constant state of transition. The prohibited and forbidden are its inhabitants. *Los atravesados* live here: the squint-eyed, the perverse, the queer, the troublesome, the mongrel, the mulato, the half-breed, the half dead; in short those who cross over, pass over, or go through the confines of "the normal." (25)

(See also our discussion of Anzaldúa in Chapter 9, Cultural Studies.)

III. POSTCOLONIAL CRITICAL PRACTICES

A. Seventeenth-Century English Colonization and "To His Coy Mistress"

Marvell composed "To His Coy Mistress" sometime in 1651–52, though it was not published until 1681, three years after his death. Before and during 1652, England experienced great turbulence in its struggles with civil war, regicide, restoration, and foreign wars for colonies and trade rights. In 1647, the Scots surrendered the deposed and fugitive English King Charles I to Parliament; though he escaped to the Isle of Wight and made another secret treaty with the Scots. In the next year when he and the Scots invaded England, they were defeated by the troops of Sir Oliver Cromwell—leader of the English anti-Royalist Commonwealth faction. In 1649, Charles I was tried and executed. The Commonwealth, a republic, was established and lasted until 1660. Cromwell dissolved Parliament in 1653 and became Lord Protector of England. During his "reign," he harshly suppressed Catholic rebellions in Ireland and continued to subdue Scotland. But there were many developments abroad as well. In addition to the ongoing "colonizing" of Scotland and Ireland by England, in 1652, Cromwell approved the First Navigation Act, which decreed that most trade goods could be imported into England only by English ships, and this led to a war with Holland. Later, in 1655, his navy seized Jamaica from Spain.

By the time Marvell's poem was written, English expansion abroad had increasingly become a primary pursuit, despite the unrest at home. Expansion and exploration of the New World meant profits from commerce in trade, and this became the key to prosperity after seemingly endless years of economic and social chaos. Not only was the spice trade with China and India critical to the growing imperial economy, but new technologies made it possible to fund more exploration and colonizing of North America. The English also encountered stiff resistance from competing European colonizers, such as Spain, Holland, France, and Portugal. In the sixteenth century, England had begun to colonize India, North America, and the West Indies; Jamestown, Virginia, was founded in 1607 and a colony on Bermuda in 1609. In 1620, the religious dissenters, the Puritan "Pilgrims" on the *Mayflower*, established Plymouth Colony. Massachusetts Bay Colony was granted a charter by Charles I in 1629. The Boston settlement began in 1630, then continued into Rhode Island, New Hampshire, and Connecticut. England vied with Spain for the spoils of the Indies. In 1652, Cape Town was founded by the Dutch East India Company in South Africa, leading to the Anglo-Dutch Wars. Unrest mounted in England over heavy taxation to support foreign expansion, as well as protests of the "blue laws" that upheld a rigid Puritan morality, anxiety over the takeover by the army, and desires for a Stuart restoration. All of this contributed to a feeling of instability with the regime and eventually resulted in the restoration of the monarchy with Charles II. Thus the trouble at home, even while "new worlds" were discovered and fought over abroad, made what historians call the Interregnum a time of extreme political, social, and religious change for all British people.

In "To His Coy Mistress," the main motifs of time and space take on new meaning within colonial and postcolonial frames of reference. The overall theme of escape from the mutable and dangerous world of the present into other times and other places parallels the feelings of many Britons about the possibility of a new start in a new world, as it demonstrates the fears they would have had about existence in their homeland. Marvell himself carefully negotiated the religious and political conflicts he faced as an adherent to Cromwell. "Had we but world enough, and time," the poet begins, we could do as we pleased and pursue life with all its pleasures, including traveling in time and space to new sites of possibility.

The reference to the "Indian Ganges" suggests the entire exotic East being rapidly colonized by Europe, even as the "humble" Humber River reference brings one back to hearth and home. Rubies are the fabled treasures of new worlds, with their promises of untold riches. The references to the beginning of "modern" time (the Flood) and the Conversion of the Jews (the end of time) posit a Western Judeo-Christian conception of history that the English, whether royalist or republican, Catholic or Protestant took for granted. The idea that history is composed of "ages" corroborates a linear, progressive view of Christian history, Christianity destined to be spread over the world. The call of the lover to his mistress to "sport us while we may" could almost sound like a call to leave this old restrictive world of time and space behind and embrace the new—as the "virginity" of the New World also serves as a metaphor for sexual conquering. The chariot is an ancient image of imperial power, but it is significantly behind them, not blocking their way. The "ball" and the "sun" at the end of the poem suggest a global frame of vision, a cosmic call to love in the here and now and not in some future promise of political or national comfort—the place many people would find themselves in during a time of such civil strife and foreign wars.

At the same time, the poem suggests that perhaps the best idea is to stay home and make love as the answer to the dangers outside one's door, and especially defend against Father Time as the emblem of inevitable institutional authority, literally devouring men and women in his quest for empire and eternity.

According to Greek mythology, the one "ball" that Cronos, the Titan Father Time, could not digest was the stone his wife Rhea fed him instead of his own son Zeus, who lived to defy and defeat him, establishing the Olympian Golden Age of Greece. (Cronos had a habit of devouring his offspring lest any of them rise up against him.) Thus the last couplet of "To His Coy Mistress" depends upon a pun against all "Father Times" or dictator figures: the "sun" (or king/dictator) will be made to "run" (or busy himself and leave the lovers alone). "Iron gates of life" at home and abroad may fall about them, but the lovers will not notice if they remain freed from their present world of uncertainty.

B. Postcolonial Adaptations of *Hamlet*

A number of scholars explore postcolonial reinterpretations in performances of *Hamlet*. Indeed its politics—particularly its postcolonial applications—is alive and well abroad if not so much "at home" in Anglo-American productions. As Laura Raidonis Bates observes, "In the oft colonized nations throughout Eastern Europe, *Hamlet* has always had a special significance." In Poland, where it was staged in 1798, it expressed political, philosophical, artistic, and intellectual attitudes. In the Ukraine, *Hamlet* was used to explore the nature of evil both as political and as a metaphysical problem. The first production of the play there took place under

German occupation and was considered a sort of proclamation of independence. Even earlier, in 1930s Soviet Georgia, under Communism, the theater "turned to Hamlet, a man who tries to survive and act within a world of the absurd." An especially notable Eastern European performance was in Riga, Latvia, in 1909. The premiere *of Hamlet* at the Riga Latvian Theatre was very well attended, as emphasized in the reviews: "At a time when German and Russian colonizers still maintained the politically strategic myth of an uneducable native peasantry, the nationalist paper *Latvija* declared this attendance was 'a sign that our people have a fully lively interest in classical literature.'" And today, Bates adds, *Hamlet* has held an extremely strong position in Eastern cultures.

Yeeyong Im relates how a well-known Korean production combined Western and Eastern elements: the director Lee Yountaek acknowledged the dilemma when he stated that the production "should be Korean, but not too Korean." He believed that tradition should be restructured according to the modern sensibility in order to be understood by the modern audience. He used deconstruction to "recover the sensibility and way of thinking inborn to Korean people that have been repressed under the imported Western structure of life." Thus, in staging Shakespeare, Lee encouraged "a partial incorporation of traditional Korean conventions, instead of transplanting Western drama completely into native theatre." His production of *Hamlet* was an intercultural hybrid, with the stage design, costumes, and music mixing both Korean and Western forms, past and present. He metaphorically combined "Western structure" and "Asiatic flesh and blood." As Im observes,

> The stage was painted ocher—symbolic of old Korea—in contrast with the gray of modern concrete buildings; the troupe got the inspiration from the graveyard nearby the theatre. A replica painting of Cheonmado (the ancient painting of a heavenly horse found at Cheonmachong, an ancient tomb of the Shilla dynasty [sixth century A.D.]) was hung on the wall surrounding the stage, as if to relate the flying horse to Hamlet as an Icarus figure. Thus the stage in general gave the impression of a gigantic ancient tomb in the old Korean style. The theme of life co-mingling with death is Lee's favorite theme, which recurs in many of his productions, because he regards it as one characteristic of traditional Korean philosophy.

As she adds, "After the fact, Lee justified the grave-like setting that he had created through intuition by invoking Hamlet's words about Alexander: 'Why may not imagination trace the noble dust of Alexander till 'a find it stopping a bunghole?' This passage seems to support Lee's Korean interpretation of the play: acceptance of death as an extension of life." In addition, "the players for the Mousetrap play wore masks and costumes that, if not authentically Korean, were reminiscent of ancient Korean dress and theatre arts. The brownish archaic robes of the clowns (later gravediggers) recalled an image of Buddhist monks, an association forti-fied by the characters' philosophical remarks on life and death.... The costume for the Ghost was made of a shroud, burnt and dyed with ocher, as if to recall the fate of the Korean past, and the Ghost's movement was expressed in dance-like, controlled steps based on the *dutbeogi* dance of Youngnam province" (264–67).

Hamlet-le-Malécite, written by Yves Sioui Durand and Jean-Frédéric Messier, was produced by Ondinnok, the only First Nations theatre company in Québec, in Montréal in June 2004. The performance, directed by Messier, was staged at American Can, an old warehouse with a view over the working-class Hochelaga-Maisonneuve district of the city in which the climactic final scenes of the play are set, even though the main action takes place in the fictional, rural village of Kinogamish. Making *ondinnok,* a Huron word for a theatrical healing ritual that reveals the secret desire of the soul, is precisely what the troupe seeks to accomplish through its theater. According to Sioui Durand, the troupe, which was founded in 1985 in order to create professional First Nations theatre, considers its work a *"théâtre de résistance parce qu'il est une tentative de décolonisation culturelle"* through the performance of *"[des] céremonie[s] pour se guérir de la violence et échapper à l'abîme du suicide"* [theatre of resistance because it's an attempt at cultural decolonization; ceremonies to heal from violence and escape the abyss of suicide]. In fact, medicine and suicide are important themes in the play: "While Dave calls out for his father to give him medicine, it is ironically the acts of this same father that provoke Ophélie to commit suicide. Failing to escape from the fate of her Shakespearean namesake, Ophélie exposes how many First Nations communities are plagued by the problem of suicide, especially among youth. According to statistics by the government of Canada, the overall rate of suicide is three times higher among Native peoples than other Canadians, and five to eight times higher among Native youth." *Hamlet-le-Malécite* "is thus marked throughout by a cynical dark humour that simultaneously resists the colonization of Native peoples through a critique of defeatism yet exposes nonetheless the sombre reality underlying that same defeatism." The doubly complicated position of seeking to overcome one's own colonized status while tacitly accepting it and one's place within the structures of power is embodied in the character of Laerte. Laerte likes fine French wine but becomes sick from eating *foie gras,* "what Homi Bhabha would call a colonial mimic man"; he is not quite "white" (or in this *case français de France).* Thus, "Dave's desperate quest for his paternal origins leads him only to disaster and the discovery that his genealogy—and the history of consanguinity of some First Nation communities, which, along with incest, is evoked throughout—is much darker than he could have imagined." Laerte, on the other hand, rejects dwelling on the past. His "cynical acceptance of the social construction of his identity by colonization harbours a critique but does not consume him to the point of immobility characteristic of Hamlet":

> *"Moi, j'ai jamais su c'était qui mon père. Pis je veux pas le savoir, i peut rien faire pour moi. Quand je veux savoir qui je suis, je sort [sic] mon portefeuille...pis dedans y'a une carte que le gouvernement du Canada m'a donné [sic], avec ma photo dessus, qui dit que je fais partie des premières nations, ce qui me confère le même statut que les poteaux de téléphones el les pare nationaux."* [I never knew who my father was. And I don't want to know; he can't do anything for me. When I want to know who I am, I open my wallet...and inside there's a card that the government of Canada gave me, with my picture on it, which says that I belong

to the First Nations, which confers on me the same status as telephone poles and national parks].

She concludes, "While the dark realization that Native peoples are little more than government property resounds with defeatism, Laerte refuses to be paralyzed by the system and attempts to exploit it as best he can" (Canadian Adaptations of *Hamlet* Project 77–78).

Daria Sito-Sucic reports on a Bosnian version: "Hamlet has become a Muslim prince at the Ottoman court in an adaptation of Shakespeare's tragedy which its Bosnian director says reflects the world after the September 11, 2001, attacks on the United States." Haris Pasovic, himself a Bosnian Muslim, told Reuters: "I think the Muslim world today is facing the question: 'To be or not to be?', and I don't mean metaphysically," he said before the show's premiere. Actors from Bosnia, Croatia, France, Serbia and Montenegro, Slovenia, Spain, and Turkey took part in the coproduction, the first time the ex-Yugoslav cities of Zagreb and Belgrade have jointly backed a project since Yugoslavia broke up in the 1990s: "Pasovic chose the Ottoman court for its resemblance to Shakespeare's Danish one, where characters vie bloodily against one another for control over the throne and the court's affairs. The play, set in obviously Eastern though minimalist scenery, was well received in Sarajevo, a traditionally multiethnic city dominated by moderate Muslims since the war. Just as Ottoman princes wore undershirts embroidered with Islamic prayers before they went into battle, Pasovic's Hamlet wears an undershirt on which the line 'To be, or not to be—that is the question' is printed in. Arabic script: 'That undershirt is important because it is like a human skin. I think that every serious man today must wear the question "To be, or not to be?",' Pasovic said." As Sucic concludes, "And so a story in a Christian setting, in which the hero questions the injustices of the world and his own personal tragedy, can just as well apply to Muslims. 'Hamlet is a universal story that concerns us all,' Pasovic said. These issues do not concern only Muslims, but all people equally, showing that we all share the same problems regardless of religion, nation and culture." Similarly, other scholars explore Arab, South African, and Indonesian productions of *Hamlet,* to name just a few.

C. *Frankenstein:* Are There Any New Worlds?

Frankenstein is often compared in classrooms to Aldous Huxley's *Brave New World* (1931), especially in terms of social ethics. Like Huxley's novel, Mary Shelley's tale, if it predicts anything for science, predicts a world in which brilliant, lone geniuses will test the limits of society's moral codes in pursuing new knowledge and enforcing it. Such a model of leadership was also the case with "New World" exploration, colonization, and government just before and during her time, the early nineteenth century. With the American Revolution, Britain lost its American colonies, but it did not end its economic and political relations with the new country of the United States of America nor with the Americas in general, especially Canada and the Caribbean. And as the later experiments of naturalists such as Louis Agassiz in the later nineteenth century attest, the "New World" remained a source of scientific as well as political (e.g., colonial) discovery.

The "New World" retains its idealistic nature, however, in *Frankenstein,* when in Chapter 17 the Creature promises Victor that if he will make a female Creature for him he will leave him and his family alone and go to South America to live in the jungle:

> "I intended to reason. This passion is detrimental to me; for you do not reflect that *you* are the cause of its excess. If any being felt emotions of benevolence towards me, I should return them an hundred and an hundred fold; for that one creature's sake, I would make peace with the whole kind! But I now indulge in dreams of bliss that cannot be realised. What I ask of you is reasonable and moderate; I demand a creature of another sex, but as hideous as myself; the gratification is small, but it is all that I can receive, and it shall content me. It is true we shall be monsters, cut off from all the world; but on that account we shall be more attached to one another. Our lives will not be happy, but they will be harmless, and free from the misery I now feel. Oh! my creator, make me happy; let me feel gratitude towards you for one benefit! Let me see that I excite the sympathy of some existing thing; do not deny me my request!"

The Creature's appeal is frank and realistic: if not in perfect happiness in their New World, he and his mate will survive, if "cut off from all the world," a distinctly anticolonialist view of the Americas. Frankenstein is moved: "I shuddered when I thought of the possible consequences of my consent; but I felt that there was some justice in his argument. His tale, and the feelings he now expressed, proved him to be a creature of fine sensations; and did I not as his maker owe him all the portion of happiness that it was in my power to bestow? He saw my change of feeling and continued." Victor speaks like a royal granting "rights" to his colonial subjects. Victor is reassured as the Creature adds,

> "If you consent, neither you nor any other human being shall ever see us again: I will go to the vast wilds of South America. My food is not that of man; I do not destroy the lamb and the kid to glut my appetite; acorns and berries afford me sufficient nourishment. My companion will be of the same nature as myself, and will be content with the same fare. We shall make our bed of dried leaves; the sun will shine on us as on man, and will ripen our food. The picture I present to you is peaceful and human, and you must feel that you could deny it only in the wantonness of power and cruelty." (129)

Again, the Creature speaks as the already colonized subject pleading for territory and autonomy, within a limited sphere. But Victor asks, " 'You propose ... to fly from the habitations of man, to dwell in those wilds where the beasts of the field will be your only companions. How can you, who long for the love and sympathy of man, persevere in this exile? You will return, and again seek their kindness, and you will meet with their detestation; your evil passions will be renewed, and you will then have a companion to aid you in the task of destruction. This may not be: cease to argue the point, for I cannot consent.' " But the Creature responds,

> "'I swear to you, by the earth which I inhabit, and by you that made me, that, with
> the companion you bestow, I will quit the neighbourhood of man, and dwell as it
> may chance in the most savage of places. My evil passions will have fled, for I shall
> meet with sympathy! my life will flow quietly away, and, in my dying moments,
> I shall not curse my maker'" (130).

Can this be the attitude of the colonized and banished? Would he come to
resent his "royal" banisher and try to reclaim his rights as a subject? We do not
know, because the Creature never escapes to the jungles, but dies on an ice floe at
the North Pole, the opposite space of his New World desire.

D. Jim's Superstitions in *Huckleberry Finn*

Beginning in Chapter 2, *Huckleberry Finn* presents Jim's superstitions as both foolish to Huck and Tom and meaningful to Jim; indeed, his powers of divination with
the hairball and nickel are the source of his high standing with other slaves. Jim
has also had experience with "witches":

> Tom said he slipped Jim's hat off of his head and hung it on a limb right over
> him, and Jim stirred a little, but he didn't wake. Afterwards Jim said the witches
> bewitched him and put him in a trance, and rode him all over the State, and
> then set him under the trees again and hung his hat on a limb to show who done
> it. And next time Jim told it he said they rode him down to New Orleans; and
> after that, every time he told it he spread it more and more, till by and by he said
> they rode him all over the world, and tired him most to death, and his back was
> all over saddle-boils. Jim was monstrous proud of it, and he got so he wouldn't
> hardly notice the other niggers. Niggers would come miles to hear Jim tell about
> it, and he was more looked up to than any nigger in that country. Strange niggers
> would stand with their mouths open and look him all over, same as if he was a
> wonder (7–8).

Tom's parody only has the effect of raising Jim's status. As Jim also (accurately)
prophesies about pap with his hairball and coin, and speaks of witches lurking again for him in the woods, Jim uses his role as conjurer to enhance his
(enslaved, colonized) status. Jim's superstitions may initially seem foolish, but
they are all authentic sources of his folk knowledge and are often borne out in
practical realities. This is in contrast to the empty promises of Christianity in
the novel—the Christianity of the white middle class of which Huck remains
skeptical to the end.

We must also remember that Huck has been taught folk superstitions by pap
and thus he ties his hair in a lock, turns around three times to ward off the devil,
and recognizes the crossed nails in pap's shoe as a sign. He worries about lost horse-
shoes and spiders in the candle flame, owls calling to the dead and the bad luck of
snakes. But Huck's folk education has not served him as well as Jim's, as is shown
repeatedly in the first few chapters. Huck often knows the story of things but not
their meaning, as with the snake and its mate. This distance between objectivity
and feeling appears in their varying interpretations of King Solomon's wisdom as
it does in their varying understandings of Jim's situation (e.g., Huck is quicker to

buy the falsehoods presented by the King and the Duke, Colonel Sherburn, the Wilks family, and the Phelps "relatives" than Jim is). Furthermore, Jim's fears of "haints" and other supernatural forces, especially the ideas of "riding" and "the woods," point to very real threats to blacks like him from the predecessors of the Ku Klux Klan. Thus Jim's superstitions are anything but "foolish"; they are means of survival, as well as a way of overcoming fear with hope—after all, Jim's hairy chest makes him a free man.

E. Salem: A City Upon a Hill?

In the Sermon on the Mount, Jesus tells his followers: "You are the light of the world. A city that is set upon a hill cannot be hidden" (Matthew 5:24), urging them to behave in such a way that others will notice and become drawn to the message of salvation. The phrase entered the American lexicon with Puritan preacher John Winthrop's sermon, "A Model of Christian Charity," given in 1630. Just as their ship, the *Arabella,* was close to land, Winthrop warned the Puritan colonists who were to found the Massachusetts Bay Colony that their experiment would be watched by the world: "For we must consider that we shall be as a city upon a hill. The eyes of all people are upon us. So that if we shall deal falsely with our God in this work we have undertaken...we shall be made a story and a by-word throughout the world. We shall open the mouths of enemies to speak evil of the ways of God....We shall shame the faces of many of God's worthy servants, and cause their prayers to be turned into curses upon us til [sic] we be consumed out of the good land whither we are a-going." Winthrop thus urged the colonists not only to be good spiritually but successful materially, for evidence of God's favor in the form of economic and social success would help demonstrate their beliefs to the rest of the world. Nathaniel Hawthorne makes the ironies of the town of Salem as a city upon a hill central to Hawthorne's exposure of hypocrisy and its critique of Puritan values in "Young Goodman Brown." The idea that the right religion will bring riches persists today, though among television evangelists who would be no match for Winthrop.

To be sure, Salem's history was hardly that of a "city upon a hill" for Hawthorne, mainly because of the Salem Witch Trials of 1692–93, in which hundreds were accused and arrested, and many executed. Such a backdrop for "Young Goodman Brown" suits Hawthorne's purpose in showing how the ideas of Calvinism could be perverted both by those who look only for perfection in people and those who look only for sin. The only people who seem successful—that is, emblems of a city upon a hill—are those at the very top of the hill, the Devil's special friends: Goodman Brown's father and grandfather, the Governor and his Lady, and highly placed members of Puritan society. In this hierarchy, one notes that Goodman Brown doesn't even have a job that is named, and he is clearly of a lower social status than these others. Who has prospered in the New World? It would appear to Brown that only the wicked have done so, but Hawthorne's larger point is that everyone, high or low, is both sinner and believer, a position Brown finds himself unable to embrace.

The postcolonial critic might explore the history of Salem and Massachusetts as colonized spaces in which old and new values would come into conflict, in which old identities might be shed in favor of hybrid ones, and in which new versions of national identity could be explored. Such issues in the story as the several mentions of Natives as in league with the Devil, shifting sexualities, and the balance of power among binaries such as men/women, dark/light, good/evil, town/forest, saved/damned, and so on, could be mapped onto the colonial space of transformation and reinvention. The overall motif of the journey across the seas and into the forest could be described as a symbol of cultural change, as well as of Brown's spiritual and psychological metamorphosis. The postcolonialist would also investigate the enduring and diverse legacy of "Salem," as in the very different works of Arthur Miller (*The Crucible*) and Stephen King (*Salem's Lot,* and the short story "Jerusalem's Lot"). They might also investigate how the phrase "city upon a hill" became even more an American idea when it was used to exhort Americans to serve their country in President John F. Kennedy's Inaugural Address in 1961.

F. The End of an Era in "Everyday Use"

In this story a world is passing away, and a new one awaits—intruding itself into the past it treasures, but not altering it. Mrs. Johnson, the mother of the two competing daughters and the narrator, acts as an intermediary between these worlds but ultimately makes a judgment in favor of the "old world" of their country house and farm. Mrs. Johnson has imagined herself as the perfect postcolonial subject, whitened to please the dominant elite (which ironically includes her daughter Dee) and appearing on the most iconically American television show of its era, "The Tonight Show," where its "smiling, gray, sporty man, like Johnny Carson" presides. Note both the "grayness" of this icon of whiteness as his being "like" Johnny Carson, as though it does not really matter to the narrator. When her daughter Dee shows up, full of back-to-Africa names, identities, and fashion, the narrator is nonplussed but steady; her decision at the end of the story to give the quilts to Maggie demonstrates her good sense, her traditional view of life, and her resistance to what the television dictates for women. Unlike the women on "The Tonight Show," she is large, black, and fit to work outdoors to run a farm without a man to help her. The narrator indicates her satisfaction with her life at the end of the story, when Dee drives off and she and Maggie enjoy a dip of snuff, but she also hints at a changing landscape by mentioning the "beef-cattle peoples" up the road. Perhaps hers will be one of the last "swept clean" front yards, bottle trees, and hand-made quilts, but the narrator and story imply that these traditional forms have a lot longer life and much more to say than postmodern, politically aware people like Dee might suspect.

IV. SUMMARY OF KEY POINTS

- Postcolonialism refers to a historical phase undergone by Third World countries following the decline of colonialism.

- Postcolonialism has strong ties to the disciplines of history and political science.
- The British Empire once ruled one-fourth of the earth.
- Key figures in postcolonialism include Edward Said, Frantz Fanon, Homi Bhaba, and Gayatri Chakravorty Spivak.
- Authors often studied by postcolonial critics include Salman Rushdie, Jean Rhys, and Norma Elia Cantú.
- Postcolonialism has been an important force in feminism, especially Third World feminism.
- Spatial studies is a new field influenced by postcolonialism that challenges Western views of Third World spaces, examines how power interacts with geographical spaces, how nations map themselves onto colonized spaces. It examines borders, diasporas, refugees and immigrants, transnational spaces, and how the separation of workplace and home has alienated workers.
- Important figures in spatial studies include Edward Soja, Mary Louise Pratt, and Chinua Achebe.

V. LIMITATIONS OF POSTCOLONIALISM

The limitations of postcolonial criticism are similar to those for any approach that takes a primarily political view of literature, such as feminism or Marxism. That is, postcolonialist approaches can elide the aesthetic properties of a work of literature in the pursuit of politically correct solutions. As of now, postcolonialism has set its own limits, since nearly all of it pertains only to Western colonization; indeed, only Euro-American colonization in Africa, Asia, and the Americas. It has not yet managed to address some objections raised to the approach: Isn't nearly all human history the history of colonization, so that it is not unique to the early modern and modern eras? What about Asians colonizing Asians or Africans Africans? Do the same sorts of power structures exist in all colonization? Are postcolonial experiences narrated in similar manners around the world? Does postcolonial status always silence indigenous cultures? Was colonialism exclusively a negative force? Many explorers, missionaries, and scientists would disagree. Do all postcolonial voices reflect primarily their postcolonial status? In addition, what really distinguishes a "subaltern" voice—if the voice is spoken, is it still "subaltern?" There are subalterns and subalterns: Salman Rushdie versus an anonymous slave narrator.

QUICK REFERENCE

Abrahams, Roger D., ed. *Afro-American Folktales: Stories from Black Traditions in the New World.* New York: Pantheon, 1985.

Achebe, Chinua. "An Image of Africa: Racism in Conrad's 'Heart of Darkness.'" *Heart of Darkness: An Authoritative Text, Backgrounds, and Sources, Criticism.* New York: Norton, 1988. 251–62.

Adorno, Theodor. *The Adorno Reader.* Ed. Brian O'Connor. London: Blackwell, 2000.

Althusser, Louis. *For Marx.* Trans. Ben Brewster. New York: Pantheon, 1969.

Ammons, Elizabeth, and Annette White Parks, eds. *Tricksterism in Turn-of-the-Century American Literature: A Multicultural Perspective.* Hanover, MA: Tufts University Press, 1994.

Anderson, Benedict. *Imagined Communities.* New York: Verso, 2006.

Anzaldúa, Gloria. *Borderlands, La Frontera: The New Mestiza.* 1987. Rpt. San Francisco: Spinsters/Aunt Lute, 1999.

Ashcroft, Bill, Gareth Griffiths, and Helen Tiffin, eds. *The Post-Colonial Studies Reader.* 2nd edn. London: Routledge, 2006.

Ashcroft, Bill, Gareth Griffiths, Helen Tiffin, and Sarah Menin, eds. *The Empire Writes Back: Theory and Practice in Post-Colonial Literatures.* New York: Routledge, 2000.

Bakhtin, Mikhail. *The Dialogic Imagination: Four Essays.* Ed. Michael Holquist. Trans. Caryl Emerson. Austin: University of Texas Press, 1981.

Baksh-Soodeen, Rawwida. "Issues of Difference in Contemporary Caribbean Feminism." *Feminist Review.* Special Issue on Rethinking the Caribbean Difference 59 (Summer 1998): 74–85.

Barthes, Roland. *Mythologies.* Trans. Annette Lavers. New York: Hill and Wang, 1972.

Bates, Laura Raidonis. "Hamlet Under Imperialist Rule" *Lituans: Lithuaniauan Quarterly Journal of Arts and Sciences* 43, 3 (Fall 1997): http://www.lituanus.org/1997/97_3_04.htm

Baudrillard, Jean. *Simulations.* Trans. Paul Foss, Paul Patton, and Philip Beitchnan. New York: Semiotext (e), 1981.

Bell, Bernard. *The Afro-American Novel and Its Tradition.* Amherst: University of Massachusetts Press, 1987.

Benjamin, Walter. *Illuminations.* Ed. Hannah Arendt. Trans. H. Zohn. New York: Harcourt, 1968.

Bhabha, Homi K. *The Location of Culture.* New York: Routledge, 1994.

———. *The Location of Culture.* London: Routledge, 1994.

Botstein, Leon. "The De-Europeanization of American Culture." In Sill et al.

Bourdieu, Pierre. *Outline of a Theory of Practice.* Trans. Richard Nice. Cambridge Studies in Social Anthropology, no. 16. Cambridge: Cambridge University Press, 1977.

Brady, Mary Pat. "The Fungability of Borders." *Nepantla: View from the South.* 1, 1 (2000): 171–89.

Brantlinger, Patrick. *Crusoe's Footprints: Cultural Studies in Britain and America.* New York: Routledge, 1990.

Brady, Mary Pat. "The Fungability of Borders." *Nepantla: View from the South* 1, 1 (2000): 171–89.

Brody, Jules. "The Resurrection of the Body: A New Reading of Marvell's 'To His Coy Mistress.'" *ELH* 56, no. 1 (1986): 53–80.

Bruce, Susan. "The Flying Island and Female Anatomy: Gynaecology and Power in *Gulliver's Travels.*" *Genders* 2 (July 1988): 60–76.

Cain, William E. "Why English Departments Should Focus on Close Reading, Not Cultural Studies." In *Chronicle of Higher Education* (13 Dec. 1996): B4.

Calderon, Hector, and José David Saldivar, eds. *Criticism in the Borderlands: Studies in Chicano Literature, Culture, and Ideology.* Durham, NC: Duke University Press, 1991.

Cantú, Norma Elia. *Canicula: Snapshots of a Girlhood en la frontera.* Albuquerque: University of New Mexico Press, 1994.

Césaire, Aimé. *Discourse on Colonialism*. 1950. Trans. Joan Pinkham, New York: Monthly Review Press, 1972.

Chatterjee, Partha. *The Nation and Its Fragments: Colonial and Postcolonial Histories.* Princeton, NJ: Princeton University Press, 1993.

Chhachhi, Amrita. "Concepts in Feminist Theory: Consensus and Controversy." In *Gender in Caribbean Development*. Ed. Patricia Mohammed and Catherine Shepard. Mona, Jamaica: University of the West Indies Women and Development Studies Project, 1988.

Childers, Joseph, and Gary Hentzi, eds. *The Columbia Dictionary of Modern Literary and Cultural Criticism*. New York: Columbia University Press, 1995.

Davidson, Cathy N., ed. *Reading in America: Literature and Social History*. Baltimore: Johns Hopkins University Press, 1989.

de Certeau, Michel. *The Practice of Everyday Life*. Trans. Steven F. Rendall. Berkeley: University of California Press, 1984.

Derrida, Jacques. *Of Grammatology*. Trans. Gayatri Chakravorty Spivak. Baltimore: Johns Hopkins University Press, 1974.

——. *Writing and Difference*. Chicago: University of Chicago Press, 1980.

DuBois, W. E. B. *The Souls of Black Folk*. 1903. Reprint. New York: St. Martin's Press, 1997.

Duran, Yves Sioui, and Edward Messer. "Hamlet-le-Malécite (2004). Canadian Adaptations of Shakespeare Project http://www.canadianshakespeares.ca/a_sioui.cfm.

Eagleton, Terry. "Foreword." In Daniel Cottom. *Social Figures: George Eliot, Social History, and Literary Representation*. Minneapolis: University of Minnesota Press, 1987.

Eisenstein, Zillah. *Against Empire: Feminisms, Racism, and the West*. London: Zed Books, 2004.

Ellison, Ralph. *Shadow and Act*. New York: Random House, 1964.

Epstein, Marcus. "Black Libertarian: The Story of Zora Neale Thurston. http://www.lewrockwell.com/orig/epstein2.html.

Fanon. *Black Skin, White Masks*. 1952. Trans. Charles Lam Markmann. New York: Grove Press, 1967.

——, Frantz. *The Wretched of the Earth*. Preface by Jean-Paul Sartre. Trans. Constance Farrington. New York: Grove Press, 1963.

Fishkin, Shelley Fisher. *Was Huck Black? Mark Twain and African American Voices*. New York: Oxford University Press, 1993.

Flores, Juan, and George Yudice. "Living Borders/Buscando America: Languages of Latino Self-Formation." *Social Text* 24 (1990): 57–84.

Florescu, Radu. *In Search of Frankenstein*. Boston: New York Graphic Society, 1975.

Foucault, Michel. "The Eye of Power." Preface to Jeremy Bentham, *La Panoptique*. 1977. Rpt. in *Power/Knowledge*. 1980.

——. "What Is an Author?" From *Discipline and Punish;* from *The History of Sexuality* (Vol. 1); and from *Truth and Power*. Reprinted in Leitch.

Gates, Henry Louis, Jr. *"Race," Writing and Difference*. Chicago: University of Chicago Press, 1986.

——. *The Signifying Monkey*. New York: Oxford University Press, 1988.

Geertz, Clifford. *The Interpretation of Cultures*. New York: Basic Books, 1972.

Gilroy, Paul. *The Black Atlantic: Modernity and Double Consciousness*. Cambridge, Mass.: Harvard University Press, 1993.

——. *The Black Atlantic: Modernity and Double Consciousness*. Cambridge, MA: Harvard University Press, 1995.

Giroux, Henry, David Shumway, Paul Smith, and James Sosnoski. "The Need for Cultural Studies: Resisting Intellectuals and Oppositional Public Spheres." *Dalhousie Review* 64, no. 2 (1984): 472–86.

Graff, Gerald, and James Phelan, eds. Adventures of Huckleberry Finn: *A Case Study in Critical Controversy.* Boston: St. Martin's Press/Bedford Books, 1995.

Gramsci, Antonio. *Selections from the Prison Notebooks.* Ed. Quintin Hoare and Geoffrey Nowell Smith. New York: International, 1971.

Granville-Barker, Harley. *Prefaces to Shakespeare.* 2 Vols. Princeton: Princeton University Press, 1946.

Greenblatt, Stephen. "Towards a Poetics of Culture." In Veeser.

Groden, Michael, and Martin Krieswirth, eds. *The Johns Hopkins Guide to Literary Theory and Criticism.* Baltimore: Johns Hopkins University Press, 1994.

Grossberg, Lawrence, Cary Nelson, and Paula Treicher, eds. *Cultural Studies.* New York: Routledge, 1992.

Haining, Peter, ed. *The Frankenstein Omnibus.* London: Orion, 1994. Reprint. Edison, NJ: Chartwell Books, 1994.

Hau'ofa, Epeli. "Our Sea of Islands." In *A New Oceania: Rediscovering Our Sea of Islands.* Ed. Eric Waddell, Vijay Naidu, and Epeli Hau'ofa (Suva, Fiji: School of Social and Economic Development, University of the South Pacific, 1993). 2–26. Rpt. in *Contemporary Pacific* 6 (1994): 147–61.

———. "The Ocean in Us." In *Voyaging Through the Contemporary Pacific.* Ed. David Hanlon and Geoffrey M. White. Lanham, MD: Rowman & Littlefield Publishers, 2000.

Hebdige, Dick. *Hiding the Light: On Images and Things.* New York: Routledge, 1988.

Hunter, J. Paul ed. *Mary Shelley, Frankenstein.* New York: W. W. Norton, 1996.

Huyssen, Andreas. *After the Great Divide: Modernism, Mass Culture, Postmodernism.* Bloomington: Indiana University Press, 1986.

Im, Yeeyon. "The Location of Shakespeare in Korea: Lee Yountaek's *Hamlet* and the Mirage of Interculturality." *Theater Journal* 60, 2 (May 2008): 257–76.

Jameson, Frederic. *The Political Unconscious: Studies in the Ideology of Form.* Ithaca, NY: Cornell University Press, 1979.

———. *Postmodernism, or the Cultural Logic of Late Capitalism.* Durham, NC: Duke University Press, 1991.

JanMohamed, Abdul R. "The Economy of Manichean Allegory: The Function of Racial Difference in Colonialist Literature." *Critical Inquiry* 13,1 (Autumn 1986): 59–87.

Jenkins, Harold, ed. *The Arden Shakespeare: Hamlet.* New York and London: Routledge, 1982. Reprint, 1989–90.

Joseph, Bertram. *Conscience and the King: A Study of Hamlet.* London: Chatto and Windus, 1953.

Kalogeras, Yiorgos, Eleftheria Arapoglou, and Linda Manney, eds. *Transcultural Localisms: Responding to Ethnicity in a Globalized World.* Heidelberg, Germany: Universitätsverlag, 2006.

Kaplan, Justin. "Born to Trouble: One Hundred Years of *Huckleberry Finn.*" In Graff and Phelan.

Katrak, Ketu H. *Politics of the Female Body: Postcolonial Women Writers of the Third World.* New Brunswick, NJ: Rutgers University Press, 2006.

Kranzler, Laura. "*Frankenstein* and the Technological Future." *Foundation* 44 (Winter 1988–89): 42–49.

Lacan, Jacques. *Ecrits: A Selection.* 1966. Trans. Alan Sheridan. New York: W. W. Norton, 1977. Revised version reprinted 2002. Trans. Bruce Fink.

Lawrence, D. H. *Studies in Classical American Fiction.* 1923. Reprint. New York: Viking/Compass, 1964.

Leavis, F. R. *Revaluation: Tradition and Development in English Poetry.* 1936. Reprint. New York: Ivan R. Dee, 1998.

Lederer, Susan E. Visiting Curator. *Frankenstein: Penetrating the Secrets of Nature.* Exhibition by the National Library of Medicine. New Brunswick, NJ: Rutgers University Press, 2002.

Leitch, Vincent, ed. *Norton Anthology of Theory Criticism.* New York: W. W. Norton, 2001.

Lester, Julius. "Morality and *Adventures of Huckleberry Finn.*" In Graff and Phelan.

Levine, George, and U. C. Knopelmacher, eds. *The Endurance of* Frankenstein: *Essays on Mary Shelley's Novel.* Berkeley: University of California Press, 1979.

———. "The Ambiguous Heritage of *Frankenstein.*" In Levine and Knopelmacher.

Lévi-Strauss, Claude. *The Raw and the Cooked.* Trans. John and Doreen Weightman. New York: Harper, 1975.

Levith, Murray J. *What's in Shakespeare's Names.* Hamden, CT: Shoe String Press/Archon, 1978.

Litvak, Joseph. "Back to the Future: A Review-Article on the New Historicism, Deconstruction, and Nineteenth-Century Fiction." *Texas Studies in Literature and Language* 30 (1988): 120–49.

Loomba, Ania. *Colonialism/Postcolonialism.* 2nd edn. London: Routledge, 2005.

Lukács, Georg. *The Theory of the Novel.* 1920. Reprint. Cambridge, MA: Massachusetts Institute of Technology Press, 1971.

Lyotard, Jean-François. *The Postmodern Condition: A Report on Knowledge.* 1979. Reprint. Manchester: Manchester University Press, 1984.

Malchow, H. L. "Was Frankenstein's Monster 'a Man and a Brother'?" *Gothic Images of Race in Nineteenth-Century Britain.* Stanford: Stanford University Press, 1996.

Mignolo, Walter. *Local Histories/Global Designs.* Princeton, NJ: Princeton University Press, 2000.

Mohammed, Patricia and Catherine Shepard, eds. *Gender in Caribbean Development.* Mona, Jamaica: University of the West Indies Women and Development Studies Project, 1988.

Mohanty, Chandra. *Feminism Without Borders: Decolonizing Theory, Practicing Solidarity.* Durham, NC: Duke University Press, 2003.

Morrison, Toni. *Playing in the Dark: Whiteness and Literary Imagination.* New York: Vintage Press, 1993.

Morton, Timothy, ed. *A Routledge Literary Sourcebook on Mary Shelley's* Frankenstein. London and New York: Routledge, 2002.

Mullaney, Steven. "Brothers and Others, or the Art of Alienation." In *Cannibals, Witches, and Divorce: Estranging the Renaissance.* Ed. Marjorie Garber. Baltimore: Johns Hopkins University Press, 1987.

Murdoch, Jonathan. *Post-Structuralist Geography: A Guide to Relational Space.* London: Sage, 2006.

Ngugi, James [Ngugi wa Thiong'o]. *Weep Not, Child.* 1964. Rpt. New York: Collier Books, 1969.

Pechter, Edward. "The New Historicism and Its Discontents: Politicizing Renaissance Drama." *PMLA* 102 (May 1987): 292–303.

Phillips, Richard. "The Geography of Robinson Crusoe." *Post-Colonial Theory and English Literature: A Reader.* Ed. Peter Childs. Edinburgh, Scotland: Edinburgh University, 1999. 120–27.

Porter, Carolyn. "Are We Being Historical Yet?" *South Atlantic Quarterly* 87 (Fall 1988): 743–86.

Portillo, Maria Josefina. *The Revolutionary Imagination in the Americas and the Age of Development.* Durham, NC: Duke University Press, 2003.

Pratt, Mary Louise. *Imperial Eyes: Travel Writing and Transculturation.* New York: Routledge, 1992.

Radway, Janice. *Reading the Romance: Women, Patriarchy, and Popular Literature.* Chapel Hill: University of North Carolina Press, 1984.

Rebolledo, Diana, and Eliana S. Rivera, eds. *Infinite Divisions: An Anthology of Chicana Literature.* Tucson: University of Arizona Press, 1993.

Reynolds, David S. *Beneath the American Renaissance: The Subversive Imagination in the Age of Emerson and Melville.* New York: Alfred A. Knopf, 1988.

Richter, David, ed. *The Critical Tradition.* New York: St. Martin's, 1998.

Roberts, John. *From Trickster to Badman: The Black Folk Hero in Slavery and Freedom.* Philadelphia: University of Pennsylvania Press, 1989.

——. "The African American Animal Trickster as Hero." In *Redefining American Literary History.* Ed. A. LaVonne Ruoff and Jerry W. Ward. New York: MLA, 1990.

Rushdie, Salman. *Imaginary Homelands: Essays in Criticism, 1981–1991.* New York: Penguin, 1992.

Said, Edward. *Orientalism.* New York: Pantheon, 1978.

——. *Culture and Imperialism.* New York: Knopf, 1993.

Schatzki, Theodore R. "Spatial Ontology and Explanation." *Annals of the Association of American Geographers.* 81, 4 (1991): 650–70.

Shelley, Mary. *The Letters of Mary Wollstonecraft Shelley.* Ed. Betty T. Bennett. 3 vols. Baltimore: Johns Hopkins University Press, 1980–88.

Sill, Geoffrey M., Miriam T. Chaplin, Jean Ritzke, and David Wilson, eds. *Opening the American Mind: Race, Ethnicity, and Gender in Higher Education.* Newark: University of Delaware Press, 1993.

Skal, David J. *The Monster Show: A Cultural History of Horror.* New York: Norton, 1993.

Sito-Sucic, Daria. "Hamlet Made a Muslim Prince in Post 9/11 Adaptation." Reuters, September 2005. *Free Republic.* http://www.freerepublic.com/focus/f-news/1485277/posts.

Smith, Johanna M., ed. Frankenstein *by Mary Shelley.* 1831 Text. 2nd ed. Boston: Bedford/St. Martin's, 2000.

Soja, Edward. "The Spatiality of Social Life: Towards a Transformative Retheorisation." *Social Relations and Spatial Structures.* Eds. Derek Gregory and John Urry. New York: St. Martin's, 1985. 90–127.

——. "History: geography: modernity." *The Cultural Studies Reader.* Ed. Simon During. New York: Routledge, 1993. 135–49.

Spivak, Gayatri Chakravorty. "Can the Subaltern Speak? Speculations on Widow-Sacrifice." *Wedge* 7, 8 (Winter-Spring 1985): 120–30. Rpt. and Expanded in *Marxism and the*

Interpretation of Culture. Ed. Laurence Grossberg and Cary Nelson. Urbana: University of Illinois Press, 1985. 271–313.

———. "Three Women's Texts and a Critique of Imperialism." *Critical Inquiry* 12 (Autumn 1985): 243–61.

———. "Three Women's Texts and a Critique of Imperialism." *Critical Inquiry* 12 (Autumn 1985): 243–61. Reprinted as "*Frankenstein* and a Critique of Imperialism." In Hunter.

———. *A Critique of Postcolonial Reason: Toward a History of the Vanishing Present.* Cambridge, Mass.: Harvard University Press, 1999.

———. "From *A Critique of Postcolonial Reason.*" In Leitch.

Stepan, Nancy Leys. *Picturing Tropical Nature.* Ithaca, NY: Cornell University Press, 2001.

Tambiah, Stanley J. "Transnational Movements, Diasporas, and Multiple Modernities." *Daedalus* 129, 1 (2000): 163–94.

Trask, Haunani-Kay. *From a Native Daughter: Colonialism and Sovereignty in Hawai'i.* Rev. edn. Honolulu: University of Hawai'i Press, 1999.

Tylor, Edward Burnett. *Primitive Culture.* New York: Holt, 1877.

Veeser, H. Aram, ed. *The New Historicism.* New York: Routledge, 1989.

Velie, Alan R., ed. *American Indian Literature: A Brief Introduction and Anthology.* New York: HarperCollins, 1995.

Vizenor, Gerald. *Fugitive Poses: Native American Indian Scenes of Absence and Presence.* Lincoln: University of Nebraska Press, 1998.

Warner, Michael. "Literary Studies and the History of the Book." *Book* 12 (1987): 3–9.

Wendt, Albert. "Towards a New Oceania." *Mana Review* 1 (1976): 49–60.

White, Hayden. *Metahistory: The Historical Imagination in Nineteenth-Century Europe.* Baltimore: Johns Hopkins University Press, 1973.

Wiget, Andrew. "His Life in His Tale: The Native American Trickster and the Literature of Possibility." In *Redefining American Literary History.* Ed. A. LaVonne Ruoff and Jerry W. Ward. New York: MLA, 1990.

Williams, Patrick, and Laura Chrisman, eds. *Colonial Discourse and Postcolonial Theory: A Reader.* New York: Columbia University Press, 1994.

Williams, Raymond. *Marxism and Literature.* New York: Oxford University Press, 1973.

———. *Culture and Society: 1780–1950.* London: Chatto, 1958.

Winthrop, John. "A Model for Christian Charity." 1630. Rpt. *The Puritans in America: A Narrative Anthology.* Eds. Alan Heimert and Andrew Delbanco. Cambridge, Mass.: Harvard University Press, 1985. 89–92.

Young, Robert J. C. *Postcolonialism: A Very Short Introduction.* Oxford, Eng.: Oxford University Press, 2003.

———. *White Mythologies: Writing History and the West.* 2nd edn. London: Routledge, 2004.

Epilogue

"How do you learn to *read* this way? *Where* do you learn this? Do you take a course in *symbols* or something?"

With a rising, plaintive pitch to his voice, with puzzled eyes and shaking head, a college student once asked those questions after his class had participated in a lively discussion of the multiple levels in Henry James's *Turn of the Screw*. As with most students when they are first introduced to a serious study of literature, members of this group were delighted, amazed—and dismayed—as they tried to unfold the rich layers of the work, to see it from perspectives of form and of psychology, to correlate it with the author's biography and its cultural and historical context.

But that particular student, who was both fascinated and dismayed by the "symbols," had not yet taken a crucial step in the learning process: he had not perceived that the practice of close reading, the bringing to bear of all kinds of knowledge, and the use of several approaches are in themselves the "course in symbols or something." What we have traced in this volume is not something only for those who have access to the inner sanctum. A poet or a dramatist embodies an experience in a poem or a play, embodies it—usually—for us, the readers; and we respond by reliving that experience as fully as possible.

To be sure, not all of us may want to respond to that extent. There was, for example, the secondary school teacher who listened to a fairly long and detailed explication of "The Death of the Ball-Turret Gunner," a five-line poem by Randall Jarrell. Later she took the lecturer aside and said, with something more than asperity, "I'd *never* make my class try to see all of *that* in a poem." Perhaps not. But is the class better or worse because of that attitude?

Clearly, the authors of this book believe that we readers are the losers when we fail to see in a work of literature all that may be legitimately seen there. We have presented a number of critical approaches to literature, aware that some have been only briefly treated and that much has been generalized. But we have suggested here some of the tools and some of the approaches that enable a reader to criticize—that is, to judge and to discern so that he or she may see better the literary work, to relate it to the range of human experience, to appreciate its form and style.

Having offered these tools and approaches, we would also urge that caution against undue or misdirected enthusiasm in their use is called far. Some read a simple poem like William Carlos Williams's "The Red Wheelbarrow" and, unwilling to see simplicity and compression as virtues enough (and as much more than mere simpleness), stray from the poem into their individual mazes. They forget that any interpretation must be supported logically and fully from the evidence within the literary work and that the ultimate test of the validity of an interpretation must be its self-consistency. Conversely, sometimes they do establish a fairly legitimate pattern of interpretation for a work, only to find something that seems to be at odds with it; then, fascinated with or startled by what they assume to be a new element, they forget that their reading is not valid unless it permits a unified picture of both the original pattern and the new insight.

Pablo Picasso, *Las Meniñas según Velázquez,* 1957

This painting is perhaps the most famous of Picasso's many interpretations of Velázquez's original. In comparing and contrasting the two paintings, one first notices how Picasso has chosen a palette of black, grey, and white. He has flattened the space onto a single plane but left the suggestion of depth through lines of perspective and an emphasis on the man coming in through the back door, which is very brightly lit. But it is what has happened to the characters in the painting that most shows the influence of modern art. Picasso was a Cubist, and his people are often composed as blocks emphasizing certain angles of the body. In this painting the maid of honor to the left is treated this way, as is the Infanta and the dwarf. The maid of honor on the right is reinterpreted cubistically as a horse's head. The two chaperones in the right rear become coffin-like boxes with faces like skeletons and tiny hands sticking out. But Picasso uses other techniques: The boy on the far right becomes a line drawing, and the painter becomes gigantic and is made up of shapes with odd symbols here and there. Picasso's palette draws attention to itself, as does the canvas, which is broken into two planes, perhaps reflecting the importance of form to Picasso, as opposed to realistic renderings of the characters. A dash of humor pervades the work, especially the Dali-like mustache drawn on the king which renders him comical. A note of mystery is introduced with the two hooks added to the ceiling.

Questions: What does it mean in terms of criticism to portray human beings this way? Can we find the careful formal relationships in Velázquez's painting also in Picasso's? Are any of their relationships changed by Picasso? Note how the source of light at the window has been dramatized—what would Picasso's purpose be here? Why no color? Finally, how can we use this interpretation to highlight the differences between "traditional" art and modern art? What are some parallels in literature and literary criticism?

Figure E.1. Pablo Picasso, *Las Meniñas*, No. 1 (1957).
Museo Picasso, Barcelona, Spain/© DACS/Giraudon/The Bridgeman Art Library International/© 2009 Estate of Pablo Picasso/Artists Rights Society (ARS), New York.

Individual readers bring their own unique experiences to the perception of a literary work of art; since these experiences may and will be vastly different, they will color the readers' perceptions. As we have shown, important recent critical theories have acknowledged and furthered this potential for more subjective and culturally based interpretations.

We must therefore remember to be flexible and eclectic in our choices of critical approaches to a given literary work. Our choices are determined by the same discretion that controls what we exclude, by our concern for the unique experience and nature of a piece of literature. Not all approaches are useful in all cases. All we can do is to draw from the many approaches the combination that best fits a particular literary creation. As David Daiches has said, "Every effective literary critic sees some facet of literary art and develops an awareness with respect to it; but the total vision, or something approximating it, comes only to those who learn how to blend the insights yielded by many critical approaches" (393).

That is why we have chosen to present a variety of approaches and why some of the chapters in this book have even blended several methods. This blending is as it should be. It is not easy—and it would be unwise to try—to keep the work always separate from the life of the author and a view of his or her times; to divide the study of form from the study of basic imageries; to segregate basic imageries from archetypes or from other components of the experience of the work. And it would be unwise to ignore how, for example, a work long known and interpreted by older, traditional methods might yield fresh insights if examined from such newer perspectives as feminism and cultural studies.

Our final word, then, is this: we admit that literary criticism can be difficult and sometimes esoteric, but it is first of all an attempt of readers to understand fully what they are reading. To understand in that manner, they do well to bring to bear whatever is in the human province that justifiably helps them to achieve that understanding. For literature is a part of the richness of human experience: it at once thrives on it, feeds it, and constitutes a significant part of it. When we realize this, we never again can be satisfied with the simple notions that a story is something only for the idler or the impractical dreamer (like Hawthorn's fiddler), that a poem is merely a pretty combination of sounds and sights, that a significant drama is equivalent to a television melodrama. As Browning's Fra Lippo Lippi puts it:

> This world's no blot for us,
> Nor blank; it means intensely, and means good:
> To find its meaning is my meat and drink.

Appendix A

Andrew Marvell
TO HIS COY MISTRESS

Had we but world enough, and time,
This coyness, Lady, were no crime.
We would sit down and think which way
To walk and pass our long love's day.
Thou by the Indian Ganges' side   5
Shouldst rubies find; I by the tide
Of Humber would complain. I would
Love you ten years before the Flood,
And you should, if you please, refuse
Till the conversion of the Jews.   10
My vegetable love should grow
Vaster than empires, and more slow;
An hundred years should go to praise
Thine eyes and on thy forehead gaze;
Two hundred to adore each breast,   15
But thirty thousand to the rest;
An age at least to every part,
And the last age should show your heart.
For, Lady, you deserve this state,
Nor would I love at lower rate.   20

But at my back I always hear
Time's wingèd chariot hurrying near;
And yonder all before us lie
Deserts of vast eternity.
Thy beauty shall no more be found,   25

Nor, in thy marble vault, shall sound
My echoing song; then worms shall try
That long preserved virginity,
And your quaint honor turn to dust,
And into ashes all my lust:
The grave's a fine and private place,   30
But none, I think, do there embrace.

Now therefore, while the youthful hue
Sits on thy skin like morning dew,
And while thy willing soul transpires   35
At every pore with instant fires,
Now let us sport us while we may,
And now, like amorous birds of prey,
Rather at once our time devour
Than languish in his slow-chapped power.   40
Let us roll all our strength and all
Our sweetness up into one ball,
And tear our pleasures with rough strife
Thorough* the iron gates of life:
Thus, though we cannot make our sun   45
Stand still, yet we will make him run.

*thorough: through

Appendix B

Nathaniel Hawthorne
YOUNG GOODMAN BROWN

Young Goodman Brown came forth at sunset into the street at Salem Village; but put his head back, after crossing the threshold, to exchange a parting kiss with his young wife. And Faith, as the wife was aptly named, thrust her own pretty head into the street, letting the wind play with the pink ribbons of her cap while she called to Goodman Brown.

"Dearest heart," whispered she, softly and rather sadly, when her lips were close to his ear, "prithee put off your journey until sunrise and sleep in your own bed to-night. A lone woman is troubled with such dreams and such thoughts that she's afeard of herself sometimes. Pray tarry with me this night, dear husband, of all nights in the year."

"My love and my Faith," replied young Goodman Brown, "of all nights in the year, this one night must I tarry away from thee. My journey, as thou callest it, forth and back again, must needs be done 'twixt now and sunrise. What, my sweet, pretty wife, dost thou doubt me already, and we but three months married?"

"Then God bless you!" said Faith, with the pink ribbons; "and may you find all well when you come back."

"Amen!" cried Goodman Brown. "Say thy prayers, dear Faith, and go to bed at dusk, and no harm will come to thee."

So they parted; and the young man pursued his way until, being about to turn the corner by the meeting-house, he looked back and saw the head of Faith still peeping after him with a melancholy air, in spite of her pink ribbons.

"Poor little Faith!" thought he, for his heart smote him. "What a wretch am I to leave her on such an errand! She talks of dreams, too. Methought as she spoke there was trouble in her face, as if a dream had warned her what work is to be done to-night. But no, no; 'twould kill her to think it. Well, she's a blessed angel on earth, and after this one night I'll cling to her skirts and follow her to heaven."

foreshadow

With this excellent resolve for the future, Goodman Brown felt himself justified in making more haste on his present evil purpose. He had taken a dreary road, darkened by all the gloomiest trees of the forest, which barely stood aside to let the narrow path creep through, and closed immediately behind. It was all as lonely as could be; and there is this peculiarity in such a solitude, that the traveller knows not who may be concealed by the innumerable trunks and the thick boughs overhead; so that with lonely footsteps he may yet be passing through an unseen multitude.

racist / (even) *historical* *context*

"There may be a devilish Indian behind every tree," said Goodman Brown to himself; and he glanced fearfully behind him as he added, "What if the devil himself should be at my very elbow!"

His head being turned back, he passed a crook of the road, and, looking forward again, beheld the figure of a man, in grave and decent attire, seated at the foot of an old tree. He arose at Goodman Brown's approach and walked onward side by side with him.

"You are late, Goodman Brown," said he. "The clock of the Old South was striking as I came through Boston, and that is full fifteen minutes agone."

symbolic? "Faith kept me back a while," replied the young man, with a tremor in his voice, caused by the sudden appearance of his companion, though not wholly unexpected.

It was now deep dusk in the forest, and deepest in that part of it where these two were journeying. As nearly as could be discerned, the second traveller was about fifty years old, apparently in the same rank of life as Goodman Brown, and bearing a considerable resemblance to him, though perhaps more in expression than features. Still they might have been taken for father and son. And yet, though the elder person was as simply clad as the younger, and as simple in manner too, he had an indescribable air of one who knew the world, and who would not have felt abashed at the governor's dinner table or in King William's court, were it possible that his affairs should call him thither. But the only thing about him that could be fixed upon as remarkable was his staff, which bore the likeness of a great black snake, so curiously wrought that it might almost be seen to twist and wriggle itself like a living serpent. This, of course, must have been an ocular deception, assisted by the uncertain light.

"Come, Goodman Brown," cried his fellow-traveller, "this is a dull pace for the beginning of a journey. Take my staff, if you are so soon weary."

"Friend," said the other, exchanging his slow pace for a full stop, "having kept covenant by meeting thee here, it is my purpose now to return whence I came. I have scruples touching the matter thou wot'st of."

"Sayest thou so?" replied he of the serpent, smiling apart. "Let us walk on, nevertheless, reasoning as we go; and if I convince thee not thou shalt turn back. We are but a little way in the forest yet."

"Too far! too far!" exclaimed the goodman, unconsciously resuming his walk. "My father never went into the woods on such an errand, nor his father before him. We have been a race of honest men and good Christians since the days of the martyrs; and shall I be the first of the name of Brown that ever took this path and kept—"

"Such company, thou wouldst say," observed the elder person, interpreting his pause. "Well said, Goodman Brown! I have been as well acquainted with your family as with ever a one among the Puritans; and that's no trifle to say. I helped your grandfather, the constable, when he lashed the Quaker woman so smartly through the streets of Salem; and it was I that brought your father a pitch-pine knot, kindled at my own hearth, to set fire to an Indian village, in King Philip's war. They were my good friends, both; and many a pleasant walk have we had along this path, and returned merrily after midnight. I would fain be friends with you for their sake."

"If it be as thou sayest," replied Goodman Brown, "I marvel they never spoke of these matters; or, verily, I marvel not, seeing that the least rumor of the sort would have driven them from New England. We are a people of prayer, and good works to boot, and abide no such wickedness."

"Wickedness or not," said the traveller with the twisted staff, "I have a very general acquaintance here in New England. The deacons of many a church have drunk the communion wine with me; the selectmen of divers towns make me their chairman; and a majority of the Great and General Court are firm supporters of my interest. The governor and I, too—But these are state secrets."

"Can this be so?" cried Goodman Brown, with a stare of amazement at his undisturbed companion. "Howbeit, I have nothing to do with the governor and council; they have their own ways, and are no rule for a simple husbandman like me. But, were I to go on with thee, how should I meet the eye of that good old man, our minister, at Salem village? Oh, his voice would make me tremble both Sabbath day and lecture day."

Thus far the elder traveller had listened with due gravity; but now burst into a fit of irrepressible mirth, shaking himself so violently that his snake-like staff actually seemed to wriggle in sympathy.

"Ha! ha! ha!" shouted he again and again; then composing himself, "Well, go on, Goodman Brown, go on; but, prithee, don't kill me with laughing."

"Well, then, to end the matter at once," said Goodman Brown, considerably nettled, "there is my wife, Faith. It would break her dear little heart; and I'd rather break my own."

"Nay, if that be the case," answered the other, "e'en go thy ways, Goodman Brown. I would not for twenty old women like the one hobbling before us that Faith should come to any harm."

As he spoke he pointed his staff at a female figure on the path, in whom Goodman Brown recognized a very pious and exemplary dame, who had taught him his catechism in youth, and was still his moral and spiritual adviser, jointly with the minister and Deacon Gookin.

"A marvel, truly, that Goody Cloyse should be so far in the wilderness at nightfall," said he. "But with your leave, friend, I shall take a cut through the woods until we have left this Christian woman behind. Being a stranger to you, she might ask whom I was consorting with and whither I was going."

"Be it so," said his fellow-traveller. "Betake you to the woods, and let me keep the path."

Accordingly the young man turned aside, but took care to watch his companion, who advanced softly along the road until he had come within a staff's length of the old dame. She, meanwhile, was making the best of her way, with singular speed for so aged a woman, and mumbling some indistinct words—a prayer, doubtless—as she went. The traveller put forth his staff and touched her withered neck with what seemed the serpent's tail.

"The devil!" screamed the pious old lady.

"Then Goody Cloyse knows her old friend?" observed the traveller, confronting her and leaning on his writhing stick.

"Ah, forsooth, and is it your worship indeed?" cried the good dame. "Yea, truly it is, and in the very image of my old gossip, Goodman Brown, the grandfather of the silly fellow that now is. But—would your worship believe it?—my broomstick hath strangely disappeared, stolen, as I suspect, by that unhanged witch, Goody Cory, and that, too, when I was anointed with the juice of smallage, and cinquefoil, and wolf's bane—"

"Mingled with fine wheat and the fat of a new-born babe," said the shape of old Goodman Brown.

"Ah, your worship knows the recipe," cried the old lady, cackling aloud. "So, as I was saying, being all ready for the meeting, and no horse to ride on, I made up my mind to foot it; for they tell me there is a nice young man to be taken into communion to-night. But now your good worship will lend me your arm, and we shall be there in a twinkling."

"That can hardly be," answered her friend. "I may not spare you my arm, Goody Cloyse; but here is my staff, if you will."

So saying, he threw it down at her feet, where, perhaps, it assumed life, being one of the rods which its owner had formerly lent to the Egyptian magi. Of this fact, however, Goodman Brown could not take cognizance. He had cast up his eyes in astonishment, and, looking down again, beheld neither Goody Cloyse nor the serpentine staff, but his fellow-traveller alone, who waited for him as calmly as if nothing happened.

"That old woman taught me my catechism," said the young man; and there was a world of meaning in this simple comment.

They continued to walk onward, while the elder traveller exhorted his companion to make good speed and persevere in the path, discoursing so aptly that his arguments seemed rather to spring up in the bosom of his auditor than to be suggested by himself. As they went, he plucked a branch of maple to serve for a walking stick, and began to strip it of the twigs and little boughs, which were wet with evening dew. The moment his fingers touched them they became strangely withered and dried up as with a week's sunshine. Thus the pair proceeded, at a good free pace, until suddenly, in a gloomy hollow of the road, Goodman Brown sat himself down on the stump of a tree and refused to go any farther.

"Friend," said he, stubbornly, "my mind is made up. Not another step will I budge on this errand. What if a wretched old woman do choose to go to the devil when I thought she was going to heaven: is that any reason why I should quit my dear Faith and go after her?"

"You will think better of this by and by," said his acquaintance, composedly. "Sit here and rest yourself a while; and when you feel like moving again, there is my staff to help you along."

Without more words, he threw his companion the maple stick, and was as speedily out of sight as if he had vanished into the deepening gloom. The young man sat a few moments by the roadside, applauding himself greatly, and thinking with how clear a conscience he should meet the minister in his morning walk, nor shrink from the eye of good old Deacon Gookin. And what calm sleep would be his that very night, which was to have been spent so wickedly, but so purely and sweetly now, in the arms of Faith! Amidst these pleasant and praiseworthy meditations, Goodman Brown heard the tramp of horses along the road, and deemed it advisable to conceal himself within the verge of the forest, conscious of the guilty purpose that had brought him thither, though now so happily turned from it.

On came the hoof tramps and the voices of the riders, two grave old voices, conversing soberly as they drew near. These mingled sounds appeared to pass along the road, within a few yards of the young man's hiding-place; but, owing doubtless to the depth of the gloom at that particular spot, neither the travellers nor their steeds were visible. Though their figures brushed the small boughs by the wayside, it could not be seen that they intercepted, even for a moment, the faint gleam from the strip of bright sky athwart which they must have passed. Goodman Brown alternately crouched and stood on tiptoe, pulling aside the branches and thrusting forth his head as far as he durst without discerning so much as a shadow. It vexed him the more, because he could have sworn, were such a thing possible, that he recognized the voices of the minister and Deacon Gookin, jogging along quietly, as they were wont to do, when bound to some ordination or ecclesiastical council. While yet within hearing, one of the riders stopped to pluck a switch.

"Of the two, reverend sir," said the voice like the deacon's, "I had rather miss an ordination dinner than to-night's meeting. They tell me that some of our community are to be here from Falmouth and beyond, and others from Connecticut and Rhode Island, besides several of the Indian powwows, who, after their fashion, know almost as much deviltry as the best of us. Moreover, there is a goodly young woman to be taken into communion."

"Mighty well, Deacon Gookin!" replied the solemn old tones of the minister. "Spur up, or we shall be late. Nothing can be done, you know, until I get on the ground."

The hoofs clattered again; and the voices, talking so strangely in the empty air, passed on through the forest, where no church had ever been gathered or solitary Christian prayed. Whither, then, could these holy men be journeying so deep into the heathen wilderness? Young Goodman Brown caught hold of a tree for support, being ready to sink down on the ground, faint and overburdened with the heavy sickness of his heart. He looked up to the sky, doubting whether there really was a heaven above him. Yet there was the blue arch, and the stars brightening in it.

"With heaven above and Faith below, I will yet stand firm against the devil!" cried Goodman Brown.

While he still gazed upward into the deep arch of the firmament and had lifted his hands to pray, a cloud, though no wind was stirring, hurried across the zenith and hid the brightening stars. The blue sky was still visible, except directly overhead, where this black mass of cloud was sweeping swiftly northward. Aloft in the air, as if from the depths of the cloud, came a confused and doubtful sound of voices. Once the listener fancied that he could distinguish the accents of towns-people of his own, men and women, both pious and ungodly, many of whom he had met at the communion table, and had seen others rioting at the tavern. The next moment, so indistinct were the sounds, he doubted whether he had heard aught but the murmur of the old forest, whispering without a wind. Then came a stronger swell of those familiar tones, heard daily in the sunshine at Salem village, but never until now from a cloud of night. There was one voice, of a young woman, uttering lamentations, yet with an uncertain sorrow, and entreating for some favor, which, perhaps, it would grieve her to obtain; and all the unseen multitude, both saints and sinners, seemed to encourage her onward.

"Faith!" shouted Goodman Brown, in a voice of agony and desperation; and the echoes of the forest mocked him, crying, "Faith! Faith!" as if bewildered wretches were seeking her all through the wilderness.

The cry of grief, rage, and terror was yet piercing the night, when the unhappy husband held his breath for a response. There was a scream, drowned immediately in a louder murmur of voices, fading into far-off laughter, as the dark cloud swept away, leaving the clear and silent sky above Goodman Brown. But something fluttered lightly down through the air and caught on the branch of a tree. The young man seized it, and beheld a pink ribbon.

"My Faith is gone!" cried he, after one stupefied moment. "There is no good on earth; and sin is but a name. Come, devil; for to thee is this world given."

And, maddened with despair, so that he laughed loud and long, did Goodman Brown grasp his staff and set forth again, at such a rate that he seemed to fly along the forest path rather than to walk or run. The road grew wilder and drearier and more faintly traced, and vanished at length, leaving him in the heart of the dark wilderness, still rushing onward with the instinct that guides mortal man to evil. The whole forest was peopled with frightful sounds—the creaking of the trees, the howling of wild beasts, and the yell of Indians; while sometimes the wind tolled like a distant church bell, and sometimes gave a broad roar around the traveller, as if all Nature were laughing him to scorn. But he was himself the chief horror of the scene, and shrank not from its other horrors.

"Ha! ha! ha!" roared Goodman Brown when the wind laughed at him. "Let us hear which will laugh loudest. Think not to frighten me with your deviltry. Come witch, come wizard, come Indian powwow, come devil himself, and here comes Goodman Brown. You may as well fear him as he fear you."

In truth, all through the haunted forest there could be nothing more frightful than the figure of Goodman Brown. On he flew among the black pines, brandishing his staff with frenzied gestures, now giving vent to an inspiration of horrid blasphemy, and now shouting forth such laughter as set all the echoes of the forest laughing like demons around him. The fiend in his own shape is less hideous than when he rages in the breast of man. Thus sped the demoniac on his course, until, quivering among the trees, he saw a red light before him, as when the felled trunks and branches of a clearing have been set on fire, and throw up their lurid blaze against the sky, at the hour of midnight. He paused, in a lull of the tempest that had driven him onward, and heard the swell of what seemed a hymn, rolling solemnly from a distance with the weight of many voices. He knew the tune; it was a familiar one in the choir of the village meeting-house. The verse died heavily away, and was lengthened by a chorus, not of human voices, but of all the sounds of the benighted wilderness pealing in awful harmony together. Goodman Brown cried out, and his cry was lost to his own ear by its unison with the cry of the desert.

In the interval of silence he stole forward until the light glared full upon his eyes. At one extremity of an open space, hemmed in by the dark wall of the forest, arose a rock, bearing some rude, natural resemblance either to an altar or a pulpit, and surrounded by four blazing pines, their tops aflame, their stems untouched, like candles at an evening meeting. The mass of foliage that had overgrown the summit of the rock was all on fire, blazing high into the night and fitfully illuminating the whole field. Each pendent twig and leafy festoon was in a blaze. As the red light arose and fell, a numerous congregation alternately shone forth, then disappeared in shadow, and again grew, as it were, out of the darkness, peopling the heart of the solitary woods at once.

"A grave and dark-clad company," quoth Goodman Brown. In truth they were such. Among them, quivering to and fro between gloom and splendor, appeared faces that would be seen next day at the council board of the province, and others which, Sabbath after Sabbath, looked devoutly heavenward, and benignantly over the crowded pews, from the holiest pulpits in the land. Some affirm that the lady of the governor was there. At least there were high dames well known to her, and wives of honored husbands, and widows, a great multitude, and ancient maidens, all of excellent repute, and fair young girls, who trembled lest their mothers should espy them. Either the sudden gleams of light flashing over the obscure field bedazzled Goodman Brown, or he recognized a score of the church members of Salem village famous for their special sanctity. Good old Deacon Gookin had arrived, and waited at the skirts of that venerable saint, his revered pastor. But, irreverently consorting with these grave, reputable, and pious people, these elders of the church, these chaste dames and dewy virgins, there were men of dissolute lives and women of spotted fame, wretches given over to all mean and filthy vice, and suspected even of horrid crimes. It was strange to see that the good shrank not from the wicked, nor were the sinners abashed by the saints. Scattered also among their pale-faced enemies were the Indian priests, or powwows, who had often scared their native forest with more hideous incantations than any known to English witchcraft.

"But where is Faith!" thought Goodman Brown; and, as hope came into his heart, he trembled.

Another verse of the hymn arose, a slow and mournful strain, such as the pious love, but joined to the words which expressed all that our nature can conceive of sin, and darkly hinted at far more. Unfathomable to mere mortals is the lore of fiends. Verse after verse was sung; and still the chorus of the desert swelled between like the deepest tone of a mighty organ; and with the final peal of that dreadful anthem there came a sound, as if the roaring wind, the rushing streams, the howling beasts, and every other voice of the unconverted wilderness were mingling and according with the voice of guilty man in homage to the prince of all. The four blazing pines threw up a loftier flame, and obscurely discovered shapes and visages of horror on the smoke wreaths above the impious assembly. At the same moment the fire on the rock shot redly forth and formed a glowing arch above its base, where now appeared a figure. With reverence be it spoken, the apparition bore no slight similitude, both in garb and manner, to some grave divine of the New England churches.

"Bring forth the converts!" cried a voice that echoed through the field and rolled into the forest.

At the word, Goodman Brown stepped forth from the shadow of the trees and approached the congregation, with whom he felt a loathful brotherhood by the sympathy of all that was wicked in his heart. He could have well-nigh sworn that the shape of his own dead father beckoned him to advance, looking downward from a smoke wreath, while a woman, with dim features of despair, threw out her hand to warn him back. Was it his mother? But he had no power to retreat one step, nor to resist, even in thought, when the minister and good old Deacon Gookin seized his arms and led him to the blazing rock. Thither came also the slender form of a veiled female, led between Goody Cloyse, that pious teacher of the catechism, and Martha Carrier, who had received the devil's promise to be queen of hell. A rampant hag was she. And there stood the proselytes beneath the canopy of fire.

"Welcome, my children," said the dark figure, "to the communion of your race. Ye have found thus young your nature and your destiny. My children, look behind you!"

They turned; and flashing forth, as it were, in a sheet of flame, the fiend worshippers were seen; the smile of welcome gleamed darkly on every visage.

"There," resumed the sable form, "are all whom ye have reverenced from youth. Ye deemed them holier than yourselves, and shrank from your own sin, contrasting it with their lives of righteousness and prayerful aspirations heavenward. Yet here are they all in my worshipping assembly. This night it shall be granted you to know their secret deeds: how hoary-bearded elders of the church have whispered wanton words to the young maids of their households; how many a woman, eager for widows' weeds, has given her husband a drink at bedtime and let him sleep his last sleep in her bosom; how beardless youths have made haste to inherit their fathers' wealth; and how fair damsels—blush not, sweet ones—have dug little graves in the garden, and bidden me, the sole guest, to an infant's funeral. By the sympathy of your human hearts for sin ye shall scent out all the places—whether in church, bedchamber, street, field, or forest where crime has been committed, and shall exult to behold the whole earth one stain of guilt, one mighty blood spot. Far more than this. It shall be yours to penetrate, in every bosom, the deep mystery of sin, the fountain of all wicked arts, and which inexhaustibly supplies more evil impulses than human power—than my power at its utmost—can make manifest in deeds. And now, my children, look upon each other."

They did so; and, by the blaze of the hell-kindled torches, the wretched man beheld his Faith, and the wife her husband, trembling before that unhallowed altar.

"Lo, there ye stand, my children," said the figure, in a deep and solemn tone, almost sad with its despairing awfulness, as if his once angelic nature could yet mourn for our miserable race. "Depending upon one another's hearts, ye had still hoped that virtue were not all a dream. Now are ye undeceived. Evil is the nature of mankind. Evil must be your only happiness. Welcome again, my children, to the communion of your race."

"Welcome," repeated the fiend worshippers in one cry of despair and triumph.

And there they stood, the only pair, as it seemed, who were yet hesitating on the verge of wickedness in this dark world. A basin was hollowed, naturally, in the rock. Did it contain water, reddened by the lurid light? or was it blood? or, perchance, a liquid flame? Herein did the shape of evil dip his hand and prepare to lay the mark of baptism upon their foreheads, that they might be partakers of the mystery of sin, more conscious of the secret guilt of others, both in deed and thought, than they could now be of their own. The husband cast one look at his pale wife, and Faith at him. What polluted wretches would the next glance show them to each other, shuddering alike at what they disclosed and what they saw!

"Faith! Faith!" cried the husband, "look up to heaven, and resist the wicked one."

Whether Faith obeyed he knew not. Hardly had he spoken when he found himself amid calm night and solitude, listening to a roar of the wind which died heavily away through the forest. He staggered against the rock, and felt it chill and damp; while a hanging twig, that had been all on fire, besprinkled his cheek with the coldest dew.

The next morning young Goodman Brown came slowly in to the street of Salem village, staring around him like a bewildered man. The good old minister was taking a walk along the graveyard to get an appetite for breakfast and meditate his sermon, and bestowed a blessing, as he passed, on Goodman Brown. He shrank from the venerable saint as if to avoid an anathema. Old Deacon Gookin was at domestic worship, and the holy words of his prayer were heard through the open window. "What God doth the wizard pray to?" quoth Goodman Brown. Goody Cloyse, that excellent old Christian, stood in the early sunshine at her own lattice, catechizing a little girl who had brought her a pint of morning's milk. Goodman Brown snatched away the child as from the grasp of the fiend himself. Turning the corner by the meeting-house, he spied the head of Faith, with the pink ribbons, gazing anxiously forth, and bursting into such joy at sight of him that she skipped along the street and almost kissed her husband before the whole village. But Goodman Brown looked sternly and sadly into her face, and passed on without a greeting.

Had Goodman Brown fallen asleep in the forest and only dreamed a wild dream of a witch-meeting?

Be it so if you will; but, alas! it was a dream of evil omen for young Goodman Brown. A stern, a sad, a darkly meditative, a distrustful, if not a desperate man did he become from the night of that fearful dream. On the Sabbath day, when the congregation were singing a holy psalm, he could not listen because an anthem of sin rushed loudly upon his ear and drowned all the blessed strain. When the minister spoke from the pulpit with power and fervid eloquence, and, with his hand on the open Bible, of the sacred truths of our religion, and of saint-like lives and triumphant deaths, and of future bliss or misery unutterable, then did Goodman Brown turn pale, dreading lest the roof should thunder down upon the gray blasphemer and his hearers. Often, awaking suddenly at midnight, he shrank from the bosom of Faith; and at morning or eventide, when the family knelt down at prayer, he scowled and muttered to himself, and gazed sternly at his wife, and turned away. And when he had lived long, and was borne to his grave a hoary corpse, followed by Faith, an aged woman, and children and grandchildren, a goodly procession, besides neighbors not a few, they carved no hopeful verse upon his tombstone, for his dying hour was gloom.

~

Appendix C

Alice Walker
EVERYDAY USE

for your grandmama

I will wait for her in the yard that Maggie and I made so clean and wavy yesterday afternoon. A yard like this is more comfortable than most people know. It is not just a yard. It is like an extended living room. When the hard clay is swept clean as a floor and the fine sand around the edges lined with tiny, irregular grooves, anyone can come and sit and look up into the elm tree and wait for the breezes that never come inside the house.

Maggie will be nervous until after her sister goes: she will stand hopelessly in corners, homely and ashamed of the burn scars down her arms and legs, eying her sister with a mixture of envy and awe. She thinks her sister has held life always in the palm of one hand, that "no" is a word the world never learned to say to her.

You've no doubt seen those TV shows where the child who has "made it" is confronted, as a surprise, by her own mother and father, tottering in weakly from backstage. (A pleasant surprise, of course: What would they do if parent and child came on the show only to curse out and insult each other?) On TV mother and child embrace and smile into each other's faces. Sometimes the mother and father weep, the child wraps them in her arms and leans across the table to tell how she would not have made it without their help. I have seen these programs.

Sometimes I dream a dream in which Dee and I are suddenly brought together on a TV program of this sort. Out of a dark and soft-seated limousine I am ushered into a bright room filled with many people. There I meet a smiling, gray, sporty man like Johnny Carson who shakes my hand and tells me what a fine girl I have. Then we are on the stage and Dee is embracing me with tears in her eyes. She pins on my dress a large orchid, even though she has told me once that she thinks orchids are tacky flowers.

In real life I am a large, big-boned woman with rough, man-working hands. In the winter I wear flannel nightgowns to bed and overalls during the day. I can kill and clean a hog as mercilessly as a man. My fat keeps me hot in zero weather. I can work outside all day, breaking ice to get water for washing; I can eat pork liver cooked over the open fire minutes after it comes steaming from the hog. One winter I knocked a bull calf straight in the brain between the eyes with a sledge hammer and had the meat hung up to chill before nightfall. But of course all this does not show on television. I am the way my daughter would want me to be: a hundred pounds lighter, my skin like an uncooked barley pancake. My hair glistens in the hot bright lights. Johnny Carson has much to do to keep up with my quick and witty tongue.

But that is a mistake. I know even before I wake up. Who ever knew a Johnson with a quick tongue? Who can even imagine me looking a strange white man in the eye? It seems to me I have talked to them always with one foot raised in flight, with my head turned in whichever way is farthest from them. Dee, though. She would always look anyone in the eye. Hesitation was no part of her nature.

"How do I look, Mama?" Maggie says, showing just enough of her thin body enveloped in pink skirt and red blouse for me to know she's there, almost hidden by the door.

"Come out into the yard," I say.

Have you ever seen a lame animal, perhaps a dog run over by some careless person rich enough to own a car, sidle up to someone who is ignorant enough to be kind to him? That is the way my Maggie walks. She has been like this, chin on chest, eyes on ground, feet in shuffle, ever since the fire that burned the other house to the ground.

Dee is lighter than Maggie, with nicer hair and a fuller figure. She's a woman now, though sometimes I forget. How long ago was it that the other house burned? Ten, twelve years? Sometimes I can still hear the flames and feel Maggie's arms sticking to me, her hair smoking and her dress falling off her in little black papery flakes. Her eyes seemed stretched open, blazed open by the flames reflected in them. And Dee. I see her standing off under the sweet gum tree she used to dig gum out of; a look of concentration on her face as she watched the last dingy gray board of the house fall in toward the red-hot brick chimney. Why don't you do a dance around the ashes? I'd wanted to ask her. She had hated the house that much.

I used to think she hated Maggie, too. But that was before we raised the money, the church and me, to send her to Augusta to school. She used to read to us without pity; forcing words, lies, other folks' habits, whole lives upon us two, sitting trapped and ignorant underneath her voice. She washed us in a river of make-believe, burned us with a lot of knowledge we didn't necessarily need to know. Pressed us to her with the serious way she read, to shove us away at just the moment, like dimwits, we seemed about to understand.

Dee wanted nice things. A yellow organdy dress to wear to her graduation from high school; black pumps to match a green suit she'd made from an old suit somebody gave me. She was determined to stare down any disaster in her efforts. Her eyelids would not flicker for minutes at a time. Often I fought off the temptation to shake her. At sixteen she had a style of her own: and knew what style was.

I never had an education myself. After second grade the school was closed down. Don't ask me why: in 1927 colored asked fewer questions than they do now. Sometimes Maggie reads to me. She stumbles along good-naturedly but can't see well. She knows she is not bright. Like good looks and money, quickness passed her by. She will marry John Thomas (who has mossy teeth in an earnest face) and then I'll be free to sit here and I guess just sing church songs to myself. Although I never was a good singer. Never could carry a tune. I was always better at a man's job. I used to love to milk till I was hooked in the side in '49. Cows are soothing and slow and don't bother you, unless you try to milk them the wrong way.

I have deliberately turned my back on the house. It is three rooms, just like the one that burned, except the roof is tin; they don't make shingle roofs any more. There are no real windows, just some holes cut in the sides, like the portholes in a ship, but not round and not square, with rawhide holding the shutters up on the outside. This house is in a pasture, too, like the other one. No doubt when Dee sees it she will want to tear it down. She wrote me once that no matter where we "choose" to live, she will manage to come see us. But she will never bring her friends. Maggie and I thought about this and Maggie asked me, "Mama, when did Dee ever have any friends?"

She had a few. Furtive boys in pink shirts hanging about on washday after school. Nervous girls who never laughed. Impressed with her they worshiped the well-turned phrase, the cute shape, the scalding humor that erupted like bubbles in lye. She read to them.

When she was courting Jimmy T she didn't have much time to pay to us, but turned all her faultfinding power on him. He flew to marry a cheap city girl from a family of ignorant flashy people. She hardly had time to recompose herself.

When she comes I will meet—but there they are!

Maggie attempts to make a dash for the house, in her shuffling way, but I stay her with my hand. "Come back here," I say. And she stops and tries to dig a well in the sand with her toe.

It is hard to see them clearly through the strong sun. But even the first glimpse of leg out of the car tells me it is Dee. Her feet were always neat-looking, as if God himself had shaped them with a certain style. From the other side of the car comes a short, stocky man. Hair is all over his head a foot long and hanging from his chin like a kinky mule tail. I hear Maggie suck in her breath. "Uhnnnh," is what it sounds like. Like when you see the wriggling end of a snake just in front of your foot on the road. "Uhnnnh."

Dee next. A dress down to the ground, in this hot weather. A dress so loud it hurts my eyes. There are yellows and oranges enough to throw back the light of the sun. I feel my whole face warming from the heat waves it throws out. Earrings gold, too, and hanging down to her shoulders. Bracelets dangling and making noises when she moves her arm up to shake the folds of the dress out of her arm-pits. The dress is loose and flows, and as she walks closer, I like it. I hear Maggie go "Uhnnnh" again. It is her sister's hair. It stands straight up like the wool on a sheep. It is black as night and around the edges are two long pigtails that rope about like small lizards disappearing behind her ears.

"Wa-su-zo-Tean-o!" she says, coming on in that gliding way the dress makes her move. The short stocky fellow with the hair to his navel is all grinning and he follows up with "Asalamalakim, my mother and sister!" He moves to hug Maggie but she falls back, right up against the back of my chair. I feel her trembling there and when I look up I see the perspiration falling off her chin.

"Don't get up," says Dee. Since I am stout it takes something of a push. You can see me trying to move a second or two before I make it. She turns, showing white heels through her sandals, and goes back to the car. Out she peeks next with a Polaroid. She stoops down quickly and lines up picture after picture of me sit-ting there in front of the house with Maggie cowering behind me. She never takes a shot without making sure the house is included. When a cow comes nibbling around the edge of the yard she snaps it and me and Maggie and the house. Then she puts the Polaroid in the back seat of the car, and comes up and kisses me on the forehead.

Meanwhile Asalamalakim is going through motions with Maggie's hand. Maggie's hand is as limp as a fish, and probably as cold, despite the sweat, and she keeps trying to pull it back. It looks like Asalamalakim wants to shake hands but wants to do it fancy. Or maybe he don't know how people shake hands. Anyhow, he soon gives up on Maggie.

"Well," I say. "Dee."

"No, Mama," she says. "Not 'Dee,' Wangero Leewanika Kemanjo!"

"What happened to 'Dee'?" I wanted to know.

"She's dead," Wangero said. "I couldn't bear it any longer, being named after the people who oppress me."

"You know as well as me you was named after your aunt Dicie," I said. Dicie is my sister. She named Dee. We called her "Big Dee" after Dee was born.

"But who was she named after?" asked Wangero.

"I guess after Grandma Dee," I said.

"And who was she named after?" asked Wangero.

"Her mother," I said, and saw Wangero was getting tired.

"That's about as far back as I can trace it," I said. Though, in fact, I probably could have carried it back beyond the Civil War through the branches.

"Well," said Asalamalakim, "there you are."

"Uhnnnh," I heard Maggie say.

"There I was not," I said, "before 'Dicie' cropped up in our family, so why should I try to trace it that far back?"

He just stood there grinning, looking down on me like somebody inspecting a Model A car. Every once in a while he and Wangero sent eye signals over my head.

"How do you pronounce this name?" I asked.

"You don't have to call me by it if you don't want to," said Wangero.

"Why shouldn't I?" I asked, "If that's what you want us to call you, we'll call you."

"I know it might sound awkward at first," said Wangero.

"I'll get used to it," I said. "Ream it out again."

Well, soon we got the name out of the way. Asalamalakim had a name twice as long and three times as hard. After I tripped over it two or three times he told me to just call him Hakim-a-barber. I wanted to ask him was he a barber, but I didn't think he was, so I didn't ask.

"You must belong to those beef-cattle peoples down the road," I said. They said "Asalamalakim" when they met you, too, but they didn't shake hands. Always too busy: feeding the cattle, fixing the fences, putting up salt-lick shelters, throwing down hay. When the white folks poisoned some of the herd the men stayed up all night with rifles in their hands. I walked a mile and a half just to see the sight.

Hakim-a-barber said, "I accept some of their doctrines, but farming and raising cattle is not my style." (They didn't tell me, and I didn't ask, whether Wangero [Dee] had really gone and married him.)

We sat down to eat and right away he said he didn't eat collards and pork was unclean. Wangero, though, went on through the chitlins and corn bread, the greens and everything else. She talked a blue streak over the sweet potatoes. Everything delighted her. Even the fact that we still used the benches her daddy made for the table when we couldn't afford to buy chairs.

"Oh, Mama!" she cried. Then turned to Hakim-a-barber. "I never knew how lovely these benches are. You can feel the rump prints," she said, running her hands underneath her and along the bench. Then she gave a sigh and her hand closed over Grandma Dee's butter dish. "That's it!" she said. "I knew there was something I wanted to ask you if I could have." She jumped up from the table and went over in the corner where the churn stood, the milk in it clabber by now. She looked at the churn and looked at it.

"This churn top is what I need," she said. "Didn't Uncle Buddy whittle it out of a tree you all used to have?"

"Yes," I said.

"Uh huh," she said happily. "And I want the dasher, too."

"Uncle Buddy whittle that, too?" asked the barber.

Dee (Wangero) looked up at me.

"Aunt Dee's first husband whittled the dash," said Maggie so low you almost couldn't hear her. "His name was Henry, but they called him Stash."

"Maggie's brain is like an elephant's," Wangero said, laughing. "I can use the churn top as a centerpiece for the alcove table," she said, sliding a plate over the churn, "and I'll think of something artistic to do with the dasher."

When she finished wrapping the dasher the handle stuck out. I took it for a moment in my hands. You didn't even have to look close to see where hands pushing the dasher up and down to make butter had left a kind of sink in the wood. In fact, there were a lot of small sinks; you could see where thumbs and fingers had sunk into the wood. It was beautiful light yellow wood, from a tree that grew in the yard where Big Dee and Stash had lived.

After dinner Dee (Wangero) went to the trunk at the foot of my bed and started rifling through it. Maggie hung back in the kitchen over the dishpan. Out came Wangero with two quilts. They had been pieced by Grandma Dee and then Big Dee and me had hung them on the quilt frames on the front porch and quilted them. One was in the Lone Star Pattern. The other was Walk Around the Mountain. In both of them were scraps of dresses Grandma Dee had worn fifty and more years ago. Bits and pieces of Grandpa Jarrell's Paisley shirts. And one teeny faded blue piece, about the size of a penny matchbox, that was from Great Grandpa Ezra's uniform that he wore in the Civil War.

"Mama," Wangero said sweet as a bird. "Can I have these old quilts?"

I heard something fall in the kitchen, and a minute later the kitchen door slammed.

"Why don't you take one or two of the others?" I asked. "These old things was just done by me and Big Dee from some tops your grandma pieced before she died."

"No," said Wangero. "I don't want those. They are stitched around the borders by machine."

"That'll make them last better," I said.

"That's not the point," said Wangero. "These are all pieces of dresses Grandma used to wear. She did all this stitching by hand. Imagine!" She held the quilts securely in her arms, stroking them.

"Some of the pieces, like those lavender ones, come from old clothes her mother handed down to her," I said, moving up to touch the quilts. Dee (Wangero) moved back just enough so that I couldn't reach the quilts. They already belonged to her.

"Imagine!" she breathed again, clutching them closely to her bosom.

"The truth is," I said, "I promised to give them quilts to Maggie, for when she marries John Thomas."

She gasped like a bee had stung her.

"Maggie can't appreciate these quilts!" she said. "She'd probably be backward enough to put them to everyday use."

"I reckon she would," I said. "God knows I been saving 'em for long enough with nobody using 'em. I hope she will!" I didn't want to bring up how I had offered

Dee (Wangero) a quilt when she went away to college. Then she had told me they were old-fashioned, out of style.

"But they're priceless!" she was saying now, furiously; for she has a temper. "Maggie would put them on the bed and in five years they'd be in rags. Less than that!"

"She can always make some more," I said. "Maggie knows how to quilt."

Dee (Wangero) looked at me with hatred. "You just will not understand. The point is these quilts, these quilts!"

"Well," I said, stumped. "What would you do with them?"

"Hang them," she said. As if that was the only thing you could do with quilts.

Maggie by now was standing in the door. I could almost hear the sound her feet made as they scraped over each other.

"She can have them, Mama," she said, like somebody used to never winning anything, or having anything reserved for her. "I can 'member Grandma Dee without the quilts."

I looked at her hard. She had filled her bottom lip with checkerberry snuff and it gave her face a kind of dopey, hangdog look. It was Grandma Dee and Big Dee who taught her how to quilt herself. She stood there with her scarred hands hidden in the folds of her skirt. She looked at her sister with something like fear but she wasn't mad at her. This was Maggie's portion. This was the way she knew God to work.

When I looked at her like that something hit me in the top of my head and ran down to the soles of my feet. Just like when I'm in church and the spirit of God touches me and I get happy and shout. I did something I never had done before: hugged Maggie to me, then dragged her on into the room, snatched the quilts out of Miss Wangero's hands and dumped them into Maggie's lap. Maggie just sat there on my bed with her mouth open.

"Take one or two of the others," I said to Dee.

But she turned without a word and went out to Hakim-a-barber.

"You just don't understand," she said, as Maggie and I came out to the car.

"What don't I understand?" I wanted to know.

"Your heritage." she said. And then she turned to Maggie, kissed her, and said, "You ought to try to make something of yourself, too, Maggie. It's really a new day for us. But from the way you and Mama still live you'd never know it."

She put on some sunglasses that hid everything above the tip of her nose and her chin.

Maggie smiled; maybe at the sunglasses. But a real smile, not scared. After we watched the car dust settle, I asked Maggie to bring me a dip of snuff. And then the two of us sat there just enjoying, until it was time to go in the house and go to bed.

Glossary of Literary Terms

Absurdist Drama. Often called the Theater of the Absurd, the term refers to particular plays written by a number of primarily European playwrights from the late 1940s through the 1960s. Influential was Albeit Camus's philosophy that life is inherently without meaning, the philosophy of *existentialism*. *Comedy* is mixed with *tragedy* and horror as characters are caught in hopeless situations and forced to carry out meaningless actions; they converse in dialogue full of clichés, wordplay, and nonsense. Playwrights include Samuel Beckett, Eugene Ionesco, Jean Genet, and Harold Pinter.

Accidentals. In textual editing, a term used not only to refer to the actual words of a text but rather to such conventions as spelling, punctuation, capitalization, etc.

Affective Fallacy. Attributing the meaning of a text to the reader's emotions.

Allegory. A work in which the surface narrative reveals a secondary, symbolic, or metaphorical meaning generally tied point by point to what it signifies; allegory is usually restricted to a single meaning because its events, actions, characters, settings, and objects represent specific abstractions or ideas. In *The Faerie Queene*, for example, Red Cross Knight is a heroic figure representing Everyman in the Christian journey.

Alliteration. The repetition of the same consonant sounds in a sequence of words, usually at the beginning of a word or stressed syllable, such as in Hamlet's initial instructions to the players: "Speak the speech, I pray you, trippingly on the tongue;.... Nor do not saw the air too much with your hand, thus, but use all gently; for in the very torrent, tempest, and, I must say, whirlwind of your passion, you must acquire and beget a temperance that may give it smoothness" (III.ii.1–8). Hamlet alliterates with the letters *s* and *t* throughout the passage.

Allusion. A brief reference to a person, place, thing, event, or idea in history or literature. Common traditional sources have included the Bible, Greek and Roman mythology, and Shakespeare. Nearly all works of literature contain allusions, since all are influenced by the author's reading and store of know-ledge. Few works are more allusive than T. S. Eliot's *The Waste Land*, which required him to provide footnotes.

Ambiguity. Allows for more than one interpretation of a word, phrase, action, or situation, contributing to the depth and richness of a work, as in the open-ended conclusion to Hawthorne's "Young Goodman Brown."

Amor de Lohn (**Provençal**). Literally, "love from afar," a style of poetry practiced by troubadours in France and Spain during the High Middle Ages, in which the poet admires a woman he has never seen and to whom he would not have access.

Antagonist. The character who opposes the *protagonist* in the conflict of the story; in *Hamlet* Claudius is antagonist to Hamlet. Colloquially: "the bad guy."

Anthropomorphism. Attributing human characteristics to a nonhuman subject. See also *personification.*

Antihero. A *protagonist* who lacks heroic qualities and actually displays the opposite of most of the traditional attributes of a *hero.* Antiheroes are most often alienated from society or from God.

Archetype. A model of a person, ideal example, or a prototype after which oth-ers are copied, patterned, or emulated, or a symbol recognized across cul-tures. Present in folklore and literature for thousands of years, including prehistoric art, archetypes illuminate certain human basics—figures such as the Great Mother or Sky Father, symbols of water or fire, sun-worship, and an endless host of other "super-symbols" found across times and cultures. Thus, in literature, certain character types or images resonate with a large audience.

Aside. In *drama*, a speech directed to the audience that supposedly is not heard by the other characters onstage at the time. When Hamlet first appears onstage, for example, his aside "A little more than kin, and less than kind!" gives the audience a strong sense of his alienation from King Claudius. See also *soliloquy.*

Assonance. The repetition of internal vowel sounds in nearby words that do not end the same; in Edgar Allan Poe's "The Bells" he uses the short "e" sound: "Hear the mellow wedding bells."

Atmosphere. See Chapter 1.

Ballad. A form of verse, often a narrative story and set to music. Ballads arose in medieval times and continued to be of interest in later years.

Bibliography. The academic study of books as physical, cultural objects. Bibliography may be in the form of a list of texts (enumerative bibliography) or in the form of a textual description of a book's features (descriptive or ana-lytical bibliography). The analytical study of bibliography can be subdivided into descriptive (or physical), historical, and textual bibliography.

Bildungsroman. German for "novel of development," in which a youth matures into an adult after a series of struggles and conflicts that lead to self-awareness.

A related type of novel, the *Künstlerroman,* is the story of the development of a young artist.

Blank Verse. Unrhymed *iambic pentameter*, as in *Hamlet.*

Blazon. A formal description of a coat of arms or flag.

Bowdlerizing. The expurgation of a portion of a text considered vulgar; a form of censorship.

Burlesque. A work designed to mock a style, literary form, or subject matter through exaggerated imitation. Burlesque can treat the exalted in a trivial way or the trivial in exalted terms. In *Huckleberry Finn* Twain burlesques Tom's ridiculous romantic ideas, especially in his treatment of Jim as a prisoner in the novel's last chapters.

Canon. When applied to literature, "canon" refers to the body of works deemed standard by scholarly authorities. The canon is constantly undergoing modification. The word may also apply to the group of works of a particular author (the "Chaucer canon").

Catalogue. In a work of literature, a list of people, attributes, places, objects extended to some length and used for dramatic effect. Examples include Walt Whitman's "Song of Myself," and Homer's *Odyssey*, especially Book XI.

Catastrophe. Occurs at the end of a tragedy, a final reversal for the protagonist.

Catharsis. The "purgation" or catharsis describes the release of the emotions of pity and fear by the audience at the end of a *tragedy,* as defined by Aristotle in his *Poetics.* By facing the fall of the tragic *hero*, the audience is both moved by pity for him but also reminded of the limitations and failures of human beings; still, the tragic hero's suffering is an affirmation of human values rather than a cause for despair. This goes back to the sacrificial and religious nature of Greek *tragedy*.

Cavalier Poets. Refers to a set of seventeenth-century English poets who included Edward Herbert, Richard Lovelace, Robert Herrick, Henry Vaughan, John Suckling, Ben Jonson, Thomas Carew, and Abraham Cowley, referencing both their general monarchist allegiances and their "cavalier," or careless, attitude toward life and poetry—the verse should not be a thing of labor but of inspiration. They used a combination of erudite and direct colloquial language to express highly individualistic personalities, and they enjoyed the casual, the amateur, the affectionate poem written on the spur of the moment. The Cavalier poets were Renaissance gentlemen, at once lovers, soldiers, wits, men of affairs, and poets.

Character. See Chapter 1.

Chorus. In fifth-century b.c. Athens, the Greek chorus was a group of twelve or fifteen actors in tragic and twenty-four in comic plays. In ancient tradition, they danced and chanted in a precise strophe/antistrophe (that is, movement and counter movement) at certain key points in the *drama*. The chorus offers background and summary to help the audience follow the performance, also commenting on themes and representing the values of the general population. The chorus can express to the audience what the main characters cannot say, and it provides other characters with the insight and judgment they need.

Climax. See Chapter 1.

Colloquialism. Casual, informal style in speaking and writing, not to be confused with localisms.

Comedy. A work intended to interest, involve, and amuse the reader or audience, in which no terrible disaster occurs and which ends happily for the main characters. High comedy refers to verbal wit, such as puns, whereas low comedy is generally associated with physical action, even slapstick. Romantic comedy involves a love affair that meets with various obstacles (disapproving parents, mistaken identities, deceptions, or other sorts of misunderstanding) that are overcome. Shakespeare's comedies usually end with a wedding.

Conceit. An elaborate, ingenious poetic comparison or image, such as an analogy or *metaphor*, a technique perfected by the seventeenth-century British *Metaphysical poets*, such as John Donne. "To His Coy Mistress" contains a conceit describing the narrator's love: "My vegetable love should grow / Vaster than empires and more slow." The Petrarchan conceit is the basis for these later conceits; it was used by Italian Renaissance poet Petrarch and was popular in Renaissance English *sonnets*. A beloved might be described in similes such as eyes cold as ice, skin white as snow, and so on.

Connotation. Associations and implications that go beyond the literal meaning of a word. For example, the word "quaint" in "To His Coy Mistress" is a sexual pun. See also *denotation.*

Couplet. Two consecutive lines of poetry that usually rhyme and have the same meter. A *heroic couplet* is a couplet written in rhymed iambic pentameter.

Courtly Love Tradition. A medieval European convention of noble and chivalrous love and admiration to a (usually remote) woman of noble standing, often in an adulterous relationship. Courtly love in some cases could have a civilizing effect on knights in literature after the eleventh century. Some tales told of men who had fallen in love with women they never met, merely on hearing of their perfection. As the etiquette of courtly love developed, the knight might wear the colors of his lady and offer her his trophies. Wandering poets called troubadours as well as Chaucer, John Gower, Dante, Chrétien de Troyes, and Sir Thomas Malory wrote about the tradition.

Denotation. The literal or dictionary meaning of a word. See also *connotation.*

Dénouement. See Chapter 1.

Dialect. A variety of a language characteristic of a particular group of the language's speakers. It is often misapplied to mean regional speech patterns. *Adventures of Huckleberry Finn* is almost completely told in dialect, and Twain was proud of his ear for it.

Dialectic. A method of argument central to both Eastern and Western philosophy since ancient times. It was used in Plato's Socratic dialogues, in which two people with different opinions try to persuade each other. Dialectic in the form of opposed forces is very important to Marxist *ideology*.

Diction. A writer's choice of words, phrases, sentence structures, and figurative language. Diction ranges from *formal* (a dignified, impersonal, and elevated use of language following the rules of syntax and characterized by complexity) to *informal,* the plain language of everyday use, which often includes idiomatic expressions, slang, contractions, and ***dialect.*** *Poetic diction* refers to the way poets sometimes employ an elevated diction that deviates significantly from the common speech and writing of their time, choosing words for their poetic qualities.

Double Entendre. A statement with a double meaning, often somewhat obscured.

Drama. A work of literature designed to be performed in a theater by actors; "drama" is derived from the Greek word *dram,* meaning "to do" or "to perform." In a broader sense it can refer to the entire genre of "plays" and to other performed media.

Dramatic Monologue. A type of ***lyric poem*** in which the speaker addresses a distinct but silent audience imagined to be present in the poem in such a way as to reveal the dramatic situation and often some aspect of himself or herself, as in Robert Browning's "My Last Duchess."

Dramatis Personae. The complete list of characters in a drama. In most plays after Shakespeare, they are listed at the beginning of the play.

Dystopian Novel. An anti-utopian novel in which instead of a paradise, the future brings a catastrophic world. See ***utopian novel.***

Elegy. A contemplative ***lyric*** poem, generally written to mourn and commemorate someone who is dead, often ending in a consolation. Tennyson's "In Memoriam," written on the death of Arthur Hallam, is an elegy. It may also be a serious meditative poem designed to express the speaker's melancholy thoughts.

Emendation. Editing to correct.

End-stopping. Ending a line that has a natural pause at the end (period, comma, etc.), typical of the heroic couplet. See also ***enjambment.***

Enjambment. When a line runs into the next couplet or line without a pause; also called a run-on line. In "To His Coy Mistress," the following lines are enjambed: "Nor, in thy marble vault, shall sound / My echoing song; then worms shall try / That long-preserved virginity."

Epic. An extended narrative poem recounting actions, travels, adventures, and heroic episodes and written in a high style of ***diction.*** (The term is technically confined to poetry but is used casually to describe an "epic novel" such as *War and Peace.*) Most epic poems are written in *hexameter* verse, especially *dactylic hexameter* (see ***meter***), and they usually have twelve books or twenty-four books. The ***protagonist*** must be larger than life, often a national ***hero.*** He is shown both in heroic deeds and in his errors. Episodes generally include battle and other heroic contests. The setting is broad, sometimes the entire world as well as heaven and hell (as in *Paradise Lost).* In classical epics, the gods play an active role. The epic usually opens with a statement of the theme and an invocation, and it often begins in the middle *(in medias res),* as in

The Odyssey. Epic **catalogues** are descriptive lists of warriors, ships, or arms. *Epithets* (descriptive names) like Homer's "wily Odysseus" or "rosy-fingered Dawn") often appear. Main characters give long formal speeches in which previous episodes in the story are recounted. There is usually a journey to the underworld. A *mock epic* treats a frivolous subject with epic gravity, as in Alexander Pope's "The Rape of the Lock."

Epistolary Novel. A novel made up of letters written by a character or characters, without an omniscient narrator, allowing for the use of multiple points of view and **ambiguity**, as well as the **frame story**.

Epistemology. Broadly, the study of how we know, especially in an empirical way. See also **hermeneutics**.

Etymology. The study of word origins. The main source in English is the *Oxford English Dictionary.*

Exponent. A word or pattern that is meaningfully structured and repeated in a text. Sometimes called an *image cluster.*

Exposition. Relating events that have transpired.

External Form. Such features of a text as stanzas, lines, rhythm, rhyme, and so on.

Fallacy. A mistake in logical reasoning. In literature, the **intentional fallacy** is the idea that one can know exactly what the author intended; the **affective fallacy** is the error of judging a text on the basis of its emotional effects on the reader.

Falling action. See Chapter 1.

Figurative Language. Language or speech containing images, especially within a comparison between different things.

Focal Character. The character from whose point of view the story is told by a third person **narrator**. Sometimes called *point-of-view character.*

Foil. A character in a work whose behavior and values contrast sharply with those of another character, especially the protagonist. In *Hamlet*, Laertes acts as a foil to Hamlet.

Folio. In bookbinding, a term referring to a full sheet of paper, parchment, or other material folded in half to make two leaves in a *codex*, usually 15 inches tall or more. A famous book printed on folio pages is the *First Folio* of William Shakespeare's plays, published by friends after his death.

Foot. The basic unit of poetic **meter**, consisting of a group of two or three syllables. *Scanning* or **scansion** is the process of determining the prevailing foot in a line of poetry by analyzing the types and sequence of different feet. Meter is expressed in feet that are unstressed (U) or stressed (/): Iamb: U /, Trochee: /U, Anapest: U U /, Dactyl: / U U, Spondee: / /, Pyrrhic: U U. See **meter** and **versification**.

Foreshadowing. A device to create expectation or to set up an explanation of later developments. Thus, Faith's protestations at the beginning of "Young Goodman Brown" foreshadow Brown's evil fate.

Frame Story. A narrative structure that provides a setting and exposition for the main narrative in a **novel** or **short story**. A narrator might claim he found the manuscript (*The Scarlet Letter*), it might consist of letters (*Frankenstein*), or it might be a story the **narrator** heard from someone else *(The Turn of the Screw)*.

Free Verse. Verse that has neither regular **rhyme** nor regular **meter**. Free verse often uses cadences rather than uniform metrical feet, as in Walt Whitman's *Song of Myself.*

Genre. Refers to the form of a work of literature formed by sets of conventions, so that **poetry** is distinct from essay, **novel** from **drama**, **short stories** from **epic** poems. These conventions can change with time but are usually clearly recognized by the culture in which they are produced.

Gothic Tale. A *novel* in which supernatural horrors and an atmosphere of unknown terror pervade the action. The setting is often dark and mysterious, peopled by ghosts and sinister humans. Supernatural events occur, creating a mystery the **hero** tries to solve. Ancient curses, dream visions, and frightening natural events such as storms take place in a ruined castle full of secrets. Generally the threat is directed toward a woman by a dangerous male who must be stopped by the hero. *Frankenstein* bears some of the elements of the gothic.

Grotesque. Dating from Renaissance Italy, when bizarre part-human part-plant paintings were found on the excavated walls of Nero's throne room, the Domus Aurea (the word comes from the Italian "grotto" or cave), the grotesque combines, exaggerates, and deforms the human figure sometimes in comical ways and sometimes in terrifying ones. In order to be truly grotesque, an image has to combine humor and horror, as in medieval gargoyles.

Hermeneutics. The study of interpretation, or, more broadly, the idea that knowledge is only an interpretation, not a matter of absolute fact. See also *epistemology*.

Hero/Heroine. The principal sympathetic character in a literary work. Heroes and heroines typically exhibit admirable traits and often carry out their actions for the benefits of others. See also **antihero**. Heroes usually leave home on a *quest*, in which they must undergo an *initiation*, and return home to help the community. A sacrificial hero is called a *scapegoat*.

Heuristic. A strategy for problem solving.

Holograph. A manuscript written by hand by its author.

Hubris. Greek for "pride," hubris describes the tragic flaw in the tragic **hero**, such as Oedipus's hubris in killing his father and marrying his mother. In Greek drama heroes are punished for undue pride in themselves, which is an insult to the gods. The concept translates well into modern **drama**, as well, as in James Tyrone, Sr.'s hubris in Eugene O'Neill's *Long Day's Journey into Night.*

Hyperbole. A figure of speech characterized by exaggeration. Hyperbole is used to evoke strong feelings or to create a strong impression, but it is not meant to be taken literally.

Iambic Pentameter. A poetic line of five feet, each with a syllable unstressed (U) followed by one stressed (*l*). *Hamlet* is mostly written in iambic pentameter. See *foot*.

Ideology. An identifiable set of aims or the body of doctrine, myth, or belief that guides an individual, social movement, institution, class, or large group of people.

Image, Imagery. A word, phrase, or figure of speech (especially a *simile* or a *metaphor)* that represents a concrete object or sense. Such a representation evokes feelings associated with the object or experience.

In Medias Res. A narrative structure that begins in the middle of the story, as, famously, in Homer's *Odyssey.*

Intentional Fallacy. The idea that the meaning intended by the author of a literary work is of primary importance. Such an assumption is a fallacy because first, one cannot know what an author intended; second, because the author may not consciously have meant a certain idea; and third, because we cannot assume that even if we knew the author's intention that would be the basis for critical interpretation.

Interior Monologue. Also known as inner voice or speech, or *stream of consciousness*, interior monologue tries to capture in words a character's private thoughts; in a sense it tries to mimic the one-sided, semi-constant internal monologue one has with oneself at a conscious or semi-conscious level, what people call "thinking about" something—and this thinking is often in the form of questions and answers: "To be, or not to be?"

Irony. A mode of expression, through words (*verbal irony*) or events (*irony of situation*), conveying a reality different from and usually opposite to appearance or expectation, often used by writers of *satire.* A writer may say the opposite of what he means or give the audience knowledge that a character lacks, making the character's words mean things to the audience not perceived by the character. The surprise recognition by the audience often produces a comic effect. In *Huckleberry Finn,* pap's rant about how his rights as a father are being denied by St. Petersburg reflects only on him and his failure to be anything like a father.

Kinesthesia. A sense of the muscles and the movement of the body.

Linguistics. Linguistics is the scientific study of natural language, divided between the study of language structure as grammar and the study of meaning as semantics, including such concepts as the formation and composition of words, called morphology; syntax or the rules that determine how words combine into phrases and sentences, phonology, and phonetics (the actual properties of speech sounds). Evolutionary linguistics considers the origins of language; historical linguistics, how languages adapt and change; sociolinguistics, linguistic variations with social structures; psycholinguistics and neurolinguistics, language in the mind and brain; language acquisition, how children acquire their first language and how people acquire and learn subsequent languages; discourse analysis, the structures of texts and conversations; pragmatics, how meaning is transmitted based on a competence in a language, nonlinguistic knowledge, and the actual context of the statement.

Local Color. Fiction or poetry that focuses on specific features—characters, dialects, customs, and topography—of a particular region, often accompanied by nostalgia and sentimentality.

Lyric. Brief poem that expresses the personal emotions and thoughts of a single speaker. There are many varieties of lyric poetry, including the *dramatic monologue, elegy, ode,* and *sonnet* forms.

Masque. A form of festive courtly entertainment in sixteenth- and early seventeenth-century Europe. (A public version of the masque was the pageant.) Masques offered music and dancing, singing and acting, with elaborate stage design and costumes. Both professionals and courtiers took part in honoring the masque's often royal patron. Edgar Allan Poe's "The Masque of the Red Death" presents a grotesque version of this celebration.

Metafictive/Metafiction. Metafiction occurs when fiction self-consciously addresses itself as fiction, exposing the fictional illusion. It describes fictional writing that self-consciously and systematically draws attention to its status as an artifact.

Metaphor. A figure of speech that makes a comparison between two unlike things without using the word *like* or *as.* Hamlet, for example, conveys his meaning succinctly when he states, "Denmark's a prison" (II.ii.262). Metaphors can be direct or merely *implied*, as when Hamlet describes how "The kettledrum and trumpet thus bray out / The triumph of his pledge" to describe salutes to Claudius's drinking that compare him to an ass. An *extended or controlling metaphor* is a sustained comparison which goes throughout the work or part of it, as with Donne's "stiff twin compasses" in "A Valediction Forbidding Mourning." *Synecdoche* is a metaphor in which a part of something is used to signify the whole, as when Hamlet reflects upon his past when he encounters Yorick's skull in Act V. *Metonymy* substitutes something closely associated with a subject and is substituted for it, such as a crown to stand for the king. See also *image, simile.*

Metaphysical Poetry. The work of British lyric poets of the seventeenth century, who shared an interest in exaggerated, often grotesque *conceits*, characterized by wit, subtle argumentations, or unusual similes or metaphors. Poets such as William Herbert, John Donne, Henry Vaughan, and Andrew Marvell wrote about sexuality and love in divine terms and religious faith in corporeal terms, denying the medieval separation of mind and body or spirit and substance.

Meter, Metrics. The rhythmic pattern produced when words are arranged so that their stressed and unstressed syllables fall into a more or less regular sequence, resulting in repeated patterns of accent (called feet). See *foot* and *versification.*

Metonymy. Figure of speech in which a thing or concept is not called by its own name, but by the name of something intimately associated with that thing or concept. For example, "The White House supports the bill."

Mimesis. The function of literature in its capacity to represent life. Aristotle termed it "imitated human action."

Mock Epic. A form *of satire* that adapts the elevated heroic style of the classical *epic* poem to a trivial subject. Jonathan Swift's "Battle of the Books" (1704) is a variation of this theme in mock-heroic prose. The outstanding English mock-epic poem is Alexander Pope's tour de force "The Rape of the Lock" (1712–14), which concerns a gentleman's theft of a lock of hair from a society lady. Pope satrized the incident as if it were comparable to events that sparked the Trojan War.

Modernism. Cultural movements arising from wide-scale and far-reaching changes in Western society in the late nineteenth and early twentieth century, especially after World War I. Modernist writers and artists felt the "traditional" forms of art, architecture, literature, religious faith, social organization, and daily life were outdated in the new economic, social, and political conditions of an emerging fully industrialized world. Associated with movements in surrealism, formalism, and various avante-garde French movements and with writers such as James Joyce, Virginia Woolf, W. B. Yeats, and William Faulkner.

Monody. A poem in which one person laments another's death.

Mood. Related to *atmosphere* and *tone*, mood refers to the elements that make up the literary work's emotional tone.

Motif. A recurring object, concept, or structure in a work of literature. A major motif in *Huckleberry Finn* is the Mississippi River.

Myth. A story that attempts to explain how the world was created or why the world is the way that it is, passed on from generation to generation and normally as part of religion. Myths were first spread by oral tradition and then were written down in some literary form. "Myth" does not mean "falsehood," as one often hears it used, but rather the opposite: a story that continues to captivate human beings whether they are part of the myth's original religious context or not. Similar myths are found across many cultures, but there are no truly "universal" myths. See also *archetype*.

Narrative. A narrative is a story, which may be true or not, with its events placed in a particular order and recounted through either telling or writing.

Narrator. The person telling the story, not to be confused with the author. *First-person narrators* tell their own stories and restrict the reader to the perceptions, thoughts, and feelings of that single "I," as in *Huckleberry Finn*. *Unreliable narrators* interpret events differently from the author, again, as in *Huckleberry Finn*. An *omniscient narrator* is all-knowing and thus cannot be a character in the story. Omniscient narrators can move from place to place and pass back and forth through time, slipping into and out of characters' points of view. Hawthorne's narrator in *The Scarlet Letter* is an omniscient narrator. *Limited omniscience* occurs when an author restricts a narrator to the single perspective of either a major or minor character. A *third-person narrator* means that the third-person pronouns he, she, and it are used instead of the first-person "I."

Naturalism. A literary movement primarily in France and the United States in which the rude facts of life are addressed as a reductive view of humanity instead of a romantic vision. Naturalist authors such as Émile Zola, Frank Norris, Theodore Dreiser, Stephen Crane, and Jack London sought to depict life as accurately as possible, without artificial distortions of emotion, idealism, and literary convention; they show characters who struggle against seemingly malevolent forces they do not understand and by which they are most often crushed. Heavily influenced by Darwinian thought, especially the "struggle to survive" that Darwin described.

Neoclassicism. Literary and artistic style of England and Europe in the eighteenth century focusing upon the *mimesis* of works—that is, their mirroring of nature—in texts that are highly formal in *diction* and organized in structure. Nature was conceived as orderly and balanced. This is the period of the Greek revival in architecture, with its insistence upon carefully ordered forms.

Novel. An extended *prose* fiction *narrative* of 50,000 words or more, in a generally realistic style concerning the everyday events of ordinary people—and especially concerned with character.

Novella. A *prose* fiction longer than a *short story* but shorter than a *novel*, thus between 20,000 and 50,000 words; a famous example is *The Call of the Wild*.

Objective Correlative. As argued by T. S. Eliot, "the only way of expressing emotion in the form of art is by finding…a set of objects, a situation, a chain of events which shall be the formula of that particular emotion; such that when the external facts, which must terminate in sensory experience, are given, the emotion is immediately evoked."

Octave. A poem or stanza of eight lines, such as the first eight lines of a *Petrarchan sonnet*. See *sonnet*.

Ode. A relatively lengthy *lyric* poem that expresses lofty emotions on a serious topic in a formal style. Perhaps most famous is John Keats's "Ode on a Grecian Urn."

Organic Form. The structure of a work that has grown naturally from the author's subject and materials as opposed to being shaped by and conforming to artificial rules. The concept was developed by Samuel Taylor Coleridge to counter the arguments of those who claimed that the works of William Shakespeare were formless. The "New Critics" of the earlier twentieth century made frequent use of the concept.

The "Other." A person different from oneself who is singled out as different; there can be racial "others" as well as gendered, class, and national "others."

Ottava Rima. An Italian rhyming *stanza* originally used for long poems on heroic themes, it also came to be popular in the writing of mock-heroic works, as with Giovanni Boccaccio. In English the stanza consists of eight iambic lines, usually *iambic pentameters*. Each stanza features three alternate *rhymes* and one double rhyme, for the a-b-a-b-a-b-c-c pattern.

Oxymoron. A condensed form of *paradox* in which two contradictory words are used together, as in "O heavy lightness" (*Romeo and Juliet*, Ii.).

Paleography. The study of ancient handwriting and the practice of reading and deciphering historical manuscripts.

Paradox. A statement that initially appears to be contradictory but then, on closer inspection, turns out to point to a deeper meaning.

Paraphrase. A prose restatement of the central ideas of a literary work in one's own words.

Parody. A satiric imitation written with the idea of ridiculing an author, an idea, or a work. The parodist exploits the peculiarities of an author's expression or an improbable plot. In *Huckleberry Finn* Emmeline Grangerford's poem "Ode to Stephen Dowling Bots" is Twain's parody of American sentimental poetry.

Pastiche. A work cobbled together from disparate sources, or an imitation of an author's style.

Pastoral. Either a literary composition on a rural theme or a reference to the presence of rustic themes and characters in *dramas, elegies*, and *lyrics*. *Huckleberry Finn* contains elements both of the pastoral and the anti-pastoral.

Pathetic Fallacy. Related to the idea of *personification*, of attributing human qualities to a nonhuman agent, the pathetic fallacy or anthropomorphic fallacy is the treatment of inanimate objects as if they had human feelings, thoughts, or sensations. It was first named and criticized in the work of English author John Ruskin (1819–1900) in his 1856 work *Modern Painters*. However Ruskin and subsequent critics have recognized the importance of the pathetic fallacy particularly in British *Romantic* poetry.

Persona. The person created by the author to tell a story, as Twain created Huck to tell the story of *Huckleberry Finn* or Satan in *Letters from the Earth*. The attitudes, beliefs, and degree of understanding expressed by the narrator will not be identical to those of the actual author.

Personification. A form of *metaphor* in which human characteristics are attributed to nonhuman things. For example, in Keats's "Ode on a Grecian Urn," the speaker refers to the urn as an "unravished bride of quietness." See also: *anthropormorphism*.

Petrarchan Sonnet. Petrarch popularized the Italian *sonnet* (an *octave* and a *sestet*); his poetry came to represent an entire *genre* of poems written to ladies who are praised and idealized in the poem.

Phallic Symbol. (from Greek *phallos*, "penis"): A phallic symbol or phallus is a sexualized representation of male potency, power, or domination—particularly through some object vaguely reminiscent of the penis, such as sticks, staves, swords, clubs, towers, trees, missiles, and rockets. Contrast with a **yonic** symbol.

Picaresque. An episodic tale about a rogue *or picaro* (a person of low social status) wandering around and living off his wits. The wandering hero provides the author with the opportunity to connect widely different pieces of plot, Miguel de Cervantes's *Don Quixote* is the classic of the genre.

Plot. See Chapter 1.

Poem, Poetry. Poetry (from the Greek "ποίησις", *poiesis,* or "making") is a form of literary art in which language is used figuratively rather than literally, with formal features such as verse form and *rhyme, imagery, assonance, alliteration, repetition, ambiguity, symbolism, irony, metaphor, simile, metonymy,* and other devices to achieve a musical as well as thematic effect. Poetry often makes connections between otherwise disparate things—generating a series of interrelated meanings which require the reader to delve deeply into form and content.

Point of View.   Who tells us a story and how it is told, the *narrator's* vantage point. It is important, for example, that *Huckleberry Finn* is told from the point of view of a homeless, untutored fourteen-year-old boy, who, despite his hard life, is remarkably naïve.

Postmodernism.   Postmodernism, like modernism, rejects boundaries between high and low forms of art and rigid genre distinctions, and emphasizes pastiche, parody, bricolage, irony, and playfulness. Postmodern art (and thought) promotes reflexivity and self-consciousness, fragmentation (especially in narrative structures), ambiguity, discontinuity/simultaneity, and an emphasis on decentered and dehumanized subject. Unlike modernists, postmodernists view these changes and doubts not with a tragic sense of loss but with a celebratory sense of play.

Proof Sheets.   Printed, unbound sheets of a text for the author's and editor's review before publication.

Prose.   Prose literature—generally novels and short stories—mirrors the language of everyday speech, distinguished from poetry by its use of unmetered, unrhymed language and logically related sentences. Prose is usually grouped into paragraphs that form a cohesive whole.

Protagonist.   The main character of a work of literature. The protagonist can be a *hero* or *antihero,* successful or failing in the end, admirable or despicable.

Pseudonym.   An alias used by a writer who desires not to use his or her real name, sometimes called a *nom de plume* or "pen name," for example, Mark Twain for Samuel Clemens and George Eliot for Mary Ann Evans.

Quarto.   A book resulting from the bookbinder's technique when four leaves of a book are created from a standard (*folio*) size sheet of paper. Many of Shakespeare's plays were printed unofficially in quarto-sized, cheap editions.

Quatrain.   A four-line stanza, the most common form in the English language. See also *meter, rhyme, stanza.*

Realism.   The depiction of subjects as they appear in everyday life. In the *novel,* the great period of realism was in English and American novels of the nineteenth century. Realism came to mean a depiction not of all classes, but primarily the middle class. See also *naturalism.*

Rhyme.   The similarity between syllable sounds at the end of two or more lines. A *rhyme scheme* is the pattern of rhyme used in a poem, generally indicated by matching letters to show which lines rhyme. The letter "A" notes the first line, and all other lines rhyming with the first line. The first line that does not rhyme with the first, or "A" line, and all others that rhyme with this line, is noted by the letter "B" and so on. A *couplet* is a pair of lines rhyming consecutively; *eye rhyme* means words whose spellings suggest that they rhyme even while they do not (lone, none or bough, though). *Feminine rhyme* occurs in a two-syllable rhyme consisting of a stressed syllable followed by an unstressed; while *masculine rhyme* refers to the similarity between terminally stressed syllables.

Rhythm. The variation of the length and accentuation of a series of sounds or other events. In poetry, rhythm refers to the number of beats per line. See *foot, versification.*

Rising Action. See Chapter 1.

Romance. An extended fictional *prose narrative* about improbable events involving characters who are quite different from ordinary people, such as knights on a quest for a magic castle, aided by fantastic characters such as wizards and fairies and opposed to a fearsome enemy such as a witch or a dragon. However, the term was also used in the nineteenth century to refer to romantic novels, such as Hawthorne's, which do not contain the supernatural but which do reflect a romantic sensibility. The word *roman* means novel in French.

Romanticism. An artistic, literary, and intellectual movement that originated in the second half of the eighteenth century in Western Europe, and gained strength during the Industrial Revolution. Partly a revolt against aristocratic social and political norms of *neoclassicism* and a reaction against the scientific rationalization of nature, it was embodied most strongly in the visual arts, music, and literature, stressing strong and individual emotion as a source of aesthetic experience.

Satire. A literary mode based on criticism through ridicule. The satirist aims to reduce the social, political, religious, or personal practices attacked by laughing scornfully at them—and being witty enough to allow the reader to laugh also. The satirist relies on an implicit moral code, understood by his audience. The satirist's goal is to point out the hypocrisy of his target in the hope that either the target or the audience will return to a real following of the code. Jonathan Swift's *Gulliver's Travels* takes aim at numerous political targets of the time.

Scansion. Reading (scanning) a line of poetry to measure its stressed and unstressed syllables and determine its meter. See *versification, meter, foot.*

Sestet. A six-line poem or *stanza*, such as the last six lines of the *Petrarchan sonnet* form.

Setting. See Chapter 1.

Shakespearean Sonnet. Shakespeare's sonnets took the form of three four-line *stanzas* (called *quatrains*) and a final *couplet* composed in *iambic pentameter.*

Short Story. A *prose narrative* that is brief and focused, usually under 20,000 words. Though it shares techniques with the *novel*, because it is short, the short story tends to be spare in developing the kind of complex detail found in a novel, but aims for a unity of effect.

Simile. A figure of speech that makes an explicit comparison between two things by using words such as *like, as, than, appears,* and *seems.* In a famous simile, Robert Burns wrote, "My love is like a red, red rose."

Soliloquy. When a dramatic character, alone onstage, utters his or her thoughts aloud. Soliloquies are a convenient way for the playwright to inform the audience about a character's motivations and state of mind. Hamlet is famous for his soliloquies.

Sonnet. A fourteen-line poem, usually in ***iambic pentameter***, with a varied ***rhyme*** scheme. The two main types of sonnet are the Petrarchan (or Italian) and the Shakespearean. The ***Petrarchan Sonnet*** is divided into two main sections, the ***octave*** (first eight lines) and the ***sestet*** (last six lines). The octave presents a problem or situation which is then resolved or commented on in the sestet. The most common rhyme scheme is A-B-B-A A-B-B-A C-D-E C-D-E, though there is flexibility in the sestet, such as C-D-C D-C-D. The ***Shakespearean Sonnet,*** (perfected though not invented by Shakespeare), contains three ***quatrains*** and a ***couplet***, with more rhymes (because of the greater difficulty finding rhymes in English). The most common rhyme scheme is A-B-A-B C-D-C-D E-F-E-F G-G. In Shakespeare, the couplet often undercuts the thought created in the rest of the poem.

Spenserian Stanza. A nine-line stanza, with the first eight lines in ***iambic pentameter*** and the last line in iambic hexameter (an Alexandrine). The rhyme scheme is A-B-A-B B-C-B-C C. The form originates in Edmund Spenser's *Faerie Queene.*

Stanza. In poetry, stanza refers to a grouping of lines, set off by blank spaces, that usually has a set pattern of ***meter*** and ***rhyme***.

Stream of Consciousness. A style of writing that tries to relay the actual experience of consciousness, in its chaotic, inclusive, incomplete, impressionist run-on form. James Joyce, Virginia Woolf, and William Faulkner were all practitioners.

Structure. See Chapter 1.

Subject-position. Subjects do not preexist as a unified essence of identity but are created within discourses. One of Michel Foucault's main concerns is the relationship between knowledge and power: it is not a subject itself who produces knowledge, but the discursive formation of which the subject is only one part.

Subjunctive. A verb mood used in dependent clauses to express wishes, commands, emotion, possibility, judgment, opinion, necessity, or statements that are contrary to fact at present. In English, the subjunctive is used when the sense is past tense, but the form of the subjunctive verb required is present: "If it be true that...."

Syllogism. A logical argument consisting of a major premise, a minor premise, and a conclusion, as in the three sections of "To His Coy Mistress."

Symbol, Symbolic. When the surface meaning of an object, event, person, place, etc., reveals another deeper meaning or even several meanings. Symbols embody ideas, so that Faith's pink ribbons in "Young Goodman Brown" symbolize both her faith (white, purity) and her humanity (red, passion).

Synecdoche. A very broad interpretive term which can mean the following: denoting a part of something to refer to the whole thing; denoting a whole thing to refer to part of it; denoting a specific class of things to refer to a larger, more general class; or, finally, denoting a general class of a thing to refer to a more specific class. Synecdoche is closely related to *metonymy* (a term denoting one thing that refers to a related thing); synecdoche is a subclass of metonymy.

Synesthesia. A literary device in which the different senses are mingled, sound with color, or color and taste. Often found in British *Romantic* poetry.

Tercet. Three lines of poetry, either forming a *stanza* or complete poem. Haiku is an example of an unrhymed tercet poem.

Textual Variants. Instances in which two or more versions of a text differ.

Theme. See Chapter 1.

Tone. The writer's attitude toward his readers and his subject, his or her moral point of view or intellectual mood. For example, diverse works of literature employ formal, informal, playful, ironic, humorous, or pessimistic tones. Hamlet's tone in his soliloquies is desperate, while he also banters playfully with the actors, a change in his tone.

Tragedy. Traditionally a *drama* that presents a courageous individual who confronts powerful forces within or outside him or her with a courage that reveals the breadth and depth of the human spirit in the face of failure, defeat, and even death. Though the traditional tragic hero begins in a high position, his *hubris,* or tragic flaw (which is usually pride) leads to his undoing. See also *drama, catharsis.*

Trickster. A character common in many cultures, from ancient Greece to traditional and contemporary Native American and African-American literature. Trickster, constantly at the mercy of his drives and desires, must use his ingenuity to defeat enemies and escape difficult situations, like B'rer Rabbit. Tricksters are most often animals, such as the spider, hare, or coyote, although they may take the form of humans as well; they are shape-shifters. Tricksters mediate between the gods and humankind, as in the case of Prometheus or the Hawaiian demigod Maui.

Trope. In Greek, a "turn"; in linguistics a rhetorical figure of speech that consists of a play on words; in literature, a common pattern, theme, *motif,* or a figure of speech in which words are used in a sense different from their literal meaning.

Typography. The art and techniques of arranging type and type design, and of modifying type, including the selection of typefaces, point size, line length, leading (line spacing), adjusting the spaces between groups of letters (tracking) and (kerning) adjusting the space between pairs of letters. In the past when type was hand-set, typography was performed by typesetters, compositors, and typographers.

Utopian Novel. A novel that presents an ideal society where the problems of poverty, greed, crime, and so forth have been eliminated, named for Sir Thomas More's *Utopia*. Charlotte Perkins Gilman's *Herland* is a Utopia of women only. See also ***dystopian novel***.

Variants. Textual variants are classified as either "substantive" or "accidental." Substantives affect the reading or interpretation of a text and consist of such things as the substitution of one word for another; an accidental is an emendation such as a typo that does not (usually) affect interpretation, or a mistaken use of upper- or lower-case letters or changes from British to American spellings.

Verisimilitude. How fully the characters and actions in a work of fiction conform to our sense of reality, its quality of being "true to life."

Vernacular. The language of everyday speech. Dante famously contributed to the early days of vernacular literature in his *Divine Comedy*, written in vernacular Italian instead of Latin. *Adventures of Huckleberry Finn* is the first great American novel written entirely in dialect, a form of the vernacular.

Vers de Société. (French: "society verse"), light poetry written with particular wit and polish and intended for a limited, sophisticated audience, flourishing in cultured societies, particularly in court circles and literary salons, in existence since the Greek poet. Anacreon (sixth century B.C.E.). The tone is flippant or mildly ironic. Trivial subjects are treated in an intimate, subjective manner, even when social conditions form the theme.

Versification. The writing of verse including *meter*, *rhyme*, and other mechanical components of a poem. The structural form of a verse is revealed by *scansion*, including metrical type and number of *feet*: a *monometer* is one foot, *dimeter* two, and so on, to *nonameter* for nine feet. The most common versification in English is ***iambic pentameter***, which is five feet with the first syllable stressed and the second unstressed.

Yonic Symbol. (from Sanskrit *yoni*, "vagina"): A sexualized representation of femininity and reproductive power—particularly through some object reminiscent of the vagina, such as cups, cauldrons, chalices, goblets, wells, caves, tunnels, circles, hoops, pots, and other containers. The grave in "To His Coy Mistress" is a yonic symbol. Contrast with a ***phallic*** symbol.

Index